LEGAL NURSE CONSULTING
PRACTICES
Third Edition

LEGAL NURSE CONSULTING PRACTICES

PRACTICES
Third Edition

Edited by

Ann M. Peterson, EdD, MSN, RN, FNP-BC, LNCC
Lynda Kopishke, MSN, RN, LNCC

Associate Editors

Cheryl E. White, RN, BS, MSHL, LNCC, LHRM, MSCC, DFSHRMPS
Claire Hoffman, MS, RNC, CDDN, CLNC
Tracy Patrick- Panchelli, BSN, RN-BC, CPN
Bonnie Rogers, DrPH, COHN-S, LNCC, FAAN

AALNC
AMERICAN ASSOCIATION OF
LEGAL NURSE CONSULTANTS

CRC Press
Taylor & Francis Group
Boca Raton   London   New York

CRC Press is an imprint of the
Taylor & Francis Group, an **informa** business

CRC Press
Taylor & Francis Group
6000 Broken Sound Parkway NW, Suite 300
Boca Raton, FL 33487-2742

© 2010 by American Association of Legal Nurse Consultants
CRC Press is an imprint of Taylor & Francis Group, an Informa business

No claim to original U.S. Government works

Printed in the United States of America on acid-free paper
10 9 8 7 6 5 4 3 2 1

International Standard Book Number: 978-1-4200-8948-6 (Hardback)

Library of Congress Cataloging-in-Publication Data

Legal nurse consulting practices. -- 3rd ed. / editors, Ann Peterson, Lynda Kopishke.
    p. cm.
  Rev. ed. of part of: Legal nurse consulting / edited by Patricia W. Iyer. 2nd ed. c2003.
  Includes bibliographical references and index.
  ISBN 978-1-4200-8948-6 (hardcover : alk. paper)
  1. Nursing consultants--Legal status, laws, etc.--United States. 2. Nursing--Law and legislation--United States. I. Peterson, Ann, 1943- II. Kopishke, Lynda. III. Legal nurse consulting.
  [DNLM: 1. Consultants--United States. 2. Nursing--United States. 3. Expert Testimony--United States. 4. Legislation, Nursing--United States. WY 90 L4954 2010]

KF2915.N8L35 2010b
344.73'0414--dc22
                                                2009047505

Visit the Taylor & Francis Web site at
http://www.taylorandfrancis.com

and the CRC Press Web site at
http://www.crcpress.com

Acknowledgment from Lynda Kopishke

Working on the third edition has been both a labor of love and an opportunity for professional growth. Having the chance to collaborate with Ann Peterson as co-senior editor was a delight. All the authors involved in this process have generously given their time and talents to make this text a success. Your words will shorten the learning curve for many as they journey through their careers as legal nurse consultants. Choosing to expand the previous edition, with specialty practice chapters, begins the process of highlighting emerging areas of legal nurse consulting practice.

No text is ever published but for the assistance and support of the behind-the-scenes professionals: the associate editors who gave selflessly of their time to communicate, edit, and support the authors, and the senior editors. This product would never have come to fruition without your efforts and support. I offer kudos to the associate editors for a job well done!

The reviewers for each chapter added a dimension of content expertise and assisted the authors in honing each topic to make it meaningful to the readers. Many thanks for the great suggestions and support of the reviewers, and especially for those who burned the midnight oil in order to turn the product around in an expedited manner to meet deadlines.

A huge thanks to the AALNC staff and particularly Emily Palmer for all the support, patience, gentle guidance, and hard work that was required to put this text in the publisher's hands. Emily handled the day-to-day internal operations and logistics of this text, allowing the rest of us to focus on the creative process. Wishing you weekends of peace and fun now Emily! This text would not have evolved to a third edition without the foundation provided by previous editors, authors, and reviewers. The specialty practice of legal nurse consulting owes its history to your persistence in the written word. Many thanks for your guidance and forward thinking.

Lastly, I want to say thank you to my family, who provided unconditional love and support during the many hours of volunteer work required to craft this edition. You deserve recognition and knowing the time you sacrificed allowing me to finish this project is a precious gift that I will cherish forever.

Lynda Kopishke, MSN, RN, LNCC
Senior Editor

Acknowledgment from Ann M. Peterson

This edition reflects the team effort of many contributors working long hours to produce a book that will provide a foundation for LNCs, attorneys, and others involved in the litigation process of health care issues. The authors provided countless hours, sharing their expertise, to the difficult labor-intensive process of revising or writing new chapters.

The reviewers provided excellent feedback to help shape the chapters as being comprehensive, yet practical.

The associate editors were key managers, providing feedback and guidance, while moving the project forward.

The AALNC Board of Directors has provided continued vision, support, and resources over the past three years to ensure this publication would be available for all nurses practicing in the medical-legal arena. It reflects the mission of our association and we are proud to present it to you.

The staff at AALNC provided support and encouragement while assisting in keeping the lines of communication open and keeping the project on course.

I particularly want to thank our families, who have supported the often arduous and time-consuming efforts spent in coordinating the project. Your patience and encouragement throughout this project lightened the task of bringing this book to publication.

Ann M. Peterson, EdD, MSN, RN, FNP-BC, LNCC
Senior Editor

Preface

From the first edition of this book published in 1998, the special practice of legal nurse consulting has grown by leaps and bounds. In the early years, practice primarily focused on the education and support of attorneys practicing in medical litigation areas. The American Association of Legal Nurse Consultants (AALNC) has supported the growth of legal nurse consulting to include a rigorously administered certification process, and a Scope and Standards of Practice published by the American Nurses' Association. Over the past 20 years, the practice of legal nurse consulting has grown to include areas such as life care planning, risk management, administration health law, criminal law, toxic torts, product liability, technical support in the courtroom, and much more. The opportunities for the education of legal nurse consultants have grown as well, with many online and college-based courses utilizing the *Principles and Practices* text as a core for curriculum development.

This third edition seeks to continue the expansion of the specialty practice with focus on emerging areas for legal nurse consultants to explore. This edition was created after a careful analysis of the current practice environment, a focus survey of membership, and a review of the practice analysis undertaken by the American Legal Nurse Consulting Certification Board (ALNCCB). Thoughtful analysis was completed to determine additions and deletions to the text that would best serve readers for several years to come.

The scope of this project was handled in an efficient and thoughtful manner. A talented group of associate editors each volunteered to take on six chapters to mentor, edit, and support. An invitation to previous edition authors was extended to allow past authors to contribute to this edition. A vetting process for new authors yielded many competent chapter authors who were willing to share their expertise in this all-volunteer project. A decision to expand the glossary and acronym sections allows the reader to quickly learn new information. The decision to evolve into a two-volume set took into consideration the needs of both novice legal nurse consultants and advanced practitioners for up-to-date information delivered in a cost-effective manner.

It has been our privilege to incorporate the skills and talents gathered for this project and shepherding them to fruition. It is indeed the opportunity of a lifetime to stand shoulder to shoulder with caring professionals, contributing to the future of nursing. On behalf of the authors, associate editors, reviewers, and staff, we invite you to read with vigor and enjoy!

Lynda Kopishke, MSN, RN, LNCC
Ann M. Peterson, EdD, MSN, RN, FNP-SC, LNCC
Senior Editors

Editors

Senior Editors

Ann M. Peterson, EdD, MSN, RN, FNP-BC, LNCC, president of Ann M. Peterson & Associates, received a diploma in nursing from Boston City Hospital School of Nursing, a Bachelor of Arts in Psychology, a Master of Science in Nursing, and a Doctorate in Higher Education Administration. Dr. Peterson is an experienced legal nurse consultant working with both defense and plaintiff attorneys on medical malpractice, nursing negligence, personal injury, and criminal cases. She has a background in health care administration and advanced clinical practice, has held an academic appointment as an assistant professor at the graduate level, and has multiple publications to her credit. She is a current member of AALNC and a past president of the Rhode Island Chapter of AALNC. She has also served on the Massachusetts Nurses Association (MNA) Congress on Nursing Practice and the Blue Ribbon Commission on Health Policy and Legislation, and is a panel member of the Massachusetts Medical Malpractice Tribunal.

Lynda Kopishke, MSN, RN, LNCC received her diploma in Nursing from St. Francis Hospital School of Nursing in Wilmington, Delaware. After many years of successful practice, Ms. Kopishke returned to Wilmington University, where she obtained a Bachelor of Science and a Master of Science in Nursing. She became certified as a legal nurse consultant in 2000. She served on the Board of Directors of the American Association of Legal Nurse Consulting at both the local and the national levels. She is past editor of the *Journal of Legal Nurse Consulting*, a reviewer for the second edition of *Principles and Practices*, and a published author and national speaker on topics associated with nursing and legal nurse consulting. Ms. Kopishke operates an independent consulting business, Forensic Matters. She has been admitted at trial in several states and at the federal level as an expert witness in standards of nursing care as well as in life care planning. She is a nurse educator, researcher, and strong advocate for nursing practice.

Associate Editors

Teddylen A. Guffey, MHSA, BSN, RN, LNCC has worked clinically in both nursing and health care administration for 8 years before entering the field of legal nurse consulting. In the years since, Ms. Guffey has worked as an independent legal nurse consultant (LNC) and as a professional staff member of the law firm team, assisting in the provision of medical malpractice representation and litigation services.

In addition to having her Master's Degree in Health Services Administration, Ms. Guffey has authored numerous articles on various topics ranging from health care rationing to the business realities of the LNC's role within the field of Law. She served 5 years on the board of the Phoenix Chapter of the American Association of Legal Nurse Consultants as president, vice president, past president, and program chair and has given numerous presentations locally and nationally concerning risk and medical malpractice management within the health care field.

Currently, Ms. Guffey is the principal of Guffey & Associates, PC, a law firm specializing in providing business, legal, and risk management services to physicians. She continues to work in the field of legal nurse consulting, risk management, and medical–legal business consulting.

Claire A. Hoffman, MS, RNC, CDDN, CLNC is the president of Hoffman Associates, a health care and medical legal consulting firm, which focuses on all aspects of geriatric care, developmental disabilities, regulatory compliance, and standards of care. She has been in legal nurse consulting for 23 years and has been retained as an expert for both plaintiff and defense law firms throughout the country to conduct record reviews, determine case merit, and consult with attorneys in preparation for depositions/trials, and as an expert witness. Ms. Hoffman has been recognized by the US Congress and professional associations for her advocacy for individuals with developmental disabilities.

Marilyn R. Mason, RN, LNCC has practiced as a legal nurse consultant since 1986. She has worked in both plaintiff and defense litigation, holding positions within law firms as well as practicing in an independent consulting capacity. Her clinical experience includes emergency room, psychiatric, medical–surgical, and administrative nursing. Ms. Mason is currently employed at Winer & McKenna, working in the areas of personal injury, medical malpractice, products liability, and employment law. She received her nursing diploma from Barnes Hospital School of Nursing in St. Louis and her bachelor's degree in health administration from St. Mary's College in Moraga, California. She is a registered nurse through the California Board of Registered Nursing. Ms. Mason has published in national journals and spoken to and consulted with nurses, paralegals, and attorneys, at both the national and the local levels, on medical issues in litigation. She has been a member of the San Francisco State University Faculty, teaching and advising for the legal nurse consulting certificate program. She is a founding member and past president of the American Association of Legal Nurse Consultants (AALNC) and is certified by the AALNC in Legal Nurse Consulting (LNCC).

Tracy Patrick-Panchelli, BSN, RN-BC, CPN has been an AALNC member since 1999 and has had an independent legal nurse consulting practice, focusing on medical malpractice plaintiff and defense work, since 2001. In 2009, she was elected president of the Philadelphia Chapter of AALNC and also became a member of the planning committee for the AALNC National Educational Conference. Tracy earned her Bachelor of Science degree in Nursing from the University of Pennsylvania in 1993 and matriculated in the Master of Science in Nursing—Health Care Administration program at Villanova University in 2009. She is a certified pediatric nurse and is also board certified in nursing professional development. She is employed by Nemours/Alfred I. duPont Hospital for Children in Wilmington, Delaware, as Coordinator of Nursing Continuing Education and as a staff nurse on the Critical Care Transport Team.

Bonnie Rogers, DrPH, COHN-S, LNCC, FAAN is a professor of Nursing and Public Health and is director of the North Carolina Occupational Safety and Health Education and Research

Center and the Occupational Health Nursing Program at the University of North Carolina, School of Public Health, Chapel Hill. She is an independent legal nurse consultant in occupational safety and health, public health, and malpractice plaintiff and defense work. Dr. Rogers is a nurse ethicist, holds a postgraduate certificate as an adult health clinical nurse specialist, and is certified as a legal nurse consultant, in occupational health nursing and in case management. She is a fellow in the American Academy of Nursing and the American Association of Occupational Health Nurses.

Dr. Rogers has conducted several funded research projects with a major focus on hazards to health care workers. She has worked on several committees with the Institute of Medicine and completed several terms as an appointed member of the National Advisory Committee on Occupational Safety and Health. She is currently on the AALNC Nominating Committee and Editor of the AALNC *Journal of Legal Nurse Consulting*.

Luanne Trahant, MSN, RN, LNCC has been a legal nurse consultant for over 9 years and is the co-owner of Consulting Concepts of Louisiana, Inc. She has been a practicing registered nurse for over 17 years in multiple nursing and administration settings, including medical surgical nursing, orthopedics, rehabilitation, long-term care, home health, hospice, pediatrics, intensive care, cardiology, and psychiatric care. Mrs. Trahant has served her profession as a staff nurse, charge nurse, director of nursing, and administrator in long-term care settings. She received her Bachelor of Science in Nursing from Northwestern State University in 1992, a Master of Science in Nursing from the University of Phoenix in 2005, and is currently completing a postgraduate certificate as a Family Nurse Practitioner. Mrs. Trahant plans to serve the elderly population as an FNP. She is an active member in national, state, and local nursing associations and forums to help advance the nursing profession. Additionally, she is an avid supporter and advocate for the advancement of nursing in long-term care and the elderly population. For the last 9 years, she has provided independent consulting and expert witness services to plaintiff and defense attorneys nationwide in the areas of long-term care, rehabilitation, orthopedics, administration, and general nursing standards.

Margaret S. Wacker, RN, PhD is the director of Nursing at Lake-Sumter Community College, and the president of Wacker and Associates. She is a nationally recognized speaker, writer, and expert witness in pain management. She is an experienced legal nurse consultant working for defense and plaintiff attorneys on issues of nursing negligence and pain management. She is active in professional organizations, received the Florida Nurses Association District 14 Nurse of the Year award in 2006, and has served on the Rhode Island Attorney General's Task Force for End of Life Care since 2001. Dr. Wacker has held academic appointments at the University of Rhode Island and Yale University. She was a graduate of Saint Catherine's School of Nursing, received her Bachelor of Nursing at New York University, a Master of Science degree from Adelphi University, a Master of Arts degree in Anthropology from the State University of New York at Stony Brook, and a PhD in Nursing from New York University.

Cheryl E. White, RN, BS, MSHL, LNCC, LHRM, MSCC, DFSHRMPS has almost 25 years of extensive legal nursing experience. She has an MS in Health Care Law, a BS in Health Care Administration, and over 30 years experience as a registered nurse. Cheryl has been a risk manager for three large health care organizations, works for the Florida Board of Medicine as an inspector of physician offices seeking licensure in levels II and III office surgery, and has worked the last eight years as an in-house legal nurse consultant to a defense firm. Cheryl is also a certified Medicare Set-Aside Consultant.

Contributors

Lori Barber, RN, MN, LNC
Barber Legal Medical Consulting, LLC
Spanish Fork, Utah

Sue Barnes, MSN, MSHCA, RN
Phoenix, Arizona

Jenny Beerman, MN, RN
Beerman & Associates
Kansas City, Missouri

Julie Bogart
Prairie Village, Kansas

Adrienne Randle Bond, JD, BA
Hughes, Watters & Askanase, LLP
Houston, Texas

Wendy Bonnar, RN, WHNP-BC, MSN
Bonnar Legal Nurse Consulting
La Mesa, California

Judith L. Bragdon
Silver Spring, Maryland

Kathleen P. Buckheit, MPH, BSN, RN,
COHN-S/CM/SM, FAAOHN
Cary, North Carolina

Rebecca S. Busch, RN, MBA, CCM, CBM,
CHS—III, CFE, FIALCP, FHFMA, CPC
MBA, Inc.
Oak Brook, Illinois

Roxanne Bush, MHSA, BSN, BA, RN
R&G Medical Consultants, Inc.
Phoenix, Arizona

Rachel Cartwright-Vanzant, RN, MS,
CNS, LHRM, FNC, LNCC
Medical Legal Concepts, LLC and
    NursingIMPACT
Palm Beach Gardens, Florida

Doreen Casuto, MRA, BSN, RN,
CCM, CRRN
Rehabilitation Care Coordination
San Diego, California

Karen Cepero
Jersey City, New Jersey

Mariann Cosby, MPA, MSN, RN,
CEN, NE-BC, LNCC, CLCP,
CCM, MSCC
MFC Consulting
Sacramento, California

Patricia Costantini, MEd, RN,
LNCC
Costantini Rehab Inc
Pittsburgh, Pennsylvania

Dolly M. Curley, RN, BS, BSN,
DABFN, LNCC
ExpertHQ
Glen Mills, Pennsylvania

Deborah D. D'Andrea, BSN, RN
D'Andrea Consulting LTD
Chicago, Illinois

Doug Davis, BSN, RN, DABFN
Arlington, Texas

Deborah Dlugose, RN, CCRN, CRNA
Wright Professional Associates PC
Oldsmar, Florida

Elizabeth Edel, MN, RN
Houston, Texas

Nancy R. Ellington, BS, RN, LNCC
Medical Review & Analysis, Inc.
Ponte Vedra Beach, California

Linda Fernandes, RN, MSN
Office of the Public Defender State
   of Delaware
Felton, Delaware

Nancy Angelo Finzar, RN, MN
Venice, Florida

Janet G. Foster, PhD, RN, CNS, CCRN
Houston, Texas

Laura E. Fox, MSN, RN, CDDN, CLCP
Fox and Associates
Fairfax, Virginia

Adella Toepel Getsch, BSN, RN, LNCC
Robins, Kaplan, Miller & Ciresi
Minneapolis, Minnesota

Agnes Grogan, RN, BS
VG Associates
Westminster, California

Judith Romanow Guidash, RNC-NIC, BSN
Newark, Delaware

Joan Hand, BSN, RN, CCM
The Hartford Group
Havertown, Pennsylvania

Amy Heydlauff , RN, LNCC, MHSA
Chelsea, Michigan

Jill Holmes
La Jolla, California

Patricia W. Iyer, MSN, RN, LNCC
Med League Support Services Inc.
Flemington, New Jersey

Paula Deaun Jackson, RN, MSN, CRNP, LNC
Philadelphia, Pennsylvania

Patricia A. Jenkins-Barnard, RN
Newtown, Pennsylvania

Geraldine B. Johnson, BSN, RN, LNCC
Medical Review & Analysis Inc.
Jacksonville, Florida

Dana Jolly, BSN, RN, LNCC
Jolly Consulting, Inc.
Richmond, Virginia

Moniaree Parker Jones, RN, MSN, COHN-S, CCM
Pelham, Alabama

Betty Joos, MED, BSN, RN
Informed Decisions Inc.
Sautee Nacoochee, Georgia

Betsy Isherwood Katz, BSN, RN, LNCC
Williams & Trine
Boulder, Colorado

Bruce Kehoe, JD
Wilson Kehoe & Winingham
Indianapolis, Indiana

Heather M. Kennedy, MSN, MBA, RN, BC, LNCC
St. Paul Travelers Insurance Company
Huntersville, North Carolina

Jo Anne Kuc, BSN, RN, LNCC
Midwest Medical Legal Resources Inc.
Schererville, Indiana

Kathleen Ryan Kuntz, MSN, CRNP, CRRN, CLCP, RN-BC, MSCC
Rehab Advantage, Inc.
Jamison, Pennsylvania

Cynthia Lacker, RN, MS, LNCC
Lacker & Associates
West Chester, Pennsylvania

Nancy LaGasse, RN, MS, CDMS, CCM, CLCP, LHRM, ARM, MSCC
Southern Catastrophic Management
    Services, Inc.
Sarasota, Florida

Mary Lanz, RN, LNCC
Tolman & Osborne
Tempe, Arizona

Melanie Eve Longenhagen, MBA, MSN, RN, CCM
Southampton, Pennsylvania

Kathleen Martin, MSN, MPA, CCRN, CS
Jersey City, New Jersey

Helen "Heather" McDaniel, RN, LNCC, CNOR, CNLCP
Seal Beach, California

Thomas B. Mendez, MSN, RN, ANP
Medical Research Consultants, Inc.
Houston, Texas

Christine Revzin Merritt, MSN, RN, LNCC
Castle Rock, Colorado

Donna Miller, BSN, LNCC
Strategic Litigation Partners, LP
Houston, Texas

Phyllis ZaiKaner Miller, RN
Robins Kaplan Miller & Ciresi
Minneapolis, Minnesota

Kathleen A. Morales, RN, C, BSN
Ellijay, Georgia

Michelle Myers-Glower, RN, MSN
Grand Rapids, Michigan

Dawn D. Nash, RN, LNCC
American Baptist Homes of the Midwest
Cottage Grove, Minnesota

Rosie Oldham, BS, RN, LNCC
R & G Medical Consultants, Inc.
Peoria, Arizona

Melanie Osley, RN, MBA, CPHRM, FASHRM
Risk Networking Solutions, LLC
Bolton, Connecticut

Judith S. Ostendorf, MPH, RN, COHN-S, CCM, FAAOHN
Raleigh, North Carolina

Valerie V. Parisi, RN, CRRN, CLCP
ValPar Consultants
Doylestown, Pennsylvania

Julie Pike, MN, BSN, RN, LNCC
Kansas City, Kansas

Ellen Plummer, DL, MJ, RN, BSN, CCRN
Chesapeake City, Maryland

Fran J. Provenzano, RN, BSN, CDMS, CCM, CLCP, MSCC
MSA Specialists
Oldsmar, Florida

Carolyn Pytlik, BSN, RN, CRNA
Vienna, Ohio

Sherri Reed, BSN, RN, LNCC
Wilson Kehoe & Winingham
Indianapolis, Indiana

Karen L. Rollo, RN, MSN
Christiana Care Health System
Newark, Delaware

Sheree M. Saroff, RN, BSN, MBA, MSCC
Saroff Consulting
Oldsmar, Florida

Paula Schenck, BSN, BS, RN
Salem, Missouri

Suzanne Schutze
Austin, Texas

Kathleen Spiegel
Pittsburgh, Pennsylvania

Cathy Weitzel, MSN, ARNP
Wichita State University
Wichita, Kansas

Tricia West, RN, BSN, MBA/HCM, CHN, PHN, LNC
P J West and Associates
Agoura Hills, California

Sharon Whidden, MSN, RN, LNCC
Bayhealth Medical Center
Frederica, Delaware

Deborah S. White, RN, BSN, LNCC
American Family Insurance
Jefferson City, Missouri

Paula Windler, MS, RN, LNCC
Tempe, Arizona

Doreen James Wise, EdD, MSN, RN
Medical Research Consultants, Inc.
Houston, Texas

Mona Yudkoff, BSN, MA, RN, MPH, CRRN, CCM, CLCP
Mona Yudkoff Rehab Consultants
Bala-Cynwyd, Pennsylvania

Elizabeth K. Zorn, BSN, RN, LNCC
Faraci & Lange
Rochester, New York

Reviewers

Tracy Albee, BSN, RN, LNCC, CLCP, FIALCP
MediLegal, A Professional Nursing Corp.
Tracy, California

Angel Boyce, RN, MSN, COHN
Christina School District

Patty Costantini, Med, RN, LNCC
Costantini Rehab, Inc.
Pittsburgh, Pennsylvania

Teri Cox, RN, MS, CLNC
TCK Consulting
Point Pleasant, New Jersey

Anna Davies, BSN, RN
Law Offices of Barry G. Doyle, P.C.
Tinley Park, Illinois

Pat DiFiglio, BSN, RN
Healthcare Solutions
Chicago, Illinois

Tamara Ellinghausen, RN
Legal RN Consulting, LLC
Wheaton, Illinois

Karon Goldsmith, RN, CLNC, NHA
Goldsmith Consulting Associates
Brevard, North Carolina

Deb Gorombei, RN, BSN, MS, LNCC
Laveen, Arizona

Deborah Hafernick, RN, LNCC
Hafernick Legal-Nurse Consulting
League City, Texas

Marianne Hallas, RN, BS, MBA, LNCC
USAA
Saint Petersburg, Florida

Jane Heron, RN, BSN, MBA, CLNC
Heron and Associates, LLC
Abderdeen, New Jersey

Christine Hoch, MSN, RN
Delaware Technical and Community College
Newark, Delaware

Suzanne Langroth, BSN, RN, LNCC
Cataula, Georgia

Pat Larimore, MSN, RN
Felton, Delaware

Sharon McAteer, BSN, MS, CLNC
McAteer Medical Legal Consulting &
 Associates
Matawan, New Jersey

Lorna Morelli-Loftin, RN, LNCC
Medical Records Review Service Inc.
Dallas Center, Iowa

Dina Morgan, BSN, RN, LNCC
CorVel Corporation
Mount Prospect, Illinois

Fran Muldoon, Deceased

Gerry Nestor, MSN, NP
Delaware Technical and Community
    College
Wilmington, Delaware

Lisa Pfeifer
Rochester, New York

Lisa Schwind, BSN
Wilmington, Delaware

Diane Toto, MSN
Delaware Technical and Community College
University, Pennsylvania

Denise Williams, RNC, MPH
Flossmoor, Illinois

Contents

Chapter 1

The Legal Nurse Consultant as Expert Witness

Mariann Cosby, MPA, MSN, RN, CEN, NE-BC, LNCC, CLCP, CCM, MSCC and Tricia West, RN, BSN, MBA/HCM, CHN, PHN, LNC

First Edition
Janet G. Foster, PhD, RN, CNS, CCRN; Patricia W. Iyer, MSN, RN, LNCC; Kathleen Martin, MSN, MPA, CCRN, CS; and Julie Pike, MN, BSN, RN, LNCC

Second Edition
Deborah Dlugose, RN, CCRN, CRNA; Elizabeth Edel, MN, RN; Janet G. Foster, PhD, RN, CNS, CCRN; and Patricia W. Iyer, MSN, RN, LNCC

Contents

Objectives

At the conclusion of this chapter, the reader will be able to:

- Discuss the foundation for nurses serving as expert witnesses
- Describe routes by which nurses may assume the role of expert witness
- List steps for record review and analysis by expert witnesses
- Delineate expectations for communications by nurse experts
- Relate the legal definition of "standard of care" to the clinical definition
- Explain the testifying nurse expert's role in deposition and trial

History of the Nurse as an Expert Witness

Legal proceedings employing expert witnesses date back seven centuries. Even then, courts called upon persons with special knowledge or experience to assist them. Early courts, however, did not specify the exact degree of experience required; it was sufficient that there were persons with expertise who could assist the court in reaching reasonable conclusions. In the 16th century, the courts designated expert "witnesses," and legislation was enacted providing for their compulsory attendance and testimony. The principal purpose of expert witness testimony was to provide the court with opinions based upon the expert's background, experience, skill, and training, just as it is today (Cohen, Rosen, & Barbacci, 2008).

Black's Law Dictionary defines an expert as "a person who, through education or experience, has developed skill or knowledge in a particular subject so that he or she may form an opinion that will assist the fact finder" (Garner, 2004). Nurses are now being called upon to function as experts in a variety of legal proceedings. The nurse expert witness will examine what occurred in a clinical setting to see if it corresponds with the standard of care for nurses. As a fact witness, the nurse offers testimony comprising information and observations from what he or she knows or observes. A key distinction between fact witnesses and expert witnesses is that an expert witness may provide an opinion. Fact witnesses must limit their testimony to facts, except for opinions that are either rationally based on an actual perception of the witness or that might otherwise aid understanding of their testimony. Nurses also serve as liability experts in insurance industry cases.

In addition to approving the expert's qualifications, the court must determine that the opinion evidence is relevant to the issues in the case, that it is reliable, and that it will assist the trier of fact. It is the specialized knowledge or skill that permits a person to form and offer opinion evidence, rather than fact evidence, and it is the ability to offer opinion testimony that distinguishes the expert witness from the fact witnesses.

Expert testimony is necessary when the judge's or jury's understanding of the science or technical facts is beyond the scope of the layperson. The landmark case that established the rule of *general acceptance* for scientific evidence is *Frye v. United States*, a federal case decided by the District of Columbia Circuit in 1923. In brief, the court in this case held that if an expert's conclusions are "generally accepted" in the scientific community, the expert's testimony is admissible evidence. "When the question involved requires special experience or special knowledge, then the opinion of the expert skilled in the particular science, art or trade to which the question relates is admissible in evidence" (*Frye v. United States*, 1923). The general acceptance standard remained in place until the Federal Rules of Evidence were adopted in 1975. The Federal Rules of Evidence adopted by the U.S. Supreme Court govern the introduction of evidence in civil and criminal proceedings in federal courts. While the Federal Rules do not apply to state court proceedings, many states model their evidence rules on the Federal specifications (Cohen et al., 2008; Croke & Fyler, 2002).

Article VII of the Federal Rules of Evidence governs opinions and expert testimony. Rule 702 applies to testimony that may be offered by an expert witness. "If scientific, technical or other specialized knowledge will assist the trier of fact (judge/jury) to understand the evidence or determine a fact at issue, a witness qualified as an expert by knowledge, skill, experience, training or education, may testify thereto in the form of an opinion or otherwise, if (1) the testimony is based upon sufficient facts or data, (2) the testimony is the product of reliable principles and methods, and (3) the witness has applied the principles and methods reliably to the facts of the case" (Federal Rules of Evidence amended April 17, 2000, eff. December 1, 2000). Rule 702 was amended in response to the 1993 U.S. Supreme Court decision, *Daubert v. Merrell Dow Pharmaceuticals, Inc.* In Daubert, the Supreme Court charged trial judges with the additional responsibility of "gatekeeper." In this role, the trial judge evaluates the methodology, reliability, and relevance of opinions presented by scientific experts. If the trial judge opines that scientific testimony is not supported by accepted scientific methodology, the judge can exclude the unreliable "scientific" expert testimony (Cohen et al., 2008).

Nursing has evolved into a profession with a distinct body of knowledge, university-based education, specialized practice, standards of practice, a societal contract, and an ethical code. The practice of nursing requires decision making and skill based upon the principles of the biological, physical, and behavioral and social sciences, as well as evidence-based research for identifying risk factors and providing specific interventions. Every state has a Board of Nursing that is the state entity authorized to regulate nursing practice. Every state legislature has promulgated licensing standards and regulations for the nursing profession in their respective Nurse Practice Acts and Advanced Practice Nursing Acts. Under the nursing act, only a nurse would meet the qualifications for sitting for a nursing licensure examination, and as such be eligible for licensure as a registered nurse (RN).

Nursing is not under the supervision of a physician. Although the physician writes medical orders for patients, which are carried out by nurses, physicians do not supervise or direct nursing care. Expert opinion is typically required to establish the applicable standard of care and the actual departure from standard practice. The expert witness must possess the necessary skill, knowledge, training, and experience to ensure that the opinion rendered is reliable. It appears self-evident that the only expert qualified to render expert opinion testimony would be a member of the same profession who practices in a substantially similar manner. However, for many years, physicians have routinely been allowed to testify to establish the standard of care for the nursing profession. On the other hand, many courts have found that while physicians are best qualified to render testimony as to standard of care for physicians, in many other healthcare professions, only a member of that profession is qualified to testify to standard of care for that discipline. Recently, the courts have acknowledged that nurses possess specialized knowledge that physicians do not have unless they have been trained and have practiced as a nurse (Cohen et al., 2008).

As discussed by Zerres, Iyer, and Banes (2007), in a landmark case in 2004, the Supreme Court of Illinois held that a board-certified internal medicine physician was not competent to testify as to the standard of care of a nurse. In 2006, the American Association of Legal Nurse Consultants (AALNC) issued a position statement emphasizing that only nurses should testify about nursing standards of care, which contains the following:

Citing the Amicus Brief submitted by The American Association of Nurse Attorneys, the court noted as follows:

> A physician who is not a nurse is no more qualified to offer expert opinion testimony as to the standard of care for nurses than a nurse would be to offer an opinion as to the physician standard of care. As a result, nurses are not permitted to offer expert testimony against a physician even if they observe that physician's practice on a daily basis and are exceedingly familiar with the procedures the physician performs. Such testimony would be, essentially, expert testimony as to the standard of medical care. (*Sullivan v. Edward Hospital*, 806 N.E. 2d 645 Ill., 2004).

Scholars and litigators have long held as follows:

> Physicians often have no first-hand knowledge of nursing practice except for observations made in patient care settings. The physician rarely, if ever, teaches in a nursing program nor is a physician responsible for content in nursing texts. In many situations, a physician would not be familiar with the standard of care or with nursing policies and procedures which govern the standard of care. Therefore, a physician's opinions would not be admissible in jurisdictions which hold the expert must be familiar with the standard of care in order to testify as an expert. (Elizabeth W. Beyer & Pamela W. Popp,

Nursing Standard of Care in Medical Malpractice Litigation: The Role of the Nurse Expert Witness, 23A[sic] J. A.[sic] HEALTH & HOSP. L. 363–365, 1990, p. 1220)

The common theme running through court decisions on this issue is that physicians have little first-hand knowledge of nursing practices and training. Physicians rarely teach nursing programs or write nursing texts. Therefore, a physician in most cases would not be familiar with the standard of care or with the nursing policies and procedures (P&P) governing the standard of care for nurses. The profession of nursing is autonomous, separate, and distinct from the profession of medicine and allied health disciplines. The profession of nursing has its own educational and licensing requirements that serve to identify RNs and, among RNs, further identify those with advanced training and certification in their nursing specialty. The nursing profession is responsible for defining its standards of practice, and indeed has published these standards of care. Therefore, licensed RNs, not physicians, are competent to address standards of nursing practice in the litigation arena.

Desirable Characteristics of an Expert Witness

Expert witnesses are represented in many venues. Because they contribute to the process of determining whether the standards set forth in their profession are being upheld and as such are a valuable tool to the trier of fact in a court proceeding, their qualifications and credibility are of paramount importance. The following set of guidelines are instructive to any expert making themselves available to the triers of fact, and may assist the expert to increase their credibility:

- Do not work with unethical attorneys
- Be wary of attorneys who are reluctant to provide all case materials to you as an expert
- Avoid attorneys whose cases are significantly underfunded
- ALWAYS tell the truth. Do not accept cases as an expert that you cannot honestly support
- Be certain that the attorney for whom you have been retained has made your role in the case clear
- Be certain to explain concepts and terminology for layman understanding
- Read all documents before you opine about the case
- Do not exaggerate
- Do not guess
- Say you do not know if you do not know
- Say you do not remember if you do not remember
- Stay within your area of expertise
- Know that everything you do inside and outside of a courtroom can and will affect your credibility
- Maintain a competent, professional, and confident decorum at all times
- Do the best job you can when forming an opinion
- Carefully review all case documents

According to Babitsky (2005), the "dangerous expert witness is an expert witness who puts fear into opposing counsel." As Babitsky further describes, this is elicited by the expert's ability to communicate, their command of factual knowledge, teaching and communication skills, and skills in persuading a jury. Being a dangerous expert witness means mastering opposing counsel's tactics and turning the tables back on them. This makes cross-examining the witness very difficult for opposing counsel.

Attorneys frequently evaluate and consider credentials or qualifications that will be carefully scrutinized when an expert witness is called to testify. Areas that the retaining attorney will consider include the expert's license and certifications, formal education and continuing education, professional experience, specialty training, membership in professional organizations, publications including peer-reviewed journals and textbooks, consulting experience, teaching and lecturing positions, and presentations.

Therefore, the successful expert should consider these qualification guidelines:

■ Avoid holes in your curriculum vitae (CV) by providing assurance that all your credentials are correct and your certifications are current
■ NEVER include certifications that you do not possess
■ State only experience that you have had and to which you can attest
■ Be aware of to whom and how you market your services
■ Assert that you market to both plaintiff and defense
■ Carefully review what is on your website in terms of not only content but also sales language, case names, and stretching the truth

Additional information regarding marketing materials and information on the expert's website is located in Volume 1, Chapter 15, "Locating and Working with Expert Witnesses."

The nurse expert witness is an integral part of the legal team. In professional negligence actions, plaintiffs' attorneys provide the court with expert testimony supporting the case allegations, and defendant healthcare providers' attorneys offer opinions that rebut the allegations. In this context, experts testify to assist triers of fact (judge or jury) in reaching a decision by offering scientific and technical information that is more than common knowledge. As a member of the nursing profession, the nurse expert witness identifies standard of care for nursing aspects of the case and objectively describes whether or not the standard of care was met or how the standard of care was breached. This role is an opportunity for nurses to integrate their professional education and knowledge with experience from clinical, administrative, educational, and research settings and apply them to situations in the legal arena. The role of the nurse expert witness must be understood to include commitment to testimony at deposition and trial.

Nurse experts are now commonly involved in litigation. Because legal qualifications for testimony as an expert witness may vary from state to state, nurses should discuss their qualifications very carefully with retaining attorneys. The major responsibilities of the nursing expert include the following:

■ Offering opinions based on the standard of care and current practice guidelines, not on the morals, motivations, or scruples of any party
■ Rendering an opinion based on their knowledge, experience, training, education, and the information reviewed
■ Basing an opinion on "a reasonable degree of nursing certainty" for each alleged act of negligence that constitutes a deviation from the acceptable standard of care
■ Offering nursing opinions on causation when state law allows it
■ Acknowledging that the nurse expert is *not* an advocate for the plaintiff or the defendant—they are advocates for the standard of care

Legal Culture versus Healthcare Culture

The legal arena is a forum that differs from healthcare culture in many ways. Nurses who propose to work as expert witnesses may find it helpful to visit the law library to peruse the textbooks and journals that attorneys use as they prepare cases. Practice-oriented journals for attorneys such as *Trial* and *For the Defense* describe specific communication techniques and strategies. Books such as *Theater Tips and Strategies for Jury Trials* by David Ball delineate drama and communication techniques for legal practice.

As members of a highly regarded profession, nurses may be shocked at the communication rules and adversarial style of the legal world. Experienced nurses are familiar and comfortable with indirect communication with physicians, such as querying potentially deleterious orders in a way that preserves the physician's ego and role in the healthcare hierarchy. Direct, powerful communication from attorneys may cause nursing professionals to feel uncomfortable. The nurse expert witness should not be intimidated by unfamiliar communication rules. Educational and professional preparations in critical thinking, and experience in clinical crises, provide a firm foundation for nurses to adapt to the foreign territory of the legal arena.

Obtaining Cases for Review

Professional reputation, clinical expertise, and communication skills are the most significant factors sought in nurse expert witnesses. Additionally, attorneys seek experts with whom they can communicate easily and candidly discuss strategies. Attorneys look for professionals with characteristics that will assist them in telling their story to the triers of fact. To win their cases, they need experts with strong teaching skills that can be adapted to the courtroom's unique environment, as well as an open, pleasant personality with a relaxed manner, and a sense of humor.

Such an expert must also possess the ability to explain rather than advocate, despite nursing's self-defined commitment to patient advocacy, as legal advocacy in the courtroom belongs to the attorneys. Experts should possess the ability to offer and defend concise, clear, and objective opinions with honesty; and impeccable integrity, professional responsibility, and ethical conviction. They must exude professional authenticity and confidence (Ross, 2000).

In some situations, novice nurse experts may have more credibility with juries than experts with extensive testifying experience. The ability to meet the requirements of the nurse expert role is more important than experience in the testifying role. It is not uncommon to find nurse experts who have worked on many dozens of cases yet have never testified at trial. This is due to the overwhelming number of cases that settle before trial.

Multiple sources exist for obtaining cases for review. Nursing colleagues may provide an expert's name to a particular attorney. Nurse expert witnesses experienced in case review may be asked to refer other nursing experts. Some legal nurse consulting firms either refer or subcontract RNs to requesting attorneys or claims adjusters who seek assistance for case review. The RN interested in expert witness review may refer colleagues to legal nurse consulting firms or may interview with a firm directly. Legal nurse consultants (LNCs) who prefer to function in a nontestifying role, may provide referrals. Attorneys may also contact potential nurse expert witnesses directly when they are not working through another firm.

Membership in AALNC is a valuable resource for obtaining cases to review. A listing on the LNC locator, a service provided on the AALNC website (http://www.aalnc.org), may result in a case being referred to the expert. Attending local and national AALNC meetings, networking with colleagues and speakers, and distributing business cards are marketing options. Demonstrating professional expertise and strong communication skills by speaking at local and national meetings or publishing in journals and books is a reliable method for increasing the nurse's visibility to other professionals who seek such expertise.

Advertising for case solicitation must be done with care and consideration. The nurse expert witness is an expert clinician serving as case reviewer and analyst. Marketing this clinical expertise as a business must be done for both defense and plaintiff to avoid the appearance of bias and a lack of objectivity.

The professional nurse expert needs to diligently avoid the perception of being a *hired gun*, a common term used to describe experts whose opinions are for sale. Unfortunately, there are those experts who can be hired to say whatever an attorney wants to hear. The ethical nurse expert witness bases case review, analysis, and opinions strictly on the standard of care and facts in the case. This speaks for itself in answering why and how an expert can testify for either side. Ethical experts simply address what happened and how, and testify accordingly. They have no allegiance to a particular side; rather, their opinions are grounded solely in standards and ethics (Cohen et al., 2008).

The ethical nurse expert's fees are strictly based on time expended on the matter. Although time-based bills are created, opinions cannot be bought. It is unethical to contract with attorneys on the basis of the outcome of the case. For this very reason, it is highly recommended that all outstanding fees be paid prior to the nursing expert providing any sworn testimony. The expert is being paid for their time, not their opinion. By being paid after an opinion is rendered, opposing counsel can accuse the expert of having been paid for their opinion. If the length of testimony is unknown upfront, it is recommended that one get a retainer to cover the longest time likely for testimony. Fees that were advanced and unused should be refunded to the attorney after the testimony concludes.

Accepting a Case

As outlined below, when accepting a case, the nurse expert should check for conflicts, and establish whether being retained as a consultant or expert witness, being cognizant of the standard of care considerations, whether the case is plaintiff or defense, and what the expectations are with regard to notes, written reports, and timelines. Additionally, services and associated fees should be clearly stated in writing.

Check for Conflicts

The first order of business is to check for conflicts of interest. The nurse expert must confirm that no bias or impropriety exists. Depending upon the situation, personal or professional relationships with the opposing side may require the expert to refer the case to another expert. Examples of conflicts would include the expert working clinically for a facility being sued or a personal or professional relationship with the plaintiff or defendant. Whenever the expert is uncertain as to whether a prior or current relationship with individuals, institutions, opposing law firms, or any other defendant could be a conflict, he or she should discuss it with the retaining attorney. If a conflict does exist, the expert can offer to refer the case or, depending upon their practice, subcontract the case to a colleague. If the expert identified a potential conflict, again the facts should be shared with counsel at the outset.

Once conflict checks are concluded, the attorney typically provides case details about the plaintiff, events, and specific expectations for the nurse expert. Acceptance by the nurse expert should be based on the appropriateness of their education, research, publications, and experience in a clinical setting similar to the case. If doubt exists, the issue should be discussed in detail with the attorney, and may include a referral to a more qualified colleague when necessary. Maintaining a network of other qualified nursing and medical experts is a sign of professional involvement.

Such referrals define the expert's integrity and invite future contact from the same attorney. Follow-up correspondence to thank the attorney for consideration in a specific case is always appropriate, even if the nurse expert does not accept the assignment.

Establishing Your Role

When the expert is first contacted by an attorney or member of the attorney's firm, it is important to ascertain whether the attorney represents the plaintiff or defense. Having this piece of information should assist the nursing expert in framing the initial conversation. The nursing expert must realize that there are differences specific to working with plaintiff versus defense counsel. Defense counsel is hired by insurance companies to defend their clients. Once a case is filed, there is no option whether or not to take the case for the defense attorney—defending the defendant their job—the defensible, or otherwise. Based upon the facts and strength of the case, defense attorneys may try to cut their losses early, fight the claim with a demurrer or Motion for Summary Judgment (MSJ), or eventually offer a settlement.

Plaintiff's counsel, on the other hand, is never obligated to take a case. They are tasked with evaluating a potential client's claim, whether or not it is meritorious, and whether it is worth taking, both ethically and financially.

Expert Witness or Consultant

The nurse needs to know what type of services the attorney is seeking: Are you being engaged to provide services as an expert witness or consultant? Bear in mind that only an expert witness' materials are discoverable. A nurse functioning as a consultant can make notes, comments, and the like that will be considered attorney work product and are privileged. However, if the attorney initially engages the nurse as a consultant and later wants the nurse to testify as an expert witness on the case, the privileged status becomes void and all documents and notes become discoverable. Therefore, when contacted by an attorney who may initially be uncertain about whether the nurse will be needed to testify, the nurse should err on the side of caution and approach the case as if retained as an expert witness.

Note Taking and Written Reports

Since all written materials created by expert witnesses are subject to discovery, the expert should discuss the creation of written materials with the attorney at the time the case is accepted, before any notes or reports are generated. Depending on the jurisdiction of the case, a report may be required. For those jurisdictions that do not require a report, the attorney may prefer that no documents be created. It is important for the nurse expert to know what the attorney needs and expects before creating any potentially discoverable documents. If a chronology is part of your method of case review, it is important to let the attorney know in advance of your intent to create a chronology.

Timelines/Deadlines

Case acceptance should be accompanied by a clear understanding of deadlines, which are important in the legal arena. The nurse should not accept the case unless there is time to receive, review, and analyze the materials appropriately. It is accepted common practice for the expert to charge a rush fee for review needed in less than 10 days. Communication channels should be clearly delineated to the attorney to avoid awkward situations for the nurse, such as receiving phone calls at clinical jobs or late at night.

Standard of Care Considerations

It is essential for the nurse expert to be sure that the attorney's intent is evaluation of nursing care. It is not appropriate for nurses to testify as to the standards for other professions. Because of the scope of their practice, and nurses' intimate working relationship with other healthcare practitioners, most nurses will have extensive knowledge about other healthcare practitioners' scope of practice. While this may benefit the attorney during case evaluation, when appropriate, the expert should suggest that counsel obtain other expert opinion in nonnursing areas where the nurse expert has identified that potential substandard care was an issue.

The nurse expert witness must base testimony on the legal standard of care. This is the ordinary degree of skill and care exercised by a like professional given the same condition in the same circumstances. Many nurses set their own personal standards of care that may be considerably higher than the legal definition. This is a pattern commonly seen in inexperienced expert witnesses. However, the standard of care is based on the reasonable average practitioner and not the expert clinician. While those higher standards certainly may benefit patient care, it is inappropriate to apply them in the context of legal case review.

The definition of *standard of care* was historically linked to the geographical community in which the event happened. However, lower local standards of care are no longer justified for current clinical practice, which now includes advanced communications, standardized educational curricula, widely distributed professional publications, and standards promulgated by professional organizations. Simply stated, a patient with an acute myocardial infarction in a rural area is entitled to the same standard of care as the patient presenting to a major university medical center. The difference, however, is that the rural provider must know when it is appropriate to transfer the patient to another facility in order to assure that the standard of care is upheld. This includes determining when the patient's needs and status exceed the level of services available at the rural facility.

The standard of care must also be matched to the date of the event associated with the incident to the patient. Rapid advances in technology may create changes in the standard of care from year to year. The nursing expert must be able to delineate standards of care for the case's time period; thus, the expert must be familiar with standards of care at the time of the alleged malpractice or accident. The expert's educational and clinical involvement in similar care may also be time sensitive. With long statutes of limitations associated with obstetric and pediatric cases, it may be challenging for attorneys to find an expert who practiced in the prior era associated with the clinical event. Changes in institutional and facility P&P, state statutes and regulations, national professional standards, certification criteria, and academic curricula must all be considered as the expert researches these sources to aid in opinion formulation.

Establishing Expert Relationship

Although a case may be accepted for initial review by telephone, the nurse expert should immediately write to the attorney to confirm details of the arrangement, fee structure, deadlines, and whether a report is being requested. This can be done most professionally with a service acknowledgment or engagement agreement confirming the terms of the attorney/expert relationship. This acknowledgment should be signed by the attorney and returned with the retainer check prior to beginning work on the case. Fee schedules should also be sent at this time, specifying what the expert is charging for time spent as well as any other charges that may be incurred during the course of the case such as travel time, mileage, copying, Bates-stamping, postage, etc.

The expert's commitment to objective evaluation should be apparent in conversation and correspondence. Although initial screening thoughts may be shared based upon facts presented during this first conversation, it must be made clear that the responses to counsel's query is based solely on the information provided and, as such, is subject to significant revision. As the attorney is not a nurse, nor a healthcare provider, the expert cannot rely completely on their facts or analysis of the medical records. Counsel may omit facts because they were unaware of their medical importance or may provide biased information, unintentionally or otherwise. Once records are provided and reviewed, the seasoned expert may identify a *smoking gun* (a fact that serves as conclusive evidence) not previously noted by counsel. Formation of opinions are to be reserved until all records are provided and appropriately analyzed. It is likely that additional records and documents will be provided as the case discovery process proceeds.

As a legal strategy, in order to preclude one from being retained by the other side, attorneys may contact a well known expert for a *curbside* opinion about a case. Having the non-retained expert provide even a verbal opinion could, as a consequence, prevent them from being designated as an expert for the other side. This strategy serves to "block" the use of a strong potential expert for the opposing attorney. Additionally, the expert should be cautious in providing opinions prior to being retained, since one would not have all pertinent information on which to base an opinion. The ethical expert should be careful to always have solid facts prior to formulating an opinion.

After Accepting a Case: The Case Review

Elements of a Case Review

Once the expert's role and relationship are established, the expert should have an understanding as to when the case materials will be provided. Case materials can include medical records, depositions of the plaintiff, healthcare providers, and opposing expert; and other documents.

The nurse expert should ascertain information about specific elements of the case. The nurse expert will be expected to look at the records with a critical eye—considering both sides of the case and keeping an open mind. Is the clinical situation one in which either liability or causation can be defended? Can any of the four required elements (duty, standard of care, causation, and damages) be explained and therefore eliminated? As the nurse begins the case review process, this provides additional information that can be helpful in determining what documents may be needed, and how best to approach and evaluate the medical records.

Inventory of Documents

Upon receipt of the documents, the nurse must verify that what counsel stated was sent in their cover letter (if provided) is in fact what was received. Additionally, as the expert begins the case review process, the expert must determine if additional records are needed, as all applicable records must be present to allow the nurse expert to develop coherent and complete opinions. Clinicians are aware of the variety of records that are created in any patient care situation, including notes and documents from a variety of physicians, nurses, and allied health personnel. Although the attorney may describe the allegations and central issues of the matter, the nurse expert and attorney should discuss which records would be essential, because the expert's opinion cannot be based on the attorney's summary.

The nurse expert should also be aware that case development can go on for several years. The records are confidential, just as in clinical practice. The nurse expert must create an organized filing system to maintain records safely and completely. Filing systems need not be elaborate but should provide for rapid retrieval and safe keeping of information.

Organizing the Medical Records

Establishing a process for reviewing the medical records assures the best rate of success for being able to identify breaches in the standard of care and decreasing the chance of omitting salient information. The nurse expert's first perusal of the documents provided should focus on identification of potential missing records. Developing a list of case specific forms and documents that one should expect to see in the medical record can assist the nurse in this process. Additionally, other health related documents such as billing records or logs can be added to the list of records to request from the retaining attorney. The reader is referred to Volume 1, Chapter 12, "Medical Record Analysis" where this topic is discussed at length.

Ideally, a complete set of all medical records associated with the event will be provided. These records should be organized by the expert in a logical manner that:

1. Corresponds to the way in which a nursing/medical expert would expect to find records in a medical chart
2. Will allow opinions to be developed
3. Provide easily retrievable data for discussion with the attorney and for testimony

It is common for legal office staff to create a master set of records which are Bates-stamped so as to minimize confusion when pages are identified. Some practitioners have devised other acceptable means of organizing the records such as utilizing character recognition software and scanning records onto compact disks.

If only abstracts or selected pages from a record are provided for the expert's initial overview, the opinion rendered should clearly express that it is based on limited information and thus subject to change if more information is provided. The nurse expert should ask whether all pages of the record have been sent, or it may be apparent from review of the Bates-stamping that some pages are missing, either accidentally or by design. In some situations, the nurse expert may decline to provide an opinion until appropriate documents are received and analyzed.

Extracting the Medical Record Information

Now that the records are organized, reading and extracting the important facts will serve to assist the nurse expert in developing opinions in the case. It will help in preparing for depositions, when opposing motions for summary judgment and pretrial motions, in settlement conferences, and during trial. It is critical for assisting counsel in putting together the facts as they relate to the standard of care.

Familiarity with medical records provides a firm foundation for the nurse expert's review. Applicable sections of the record are examined in detail, with the framework of the nursing process and standard of care kept in mind to ensure objective evaluation. Time frames, nursing care (including all the elements of the nursing process), patient responses, and continuity of care are significant elements for meeting the standard of care. Validation of data from other healthcare providers (such as physicians, pharmacists, and other ancillary departments) is essential.

Documentation from other providers that may support or diminish the nurse's initial opinion must be considered as case analysis progresses. In order to be as unbiased as possible, opinion formulation should be based on findings in the medical record, perhaps supported by information from published standards of care sources.

Some experts prefer to make notes on temporary stickers such as Post-it® notes; some may create detailed notes, outlines, and chronologies. Others may prefer to read the material and formulate opinions without creating written materials of any kind. Since all written materials created by expert witnesses are subject to discovery, the expert should discuss the creation of written materials with the attorney at the time the case is accepted before any notes or reports are generated. Many attorneys prefer that no documents be created.

Chronologies

Most experts find chronologies very beneficial as they are thinking tools. The very act of logically organizing the facts clarifies thinking and makes the facts of the case clear. With a well-developed chronology, the key points and issues can become evident very quickly as can other challenges. From the first documents received, assembling case facts in an accessible format can put you on track to assist the attorney with a courtroom victory. A fact chronology can be a tremendous asset as you prepare for trial.

A chronology is also a communication aid. A good chronology makes it easy for everyone on the trial team to share case knowledge as well as brainstorm strategies. Chronologies can also help ensure complete discovery. What facts are disputed? Which facts will still need sources that will be acceptable in court?

There are several methods by which an expert can create a chronology. Perhaps the simplest is written notes. Moving up a level in technology, a word document table or spreadsheet can be set up and used to develop a basic chronology that focuses on the events of the case that are of particular importance to the expert's review and opinions. Nurse experts will most likely have these software programs already, without further financial investment.

Moving to the next level of technological sophistication, one can employ specific software and legal programs designed for the development of comprehensive chronologies and timelines that utilize database functions. With database capability, the nurse expert can create a chronology that keeps the facts in chronological order yet offers the option of creating other documents and can include graphs and charts, which can be useful when focusing on a specific provider or care activity (West, 2006).

It is also important to include disputed facts that opposing counsel may present. Recording these in a chronology or database may make it easy to identify those facts that support or negate opposing counsel's position. A chronology can also be an aid as one is reviewing the facts and information of the case, without spending time redoing notes. Further, it helps tremendously in conveying the essence of the case, supporting the opined conclusions when the time comes. However one establishes a chronology, such a document is vital to making the case clear and coherent.

Formulating the Expert Opinion

Determining the Standard of Care

The nursing process defines each patient as unique, requiring individual assessment, nursing diagnosis, planning, interventions, and ongoing evaluation and re-evaluation. Although many professional commonalities are involved in meeting the standard of care, the expert must define standards for the patients and clinical scenarios presented for review, assuring that the time frame that pertains to the case is utilized.

Written standards are developed by several sources such as the following.

- State and federal statutes and regulations, including nurse practice acts and position statements
- Accreditation agencies such as The Joint Commission
- National nursing associations, including specialties
- Academic curricula
- Professional literature, particularly peer-reviewed publications
- Institutional P&P

Use of published standards reduces subjectivity of opinion in judgments of whether the standard of care was met. However, many documents accepted as standards contain disclaimers that point to their use as guidelines that are neither comprehensive nor limiting. In some ways, these disclaimers may seem to dilute the strength of the information as published; however, such disclaimers also refer to the importance of tailoring care to individual patient circumstances and to the fact that professional responsibility requires a *thinking cook*, as the American Heart Association (2000) describes in its discussion of application of algorithms to clinical care. If patient care could be reduced to a set of objective *cookbook* requirements, there would be no need for analysis by nurse expert witnesses. The nurse expert needs to utilize and apply critical thinking skills when analyzing the records and care for adherence to or deviation from the standard of care.

When performing the medical record review, the nurse expert should also consider the following as part of the analytical process to determine whether the standard of care was met or breached:

- Standards of practice
- Facility policies, procedures, and protocols
- Medications and treatments being administered to the patient
- Equipment used on patients
- Pathophysiology of common disorders seen with patients in general and specifically the pathophysiology of the condition of the case-specific patient

Depending upon the circumstances of the case, the LNC is expertise in the field of nursing will be advantageous when reviewing the medical records. As the expert, their needed to evaluate the signs, symptoms, treatment, and outcomes in order to opine within their scope of practice and determine whether the standard of care was met. It is incumbent upon the expert to address the following three questions: What constitutes being below the standard of care? Where does the reasonable and prudent nurse test apply? What are considered known potential complications?

Deciphering the Medical Record

Deciphering what is actually charted in the medical record is a talent unto itself. Knowing what is reasonable and expected in a medical record makes reading the records possible. If at some point what is written cannot be read or deciphered it should be gone back to later. Sometimes what is difficult to decipher or read becomes clear as the context of the case and other portions of the medical record are read and analyzed. Remember that ignoring charting because it cannot be read may be tempting but unwise. The expert may identify a *smoking gun* that had not previously been noted by counsel, an oversight that could be germane to the case.

The expert should be aware that there may be inaccuracies or conflicting information in the record. This may occur when a healthcare provider makes a mistake in a history and physical, and others involved in the patient's care read and carry the error forward, perhaps compounding it with their own misunderstanding of care previously rendered. While these errors may frequently have little bearing on the case, there are times when there is a major impact. There may be prior treatment received, or not received, to which one needs to pay close attention and then validate or invalidate what the chart reports.

Documentation Scrutiny

As medical records are read and analyzed, the nurse expert should be cognizant of the mantra from nursing school: *If it wasn't charted, it wasn't done.* The expert should keep in mind that there are some gray areas of this dictum. The nurse expert should analyze documentation deficiencies very carefully. The nurse should look for trends in the documentation that reflect the expected standard of care as it relates to the case issues. Conversely, inadequate or absent documentation may be a reflection of a pattern of inadequate care, case-specific or otherwise. This is an essential part of the expert's medical record review. Oftentimes, what is not said or is omitted in a medical record is just as important or more so than what is documented. For example, the medical record of a patient who was to receive a specific type of intravenous (IV) fluid to replace a low sodium level contained documentation of the type of IV fluids administered and the rate. On the surface, the documentation appeared consistent with the orders and the standard of care. However, upon further review of other evidence in the record and additional scrutiny and analysis of the IV fluid documentation, it was apparent that the records were missing documentation of several liters of fluid that had to have been administered to the patient to result in such a rapid increase in her serum sodium level. As a result of identifying the incomplete documentation, causation was identified. In this case, although the additional IV fluids were not charted, based on case analysis, they were given, and ultimately led to the patient's demise. So, even though it was not charted, it was done.

There are often state and federal regulations that mandate adequate charting in the healthcare setting. For example, in California one would check California Code of Regulations Title 22 Division 5 Licensing and Certification for regulations regarding the content of health records. Information such as this is specific to each state and available by using an Internet search engine, such as Dogpile or Google, to find the official code of regulations site. There, one would find the following excerpt (for California) regarding skilled nursing facilities:

§ 72547 Content of Health Records.
   (a) A facility shall maintain for each patient a health record which shall include
        (5) Nurses' notes which shall be signed and dated. Nurses' notes shall include
             (B) Meaningful and informative nurses' progress notes written by licensed nurses as often as the patient's condition warrants. However, weekly nurses' progress notes shall be written by licensed nurses on each patient and shall be specific to the patient's needs, the patient care plan, and the patient's response to care and treatments.

Similarly, the federal regulations, which apply to all states, can also be found by doing an Internet search.

When identifying deficits, it is important to identify what was not charted (and presumably not done). At the same time, it is crucial to look for behaviors such as assessments, treatments, and medication administration that may have been done although they are not evident in the chart documentation. For example, although urinary catheter insertion may not be documented, the output and monitoring of such is documented. Therefore although not documented as inserted, it was done.

Obviously, not every single thing that is done for a patient and every conversation can be charted, as the nurse would be left with no time to actually care for the patient. Key care, instructions, and patient teaching, however, are essential to chart. An example would be the following: if a patient is at risk for a pressure ulcer, it is critical that nurses document the patient's nutritional status, position changes, and communication to the physician about any wound development, consultation by a wound care specialist, and care planning to address pressure ulcer prevention, as well as the patient's response to all of the above.

Reviewing Depositions

Reviewing depositions is an important component of case review. Depending on where the case is in the discovery process when the nurse expert is retained, depositions may or may not be provided to the nurse expert as part of the initial review process. If depositions were included in the initial records package from the attorney, the nurse expert should consider reviewing them prior to providing the initial report to the attorney. If not provided initially, the nurse expert can expect to receive and review various depositions as they are taken and made available.

The following outlines what the nurse expert may expect in terms of content of the depositions depending on whether the deposition is from the plaintiff, defendant, percipient witnesses, or opposing nurse experts (see glossary for percipient witness).

All Depositions

Depositions constitute sworn testimony. Although in a less formal environment than a courtroom, the deponent is under the same oath as in a court of law. A court reporter creates a record of the questions and answers. The court reporter's transcript is utilized by the expert to evaluate the case. Although it is acceptable to use highlighting, Post-it® notes, or other methods of flagging pertinent information in the transcripts, the expert should be aware that an explanation about the flagging may need to be provided when deposed. This is neither negative nor positive, but the experienced expert will have an answer ready.

Depositions typically begin with an explanation of the process by the deposing attorney. The attorney may instruct the witnesses to speak their responses; nods, uh-huh, and shrugs of the shoulders are not acceptable as answers. Witnesses should not interrupt the attorney's questions. It is important to wait until the question is completed before answering. One must refrain from answering in anticipation of the question. After hearing the entire question, the expert should think about it carefully before answering. This also allows time for the attorney defending the deposition to comment or object. If a question is unclear, a request for clarification should be made. The expert should not attempt to answer a question that is not understood. Once the question is answered, it is assumed that the witness understands the question.

The pattern of the deposition may vary from one attorney to the next. Sometimes, in complicated cases where the deposition may go on for many hours, additional sessions with the deponent or witness may need to be scheduled if all the questioning cannot be accomplished in one sitting.

This can also happen with experts due to time constraints and scheduling. Questions previously asked in the deposition may not be revisited during the subsequent sessions. This may vary by state code.

Plaintiff Deposition

The plaintiff may be either the injured patient or a family member who filed the suit on behalf of a deceased or incompetent patient. The plaintiff's deposition often begins with background questions, such as address, number of children, and so on. Next, the plaintiff is asked questions about the patient's care leading up to the incident or care in question. Details concerning the incident are solicited. The last part of the plaintiff's deposition typically consists of questions that determine the nature of the injuries and their impact on the plaintiff's life.

Percipient Witness

Depositions of percipient witnesses or other experts may be provided to the nurse expert at the beginning of the case or at any time during the discovery. The receipt of these depositions for review will depend upon the point in the case the expert services are engaged. When providing an opinion, nurse experts should always reserve the right to modify their opinion should discovery provide additional information. Such information may include deposition testimony, new documents, newly identified medical records, or witness statements.

Any healthcare provider involved in the care of the plaintiff may be deposed. Their depositions include questions about their background, education, employment, and experience. The plaintiff attorney will ask questions about the care of the plaintiff. Any recollections of the witness will be explored. The medical records are referred to in the deposition and most often are entered as exhibits. The institution's P&P may also be referred to and entered as exhibits. If the exhibits are not provided with the transcript, the expert may request the attorney's office to supply them. The healthcare provider's deposition transcripts should be reviewed for discrepancies with the plaintiff's testimony and the medical records for all disciplines (i.e., physician progress notes, physician orders, nursing records, respiratory therapist (RT), physical therapist (PT), etc.). The nurse expert evaluates descriptions of the care or incident, and analyzes testimony for the witness's understanding of the standard of care. Admissions of mistakes, lapses in judgment, and lack of knowledge of the facility's policies are identified.

Opposing Nurse Expert Deposition

The opposing nurse expert witness deposition testimony often begins with an exploration of the expert's background (education and clinical experience) as well as prior experience in reviewing cases and testifying. Depending upon the state in which the suit was filed, an expert report may have been created by either or both sides. If a report is provided, the deposing counsel will explore the testifying expert's opinions as contained in the expert's report. If a report is not provided, opposing counsel will ask the expert about their opinions. Counsel will ask about the expert's familiarity with the care delivered and standards in the case. The expert will be expected to opine on both the care and basis for that care.

When reviewing the opposing nurse expert's deposition, it is important for the nurse expert to analyze the deposition and the expert's report, should one exist, with a critical eye, looking for discrepancies both within the deposition and from other case evidence. Did the opposing expert alter and misstate the facts in any way? Are the opinions supported based upon facts in the medical records or other depositions taken in the case?

Witness Statements and Other Documents

At times, attorneys obtain written statements from the plaintiff or witnesses to an incident. These statements do not constitute sworn testimony and do not carry the same weight. The expert witness may be asked to review these as part of the case file.

Communication with the Attorney

Once the initial records are organized and reviewed, additional questions will often arise. The timing of the communications with the attorney will vary from case to case. The nurse expert may want to initiate a call to the attorney early on, before completing the entire review, in order to get some questions answered. At other times, a follow-up interview with the attorney may be in order once the bulk of the review is completed.

The experienced nurse expert may suggest that counsel serve a request for the production of additional documents. Almost without exception, this will include the facility's policies and procedures (P&P). Rather than request entire volumes of P&P, which is time consuming and expensive to provide and review, it is more cost-effective for counsel to have the expert suggest which specific P&Ps are necessary. Again, what is requested is case-specific.

More often than not, a response to a request for medical records omits certain types of documents. The nurse expert should suggest to the attorney what additional records to request. For a comprehensive list of documents to request for production, please refer to Volume 1, Chapter 12, Medical Record Analysis.

Initial Report to the Attorney

After initial case review, a conversation with the attorney provides the expert with an opportunity to ask questions, discuss opinions, and review case strategy. The nurse expert's clinical experience and education should be apparent in this conversation, as elements of nursing care are reviewed with the attorney to support opinions about the standard of care being met or breached. The expert's initial verbal report also provides more details of record analysis to assist the attorney, including suggestions for additional document requests, advice about other areas to investigate in the patient's care, and provision of literature pertinent to the case.

If the expert hired by a plaintiff's attorney believes that no breach occurred, those opinions should be conveyed to the attorney as soon as possible to allow the attorney to make a decision about continuing with the case. This is especially true as most of the time the plaintiff attorney pays all costs up front, recouping them only when and if a verdict or settlement for the plaintiff is found. On the defense side, if the defensibility is questionable, a conversation with defense counsel about settlement should ensue. Other times, the nurse expert may identify challenges in the case's fact pattern, which require reformulating the case strategy or taking an alternative approach. No matter which side retains the nurse expert, opinions should reflect a knowledge and understanding of the standard of care and how the medical record substantiates or refutes whether the nursing actions were within the standard of care.

The nurse expert must show personal and professional integrity at all times. Most attorneys appreciate a frank discussion of case merits. If the expert's opinion is not strong, grounded in experience, education, literature, and clinical practice, it is inappropriate to continue as an expert in the case. Weak opinions are a disservice to all involved. It goes without saying that any specific opinion should never be given because of counsel's request and should always be based on the evidence as identified from the case review.

At times the merits of the case may not be in alignment with the expert's opinions and the attorney may determine that the role as an expert witness is concluded. This may not necessarily require withdrawal as a member of the legal team, but could potentially shift the nurse services to that of consultant.

Written Reports

A report should not be written unless it is specifically requested by the attorney. If a report is requested, the expert may choose to ask the attorney if a specific format or style is preferred. Whatever the format or style, the professional content must be defined by the expert's own opinion (Carter, 2001). It may be helpful to look at similar reports from other cases supplied by the attorney for writing and format techniques, but the final result must not be tainted by the attorney's input. Individual states may promulgate specific rules for expert reports that the attorney should clearly explain to the nurse expert.

Most expert reports include a list of documents that were reviewed, a description of the events that led up to the incident, a definition of the standard of care, and the actual opinion about whether the standard of care was met or breached. Such opinions must be supported with specific nursing behaviors identified for each area of concern, and an explanation of the standard of care's relationship to the action.

Reports should be concise, carefully organized, and clear and should have perfect spelling and flawless grammar. Rambling writing dilutes and muddles opinions. The five elements of the nursing process: assessment, nursing diagnosis, planning, interventions, and evaluation; provide a simple framework that allows a variety of nursing activities, events, and outcomes to be described cogently. If more than one breach of the standard of care is identified, effort should be made to assure that each element discussed follows the same written format.

References to professional literature should be carefully considered before they are included in written reports to assure that the elements of the literature apply. Although the nurse expert may examine such documents as part of opinion formulation, the expert's background, education, and experience in similar clinical situations constitute the strongest foundation for opinions.

Deposition Process and Trial Testimony for the Nurse Expert Witness

Predisposition Process

The deposition process for the nurse expert witness begins with predeposition planning, which includes a careful review of the documents and a meeting with the retaining attorney. Although the nurse is not expected to have all of the records memorized, the expert is expected to know what is in the records and be able to locate relevant records without much difficulty. This clearly indicates the utility of having the records organized and numbered/Bates-stamped along with a chronology that allows the expert to quickly find the relevant records germane to the opinions. The ability to meet this goal is enhanced by strong professional background, personal confidence, calm demeanor, and careful attention to every word heard and spoken during the deposition. The expert needs to keep in mind that the court reporter's transcription of the deposition creates a permanent record that may be used at trial.

All depositions should be approached from the perspective that you are at trial. In preparing for the deposition, the nurse expert should consider the deposition testimony equivalent to trial testimony. The expert should spend the time needed to thoroughly review the case materials and formulate all opinions based on those materials.

Prior to the deposition, the retaining attorney should meet with the nurse expert to prepare. The meeting may occur days in advance or an hour or so just prior to the deposition testimony. The nurse expert should discuss the timing of this meeting in advance so that it best meets the needs of both parties. The attorney may discuss the formality and strict rules of deposition. This can create an environment that may be intimidating to the new nurse expert who is comfortable with clinical expertise, patient care, and healthcare culture and communication, yet a stranger to the legal world. Rules of discovery require that attorneys should not coach witnesses or obstruct information. The nurse expert must be able to explain opinions clearly, defending them in the face of a variety of questioning strategies from the opposing attorney. Above all, the expert must focus on the goal of this event—to clearly articulate opinions about the standard of care for the particular case.

Retaining counsel should be consulted about personal and professional items to be brought to deposition, in view of the fact that everything in the expert's file is discoverable. It is common to bring two copies of an updated CV. The court reporter appreciates receiving a nurse expert's business card to verify identifying information that is part of the deposition, as well as a list of any technical words one might expect to be used during the deposition.

On the day of the deposition, the nurse expert should exhibit professional demeanor from the moment of arrival at the deposition, because attorneys from both sides will evaluate the expert's potential for strong courtroom appearance and testimony. The nurse expert should mentally rehearse good posture, pleasant facial expressions, and positive body language. Conservative business attire and accessories should be selected. A good night's rest, a healthy breakfast, and allowing extra travel time will help in decreasing stress. Electronic devices such as cell phones and pagers should be turned off.

Since most cases will settle prior to going to trial, the nurse expert should remember that his or her deposition is an important factor in the outcome of the case. A strong and credible nurse expert is likely to have a positive impact.

Deposition Questioning

Opposing counsel conducts the deposition to discover information about the case and to develop the case for trial. Nurse experts should not minimize the importance of discovery and case development. Opposing attorneys craft specific strategies to discredit testimony or individuals. Experts take an oath to be truthful when testifying. Nurse experts can expect to have any element of their professional practice queried, often in a negative style, which is designed to intimidate and reduce the expert's credibility. Education, clinical experience, research, publications, and fees are often discussed. Part of the opposing counsel's job is to minimize the impact the expert's testimony provides in the case. Careful consideration of the exact question asked and formulation of an answer that is responsive to the question are essential. A responsive answer provides only the information requested by the single question. Rambling explanations should be avoided because this may provide points for reducing credibility. Familiarity with attorney questioning strategies described in legal practice literature can be very helpful for nurses entering the legal arena (Morris, 2000). For additional tips on deposition testimony, the reader is referred to Zimmerman (2008).

The nurse expert should be careful to keep testimony focused on nursing practice without venturing into practice areas of other healthcare providers. If opposing counsel asks hypothetical questions, the expert should provide hypothetical answers. Hypothetical questions sometimes lead to complicated lines of questioning and potential for confusion. It is always appropriate to request that the question be repeated or clarified. This is especially true when the question is hypothetical rather than about the specific circumstances of the case. Questions about authoritative literature must also be carefully considered, in light of the multiple factors that create the standard of care and the fact that no author's every word is completely authoritative. All answers should be visualized in their future black-and-white transcript format. Playful playful quips or humorous remarks are likely to diminish the expert's credibility when the opposing attorney reads them aloud later in the courtroom. Fine distinctions of language and meaning that are minimized in daily life become paramount in the legal system.

Other attorneys who are present at the deposition may object to certain questions or answers. The nurse expert should be prepared for this eventuality with instructions from the retaining attorney in the predeposition meeting. Objections constitute a legal procedure for the record; they may be distracting to the expert, who may request that the question be reread by the court reporter. An objection does not negate the need to answer the question; however, it may impact the wording and timing of the answer. The retaining attorney may choose to withhold questions or may ask questions that further clarify the expert's opinions. The nurse expert or any of the attorneys may request a break at any time. The deposition ends when all the attorneys, including the retaining attorney, are finished with their questions.

The expert should always remember to reserve the right to modify opinions or add any additional opinions based on new material reviewed whether or not a report was written. Acquisition of other information from depositions or opposing experts' reports may support the expert's opinion or may serve as a foundation for reanalysis of the records. The receipt of more medical records may also affect the expert's initial opinion. Thus, it should be clear at all times that the nurse expert's opinion is based on currently reviewed information and is potentially subject to change. If this possibility arises after the deposition, it is the expert's responsibility to contact the attorney immediately to discuss the matter and, if appropriate, consider a revision of the opinion. The deposition may be videotaped, especially if the expert is not available for trial.

While the presence of the camera may be intimidating at first, the nurse expert should consider that the film will preserve a verbal and visual record of the testimony. Maintaining a calm demeanor and a professional presentation of information is essential. Remember to refrain from covering your face with your hands or papers, and look at the attorney who is doing the questioning. Videotaped testimony can create a positive record of the nurse's opinions and communication skills, which is especially noteworthy when faced with negative or badgering behavior by opposing counsel.

Reviewing the Transcript

Following the deposition, the transcription of the deposition will need to be reviewed by the nurse expert. It should be closely checked for accuracy. Any changes should be noted on the corrections form, including the rationale for each change (such as spelling error, typographical error, or obvious omission of a word). Such errors may be corrected, but the substantive nature of the content must not be changed by this process. If the nurse expert believes that a change in the substance of the testimony must be made, the retaining attorney should be contacted immediately before notating any change on the form.

Trial Testimony Preparation

Most cases settle prior to trial. If the case proceeds to trial, the nurse expert's testimony is required. Since a time lapse between deposition and trial is common, the expert must prepare with another review of all the case material, with particular attention being given to one's own deposition. Well-organized files and a strong chronology, as well as consultation with the retaining attorney, will simplify this process. The retaining attorney will appreciate the organized expert in that this secondary review will be far less time consuming and therefore less expensive.

Personal and professional preparation for trial follows the same rules as for deposition, with even more emphasis on appearance, demeanor, communication, and unequivocal testimony. The nurse expert must be prepared for the content of testimony as well as for trial-scheduling uncertainties, anxiety that may be associated with the unfamiliar environment of the courthouse, and development of techniques to enhance communication with the jury.

The Witness Stand

The witness starts testimony by swearing or affirming to tell the truth. The retaining attorney does the initial questioning, starting with credentials and CV to establish credibility as an expert. These supporting data are then offered to the court to accept the nurse as an expert who is qualified to testify at trial. Opposing counsel may question credentials at this time or wait until cross-examination.

After the judge accepts the nurse as a qualified expert, the retaining attorney asks specific questions about the circumstances relevant to the case. The nurse expert's testimony then addresses the standard of care and the specific issues that are in question for the jury. At this point, the nurse expert may feel quite comfortable in the teaching role, which is an inherent part of nursing care, as explanations are made to help the jury of laymen understand the intricacies of healthcare and patient outcomes. The opposing attorney then questions the nurse in cross-examination, which is often focused on eliciting information that discredits the nurse expert. At this point, the nurse expert must display an extremely calm demeanor, focus on the elements of the case, and communicate clearly in the face of hostility. Although cross-examination is not comfortable to endure, it gives the well-prepared expert an opportunity to show true professionalism to the jury. The retaining attorney then has the chance to redirect, questioning answers or ideas that need to be emphasized to the jury. Finally, the opposing attorney has the opportunity for re-cross-examination. The appendix provides information about common cross-examination strategies.

In *Theater Tips and Strategies for Jury Trials*, attorney David Ball discusses how witnesses can look and sound good for the jury. Confident eye contact, word delivery, and body language make witnesses look good. Talking into space or down to the floor or shirtfronts reduces communication. Vocal support with full, relaxed breathing techniques, as well as clear and strong speech articulation and volume, enhances communication. Speech volume should not fade at the end of sentences. Ball recommends practicing these techniques with a warning that *practice* does not mean *memorize*. The expert should become comfortable with expressing the substance of testimony utilizing a variety of wording.

Demonstrative evidence and visual aids may be helpful to the judge and jury because they provide emphasis and concreteness, and also memorialize evidence. The nurse expert may play an important role in developing this evidence which may be as simple as an enlargement of a medical record page or as complicated as computer-generated graphics that demonstrate physiology or mechanism of injury. Pieces of medical equipment may also be shown in action. Part of the nurse expert's testimony may include teaching the jury about the role of these pieces of evidence in the case. Visual aids should follow rules of simplicity, readability, and easy comprehension.

Summary

Although professionals set their own personal standards of care, one needs to remember that this is not necessarily the same as the legal definition for standard of care. The courts use expert testimony to define and examine these standards as they relate to specific clinical events. Nurses are well prepared to assume the role of expert witness, with appropriate consideration of the demands and challenges of the role. Education of the judge and jury about the standard of care and how it was met or breached allows the plaintiff's counsel to build a case and the defense counsel to rebut allegations. This role in the legal arena is a natural extension of the professional responsibility of nurses to uphold standards of care.

References

American Heart Association. (2000, August 22). Guidelines 2000 for cardiopulmonary resuscitation and emergency cardiovascular care. Part 6: advanced cardiovascular life support: section 7:algorithm approach to ACLS emergencies: section 7A: principles and practice of ACLS. *Circulation, 102* (8 Suppl.): I136–1139.

Babitsky, S. (2005). *How to become a dangerous expert witness: Advanced techniques and strategies.* Falmouth: MA: SEAK.

Ball, D. (1997). *Theater tips and strategies for jury trials* (2nd ed.). Notre Dame, IN: National Institute for Trial Advocacy.

Carter, B. (2001). Drawing the line: Attorney involvement in preparing expert reports. *For The Defense, 86,* 15–19.

Cohen, M., Rosen, L. F., & Barbacci, M. (2008). Past, present, and future: The evolution of nurse expert witness. *The Journal of Legal Nurse Consulting, 19*(4), 3–8.

Croke, E., & Fyler, P. (2002). Nurse experts: Contributing members of today's litigation team. *Journal of Legal Nurse Consulting, 13*(1), 8–12.

Frye v. United States, 293 F.1013 (D.C. Cir. 1923).

Garner, B. (Ed.). (2004). *Black's law dictionary.* St. Paul, MN: West.

Morris, C. (2000, July). Effective communication with deposition witnesses. *Trial,* 70–75.

Ross, J. (2000, June). How jurors perceive expert witnesses. *Trial,* 51–57.

West, T. (2006). Deciphering medical hieroglyphics: The "how to's" of making the most of your medical discovery documents. *Journal of Consumer Attorneys Association for Southern California, Advocate.* Retrieved January 24, 2009, from http://www.theadvocatemagazine.com/West%20article.

Zerres, M., Iyer, P., & Banes, C. (2007). Working with nursing expert witnesses. In P. Iyer and B. Levin (Eds.), *Nursing malpractice* (3rd ed.). Tucson, AZ: Lawyers and Judges.

Zimmerman, P. G. (2008). Providing expert witness testimony: Lessons learned. *The Journal of Legal Nurse Consulting, 19*(4), 15–17.

Test Questions

1. Marketing nurse expert witness services is best achieved by:
   A. Commercial advertising in legal journals
   B. Networking with LNC colleagues
   C. Paying attorneys for referrals to their colleagues
   D. Purchasing listings in commercial expert witness directories

2. Fees for expert witness work should:
   A. Depend on the outcome of the case
   B. Include a bonus for the nurse expert if the retaining attorney wins the case
   C. Be negotiable depending on the potential award amount
   D. Be completely time-based

3. Which is true about deposition testimony?
   A. It is an opportunity for opposing counsel to discover the nurse expert's opinions
   B. It is considered unimportant except as a partial rehearsal for trial
   C. It may not be admitted into the evidence at trial
   D. The retaining attorney conducts the deposition to allow the nurse expert witness to clarify opinions

4. Record review and analysis by the nurse expert witness should include:
   A. Detailed note-taking and outlining of all case elements in a timeline
   B. Colored highlighting of critical elements of the original medical record
   C. Ensuring that all appropriate pages of the record are present
   D. Advising the attorney that a detailed written report is essential

5. The nurse expert witness's case analysis should hold nursing actions to which standard?
   A. Actions expected of a reasonably prudent nurse in similar circumstances
   B. Actions expected of advanced-practice clinicians in the same specialty
   C. The universal standards for all healthcare providers
   D. The highest possible standards in order to improve patient care

Answers: 1. B, 2. D, 3. A, 4. C, 5. A

Appendix: Cross-Examination Techniques

The expert witness will encounter a number of strategies used by attorneys in cross-examination. This appendix provides an overview of some of the more common techniques. The expert can become more skilled at identifying and reacting to these techniques by anticipating them and knowing effective ways of responding. Each strategy is briefly explained, followed by sample dialogue. "A" stands for "Attorney" and "E" stands for "Expert." Comments in parentheses are provided by the authors.

   1. Expect detailed probing into the expert's background, fee structure, and experience as an expert. The expert should calmly, and without being defensive, provide the answers to these questions.

A: Nurse __, where did you go to nursing school?
E: University of Louisiana.
A: Do you have any advanced degrees in nursing?
E: Yes, I have a master's of science in nursing.
A: You don't have a doctorate in nursing?
E: No.
A: And yet you feel qualified to be an expert in this case?
E: Yes, I do, based on my experience as a nurse and my education. (A doctorate in nursing is not the entry-level degree for expert witness review.)
A: Where have you worked as a staff nurse?
E: Baton Rouge Medical Center and University of Alabama Hospital.
A: You realize that the nurses who were sued in this case worked in Denver?
E: Yes.
A: And yet you have never worked in Denver, have you?
E: I have not.
A: Why do you feel qualified to comment on the standard of care for nurses who work in Denver?
E: I believe the standard of care is a national one. The nurses in Denver are expected to adhere to the same standards as the nurses in the state in which I work.
A: How much do you charge per hour to review a case?
E: $200 per hour.
A: How much? The attorney acts (shocked).
E: $200 per hour. (The expert repeats answer calmly.)
A: Do you know how much nurses earn who work in hospitals in Denver?
E: Not precisely.
A: Why are your fees so much higher?
E: They reflect my education, training, and expertise.
A: How much are you being paid for your testimony today?
E: I am being paid for my time at the rate of $200 per hour. (The expert should be clear that his/her time is being paid for, not his/her opinion.)
A: How many cases have you reviewed as an expert?
E: Twenty.
A: So, you are really a novice at this work, aren't you? (This question is an effort to intimidate the expert.)
E: I have reviewed a fair number of cases.
A: How much money did you earn last year doing expert witness work? (The courts generally permit the expert to provide a percentage of income rather than have to reveal the expert's income.)

E: My expert witness earnings represented about 15 percent of my income.

A: Are you going to be paid a percentage of the recovery that plaintiff hopes to get in this case?

E: No. (It is illegal for experts to work on contingency.)

2. Asking questions in no obvious order—this is designed to prevent the expert from seeing a pattern in the questions. The expert should answer each question as clearly as possible.

A: Let's talk about your opinions in this case, all right?

E: All right.

A: What is your understanding about the responsibilities of the nurse for keeping the doctor informed of changes in the patient's condition?

E: The nurse should report significant changes in the patient's condition.

A: What is the purpose of giving insulin to diabetics?

E: It is to provide a medication that will control blood sugar.

A: What is a patient acuity system?

E: It is designed to help determine how to staff a nursing unit.

3. Deliberate mispronunciation of words—the attorney is trying to present an uneducated air so that the expert's guard will be let down. The expert should ignore the mispronunciations.

A: Nurse___, this case is about a patient who had hypertrophy of the ventricles. (Mispronounces words.) Is that right?

E: Yes. The patient's echocardiogram showed that the patient had hypertrophy of the left ventricle. (Pronounces it correctly.)

A: What is that?

E: (The expert gives an explanation of this term.)

4. Flattery—the opposing attorney acts impressed with the expert's credentials in order to lower the expert's guard. The expert should politely acknowledge the flattery and wait for the next question.

A: You went to nursing school, right?

E: Yes, I did.

A: You went to one of the finest nursing schools in the country to get your degrees, didn't you?

E: Yes.

A: You have written a number of articles that have been published in prestigious journals, correct?

E: Yes.

A: Why, I bet you know more than about 99 percent of the nurses in this country, don't you?

E: I don't know about that, but I do know the standard of care and how it applies to this case.

5. Goading the expert—the attorney is hoping the expert will lose his or her temper or respond in a flippant way. The expert should remain calm.

A: Did you speak to any of the nurses who were sued in this case? (This is a misleading question to ask in front of a jury, because it implies that the nursing expert was not being fair to the defendants by not allowing them to tell the expert their side of the story.)

E: I did not, as it is my understanding that I am not permitted to contact the defendants.

A: Did you think it was important to know what they had to say about how this incident occurred?

E: I did, and that is why I read their deposition transcripts.

A: Have you heard the expression that hindsight is 20/20?

E: Yes.

A: Wouldn't you agree that the nurses taking care of the patient did not have the benefit of hindsight?

E: I agree with that statement, but it is my position that the nurses should have followed the standard of care.

A: You have testified that it is your opinion that the nurses did not follow the standard of care, isn't that right?

E: Yes, I have.

A: This is only your opinion, isn't it?

E: It is my opinion based on my education, training, and knowledge of the standard of care.

A: You are telling this jury that these dedicated nurses, who work day in and day out, made a mistake, aren't you?

E: Yes, they deviated from the standard of care.

A: You want the jury to believe that these nurses were negligent, don't you? (This is a blatant effort to attack the nursing expert. The expert must remain firm in his or her convictions.)

E: Yes, I do.

6. Using body language to intimidate—pointing fingers, shouting, and leaning into the expert's space are often tactics that the attorney who retained the expert can bring to a halt by objecting.

7. Asking questions in a rapid manner—the attorney may be hoping that the expert will mimic the pace of questioning and give a careless answer in haste. The expert should think through the answer to each question and establish a pace that is comfortable for the expert, remembering that a pause does not show up on a transcript.

8. Asking repetitive questions—the expert should provide consistent answers to the same question asked several times.

A: Now, let me be sure I have this right. You are saying that you don't think the nurses did anything wrong with respect to the care that was provided to my client, right?

E: Yes, I am.

A: And you believe, in your professional opinion, that the standard of care was met?

E: Yes, I do.

A: There was nothing that should have been done differently, is that right?

E: That is true.

A: You are very sure about that?

E: Yes.

9. Asking vague or complex, convoluted questions—whether on purpose or because of difficulty framing questions, the attorney should be asked to rephrase the question so that it is clear.

A: What is nursing all about?

E: I don't understand your question.

A: What do you do as a nurse?

E: In what context?

10. Questioning the expert about details in the medical record to test the expert's memory—the expert is allowed to refer to the materials that were reviewed and does not have to answer questions based on memory alone.

11. Use of silence—the attorney may pause after the expert's answer, hoping the expert will elaborate on the answer. The expert should answer the question and wait for the next one.

12. Asking about nursing literature to identify "authoritative texts"—the attorney should prepare the expert to answer these questions based on the jurisdiction's case law.

A: Nurse ___, what texts do you have in your library?

E: Luckmann and Sorenson Medical Surgical Nursing, Barker's Neuroscience Nursing.

A: What texts do you believe are authoritative in the field of medical surgical nursing?

E: I find several to be generally reliable.

A: Do you rely on those texts for information?

E: Yes, but no text is completely up to date because of the lag time from sending it to the publishers and getting it into print.

13. Hypothetical questions—the expert needs to be sure that the details included in the hypothetical question match the case issues.

A: Now, Nurse ___, I'd like you to assume that the following is true. The patient has been admitted to the hospital for a breast reduction. She tells the nurses that she has numbness and tingling in her legs after surgery. She complains each shift to each nurse. What is the standard of care regarding notifying the physician of these changes?

E: I am having difficulty with your hypothetical because it is not based on the facts of this case. My review of the medical record and the depositions of the nurses show that the patient complained on only two shifts.

A: You are aware of my client's testimony that she complained to each nurse who took care of her?

E: I read her testimony to that effect, but it is contradicted by the nurse's testimony.

A: Can you answer my question?

E: If I accept the facts of your hypothetical, I would want to know how often her physicians were visiting her and what they were documenting about her legs.

A: Nurse ___, I am not asking you about what the doctors were doing. I am asking you about the nursing standard of care. Do you understand that?

E: Yes.

A: Now can you answer my question?

E: I would have to say, if I accepted your hypothetical, that I would expect the nurses to report this finding to the doctor if it was a new one, but I understand from the testimony of the nurse that the patient said this was not new.

14. Failing to bring materials to the deposition will make it more difficult for the expert to answer questions. This dialogue illustrates the difficulties in not bringing the materials.

A: Do you have with you the copies of materials that were provided to you for review in this case?

E: I do not have a copy with me, but Ms. Wilson does have the materials that you reviewed in order to supply this expert report.

A: When you say Ms. Wilson has copies of those materials, did you bring your copies with you today?

E: Ms. Wilson has a copy of my nurse expert report and she has copies of all of the material that was sent to me from her office that I reviewed in compiling the report.

A: I realize that she has copies of those materials, but does she have your copies of the materials?

E: No, my copies are at home.

15. Making derogatory remarks on the material that was reviewed is not advisable. The attorney has the right to look at anything in the expert's file.

A: Did you make any notations or marks of any kind on the materials you reviewed?

E: Yes, I did.

A: May I see your file? (Looks at materials.) Why did you highlight this sentence in Nurse Perry's deposition?

E: I thought it was significant.

A: What was significant about it?

E: It was in conflict with what the doctor said happened.

A: I see a comment in the margin of the report that was prepared by Nurse Watson, who is the expert for the plaintiff. What does this mean: "She should stick to obstetrics where she belongs and not review this case?"

E: I thought the expert was not qualified to review this case.

A: What does this comment mean: "What a jerk?"

E: I thought his conclusion was not correct.

16. Failing to read and consider all information—the expert should ask for pertinent documents, depositions, and other records needed to formulate an opinion.

A: When you undertook this assignment, did you want to render a fair opinion? The following dialogue illustrates the problems that can occur.

E: Yes, I did.

A: And in order to render a fair opinion, did you think it was important to know as much as you could about the facts of this case?

E: Yes.

A: Did you read the depositions of the nurses?

E: No, I did not.

A: Why did you not read them?

E: They were not sent to me.

A: Did you ask the attorney for them?

E: No. (This question is designed to make the expert look unfair. The expert is placed in an awkward position if the attorney does not provide him or her with the depositions. The expert can prevent this type of trap by asking the attorney for all relevant material.)

17. Failing to listen to the question and failing to stay focused are shown below.

A: Could you explain to the jury why Mrs. Queen was admitted to the hospital?

E: She stayed in the hospital after her fractured hip because they were trying to find a nursing home bed.

A: I asked you why she was admitted. What caused her to be hospitalized?

E: She was unsteady on her feet and falling frequently.

A: Can we agree that there does not appear to be an order for taking these compression stockings off this patient?

E: No.

A: No, we can't agree or —

E: We can agree.

18. Failing to be responsive, especially giving more explanation or more information than is asked for, is not recommended.

A: Did the job as an instructor involve teaching emergency nursing to students?

E: Yes, I took the students into the emergency room for one semester. They were assigned to observe the triage nurse and to perform simple treatments. At times, they would observe cardiac arrests, of course always standing in the back of the room where they would not be in the way. Many of them found this to be the most traumatic experience they had as students, although I did have one student one time who fainted when the doctor started suturing a head laceration on a child. (This was a yes-or-no question.)

19. Failing to stand behind the expert report is ill-advised.

A: It says in your report that Nurse Williams did not deviate from the standard of care when she administered morphine to my client.

E: Yes, that is what it says.

A: Do you hold that opinion today?

E: Actually, I have changed that opinion.

A: What have you changed about your opinion?

E: I now believe that she should not have given 35 mg of morphine at one time, when the doctor ordered 10 mg. (This expert should have come to this realization long before the deposition.)

20. Going too far out on a limb—not being flexible—creates problems for the expert.

A: How often does the tube-feeding bag need to be changed?

E: It should be changed every 24 hours.

A: What is the purpose of changing the tube-feeding bag?

E: It is to keep the bag sanitary.

A: You have heard testimony that Mrs. Viglione's family saw fungus growing on the inside of the tube-feeding bag, correct?

E: Yes, but that does not really matter.

A: Why is that?

E: The stomach is not sterile, so fungus will not hurt it.

A: Would you eat bread that has mold growing on it?

E: No.

A: Why is that?

E: (long pause) I would not want to get sick.

A: If a fly flew into the tube-feeding solution, would you feed the fly to the patient?

E: Yes, I would, because the stomach is not sterile. (This is actual testimony by a nursing expert.)

21. Testifying to issues outside his or her expertise is inappropriate.

A: Do you have an opinion as to whether or not Dr. White should have prescribed Keflex® to this patient?

E: Yes, I do.

A: And your opinion is?

E: Even though I am not an orthopedic surgeon my opinion is that he should not have prescribed the Keflex, based on the fact that the patient herself had requested that she not be given this drug.

Defense attorney #1: Can we just take a two-minute break? I want to talk to her outside.

Defense attorney #2: I object to any break.

A: Are you through with your response?

E: I still believe that Dr. White should have, based on his medical judgment, not given Keflex to the patient.

(Attorney #1 puts his hand on expert's arm, whispers in her ear, and forces her to stand up.)

Defense attorney #2: Let the record reflect that the attorney is coaching the expert during this deposition. His witness did not ask to speak to counsel. Counsel has asked to speak to his expert. The expert and her attorney are leaving the room.

Defense attorney #1: I object to the use of the word "coach" in terms of characterizing because I want to speak to my expert witness. I just want to talk to my expert in private with regard to the scope of her testimony that we will hope to use at the time of trial. I would like to clarify with her, and I don't consider that coaching at all with regard to anything. We will be back in a few minutes after I have had that opportunity to speak with her.

Defense attorney #2: "Coaching" is a good word, and I stand by my description of what you are doing here, Counsel.

A: Before you leave, are you able to put on the record the scope of this witness's intended testimony?

Defense attorney #1: I intend to do that when I come back.

A: You can't do that beforehand?

Defense attorney #1: I will come back and do it.

Defense attorney #2: That's after he coaches her.

(Expert and defense attorney #1 leave room for a minute, then return.)

Defense attorney #1: Before we begin, I would like to put a statement on the record with regard to my conversation with the witness.

A: Which the record should reflect was three minutes.

Defense attorney #1: I have had the opportunity to discuss with the expert the scope of her review. I was concerned that she might have some questions about her role. She is being offered as a nursing expert who will address the standard of care for the nurse. At the end of her report, she has a paragraph that seems to conclude that Dr. White prescribing Keflex may have been a cause of the problems.

A: Let me ask you this.

Defense attorney #1: Go for it.

A: Will this witness be testifying about causation? In other words, what damages, if any, were caused by administering Keflex?

Defense attorney #1: We are offering her as an expert witness as to the standard of care of the nurse. We are going to limit her testimony to the duty of the nurse.

Defense attorney #2: Exactly! (The nursing expert may not testify about the physician standard of care.)

22. Failing to know the topic is problematic.

A: What is the nursing process?

E: It is the process by which we give nursing care.

A: Can you be more specific?

E: No, I can't.

A: Can you list any of the steps of the nursing process?

E: No.

23. Using terms such as "always" and "never" can be too sweeping and trap the nurse.

A: Does a nurse read the entire medical record before she takes care of a patient?

E: Yes, nurses always read the chart.

A: So, without exception, nurses always read about the patient before they take care of him, is that correct?

E: Yes.

A: The standard of care requires the nurse to always read the medical record, is that what you are saying?

E: Yes, it is.

A: Can you give me a reference to an article or textbook that says that the nurse should always read the medical record before taking care of the patient?

E: No, I can't.

A: So this is your opinion on what the nurse should do?

E: Yes, it is.

A: In your practice as a nurse, have you seen nurses sit down before taking care of the patient and read the entire medical record?

E: No, I have not. But they should do it. (It is difficult to maintain that this is the standard of care if the expert cannot support her opinion with a text or common practice.)

24. Trying to be a lawyer is not advisable. The nursing expert should avoid adopting legal language.

A: Do you believe that the patient did anything wrong?

E: Yes, I believe she was contributorily negligent.

25. Being biased or an advocate is to be avoided. The expert's role is to be objective and an educator about the standard of care.

A: Nurse __, you have been retained to be an expert in this case, isn't that correct?

E: Yes, I was hired to defend the nurses.

A: I'm confused; isn't Ms. Corner the defense attorney?

E: Yes, she is.

A: What do you see as your role?

E: My role is to make sure that these nurses don't have to pay for something that was not their fault. It was not their fault that the patient did not follow instructions. There would be far fewer lawsuits if patients just did what they were told!

26. Being argumentative, evasive, aggressive, or too clever is not recommended. The expert often comes out on the losing end of this type of tactic.

A: It is your opinion that the nurses at Major Hospital did nothing wrong, is that right?

E: Yes, it is. I think the nursing care was perfectly fine.

A: Do you have an opinion about whether this order sheet existed?

E: (Smiling) I have an opinion that will remain private.

A: Why?

E: I find it interesting that this order sheet was supposed to be in the chart, and it is the most crucial document in this case and it is missing. I find it unusual that it is missing because it should be there. I mean, I have never seen this type of patient being cared for in the hospital without that type of order sheet in place.

A: I don't think you have answered my question as to what your belief is as to whether that order sheet ever existed.

E: I cannot testify with any certainty that the document existed because I was not there to see it. Based on my review of the deposition of the nurse and her answers to interrogatories, I feel that a possibility does exist that this order sheet was there, and then destroyed.

A: When I asked you the question originally, and I know that the reporter can't take this down, but you gave a little smile as to indicate that perhaps you did have an opinion as to whether or not this existed. What is your opinion about whether or not it really existed?

E: I think anything is possible at this point since we have so many pieces of paper involved in this case.

A: Yes or no? In your opinion do you believe is it more likely than not that the paper existed?

E: I would say no, that it probably did not exist. It is a possibility either way, 50/50. (This response is completely ambiguous and not helpful.)

27. Answering two-part questions with one answer—each part of the question should be answered separately or the attorney should be asked to rephrase the question.

A: Do they read the whole chart or just portions of the chart?

E: Yes.

28. Speculating about the actions of others is dangerous.

A: What is the purpose of the medical record?

E: It is to document the significant aspects of patient care.

A: Would you expect the physician to document significant observations about the patient?

E: Yes, I would.

A: You are aware that the house doctor recorded that there was a strong pulse in the patient's right leg at 10:00 a.m.?

E: Yes, I read that.

A: You are also aware that the vascular surgeon came in at 10:45 a.m. and recorded that the patient had compartment syndrome in the right leg?

E: Yes.

A: Is it possible that the patient had a strong pulse in the right leg at 10:00 a.m.?

E: Anything is possible. (The expert may find it more useful to say that it is highly unlikely.)

A: Do you believe that it was likely that the patient had a strong pulse at 10:00 a.m.?

E: No, I do not.

A: Why do you believe the house physician documented the presence of a strong pulse?

E: Sometimes when there is a bad outcome there is a cover-up. (This may be viewed as an inflammatory statement.)

29. The attorney may ask the expert to speculate. The expert has to analyze information provided to him/her and should not speculate.

A: Do you know how long the nurse was with this patient?

E: I don't know for a fact, no.

A: Do you have an opinion as to when the nurse saw this patient?

E: I have an opinion that she saw her at the end of the evening shift rather than at the beginning of the evening shift, based on her testimony at the deposition.

A: Is there anything in the medical record to indicate that valuables had been taken from the patient?

E: I did not find anything to that effect.

A: If valuables are taken from a patient, does that usually include jewelry?

E: Not necessarily.

A: What does that usually include?

E: It depends on what the patient has.

A: Could that include rings, necklaces, and money?

E: It depends on what the patient comes into the hospital with.

A: In a situation when a patient comes in with a drug overdose, when a hospital will take valuables from a patient, what does that generally include? (The expert is being asked to speculate.)

E: I can't answer that question.

A: Why not?

E: Because I don't know what the patient had. Patients come into the hospital with all kinds of things.

A: You have no understanding what general hospital procedure would be in terms of removing a patient's valuables under those circumstances?

E: No. The definition of "valuables" is highly variable.

30. Do not charge fees that are difficult to justify to the jury.

A: What do you charge to come to court for the day?

E: My trial fee is $5000 per day.

A: Do you know how much nurses make at General Hospital?

E: The nurse working in a hospital makes between $22 and $35 per hour.

A: So, that is $176 per day if we use $22 per hour and $320 per day if we use $35 per hour, right?

E: Yes.

A: And you charge $5000 per day, correct?

E: Yes, I do.

31. Explain medical terms in the language of laypersons to avoid talking over the heads of the jury. Avoid doing what this expert did:

A: Could you explain to the jury what type of surgery Mrs. Wilson had?

E: She had a bilateral salpingo-oophorectomy and a vaginal hysterectomy with fulguration of areas of endometriosis. (The jury will have no idea what she just said.)

32. Avoid talking down to the jury.

A: Could you explain to the jury what type of surgery Mrs. Wilson had?

E: Every woman has a uterus, ovaries, and tubes. The eggs are made in the ovaries. The male seeds are called sperm. The male seeds meet the egg in the tube and the egg travels down the tube to the uterus or womb. The fertilized egg stays in the uterus until the baby is ready to be born. The baby comes out the birth canal or vagina. The patient had removal of her ovaries and tubes. Her womb was removed through her vagina. She had areas of endometriosis, which are made up of cells from the uterus that travel outside of the uterus. Each month when a woman has her menses, these cells swell and this causes pain. The doctor used electricity to burn these cells.

33. Avoid making statements that defy the common sense of jurors.

A: Do you accept as true everything that the nurse said happened?

E: Yes, I do. I believe in her honesty.

A: So if I told you that she testified yesterday that she took care of the patient on February 30, would you believe her testimony was true?

E: Yes, I would.

34. Referring to the insurance company is to be avoided.

A: Have your bills been paid by my firm?

E: No, I have gotten my checks directly from the insurance company. (The jury is not supposed to know that an insurance company is involved in the case.)

35. Being able to cite sources of information makes the expert's testimony stronger.

A: What do you base your opinion on that restraints may not have been mandated on the evening shift?

E: I based my opinion on the testimony of the plaintiff and on the medical record. Both stated that the patient was cooperative, awake, alert, and oriented.

36. The attorney may ask questions of the expert to trap the expert into admitting that she has committed malpractice.

A: Have you ever been a staff nurse assigned to a patient who was in restraints of any nature where the patient sustained an injury?

E: No.

A: Have you ever been a staff nurse assigned to a patient who sustained an injury as a result of not being restrained?

E: No.

A: Have you ever been a staff nurse assigned to a patient who sustained an injury in a hospital?

E: Yes.

A: Tell me about those circumstances. First of all, on how many occasions?

E: Do you mean when I was caring for the patient?

A: Yes.

E: I can recall taking care of an elderly person with frail skin. I inadvertently applied pressure to the skin and the skin tore. I recall that situation. Other than that I don't recall other situations.

A: Okay. Have you ever cared for a patient where a patient fell out of bed?

E: No.

A: Have you ever committed malpractice?

E: Not that I know of.

A: Have you ever been sued for malpractice?

E: No.

37. The expert should avoid being backed into a corner.

A: Is it your opinion that any time the patient sustains an injury while in four-point restraints, malpractice has occurred?

E: I would be hard pressed to agree to a blanket statement like that. I would have to know the circumstances.

A: Have you cared for patients who were in four-point restraints because they were being abusive, combative, and at risk to themselves or others if they were not restrained?

E: Yes.

A: And in those situations, is it possible that the patient could sustain an injury while in four-point restraints, in the absence of nursing malpractice?

E: I personally have not seen it happen. I've seen many efforts to try to avoid friction, irritation, tightness, and problems with circulation. It's my opinion that if the standard of care is followed, the probabilities of the patient sustaining injury are greatly reduced.

A: So, would that allow for the possibility that even if the appropriate standard of care was followed for monitoring a patient in four-point restraints, an injury may happen in any event?

E: It would be a very remote possibility.

A: Is it possible that a combative patient in restraints can create a friction burn?

E: Yes, it is possible, if the patient was continuously pulling.

A: Okay. So even if they are being monitored to make sure that the restraints are not too tight, and they are being released from them periodically as the protocol requires, that could occur?

E: The answer to that question is not simple because when a nurse observes that type of continuous friction and pulling against the restraint, the nurse is obligated to consider alternatives to avoid the friction. These could include putting padding under the restraint to prevent the abrasion, to considering the fact that the very act of restraining the patient can cause combativeness. The combativeness can be independent of the underlying medical reason that the combative behavior might have existed. There must be some efforts at problem-solving with respect to how to avoid damage to the skin. So, your question was can it cause abrasion? Yes, it can, but there are multiple interventions to avoid that outcome, and I do not see that those were taken in this situation.

38. The attorney may question the knowledge of the expert or realize that he has just laid a trap for himself.

A: Your criticism that Ms. Winters failed to release the restraints is based on the patient's testimony, correct?

E: Well, Ms. Winters also testified that she did not release the restraints.

A: That's your recollection? Let's strike that.

E: Would you like me to show her testimony to you?

A: No.

Chapter 2

The Expert Fact Witness
Noneconomic Damages Testimony

Sheree M. Saroff, RN, BSN, MBA, MSCC

First Edition and Second Edition
Jenny Beerman, MN, RN and Patricia W. Iyer, MSN, RN, LNCC

Contents

Objectives

■ To describe the role and purpose of an expert fact witness
■ To discuss foundation issues for the role
■ To describe the approach to organization and presentation of medical records to a jury
■ To identify steps in preparing to testify as an expert fact witness

Introduction

Most laypersons have little understanding of what occurs within the healthcare system. The triers of fact (judges, mediators, and jurors) as well as attorneys need to understand the injuries, treatment, and responses of the patient. Medical records used as evidence during a trial are often incomprehensible to the average juror, since abbreviations and symbols used by healthcare providers are often meaningless to laypersons. To overcome this obstacle, attorneys have attempted to educate the triers of fact by using treating physicians to explain medical treatment to the jury. Although a treating doctor may have an understanding of care provided to the patient, it is rare that this doctor will have read all the medical records from beginning to end. Even if requested to do so, few practicing physicians have time to read a medical record thoroughly and prepare a detailed report. The cost of having a physician do so would be beyond the resources of many plaintiff attorneys.

At trial, family members may describe what they observed during the patient's treatment, but these persons typically have no medical training and cannot provide cogent medical explanations for the triers of fact. The nursing expert fact witness is the ideal person to present a comprehensive picture of the patient's injuries, treatment, and reactions. This chapter discusses the role of the nurse as an expert fact witness who conveys this information in a teaching role.

Definition of the Role

Legal nurse consultants (LNCs) have developed new testifying roles as "expert fact witnesses" (Bogart & Beerman, 1995). The expert fact witness is one who by virtue of special knowledge, skill, training, or experience is qualified to provide testimony to aid the fact-finder in matters that exceed the common knowledge of ordinary people, but does not offer opinions on the standard of care. The expert fact witness is not engaged to express opinions about the quality of care and treatment rendered but to educate the judge or jury about that care and the plaintiff's response to it. In this role, an LNC evaluates, summarizes, and explains the contents of medical records. A report is submitted to the attorney who hired the LNC, and then provided to opposing counsel. The nurse may offer testimony at mediation or deposition. If the case proceeds to trial, the nurse's testimony aids in understanding the extent of a plaintiff's injuries, treatment, pain, and suffering.

The term "expert fact witness" does not yet appear in standard legal dictionaries. The expert witness provides testimony to aid the fact-finder in matters that exceed the common knowledge of ordinary people, typically addressing liability or damages issues. Specifically, a liability expert witness forms an opinion about adherence to the standard of care. However, a nurse who acts in the role of a damages expert witness typically provides a life care plan that defines the expected cost for caring for the patient. A fact witness may be a nurse or anyone who is not a defendant but has knowledge of the events that occurred, thereby acting as a witness to the events.

The expert fact witness's expertise is also helpful for a detailed explanation of events from initial hospitalization following an injury through discharge and rehabilitation. Injuries, care, and related pain and suffering often represent substantial damages. Often the patient's past medical and surgical history has a major impact on injuries, care, and treatment. An expert fact witness's concise and simple explanation of the patient's past history from the medical records assists with the judge and jury's understanding of the medical information. Also, these explanations can be applicable to increase the understanding of information presented by other experts in the case. This testimony is particularly useful in cases in which the plaintiff is unable to testify clearly due to cognitive impairment, language barrier, young age, or death.

At trial, the expert fact witness's presentation of medical record details bridges the gap in testimony between liability for the accident or medical malpractice and the life care plan. The jury needs a clear, concise, and understandable accounting of events based on medical records. Frequently, this testimony concentrates on presenting facts in the medical records that support the allegation of the plaintiff's pain and suffering, which is a key component of damages important for the judge or jury to understand. The expert fact witness may be retained by the defense to refute claims that the patient experienced extensive pain and suffering. By virtue of the plaintiff's need to prove that damages occurred, it is more common for plaintiffs' attorneys to hire nursing expert fact witnesses.

Federal Rules of Evidence

The Federal Rules of Evidence govern the conduct of cases tried in federal courts. Many state courts model their rules of evidence after the federal rules. Federal Rule of Evidence 702 states: "If scientific, technical, or other specialized knowledge will assist the trier of fact to understand the evidence or to determine a fact in issue, a witness qualified as an expert by knowledge, skill, experience, training, or education may testify thereto in the form of an opinion or otherwise, if (1) the testimony is based upon sufficient facts or data, (2) the testimony is the product of reliable principles and methods, and (3) the witness has applied the principles and methods reliably to the facts of the case" (http://www.law.cornell.edu/rules/fre/rules.htm#Rule702). The nurse with specialized knowledge, skill, experience, training, and education thus qualifies as an expert according to the Federal Rules of Evidence. The nurse has a greater understanding of medical details than laypersons and thus is able to assist the trier of fact in understanding what occurred to the patient.

A second Federal Rule of Evidence helps support the use of a nurse in this expert role. Federal Rule of Evidence 1006 states: "The contents of voluminous writings, recordings, or photographs which cannot conveniently be examined in court may be presented in the form of a chart, summary, or calculation. The originals, or duplicates, shall be made available for examination or copying, or both, by other parties at reasonable time and place. The court may order that they be produced in court" (http://www.law.cornell.edu/rules/fre/rules.htm#Rule1006). The report prepared by the expert fact witness constitutes a summary of medical records. Although no precise definition of "voluminous records" exists, the records generated when the patient has sustained significant injuries would usually meet this definition.

Expert fact witness reports and testimony are based on medical records. Medical records are considered business records, recorded contemporaneously with events, and as such are admissible as evidence. Although not a witness to the actual events, the expert fact witness is allowed to act as a conduit of medical record information to the judge or jury.

Expert Witness Qualifications for the Role

Several attributes strengthen the role of the expert fact witness. Above all, the expert fact witness must be an analytical thinker. The ability to interpret and analyze medical records is essential for the expert witness role. Analysis of medical records requires the ability to be extremely detail-oriented. The expert must be able to identify missing records, extract essential data from the records, and prepare a clear report that articulates the events and injuries. The ability to prepare clear, logically organized, and accurate reports is essential.

Although any registered nurse may possess the skills defined in the previous paragraph, those with advanced degrees, at the master's or doctorate level, have undergone education with the emphasis on writing that is integral to graduate studies, which is valuable preparation for developing reports. However, experts at any academic level, with any certification or specialty, can expect to have their credibility challenged by opposing counsel in an attempt to disqualify their testimony.

The expert fact witness should be familiar with the clinical specialty relative to the patient's alleged injuries. It is not necessary for the expert to have experience in the exact type of nursing specialty, but an expert who has never worked in acute care, for example, may have difficulty explaining medical and nursing issues without some firsthand knowledge.

The expert fact witness must possess expertise to explain healthcare and medical records without providing opinions about the facts. The expert fact witness must have a thorough understanding of different types of medical records. In order to suspect missing records, inconsistencies, or tampering, the expert fact witness must know the elements typically found in each type of record.

Applicable Cases

The expert fact witness may be retained to review records, prepare a report, and testify about injuries and treatment associated with bodily injury, medical or nursing malpractice, product liability, domestic violence, and criminal cases. This role is appropriate whenever a person sustains significant injuries that are documented in medical records. Examples of the types of cases prepared by expert fact witnesses include:

- Surgical errors
- Chemical and thermal burns
- Paralysis
- Closed head injury
- Major trauma from motor vehicle accidents, pedestrians hit by cars, or those with work injuries
- Worsened prognosis caused by delay in the diagnosis of cancer
- Death or injuries from surgical or treatment errors
- Battering during domestic violence
- Death or permanent injuries caused by medication errors
- Perinatal death or permanent injury
- Anesthesia errors

Cases in which the services of an expert fact witness would usually not be needed include those in which records are not voluminous, or injuries are insignificant or nonexistent. As a practical matter, many plaintiff attorneys who try cases with significant injuries but have great difficulty in proving liability may not wish to incur the expense of retaining an expert fact witness.

Marketing the Role to Attorneys

The success of the expert fact witness depends on effective marketing of the role. Armed with an understanding of this specialized role, it may fall to the expert fact witness to convince an attorney to retain a nurse in this capacity. Attorneys may have little or no understanding of the advantages of using a nurse for this role. Common responses are "I'll have the treating doctor testify" or "I'll find the treating nurses and bring them to court." The expert fact witness may point out the expense of having a doctor prepare a detailed report. If the attorney has previously used a doctor to explain treatment, the expert fact witness may want to show the attorney an example of an expert fact witness report (with identifying information redacted) to explain the differences in scope and content, which are valuable in case presentation. Another advantage of employing nurses as expert fact witnesses is that their reports are often broader in scope. Nurses have greater knowledge of the elements of pain and suffering as well as the intricacies of the healthcare system.

It is often impractical and expensive to use treating professionals to testify about the patient's ordeal. Treating healthcare professionals may be difficult to locate and they may be unable to remember the patient, they may not be analytical thinkers, and they usually do not have the communication skills to testify. They may be intimidated by the legal system or even antagonistic to the plaintiff attorney. Often they may have no prior experience in testifying or presenting clear, logically organized, and accurate reports.

When marketing the expert fact witness role, the expert should be prepared to answer questions about the likely cost of such a service. Attorneys often ask for an estimate of the cost for preparing a detailed report. Given the amount of information to be extracted, illustrated, and compiled, these reports are time-consuming and therefore usually expensive for the attorney. The wise expert attempts to determine in advance whether the attorney has the resources to pay for this service. Tailoring the report down to the bare bones may be needed when the attorney is unable to fund an extensive report. A signed fee agreement and a large retainer are recommended.

As with any product or service, gaining new clients for an expert fact witness should include consideration of the main elements of marketing. First, consider your target market, in this case attorneys. Not all attorneys will need the assistance of an expert fact witness. Determine which geographic part of the United States or cities on which to focus. Next, consider focusing on plaintiff attorneys with medically related cases for substantial injuries. The internet can assist in locating law firms that focus on particular cases. For example, a search for "medical malpractice catastrophic injury cases" provides a list from which to start marketing.

Second, select methods to reach the researched set of attorneys. Telephone calls should be planned for content and the best time of day. Be prepared, as previously discussed, to review the benefits of an expert fact witness over physicians and treaters and the difference between an expert fact witness and an expert witness. Prepare simple, brief information to discuss on the telephone and in e-mails. Placing telephone calls at nonlunch times and earlier in the workday increases the chance of talking with a person instead of leaving a message. Also, consider time zones when placing telephone calls.

The prepared information can also be used in a brochure and on a website. An example of the work product, as previously stated, is an excellent visual method. Since presentation is a key component to being an expert fact witness, marketing materials and how the expert fact witnesses present themselves should reflect a very professional, consistent, organized, and concise package. Anything sent by e-mail or mail should also reflect these qualities.

In addition to calling new potential clients, there are two key marketing methods in which to gain new attorney clients. Receiving referrals from present attorney clients is a great way of opening a new door. And the commonly used word "networking" is the other method. It is not only who you know, but what you do with who you know. This implies being prepared when meeting or speaking with attorneys, new acquaintances, friends, and relatives. Have a prepared brief "30-second elevator speech" as an introduction regarding what you do. Many times people are asked, "So what have you been doing?" This is an opportunity to mention expert fact witness services. You never know when a friend or relative knows of someone who could use your assistance. Your business cards should be readily available whenever you travel for business or socially.

The third part of a marketing plan to promote an expert fact witness service includes follow-up and repetition. An expert fact witness should demonstrate reliability by returning calls precisely, as promised. For potential attorney clients with an interest in your services, call periodically to see whether there is any case on which you can assist. If you are requested to mail the attorney information, follow up with a call to confirm the receipt of the information and answer any questions. Occasionally, mail does not reach its destination and the information needs to be resent. Also, follow up if information is sent by e-mail since some e-mails accidentally end up blocked or in a spam folder. Remember potential attorney clients at the holidays and send a professional-looking card. This is another way of increasing the repetition of your name so that you can be selected to assist their firm when a case requires an expert fact witness.

Finally, as with any marketing plan, evaluate how the plan is working. Have the marketing materials and other communications reviewed by successful professionals and marketing specialists to determine if a change needs to be made. When potential clients contact an expert fact witness for new work, confirm how they heard about you and your services. This can guide you in what works and what does not work as well in your marketing strategies. Marketing to gain new clients takes time, and since an expert fact witness is very specialized, it can take longer to find new clients than general legal nurse consulting services. Expert fact witness services can be packaged as part of your services or used as a main focus.

Record Organization and Report Preparation

The expert fact witness starts by organizing the records. Medical records received from a variety of facilities and providers may span a considerable period of time. Use of indexes, medical record tabs, and binders help control the paper and enable the expert fact witness to locate information quickly. The expert fact witness's familiarity with medical records allows early recognition of missing records. Since records are often delivered in a disorganized state, evaluation of completeness is essential. Missing records should be requested as soon as possible. The attorney may have unknowingly requested only the records that the client or family remembered, or believed that an abstract instead of the full certified copy of the medical record would suffice.

As with other expert witness work, writing on the records or using a highlighter is not recommended. Being able to refer to Post-it® notes on significant entries is helpful when writing the report. To save time while reviewing records and preparing the report, the expert may wish to use voice-activation software or to type the report as the records are being read.

When condensing and summarizing the records, the expert fact witness should not alter the facts. The expert witness must not speculate about what the patient was thinking or feeling. For example, the report should not contain statements such as "She must have been scared to wake up in the emergency room with no recollection of the accident." Instead, the report might contain the statement: "The nurse described the patient as anxious, and asking, 'Where am I?'"

The expert fact witness must differentiate preexisting conditions from those caused by the accident. At the same time, preexisting conditions exacerbated by the injuries should be noted. All damages or potential damages found by the expert fact witness should be listed and discussed with the attorney. Examples of damages that attorneys may not be aware of are cognitive delays in head-injured children (which may require yearly psychological testing) or a torn diaphragm (which may have the potential to rupture repeatedly and require future surgeries). If permanent disabling injuries have resulted, a colleague may be recommended to formulate a life care plan. A treating or expert witness physician may be needed to testify about the permanency and prognosis related to damages.

The expert has an ethical obligation to tell the attorney about potentially damaging information that is found in the medical records, such as substance abuse or data that contradict the attorney's theories of liability. This is particularly important if the patient did something that contributed to the accident or injury. The attorney is responsible for determining how to use this information in the process of litigating the case.

The expert fact witness should not lose sight of the fact that the report will be read by laypersons. This requires the ability to view the healthcare experience from the layperson's perspective. A foundation in patient education assists the expert fact witness in preparing the report. Concepts contained in the report should be explained in lay terms. Complex medical terms should be broken down into simple language, avoiding slang, abbreviations, and incomplete sentences.

The expert fact witness's report may be used as the basis for preparing demonstrative evidence. Timelines made from the narrative chronology are effective, serving as a representation of the chronology and as a useful visual aid for the jury. Exhibits can also include lists, charts, or illustrations of medications, tests, operations, treatments, complications, damages, and healthcare providers. The report may be illustrated with images of normal anatomy, medical procedures, schematic drawings of pain medications, graphs, changes in laboratory values, or quotations from the medical record. Keep the report and other demonstrative evidence simple, visual, and free of complex terminology and concepts.

Opposition to the Expert Fact Witness Role

Even before the mediation or trial begins, the opposing counsel, usually the defense attorney, may object to the testimony of the expert fact witness. The opposing counsel may prepare a brief after the expert fact witness's report has been received. The expert fact witness should help the attorney who has requested the services of the expert to anticipate opposing counsel's strategies. The expert may assist the retaining attorney in responding to the brief:

- With permission, supplying the names of clients who have successfully used the expert fact witness in court
- With permission, supplying briefs written by attorneys who have defended the use of an expert fact witness (with the names of the patients redacted)
- Supplying the text of the Federal Rules of Evidence and applicable state law

As is required for the acceptance of other expert witnesses, the attorney must offer proof to the court that the nurse is qualified to testify in this role. Opposing counsel and judges may not understand that nurses are qualified to present medical record evidence by virtue of their specialized education and certification, familiarity with hospital procedures and processes, medical records, medical terminology, and clinical education and experience. As key members of the healthcare team, nurses spend more time with patients and medical records in the clinical setting than any other care provider. With the exception of advanced practice nurses, nurses do not make medical diagnoses or prescribe medical treatment. They do teach patients about health and diseases, medical terminology, diagnostic tests, procedures, and a wide variety of treatment modalities. Nurses are qualified to provide this same information to educate jurors. Ultimately, acceptance of the qualifications of the expert fact witness is at the judge's discretion after review of the brief, or after hearing a motion in limine at the time of trial.

The appendix incorporates examples of the kinds of objections raised by opposing counsel. This material, based on briefs prepared by defense and plaintiff attorneys in an actual case, was presented at the 2001 American Association of Legal Nurse Consultants conference. The case settled before trial.

Deposition of the Expert Fact Witness

Depositions of expert fact witnesses are taken less frequently than depositions of liability expert witnesses. The purpose of taking the deposition of a liability expert witness is to evaluate the expert's ability to assert and defend opinions, and to maintain composure under questioning. There should be little question about what the expert plans to say in the courtroom.

If depositions of the expert fact witness are scheduled, they are typically short. Attorneys who have not previously encountered the expert fact witness role may be initially puzzled by the report and the role. The expert fact witness's prior experience in preparing such reports may be explored, and the outline of the testimony defined. Opposing counsel often need assurance that no liability opinions will be offered by the expert fact witness. Efforts to prevent the expert fact witness from being able to testify at trial may be instituted by opposing counsel after the deposition. Detailed reports explaining graphic injuries, treatment, and response to care may stir up most resistance from opposing counsel. This reaction can be a measure of the report's success in conveying a vivid picture of the patient's injuries, treatment, pain, and suffering.

As in depositions by other involved parties, deponents should answer the question presented briefly. In the deposition of an expert fact witness, they answer using the information previously planned with their retaining attorney. Since their purpose is to present the medical information in a clear, concise, and simple manner, their discussion should not include anything related to liability or the evaluation of healthcare provider care. Therefore, they explain the preexisting conditions, injuries, treatment, and results of treatment. As with other depositions, it is essential to tell the truth, not to guess, and keep it short and simple. The area of guessing can be expanded into questions that ask an expert fact witness to speculate regarding various created situations. This line of questioning is usually classified as guessing and should be avoided. Refocus back to the facts and not the "what ifs."

If there is any uncertainty as to what is being asked in the question to the expert fact witness, request the questioning attorney to rephrase the question. If the expert fact witness is unable to remember the question asked after objections are stated or the question is extensive, request the question to be repeated.

Anything stated in the deposition room will be recorded unless both sides have agreed to being "off the record." There are times when experts may need to ask a question of their retaining attorneies. This would be a good time to request for a break and step outside the deposition room, far away from anyone who could overhear your discussion.

Preparation for deposition should be similar to preparation for trial since the information provided at deposition can be used at trial, if the case goes to trial. The expert fact witness should have at least one meeting with your retaining attorney prior to your deposition to review what can be discussed and how it will be presented. Trial runs of all your information are advisable prior to the deposition. Some depositions will be videotaped, making your preparation with trial runs very important.

Trial Preparation

The expert fact witness should understand from the outset that the case may go to trial. The report may be used by the attorney to focus on key details and to prepare other witnesses for trial. After the report is submitted, the expert fact witness can provide further assistance to the attorney, as described below.

Drafts of Trial Exhibits and Demonstrative Aids

The jury remembers images, diagrams, and pictures long after an expert has left the stand. Collaboration with the attorney allows creative planning and development of effective exhibits. The attorney may have ideas from past trials or from colleagues. The expert fact witness should know where to get equipment and demonstrative evidence. Exhibits must then be created, enlarged, and mounted for the courtroom; demonstrative aids are collected and prepared. See Iyer, Appelbaum, and Parisi (2003) for more information on planning demonstrative evidence.

As computerized technology in the courtroom becomes increasingly accepted, the use of presentation software, like PowerPoint®, with a laptop computer is becoming more common. Telling an effective story becomes even easier with this medium. Enlarged photographs, medical illustrations, pictures of medical equipment, and scanned pages from the medical record enhance the jurors' understanding. Exhibits that will be a part of the testimony may be printed out as slides and supplied to opposing counsel in advance of the trial, as required by court rules. See Chapter 19 for more information.

The expert fact witness reviews exhibits for correctness, simplicity, and readability at every stage of production. As the trial date draws near, all equipment should be checked for proper functioning. Extra supplies, such as colored markers, pointers, and easels to display the exhibits, should be gathered. Bulbs for projectors, extension cords, and other equipment needed for a laptop presentation should be available. Technical problems should be anticipated and backup plans formulated. See Volume 1, Chapter 14 for further information on trial preparation.

Practice of the Presentation

The expert fact witness is often consulted by the attorney prior to testifying at a mediation or trial. They discuss the content of the expert's testimony, plan visual aids, and attempt to anticipate cross-examination. The expert fact witness and attorney should plan the presentation prior to trial. Strong, effective teaching in the courtroom derives from basic principles of patient education and does not differ greatly from bedside teaching for patient and family.

It is important to practice the final presentation in front of a layperson rather than an attorney, nurse, or doctor. Because testimony may have to be altered extemporaneously, the expert fact witness should concentrate on the main events of the injury. Memorizing word-for-word texts is risky because the courtroom's climate may differ greatly from the privacy of rehearsal.

Supervision of Exhibit Setup

It is advisable to bring backup equipment, batteries, cables, etc. to prevent any equipment malfunction impacting the trial and the reputation of the expert fact witness. When traveling to locations by air, use FedEx or UPS to deliver your backup equipment to your hotel room, if you are not carrying the equipment on the plane with you. When shipping equipment, track the package to ensure its arrival. The package should be labeled with a message stating to "hold for arrival of hotel guest Jane Doe on (date)." If the package arrives prior to your arrival at the hotel, call the hotel to confirm the arrival of your package. Often packages are lost inside a hotel. Do not use the U.S. mail due to an insufficient tracking system and lack of assurance of on-time delivery.

The expert fact witness should arrive early at court to assist in exhibit arrangement in the courtroom. Sitting in the jury box and witness chair before anyone arrives, if possible, is recommended in order to help the expert fact witness become familiar with the courtroom's layout. In the witness chair, note shelf space, microphone, and distance between the attorney and the jury. If the expert fact witness uses exhibits mounted on Foamcor® board, each exhibit should be placed on the easel and viewed from several jurors' chairs to test readability. The expert fact witness should verify delivery and setup of all equipment and safety of cords and wires.

Trial Testimony

A motion in limine may be made at the trial's start to prevent the expert fact witness from testifying. If the expert is accepted as qualified, the judge may either restrict testimony to strict and narrow boundaries or extend liberal boundaries for testimony. It is important to understand and abide by any limits imposed by the court. The goal is to present the facts of the medical record clearly and accurately.

At trial, the expert fact witness may testify after the liability issues have been presented. The expert fact witness may be the first of the damage witnesses. This testimony lays the foundation for other healthcare professionals. The expert fact witness may be the only person who has read the medical records completely. After review of the nursing expert fact witness's report, treating physicians may be prepared by the attorney to highlight specific areas or events in the medical record. All experts must understand their specific roles in the outline of the medical testimony. For example, in a complicated trauma case, the nurse defines and explains the anatomy of the injured areas, management of the patient in traction, the amount and frequency of pain medication, and weekly physical therapies. The trauma surgeon then explains the complicated surgery, elaborating on complications, causes, treatment, and long-lasting disabilities.

The expert fact witness serves to educate the court about the technical facts, issues, and events of the medical record. The first few minutes on the stand are critical to establishing rapport with the jury. As the attorney asks questions, the expert fact witness should be attentive. Eye contact with each juror is vital. Testimony under oath requires accurate reporting without embellishment or deletion. Meticulous, accurate, and complete testimony is difficult for the defense to discredit.

The expert fact witness should listen carefully to each question, answering only the question asked. However, some attorneys prefer a free flow of information as the expert teaches the jury.

Descriptions of the timeline of events of the hospitalization or the patient's pain and suffering should be animated without boring the jury with too much detail. Exhibits and demonstrative evidence can keep the jury interested, as long as they can see demonstrations clearly. Everyday analogies, visual aids, and lay terminology are essential, with the main points of the case always in mind.

Presentation skills are critical. Remember the audience is made of jurors, who are laypeople. The presentation should be totally geared toward nonmedical people's level of understanding. In complex cases with a large volume of information to present, begin with an overview of the areas to be presented. Proceed to details, and finish with a summary. The information should flow logically from one topic to the next. Throughout the presentation, intersperse the various types of medium. Medium types can include verbal explanation, timelines, graphs, charts, photographs, anatomical exhibits, and PowerPoint® presentations. Changing the method of presentation throughout your discussion assists in holding the interest of the jurors and increases the likelihood of them remembering the information.

Rapport development is also a key part of presenting. Videotaping your presentation prior to deposition and trial assists in perfecting how you are perceived. Nurses provide education to patients and their family members. These teaching and education skills are expanded when presenting to a group. Repetition of practice sessions assists in more comfort with the presentation under pressure and the potentially changing environment at trial.

The opposing attorney may cross-examine the expert fact witness. In contrast to the extensive cross-examination that the liability nurse expert has come to expect, this cross-examination may be brief. Accurate introduction of medical record evidence and clear explanations of treatment and medical terminology leave little room for questions. The opposing attorney may try to discredit or diminish the effectiveness of testimony by asking detailed questions regarding the expert's professional background to imply that the expert fact witness may not be qualified. The expert fact witness's pretrial preparation should include review of relevant clinical practice experience and professional positions to enhance such testimony.

Summary

LNCs who undertake to present medical record evidence testimony at trial should have an extensive background in clinical practice and teaching experience. While physicians tend to concentrate on explanations of specific medical treatments and procedures, LNCs are more likely to present a broader, more comprehensive view of the events described in the medical records to improve the court's understanding of the case.

Serving as an expert fact witness may be rewarding for nurses because it is not associated with the more adversarial, confrontational nature of nursing malpractice testimony. The testifying nurse provides the jury with an understanding of the pertinent issues in an organized, systematic, and memorable format. Opportunities for nurses to testify as expert fact witnesses are expanding as attorneys and judges are educated about financial, educational, and strategic advantages of this role.

References

Bogart, J., & Beerman, J. (1995). Expert fact witness: A testifying role for the legal nurse consultant. *Journal of Legal Nurse Consulting, 6*(4), 2–8.

http://www.law.cornell.edu/rules/fre/rules.htm#Rule702
http://www.law.cornell.edu/rules/fre/rules.htm#Rule1006
Iyer, P., Appelbaum, S., & Parisi, J. (2003). Trial exhibits: Types and uses in demonstrative evidence. In P. Iyer (Ed.), *Medical legal aspects of pain and suffering*. Tucson, AZ: Lawyers and Judges Publishing Company.

Additional Reading

Iyer, P., Bogart, J., & Beerman, J. (1996). The legal process: A view from the expert witness's hot seat. *NeuroRehabilitation*, *7*(137), 137–149.

Test Questions

1. Which of the following statements is NOT true?
   A. A judge may prevent a nurse from testifying as an expert fact witness
   B. The expert fact witness presents opinions about the standard of care
   C. A nurse who is not named as a defendant in a case may be a fact witness
   D. An attorney may resist using a nurse to explain medical records

2. Which of the following statements is true?
   A. Defense attorneys commonly hire an expert fact witness to explain the patient's pain and suffering
   B. The term "expert fact witness" is widely understood by attorneys
   C. The use of expert witnesses at any academic level of training may be challenged by opposing counsel
   D. Use of treating professionals to testify provides the same benefits as using an expert fact witness

3. Which of the following statements is NOT true?
   A. The expert witness may write notes on medical records
   B. The physician is the appropriate expert to testify about permanency of injuries
   C. The expert fact witness's report may contain trial-appropriate exhibits
   D. The expert fact witness is rarely deposed

4. Which of the following statements is true?
   A. Few trials require demonstrative aids.
   B. Memorizing testimony is an effective way to prepare for testimony
   C. Knowledge of patient education principles is useful when testifying as an expert fact witness
   D. The expert fact witness should proofread demonstrative evidence thoroughly when arriving at the witness box

5. Which is the most essential way to prepare for the role of the expert fact witness?
   A. Develop strong written and oral communication skills
   B. Prepare a concise marketing package
   C. Locate attorneys who handle personal injury cases
   D. Visit local hospitals to view medical equipment

Answers: 1. B, 2. C, 3. A, 4. C, 5. A

Appendix 2.1: Motion in Limine Regarding the Expert Fact Witness's Role

Opening Statement by Paul Pierson, Esq., Plaintiff Attorney

Ladies and gentlemen of the jury, thank you for your attention. The evidence will show that my client, Lisa Miller, was 34 years old on a beautiful day in June in 1997. Lisa was a star athlete who loved to participate in triathlons during her free time. She prided herself on her strength and fitness. Lisa worked at a children's center taking care of emotionally disturbed kids. Her job involved being on her feet all day, bending and lifting. She had to be able to respond quickly if the children needed holding or to prevent them from hurting each other.

Lisa is an only child. After going to college, Lisa moved into her own home, a mobile home. She was proud of her independence. Although she had a loving relationship with her parents, she enjoyed having a place of her own.

On June 10, 1997, Lisa was riding her bike on the shoulder of a country road. The evidence will show that the bus left the travel portion of the road surface. Lisa was hit from behind by a 30,000-pound bus that was traveling at 55 miles per hour. She was thrown 15 feet through the air and landed in a nearby field. The medical evidence that we will present will show that Lisa suffered devastating injuries to her pelvis, hip, and knee. She had multiple other broken bones. She underwent months of rehabilitation and physical therapy. You will hear testimony from Lisa that she was forced to move back with her parents when she first got out of the rehabilitation hospital. She had to give up her independence and become dependent on her parents for her most basic needs. She was unable to walk without the assistance of a walker, and then a cane. It took months before she was able to drive again and almost a year before she was able to get back on a bike.

The evidence will show that the bus driver, Richard Felton, did not see Lisa before he hit her. He has admitted that he was at fault. We are here to decide how Lisa should be compensated for the loss of her health, for her months of treatment, and for her permanent pain and limitations in her knee. Lisa would love to turn the clock back and have her fitness again. She would give anything to be able to alter the events and relive that day, and not be on that road at the time Richard Felton was driving down the road. However, Lisa cannot change what happened. She cannot turn back the clock.

You will hear her orthopedist, a world-famous doctor, testify that Lisa's injuries will get worse as she ages. She already has signs of posttraumatic arthritis, and can expect to have prosthetic knees and hips in the future. You will hear that Lisa had $125,000 in medical bills and had a wage loss of between $300,000 and $1.2 million. You will hear that she lost out on a promotion at work, and that there are limitations to what she can do now.

You have been asked to participate in helping Lisa resolve this accident. Lisa does not want your sympathy. You are the only people in the world who will hear the full story of what happened to Lisa after the accident. You are the only people who are in a position to compensate Lisa for what she has lost. This is Lisa's only chance to obtain compensation for her injuries. She won't be able to come back in 15 years when she requires her total knee replacement or her total hip surgeries. This case is about pain and suffering. It is about the destruction of bones by a bus. It is about months and years of pain. This case is simply entitled Bus versus Bike. When a bus and a bike collide, the person on the bike always loses.

At the end of our testimony, we will ask you to make a decision about how Lisa will be compensated for her devastating injuries. It is my hope that you will be fair and generous in your decision-making. My client is entitled to recover for pain and suffering, embarrassment and humiliation, for her medical costs and lost income, and for everything else that she endured as a proximate result of the bus striking her.

Opening Statement by Diane Dunne, Esq., Defense Attorney

Ladies and gentlemen of the jury, I represent the bus driver. We are here today because of an unfortunate accident. Accidents are just that—accidents. My client did not get up that morning saying to himself, "Who can I hit today?" The very unfortunate accident was our fault. We admit that. We are here to decide what to do about Lisa. You will hear testimony that Lisa has made an excellent recovery. She rides her bike and drives her car. Lisa is very active today—perhaps more active than many people. She is not in a wheelchair, and she can work. I would ask that you keep that in mind when you complete your job on the jury.

Motion in Limine

Judge: Mr. Pierson, before you call your first witness, I understand that there is a motion to be heard. Jury, you may be excused. When you return to the jury room, remember my earlier instruction that you are not to discuss this case amongst you. Mrs. Dunne, I understand that you have filed a motion in limine to preclude the testimony of Nurse Iyer. You may present your position.

Diane Dunne: Your Honor, the defense objects to the use of Nurse Iyer as an expert in this trial. She was not involved in the plaintiff's treatment in any way. There are no nursing issues involved in this case. There are no claims of medical malpractice in the care of this patient. Since plaintiff intends to call her treating physicians as witnesses, Nurse Iyer's testimony is cumulative of the testimony of her doctors and the plaintiff herself. Nurse Iyer's report, exhibits, and slide show are highly prejudicial and inflammatory, and given the cumulative nature of the report, that prejudice far outweighs any marginal probative value.

Nurse Iyer's background and expertise are strictly in nursing. She lacks any specialized medical education or experience. The practice of professional nursing is defined as "diagnosing and treating human responses to actual or potential health problems through such services as case finding, health teaching, health counseling, and provision of care supportive to or restorative of life and well being, and executing medical regimens as prescribed by a licensed physician or dentist." Nurse Iyer lacks the skill, training, knowledge, or experience to summarize plaintiff's medical records. The medical records consist of medical diagnoses, treatments, and prognoses. A medical doctor, and not a nurse, is competent to provide analysis and summary of medical records. Nurse Iyer cannot provide such a summary. She is merely a nurse. Plaintiff's treating physicians are the appropriate personnel to explain the surgical procedures, diagnoses, and other purely medical details, as distinguished from nursing events. Nurse Iyer's mere familiarity with these matters does not qualify her to provide an appropriate, accurate, and reliable medical summary.

The primary purpose of expert testimony is to assist the trier of fact in understanding complicated matters, not simply to assist one party in winning their case. An examination of Nurse Iyer's report, exhibits, and slide show clearly demonstrates that she anticipates doing nothing more than selectively repeating the medical record without bringing any nursing expertise to bear upon issues pertinent to the fact-finder. Nowhere in the report does Nurse Iyer comment upon plaintiff's nursing regimen or any nursing-care-related issues. Plaintiff is perfectly capable of testifying about her course of treatment and symptoms.

Finally, Nurse Iyer's report and slide show contain photographs of the injuries of Lisa Miller. These photographs are highly prejudicial. Her report contains a diagram of Ms. Miller's fractured hip. This drawing is so rudimentary that it cannot properly be qualified or explained except by its author. Without the exhibit's caption, it is questionable whether anyone would know what it is.

Judge: Counsel, are you finished?

Diane Dunne: Yes, Your Honor.

Judge: Mr. Pierson, you may respond.

Paul Pierson: My esteemed adversary argued earlier that Nurse Iyer was not qualified to summarize medical records. As Ms. Dunne herself noted, the practice of nursing includes health teaching and the provision of care supportive to or restorative of life and well-being, and executing medical regimens as prescribed by a licensed physician. In order for Nurse Iyer to function as a nurse, she must be able to interpret and analyze medical records. Part of the role of the registered nurse is to be able to use and explain equipment such as Foley catheters, Hoyer lifts, Rotorest beds, nasogastric tubes, and the other equipment that is explained in her report. Patient education is a basic function of all nurses. Nurse Iyer will be applying her expertise in patient education to help the jury understand the medical and nursing details of Lisa Miller's care.

Nurse Iyer's testimony is permitted under Rule 702. It states: "If scientific, technical, or other specialized knowledge will assist the trier of fact to understand the evidence or to determine a fact in issue, a witness qualified as an expert by knowledge, skill, experience, training, or education may testify thereto in the form of an opinion or otherwise." As a registered nurse with 30 years of experience, Nurse Iyer has specialized knowledge beyond that possessed by the jury. She has expertise in understanding and interpreting medical records.

Your Honor, my adversary has argued that nowhere in Nurse Iyer's report does she comment on nursing-care-related issues. As you will note from reviewing her report, she comments on several nursing-care-related issues, including the symptoms my client experienced after she was run down by the bus driven by Mr. Felton.

Judge: Now, Mr. Pierson, let's stick to the arguments. Save the dramatics for the jury.

Paul Pierson: I'm sorry, Your Honor. Nurse Iyer's report describes the many sources of discomfort my client experienced, her difficulty eating, her emotional distress, her dependence on others, just to name a few. These are all issues that nurses are educated to treat as part of their role in providing care to patients such as my client. Further, my adversary has argued that my client, Lisa Miller, is capable of testifying about her medical treatment and symptoms. My client was sedated for part of her admission, although capable of feeling and reacting to her medical treatment. She lacks the specialized knowledge and training that Nurse Iyer has, and is unable to explain to the jury why certain treatments were performed on her. Nurse Iyer has the educational background to be able to explain the drawing of Miss Miller's fractured hip, one that my adversary objected to as rudimentary. Clearly Nurse Iyer was able to understand it, when my adversary could not! This is exactly why the jury needs Nurse Iyer to help them understand what happened to my client. It is unclear how the defense can assert that Ms. Iyer serves no useful purpose whatsoever when, in fact, she has just assisted the defense counsel to understand the nature of Ms. Miller's pelvic fractures.

Further, the defense has had five months to obtain a counter expert, and they have no one. There is not a single defense expert who in any way questions the accuracy, appropriateness, or reliability of the medical information in Ms. Iyer's report. The defense's orthopedic surgeon reviewed Ms. Iyer's report as part of his medical opinion. He does not, in any manner, criticize her report. I'd like to stress that the defense argues that the plaintiff can testify to her course of medical treatment. My client, who had just been struck by a 30,000-pound bus going 55 miles per hour, was in no condition to even think! In a case such as this, where the plaintiff was in the hospital for three weeks, there would be testimony from at least 25–30 different health care professionals, including doctors, nurses, and therapists, to accurately convey that which Ms. Iyer is conveying in the course of approximately one hour's worth of testimony. To request that photographs of the plaintiff's injuries not be utilized at the time of the trial under the guise that they are prejudicial is simply wrong. In fact, it would be prejudicial to the plaintiff to not be able to accurately display the full extent of her injuries to the jury. These are simply photographs of bruises. Simply because the bruises may be a foot in circumference does not make them more prejudicial to the defense.

I would also cite Rule of Evidence 1006, which states that the "contents of voluminous writings, recordings, or photographs which cannot conveniently be examined in court may be presented in the form of a chart, summary, or calculation." Nurse Iyer's report and testimony will assist the jury in understanding my client's voluminous medical records.

Judge:	Are you finished?
Paul Pierson:	Yes, Your Honor.
Judge:	Mrs. Dunne, do you have anything further?
Diane Dunne:	Yes, if the court please. I want to add that Nurse Iyer continually states her personal interpretation of plaintiff's medical treatments. She frequently comments on plaintiff's injuries, using such terms as "large amounts of bruising," "extensive bruising," "fortunately did not disrupt her elbow joint," "maximum assistance," "moderate assistance," and "minimal assistance." The subjective nature of Nurse Iyer's characterization of plaintiff's injuries demonstrates that the sole purpose of this testimony is to excite the passions of the jury rather than to provide an accurate, brief, and objective summary of the medical record, which is too voluminous for the jury to otherwise comprehend.
Judge:	Are you now finished?
Diane Dunne:	Yes, Your Honor.
Judge:	Counsel, any response?
Paul Pierson:	Yes, Your Honor. The comments that my esteemed colleague has just cited are taken directly from the medical records of my client. The terms are not Nurse Iyer's but those of the doctors, nurses, and therapists who attended my client. Why, if Mrs. Dunne would like to see, I can point out each term and where it is located in the medical record.
Judge:	That will not be necessary, Mr. Pierson. I am satisfied that Nurse Iyer has performed a thorough review of the medical record. I agree that she possesses specialized skill, knowledge, experience, and training well beyond that of the average

layperson. She is familiar with medical terminology and has worked with medical records in the course of her duties as a nurse. She has taken direction from medical professionals and implemented instructions and orders. I do not wish to spend excessive court time bringing in a parade of doctors and nurses to testify about the treatment they rendered to the plaintiff.

Furthermore, I agree that the medical records are voluminous in this case and filled with symbols, abbreviations, and terms not understood by the average layperson. I find that the medical records are difficult to interpret without Nurse Iyer's testimony. I do not believe that Lisa Miller's doctors are prepared to render such detailed and extensive testimony as Nurse Iyer will in this case. I find that the Pennsylvania Rules of Evidence permit this type of witness to testify. Further, I do not find the photographs of the plaintiff to be prejudicial. The images of normal anatomy are also acceptable, as they are intended to provide the jury with an understanding of the issues in this case. Her testimony is permitted, and I will allow the jury to hear her. Further, I will allow the jury to see the photographs of the plaintiff that are part of the slide presentation. Anything further, Mrs. Dunne?

Diane Dunne: Judge, Nurse Iyer's report does not constitute evidence in this case. We respectfully ask the court to prohibit Nurse Iyer's report from being entered into evidence or being placed with the jury while they deliberate.

Judge: I disagree. Nurse Iyer may testify, and her report will be placed into evidence. Mr. Pierson, you may call Nurse Iyer to the stand.

Chapter 3

The Independent LNC

Cathy Weitzel, MSN, ARNP

First Edition
Sue Barnes, MSN, MSHCA, RN; Julie Bogart; Judith L. Bragdon; Karen Cepero; Patricia Costantini, MEd, RN, LNCC; Doug Davis, BSN, RN, DABFN; Jill Holmes; Doreen James Wise, EdD, MSN, RN; Adrienne Randle Bond, JD, BA; Paula Schenck, BSN, BS, RN; Suzanne Schutze; Kathleen Spiegel; and Adella Toepel Getsch, BSN, RN, LNCC

Second Edition
Roxanne Bush, MHSA, BSN, BA, RN; Deborah D. D'Andrea, BSN, RN; Nancy R. Ellington, BS, RN, LNCC; Doreen James Wise, EdD, MSN, RN; Geraldine B. Johnson, BSN, RN, LNCC; Betty Joos, MED, BSN, RN; Jo Anne Kuc, BSN, RN, LNCC; Rosie Oldham, BS, RN, LNCC; Adrienne Randle Bond, JD, BA; and Paula Windler, MS, RN, LNCC

Contents

Objectives

- Recognize the benefits of being an independent LNC
- Differentiate between work products offered to attorney clients
- Identify essential equipment needed to start an independent LNC business

Guidelines for Starting an Independent LNC Practice

For many individuals, starting a business is the culmination of a life's dream. Years of education and experience are brought to bear on what many regard as the ultimate financial freedom: the right to plan and benefit from the direct results of your own hard work. Nurses that traditionally have been employees of large corporations are understandably enticed by the concept of working for themselves. For some there is the hope of financial success; others see starting a business as the opportunity to achieve a higher standard of patient care that is unhampered by the political realities of today's corporate health systems. Additionally, more nursing programs are including curricula that focus on systems theory, business, management, and leadership concepts.

It is important to consider a few personal attributes necessary to make a start-up business successful: realistic self-confidence, a positive mental attitude, internal drive, self-discipline, and perseverance to follow through on problems or plans. The experienced nurse uses critical thinking ability to determine which data are meaningful and which take priority in the legal arena. Legal nurse consultants (LNCs) continue to use the nursing process to incorporate their experience and knowledge into the attorney's work product. The ability to manage finances responsibly and tolerate times when cash flow may be less than projected is also crucial. LNCs are most beneficial to attorneys when they make every effort to stay informed of current nursing and medical issues that pertain to healthcare practice. This includes maintaining continuing education credits and any relevant national certifications. Business-savvy LNCs remember that doing more than what is expected helps form a lasting impression of one's skill and work product.

The infancy stage of any business requires the owner to be an entrepreneur, manager, and work producer. The entrepreneur produces the creative ideas for marketing and growing one's business. The manager sets goals and makes sure the new ideas and services "happen." The worker bee must produce work acceptable to the client, often adapting to changing client needs. The art of an independent LNC's business is identifying products and services that are sought by the marketplace. To some degree, the independent LNC must be able to tolerate uncertainty and anxiety. Careful self-analysis of one's strengths and weaknesses helps guide the development of a business plan, enabling the LNC to make a long-term commitment to the clients and the business.

During the development phase, defining business goals and principles through a mission or vision statement helps to move the LNC forward. By focusing on consistent, quality work, the vision statement can be a strong marketing tool that sets one's practice apart from others.

Professional Ethics and the Independent LNC

The American Nurses Association Code of Ethics requires LNCs to maintain the highest standards of personal conduct that reflect honorably on the nursing profession. Accurate information about one's education and experience should always be provided. Assignments should only be accepted when the LNC is qualified and has sufficient time to complete it. As with the nursing/medical profession, strict patient and client confidentiality is paramount. Any appearance of a conflict of interest must be recognized and disclosed. A conflict of interest refers to a situation where the LNC has information that could potentially cause harm, injury, or prejudice to the client. Performing work that might represent a conflict of interest can put the LNC at risk for legal action. It is never appropriate for an LNC or expert to work on a contingency basis. In many states, statutes ban this arrangement. The LNC should be familiar with formal documents within the nursing profession, such as the American Nurses' Association Code of Ethics. Many professional organizations and nursing specialties publish ethical guidelines for practice. The American Association of Legal Nurse Consultants (AALNC) has developed a Code of Ethics and Conduct for the specialty practice of the LNC. In addition, the American Bar Association's (ABA) Canons of Ethics for attorneys can be found in the publication ABA Compendium of Professional Responsibility. These rules and standards can provide information regarding ethical issues in the legal arena. Websites for these valuable resources are included at the end of this chapter.

Role and Function

LNCs provide a variety of services to attorneys, facilities, organizations, and employers. Some of the specific services that can be provided by the independent LNC include

- Nursing and medical–legal research
- Reviewing medical records, including lab results and autopsy reports
- Determining the nursing standard of care issues
- Preparing affidavits
- Analyzing records for product liability cases
- Reviewing depositions of family members, physicians, and nursing and ancillary staff (OT, PT, nutritionist, etc.)
- Reviewing staff use of standardized psychiatric or other forms
- Reviewing standards of care regarding restraint application and use
- Reviewing defense exhibits
- Developing contracts
- Reviewing facility policy and procedures
- Preparing chronological chart summaries
- Providing consultation and education on the nursing process and standards of care
- Providing definition of nursing and medical terminology
- Reviewing and evaluating nursing assessments
- Testifying as expert witnesses

The specialty practice of legal nurse consulting grows daily. The above services will be expected to expand as the continued development of the practice grows. Through networking and attendance at educational conferences, LNCs learn novel ways of pushing the envelope and developing new business lines to their clients.

Networking for the LNC

A key component in business development requires the LNC to develop a keen networking ability. Networking is considered a form of marketing, involving building and developing professional relationships that are crucial to any successful business. As nurses, LNCs already use interpersonal and social skills to build on their knowledge. This is evident through mentors or other professionals who provide supervision to the LNC. Networking provides an opportunity for the education of others regarding the LNC's professional practice. Examples of networking include attending local and community business meetings, attending state bar association meetings, and membership in specialty nursing organizations. In addition to word-of-mouth advertising, membership in a state bar association may allow the LNC to place classified ads at little to no cost in monthly newsletters.

Multiple other strategies exist for increasing networking experience and exposure. For the LNC working in a hospital setting, volunteering to be involved in risk management or utilization review committees may provide a unique perspective on medical–legal issues in acute care. Offering to help develop or update policy and procedure manuals provides exposure to evidence-based practice guidelines. Becoming actively involved in a facility's preparation for Joint Commission accreditation or regulatory inspection provides the opportunity to educate other nurses about defensive documentation. These activities serve to enhance the LNC's CV and make him or her more marketable.

Honing Your Marketing Package

As important as an LNC's work product and networking skills is the presentation of a cohesive, professional company image. Investing in professionally prepared business cards and stationery is essential. After meeting a prospective client, these materials are all that may be left behind through which the LNC can be remembered. Use of a high-quality laser printer for printing and mailing statements and any additional correspondence is recommended.

With increased experience, the LNC may locate opportunities of sharing expertise at a function that targets a specific clientele. For example, state bar associations may welcome a presentation on product liability or nursing home litigation. This face-to-face contact acquaints potential clients with the services offered by an LNC and how these services can benefit the attorney's practice. Although public speaking can initially be anxiety-provoking, an organized presentation on a familiar topic can go a long way toward enhancing one's marketability. In preparation for such a presentation, developing an outline and then audiotaping the presentation of the topic helps in organizing the material and provides a self-critique prior to a formal presentation.

Writing a professional journal article is another effective way for LNCs to market their services. Reading data and published literature on the subject of interest is the recommended initial step. A letter of inquiry to a nursing journal can help determine a specific approach to writing such an article. An ever-growing demand for current articles about practice issues makes writing for publication a worthwhile endeavor.

Educating the public and potential clients about the LNC's role is another effective marketing strategy. In coastal areas of the country, LNCs are utilized more extensively than in other areas such as the Midwest. Research about these geographic areas along with how LNCs are specifically utilized there can be incorporated into a marketing strategy. As the LNC's practice grows, a list of services can be included along with a formal letter of introduction to potential clients (e.g., in a mass mailing). Maintaining a current resume or CV is helpful in providing quick responses to inquiries about one's qualifications.

Analysis of business problems and seeking solutions maximize the opportunity for success. Creating an LNC business from scratch, and then succeeding at it, requires serious motivation and perseverance. The core elements of any successful entrepreneurship include (1) developing a strategic business plan, (2) knowing individual business goals and philosophy, and (3) seeking professional consultation in legal, financial, accounting, and liability issues.

Imperative to starting any new business is the documentation of a business plan (refer to Wichita State University Small Business Development Center, 2008). The business plan is similar to a nursing care plan in that it drives the business decision-making process and orchestrates a systematic, goal-oriented approach. Clear articulation of business goals makes a significant difference in the outcome of business efforts.

The main components of a business plan include the executive summary, description of business, market analysis, marketing strategy and implementation, human resources, and an appendix that includes personal resumes, personal financial statements, any letters of intent, copies of important documents, etc. Remember that a business plan is essentially a road map for the development of a new company.

Many resources are available to help the business owner with strategic planning and developing the actual business plan. Creative use of these resources enhances your vision for the business. There are resources in local communities that give direction and mentoring at little or no charge. These include local chambers of commerce, state and community college adult education programs, and local small business administration agencies. The U.S. Small Business Administration (SBA) offers assistance in determining requirements for obtaining government loans or grant funding. Although it involves completion of several forms and has strict guidelines, the SBA is an invaluable resource. The SBA offers educational programs and counseling on how to obtain a business loan or navigate other business-related issues. The SBA also supports an organization, Service Corp of Retired Executives (SCORE), which provides one-to-one consultation and small group sessions on business development and management. Local chambers of commerce have information about obtaining funding other than from government sources. Membership in local or national organizations of business owners is another resource that helps build and structure a personal business framework.

Home Office Essentials

Getting organized and staying organized are key ingredients for the successful operation of any business, but especially important in the paper-rich environment of the LNC. Dedicated workspace separate from living quarters is essential, allowing the LNC to focus completely on the task at hand without interruption, and shifting the mental frame to one of work versus play or doing household chores. Workspace must ensure privacy and allow uninterrupted time for long intervals. Because client work products are highly confidential, Health Insurance Portability and Accountability Act (HIPAA) guidelines must be followed, necessitating a secure home office. The need for adequate desk and file space should also be considered.

Dependable high-speed Internet access is imperative. A separate, established, and secure high-speed Internet connection expedites day-to-day business needs. Having wireless access is ideal for promoting the ability to move around one's home or office. A laptop computer provides Internet access and has several convenient features compared with a traditional PC. Always purchase and install antivirus protection software and take steps to ensure privacy.

The independent LNC also needs reliable phone access to take calls and discuss cases, sometimes for long periods. Because cellular phones charge for minutes used (depending on the plan and billing cycle), establishing a dedicated landline should be considered. All receipts for purchases and even bills for cell phone use or long-distance minutes should be retained because home office necessities are tax deductible. Highlight phone numbers and minutes that were used for business purposes and keep track of the time spent on the Internet doing work, saving the monthly bills for high-speed Internet service. Each of these expenses (or a portion) can be subtracted from annual gross income, providing a reduction in tax owed.

A procedure manual kept in a hardbound notebook, on a computer disk, or on a flash drive can include any form letters, blank releases of information, templates for affidavits or other legal documents, examples of marketing letters, fee schedule/statements for reimbursement, and a list of valuable Internet websites. Include in the notebook a list of important names, addresses, and phone numbers. Keeping this available at hand's reach eliminates searching when a new client request expedited information.

Many LNCs start their business as sole proprietors and often do not seek the help of a legal professional. Although this type of business may not require a legal professional, it does require a thorough knowledge of principles in meeting state and local requirements as well as evaluation of liability issues. The LNC will want to consider both business insurance and errors and omissions insurance. The AALNC has information on its website regarding professional negligence insurance (www.allnc.org). As independent LNC practice continues to grow and change, it will be necessary to periodically reassess the legal needs of the business entity.

Working as an Independent LNC: What it Means to be a Sole Proprietor

Most independent LNCs start as sole proprietors. This means that the individual LNC is in his or her own business and has no separate legal identity. The purpose of forming a business entity is to separate personal from business assets. The LNC is the only owner and likely will be the only employee. To undertake this approach, the LNC files a "DBA" or "doing business as" or assumed-name certificate. That name is then registered in the specific county, assuring the LNC of being the only business entity with that name. For example, the person Florence N. Gale could do business as "LNC Enterprises." Personal tax returns report the LNC owner's annual income generated from all professional activities, including the sole proprietorship. For legal purposes, the LNC is the responsible individual and personal assets are not protected legally as separate from the business. Therefore, the main disadvantage to being a sole proprietor is that the LNC's personal assets are unprotected in respect to any potential future liability issues.

In contrast, several LNCs have started to incorporate their business. Corporations are relatively easy to form and operate [absent permission from the Internal Revenue Service (IRS) to the contrary] and are taxed separately from the individual owner. This means that the owner faces double taxation on income earned in the corporation, once on the corporate level and again as an individual "shareholder." However, it is possible to avoid the double taxation through a federal tax election as a subchapter S corporation. This type of corporation is a regular corporation under state law that qualifies and affirmatively files a written election to be taxed similarly to a partnership. The S corporation has strict qualifying requirements about which an attorney can advise. Corporations are generally more cost-effective because the cost of filing fees is less and standardization of forms for incorporation lowers the setup costs. Because of standardization, business owners are usually more familiar with standard day-to-day operations that lower the cost basis. For a Limited Liability Corporation (LLC), documents are essentially the same but bear different names and serve slightly different functions. Although the forms are similar, they are not dictated by state statute and take into account tax matters applicable to partnerships (versus corporations). To choose which of these entities is best means weighing the risks and benefits in relation to projected business needs. In addition, there is a wealth of information about setting up a legal business entity available in community law libraries and on reputable Internet websites.

Professional Organizations

The independent LNC will want to consider which professional organizations would most benefit continuing professional and business development. As discussed earlier, there are a number of local resources available to the LNC for business development. Leading groups such as Business Network International (http://www.bni.com/) provide opportunities for the LNC to develop business relationships in the local community. The U.S. Chamber of Commerce (http://www.uschamber.com) has a wealth of information regarding local events and opportunities for small business owners. The AALNC has information regarding resources for networking both in person and online. Joining AALNC allows the LNC to gain information from leaders in the specialty practice and provides an opportunity to market the LNC's business through the *LNC Locator*.

Billing

One of the hardest things new LNCs must struggle with is billing and collections. In a traditional nursing role, someone else is responsible for billing for services. A clearly defined fee schedule should be developed and be available for potential clients upon request. The fee schedule includes, the date fees were implemented or updated, the amount in dollars for services billed hourly, and the specific services offered. Written documentation of time spent working on a case should be maintained, including time spent on phone calls and correspondence. Statements for services provided should be mailed to the client monthly, at either the first or the last of the month. Payment expectations are included in the fee schedule as well, including a late fee percentage if invoices are not paid within a 30-day period.

Some LNCs charge a higher hourly rate for being deposed as expert witnesses or for court appearances. It is traditional for consultants, including LNCs, to ask for a fee deposit or retainer fee prior to commencing work on a case. An example of a fee schedule for services is included in the appendix of this chapter.

Summary

LNCs wishing to start an independent LNC practice would be wise to consider all aspects of business development and maintenance. Spending time on the front end of development in generating a business plan, identifying services to be provided, and looking at the market for potential clients will eliminate surprises and delays in the business launch. Being independent is exciting and exhilarating, and many LNCs choose this option for their practice with great success.

Additional Readings

Berg-Pugatch, M. (2008). Federal tort claims and military medical malpractice. *Journal of Legal Nurse Consulting*, *19*(2), 3–6.

Egan, C., McCracken, C., & Zorn, E. (2008). LNCExchange: a networking and educational forum for LNCs. *Journal of Legal Nurse Consulting*, *19*(3), 17–20.

Ellington, N., Johnson, G., & Joos, B. (2003). Successful marketing for the legal nurse consultant. In P. W. Iyer (Ed.), *Legal nurse consulting: Principles and practice* (chap. 44, 10, 2nd ed., p. 231). Sautee, GA: Sky Lake Publishing.

Fiesta, J. (1994). Failing to act like a professional. *Nursing Management*, *25*(7), 15–17.

Joos, B. (2000). *Marketing for the legal nurse consultant: A guide to getting all the clients you can handle using proven, low cost strategies*. Sautee, GA: Sky Lake Publishing.

Oldham, R., Windler, P., & Bush, R. (2003). Growing a business. In P. W. Iyer (Ed.), *Legal nurse consulting: Principles and practice* (chap. 45, 2nd ed.). London: CRC Press, Taylor and Francis.

Wichita State University Small Business Development Center. (2008, Summer). Why write a business plan? Retrieved from WSU SBA website.

Test Questions

1. Which of the following is the most important asset the independent LNC possesses?
   A. Self-discipline
   B. Critical thinking skills
   C. Ability to communicate effectively
   D. Excellent writing and research skills

2. Which of the following initially is key to business success for the independent LNC?
   A. Products and services offered
   B. Self-analysis of skills
   C. A business plan with goals
   D. Professional contacts

3. Which of the following represents the independent LNC's awareness of ethics?
   A. Referral of cases outside the LNC's area of expertise
   B. Commenting negatively in a report regarding others' reputations
   C. Billing independently for work while under subcontract to others
   D. Accepting work while recognizing a conflict of interest

4. Which of the following would be *excluded* from the role of the independent LNC?
   A. Medical chronology and research
   B. Expert testimony at deposition and trial
   C. Assisting the attorney in preparation of clients for testimony
   D. Definitively determining the merits of cases for the attorney

5. Which of the following are logistical requirements for the independent LNC? (*Choose all that apply*)
   A. Preparing a secure location for confidential information
   B. Developing a system for capturing business expenses
   C. Maintaining current clinical experience
   D. Following a structured marketing plan

Answers: 1. B, 2. C, 3. A, 4. D, 5. A, B, D

Appendix

Fee Schedule Template

Your name and credentials

Mailing address

Phone number

Fax number

E-mail address

Fee Schedule as of 1/01/2009

All services are billed at $____ per hour. These include, but are not limited to, the following:

- ◼ Review of medical records, summaries, depositions, reports, and abstracts/time lines
- ◼ Preparation of medical/nursing summaries or reports of the above
- ◼ Assisting with discovery, interpreting medical or nursing issues
- ◼ Medical research
- ◼ Drafting panel submissions, replies, and settlement brochure
- ◼ Serving as a nurse expert and testifying at trial
- ◼ Preparation of affidavits
- ◼ The cost of obtaining medical articles is dependent on the length of the article

Payment

Unless previously agreed to, all work is done on a retainer basis of $____. Invoices not paid within 30 days are subject to a ____% late fee.

Chapter 4

Legal Nurse Consultant Practice within a Law Firm

Elizabeth K. Zorn, BSN, RN, LNCC and Mary Lanz, RN, LNCC

First Edition
Phyllis ZaiKaner Miller, RN

Second Edition
Betsy Isherwood Katz, BSN, RN, LNCC and
Phyllis ZaiKaner Miller, RN

Contents

Objectives

- To describe the variable structure of law firms, types of legal services provided, management, and task delegation
- To describe the possible personnel in a law firm and their roles in carrying out the mission and work of the firm
- To describe the variable culture and politics of law firms as they relate to the role of an in-house legal nurse consultant
- To explain by example the fees, costs, and productivity measurements in plaintiff and defense firms and how they impact the role of the in-house LNC
- To identify in detail the role of the in-house LNC in the delivery of high-quality legal services at defense and plaintiff firms
- To identify the essential skills and personality traits of successful in-house LNCs
- To identify the key practice and ethical issues impacting in-house LNCs
- To discuss compensation and benefits packages for in-house LNCs

Introduction

The role of a legal nurse consultant (LNC) in a law firm may vary considerably, depending on the location and size of the firm, the nature of the work that is done, whether the firm does primarily defense or plaintiff work, whether the firm has had prior experience working with an LNC, and the extent to which a particular legal community uses and values LNCs. In most areas of the country that utilize LNCs, the responsibilities of the LNC in a law firm have evolved significantly over the past 20–25 years. Now, most LNCs not only participate in the organization, review, and summary of medical records, but also play an integral role in more complex and sophisticated activities, such as the analysis of liability in medical malpractice cases, determination of proximate cause, assessment of damages, case strategy, identification and vetting of medical and nursing experts, and trial preparation. This chapter discusses these roles and provides a general orientation to the law firm environment.

Structure of Law Firm Personnel

The categories of personnel in a law firm depend on the size of the firm. Small firms (fewer than 25 attorneys) typically have partners, associate attorneys, LNCs, paralegals (also known as legal assistants), secretaries, a receptionist, and a bookkeeper. Large firms (75 attorneys or more) typically have an array of additional support staff and services, such as librarians; word processors; private investigators; messengers; process servers; large-volume copying departments; audiovisual personnel; computer technicians; document coders and data entry persons; human resource, payroll, and benefits departments; continuing legal education and special-event coordinators; a business manager; marketing and public-relations staff; and office-supply and kitchen staff. In addition to LNCs, large firms may also have other nonattorney professionals, such as certified public accountants and environmental engineers. Generally speaking, the larger the firm, the more the support persons and services in-house. Many firms, especially small- and medium-sized firms, contract with outside vendors for support services. The purpose of employing ancillary staff is to support attorneys, paralegals, and nonattorney professionals in the delivery of legal services and in the underlying business operation of the firm.

Among lawyers, there are distinctions in rank depending on the size, structure, and economics of the firm. Generally speaking, lawyers are either partners or associates. Partners are more experienced in the practice of law, may have voting rights in the running of the firm depending on how the partnership is structured, and have a monetary compensation formula different from associates. Partners typically have practiced law for at least 8–10 years. Lawyers are invited into the partnership of a given firm once they have proven their worth to the firm. This generally requires bringing in new business and demonstrating legal skill by managing cases effectively. In large firms there may be different levels of partnership, such as senior and junior partners or voting and nonvoting partners. Some partners are recruited from outside the firm if the firm is looking for someone with a particular area of expertise. This is known as a lateral move. Another type of experienced attorney is one who is "of counsel" to a firm. This means that the attorney is associated with the firm, but is not a member of the firm. Examples are a retired attorney who still consults with the firm and an attorney who has a mutual referral relationship with a firm. There may or may not be a business arrangement of some sort between the firm and an "of counsel" attorney.

Associates are nonpartner attorneys. They range in experience from recent law-school graduates to attorneys with 6 or more years of experience on the verge of becoming partners. It is useful to compare associates to medical-school graduates. First-year associates are much like new interns. They are rarely in a position to bring in new business and generally have no prior legal experience, other than possibly summer internships at a law firm during law school or prior work as a paralegal before attending law school. Most new associates spend a large proportion of their time doing legal research. They also work on specific case projects under the close supervision of a more senior associate or partner. Although they may be gradually permitted to take depositions in cases, associates are not often asked to handle trials by themselves until they have gained considerable experience doing depositions, arguing motions before the court, and assisting senior attorneys at trial. New associates in the larger full-service firms may rotate through the different practice groups so as to help them decide which area of the law they wish to pursue. Once they have completed their rotation, they typically become part of one particular practice group, working under the supervision of the partners in that practice group.

With time and experience, associates on a "partner track" move up the ladder toward partnership, just as the medical intern eventually moves to senior resident, fellow, and attending physician. As the associates advance, they have more responsibility for the overall management and outcome of the cases assigned to them. They also have increasing responsibility to engage in direct client contact and to bring in new clients to the firm. The structure of some firms is such that associates may have the option of pursuing a "nonpartner track." An example of this is an associate in a litigation firm who is involved in the preparation of cases for trial, but does not actually try cases in the courtroom, or an associate who is hired to primarily do legal research.

Paralegals work under the supervision of an attorney or nonattorney professional. They typically have a 2- or 4-year college degree and multiple job responsibilities that vary greatly with the particular practice group to which they are assigned and their level of experience. Often their responsibilities deal with organization and review of large numbers of nonmedical and medical documents, entry of case information into a computer database, preparation of draft legal pleadings for the attorney, investigative research, summarizing depositions, interviewing prospective clients with the attorney, preparing exhibits and computerized presentations for trial, sending out correspondence, and organizing files. Some firms even utilize paralegals to do legal research. Many paralegals eventually go on to attend law school. Others become career paralegals, sometimes periodically changing their area of practice or taking on a supervisory role as a paralegal manager or coordinator.

Although historically, nurses who worked in law firms were often called nurse paralegals, it is increasingly common for LNCs to be considered nonattorney professionals, bestowed with the "legal nurse consultant" title and to receive commensurate respect, pay, and benefits. While some larger firms may be more hierarchical than smaller firms in their formal structure and in the distinctions they make between the status of attorneys and nonattorneys, the contributions of the skilled LNC as a valued member of the team are increasingly recognized. Most attorneys who become accustomed to working with experienced LNCs are cognizant of the important role the LNCs play in assisting the attorney to provide high-quality legal services in a cost-effective manner. The LNC has a large body of knowledge about anatomy, physiology, and medical and nursing practice that the attorney may not have. This allows the LNC to function as an educator, especially for less-experienced attorneys.

Delegation

Task delegation in a law firm varies with the size and structure of the firm. Generally, partners delegate tasks to any (nonpartner) employee of the firm. If a partner is the chairperson of a department or practice group, he or she may even delegate responsibilities to another partner in the same practice group. Large firms are also likely to have committees that delegate tasks to all categories of personnel in the firm.

Most firms, regardless of size, have a hierarchical order of task delegation. Typically, a partner or senior associate delegates tasks to those people with whom he or she directly works. For a given case, this would likely include a junior associate, paralegal, LNC, and secretary. Associates delegate work to paralegals, secretaries, and LNCs. LNCs delegate work to paralegals and secretaries. Paralegals delegate tasks to their secretaries. Paralegals and secretaries typically delegate tasks to in-house or outside ancillary support personnel, although anyone else higher in the hierarchy could also do this if appropriate. An effective partner or senior associate responsible for a given case will periodically confer with the team working on the case to make sure that assigned tasks are getting done in a proper and timely manner.

Although task delegation usually follows a predictable order, the nature of work in most law firms is such that during intensely busy times or when an important deadline is looming, roles overlap, the usual hierarchical order is temporarily disbanded, and everyone in the team does whatever he or she can to complete the job. It is not uncommon to see some overlap of tasks between the LNC and a paralegal. For example, in some firms the paralegals organize, review, and summarize the medical records in the simple personal injury cases, while the LNCs focus on the medical malpractice and other complex personal injury cases. Given that the roles of the paralegal and the LNC vary considerably among firms, it is very important that within a particular firm, each member of the litigation team understands the tasks for which they are responsible. The importance of this cannot be overstated. Failure to define each person's role on the litigation team can lead to tasks being done twice, wasting valuable time as the case moves through the system. The alternative, an important task not being done in a timely manner, or not being done at all, can lead to unfavorable court rulings including case dismissal, or sanctions by the court. Thus, some firms develop firm "protocols", which set forth who is responsible for the many tasks that must be done in a litigation firm.

As in all businesses, rank distinctions among the employees and partners of a firm do exist and are generally related to title, longevity, compensation and benefit packages, productivity, and responsibilities within the firm. In a well-functioning law firm, all personnel understand the importance of teamwork and have a common goal of providing quality legal services to their clients. This is most likely to occur in firms that value the role that each person plays in the delivery of client services.

Management of a Law Firm

The management of a law firm has traditionally been a function of the partnership, which votes on all significant personnel and operational decisions at regular partnership meetings. Most firms appoint a managing partner to handle the many administrative tasks that must be dealt with on a day-to-day basis. Typically, the managing partner will set the agenda for the partner meetings and make administrative decisions that do not require a formal vote by the partnership. In smaller firms, the managing partner may also attend to personnel and financial matters. Larger firms may hire a business manager to coordinate the financial operation of the firm. Typically, this person's compensation package is tied to the financial success of the firm during a given year. In addition, larger firms typically have a Human Resources Department that handles benefits and personnel issues. It is very common for firms of all sizes to outsource their payroll activities.

Mission and Work of the Law Firm

The fundamental mission of any law firm is to act in the best interest of its clients in the provision of high-quality, ethical legal services. The type of work done at a law firm depends upon the particular work generated by that firm's clients. The practice of law is as diversified as the practice of medicine. Medium and large firms offer a wide range of legal services, with separate practice groups for different areas of the law. These may include litigation, intellectual-property matters, real-estate transactions, environmental law, estate law, commercial law, bankruptcy law, family law, and employment-discrimination matters, among others. Some firms may have satellite offices in different parts of the state, country, or world. Most firms that hire LNCs either are engaged solely in medical–legal litigation or have a medical–legal litigation practice group.

Typically, litigation firms specialize in either plaintiff or defense work. Plaintiff personal injury firms or practice groups represent individuals who have been injured and wish to commence medical malpractice, personal injury, toxic tort, product liability, workers' compensation, or social security disability claims. Defense firms represent the individuals or entities being sued. For example, in medical malpractice cases, defense firms represent the defendant physician, healthcare facility, nurse, or other healthcare provider (chiropractor, dentist, podiatrist, physician's assistant, nurse practitioner, etc.). Defense firms may also represent physicians or other healthcare providers who are being investigated by a state health department or involved in credentialing disputes with the hospital where they practice. In product liability cases, defense firms represent the manufacturer, distributor, or designer of a particular product, drug, or medical device. In a motor vehicle accident case, the defense represents the individual allegedly at fault for the accident. In toxic tort cases, the defense represents those entities allegedly responsible for environmental contamination, illness, or property damage resulting from exposure to toxic substances.

Most defendants in personal injury actions carry liability insurance, and thus working for the defense usually means being retained by an insurance company to represent the interests of the healthcare provider or other insured. Claim agents at the insurance company assign cases that are in litigation to one of a number of defense firms, monitor the work and billing of the assigned defense firm, and authorize settlement of claims. Some defense firms represent individuals directly, including those involved in criminal matters.

Culture and Politics of the Law Firm

Like most business cultures, law firm culture can vary tremendously from firm to firm. Generally, large established firms are more formal, structured, and hierarchical. In these firms, decisions about pending issues may take a long time due to the need to pass through several layers of approval. The larger the firm, the more likely it is that politics plays a role in the decision-making process. The relationships among partners and employees may be more informal in small firms. For example, it is not unusual for all employees in a small firm to have access to the managing partner when an issue arises. Medium-sized firms may fit anywhere along this continuum. A practice group within a large firm may have its own distinct culture. As in other sectors of the business world, there has been a trend toward less-formal attire in most law firms.

The best way to get a sense of the culture of a particular firm or practice group is to speak with past or current employees of the firm. Information about the culture and politics of a firm can also be obtained through the interview process. Typically, a prospective LNC interviews with one or more partners, associates, and LNCs already employed at the firm. Of particular interest to the LNC is the extent to which the LNC role and work are valued by the partners, associates, and clients. This includes whether LNCs have adequate secretarial support, especially in firms where LNCs have fairly heavy caseloads. Another indication is whether the firm profiles its LNCs on the firm's website and letterhead. LNCs currently employed at the firm are the best source of this information. For LNCs applying for the first LNC position at a firm, developing a new role in the firm can be exciting and very rewarding. It can also be quite challenging, especially if the LNC has not had any prior experience in the legal field. Networking with other nurses who work at law firms is especially important in this situation. A prospective LNC employed by firms with other LNCs derives great benefit from the orientation and ongoing mentoring of other LNCs familiar with the expectations at that firm.

Economics of the Law Firm

For the in-house LNC, a reasonable understanding of the economics of the firm is vital to any understanding of productivity measures. A law firm is a for-profit enterprise that brings in gross annual revenue, out of which overhead expenses, capital improvement expenses, and salaries are paid. The remaining profits are distributed among the partners according to the partnership agreement. The salaries, bonuses, benefits, and hourly rates of employees are determined by the partnership based upon position in the firm, longevity, and performance. LNCs are evaluated by the associates and partners with whom they work. Partners evaluate associate attorneys. All attorneys and nonattorney professionals evaluate their staff, including secretaries and paralegals.

The economics of a law firm varies with its size and whether or not it is primarily a defense firm or plaintiff firm. Large firms have more complicated economic structures than small firms. Defense firms are usually paid on an hourly basis or sometimes have a flat-fee arrangement for certain legal work. Plaintiff firms usually generate income on a contingency-fee basis. This means that they generate legal fees only when they settle a case or obtain a favorable jury verdict for their clients.

The economic success of all firms depends upon satisfying and retaining existing clients, as well as bringing in new clients through various types of practice development activities and advertising. Many insurance carriers and self-insured businesses utilize a number of defense firms to handle their litigation claims. Thus, defense firms may compete for a proportion of business from a particular client. Many firms engage in practice development, such as networking and advertising activities, in order to bring in new business. For most firms, a certain percentage of their business comes from referral-based sources, such as other attorneys and existing clients. Learning to network and bringing in one's own clients may be part of the equation when associates are considered for partnership. Networking activities include speaking engagements at continuing legal education seminars, participation in state and local bar association committees, and serving on not-for-profit boards of directors. Attorneys with the ability to bring in new profitable business consistently, often referred to as "rainmakers," are very valuable to a firm.

The LNC can contribute to the economic success of a firm by providing the attorneys with high-quality work products and educating them about the medical issues in their cases. The LNC can enhance client satisfaction by regular contact with clients to update them about the status and progress of their cases. This is especially true in plaintiff firms, where LNCs typically have a great deal of contact with clients. The LNC can also assist the attorney to nurture and satisfy relationships with referring attorneys by keeping them updated on the status of cases that they have referred to the firm. Finally, the LNC can bring new business into the firm directly by networking with other LNCs and attorneys, and joining professional groups and committees in his or her legal community.

Fees and Costs in Litigation

At the most basic level, attorneys are paid a fee for their services in one of two ways: contingency, meaning a percentage of any recovery, or hourly. Plaintiff attorneys most often work on a contingency-fee basis, and defense firms work on an hourly basis. Legal fees cover the time and expertise of the lawyers and nonattorney professionals, the support staff's time, and the overheads of the firm. They do not cover costs or disbursements, which are out-of-pocket expenses that the firm incurs in the prosecution or defense of a case. Examples of disbursements are expert fees, copying charges, court-reporter and transcript charges related to depositions, and travel expenses.

Ultimately, payment of disbursements is the responsibility of the client, whether a case is won or lost. Some plaintiff firms advance payment of disbursements until the conclusion of a case. Other firms bill clients for disbursements on a monthly or quarterly basis. Disbursements in personal injury matters, especially medical malpractice claims, can be sizable. Thus, plaintiff attorneys and their LNCs must consider whether or not the potential economic recovery substantially outweighs the likely cost of prosecuting the claim.

Fees and Productivity Measurements in Defense Firms

Defense firms are paid for their time, regardless of case outcome. Most defense firms bill their clients by the hour for time spent on a case by all timekeepers. Attorneys, LNCs, and paralegals, with few exceptions, generate billable hours that translate into revenue for the firm. Secretaries, copy clerks, and other support personnel do not generate billable-hour revenue for the firm. Each category of billable personnel has an assigned billing rate for each single hour of time or part thereof. For example, a partner's time might be billed at $300 per hour or more, an associate between $150 and $250 per hour, and the LNC between $100 and $150 an hour. Billing rates are dependent upon the title, expertise, and experience of the timekeeper, and on what a particular client is willing to pay. Thus, the billing rate of a timekeeper may vary from client to client or among different types of cases for the same client. Generally, large established firms in metropolitan areas have higher billing rates than their counterparts in smaller cities or outlying areas. Some clients negotiate flat-fee arrangements for a portion of their legal services. For example, an insurance carrier might pay a set fee in malpractice cases for time spent from inception of the case through conclusion of depositions.

Timekeeping by all billable personnel is documented on a daily time sheet, customarily in blocks of a tenth of an hour (.1- or 6-min increments) or sometimes a quarter of an hour (.25- or 15-min increments). The particular requirements for timekeeping records, including how much time must be accounted for each day, vary from firm to firm. The client may have specific requirements regarding the descriptive nature of time-sheet entries. Time sheets also provide a basis for measuring the productivity of the timekeeper. Typically, there are certain minimum monthly or annual billable-hour expectations for each timekeeper. If the firm has an annual bonus program, the bonus may in part reflect billable hours in excess of the minimum requirement. Nonbillable hours are also accounted for each day. Nonbillable time might include time spent attending educational seminars, participating in department meetings, or organizing medical research or expert files (see Table 4.1).

Defense firm clients often scrutinize their bills carefully when it comes to time records and may dispute certain entries or refuse payment for others. For example, the client may feel that he was billed for a task that should have been done by ancillary personnel. Or the client may dispute the amount of time billed for a particular project or task. Some clients impose billing guidelines on firms that may restrict the types of LNC projects for which they are willing to pay. It is critical that all timekeepers, including LNCs, generate accurate time sheets that reflect the exact nature of the work done. If allowed, being more descriptive in time entries may help explain why a particular task took as long as it did. Typically, each client has an assigned billing attorney who reviews the bills for content and accuracy before they are sent to the client. The billing attorney knows the specific billing requirements of a particular client and should relay this information to all timekeepers. The billing attorney also has the authority to "write off"

Table 4.1   Sample Time Sheet

Client/Case Name	File Number	Billable Hours	Nonbillable Hours	Description
Johnson, Clyde	12,345	0.4		Telephone conference w/client
General Office	99,999		1.25	Label medical library shelves
Henderson, Charlene	67,890	5.3		Research preeclampsia
Anderson, James	34,567	0.2		Prepare correspondence to client

time before the bill is sent to the client or reduce billable time if a dispute ensues after the client receives the bill. Unfortunately, time that is written off translates into lost revenue for the firm. A firm that utilizes time efficiently to generate high-quality services will ensure profits, as well as future business from clients.

Most defense firm clients are insurance companies, self-insured hospitals, or other self-insured businesses. Instead of working with one firm exclusively, each client typically has an approved list of several defense firms with which it works. This allows the client to utilize the expertise of a particular attorney for a given case, manage conflicts that may arise (e.g., between codefendants), and reap the benefits of competition among defense firms. Like any consumers, defense clients want high-quality service at reasonable rates.

Most clients recognize the value of having the LNC as an integral part of the legal team. LNCs possess a body of medical knowledge based upon their education and clinical experience. They also have the ability to research medical issues and communicate effectively with medical experts. In many firms, LNCs perform work formerly done by attorneys at higher rates. This is cost-effective for the client and allows the attorney more time to engage in activities that only attorneys can conduct. Timelines, medical literature research, and other work product generated by the LNC enhance the attorney's knowledge and organization of the medical issues in a case. This assists the attorney in providing high-quality legal work for the client and increases the chances for a favorable outcome for the client.

In a well-run, successful defense firm, the fees generated by the billable personnel are more than sufficient to cover the overheads of the firm, including employee salaries and benefits, rent, supplies, computer expenses, and capital improvements. Any income generated in excess of the firm's overheads is profit for the partnership.

Fees and Productivity Measurements in Plaintiff Firms

Most plaintiff personal injury firms take cases on a contingency-fee basis. This means that the firm is entitled to a percentage of any verdict or settlement. The percentage varies from state to state and sometimes with type of case. Cases against the Federal Government have a predetermined percentage that the plaintiff attorney can charge. In New York, state statute requires a sliding-scale contingency fee in medical malpractice cases, which reduces the percentage of the attorney fee initially and again in incremental amounts for all awards in excess of $250,000 (30% of the first

$250,000, 25% of the next $250,000, 20% of the next $500,000, 15% of the next $250,000, and 10% of everything above $1,250,000). In addition to legal fees for time spent on a case, plaintiff firms are also entitled to recover any disbursements not already paid by the client. Many firms deduct these costs from the total award and then calculate their percentage on the remaining amount. Other firms deduct their fee from the total amount of the award and then deduct their costs. The client collects the remaining amount of the award, assuming there are no liens on the recovery, such as Medicare, Medicaid, Workers Compensation, or from third-party health insurance carriers. If a lien is involved, the attorney has to consider this in any settlement negotiations. The attorney may be able to negotiate a reduction in the lien, especially if settlement of a case is economically beneficial to the lienholder.

Example 4.1

A case has settled prior to trial for the sum of $100,000. The plaintiff's lawyer has a contingency agreement with the client for 40% and has spent $15,000 in out-of-pocket costs. $100,000 minus $40,000 (the attorney fee) minus $15,000 leaves the client with $45,000. If costs are first deducted, $100,000 minus $15,000 leaves $85,000, minus 40% equals $34,000 for the attorney's fee, leaving the client with $51,000. Some cases involve a split-fee arrangement with the referring attorney. While this reduces the fee of the attorney handling the case, it does not affect the amount of money that the client collects.

Unlike defense firms that are paid for their time whether they win or lose a case, plaintiff firms doing contingency work generate revenue only when they settle a case or obtain a favorable jury verdict. The amount of revenue generated from these cases depends upon the amount of the award and the costs associated with prosecuting the case. Keys to profitability in a plaintiff firm include maintaining continual sources of new clients, effectively screening cases, properly managing costs, and moving cases toward resolution in an effective and timely manner.

Many plaintiff firms do not utilize timekeeping records to track the productivity of attorneys, LNCs, and paralegals. They use a number of other ways to measure productivity. Assessment of partner productivity and related compensation is complex and varies greatly among firms. Typically, partner compensation is based upon preset percentages or agreed-upon criteria (effort, cases resolved, and responsibilities) for allocation of profits as defined in the partnership agreement. Productivity of associate attorneys is based upon criteria set by the partners and is reflected in the associate's annual performance evaluation. Criteria may include number of cases resolved, new cases brought into the firm, quality of written work, and perceived effort. Associate salaries and bonuses are determined by the partners and are typically based upon seniority and performance. Likewise, LNC productivity is usually measured by the extent to which the associates and partners value the contribution of the LNC, as reflected in annual performance evaluations. In some firms, LNCs may also be asked to maintain an assignment or task list in which the LNC records assignments, deadlines for completing the assignment and time spent on each project. In addition to tracking individual LNC productivity, such an assignment list can be utilized by the managing partner to determine whether LNC time is being appropriately and fairly shared among attorneys and for those cases that merit the assistance of an LNC. In addition, timekeeping records kept in a plaintiff practice may be used to justify the contingency fees to the court when a settlement or verdict is awarded to a minor or incapacitated individual.

A more detailed discussion of effective LNC performance in the context of key factors impacting plaintiff firm profitability follows.

Client Base

Plaintiff firms depend upon the continual referral of new cases. LNCs who network in the legal community by joining bar association committees, speaking at medical–legal seminars, publishing relevant articles, or joining professional LNC groups may generate referral of cases to their firms. Existing clients are likely to refer friends and family members to a firm if their satisfaction is enhanced by regular contact with the LNC. LNCs who assist the attorney in nurturing referring-attorney relationships help ensure continual referral of cases from that attorney.

Screening Cases

Effective screening of potential cases is critical to the profitability of a plaintiff firm and thus is discussed in detail later in this chapter. Many plaintiff attorneys rely heavily on the knowledge, research, and advice of their LNCs when screening cases involving medical issues, especially medical malpractice cases. While ultimately it is the attorney's decision whether to accept or reject a case, the in-house LNC may be in the best position to help weed out claims that are nonmeritorious or economically nonviable. An effective LNC is able to assist the attorney to reject nonviable cases expeditiously. Discovering a major obstacle or a series of small ones at the outset results in less time spent on unprofitable cases. The productive LNC in the contingency-fee setting recognizes how much information must be obtained to make a fair assessment of the merits of a case.

Cost Containment

Disbursements are associated with the pursuit of virtually all personal injury claims. Typical costs include those for copies of medical records, deposition transcripts, private investigator fees, and expert fees. These costs are especially high in medical malpractice cases, which may require the services of several experts and multiple depositions. A profitable firm must contain costs in proportion to the anticipated economic recovery; otherwise, expenses will consume a disproportionate share of either the client's recovery or the attorney's fee. The LNC can assist the attorney to achieve this balance by first providing a thorough assessment of the client's damages, including physical or emotional pain and suffering, functional limitations, lost income, and loss of services related to derivative claims. This allows the attorney to determine the likely settlement and verdict range in the venue for each case, assuming liability can be established. Second, the LNC can assist the attorney in deciding whether a particular expense is necessary to litigate the case properly, whether it is reasonable in light of the expenses that have already been incurred, and whether the timing of a particular expense is appropriate. For example, if a particular case moves toward settlement negotiations at the conclusion of depositions, it may be prudent to cease incurring additional costs unless settlement talks fail. Ultimately, the management decisions of a case rest with the attorney. However, a knowledgeable LNC can guide the attorney to make prudent economic decisions that benefit both the firm and its clients.

Timely Resolution of Cases

Firms that accept cases on a contingency-fee basis do not generate revenue from those cases until they negotiate a settlement or achieve a favorable jury verdict. The gross revenue of a firm is directly related to the number and value of cases that it successfully resolves annually. Productive

LNCs accept responsibility for assisting the attorneys to move their cases toward resolution at each phase of litigation, much like a case manager. A skilled LNC has all the tools to fulfill this role. This means providing the attorneys with timely work products at key points of the process and trying to stay one step ahead of the attorneys so that they always have the information they need to move the case to the next phase of litigation. This may involve maintaining a chart that tracks the progress of an attorney's cases and setting up regular conference times with the attorney to review the status of all the attorney's cases, discussing cases that need attention in more detail, including the tasks that need to be done, who is going to be responsible for completing each task and an agreed-upon time frame for completing each task.

The Role of an In-House LNC

Legal nurse consulting is a relatively nascent profession. The role of the in-house LNC is still evolving at most law firms. In many firms, the LNC performs much of the initial medical analysis traditionally done by the attorney. The roles may vary greatly among firms depending upon the firm's prior experience working with LNCs and the locality, culture, and size of the firm. The role of the LNC at plaintiff and defense firms is very similar, with the exception that LNCs at plaintiff firms are usually involved in the initial screening of cases, especially medical malpractice cases. The role of a plaintiff LNC in screening cases is a very important one, given that the economic success of a plaintiff firm, which almost always takes cases on a contingency-fee basis, is directly related to making good choices about the cases they accept. The following section is devoted to this topic, along with a discussion of the roles that both plaintiff and defense LNCs play once a case is in suit.

LNCs at plaintiff firms are usually very involved in the initial screening and investigation of potential medical malpractice cases. The screening process begins when a client or the client's representative (friend, family member, or referring attorney) contacts the firm about a potential case. While the actual screening process may vary from firm to firm, typically, a paralegal or LNC obtains the initial intake information on the phone, and records it on an intake sheet. Sometimes, a client or client's representative calls the attorney directly. The LNC then consults with an attorney about the disposition of that claim. The goal at this phase of the screening process is to obtain enough information to either reject the case right away or accept it for preliminary investigation. It is common for plaintiff firms to reject many more cases than they accept, due to lack of merit, conflicts, expired statutes of limitations, insufficient damages, or facts that make it unlikely that the attorney will prevail on the liability issues. For cases that are rejected, the LNC may draft a "reject" letter for the attorney's signature.

If the attorney decides to pursue an investigation of a potential claim, the LNC and the attorney typically meet with the client or representative to gather more in-depth information about the facts of the case and the nature of the alleged injuries, including current medical status and prognosis. It is also important to obtain a complete medical history and a list of all prior and current healthcare providers and hospitalizations. The LNC should also obtain information about potential liens. In death cases, it is important to inquire whether an autopsy was done. It is also helpful to request the client and family members to prepare a written narrative of their recollection of key events, because over time memories become less clear. On occasion, clients or their family members may already have prepared a journal of events as they unfolded or a diary related to the client's injuries and functional limitations.

The next step in the investigation of a potential medical malpractice claim is to request the relevant medical records. The LNC identifies all records needed for the managing attorney and medical/nursing expert(s) to render an opinion about the merits of the case. Typically, the LNC's secretary or a paralegal sends out correspondence requesting the medical records that have been identified by the LNC. It is important to have a tickler system, a manual or computerized reminder system, in place so that records are received in a timely manner. If the case involves a lengthy hospitalization and hence significant expense to obtain the records, the LNC may decide to review the entire chart at the hospital, selecting only those portions of the record needed for the initial investigation.

Once all the medical records are received, the LNC organizes and reviews them to form an initial impression about the merits of the case. The LNC is in a unique position to readily extract and analyze the relevant information in the medical records pertaining to liability, proximate cause, and damages. Sometimes, the end result of the LNC's review is a recommendation not to proceed any further with the case if the claim likely lacks merit or if the potential economic recovery does not justify the great time and expense involved in pursuing a medical malpractice claim. In this situation, the LNC may prepare a brief summary of his or her rationale for rejecting the case to use when conferring with the attorney about the case. The attorney decides whether to accept the LNC's recommendation to reject the case or to move forward with an expert review.

If the case appears to have merit, the LNC may prepare a summary of the relevant documentation in the medical records. The format of the summary depends upon the nature of the case. It may be a narrative in paragraph form, a medical chronology of a sequence of events, or a multicolumn chart with very detailed information from a hospitalization. In addition to preparing a summary of the medical documentation, the LNC conducts a preliminary medical literature review, focusing on the medical conditions, signs and symptoms, and treatment options as they relate to the applicable standard-of-care issues relevant to the case. The LNC also prepares a list of the potential defendants for review with the attorney. Once this process is complete, the LNC may either discuss or prepare a memo regarding his or her findings, including an analysis of the strengths and weaknesses of the case, with the assigned attorney. This includes an evaluation of the plaintiff's credibility, contributory negligence, and failure to mitigate damages, and of how the plaintiff is likely to be perceived by a jury. It also includes an evaluation of whether or not the plaintiff's injuries meet the firm's damage threshold. Armed with a thorough workup by the LNC, the attorney either rejects the case at this point or decides to send it out for review by the appropriate medical/nursing experts.

The expert medical review is the last phase in screening potential medical malpractice cases. If the attorney decides to proceed with one or more expert reviews, the LNC plays an important role in this phase of the investigation by identifying the appropriate specialty and individual physician or nurse to review the case. This includes a standard vetting of any potential expert regarding any conflicts and their clinical credentials and certifications. The LNC also consults with the attorney about whether more than one expert is necessary to address both the liability and causation issues.

Once the LNC identifies an appropriate expert who is willing to review the case, it is the LNC's responsibility to prepare a package of materials for the expert's review. This includes an organized copy of the medical records, a summary of the facts as claimed by the plaintiff, photographs or other documents, if applicable, and generally a retainer check. A list of questions or issues for the expert to consider may be included in the letter or prepared for the attorney and a summary of the LNC's verbal discussion with the expert, depending upon attorney preference. In some cases, the attorney may decide to send the expert the LNC's medical chronology or timeline, which should always be a version of the document containing only excerpts from the medical records, as it is likely discoverable by the opposing side. Any such chronology should only be used as a reference guide for the expert, who must always review the relevant medical records in their entirety prior to forming opinions. The LNC's analysis memo is never sent to a potential expert as it is discoverable and contains areas that are to be explored with an expert, which may not become issues in the case after it is filed. Attention to a detailed, organized package for the expert cannot be overemphasized. This facilitates a thorough review by the expert, whose primary job is to provide the attorney and LNC with an objective opinion about the merits of the case regarding liability, causation, and/or damages. The expert's time is very costly and should not be spent on organizing medical records. For more detailed information about identifying, vetting, and working with experts, see Volume 1, Chapter 15.

Once the expert has completed his or her review, the attorney and the LNC confer with the expert about the merits of the case, including a detailed discussion about all aspects of the case. For a more detailed discussion on working with experts, see Volume 1, Chapter 15. Based on the expert review, the case will be either rejected or pursued. In some cases, the expert may recommend review by an additional expert if some issues in the case are not within his or her area of expertise. If the expert feels that the case is meritorious, it is essential that the expert has a sound basis for his or her conclusions that will hold up under intense cross-examination. Thus, the attorney and LNC should effectively "cross-examine" the expert about the basis for his or her opinions. An effective LNC is able to discuss the medical issues in detail with the expert and serve as a liaison between the expert and the attorney, using the analysis memo prepared by the LNC as an outline, and make sure that the expert has addressed all areas of concern.

Before putting a meritorious case into suit, the attorney may decide to approach the defendant's insurance carrier to solicit interest in discussing settlement prior to suit. If so, the LNC may draft a demand letter for the attorney, summarizing the facts, liability, and damages issues. Or the attorney may use the LNC's work product to prepare the letter himself.

The LNC at a plaintiff firm plays a prominent role in the overall management of medical malpractice cases under investigation. The goal in such cases is to conduct a thorough investigation in a timely manner well before the statute of limitations expires. This means that the LNC must have a system for tracking cases that are under investigation to make sure that progress is made in the timely disposition of each case, including regular conferences with the assigned attorney. The LNC may also have frequent contact with the client to keep him or her informed about progress in the investigation of the case.

Once a plaintiff attorney commences a personal injury claim by the filing and serving of a summons and complaint, the insurance carrier assigns a defense firm to represent the interests of its insured. Depending upon the number of defendants, more than one defense firm may be involved in a given case. LNCs who work in defense firms that handle medical malpractice cases usually become involved in these cases as soon as the firm receives them. Both plaintiff and defense LNCs may assist attorneys with portions of the initial legal pleadings that are exchanged. For example, defense LNCs may draft the initial responsive pleadings, such as the answer, interrogatories (in some states a demand for a bill of particulars), and other discovery demands. The plaintiff LNC may draft portions of the bill of particulars or interrogatories that articulate specific claims of negligence and injuries resulting from the alleged malpractice. The attorney may also confer with the plaintiff LNC about which nonparty witnesses should be deposed.

As soon as the plaintiff provides medical authorizations and a list of healthcare providers to the defendant, the defense LNC goes through the same process conducted by a plaintiff LNC investigating a potential claim. The LNC requests, organizes, and summarizes the medical records; confers with the attorney about the relevant medical issues in the case; and does some preliminary research about the relevant medical conditions and applicable standard of care. The defense LNC also helps the attorney to identify experts and prepares a package of materials for the expert's review. In many defense law firms, the LNC will conduct a search for the appropriate expert and interview them for current qualifications and any possible conflicts.

Following the initial exchange of legal pleadings in medical malpractice cases, the role of the LNC in both plaintiff and defense firms is much the same. The LNC often helps the attorney prepare for depositions. For example, the LNC may help the attorney prepare for the deposition of the defendant healthcare provider or providers by educating the attorney about the medical issues in the case. This might include the relevant anatomy and physiology, a detailed explanation of a particular surgical procedure, or medical literature research about the applicable standard of care. In addition, the LNC should conduct a background check and author search regarding any defendant physician or other healthcare provider who is a named defendant. The LNC may also attend the deposition of the defendant healthcare provider to assist the attorney with unanticipated medical issues that may arise during the course of the deposition. This is especially helpful for those attorneys who are less experienced in dealing with the complex medical issues that often exist in medical malpractice cases.

The LNC may help the attorney prepare for the plaintiff's deposition by reviewing and preparing a summary of all past and current medical records and informing the defense attorney about any factors that might impact the liability, causation, damages, or contributory-negligence issues in the case. The LNC should also provide the defense attorney with any inconsistencies found in the statements of the plaintiff (interrogatories, letters) and documentation in the medical records, employment, or insurance claim files. Prior depositions and publications of the plaintiff's expert should be reviewed for any contradictory opinions expressed by that expert. In addition, a general background search should be conducted on plaintiff's expert for the purpose of determining the validity of the expert's credentials and general standing within the medical community.

Once depositions are completed, the LNC may provide transcripts of the depositions to the experts, after which the LNC and attorney confer with the experts to discuss any significant new information that was obtained during depositions.

Throughout the discovery phase of a medical malpractice claim, LNCs at both plaintiff and defense firms regularly update the client's medical records, conduct more in-depth research about the standard of care, identify and communicate with experts, regularly confer with the attorney about the strengths and weaknesses of the case, and often participate in case strategy sessions.

In addition to conferring with the attorney about the liability issues in the case, the LNC may provide a detailed assessment of the proximate cause and damages issues in the case based upon information contained in the medical records, the expert's review, and information obtained from the client at depositions. This may include an assessment of

- The nature of the injuries (both physical and emotional)
- Which injuries are likely to be permanent
- Whether there has been aggravation of a preexisting injury
- The nature of any functional impairment
- Whether the plaintiff is partly responsible for his or her injuries
- Whether the plaintiff has failed to mitigate his or her damages
- Contributing causes for the plaintiff's alleged injuries
- Apportionment of liability when there is more than one defendant

Settlement negotiations may ensue at any time during the course of a personal injury lawsuit. If this happens, the attorney may ask the LNC and colleagues for their opinions about a good settlement range for a particular case. Many factors are considered when valuing a case, including physical and emotional pain and suffering, functional limitations, the age of the injured party, lost wages, previous awards for similar injuries in the same venue, and how a particular plaintiff or defendant is likely to be perceived by a jury. If both sides agree to an alternative dispute resolution procedure such as mediation in an effort to resolve the case, LNCs for both sides assist the attorneys to prepare for this procedure by preparing summaries and anatomical drawings that are part of a submission to the mediator setting forth their arguments.

Many LNCs also play a key role in setting up and participating in focus group case evaluations. A focus group usually consists of 8–12 people from a community that is similar to the community where the case will be tried. Law firms can hire companies to find a location, advertise for the participants, and video tape the process. The participants are paid a nominal fee to hear brief versions of both sides of the case, deliberate based on what they have heard and then render a verdict. Normally, the participants are not told if the case is being presented by the plaintiff or the defense. They hear the arguments both sides are likely going to use at trial. These groups allow the attorney insight into how a jury may perceive their arguments and the arguments they believe the opposing side is going to make at the time of trial. The LNC may assist the attorney by preparing demonstrative evidence for the attorney's use, evaluating how the focus group reacts to various arguments and then reviewing the video tapes of the deliberations with the attorney. A focus group can help both the attorneys and the clients understand how a jury may react to different issues in the case as well as give both sides an idea of the potential value if a plaintiff verdict is reached. Often, these focus groups bring completely unexpected issues to light, helping the attorneys better prepare for trial.

Plaintiff LNCs may also be asked to co-ordinate the creation of a "day in the life" film that can be used for settlement purposes or perhaps at trial. The LNC may be asked to screen and choose a film company to make the film; give direction to the film company as to what should be included in the film and the length of the film; and be present during the filming and editing of the film as well. These films are powerful visual tools that show a typical day in the life of a catastrophically injured client who may be unable to sit through a trial due to their injuries.

For cases that go to trial, the LNC plays an important role in assisting the attorney to prepare for trial. This may include identifying potential medical exhibits, preparing additional medical charts or summaries, preparing demonstrative evidence, conducting further medical literature research, and obtaining and reviewing updated medical records. It may also include analysis and research related to the opposing side's expert medical opinions, testimonial history, publications, and disciplinary actions. During a trial, the LNC may assist in jury selection (i.e., review jury questionnaires), attend trial to help evaluate the testimony of key witnesses, or evaluate the jury's reaction to certain witnesses. The LNC may also assist the attorney with medical literature research or issues that arise unexpectedly during the course of trial. The LNC should also provide the defense attorney with any inconsistencies found in the statements of the plaintiff (interrogatories, letters) and the facts in the medical records, employment, or insurance claim files.

In other personal injury actions (auto, toxic tort, workers' compensation, slip and fall, etc.), the LNC's role is much the same as in medical malpractice actions except that typically, the LNC does not focus much on nonmedical liability issues, but focuses instead on the proximate cause and damage issues. In personal injury claims, plaintiff LNCs often accompany their clients to defense medical examinations arranged by the defendant. The purpose is to provide emotional support to the client and to provide the attorney with a summary of the doctor's examination. This includes the time spent on each aspect of the examination, the history elicited by the doctor from the client, and the exact nature of the physical examination. Such information is very useful if the examining doctor's report is inconsistent with what actually occurred during the Defense Medical Examination (DME). The LNC attending the DME should be aware of the procedural rules related to DMEs, which vary by state. Should the LNC encounter any problems during the DME she should contact a firm attorney for guidance. Prior to the DME, it is helpful for the LNC to attend a meeting with the client in which the attorney and LNC prepare the client for what to expect during the DME. See Volume 1, Chapter 9, "Communication with Clients in the Medical Malpractice Arena" for additional information.

Market Expectations for LNC Salaries and Benefits

Prior to considering or interviewing for an in-house position, the prospective LNC should network with other LNCs in the area to get a feel for local benefits and salary packages. They may vary significantly from firm to firm, even in the same region. Most in-house LNCs are now salaried employees. LNC salary and benefits packages differ greatly with the size and locality of the firm, whether it is a defense or plaintiff firm, and the extent to which the partnership values the LNC role. Firms that have worked with skilled LNCs typically offer higher salaries than firms hiring an LNC for the first time. Full-time LNCs often work in excess of 40 hr per week, but usually have the flexibility to work evenings, weekends, or at home and take time off during the week when necessary. Many successful plaintiff and defense firms realize that an LNC can do the work of an associate and more, and are willing to offer a salary in the range of an associate attorney, assuming that the LNC is experienced, skilled, and takes an active management role in the firm's cases. In this setting, the average annual salary range is $50,000–$75,000 in many parts of the country, with some firms offering salaries outside this range.

The American Association of Legal Nurse Consultants (AALNC, 2004) conducted another compensation survey. A total of 1,089 LNCs completed the survey, of which 165 indicated they worked full time in a law firm. Of these, 9% reported a base salary of $40,000 or less; 66% reported a salary between $40,000 and $70,000; 31% reported a salary between $70,000 and $90,000. Four percent of LNCs responding to the survey reported a full-time salary of over $90,000. Some firms have bonus programs. A bonus is a portion of the firm's profits that is awarded to some or all employees. Calculation of bonus awards varies greatly from firm to firm. Typically, bonuses are utilized to reward superior performance or productivity. However, they may also be awarded solely on the basis of seniority, be a percentage of salary, or be equal for different categories of employees.

Most salaried LNCs receive paid vacation and sick time. Additional benefits may include health and dental insurance, life insurance, retirement or pension plans, profit sharing, and flexible compensation plans. Some firms also pay the LNC's costs for RN state licensure renewals, AALNC national and local chapter dues, continuing legal or nursing education seminars, and membership in nursing specialty organizations and bar associations.

Prior to accepting an offer, the prospective LNC should obtain detailed information about the firm's LNC salary, billing requirements, benefits, and bonus programs. It is also important to request a job description, and an overview of the process for evaluating performance and productivity, especially given this may impact compensation.

Skills of the Successful In-House LNC

At the most basic level, job security for the in-house LNC depends upon the firm's maintaining an adequate volume of cases with medical issues. Beyond this, job security is directly related to performance. The LNC who develops the knowledge and experience to become a valuable and indispensable asset to attorneys in the delivery of high-quality legal services is most likely to enjoy long-lasting job security and a favorable compensation package. Although the skills required of the successful in-house LNC vary somewhat depending on the types of work done at the firm and the nature of the LNC role that exists at a given firm, the following are the basic skills of all highly effective LNCs.

Writing

LNCs and attorneys spend a large portion of their time researching and writing. The LNC's ability to prepare well-written documents in a timely fashion is a key component of successful performance. Having the skill to draft succinct medical-record summaries, informative research summaries, properly constructed correspondence, comprehensive interrogatories or bills of particulars, and persuasive summaries regarding the merits of a case is a tremendous asset to the attorney in the delivery of high-quality legal services. For example, the attorney can use a detailed, accurate, and updated medical summary or timeline that contains the relevant documentation from the medical records at key points throughout the life of the case, such as during preparation of pleadings, deposition outlines, and demand letters, and at trial or alternative dispute resolution proceedings.

The quality of written documents submitted to clients, judges, experts, and opposing counsel is a reflection of the depth of analysis and competence of its author and of the firm. Written documents should be well reasoned, factually accurate, and carefully proofread for spelling and grammatical errors. These include documents that are drafted by the LNC for the attorney to send out as his or her work product. The fewer the revisions required of the attorney, the more valuable the work of the LNC. Learning and adopting the writing style of the attorney who will sign the ultimate product is also very helpful. LNCs who feel that they need to improve their writing skills should consider engaging the help of a mentor or enrolling in a writing course. Several books designed to improve writing skills may be useful references for the LNC. See Volume 1, Chapter 10 for more information about legal writing.

Medical Literature Research

All personal injury attorneys rely heavily on the medical literature research done by LNCs to prepare their cases. Medical malpractice matters in particular often require that the attorney have an in-depth understanding of the anatomy, physiology, clinical presentation, treatment options, and prognosis for a given medical condition. The LNC must develop the means to gather this information from sources such as peer-reviewed medical journals, medical textbooks, and clinical guidelines promulgated by professional organizations. In recent years, the Internet has become an invaluable means for readily obtaining much of this information. The LNC must learn to conduct effective medical literature searches online and navigate the wealth of other professional medical information that is available on the Internet. Helpful websites relating to different medical topics should be categorized and saved for future use. Joining legal and medical listservs on the Internet is another way to gather medical information by networking with LNCs, physicians and other healthcare providers, and attorneys nationwide. See Volume 1, Chapter 11, "Researching Medical Information and Literature" for more information.

Teaching

Once the LNC gathers relevant information, he or she must decide how best to convey it to the attorney. The LNC may prepare a notebook with the relevant medical literature highlighted and organized by topic or date or prepare a written summary, such as an annotated bibliography, of the research results. The LNC must be prepared to teach the attorney any aspect of medicine that he or she does not fully understand. Teaching aids such as anatomical drawings, charts, and models are very helpful. The degree of instruction that is necessary will vary greatly with the experience of the attorney and the particular medical issues involved. A young associate may need a lesson in basic anatomy and physiology before he or she can even understand the medical literature, whereas a senior partner may need explanations regarding only very esoteric or complicated medical issues. The LNC's role in educating the attorney about all the relevant medicine is critical. Medical malpractice attorneys in particular, must be able to interact effectively with their own medical experts, depose and cross-examine the opposing side's medical experts, and make persuasive oral arguments to a judge or jury about the medical issues in the case. Medical experts also play a role in educating the attorney, but generally their availability to the attorney is somewhat limited (and expensive), whereas the attorney typically has frequent contact with the LNCs in his or her firm.

Analytical Skill

Evaluation of medical issues in the context of applicable legal standards is the essence of the work done at both plaintiff and defense personal injury firms. Effectively analyzing the liability (in medical malpractice cases), proximate cause, and damages issues in a personal injury case is a very high-level skill that can be acquired only over time. It is imperative that the LNC understand the relationship between liability, proximate cause, and damages. All of these elements must be present for a case to have merit. In addition, many states require the attorney to file an affidavit of merit when commencing a medical malpractice claim. This is, in essence, a legal document which establishes that the plaintiff attorney has had the case reviewed by a qualified expert who has opined that there is a good faith basis for filing a claim. To learn and understand the legal standards, the LNC can engage in discussions with the attorney about the applicable legal standards throughout the life of a case. This allows the LNC to differentiate more effectively between the relevant and irrelevant information contained in the medical records or literature and to understand statute of limitation issues, one of many legal issues that can impact the viability of a potential claim. It also allows an LNC working on behalf of the plaintiff to prepare a persuasive draft demand letter to an insurance carrier, or an LNC helping to defend a case to draft a case status report for the client. See Volume 1, Chapter 4 for more information about medical record analyses.

Organization

The LNC in a personal injury firm must keep track of tremendous amounts of information and large volumes of medical records. Most firms have a system for recording new information, maintaining files, and organizing documents. Some litigation firms utilize computer databases in addition to hard copy files to maintain case information. It is essential that the LNC adhere to the organizational system in place at the firm so that information and documents are readily available when needed. It is very helpful to organize medical records chronologically into notebooks, with tabs and dividers for each care provider and hospitalization. A large hospital record can be subdivided with preprinted medical index tabs for the different categories of records. Organized medical records are essential to an effective analysis of their contents by both the LNC and the medical and nursing experts. Personal injury firms request large volumes of medical records. Thus, it is essential that the LNC have a tickler system in place so that requested medical records are received in a timely manner. This can be a system maintained by the LNC, the secretary, or a records-acquisition service. See Volume 1, Chapters 4, 5, and 12 for more information about obtaining medical records.

Prioritizing

An effective LNC must have the ability to balance multiple tasks on a daily basis. The LNC at a thriving personal injury firm typically has responsibility for a large volume of existing cases and potential new claims, resulting in dozens of tasks and attorney requests competing for the LNC's time on a daily and weekly basis. Balancing these tasks requires that the LNC develop a system for keeping track of and prioritizing the projects that need to be done. First, the LNC must maintain a current "to do" list of all pending tasks and projects. One way to accomplish this is to keep all cases in a database. Reports can be printed out weekly and reviewed for deadlines and tasks that need to be accomplished. This system can also incorporate case notes that keep track of the status of the case. It is also helpful to categorize projects in some way, such as by type of task (medical summary, literature research, organization of records, etc.) or amount of time required to complete the task (small vs. large projects). Some LNCs prefer to create a comprehensive case list that includes the assigned attorney, procedural status of the case, and pending projects. Whatever the form of the list, it must be updated whenever the LNC identifies or is assigned new cases or projects. It should also be updated to reflect those projects that have been completed.

Second, it is critical that the LNC have a system for prioritizing the numerous pending projects and tasks. All cases being evaluated or managed in a litigation firm have statutory, procedural or court-ordered deadlines. Failure to meet some of these deadlines may result in dismissal of a claim, sanctions, or even a legal malpractice action. All litigation firms have a system for tracking deadlines, and ultimately it is the responsibility of the managing attorney to meet them. However, the LNC must also be aware of deadlines and procedural dates (of depositions and trials) so that he or she can complete any projects needed by the attorney well in advance of the deadline. This maximizes the value of the work product to the attorney. Also, an LNC working in a plaintiff firm must consult with the attorney about the applicable statute of limitations in cases under investigation. Some medical malpractice cases require review of certain medical records or even legal research before the applicable statute of limitations can be determined. Projects with these types of deadlines have priority over all other projects. Projects without specific or impending deadlines should be completed in as timely a manner as possible and roughly in the order in which the projects were received. This promotes a sense of fairness when the LNC takes direction from multiple attorneys. As previously mentioned, LNC task lists may be utilized by the managing partner for assisting the LNC to communicate with multiple supervising attorneys about prioritization of their LNC projects.

Computer Skills

The vast majority of law firms (small and large) provide computers for each member of the litigation team, including secretaries, paralegals, LNCs, and attorneys. Computers are the primary means for creating written documents in a law firm. It is imperative that LNCs master the word processing programs utilized at the firm, typically either Word or Word Perfect. In addition, LNCs must be able to create multicolumn charts and chronologies, which are typically done in Excel, Access, or the table format in Word. Some LNCs utilize various chronology software products or voice recognition software to create their timelines and chronologies.

The Internet is the primary means of doing various types of research in medical–legal cases, including medical literature searches; obtaining peer-viewed journal articles; conducting background checks of witnesses, parties, and experts; and doing legal research. LNCs must learn to effectively navigate the vast amount of information on the Internet, bookmarking and organizing those Internet sites that are most useful, and determining the reliability of the sites for peer review or professional association versus nonauthoritative sites or personal postings/blogs. The LNC is key in identifying and determining the reliability of the sites for the attorney.

Law firms are increasingly obtaining medical records and radiology studies in electronic form. Thus, it has become necessary for LNCs to learn to navigate, bookmark and highlight medical records in PDF format, and create chronologies while reading medical records viewed on a computer screen. This is sometimes accomplished with side-by-side computer monitors, with the records on one screen and the chronology on the other screen. LNCs now frequently need to review, catalogue, and navigate digital x-rays, MRIs, and CT scans on CDs and DVDs. The cost of obtaining and mailing radiology studies in this format is significantly less than that of studies obtained on radiology film. In addition, this allows radiology studies to be sent to experts electronically. Each radiology group uses one or more of various software programs to view and manipulate electronic studies. The LNC must become familiar with using programs used by radiology groups in a particular area.

Other Attributes of the Successful In-House LNC

Personality Traits

Highly successful LNCs possess the personality traits that one would expect in lawyers, physicians, and other professionals. This includes a strong work ethic, dedication to the mission of the work that is done at the firm, and a willingness to accept responsibility for seeing projects through to their conclusion. Litigation practice may involve the need to do research or produce a work product unexpectedly within a short time period, particularly when a case is at trial. This requires flexibility, including the willingness to work additional hours and reprioritize work projects during a crisis. Attorneys value the LNC who is independent, takes initiative to be aware of the procedural status of a case, anticipates work that needs to be done to move the case forward, and suggests ways to improve the management of cases. They also value LNCs who take the initiative to learn applicable legal standards and strategy.

LNCs spend a good deal of time communicating with many different people, including clients, medical experts, attorneys and LNCs outside the firm, and many personnel within the firm. Good interpersonal, conflict-resolution, and communication skills are essential. The LNC who supports and engages the staff that he or she supervises is likely to enhance their productivity. The plaintiff LNC must communicate empathetically with the injured client and their family members. The LNC in a defense firm has to be cognizant of the emotional toll of litigation on the defendant healthcare providers.

LNCs serve in a consulting capacity and thus must have the ability to express ideas and thoughts logically and coherently. LNCs must also possess enough self-confidence and assertiveness to express their views and debate issues with highly educated attorneys and physicians. Sometimes, the LNC is most valuable when playing devil's advocate or analyzing the case from the opposing side's viewpoint. Attorneys need as much information about the weaknesses of their cases as they do about their strengths. This is a high-level skill that can be acquired only over time through frequent discussions with the attorney about all aspects of a case.

Prior Clinical Practice

Most registered nurses with at least 5 years of prior clinical practice can learn to function effectively as LNCs. Because case analysis in personal injury firms requires evaluation of a wide range of medical conditions, in-depth knowledge of anatomy and physiology is essential. It is also helpful to have a clinical background in specialties requiring knowledge of many body systems and processes, such as critical care, trauma, and emergency room nursing. Firms with several LNCs may prefer to employ nurses with different areas of clinical expertise, including obstetrics and orthopedics.

Professional LNC Responsibilities and Practice Issues

Mentoring

In-house LNC positions are commonly held by long-term, experienced LNCs who are often integrally involved in every aspect of a firm's legal cases. This includes not only medical record analyses and medical literature searches, but also regular conversations with attorneys related to the legal standards, case strategy, and case management. Thus, in-house LNCs are in a unique position to mentor other LNCs, especially those new to the profession. This includes not only orienting and teaching LNCs new to the firm, but also reaching out to new LNCs in the community through speaking engagements, local AALNC chapters, and being available to field questions from local LNCs about LNC practice and employment opportunities. In-house LNCs should also consider approaching the firm partnership about offering internships to LNCs seeking a mentoring experience. Ultimately, the success of the LNC profession rests with providing high-quality work products and advice, something which is learned through extensive experience working on actual medical–legal cases. Experienced LNCs have a responsibility to share their knowledge with less-experienced LNCs and facilitate the advancement of the LNC profession within the legal community.

Practice Development

In-house LNCs are increasingly being profiled on firm websites, listed on firm letterheads, and included in firm advertising campaigns as attorneys realize the client and public appeal of having in-house LNCs. In-house LNCs who network within the legal community by joining their local bar association, serving on committees and procuring speaking engagements to groups of attorneys assist their firm to become recognized as having special expertise handling medical–legal cases.

Ethical and Scope of Practice Considerations

The firm is legally responsible for the conduct of all its employees, including its in-house LNCs. Nevertheless, it is very important that LNCs understand they must maintain client confidentiality and refrain from activities that could be construed as the practice of law.

In addition, LNCs should be familiar with and follow AALNC's Code of Ethics and Conduct and Scope of Practice documents (AALNC, 2006), which are voluntary practice guidelines developed to assist LNCs in their practice and advance the LNC profession within the legal and nursing communities.

In addition, all in-house LNCs should be familiar with the ethical considerations in Canon 3 of the ABA Model Code of Professional Responsibility, which states that "A lawyer should assist in preventing the unauthorized practice of law." While this canon does not specifically define what constitutes the practice of law, it does state that "functionally, the practice of law relates to the rendition of services for others that call for the professional judgment of a lawyer." Thus, for example, LNCs are prohibited from giving legal advice to clients and engaging in procedural activities (such as arguing motions before the court and questioning witnesses at deposition and trial).

In-house LNCs practice under the supervision of the firm's attorneys. As noted in section EC 3–6 of Canon 3 of the Model Code of Responsibility, "A lawyer often delegates task to clerks, secretaries, and other lay persons. Such delegation is proper if the lawyer maintains a direct relationship with the client, supervises the delegated work, and has complete professional responsibility for the work product." Thus, although experienced in-house LNCs may engage in any number of higher-level skills, the attorney is ultimately responsible for any work product and managing his or her cases. In 1983, the ABA House of Delegates adopted the Model Rules of Professional Conduct. Rule 5.3 relates to attorney responsibilities regarding non-lawyer assistants, stating that partners and other lawyers having direct supervisory authority over a nonlawyer must ensure that the nonlawyer's conduct is compatible with the professional obligations of the lawyer. In addition, rule 5.7 requires that law-related services provided by the firm must not constitute the unauthorized practice of law when provided by a nonlawyer.

Summary

In-house LNC practice is associated with both advantages and challenges. The in-house LNC benefits from frequent contact with the attorneys in the firm. Regular discussions between the LNC and the attorneys regarding the procedural status of cases, strategy, and the applicable legal standards allow the LNC to gradually develop the skills and knowledge necessary to analyze medical issues in the context of legal standards. This is an evolving process that takes time. A prospective LNC joining a firm with other LNCs has the advantage of being mentored by other LNCs familiar with the LNC role in that firm. With more than one LNC on staff, cases can be distributed more flexibly to prevent a single LNC from being overburdened.

The in-house LNC benefits from a steady income, with job security dependent upon the LNC's performance and ability of the firm to maintain an adequate caseload of civil litigation cases. The first LNC at a firm has the challenge of developing a new role that will be valued by the partnership. It can be a very rewarding and satisfying experience. Successful LNCs at all firms must continually strive to function at higher levels, including suggesting new ways to enhance the firm's delivery of high-quality services to their clients. The prospective in-house LNC should consider all the variables of in-house work at a particular firm, including plaintiff versus defense work, size and culture of the firm, types of cases, and compensation and benefits packages, in selecting an environment most compatible with the LNC's goals, philosophy, and expectations.

References

American Association of Legal Nurse Consultants (AALNC) (2004). *Compensation survey*. Chicago, IL: American Association of Legal Nurse Consultants,.

American Association of Legal Nurse Consultants (AALNC) (2006). Legal Nurse Consulting: Scope and Standards of Practice. Silver Spring, MD: nursebooks.org, the Publishing Program of ANA.

ABA Model Code of Professional Responsibility, Canon 3 (1969);

ABA Model Rules of Professional Conduct, Rules 5.1-5.7 (1983)

Test Questions

1. In-house LNCs working for the plaintiff represent
   A. The insured
   B. The physician
   C. The hospital
   D. The injured person

2. In a defense firm, all the following personnel generate billable-hour income for the firm EXCEPT
   A. Paralegals
   B. Secretaries
   C. Legal nurse consultants
   D. Associate attorneys

3. In a plaintiff firm, clients are usually retained on what basis?
   A. Hourly
   B. Contingency fee
   C. Cost
   D. Tentative

4. When prioritizing work projects, the LNC should give the least priority to
   A. Procedural deadlines
   B. Statutory deadlines
   C. Date the request was made
   D. Court-ordered deadlines

5. Elements of damages include all of the following EXCEPT
   A. Functional impairment
   B. Pain and suffering
   C. Liability
   D. Permanency of injuries

Answers: 1. D, 2. B, 3. B, 4. C, 5. C

Appendix: Legal Nurse Consultant Position Description*

Faraci Lange, LLP
Legal Nurse Consultant Position Description

Position: Legal Nurse Consultant (LNC)

Reports to: Supervising attorneys and managing partner

FLSA Status: Exempt

Revised: March 2009

POSITION PURPOSE

The essential role of the LNC is to analyze medical issues in the context of the applicable legal standards and to play a supportive role to Faraci Lange attorneys in the delivery of high quality legal services consistent with Faraci Lange's Mission Statement and Core Values.

LNC RESPONSIBILTIES

LNC responsibilities are performed under the supervision of the attorneys and are carried out based upon the discretion and preference of the attorney and established firm protocols for management of the firms' cases.

LNC responsibilities include but are not limited to:

Assist the attorneys to screen the merits of potential medical malpractice cases

*Participating in initial client interview, obtaining prior medical history, client's version of the facts, and a list of all relevant hospitalizations and health care providers

*Provide complete list of medical records that need to be obtained for initial case review

*Conduct preliminary medical literature search related to primary liability and causation issues

*Organize and review relevant medical records and prepare case screening memo for attorney

*Identify and vet potential medical and nursing experts

*Prepare package of materials for the expert, including an organized copy of the relevant medical records and letter to the expert setting forth the facts and a list of questions for the expert to consider.

*Participate in the discussion with the expert to review the expert's analysis of the merits of the case.

Assist in the management of meritorious medical malpractice cases

*Organize and review medical records

*Prepare narrative summaries, chronologies, time lines and charts reflecting relevant medical records documentation

*Draft medical portions of Bills of Particulars/Interrogatory Answers

*Keep abreast of client's current medical status and periodically update client's medical records

*Assist attorney to prepare for depositions; attend depositions as requested

*Conduct more in-depth medical literature searches as issues in case become more focused

*Provide attorney with relevant anatomical drawings and procedure descriptions relevant to case

*Draft letter for attorney summarizing the medical issues including liability and damages, as requested

*Attend selected defense medical exams and prepare memo summarizing exam

*Review and analyze opposing sides' Expert Witness Disclosures

*Assist attorney to prepare for trial, including selection of demonstrative evidence and preparation of additional charts and timelines for use at trial; attend trial as requested

*Participate in monthly meetings with attorneys to review the status of all medical malpractice cases

*Assist with focus groups

Assist in the management of selected products liability and toxic tort cases

*Identify and request client's medical records

*Organize and review medical records

*Prepare medical chronology

*For mass tort claims, assist with the medical portions of any required court documents

*Conduct medical literature searches related to the drug, device or toxic substance

Assist in the management of other personal injury cases (auto, slip & fall, labor law, etc)

*Organize and review medical records

*Prepare narrative summaries, chronologies, time lines and charts reflecting the relevant documentation in the medical records

*Draft medical portions of Bills of Particulars

*Keep abreast of client's current medical status and periodically update client's medical records

*Attend selected defense medical exams and prepare memo summarizing exam

Other

*Complete weekly projects sheets, indentifying projects completed the prior week and planned projects for the upcoming week

*Record case notes, including all communications with client, in Needles

*Maintain data bank of potential medical and nursing experts

*Work as a team player with other support staff and the attorneys

Required Skills

*Strong work ethic and dedication to the mission of the work that is done at the firm

*Willingness to accept responsibility for seeing projects through to their conclusion

*Good analytical skills; ability to express opinions logically and coherently

*Good reading and writing skills

*Good communication, teaching and interpersonal skills

*Good organizational skills and ability to prioritize pending work projects

*General working knowledge of the laws and rules applicable to medical malpractice, products liability and other personal injury cases

*Proficiency in computerized medical literature searches

*Proficiency in Word and Adobe Acrobat

*Proficiency in use of internet to conduct background searches on defendant health care providers and opposing side's experts

*Ability to work independently with minimal supervision and direction

*Strong problem solving skills

Educational and Experience Requirements

*Registered Nurse with four year BA or BS degree

*Minimum five years prior clinical nursing experience

Chapter 5

Role of the LNC
in Criminal Cases

Linda Fernandes, RN, MSN

Contents

Objectives

- To describe the roles and responsibilities of a legal nurse consultant (LNC) when consulting on criminal cases
- To differentiate between the different types of charges and the levels of those charges
- To describe the process by which an LNC would review a criminal case

- To describe the consequences of a criminal conviction and registries
- To provide an overview of the advances in forensic science that can assist an LNC when consulting on criminal cases
- To explain the types of mitigation that can be used in criminal cases
- To identify theories used by the defense and prosecution
- To provide an overview of the Innocence Project

Introduction

Forensic nurses generally work in roles that involve evidence collection, documentation of medical forensic evidence, expert or fact testimony, consultation, and education of legal professionals. A forensic nurse may be hired by either the prosecution or defense in criminal cases. When considering the role of a forensic legal nurse consultant (LNC), there are some basic educational considerations. As a clinical nurse, the specialties that will best prepare a nurse for working on criminal cases are critical care, trauma, or emergency nursing. Additional foundational knowledge includes training in sexual assault examination of adults and children, death investigation, and some basic or introductory education on other areas of forensic science. The amount of education and training that will be needed will depend on whether the LNC is being hired as an expert for the purpose of testifying or for the purpose of screening criminal cases for potential forensic evidence.

Experience as a practicing Adult or Pediatric Sexual Assault Nurse Examiner will be extremely helpful but is not absolutely necessary when considering a career as an LNC. Training as Sexual Assault Nurse should also not be the only medical forensic training that is used as the basis for employment as a forensic LNC. In order to expand one's practice and competency as a forensic LNC outside of cases that involve sexual assault reports or medical records, training in analysis of deoxyribonucleic acid (DNA), toxicology, and interpretation of forensic evidence is necessary. With generalized medical and forensic training, a forensic LNC can be involved in reviewing and screening criminal cases such as murder, attempted murder, assault, sexual assault, child abuse, vehicular murders and assaults, and DUI.

In the United States, the justice system and court structure are broken down into two separate processes, the criminal and civil justice system. As an LNC, you may be asked to consult on cases in either or both. The criminal and civil justice system have both similarities and distinct differences. Both systems are adversarial systems, meaning there are two opposing sides. There is also a difference in the standard necessary for a person or party to be found culpable. In the criminal justice system, it is "guilty beyond a reasonable doubt." In the civil justice system, it is a "preponderance of evidence." The focus of this chapter will be on the role of the LNC in the criminal justice system.

Criminal Charges and Criminal Charge Levels

A crime, by definition, is "the commission or omission in violation of a public law forbidding or commanding it and for which punishment is imposed upon conviction" (http://www.lawinfo. com/index.cfm/fuseaction/Client.lawarea/categoryid/137). A criminal case is created as a result of an individual committing a criminal act as defined by Congress, jurisdiction, or state legislation. Crimes are categorized as petty offenses, misdemeanors, or felonies.

Petty offenses, or violations, are a subcategory of misdemeanors. No jail time is typically associated with these crimes and punishment is usually a fine. Sometimes, probation may be imposed. Petty offenses usually include the issuance of ticket or citation. These types of crimes are tried before lower courts referred to as magistrates in some jurisdictions. The right to a jury trial varies within these jurisdictions depending on the offense.

Misdemeanors are less serious crimes than felonies. Punishment for committing a misdemeanor in most jurisdictions can be a fine or incarceration of less than 1 year. A grand jury indictment is not necessary to investigate or charge misdemeanors. However, misdemeanor charges could come about through a grand jury indictment if the charges are associated with a felony indictment. In most jurisdictions, defendants who cannot afford an attorney are not entitled to a court appointed attorney or Public Defender. Misdemeanor charges are sometimes resolved in specialized courts with abbreviated procedures, such as traffic court or drug court. Consequences of conviction of a misdemeanor are less serious than the consequences of a felony conviction. After a misdemeanor conviction a person can still vote, serve on a jury, serve in the military, and practice in licensed professions.

Felonies are the most serious crimes in any system of criminal law. By definition, a felony is "a crime that is punishable by more than one year in prison or by death for capital offenses in first-degree murder" (http://www.lawinfo.com/index.cfm/fuseaction/Client.lawarea/categoryid/137). However, the punishments are different depending on the state and jurisdiction. State courts also have the ability to label a crime as a "gross" or "aggravated" misdemeanor, which would allow the court to provide sentences of more than 1 year, in essence allowing the court to ensure that a more serious misdemeanor is managed as a felony (http://www.lawinfo.com/index.cfm/fuseaction/Client.lawarea/categoryid/137).

In most jurisdictions, grand jury indictments are necessary to charge an individual's criminal action as a felony. When a person is charged with a felony, they have the right to a court appointed attorney, or Public Defender, when they cannot afford one. A person convicted of a felony has greater restrictions to their rights than a person convicted of a lesser crime. A person convicted of a felony cannot serve on juries, cannot vote, and may be limited to practice in licensed professions (lawyer, teacher). They are also prohibited from owning firearms and cannot serve in the military. Persons convicted of a felony may also be required to register on specific registries as offenders such as the Sex Offender Registry, Child Abuse Registry, and Narcotics Offender Registry (specific to California) (http://www.lawinfo.com/index.cfm/fuseaction/Client.lawarea/categoryid/137).

Upon conviction, a sentence is imposed based on the crime, sentencing guidelines, and offender status. In 1987, the federal government issued the federal sentencing guidelines and minimum mandatory sentencing laws. Similar minimum mandatory sentencing laws exist in some jurisdictions. A minimum mandatory sentence is based on the sentencing guidelines that are set by the state legislator. These guidelines govern the amount of time that a judge may impose for a crime (United States Sentencing Commission, 1991). In essence, the judge is forced to impose a minimum mandatory sentence that complies with those guidelines for specific crimes such as rape, murder, and some drug offenses just to name a few. Every state has guidelines for crimes committed against their state. Crimes committed against the country are sentenced based on the federal sentencing guidelines.

There are opponents to minimum mandatory sentencing that believe it has had no positive impact on the criminal justice system or in deterring criminal activity. The opponents believe that the minimum mandatory sentencing laws do not allow the judge to take into consideration each defendant's individual circumstances. This includes the defendant's prior record, family history, education, employment status, record of service in the community, the specific facts of the case, the actual injuries caused to the victim, and the likelihood that the defendant will reoffend (ACLU, 2007). Opponents to the minimum mandatory sentencing laws also feel that the regulations give the prosecutors unfair advantage in the criminal proceeding because it allows the prosecutors to charge defendants based on which criminal acts would provide the heaviest minimum mandatory sentence (ACLU, 2007).

Another sentencing consideration is the status of the offender, meaning is the defendant a repeat felony offender (also known as a habitual offender)? A habitual offender is a person who has committed two or three previous felonies or numerous misdemeanors. Penalties for persons labeled as habitual offenders are more severe and are applied to any subsequent criminal acts. Habitual offender status may also result in the degree of crime itself being elevated to a more serious crime. In other words, a third-degree offense may be elevated to a second- or first-degree offense. Habitual offenders have longer prison terms with less opportunity for reduction in sentence for good behavior. Habitual offender laws differ by state and some states have now adopted the "Three Strikes" law. The "Three Strikes" law states that if an offender has two previous felony convictions, a third conviction would result in a mandatory life prison sentence with no possibility of parole (Travis, 1997). The application of the "Three Strikes" law is based solely on felony convictions and not misdemeanor convictions.

According to the Bureau of Justice Statistics Special Report, "Truth in Sentencing in State Prisons," defendants convicted of a criminal act may serve only a portion of the sentence imposed by the court (Delaware criminal and traffic law manual, 2006–2007). Due to the discrepancy in time being served by convicted criminals, truth-in-sentencing laws have been enacted in the majority of states. Truth-in-sentencing laws insure that defendants committed of a criminal act ultimately end up serving a more substantial portion of their sentence. States that offer parole and good-time credits to convicted criminals, which would allow early release from prison, have been either greatly restricted or have had these facilities eliminated completely. At the time of the 1996 study, the amount of time served by violent criminal offenders increased by an average of 15 months as opposed to the amount of time served prior to the implementation of truth-in-sentencing laws (Delaware criminal and traffic law manual, 2006–2007).

How a crime is charged and the degree of that charge vary based on each state's own set of rules and regulations. In general, criminal charges such as assault, murder, rape, kidnapping, and burglary all have similar elements for every degree of the criminal act such as injury, death, nonconsensual sexual intercourse, theft, or unlawful entry. The degree of the criminal charge will depend on intent, premeditation, use of a deadly weapon, the type of instrument used to commit the criminal act (person versus car), and the seriousness of inflicted injuries. The more serious the crime, the lower the degree and the greater the fines and jail time. In other words, assault first is a more serious crime than assault second.

In most states, first-degree murder is defined as "the unlawful killing of another person that is both willful and premeditated" (Delaware criminal and traffic law manual, Title 16). In other words, the elements necessary to meet the level of first-degree murder include thoughtful planning or "lying in wait" for the victim. Another common legal concept used by most states is the felony murder rule. Under the felony murder rule, a person has committed first-degree murder if "any death, even an accidental one, results from the commission of certain violent felony crimes such as arson, burglary, kidnapping, rape, and robbery" (Delaware criminal and traffic law manual, Title 16). Second-degree murder is usually defined as "an intentional killing that is not premeditated or planned, nor committed in a reasonable heat of passion; or a killing caused by dangerous conduct and the perpetrator's obvious lack of concern for human life" (Delaware criminal and traffic law manual, Title 16).

Voluntary manslaughter, sometimes called criminally negligent homicide, is usually defined as "an intentional killing in which the perpetrator had no prior intent to kill, such as killing that occurs in the heat of passion" (Delaware criminal and traffic law manual, Title 16). In order for the criminal act to be charged as voluntary manslaughter and not first-degree murder, the act that led to the killing needs to be the kind of act that would cause a reasonable person to become emotionally or mentally disturbed. Involuntary manslaughter commonly refers to "an unintentional killing that results from recklessness or criminal negligence or from an unlawful act that is a misdemeanor or low-level felony" (Delaware criminal and traffic law manual, Title 16). The difference between voluntary and involuntary is usually whether or not the victim's death is accidental or intentional.

The crime of rape generally refers to the act of nonconsensual sexual intercourse in which the perpetrator forces the victim by using physical force, threat of harm, or other duress. The victim's inability to consent to the sexual intercourse may be due to an impairment which makes the victim unable to say "no." Impairment that may lead to the victim's inability to consent could be the result of drugs or alcohol, age, or development disability. An established relationship between a perpetrator and victim does not preclude the possibility of rape such as a husband and wife or boyfriend and girlfriend. Most states have an additional provision in the law, which is used to determine the criminality of consensual sexual intercourse between an adult and an underage person who is considered to be too young to be able to consent. This provision is referred to as "statutory rape."

Most states define first-degree rape as when a perpetrator "engages in forcible sexual intercourse with another person either by using or threatening to use a deadly weapon, kidnapping the victim, inflicting serious physical injury, or during the commission of a felony" (Delaware criminal and traffic law manual, Title 16). Rape in the second degree is generally defined as "forcible sexual intercourse either when a person is incapable of consent by reason of being physically helpless or mentally incapacitated, when the victim is a person with a development disability, when the perpetrator has supervisory authority over the victim, when the perpetrator is a healthcare provider and the victim is a client or patient, when the victim is a resident of a facility for persons with a mental disorder or chemical dependency, and when the victim is elderly or a vulnerable adult" (Delaware criminal and traffic law manual, Title 16). Rape in the third degree is defined as "nonconsensual sexual intercourse that does not rise to the degree of first- or second-degree rape" (Delaware criminal and traffic law manual, Title 16). In cases of inappropriate, unwanted sexual contact that does not include sexual intercourse, a perpetrator can be found guilty of unlawful sexual contact (Delaware criminal and traffic law manual, Title 16).

Assault in the first degree is defined as "the infliction of serious physical injury to another person; use of a firearm or deadly weapon or by any force or means likely to produce serious physical injury or death" (Delaware criminal and traffic law manual, Title 16). Assault second is defined as the "intentional physical injury of another person due to recklessness; intentionally causing substantial bodily harm to an unborn child by intentionally and unlawfully inflicting any harm upon the mother; assault with a deadly weapon; causing physical injury during the commission of a felony; or, causing physical injury to a member of law enforcement or other civil servant such as nurses, doctors, emergency medical personnel, firefighters" (Delaware criminal and traffic law manual, Title 16).

Assault in the third degree is defined as the "infliction of physical injury due to criminal negligence, use of a weapon or any other instrument likely to produce bodily harm; or, causing physical injury due to criminal negligence that is accompanied by substantial pain that extends for a period sufficient to cause considerable suffering" (Delaware criminal and traffic law manual, Title 16).

Fourth-degree assault, or offensive touching, is a misdemeanor charge that is defined as "the assault of another that does not rise to the degree of assault first, assault second, or assault third." Even if the injury is very minor and there are no marks or injuries evident, a person can be charged with assault fourth or offensive touching.

National and State Registries

As previously mentioned, the consequences of a felony criminal conviction can result in the mandatory registration of the offender on specified registries such as the Sex Offender Registry, the Child Abuse Registry, or the Narcotic Offender Registry (specific to California). Most people know that each state maintains a Sex Offender Registry, but very few people are aware that each state also maintains a child abuse and neglect registry. Today, all 50 states and the District of Columbia have Sex Offender Registries. However, due to new federal laws states can no longer use their discretion in determining who must register as a sex offender and how long the offender must stay on the registry.

The Jacob Wetterling Crimes Against Children and Sexually Violent Offender Registration Act was passed by the U.S. Congress in 1994. The law required that states establish Sex Offender Registries and any state that did not comply was subject to a loss of a percentage of federal funding (Jacob Wetterling Crimes against Children and Sexually Violent Offender Registration Act). Under this law, offenders who were convicted of the sexual abuse of a child or a sexually violent crime against an adult were required to register their current address with local law enforcement for 10 years following their release from prison (Jacob Wetterling Crimes against Children and Sexually Violent Offender Registration Act). Initially, the information provided by sex offenders to the state or jurisdiction where they were convicted was not required to be released to the public. Under this law, the state or jurisdiction was allowed to use their discretion in deciding what information would be released to the public.

The length of registration time for offenders convicted of "aggravated" sexual violence or repeat sex offenders was extended to life by Congress in 1996 (Ditton & Wilson, 1999). For the purpose of the new law, an aggravated sexual act is defined as "(1) engaging in sexual acts involving penetration with victims of any age through the use of force or the threat of serious violence; and (2) engaging in sexual acts involving penetration with victims below the age of 12" (Ditton & Wilson, 1999).

In 2006, when President Bush signed the Adam Walsh Child Protection and Safety Act, the state Sex Offender Registries were incorporated into a National Sex Offender Registry and the National Child Abuse Registry was formed. The new federal requirements expanded the groups of convicted sex offenders who were mandated to register and the federal legislation now specified the length of time that a sex offender would have to stay on the registry. And for the first time, the federal law under the Adam Walsh Act required some convicted juveniles to register as sex offenders (Adam Walsh Act). The Adam Walsh Act defines a sex offense as a "criminal act that has an element involving a sexual act or sexual contact with another" (Adam Walsh Act).

In addition to the National Sex Offender Registry and the National Child Abuse Registry, the Adam Walsh Child Protection and Safety Act of 2006 also bolstered federal penalties for crimes against children by imposing more stringent minimum mandatory sentences for the more serious crimes against children (The Adam Walsh Child Protection and Safety Act of 2006). Grants were provided to states to assist with the development of federal procedures for obtaining the civil commitment for sex offenders who have shown a propensity for reoffending (The Adam Walsh Child

Protection and Safety Act of 2006). Finally, the Act also makes it more difficult for sexual predators to reach children through the Internet.

The Internet Safety Act is a subtitle of the Adam Walsh Nation Child Protection and Safety Act of 2006. The Act established federal offenses and penalties for child exploitation and for criminal acts that included embedding words or digital images into web source code for the purpose of deceiving minors into gaining access to material constituting obscenity (The Adam Walsh Child Protection and Safety Act of 2006). Through this act, attorney generals were now required to increase the number of computer forensic examiners that were employed to specifically investigate crime involving the sexual exploitation of children and to form additional Internet Crimes against Children Task Forces (The Adam Walsh Child Protection and Safety Act of 2006).

The Adam Walsh Child Protection and Safety Act states that within 3 days of being released from prison, a convicted sex offender must register on the Sex Offender Registry. This holds true for convicted offenders who have received a nonimprisonment sentence.

Each sex offender is required to provide the following registration information to the state or jurisdiction where they reside: the offender's name, social security number, all addresses, employer and employer address, school (if student) and school's address, license plate number and description of any vehicle owned or operated by offender, and any other information required by the attorney general (The Adam Walsh Child Protection and Safety Act of 2006). The following information is required to be made public by each jurisdiction for each sex offender on the registry: physical description, criminal offense, the criminal history of offender, including dates of arrest and convictions and correctional or release status, and current photograph. Additional information maintained by the state or designated jurisdiction includes fingerprints and palm prints, a DNA sample, a photocopy of a valid driver's license or ID, and any other information required by the attorney general (The Adam Walsh Child Protection and Safety Act of 2006).

The Adam Walsh Child Protection and Safety Act mandated that a three-tier classification system for sex offenders be developed. It also defined the requirements for maintaining the registry. In this classification system, tier-I offenses are the least serious and tier-III offenses are the most serious. The tier levels are as follows:

■ Tier-III sex offenses are offenses punishable by imprisonment for more than 1 year. The offenses are comparable or more severe than the federal offenses of sexual abuse or aggravated sexual abuse, abusive sexual contact against a minor less that 13 years old, offense involving the kidnapping of a minor (except by parent or guardian), or any offense committed by a person already designated as a tier-II sex offender (The Adam Walsh Child Protection and Safety Act of 2006).

■ Tier-II sex offenses are more serious offenses than tier I that are punishable by imprisonment of more than 1 year. The offenses are comparable to or more severe than the following federal offenses involving a minor: sex trafficking, coercion and enticement, transportation with intent to engage in criminal sexual activity, and abusive sexual contact. Tier-II sex offenses also include any offense involving use of a minor in a sexual performance, solicitation of a minor to practice prostitution, or production or distribution of child pornography (The Adam Walsh Child Protection and Safety Act of 2006).

Tier-I sex offenses are those offenses that do not meet the criteria for tier II or tier III (The Adam Walsh Child Protection and Safety Act of 2006).

Tier-III sex offenders must register for life unless they are a juvenile delinquent, in which case registration is for 25 years as long as they maintain a clean record. Tier-III sex offenders must appear in person to have a picture taken and verify registration information every 3 months. Tier-II sex offenders must register for 25 years and offenders must appear in person to have a picture taken and verify registration information every 6 months. Tier-I sex offenders must register for 15 years, but with clean records, the registration may be reduced to 10 years. Tier-I sex offenders must appear in person to have a picture taken and verify registration information yearly.

Of note, the Human Rights Watch discovered during a review of state sex offender laws that some states require individuals to register as sex offenders even when their conduct did not involve coercion or violence, and for criminal acts that may have little or no connection to sex (http://www.pbs.org/wgbh/pages/frontline/shows/crime/trial/faqs.html). So, while most people assume that a registered sex offender is someone who has sexually abused a child or engaged in a violent sexual act with an adult, this is not always the case. For example,

- At least five states require registration for prostitution-related offenses (http://www.pbs.org/wgbh/pages/frontline/shows/crime/trial/faqs.html).
  - At least 13 states require registration for public urination; of those, two limit registration to acts committed in view of a minor (http://www.pbs.org/wgbh/pages/frontline/shows/crime/trial/faqs.html).
  - At least 29 states require registration for consensual sexual intercourse between teenagers (http://www.pbs.org/wgbh/pages/frontline/shows/crime/trial/faqs.html).
  - At least 32 states require registration for exposing genitals in public; of those seven states require the victim to be a minor.
  - Approximately half of states in the United States have formal Child Abuse Registries as required by the Adam Walsh Child Protection and Safety Act. The majority of other states have an informal database where information regarding substantiated cases of abuse and neglect can be obtained.

For the purpose of this chapter, the following information has been taken from the Delaware Code Title 16: Health and Safety Regulatory Provisions Concerning Public Health, Chapter 9: Abuse of Children, Subchapter II: Child Protection Registry. When conducting research on the Child Abuse Registry, the LNC should refer to the specific code for the state or jurisdiction where they are working.

When a person's actions have been substantiated as child abuse or neglect, their information is placed on the Delaware Child Protection Registry. The registry was created to protect and ensure the safety of children in child-care settings, healthcare settings, and public education facilities. Under the Delaware Code, the substantiation of abuse or the substantiation of neglect results from the following:

- Conviction on a criminal offense related to abuse or neglect (Department of Justice Office of the Attorney General, 1998).
- Conviction by the preponderance of evidence in a family court child welfare proceeding brought by the division of family services (DFS) (Department of Justice Office of the Attorney General, 1998).

Once there has been a substantiation of abuse, a child protection level is assigned similar to the way tiers are assigned to sex offenders on the Sex Offender Registry. Child protection levels are regulations that assess the risk of future harm to children from acts of abuse and neglect.

The criteria for Level I are a person substantiated of abuse or neglect for any of the following:

- An incident of abuse or neglect that presents a low risk of future harm to children (Department of Justice Office of the Attorney General, 1998).
- Conviction or violation of compulsory school attendance or truancy based on abuse or neglect (failure of a parent or guardian to ensure their child's attendance at school and/or failure to bring their child to school on time) (Department of Justice Office of the Attorney General, 1998).

Persons designated as Level-I offenders are not entered on the Child Protection Registry and are not reported in response to a Child Protection Registry inquiry. They remain eligible for employment in child-care facilities, healthcare facilities, and public schools.

The criteria for Level II are a person substantiated of abuse or neglect for any of the following:

- An incident of abuse or neglect that presents a moderated risk of future harm to children (Department of Justice Office of the Attorney General, 1998).
- Conviction of interference of custody when based on the same incident of abuse or neglect (Department of Justice Office of the Attorney General, 1998).

Persons designated as Level-II offenders must remain on the registry for 3 years. For those 3 years, the response to any inquires to the Child Protection Registry by a potential employer or any other agency will be "substantiated for abuse or neglect." However, these persons will still be eligible for employment in child-care facilities, healthcare facilities, or public schools. If there are no other additional incidents of substantiated abuse or neglect while on Protection Level II, a person will automatically be removed after 3 years and will no longer be reported during a Child Protection Registry check based on the incident or conviction.

The criteria for Level III are a person substantiated of abuse or neglect for any of the following:

- An incident of abuse or neglect that presents a high risk of future harm to children including but not limited to physical injury, nonorganic failure to thrive, malnutrition, or abandonment of a child between the ages of 13 and 17 (Department of Justice Office of the Attorney General, 1998).
- Conviction of the following crimes based on the same incident of neglect or abuse: offensive touching, menacing, reckless endangering, assault third, terroristic threatening, unlawful administration of drugs or controlled substances, indecent exposure in the first or second degree, sexual harassment, unlawful imprisonment, abandonment of a child, or misdemeanor endangering the welfare of a child (Department of Justice Office of the Attorney General, 1998).

Persons designated as Level-III offenders must remain on the registry for 7 years. For those 7 years, the response to any inquires to the Child Protection Registry by a potential employer or any other agency will be "substantiated for abuse or neglect." These persons are not eligible for employment in child-care facilities, healthcare facilities, or public schools. If there are no other additional incidents of substantiated abuse or neglect while on Protection Level III, a person will automatically be removed after 7 years and will no longer be reported during a Child Protection Registry check based on the incident or conviction.

The criteria for Level IV are a person substantiated of abuse or neglect for any of the following:

- An incident of abuse or neglect presenting the highest risk of future harm to a child including but not limited to serious physical injury, sexual abuse, torture, criminally negligent treatment, or abandonment of a child 12 years of age or younger (Department of Justice Office of the Attorney General, 1998).
- Conviction of any of the following crimes when based on the same incident of abuse or neglect: vehicular assault, vehicular homicide, criminally negligent homicide, assault in the first degree, assault in the second degree, murder, manslaughter, murder by abuse or neglect, incest, rape, unlawful sexual contact, sexual extortion, sexual solicitation of a child, bestiality, continuous sexual abuse of a child, possession of child pornography, unlawfully dealing in child pornography, felony endangering the welfare of a child, dangerous crimes against a child, kidnapping, coercion, dealing in children, unlawful dealing with a child, sexual exploitation of a child, or promoting suicide (Department of Justice Office of the Attorney General, 1998).

Persons designated as Level-IV offenders will remain on the registry for life. The response to any inquires to the Child Protection Registry by a potential employer or any other agency will be "substantiated for abuse or neglect." These persons are ineligible for employment in child-care facilities, healthcare facilities, or public schools.

Removal from the Child Protection Registry is possible in certain circumstances. Persons who have been placed on the Child Protection Registry at Child Protection Level II or Level III will be automatically removed from the registry as long as there have been no additional incidents of substantiated abuse or neglect while on the registry (Department of Justice Office of the Attorney General, 1998). However, a person who has any additional substantiated incidents of abuse or neglect while on the Child Protection Registry is ineligible for automatic removal, but may be removed from the registry by a family court order. Once a person has been removed from the Child Protection Registry, they will no longer be reported through a Child Protection Registry check. The offender's name and the case information will, however, remain in an internal information system as substantiated for all other purposes such as child-care licensing decisions, and foster and adoptive parent decisions regardless of their removal from the Child Protection Registry (Department of Justice Office of the Attorney General, 1998).

Evidentiary Review

In the United States criminal justice system, probable cause is defined as the presence of facts or evidence that would make a reasonable person believe that a crime or wrong doing has been, is being, or will be committed. The term "probable cause" was extracted from the Fourth Amendment of the U.S. Constitution, which states: "the right of the people to be secure in their person, house, papers, and effects against unreasonable searches and seizures, shall not be violated, and no Warrants issued, but upon probably cause, supported by oath or affirmation, and particularly describing the place to be searched, and the persons or things to be seized."

A probable cause sheet is a document generated by law enforcement, using the minimum necessary facts, to secure an arrest warrant for the suspected perpetrator of a criminal act. The probable cause sheet may be the first legal documentation reviewed by a forensic LNC, and can provide an initial impression regarding what evidence might exist. The request for an arrest warrant may be days, weeks, months, or years after the initial criminal incident, dependant on the statute of limitations.

Types of evidence include circumstantial evidence and direct evidence. Circumstantial evidence can be used to infer a conclusion about something unknown using a collection of facts that is collectively taken into consideration. Circumstantial evidence is usually a theory, supported by a significant quantity of corroborating evidence. Circumstantial evidence is used to establish guilt or innocence in a criminal proceeding through reasoning. Taking these facts into consideration may strongly point to a certain conclusion. Circumstantial evidence can be a useful guide for further investigation. However, circumstantial evidence is not considered to be proof that something happened. Circumstantial evidence can be persuasive, and therefore may be more certain and satisfying than direct evidence. For example, a receipt for purchasing a gun is direct evidence that a certain person owned the gun but, indirect evidence would be that the gun was used to commit a crime.

Direct evidence, on the other hand, is factual evidence based on a witness's personal knowledge or observation of that fact. Direct evidence does not require inference or presumption to prove the existence of the fact at issue. A person may be found guilty of a charged crime by direct evidence alone, if that evidence satisfies a jury beyond a reasonable doubt that the defendant committed the criminal act. An example of direct evidence would be the surveillance video of a person robbing a convenience store, or a witness who saw a person stealing a car. Evidence that comes from a person who testifies to having direct knowledge on the main or ultimate fact or testimony from a person who saw or heard the criminal act is direct evidence.

In terms of weight or importance, the law draws no distinction between circumstantial evidence and direct evidence. Direct evidence or circumstantial evidence may be enough to establish guilt beyond reasonable doubt, depending on the jury's interpretation of the facts of the case. In order for evidence to be admissible, it must be relevant and reliable. Evidence obtained illegally will be inadmissible under the "exclusionary rule." The exception to this rule would be if the officer who collected the evidence acted in good faith, then the court will make a decision regarding the admissibility of the evidence.

Other types of evidence include testimonial, physical, and scientific evidence. Testimonial evidence is an oral or written statement offered during a criminal proceeding as evidence that what is being stated is the truth. Testimonial evidence includes both direct testimony and hearsay. Hearsay evidence is an oral or written statement about an out-of-court declaration attributed to someone other than the testifying person. Such evidence is generally inadmissible because the person to whom the statement is attributed cannot be cross-examined to ascertain its factual basis, which is a violation of the defendant's Sixth Amendment rights.

The hearsay rule permits the admittance of hearsay into evidence during a criminal proceeding when there are substantial guarantees of the reliability and trustworthiness of the evidence, which would be a substitute for the guarantees of cross-examination at trial (Rule 11-803(D) NMRA, 1999). The admissibility of statements for purposes of medical diagnosis or treatment is another exception under the hearsay rule even though the declarant is available as a witness (Rule 11-803(D) NMRA, 1999). For this exception to apply, there must be an assurance that the statement was "reasonably pertinent" for medical diagnosis or treatment. Such statements include those "made for purposes of describing a medical history, or past or present symptoms, pain, or sensations, or the inception or general character of the cause or external source thereof insofar as recently pertinent to the diagnosis or treatment" (Rule 11-803(D) NMRA, 1999). The basis for the medical diagnosis or treatment exception to the hearsay rule is that the patient's self-interest in obtaining proper treatment makes a patient's description of past and present physical symptoms inherently more likely to be trustworthy.

The special circumstances surrounding the sexual or physical abuse of a child allow for another exception to hearsay. Child abuse involves not only the physical injury but also the emotional and psychological injuries that accompany this crime; therefore, it is important to be attentive during the examination of these children. When treating children who have been physically and sexually abused in the home, the most paramount concern should be the prevention of recurrence of the injury. This consideration is expressed in the legislatively imposed duty placed on healthcare providers to report suspected cases of child abuse and the obligation on the healthcare provider to prevent the abused child from being returned to an environment in which he or she cannot be adequately protected from recurrent abuse (Ark. R. Evid. 803[4]).

For example, a child's statements to a healthcare provider identifying their abuser would fall within the medical-treatment exception and would be admissible in court. The child's identification of their abuser would allow the healthcare provider to take steps to prevent further abuse by that family member. Their identification of their abuser would allow the healthcare provider to take steps to treat the emotional and psychological injuries that accompany the physical or sexual abuse by a healthcare provider who specializes in treating abused children. The child's identification of their abuser permits the healthcare provider to fulfill their legislatively imposed duty of calling the child-abuse hotline and reporting the crime (Ark. R. Evid. 803[4]).

There are some additional statements that are defined as hearsay, but may nevertheless be admissible as evidence in court. These statements are referred to as an "exception" to the general rules of hearsay. Some, but not all, exceptions to the hearsay rule apply only when the declarant is unavailable for testimony at the trial or hearing. Hearsay exceptions that apply even when the declarant is available:

Excited utterances: Statements relating to startling events or conditions made while the declarant was under the stress of excitement caused by the event or condition. This is the exception that may apply to the "police officer" scenario. A victim's cries of help were made under the stress of a startling event, while the victim is still under the stress of the event, as is evidenced by the victim's crying and visible shaking. An excited utterance does not have to be made at the same time of the startling event. A statement made minutes, hours, or even days after the startling event can be an excited utterance, so long as the declarant is still under the stress of the startling event. However, the more the time elapses between a startling event and the declarant's statement, the more the statements will be looked upon with disfavor (Freedman, 2003).

Present-sense impressions: A statement expressing the declarant's impression of a condition existing at the time the statement was made, such as "it's hot in here," or "we're going really fast." Unlike an excited utterance, it need not be made in response to a startling event. Instead, it is admissible because it is a condition that the witness would likely have been experiencing at the same time as the declarant, and would instantly be able to corroborate (Freedman, 2003).

Declarations of present state of mind: Much like a present-sense impression describes the outside world, declarant's statement to the effect of "I am angry!" or "I am Napoleon!" will be admissible to prove that the declarant was indeed angry, or did indeed believe himself to be Napoleon at that time. Used in cases where the declarant's mental state is at issue. Present-state-of-mind statements are also used as circumstantial evidence of subsequent acts committed by the declarant, like his saying, "I'm gonna go buy some groceries and get the oil changed in my car on my way home from work" (Freedman, 2003).

Hearsay exceptions that apply only where the declarant is unavailable:

- *Prior testimony:* If the testimony was given under oath and the party against whom the testimony is being proffered was present and had the opportunity to cross-examine the witness at that time. This is often used to enter depositions into the court record at trial (Freedman, 2003).
- *Admission of guilt:* If you make a statement, verbal or otherwise, as an admission of guilt of the matter at hand, that statement would not be regarded as hearsay. In other words, self-incriminating statements (confessions) are not hearsay (Freedman, 2003).
- *Forfeiture by wrongdoing:* The party against whom the statement is now offered (1) intentionally made the declarant unavailable; (2) with intent to prevent declarant's testimony; (3) by wrongdoing (Freedman, 2003).

The prior statement of a witness is not hearsay if their previous statement can be used during cross-examination to impeach them or attack their credibility at a future court proceeding such as a trial or hearing. For example, it can be used when the prior statement is *inconsistent* with the declarant's testimony at the trial, or when the prior statement was given under oath at a trial, hearing, deposition, or other proceeding. Conversely, it can be used when the prior statement is *consistent* with the declarant's testimony, it can be offered to rebut a charge that the declarant has made a recent fabrication, or a charge of the declarant's improper influence or motive. Finally, it can be used when the prior statement was an identification of a person made after perceiving that person.

Evidence introduced during a criminal proceeding, which is a physical object intended to prove the demonstrative physical value of the fact in issue is physical evidence. Physical evidence can conceivably include all or part of any such object. This would include things such as a murder weapon, victim clothing, bullet, or drugs.

Evidence developed from a scientific procedure intended to help the trier of fact to understand evidence or to understand the facts in question during a criminal procedure is scientific evidence. Many scientific procedures are no longer disputed and are accepted by courts with little or no challenge to their validity. Examples include fingerprint testing for purposes of identification, blood testing, breathalyzer testing to determine alcohol consumption, and ballistics testing of bullets and their area of impact. Some scientific tests and examinations that are not universally accepted are nevertheless generally considered reliable. Some examples are neutron activation analysis to determine the identity of goods, and voiceprints to determine a person's identity. These types of scientific procedures may not be accepted in the medical communities, but they are well established such that they may be judicially noticed as automatically valid sources of scientific evidence.

Another important concept related to evidence collection and preservation is chain of custody. Chain of custody refers to the procedure used to document every person who has come in contact with the evidence. Chain of custody records are maintained in order to establish the integrity of evidence, proving it has been preserved from the time of collection to the time it is produced in court. Persons involved in the collection, processing, and transportation of evidence, all persons involved with the evidence collection, whether internal, external, or third parties, should document the procedure for accepting, storing, and retrieving the evidence (http://www.ninds.nih.gov).

A proper chain of custody requires three types of testimony: (1) testimony that a piece of evidence is what it purports to be (e.g., a litigant's blood sample); (2) testimony of continuous possession by each individual who has had possession of the evidence from the time it is seized until the time it is presented in court; and (3) testimony by each person who has had possession that the particular piece of evidence remained in substantially the same condition from the moment one person took possession until the moment that person released the evidence into the custody of another (Giannelli, 1996). Chain of custody documentation should be maintained throughout the life of the evidence and must include every instance of contact with the evidence and the action performed on it.

Elements important to establishing an accurate and defensible chain of custody include audit history logs, which should include a simple means of reporting on searches by custodian, operator, keyword/phrase/concept, and project; detailed documentation for any collection method; and allowances for original media, such as hard drives, backup tapes, and DVDs (http://www.ninds. nih.gov). Chain of custody information for original media may include information such as a unique media ID, date/time of the receipt or collection of the evidence, a description of the type and contents, exact label information, the amount of data, write-protection status, serial numbers, and a description of the data collection procedure (http://www.ninds.nih.gov). Any problems encountered should also be thoroughly documented. In instances of large collection projects that are conducted over a long period of time and may involve numerous custodians, tracking methodology, such as a database or spreadsheet, can be useful. Tracking information about the collected data would provide a thorough log of all activities, including any refusal on the part of a custodian to release data.

The police report is a more detailed document that includes victim information, victim statements, witness information, witness statements, and investigational statements of all law enforcement officers who respond to the crime scene and who collected evidence from the crime scene. The police report will confirm if victims were taken to the hospital for treatment, what evidence was collected, where the evidence is being stored, and if any of the evidence has been sent out for forensic testing. The defense's copy of the police report is generally redacted with the names and addresses of witnesses removed. It is sometimes possible to find out the redacted information from the alleged perpetrator of the crime, otherwise, the information is provided at the time of trial. In some jurisdictions, the police report is not provided until the trial, while in other states it may be provided at the time of the preliminary hearing.

The initial information provided to an LNC will depend on whether the LNC was hired by a private criminal attorney or whether they are employed full time with a legal firm. If consulting privately, the LNC may need to request additional documents such as the police report or the probable cause report from the attorney. Once the necessary reports and documents have been provided, the LNC will need to review the records to determine if there are inconsistencies in victim, witness, or perpetrator statements. Inconsistencies could include variances between perpetrator statements to law enforcement and the criminal defense attorney or variances of a victim in statements to the police and then to healthcare providers. Witnesses will also often change their statements depending on their relationship with the perpetrator such as in gang-related cases, domestic violence, or drug-related cases. Inconsistencies in statements can be used at trial to impeach a witness, victim, or perpetrator. In the case of an expert witness, the credibility of that expert could be damaged and that in turn might affect the ability of the expert to consult on future criminal cases.

The types of medical forensic evidence collected will depend on the type of case and the facts of that case. Medical forensic evidence would include medical records in assault cases, autopsy reports in murder cases, toxicology reports in DUI cases, specialized medical records in adult and pediatric sexual assault cases, DNA analysis reports in an assortment of felonies, and child advocacy center interviews of children alleging sexual abuse. The medical forensic evidence that a forensic LNC is qualified to review will depend on their training and their area of expertise. Also keep in mind that some of the medical forensic evidence will be DVDs, CDs with photographs, or crime scene videos. It may be necessary to inform a criminal defense attorney that such type of evidence exists as they may not be aware of it if that information is not intimated in the initial discovery packet.

Advances in DNA Analysis

Forensics is "a field of science dedicated to the methodical gathering and analysis of evidence to establish facts that can be presented in a legal proceeding" (James & Nordby, 2005). Forensic science includes disciplines such as pathology, serology, fingerprint analysis, trace evidence, DNA evidence, weapons identification, and questioned document examination. The methods and tools used to apply this scientific knowledge are referred to as forensic technology. In a criminal case, the more the evidence collected, the greater the chance that the prosecutor will have a strong case. Additionally, the more accepted the forensic technology, the more likely the prosecutors will be able to use the evidence during a criminal proceeding to strengthen their case.

DNA is the fundamental basis for the human body, and almost every cell in the human body has DNA. DNA is not an effective investigational technique when analyzing the DNA of twins since twins have identical DNA. DNA analysis is probably the most widely known type of forensic evidence due to its increased exposure in television shows and mystery novels. DNA analysis is also the most widely scrutinized forensic science technology being used today. The advances in forensic DNA analysis contributed to the progression of a protracted process that took weeks or even months to complete a process that can be completed as quickly as in 2 days (National Districts Attorneys Association, 1994). DNA analysis involves the extraction of genetic material from the cells of human blood, bloodstains, seminal stains, and other biological fluids and tissues (National Districts Attorneys Association, 1994).

Dr. Henry Lee has stated that "DNA analysis has ended the careers of serial rapist and serial killers, identified the remains for soldiers missing in action, established paternity in many instances, helped medical detectives to track diseases, and illuminated countless other controversies involving biological issues" (Henry, 2004). Previously, DNA samples that were small or degraded could not be analyzed by available DNA techniques. With the current advances and new technologies, it is now possible to test older and smaller samples. This type of testing has been made possible with the introduction of polymerase chain reaction (PCR) methodology. PCR testing has made it possible for DNA obtained from coffee cups, a single hair root, or saliva on an envelope to be reproduced into larger quantities so that DNA testing and comparison can be done (Henry, 2004).

With the creation of the combined DNA indexing system known as CODIS, DNA evidence from separate criminal cases can now be linked together to identify perpetrators who have committed other criminal acts in cases that are unsolved. The changes and advancements in DNA analysis have allowed it to be used in other serious crimes such as murder and rape. Other cases where DNA evidence can now be collected for potential DNA analysis include hit-and-run, burglary, robbery, and assault.

Mitochondrial DNA is the portion of the DNA that each individual receives from their mother. Individuals share their mitochondrial DNA with other siblings, so it can be used to identify mother–child and sibling relationships. Mitochondrial DNA analysis is quickly becoming the more commonly used and more widely accepted technique of DNA analysis since mitochondrial

DNA is abundant in all cells; so, it is extremely valuable in cases where there is only a small amount of DNA available (National Districts Attorneys Association, 1994). As of late, mitochondrial DNA analysis has become accepted in criminal courts as valid and reliable scientific evidence.

There are several issues when evaluating the admissibility of forensic evidence in a criminal proceeding. Guidelines for conducting quality assurance audits were developed in response to challenges of DNA admissibility. These guidelines were developed by the National Research Council, the FBI, and the technical working group on DNA analysis (James & Nordby, 2005). The admissibility of DNA analysis as scientific evidence and the scope of expert testimony have been challenged based on the Daubert and Frye standard to determine if the scientific evidence and expert testimony are relevant and reliable, and accepted by the scientific community (James & Nordby, 2005). After many rigorous legal arguments, DNA evidence is now generally accepted in most states and jurisdictions as admissible in a criminal proceeding and is rarely challenged.

If the admissibility of DNA analysis is challenged, it is being challenged based on the following reasons. Firstly, the integrity of the evidence sample might be challenged. For example, was the chain of custody maintained, was the sample mixed up with another sample, or was the sample contaminated (James & Nordby, 2005). Secondly, the integrity of the laboratory may be challenged. For example, was the laboratory accredited, was quality assurance being conducted, or was the laboratory in compliance with established guidelines and standards (James & Nordby, 2005). Thirdly, there may be challenges to the interpretation of the results or the statistical inferences made based on the results. For example, was the DNA able to be separated or was it a mixed sample when it was tested, or was a forensic profile more common than reported by the forensic laboratory (James & Nordby, 2005).

The potential DNA evidence collected will depend on the facts of the case. DNA evidence can be in the form of semen, red blood cells, hair shaft, and epithelial-containing cells such as saliva and hair roots. Potential DNA samples can be collected from bite marks, fingernail scrapings, blankets, sheets, pillows, clothing, hat, bandanna, tissue, washcloth, cigarette butt, toothpick, rim of bottle or glass, dental floss, tape, or ligature. Another aspect of DNA collection in criminal cases is the collection of elimination samples to rule out potential suspects. If potential DNA evidence is not collected at the time of the criminal act, then it may be lost or degraded.

When interpreting a DNA analysis report, there can be three types of results. Firstly, inclusion of the suspect, which means they are a possible source of the DNA profile (NIJ, 2000). However, before the results can be admissible in a court proceeding, the strength of the inclusion must be reviewed. The strength of the results depends on the specific profile at each loci site. The fewer the number of loci matches at each site, the weaker the strength of the results and conversely, the greater the number of loci matches at each site, the stronger the strength of the results.

Secondly, the results could be exclusion, which means that the DNA profile of the suspect does not match the DNA profile generated from the evidence collected from the crime scene (NIJ, 2000). However, exclusion does not mean that the suspect did not commit the crime only, but that the suspect may have done something to ensure that his DNA was not left behind. For example, a suspect may have worn gloves or the suspect may have worn a condom.

Finally, the results could be inconclusive. Inconclusive results mean that when the DNA was analyzed, it could neither include nor exclude an individual as the source of the biological evidence (NIJ, 2000). Inconclusive results can occur as a result of poor quality or quantity of biological material, the sample could be contaminated, or the sample may be a mixed sample containing biological material from multiple individuals (NIJ, 2000).

Prosecution and Defense Strategies

In a criminal case, defense strategy is one of the most critical components. An effective defense strategy can make the difference between incarceration and freedom. The development of a defense strategy will depend on the facts of case and usually emerges once information about the case begins to surface. This includes discovery material provided by the prosecution and the defendant's account of the criminal act (http://www.criminal-law-lawyer-source.com/tips/defense.html). The defendant's account of the events is most often dependant on their version of the facts. It is important to keep in mind that just because there are different accounts of the event it does not mean that each account is inaccurate. Important elements will include the consistency of verifiable evidence, the defendant's potential for getting jury sympathy, and explaining the reason for events that relate to the defendant's account (Human Rights Watch, 2008).

A defense attorney must take certain factors into consideration when developing a defense strategy, or "theory of the crime." The defense attorney must consider the prosecution and defense witnesses, the community's perception of the crime and law enforcement, and the defendant's moral responsibility (Human Rights Watch, 2008). The goal of any defense strategy would be to obtain an acquittal or to place doubt on the prosecutions evidence in order to pursue a plea bargain that would be in the best interest of the defendant.

Competency to stand trial hinges on a defendant's mental state at the time of trial and not their state of mind at the time of the criminal offense. Competency is generally a low-level standard that requires merely that a defendant understands the criminal proceeding process—that he is being tried for a crime and the relative roles of prosecutor, defense attorney, and judge—and be able to assist his attorney in his defense (http://www.aap.org). The low standard reflects an attempt to allow as many people as possible to have their day in court, while excluding those individuals who are so sick as to be completely unable to comprehend the criminal proceeding or to assist their attorneys (http://www.aap.org). There is a common misperception that if an individual is found incompetent, it is the same as being found not guilty. In reality, if the defendant is deemed incompetent, there is no trial, nor is there a conviction or acquittal.

A finding of incompetence merely signals a hiatus in the criminal proceeding. In the majority of cases, a mentally ill defendant deemed incompetent receives treatment until he is deemed "restored to competence," and returns to court (http://www.aap.org). Until 1972, defendants found incompetent to stand trial often ended up being institutionalized automatically and indefinitely. In that year, the U.S. Supreme Court ruled that such institutionalization was unconstitutional, and that defendants deemed incompetent may not be held for a longer period than is reasonable to determine whether they will be deemed competent in the foreseeable future (http://www.aap.org). If the determination is made that he will not, commitment proceeding must be initiated or the defendant must be released.

Conversely, the insanity defense has nothing to do with a defendant's current mental status; to be found not guilty by reason of insanity (NGRI), a judge or jury must evaluate the defendant's state of mind at the time of the offense (http://www.aap.org). Each state, and the District of Columbia, has its own statute setting out the standard for determining whether a defendant was legally insane, and therefore not responsible, at the time his crime was committed (http://www.aap.org). In general, the standards fall into two categories.

About half of the states follow the "M'Naughten" rule, based on the 1843 British case of Daniel M'Naughten, a deranged woodcutter who attempted to assassinate the prime minister (http://www.aap.org). He was acquitted, and the resulting standard is still used in 26 states in the United States. Simply, the M'Naughten rule states that a defendant may be found NGRI if "at the time of committing the act, he was laboring under such a defect of reason from disease of the mind as not to know the nature and quality of the act he was doing, or if he did know it, that he did not know what he was doing was wrong" (http://www.aap.org). This test is also commonly referred to as the "right/wrong" test.

Twenty-two other jurisdictions use some variation of the "Model Standard" set out by the American Law Institute (ALI) in 1962. Under the ALI rule, a defendant is not held criminally responsible "if at the time of the criminal act, his conduct was a result of mental disease or defect limiting by substantial capacity his ability to either appreciate the criminality (wrongfulness) of his conduct or to conform his conduct to the requirements of law" (http://www.aap.org). The ALI rule is generally considered to be less restrictive than the M'Naughten rule. Some states that use the M'Naughten rule have modified it to include a provision for a defendant suffering under "an irresistible impulse," which prevents him from being able to stop himself from committing an act that he knows is wrong (http://www.aap.org).

A major 1991 eight-state study commissioned by the National Institute of Mental Health found that less than 1% of county court cases involved the insanity defense, and out of those, only around one in four was successful (Way, Dvoskin, & Steadman, 1991). The vast majority of those that were successful were the results of a plea agreement in which the prosecution and the defense agree to an NGRI defense (Way et al., 1991). Ninety percent of defendants found to be NGRI had been diagnosed with a mental illness. About half of the cases had been indicted for violent crimes; 15% were murder cases (Way et al., 1991). Three states—Montana, Idaho, and Utah—do not allow the insanity defense. Defendants must still be found competent to stand trial, and they may introduce evidence of a mental disease or defect as proof that they did not possess the requisite intent or state of mind (mens rea) to be found guilty (http://www.aap.org).

A defense of guilty but mentally ill (GBMI) does not eliminate the insanity defense; it is merely an alternative for defendants who are found to be mentally ill, but whose illness is not severe enough to relieve him of criminal responsibility (http://www.aap.org). A defendant who receives a GBMI verdict is sentenced in the same way as if he were found guilty. The court then determines whether the defendant needs treatment for mental illness and if so, to what extent. When, and if, the defendant is deemed "cured" of his mental illness, he is required to serve out the rest of his sentence in a prison, unlike a defendant found guilty by reason of insanity who would be released from psychiatric commitment once he is deemed to be no longer dangerous, without completing his entire sentence (http://www.aap.org). Proponents of the GBMI plea argue that it provides for necessary treatment of mentally ill defendants, while still ensuring that those defendants are punished for their crimes (http://www.aap.org). They say that the GBMI verdict protects the public because mentally ill defendants would not be released if they are deemed no longer dangerous, as would a defendant who was acquitted by reason of insanity (http://www.aap.org).

Critics, including the American Psychiatric Association, claim that the GBMI verdict takes away the hard choices that juries and judges are supposed to make: "While the 'GBMI' category may seem to make juries' jobs easier, it compromises one of our criminal system's most important functions— deciding, through its deliberations, how society defines responsibility" (http://www.aap.org). A GBMI plea absolves the judge or jury of this obligation. Mental health resources in prison are scarce, and because most statutes grant substantial discretion to the facility directors to provide a level of treatment that they determine is necessary, there is no guarantee that an inmate will receive adequate treatment (http://www.aap.org). In 2000, at least 20 states had enacted "GBMI" provisions.

"Rape trauma syndrome" was first defined by Burgess and Holstrom in 1974. Rape trauma syndrome describes the acute and long-term problems related to sexual assaults (Burgess & Holstrom, 1974). Rape trauma syndrome has two phases: the acute and long term (Burgess, 1986).

These phases are further broken into the disorganization, reorganization, and resolution and integration phases. The acute phase is used to describe a victim's initial reactions in the first few hours following the sexual assault. When reviewing medical forensic records for sexual assault victims or interviewing sexual assault victims, it is important to keep in mind that how victims present their feelings following the assault may vary. Some victims may be more expressive and display feelings of crying, sobbing, smiling, restlessness, tenseness, and/or joking (Burgess & Holstrom, 1974). Other victims may present in a more controlled style appearing calm, composed or subdued (Burgess & Holstrom, 1974). During the acute phase, victims may experience somatic symptoms, physical trauma, and gastrointestinal irritation (Burgess & Holstrom, 1974). Emotionally, victims may experience shock, numbness, guilt, powerlessness, loss of trust, fear, anxiety, anger, shame, depression, and denial (Burgess & Holstrom, 1974).

During the reorganization phase, the victim will continue to have generalized anxiety and fear but may also start to experience sleep disturbance, eating disturbances, and relationship disturbances (Burgess & Holstrom, 1974). Victims may experience a change in their social functioning. They may isolate themselves from significant others, friends, and coworkers. Victims will also have difficulty establishing new relationships (Burgess & Holstrom, 1974). Unfortunately, victims will often feel guilty for not preventing the sexual assault and are disappointed or frustrated with the legal process.

In the intermediate phase, victims may move or change jobs and become increasingly reliant on family. Victims may develop phobias of going out or being alone (Burgess & Holstrom, 1974). The victim's sexuality can also be damaged by change in body images and thoughts of being "damaged goods" (Burgess & Holstrom, 1974). Victims can have long-term reactions that last for years, and experience a reduced ability to enjoy life. Finally, in the third phase, victims begin to re-establish emotional equilibrium, and learn how to readapt to their lifestyle (Burgess & Holstrom, 1974).

In criminal cases, testimony on rape trauma syndrome is admissible for the purpose for refuting an inference that the victim's postassault behavior was inconsistent with the expected reaction of a victim of sexual assault or incest (Pretty, Schroeder, Brueggemann, & Clark, 1990). The expert's testimony cannot be used to prove or disprove that the crime occurred. The expert's opinion also may not include any statements regarding the truthfulness or credibility of the victim (Pretty et al., 1990). Clinical studies have shown that rape trauma syndrome is a form of post-traumatic stress disorder (PTSD). Rape trauma syndrome is recognized as a mental health disorder in the "Diagnostic and Statistical Manual of Mental Health Disorders, Third Edition." Therefore, expert testimony on rape trauma syndrome meets the standard of general acceptance by the scientific community.

The term "battered women syndrome" was defined by Dr. Lenore E. Walker, the nation's most prominent expert on battered women in 1984. Battered women syndrome is defined as having three phases: the tension building phase, the explosion or acute battering phase, and the "honey-moon" phase where the perpetrator is loving and gives the victim gifts in effort to show that he/she is sorry (Campbell, 1990). Only about two-third of the states in the United States allows expert testimony on battered women syndrome for two reasons. Firstly, there is no clear definition of the criteria for the diagnosis of battered women syndrome. Secondly, like rape trauma syndrome, battered women syndrome is considered a form of PTSD. However, battered women syndrome is not recognized in the Diagnostic and Statistical Manual (DSM) IV.

The symptomology of battered women syndrome includes the following:

■ Re-experiencing the battering:
  – Avoidance of people, activities, and emotions in order to limit the psychological affects of the battering
  – Hyperarousal and hypervigalance

- Disrupted interpersonal relationships
- Body image changes
- Sexuality and intimacy problems (Walker, 2006)

A victim of battering may exhibit some or all of the previous symptoms. Due to its frequent inadmissibility, many attorneys, especially defense attorneys, have stopped using battered women syndrome as the foundation to explain the actions of battered women who commit violent crimes.

A perpetrator of battering acts in certain ways to control and isolate their significant other. These are a few examples. The perpetrator will intimate the victim by causing the victim to fear them through destroying the victim's property, displaying weapons, and at times harming family pets (Campbell, 1990). To isolate the victim, the perpetrator will limit the victim's contact with family and friends, make the victim financially dependant, and control who the victim talks to and what the victim reads (Campbell, 1990). The perpetrator will also use the victim's children to control them by threatening to take the children away, making the victim feel guilty about causing the abuse to occur in front of them, and even if the victim is able to get away from the batterer, the batterer may still use child visitation as a way to harass the victim (Campbell, 1990).

In jurisdictions where testimony on battered women syndrome is admissible, the expert opinion can be used to show that a person exhibits the symptomology of battered women, to explain the battered women's state of mind at the time of the criminal incident, and to support an affirmative defense of self-defense or extreme emotional distress (Dixon, 2002). Expert testimony can also be used to explain why the battered women often recants and is resistive to having her significant other prosecuted, and to strengthen her credibility in these situations (Dixon, 2002). When abused women kill their abuser, they are often charged with murder. Finally, expert testimony can be used as a mitigating factor when sentencing a battered woman after conviction.

Even though testimony on battered women syndrome is not allowed in some states and jurisdictions, there is an organization that exists to help defend battered women who commit violent crimes. The National Clearinghouse for the Defense of Battered Women was founded in 1987. The National Clearinghouse provides assistance, resources, and support for women who have killed their abuser while trying to defend themselves. The National Clearinghouse acts in collaboration with battered women advocates, criminal defense attorneys, prison advocates, and social scientist. Information available through the National Clearinghouse can be found at their website: http://www.ncdbw.org/about.htm.

Battered child syndrome was first described by Professor Henry Kempe in 1962. He coined the phrase to describe the most severe form of child abuse (Campbell, 1993). However, Dr. John Caffey identified suspicious injuries in children through some of the first widely recognized studies in children in 1946 (Caffey, 1946). Professor Kempe developed a diagnostic tool that could be used during the examination of children to help in determining and identifying a pattern of injuries that can only occur from physical abuse. In 1972, Professor Kempe changed the definition of battered child syndrome emphasizing that a "battered child is any child who received nonaccidental physical injures as a result of acts or omissions on the part of parents or guardians" (Kempe & Helfer, 1972). In 1974, the Child Abuse Prevention and Treatment Act was signed into law.

Professor Kempe identified injuries that he believed were suspicious of abuse. These included certain types of fractures such as spiral fractures, subdural hematomas, multiple soft tissue injuries, and skeletal injuries in various locations in different stages of healing (Kempe, Silver, Steele, Broegemueller, & Silver, 1962). Professor Kempe also felt that children diagnosed with failure to thrive should also be thoroughly screened for suspected child abuse (Kempe et al., 1962).

Abused children, like abused women, have been known to kill their abusers during nonconfrontational periods and they also learn how to detect subtle changes in their abuser's behavior. The most common defense in cases of child physical abuse is that the injuries were accidental. Expert testimony can be used to explain the difference between accidental and nonaccidental injuries. By 1983, expert testimony about battered child syndrome was well accepted in the legal community.

Shaken baby syndrome, also known as abusive head trauma or Whiplash infant syndrome, was first described by Dr. John Caffey in 1946. Dr. Caffey identified a triad of symptoms that should make a healthcare provider suspicious of abuse. They include subdural hematoma, brain swelling, and retinal hemorrhage (Caffey, 1946). Dr. Caffey also described several other suspicious injuries in children: long bone fractures, rib fractures, and little to no evidence of external trauma to the head (Caffey, 1946). Perpetrators can be fathers, mothers, boyfriends, or babysitters. There may be minimal to no external injuries and the history provided by the caregivers is often inconsistent with the injuries (Reese & Ludwig, 2001).

Currently, the legal and medical communities have begun to challenge Dr. Caffey's theory regarding the identification of shaken baby syndrome. The American Academy of Pediatrics declares on its website that "shaken baby syndrome is a serious and clearly definable form of child abuse." (http://www.criminal-law-lawyer-source.com/tips/defense.html) The National Institute of Neurological Disorders and Strokes states that "because of a baby's relatively heavy head and weak neck muscles, shaking makes the fragile brain bounce back and forth in the skull causing bruising, swelling, and bleeding which can lead to permanent, severe brain damage and even death" (http://www.law.com/jsp/legaltechnology/roadmapArticle.jsp?id=1158014995389&hubpage=Collection). A 2001 article in the *American Journal of Forensic Medicine and Pathology* concluded that it was possible for an infant to suffer a fatal injury from a short fall. The article stated that an injury from a short fall could cause periods of lucidness along with bilateral retinal hemorrhages mimicking symptoms of shaken baby syndrome (Schaber, Hart, Armbrustmacher, & Hirsch, 2001). The article suggested that symptoms can also be delayed after a short fall. They stated that they found an alternative accidental source for at least one of the symptoms in the "triad" of shaken baby syndromes (Schaber et al., 2001).

In another study conducted in 2004, researchers found that the velocity and acceleration needed to cause the symptoms of shaken baby syndrome would far exceed the limits of the cervical spine and cause structural failure (Bandak, 2004). An additional study carried out in 2003 by researchers at the University of Pennsylvania used biofidelic models to simulate a one-and-a-half-month-old infant. They then shook the model and dropped the model from various heights. Researchers found that symptoms that resulted from vigorous shaking were "statistically similar" to the symptoms following a 1 ft fall onto concrete or concrete with carpet padding (Margulies et al., 2005).

Child sexual abuse accommodation syndrome was first articulated by Dr. Roland Summit in 1983. Dr. Summit was attempting to explain the apparently contradictory behavior of child who had been sexually abused. He defined a group of five reactions that children exhibit after being sexually abused (Summit, 1983). He identified and defined the following common reactions:

- Secrecy: often ensured by threats of negative consequences or harm
- Helplessness: emotional inability to resist or complain
- Entrapment: child sees no way to escape ongoing abuse and thus learns to adapt
- Delayed, conflicted, and unconvincing disclosure:
    - Retraction/recantation—attempts to restore order in the family structure when the disclosure threatens to destroy it (Summit, 1983)

Dr. Summit followed up his initial article on the child sexual abuse accommodation syndrome with a second article in 1992. Dr. Summit wrote that he felt the Child Sexual Abuse Accommodation Syndrome (CSAAS) was being misused in the courts (Summit, 1992). He wrote that he would not have used the term "syndrome" had he known how it would be exploited (Summit, 1992). Dr. Summit clarified that the CSAAS was the result of his clinical observations and not a scientific study. He wrote that the CSAAS described a pattern of behaviors and was not a diagnostic tool meant to identify an illness or disorder. Dr. Summit believed that expert testimony on CSAAS was meaningless in court proceeding unless there had been a disputed disclosure (Summit, 1992). Expert testimony on CSAAS is appropriate when it is used to rebut the myths surrounding delayed or inconsistent reporting, and to explain a child's reaction to sexual abuse when it appears to be the opposite of expected behavior (Summit, 1992). The ultimate decision about whether a child was or was not sexually abused is the sole responsibility of the trier of fact.

Two additional and frequently used affirmative criminal defenses are self-defense and consent in sexual assault cases. In case of self-defense, the LNC will need to scrutinize any medical records, forensic reports, and witness statements for information that may prove or disprove the defendant's claim of self-defense. In case of sexual assault, when the perpetrator argues that the victim consented to sexual intercourse, the LNC should ensure that expert testimony regarding consent should be excluded since the ultimate decision should be made by the trier of fact.

Postconviction Relief

Once a defendant has been convicted of criminal offense either by a jury of his peers or the judge during a bench trial, there are several motions and appeals that the defendant can file. They are used in an attempt to reverse a judicial decision that was either granted or denied during the trial in order to get a new trial or have the verdict dismissed. The first motion filed during this process is a motion asking the trial court to reconsider its decision or set aside the jury verdict. The second would be a motion for a new trial due an error at the court level. "Errors" at the court level are possible errors made by the judge during the course of the trial.

There are four types of errors. The first is a harmless error. A harmless error refers to a judicial decision during the course of the trial that probably would not have affected the outcome of the trial (Larson, 2000). The second is a harmful error. A harmful error refers to a judicial decision made during the course of the trial that probably would have affected the outcome of the trial (Larson, 2000). The third is an invited error. An invited error refers to an error caused by the defendant asking the trial court to make a ruling that is inherently erroneous (Larson, 2000). The final error is a reversible error. A reversible error is an error that causes the appellate court to overturn a lower courts decision (Larson, 2000).

An appeal is another right of convicted defendants to request a higher court to review their case. Defendants are guaranteed the right to at least one appeal. However, defendants who have pled guilty have waived their right to appeal when they entered their plea into the court record (Larson, 2000). The purpose of an appeal is to address "errors of law." (Larson, 2000) The appellate court does not review any new evidence or re-evaluate evidence that was admitted in the original trial (Larson, 2000). A decision by the appellate court to grant a new trial is based solely on the court record made at the time of the trial.

Appeals can be made on the basis of Constitutional Amendment violations. The most common Constitutional Amendments used during the appeal process are the Fourth Amendment, the Fifth Amendment, the Sixth Amendment, and the Eighth Amendment. The Fourth Amendment protects the public from unlawful search and seizures. Defendants will challenge the soundness of any warrants used during the criminal proceeding and any evidence that was collected on the basis of those warrants. In criminal court proceeding, if a warrant is deemed to be unconstitutional, then any evidence obtained based on the warrant may be inadmissible in a court of law.

The Sixth Amendment protects a person's right to due process and self-incrimination. Due process refers to, but is not limited to, the right to a fair and speedy trial, the right to a public trial, the right to an impartial jury, the right to counsel, and the right to testify at trial on their own behalf. Self-incrimination challenges most often have to do with Miranda rights and a violation of those rights. Sixth amendment violations also entitle the defendant to challenge his representation by claiming ineffective assistance of council. In other words, the defendant believes that the attorney did not represent him zealously. Eighth Amendment violations refer to excessive bail, excessive fines, or cruel and unusual punishment.

Mitigation

Mitigation is a term used to describe the process of gathering facts about a defendant during the criminal process. Once defendant has been arraigned and a defense attorney has either been hired or appointed, the process for collecting information regarding the defendant's medical and mental health background can begin. An LNC can begin to gather information about any chronic medical conditions, any acute medical conditions, and any medications the defendant might be taking. Experienced mental health providers can begin to collect information concerning any mental health issues and any psychotropic drugs the defendant might be taking.

The information gathered about the defendant's medical and mental health status can be used by the attorney to argue for a lesser punishment such as minimal to no incarceration and treatment rather than incarceration. Mitigation also has a specific role in capital murder trials.

According to the American Bar Association (ABA), a capital defense team must consistent of at least two attorneys, an investigator, and a mitigation specialist (Frajola, 1993). The mandate that a mitigation specialist must be involved is a result of a decision in the *Wiggins v. Smith* (2003) case. At that time, it was mandated that a thorough life history investigation must be done. The mitigation specialist would be responsible for providing supportive research and a documented history to the defense team. The mitigation specialist would be accountable for the preparation and presentation of the mitigation evidence during the penalty phase of a capital murder trial. The responsibilities of a mitigation specialist would be to obtain a complete and thorough history of the defendant's life history by identifying and interviewing lay witnesses, family members, peers, coworkers, teachers, and other social contacts; obtaining any medical or mental health records to investigate any potential biological, sociological, or psychological issues; and determining if any expert services are needed for areas such as psychological and mental health (Frajola, 1993). The ultimate goal of mitigation is to enable the judge and jury to see the defendant as a human being and not a "monster."

Research Evaluation

Whether hired as a consultant or employed by a law firm fulltime, an LNC will need to be current on medical and forensic research. Because of this, it will be necessary for an LNC to know how to evaluate the reliability and validity of a research article. When reviewing a research article, the

LNC will need to scrutinize certain areas such as the type of publication, the author, and the references used. Some questions about the journal would be who published the journal, is it a peer reviewed journal, and how frequently the journal is published. When evaluating the author, the LNC will want to look at the credential of the author, the author's affiliations and potential biases, and whether the author has been referenced in any other sources. The article's references should be current and the number of references should be appropriate for the article. The only exception would be the inclusion of any prior research on the topic that is considered to be the "classic" resources such as the original articles by Kempe, Silverman, Steele, Droegemuellar, and Silver (1962) that, for the first time, defined battered child syndrome. And finally, how the information in the article compares with other information in other sources on the same topic.

The LNC will also need to keep in mind that research is not generalizable and that all research has limitations. Research is usually not generalizable because the methodology involves a specific location, rural or urban, and a specific population, and it is done at a specific time. Research done in rural Kansas would not necessarily apply to inner-city Detroit. Most reliable research articles will have a section that describes the limitations of the study. Limitations could include the lack of a control group or a very small control group, poor compliance, drop-out rates, and incomplete data. The LNC should also familiarize themselves with the different types of statistical analysis. The type of statistical analysis used will lend itself to the weight of any statistically significant findings.

Process of Criminal Case Review

When reviewing a murder case, the LNC will need to review certain aspects of the case. First and foremost would be the autopsy report, possibly in conjunction with the victim's medical records. The autopsy report will include the cause and mechanism of death. The LNC will need to verify that the mechanism and cause of death match the facts of the criminal act. Additional forensic reports will depend on the facts of the case. If the murder involved a firearm, then there might be ballistics reports, gunshot residue reports, or possible DNA evidence from the firearm if it was collected as evidence. In these types of cases, the LNC's responsibility would include the identification of potential forensic issues and recommendations regarding experts as needed.

For example, the LNC may be hired to review the autopsy report and medical records for a victim initially treated at the hospital, who dies a few days later. The autopsy report determines the cause of death to be hemorrhage. Upon review, the LNC notices that the blood count taken at the time of his cardiac arrest showed a stable blood count. The LNC further notices that the medical examiner documented that there was 1,000 cc of fluid in the left and right pleural spaces. From the perspective of the prosecution, the LNC will need to inform the prosecutor so that the medical examiner can be properly prepared for court and the possible challenge to their findings. From the perspective of the defense, the findings of the LNC could be used to impeach the credibility of the medical examiner.

When reviewing an assault case, the LNC's primary responsibility will be to review the medical records and provide an opinion on the nature and severity of the injuries. In assault cases, the seriousness of the crime is determined based on the nature and severity of the victim's injuries. Following are the types of questions to be asked when doing the medical records review: how long was the victim in the hospital; how much direct treatment did the victim receive; was the victim medicated for pain; what other medication did the victim receive; and, was the victim admitted to the hospital and if so, why were they medicated and to what type of floor where they admitted to. The LNC's opinion will have the same purpose regardless of whether the LNC is working for the prosecution or defense. In both situations, the medical records will be used to either charge the crime or argue for a lesser degree of the charge.

For example, the LNC may be hired to review the medical records for a victim brought into the emergency department (ED) after being assaulted. There are two possible scenarios. First, a victim is brought into the ED after being assaulted by a perpetrator with a knife. The victim tells police that he was stabbed and the police have noted that the victim is bleeding. When the medical records are reviewed, the LNC learns that the victim's wound was superficial and closed with a couple of steri-strips. From the perspective of the prosecution, the LNC's opinion could be used in determining how the crime is charged. From the perspective of the defense, the LNC's opinion could be used by the defense attorney to obtain a plea bargain with a more appropriate charge.

The other scenario might be a case where the victim was taken to the hospital after saying that they had been stabbed in the abdomen. The police document reveals that there is a small puncture wound with no active bleeding. While being examined at the hospital, the healthcare providers find that the victim had sustained serious internal injuries and required immediate surgery. From the prosecution perspective, if the prosecutor has charged the perpetrator with a lower degree of assault, they can reindict the perpetrator on a higher count. From the defense perspective, the attorney can push for an early plea before the prosecution has a chance to reindict the perpetrator.

When reviewing sexual assault cases, the LNC will first need to determine if the victim is an adult or a child. The available medical forensic reports will vary depending on the victim. If the victim is an adult, then the most likely medical forensic reports are a Sexual Assault Nurse Examiner (SANE) report, medical reports, photographs, and a DNA analysis report. If the sexual assault examination was not done within the first 3–5 days, then it is possible that there was no attempt to collect DNA evidence. It is also possible that if the perpetrators' defense is consent, then the sexual assault kit may not have been processed. There should always be medical records at a minimum regardless of the time between the assault and the examination. As with medical records, there should also always be photographs. At a minimum, the photographs should include an identifying face shot of the victim. Regardless of the presence or absence of genital injury, there should still be photographs to either document that the genitalia was normal or to document the location of any injuries, although this is not the practice in all jurisdictions.

Specific areas to scrutinize when reviewing the sexual assault report include the history of events, what evidence was collected, was the appropriate evidence collected based on the history, were there any injuries and if so, was the documentation complete (size, color, exact location), are there any photographs and where are the photographs being stored, and was toulidine dye used. Other information that may be of use include was the victim menstruating, did the victim report having had consensual sex within 72 hr of the sexual assault, and what are the policy and procedures for the SANE program. From both the prosecution and defense perspective, the responsibility of the LNC will be to request the CV for the SANE nurse from counsel; defense counsel may have to subpoena this document. Other responsibilities include the following: determine what the SANE nurse's opinion will be, assist the prosecutor or defense attorney with the development of direct and cross-examination questions, educate the attorneys about the most current research and the most current case law, and be available for the attorney during any criminal proceedings.

Another major issue with regard to reviewing sexual assault cases is the issue of consent. The first article to have a significant impact on the expert testimony of SANE nurses following a medical forensic examination of a victim was the Slaughter, Brown, Crowley, and Peck article. The research study conducted by Slaughter, Brown, Crowley, and Peck found that of the 200 victims they had examined, 94% of the victims had "trauma at one or more of four locations, as follows: posterior fourchette, labia minora, hymen, fossa navicularis" (Slaugher, Brown, Crowley, & Peck, 1997). They reported the most likely types of trauma as tears to the posterior fourchette and fossa, abrasions to the labia, and ecchymosis to the hymen (Slaugher et al., 1997). Slaughter, Brown, Crowley, and Peck concluded that a localized pattern of genital trauma can frequently be seen in women reporting nonconsensual sexual intercourse (Slaugher et al., 1997).

As of late, extensive research has been done to challenge the findings in the Slaughter, Brown, Crowley, and Peck research study. In 1998, Biggs, Stermac, and Divinsky conducted a research study to determine if there were any differences in the genital findings of sexually assaulted women who did and did not have prior sexual experience. The results of their research study suggested that women without prior sexual intercourse experience were more likely to have genital injuries than those with experience (Biggs, Stermac, & Divinsky, 1998). Biggs, Stermac, and Divinsky further noted that a significant number of women did not have any visible signs of injury, regardless of their prior sexual experience at the time of assault (Biggs et al., 1998).

There are also additional articles challenging the early research that opined that genital injury was consistent with nonconsensual sexual intercourse. Research done by Jones, Rossman, Hartman, and Alexander in 2003 found that "anogenital trauma was documented in 73% of adolescent females after consensual sexual intercourse versus 85% of victims of sexual assault." The localized pattern and severity of anogenital injuries were significantly different when compared with victims of sexual assault (Jones, Rossman, Hartman, & Alexander, 2003). A 2003 research study by Adams, Girardin, and Faugno found that hymenal tears were rare in girls who reported no prior sexual experience (Adams, Girardin, & Faugno, 2000). They concluded that prompt examination of adolescent victims is essential for documenting injuries, but even with prompt examination many victims may have only nonspecific examination findings (Adams et al., 2000). Finally, the most recent research study conducted by Anderson, McClain, and Riviello reported that there was no statistical significance between the genital findings of women after consensual and nonconsensual sexual intercourse (Anderson, McClain, & Riviello, 2006).

The LNC will also need to familiarize themselves with the case law surrounding the testimony of experts in the area of sexual assault. In Fairfax County, Virginia, the case of *Commonwealth v. Johnston* challenged expert testimony on the subject of the human sexual response (HSR) (Canaff, 2004). The expert in the Johnston case was an experienced SANE nurse who was expected to offer an opinion that severe injuries are those injuries that are evident through gross examination, which in turn would support the opinion that there was a lack of HSR (*Commonwealth v. Johnston*, 2000). A hearing was conducted where the prosecution and defense had the opportunity to present testimony regarding the SANE nurse's anticipated opinion. The attorneys used the available scientific research to make their arguments regarding the admissibility of the expert testimony. The judge ultimately ruled that "there was an insufficient scientific basis for the opinion that consensual and nonconsensual sex can be distinguished based on the concept of HSR" (*Commonwealth v. Johnston*, 2000). In other words, the SANE nurse's expert testimony could not link an injury to the likelihood of consent.

A similar case was the *Velasquez v. Commonwealth* case, which reached the Virginia Supreme Court. The defense challenged the testimony of the SANE nurse based on two issues (Canaff, 2004). Firstly, the defense argued that even if a SANE nurse is qualified as an expert, their testimony should still be limited to describing any injuries but should not include an opinion of the possible cause of those injuries (*Velasquez v. Commonwealth*, 2002). The defense asserted that an opinion about cause would amount to making a medical diagnosis. Secondly, the defense argued that the SANE nurse's expert testimony about the cause of genital trauma took away the trier of fact's responsibility to make the ultimate decision about the facts of the case (*Velasquez v. Commonwealth*, 2002).

The Virginia Supreme Court disagreed with the defense's first argument, but did grant the defense a new trial based on the second argument (*Velasquez v. Commonwealth*, 2002). As a result of the Virginia Supreme Court's ruling, a SANE nurse cannot provide expert testimony that would address the ultimate issue in the case. The ruling would allow the expert SANE nurse to testify that certain injuries are consistent with consensual sexual intercourse but would not allow any expert testimony on any other possible causes of genital injury (*Velasquez v. Commonwealth*, 2002).

Child sexual abuse cases have an additional dimension. Studies have indicated that child sexual abuse affects approximately 10–28% of children, making it more common than pneumonia and urinary tract infections (Federal Rules of Evidence, 2007). In most cases, the only medical forensic evidence will be medical records or a SANE report if the victim was examined. Since most cases of child sexual abuse are not reported until days, weeks, months, or years after the incident, the chance of finding any forensic evidence is extremely limited. Whether working for the prosecution or the defense, the medical records, if available, will need to be closely scrutinized. The two main issues are (1) what is the significance of the presence or absence of injuries; and (2) are there any medical conditions that could mimic abuse.

Since the findings of a medical forensic examination are most often negative for physical injures or injuries that are nonspecific, it may be necessary to assess the victim for the presence of behavior or psychological problems. Sexually abused children may also develop the following:

- Unusual interest in or avoidance of all things of a sexual nature
- Sleep problems or nightmares
- Depression or withdrawal from friends or family
- Seductiveness:
  - Statements that their bodies are dirty or damaged, or fear that there is something wrong with them in the genital area
- Refusal to go to school
- Delinquency/conduct problems
- Secretiveness
- Aspects of sexual molestation in drawings, games, fantasies
- Unusual aggressiveness
- Suicidal behavior (American Academy of Child and Adolescent Psychiatry, 2008)

Conditions that could potentially mimic child sexual abuse include dermatological conditions, congenital conditions, urethral conditions, anal conditions, traumatic conditions, and infectious diseases. The most common skin disease mistaken for child abuse is lichen sclerosis. Other possible skin conditions include poor hygiene, diaper rash, intertigo, sensitivity to bubble bath, dyes used in toilet products, pinworms, and *Candida* infection. Congenital conditions include the following: hemangioma of the hymen, vulva, vagina, or perinial body is often confused with erythema from child sexual abuse. The variations in congenital structure are another commonly confused normal condition. For example, periurethral bands, hymenal tags, hymenal septa, septal remnants, intravaginal ridges, tissue bridges, hymenal clefts, and hymenal mounds. An LNC should also familiarize themselves with normal hymenal variants such as fimbriated, annular, cresentic, navicular, cribiform, or septate.

Clator, Barth, and Shubin (1989) conducted a research study where they reviewed the records of 944 children examined by the same pediatrician for alleged sexual abuse. The study found that

64% of the females and 34% of the males had positive findings suggestive of anogenital injury (Clator et al., 1989). Adams and Knudson (1996) discovered while conducting research on adolescents girls that normal or nonspecific results of genital examinations are commonly found in adolescents who have been sexually abused, unless the abuse was very recent (Adams & Knudson, 1996). Research conducted by Heger, Ticson, Velasquez, and Bernier found while reviewing past research that the findings of the medical examination are relied upon heavily by medical, social, and legal professionals when attempting to diagnose child sexual abuse instead of focusing on the child history, which remains the single most important diagnostic feature (Heger, Ticson, Velasquez, & Bernier, 2002). They also noted that abnormal findings were only present in about 4% of the medical forensic examinations conducted on children referred for suspected child abuse (Heger et al., 2002).

The LNC may be hired to review Driving While Intoxicated/Driving Under the Influence (DWI/DUI) cases that involved alcohol or prescription drugs. For the purpose of this chapter, DWI/DUI related to illicit drugs will not be discussed. When evaluating a DWI/DUI case, the LNC consultant will need to review the drug and alcohol analysis reports from the medical examiners office or other laboratory testing facility. Once again, there will be similarities in the information provided to the attorney regardless of whether it is for the prosecution or defense. It should also be noted that the alcohol and drug analysis reports should not be analyzed independently. The LNC may need to evaluate the police records of any field sobriety testing done such as an alcohol involved incident report (AIIR).

From the prosecution perspective, the LNC may need to educate the attorneys about diabetes when it is being considered as a defense for a DUI charge. The defense will try to claim that the defendant was not drunk at the time of the offense but was instead suffering from a diabetic reaction. Diabetics who do not follow a proper diet regimen or drinks alcohol may experience a drop in their bloods sugar, or a hypoglycemic reaction. The symptoms of a hypoglycemic reaction can mimic the behaviors of someone who is drunk: slurred speech, uncoordinated movements, confusion, and an altered odor to the breath. The diabetic defense also has an explanation for an elevated breathalyzer readings claiming that the acetone emitted by diabetics while in a hypoglycemic state interferes with the breathalyzer sample (National Institute of Justice, 1998).

In September 1985, the National Highway Traffic Safety Administration (NHTSA) issued a report regarding the interference of acetone in standardized breath alcohol measurement devices. The NHTSA concluded that higher than normal acetone levels experienced from "uncontrolled" diabetes would render an actual diabetic to be so sick that they would be unable to drive and would require hospitalization (National Institute of Justice, 1998). They further stated that the amount of acetone necessary to interfere with a breath alcohol measurement could not be generated by diabetics who have their condition under control (National Institute of Justice, 1998). To determine if the defendant may have a valid diabetes defense, a prosecutor should ask the following questions:

■ Does the defendant's medical records indicate that he/she is a diabetic?
■ Was the defendant diagnosed with diabetes prior to or subsequent to his arrest?
■ Does the defense plan to call an expert witness to testify that the defendant was suffering from low blood sugar at the time of the arrest?
■ Is the expert witness the treating physician? Did he/she examine the defendant on the date of the arrest? Did the expert ever examine the defendant?
■ Is the defendant an insulin-dependent or noninsulin-dependent diabetic? Noninsulin-dependent diabetics are unlikely to even emit acetone from their breath (National Institute of Justice, 1998).

There is another common argument in alcohol-related criminal acts that could affect both the prosecution and the defense. The LNC should familiarize themselves with the current research related to the accuracy of blood alcohol content (BAC) results based on whether the sample analyzed was whole or serum blood. Blood samples are generally drawn and tested for alcohol content in two situations, when requested by law enforcement officers in connection with a suspected DUI case or by hospital medical personnel in connection with patient diagnosis and treatment. A legal blood-alcohol concentration is often expressed as the percentage of alcohol by weight (i.e., grams of ethanol in 100 mL of blood) (Roehrenbeck & Russell, 1993).

Clinical laboratories generally report ethanol concentration in mg per dL of blood. In order to convert the laboratory results to a legal blood-alcohol concentration, move the decimal point three places to the left. For example, 135 mg/dL becomes 0.135% wt/vol. The water content of serum blood is 98%, while the water content of whole blood is 86%. Understanding this discrepancy is vital when evaluating blood-alcohol concentration results. Serum and plasma levels average 1.09–1.18 times higher than whole blood levels (Roehrenbeck & Russell, 1993).

In order for an attorney to challenge the results of a serum blood-alcohol result, they must become familiar with the accepted procedures used to arrive at the results for both substances. The admissibility of blood-alcohol tests as evidence at a trial depends on the wording of the relevant state statute and on the attorney's ability to provide evidence that the test results are unreliable (Roehrenbeck & Russell, 1993).

The defendant will commonly use one of the following three arguments when challenging the conversion of serum blood results to whole blood: (1) every individual has a different conversion ratio; (2) the defendant was on medication; (3) the defendant was dehydrated (Roehrenbeck & Russell, 1993). Individual conversion ratios may vary, but experts have found that most people's conversion rates fall within a known range (Roehrenbeck & Russell, 1993). Attorneys, both prosecutor and defense, may need to consult with an expert toxicologist to discuss conversation ratios since the process of converting a serum reading to a whole blood reading does involve complex equations (Roehrenbeck & Russell, 1993). This is where the knowledge and expertise of LNC can be useful. The LNC can help prosecutors to respond to the defense counsel's attempts to challenge conversion ratios by preparing them and the expert witness in advance.

Additional research articles of interest include the following: (1) Hodgon and Shajani (1985) concluded that blood-alcohol concentration in plasma was approximately 11% higher than that of whole blood (Hodgon & Shajani, 1985); (2) Winek and Carfagna (1987) found that a "person with an ethanol concentration of .09 in whole blood could have been reported as a concentration above .10 if serum or plasma was analyzed" (Winek & Carfagna, 1987); (3) Frajola concluded that the serum alcohol concentrations can be up to 20% higher than whole blood-alcohol concentrations (Feldman et al., 1991). The LNC will also want to review the most current case law, for example, *Commonwealth v. Wanner* 605 A.2d 805 (Pa. Super 1992) (*Commonwealth v. Wanner*). In this case, the defendant appealed his DUI conviction on the grounds that the evidence of his blood-alcohol concentration was based on tests conducted on blood plasma rather than whole blood. The appellate court agreed. As a final note, the court reported that it found testing on plasma resulted in BAC 15–20% higher than tests on whole blood. In *Melton v. state*, 597 N.E 2d 359 (Ind App 1992), the appellate court reversed a defendant's DUI conviction after hearing evidence that the BAC presented to the jury was based on test performed on blood plasma and therefore it was inaccurate (*Melton v state*). The court said that tests on blood plasma samples register 18–20% higher than test on whole blood. Conversion factor in translating serum results to whole blood results range from 0.88 to 1.59, with a median of 1.15 (Feldman et al., 1991). Currently, labs are using the uniform ratio of 1.16:1.

Similar to alcohol-related DUIs, prescription DUIs have issues that will need to be examined by the LNC. In DUI cases involving prescription drugs, a report from the medical examiners office or forensic laboratory should be provided. Once the report has been provided, it should be reviewed to determine what prescription drugs are present and in what quantity. If the results have not been quantified by the laboratory, then consult with the attorney regarding having the results quantified. From the prosecution perspective, it may be helpful to have the results quantified in order to potentially argue that the elevated level is a sign of intoxication. However, a normal or low value could allow the defense to argue the opposite, that the result is evidence that the defendant was not intoxicated. Two possible resources are the Toxic Drug Concentrations Data Chart from the office of the chief medical examiner in Chapel Hill, North Carolina or Winek's Drug and Chemical Blood-Level Data 2001. Those resources will provide information on prescription drugs and the blood value ranges for therapeutic, toxic, or lethal levels. As noted when alcohol DUI cases were discussed, a laboratory value is not sufficient evidence when it comes to proving or disproving intoxication. The defendant's behavior and actions at the time of the alleged criminal act should also be taken into consideration.

Summary

The LNC is an appropriate and valuable member of the criminal justice system. An LNC can provide effective assessments of medical and forensic reports. They are capable of doing extensive medical and forensic research. LNCs are proficient in reviewing medical records for both the civil and criminal justice systems. They are also capable of reviewing specialized medical forensic reports such as SANE reports, DNA reports, and some toxicology reports. LNCs can assist with gathering medical information for mitigation purposes in a variety of criminal cases, including capital murder cases. The most important thing for LNCs to remember is that they should only consult within those areas in which they are trained and qualified.

References

ACLU. (2007, April). Why I oppose mandatory minimum sentencing laws. Retrieved September 2008, from http://aclupa.blogspot.com/2007_04_01_archive.html.

Adam Walsh Act, Title I, Sec. 111(5)(A)(i.).

Adams, J. A., & Knudson, S. (1996). Genital findings in adolescent girls referred for suspected sexual abuse. *Archives of Pediatric and Adolescent Medicine, 150*(8), 850–857.

Adams, J. A., Girardin, B., & Faugno, D. (2000). Signs of genital trauma in adolescent rape victims examined acutely. *Journal of Pediatric and Adolescent Gynecology, 13*(2), 88.

American Academy of Child and Adolescent Psychiatry. (2008). *Child Sexual Abuse*, No. 9, updated May 2008.

Anderson, S., McClain, N., & Riviello, R. J. (2006). Genital findings of women after consensual and non-consensual intercourse. *Journal of Forensic Nursing, 2*(2), 59–65.

Ark. R. Evid. 803(4).

Bandak, F. A. (2004). Shaken baby syndrome: A biomechanics analysis of injury mechanisms. *Forensic Science International, 151*(1), 71–79

Biggs, M., Stermac, L. E., & Divinsky, M. (1998). Genital injuries following sexual assault of women with and without prior sexual intercourse experience. *Canadian Medical Association Journal, 14, 159*(1), 33–37.

Burgess, A. W. (1986). *Rape: Crisis and recovery*. West Newton, MA: Awab.

Burgess, A. W., & Holstrom, L. L. (1974). Rape trauma syndrome. *American Journal of Psychiatry, 131*(9), 981–986.

Caffey, J. (1946). Multiple fractures in the long bones of infants suffering from chronic subdural hematoma. *American Journal of Roentgemology, 56,* 163–173.

Campbell, H. (1993). *Nursing care of survivors of family violence.* St. Louis, MI: Mosby.

Campbell, J. C. (1990). *Violence Update, 1*(4), 1, 4, 10–11.

Canaff, J. D. (2004). Limits and lessons: The expert medical opinion in adolescent sexual abuse cases. *National District Attorneys Association Update, 17,* 3.

Clator, R. N., Barth, K. L., & Shubin, C. I. (1989). Evaluation child sexual abuse: observations regarding ano-genital injury. *Clinical Pediatrics, 28*(9), 419–422.

Commonwealth v. Johnston, WL 3317722 (2000).

Commonwealth v. Wanner, 605 A.2d 805 (Pa. Super 1992).

Delaware criminal and traffic law manual, 2006–2007, University of Delaware (Vol. 11, pp. 636). LexisNexis.

Delaware criminal and traffic law manual, Title 16. Chapter 9: Abuse of Children. Subchapter II: Child Protection Registry, University of Delaware. Retrieved on September 1, 2008, from http://delcode. delaware.gov/title16/c009/sc02/index.shtml.

Department of Justice Office of the Attorney General. (1998, December). Megan's law; Final Guidelines for the Jacob Wetterling Crimes against Children and Sexually Violent Offender Registration Act, as amended.

Ditton, P. M., & Wilson, D. J. (1999). *Truth in sentencing in state prisons.* Bureau of Justice Statistics. Retrieved September 1, 2008, from http://www.ncjrs.gov/App/Publications/abstract.aspx?ID=170032.

Dixon, J. W. (2002). Battered women syndrome. Retrieved on September 1, 2008, from http://www. expertlaw.com/library/domestic_violence/battered_women.html.

Federal Rules of Evidence. (2007). Article VII Hearsay, Title 803.

Feldman, W., Feldman, E., Goodman, J. T. et al. (1991). Is childhood sexual abuse really increasing in prevalence? An analysis of evidence. *Pediatrics, 88,* 317–322.

Frajola, W. J. (1993). Blood alcohol testing in clinical laboratories: Problems and suggested remedies. *Clinical Chemistry, 39*(3), 377–379.

Freedman, E. M. (2003). American Bar Association: Guidelines for the appointment and performance of defense counsel in death penalty cases, 31 Hofstra L Rev. 913.

Giannelli, P. (1996). Criminal Law Bulletin 32.1983. Chain of custody and the handling of real evidence. *American Criminal Law Review, 20,* 447–465.

Heger, A., Ticson, L., Velasquez, O., & Bernier, R. (2002). Children referred for possible sexual abuse: medical findings in 2384 children. *Child Abuse and Neglect, 26*(6–7), 645–659.

Henry, L. (2004). Advances in forensic science. *Bulletin of the Connecticut Academy of Science and Engineering, 19,* 1–2.

Hodgson, B. T., & Shajani, N. K. (1985). Distribution of ethanol: Plasma to whole blood ratios. *Forensic Science Journal, 18,* 73–77.

Human Rights Watch. (2008). Sex offender registration laws. Retrieved September 1, 2008, from http:// www.hrw.org/reports/2007/us0907/5.htm.

http://www.aap.org.

http://www.criminal-law-lawyer-source.com/tips/defense.html.

http://www.law.com/jsp/legaltechnology/roadmapArticle.jsp?id=1158014995389&hubpage=Collection.

http://www.lawinfo.com/index.cfm/fuseaction/Client.lawarea/categoryid/137.

http://www.ninds.nih.gov.

http://www.pbs.org/wgbh/pages/frontline/shows/crime/trial/faqs.html.

Jacob Wetterling Crimes against Children and Sexually Violent Offender Registration Act. (1994). Pub. L. 103–322, Title XVII, Subtitle A, § 170101, September 13, 1994, 108 Stat. 2038, 42 USC. § 14071.

James, S. H., & Nordby, J. J. (2005). *Forensic science: An introduction to scientific and investigative techniques.* Boca Raton, FL: CRC Press.

Jones, J. S., Rossman, L., Hartman, M., & Alexander, C. C. (2003). Anogenital injuries in adolescents after consensual sexual intercourse. *Academy of Emerging Medicine, 10*(12), 1378–1383.

Kempe, C. H., & Helfer, R. E. (1972). *Helping the battered child and his family.* Philadelphia, PA: Lippincot.

Kempe, C. H., Silver, F., Steele, B., Broegemueller, W., & Silver, H. (1962). *The battered child syndrome.* Journal of the American Medical Association, 181, 17–24.

Larson, A. (2000). Appealing criminal conviction. Retrieved September 1, 2008, from http://www.expertlaw.com/library/criminal/criminal_appeals.html.

Margulies, S., Prange, M., Myers, B., Maltese, M., Ji, S., Ning, X., Fisher, J., Arbogast, K., & Christian, C. (2005). Shaken baby syndrome: A flawed biomechanical analysis. *Forensic Science Internation, 164*(2–3), 71–79.

Melton v. state, 597 N.E 2d 359 (Ind App 1992).

National Districts Attorneys Association. (1994). *National Traffic Law Center—Resource clearinghouse: Between the lines* (Vol. 2, p. 1). Alexandria, VA: American Prosecutors Research Institute.

National Institute of Justice. (1998). *National Law Enforcement and Correction Center Technology Center Bulletin.* Washington, DC: The National Institute of Justice and Advances in Forensic Science and Technology.

National Institute of Justice. (2000). *Understanding DNA evidence: A guide for victim services provider.* Rockville, MD: National Institute of Justice Office of Science and Technology.

Block, A. P. (1990). Rape trauma syndrome as scientific expert testimony. *Archives of Sexual Behavior, 19*(4), 309–323.

Reese, R. M., & Ludwig, S. (2001). *Child abuse medical diagnosis and management.* Philadelphia, PA: Lippincott.

Roehrenbeck, C. A., & Russell, R. W. (1993). Blood is thicker than water: What you need to know to challenge a serum blood alcohol result. *Criminal Justice, 3*(8), 14–18.

Rule 11-803(D) NMRA 1999.

Schaber, B., Hart, A. P., Armbrustmacher, V., & Hirsch, C. S. (2001). Fatal pediatric head injuries caused by short distance falls. *American Journal of Forensic Medicine and Pathology, 23*(1), 101–103.

Slaugher, L., Brown, C. R., Crowley, S., & Peck, R. (1997). Patterns of genital injury in female sexual assault victims. *American Journal of Obstetrics and Gynecology, 176*(3), 609–616.

Summit, R. C. (1983). The child sexual abuse accommodation syndrome. *Child Abuse and Neglect, 7,* 177–193.

Summit, R. C. (1992). Abuse of the child sexual abuse accommodation syndrome. *Journal of Child Sexual Abuse, 1*(4), 153–163.

The Adam Walsh Child Protection and Safety Act of 2006. NCSL Summary P.L. 109-248 (HR 4472). Retrieved September 1, 2008, from www.ncls.org/standcomm/sclaw/walshact.htm.

Travis, J. (1997). "Three strikes and your out": A review of State legislation. National Institute of Justice Research Brief. (Michigan State University). Retrieved September 1, 2008, from http://www.lib.msu.edu/harris23/crimjust/sentence.htm.

United States Sentencing Commission. (1991). Special report to congress: Mandatory minimum penalties in the federal criminal justice system. Retrieved September 1, 2008, from http://www.ussc.gov/r_congress/MANMIN.PDF.

Velasquez v. Commonwealth, 263 Va. 95, 557 S.E.2d. 213 (2002).

Walker, L. E. (2006). Battered women syndrome: Empirical findings. *Annuals of N Y Academy of Science, 1087,* 142–157.

Way, B. B., Dvoskin, J. A., & Steadman, H. J. (1991). Forensic psychiatric inpatients served in the United States: Regional and system differences. *Bulletin of the American Academy of Psychiatry and the Law, 19* 405–412.

Wiggins v. Smith, 539 U.S. 510 (2003).

Winek, C. L., & Carfagna, M. (1987). Comparisons of plasma, serum, and whole blood ethanol concentrations. *Journal of Analytical Toxicology, 11*(6), 267–268.

Test Questions

1. What type of crime is the most serious?
   A. Misdemeanor
   B. Felony
   C. Petty
   D. Citation/ticket

2. The Child Abuse Registry was created as a result of which piece of legislation?
   A. Constitution
   B. Megan's Law
   C. Adam Walsh Child and Safety Act
   D. Human Rights Act

3. Which of the following statements is NOT true?
   A. The Sex Offender Registry was created as a result of the Adam Walsh Child and Safety Act
   B. "Truth-in-sentencing" is a law that ensures that convicted defendants serve the major portion of their sentence
   C. "Three Strikes" law applies to defendants who have committed three or more misdemeanors
   D. Hearsay evidence is an oral or written statement about an out-of-court declaration attributed to someone other than the testifying person

4. Which of the following is NOT a postconviction challenge?
   A. Defendant did not like the outcome of the trial
   B. Constitutional violation
   C. Trial error
   D. Judicial error

5. Which affirmative defense is used to help explain why a woman might kill her spouse while he is sleeping?
   A. Rape trauma syndrome
   B. Battered woman syndrome
   C. Battered child syndrome
   D. PMS syndrome

Answers: 1. B, 2. C, 3. C, 4. A, 5. B

Chapter 6

The LNC's Role in Healthcare Risk Management

Dolly M. Curley, RN, BS, BSN, DABFN, LNCC and
Sharon Whidden, MSN, RN, LNCC

First Edition and Second Edition
Thomas B. Mendez, MSN, RN, ANP

Contents

Objectives

- Describe a risk management program structure with risk reduction strategies associated with the safety of patient care
- Discuss the systems used for risk identification
- Identify at least four examples of sentinel events that must be reported
- Discuss the difference between a root cause analysis and failure mode effects analysis

Introduction

An interesting and challenging role for the legal nurse consultant (LNC) is providing services in the area of healthcare risk management. Both risk management and legal nurse consulting offer a variety of overlapping roles within each specialty that require comparable, specialized skills and attributes. LNCs can apply their experience and knowledge as transferable skills gained from clinical practice, management, and/or administrative roles to this stimulating field. Experience with accreditation, compliance, contracts, insurance, and licensing issues, as well as knowledge of the legal process and system is of tremendous benefit when entering into risk management. It is, however, essential for the risk manager to know and understand the organizational hierarchy, history, and culture as this determines specific operations and reporting processes.

The role of the LNC as an employee in healthcare risk management is widely diverse and is influenced by the size and structure of the organization. The sophistication level of the risk management model is dependent on the institutional commitment. An LNC may also be requested to serve as a risk manager consultant to the organization depending on his/her background. Regardless of the position, the functions performed may range from taking responsibility for risk management activities in prevention, reduction, and control of loss to educating staff and physicians about risks, patients' rights and disclosure, documentation, regulatory, licensing, accreditation compliance, and ethical issues. The experienced risk manager may also become credentialed in claims management activities and have responsibilities in managing actual or potential claims by determining the liability exposure and negotiating resolution when possible, prior to initiation of a lawsuit.

As health care is redefined and becomes more competitive, all healthcare providers are charged with managing costs of care and driving quality improvements. Patient satisfaction, provider productivity, and quality management are critical to successful cost containment; therefore, healthcare entities must explore new ways to reduce direct and indirect liability exposure and cost. According to the Agency for Healthcare and Quality (AHRQ), widespread consensus exists that healthcare organizations can reduce patient injuries and liability exposure by improving the environment for patient safety, implementing technical changes, such as electronic medical records, improving staff awareness for patient safety risks, and developing clinical process interventions that have strong evidence for reducing the risk of adverse events related to patient exposure to hospital care (AHR Quality Indicators, 2006). Patient safety has been a main focus and priority in the healthcare industry since the beginning of 2000 and has led to the development of a patient safety officer position. In many states, the position of patient safety officer is mandated by statute. The individual designated as the safety officer, who also could be the risk manager, should be one commanding trust and respect, and possessing integrity as she/he has oversight of the facility-wide safety program in the reduction of healthcare errors and litigation.

Consumers of healthcare are savvier than ever in their selection of providers of care and in their overall awareness and expectations since insurance companies required second opinions and since massive amounts of information became available at the click of a mouse. Risk managers are charged with staying current with new initiatives. Changes to the Joint Commission standard that went into effect July 21, 2001 dictate disclosure of unanticipated outcomes to patients and family members (Joint Commission on Accreditation of Healthcare Organizations, 2001). Patient and family responses to these disclosures increased public awareness of medical errors and have had an impact on healthcare organizations' liability exposure. Patients clearly expect open disclosure to include an explanation of what happened, an apology for harm done, an assurance that appropriate remedial action will be taken, and an explanation of what will be done to learn from the event and to prevent recurrence. A process for addressing the emotional needs of healthcare professionals following an adverse event is another consideration (Manser & Staender, 2005). Obviously, significant commitment is required from the organizations to make disclosure and follow-up occur timely and appropriately. To further improve and enhance for safe care, Pennsylvania has passed a new law, Act 52 of 2007, the Health Care-Associated Infection Prevention and Control Act, that amends the Medical Care Availability and Reduction of Error Act (Act 13 of 2002) to better protect patients, healthcare workers, and the public in the reduction and prevention of healthcare-associated infections. Senate Bill 968 was signed into law on July 20, 2007. The bill reflects the Hospital and Health System of Pennsylvania's (HAP) influence in requiring the adoption of the Centers for Disease Control and Prevention (CDC), National Healthcare Safety Network (NHSN), Internet-based surveillance system as a primary framework for hospitals to report healthcare-associated infections to the Department of Health (DOH), Health Care Cost Containment Council (PHCC), and Patient Safety Authority (The Hospital and Healthsystem Association of Pennsylvania, 2008). The above changes in legislation call for a sophisticated and well coordinated risk management program.

The level of expertise of the individual charged with risk management responsibilities and the availability of resources such as staff and computer support will affect the program's success. Often, the individual charged with risk management is given additional areas of responsibility, such as corporate compliance, quality assurance, patient safety, and professional staff credentialing. It can be difficult for the risk manager to juggle the various roles. When this occurs, the LNC can be of great benefit to a healthcare organization by providing consultative services, performing risk assessments, and developing educational programs for the risk manager's use. With the evolution of enterprise risk management (ERM), organizational commitment, and the trend for transparency in healthcare, the healthcare industry may be better prepared in the future to prioritize roles and responsibilities.

Principles of Risk Management

Risk management is the systematic process of managing an organization's risk from physical harm and financial exposure. The principles of risk management and the nursing process are quite similar, each requiring knowledge in the process of decision-making through assessment, planning, implementation, and evaluation. A risk manager must understand what a risk is and the impact it will have on the organization in order to accomplish effective risk management. Risk identification asks what can go "wrong" while risk control asks what can we do to prevent something from going "wrong" and risk financing asks how we pay for it if something does go wrong. According to Levick (2002), there are four basic steps in the risk management process:

1. Identification of sources from which losses may arise
2. Evaluation of the financial risk involved in each exposure in terms of expected frequency, severity, and impact
3. Management of risks by elimination, reduction, or control of risk factors, transfer of responsibility for risk to other parties, and funding through the operation of a coordinated and effective program
4. Continuous and systematic monitoring of risks

Ultimately, the goal focuses on identification of problems, prevention of exposure to liability, and promotion of patient safety.

Risk Identification

Accurate and complete risk identification of potential and actual areas of risk is similar to the assessment phase of the nursing process and is vital for effective risk management. Risk identification is discovering and communicating risks before they become problems. The risk and quality departments are responsible for developing systematic methods for timely incident reporting of adverse events. Providing uncomplicated tools and instructions to both clinical staff and physicians regarding what is an incident and who should report it, increases awareness and opportunities for correct reporting. There are various techniques that can be used for risk identification assessment. Among them include

- Internal audits, staff and patient interviews, patient complaints, and satisfaction surveys
- Committee minutes from in-house quality and risk-related meetings including sentinel events
- Survey reports and recommendations from the Joint Commission (TJC), Department of Health (DOH), National Committee on Quality Assurance (NCQA), Commission on Accreditation of Rehabilitation Facilities (CARF), and Occupational Safety and Health Administration (OSHA)
- Security, hazard, and insurance company reports
- Passive surveillance predicts near misses
- Chart reviews and computerized screening
- Policies and procedure updates to assure best practices
- Root cause analysis (RCA)

- Failure mode effects analysis (FMEA)
- Medical malpractice claims relative to facility

Brainstorming with individual departments and developing teams who understand risk and process analysis will serve to improve risk identification. Making risk management an integral and vital part of the entire organization will move healthcare leaders toward achieving a common goal of patient safety and error reduction.

Creating a Proactive Risk Management Plan

Following a thorough risk identification process and aligning with the overall integrated organizational strategies, a comprehensive risk management plan addressing purpose, structure, and process can be created with clear, documented goals and objectives. The final product becomes a road map outlining organizational strategy, allocation of appropriate risk resources with defined positions, the assessment process, delineation of procedures, handling of risk issues, identifying priority risk issues, monitoring/tracking processes, evaluating loss control activities, and monitoring equipment. Several factors shape a successful risk management program. Visibility, accessibility, and quick response of the risk management department staff to all departments can greatly increase the likelihood that a program will succeed. Setting the standard for "mindfulness" of patient safety in the organizational culture must be absolutely fostered if it is the expectation. A risk manager's level of knowledge and expertise definitely has an impact on the success of a risk program, but one cannot underestimate the need for excellent interpersonal skills with an appreciation of overall organizational and individual departmental issues. Staff responds positively to a risk manager who is a team player, listens objectively, remains calm, and is an effective communicator. If the employees and medical staff of an organization visibly see and interact with a risk manager only following a negative event, staff and physicians alike tend to move in the opposite direction. Partnering with staff at all levels and developing ongoing positive relationships throughout the organization is key to a successful program.

Implementing the Risk Plan

Risk management is not an isolated entity in any institution. The risk manager who realizes the importance of integrated decision-making throughout the organization will incorporate interdepartmental suggestions and strategies for prevention of medical errors and injuries. Education is a necessary component to any change. Advanced publicized notification of mandatory educational programs demonstrates a commitment to the organization, which in turn will promote learning and compliance. Through the process of risk identification and data collection, individual units such as Rehab may encounter an increase in the number of fall events, while the Intensive Care Unit (ICU) may have issues relative to interdisciplinary communication with transferring patients. Each area will require an independent plan of action to reduce the frequency of adverse events. Implementing a plan with new safety initiatives that provide well-defined outcomes and encourage team support is more readily received when staff and physicians are recognized for their participation and contribution. The overall risk plan for the organization needs leadership commitment at all levels. The plan must be fully integrated with purpose, goals and desired outcomes, and time frames. If an organization hears the risk department concentrating only on numbers versus patient- and staff-care issues, their perception could have a negative impact on supporting the plan. Therefore, the popularity of benchmarking and loss controls should not be the only focus of the risk plan. Rather, the measurement must be combined with leadership commitment to a positive culture change in both attitude and awareness toward patient safety.

Evaluating the Effectiveness of the Risk Management Process

The evaluation portion of the risk management program is a continuous process and requires continual vigilance to identity risks and trends of events, potential and actual claims, and educational needs. The type and frequency of events, potential claims, actual claims, and the value of each provide excellent yardsticks to evaluate the program and identify needs for improvement. The specialty of risk management is an evolving industry demanding more accurate and consistent methods of data collection and categorizing medical events. The Patient Safety and Quality Improvement Act of 2005 was a direct response to the Institute of Medicine report of 1999, "*To Err is Human: Building a Safer Health System*," which concluded that up to 98,000 patients die each year as a result of "medical error." The Institute of Medicine serves as adviser to the nation to improve health. Established in 1970 under the charter of the National Academy of Sciences, the Institute of Medicine provides independent, objective, evidence-based advice to policymakers, health professionals, the private sector, and the public (Kohn, Corrigan, & Donaldson, 2000). The Patient Safety and Quality Improvement Act of 2005 (Public Law 109-41) emphasized that future healthcare models need to be designed for and aimed at reducing the number of medical errors and improving patient safety. Development of a patient safety taxonomy that captures and describes events using common language is the first step toward providing improvement in data-driven outcomes, assisting in benchmarking against other risk departments, and supporting data analysis to accurately identify and classify the risks.

Practicing Proactive Risk Management

As health care is redefined and becomes more competitive, all healthcare providers are charged with managing the costs of care and driving quality initiatives. Patient satisfaction, provider productivity, and quality management are critical to successful cost containment; therefore, healthcare entities must explore new ways to reduce direct and indirect liability exposure and cost. According to the AHRQ, widespread consensus exists that healthcare organizations can reduce patient injuries and liability exposure by improving the environment for patient safety, implementing technical changes, such as electronic medical records, improving staff awareness for patient safety risks, and developing clinical process interventions that have strong evidence for reducing the risk of adverse events related to patient exposure to hospital care. Patient safety and patient satisfaction ultimately have a direct impact on each other (ASHRM Task Force, Monograph, 2008). It almost never fails that when patients are asked about the care they received, their answer is a result of an association between the caregivers being compassionate to the perceived quality of care. Open communication is another fact conducive to patient satisfaction.

ERM includes the methods and processes used by an organization to manage risks. It can be described as a risk-based approach to managing an enterprise integrating concepts of strategic planning, operations management, and internal management (Agency for Healthcare Research and Quality: The Patient Safety & Quality Act). All business entities track revenue as the driver of success and continued operation. Historically, hospitals were not recognized as a business but as an expected provider of care. Today, hospitals must run as any other business while meeting numerous regulatory requirements and maintaining a quality patient-care focus. Balancing this act is both complex and multifaceted; however, the consumers of healthcare are now demanding quality. Systems and techniques such as Failure Mode Effects Analysis (FMEA) have been adopted by healthcare organizations from other industries to prevent errors prospectively. Risk managers need to become familiar with these concepts.

The Role of the LNC in Risk Management

The LNC who selects healthcare risk management as their area of interest will discover that the skills and attributes necessary in legal nurse consulting have a mirror image to that of a risk manager. The role of the LNC's area of practice is a recognized specialty by the American Nurses Association. Entering this field affords the LNC numerous opportunities in which one can professionally advance. LNCs can bring clinical specialization together with knowledge of the litigation process, being an invaluable resource to any organization. The risk professional is not limited to hospital risk management. Risk management is an essential business entity that crosses the continuum of care into other venues that include, but are not limited to, home care, ambulatory services, behavioral health, long-term care, insurance companies, broker companies, physician groups, legal practice, and managed care organizations. In any healthcare setting, risk management is a challenging specialty that is evolving into a field of increasing opportunity.

Loss Prevention

Loss prevention is the proactive use of programs or activities to reduce or eliminate the chance of loss or to decrease the severity of a loss. One pivotal activity for the risk manager is to focus on regular formal education programs to teach physicians and nurses about risk management and the role of the risk manager. Employee orientation is an excellent example of an educational loss-prevention opportunity. Providing employees with guidelines, policies, and procedures makes them aware of their responsibility for loss control and prevention, as well as giving them an understanding of the responsibility of the organization overall.

A proactive safety program is also an excellent loss-prevention technique. Such a program should include active participation by the safety officer or designee in the employee orientation program. The orientation should include the following:

- Identification of the individual responsible for safety.
- Review of pertinent safety and security policies and procedures, with emphasis on electrical and fire safety.
- Education of hospital employees about the annual Joint Commission Patient Safety Goals established in 2003 and added to the accreditation process. Emphasis is placed on exactly what the organization is doing to meet these goals. Staff must know this information for their Joint Commission Survey. For example, what is being done to improve the effectiveness of communication among caregivers? The reading back of verbal orders and timely communication of critical test results are two of the mandated requirements for this safety goal.
- Review of the Preventive Maintenance program for all equipment, including furniture.
- Review of disaster preparedness.

- ◼ Review the location of the material safety data sheet (MSDS) manual.
- ◼ Identification of the employee's role in the safety program.
- ◼ Review of the method for reporting safety or security concerns.
- ◼ Ongoing education should include frequent walking rounds or site visits and annual risk management in-service employee education.

Loss Control

Two essential components of an effective risk management program are loss control and loss prevention. Loss control is the application of techniques designed to minimize loss in a cost-effective manner. Components of loss control are described below.

Risk Avoidance

One of the most common techniques is risk avoidance. In risk avoidance, known high-risk or problem-prone areas are avoided. Generally, obstetrical services are considered high risk or problem prone. An example of risk avoidance is a hospital's decision not to provide obstetrical services.

Risk Transfer

Risk transfer is another means of loss control. The three basic elements of risk transfer are purchase of insurance, contractual transfer, and segregation of risk exposures.

Purchase of Insurance

The first element of risk transfer involves purchasing insurance to cover identified risks. A hospital has an economic responsibility in the event of an injury to a patient, visitor, or employee. To transfer a portion of that responsibility, the facility should purchase insurance such as general liability insurance from an insurance company, which would then assume some or all of the risk in return for an amount to be paid (premium) by the facility.

Contractual Transfer

The second element of risk transfer is known as a noninsurance transfer of risk or a contractual transfer. With this technique, the transfer of risk is effected by a contract, other than insurance, in which one party transfers to another party legal responsibility for losses. One of the most common examples is the use of contractors who subcontract to perform certain functions. In this scenario, the subcontractors hire their own employees. The contract contains a hold-harmless clause releasing the contractor of any responsibility in the event of a loss. As a result, responsibility for the employees, by contract, transfers to the subcontractors, who then assume responsibility and are obligated to pay for any losses arising from their services.

A more complex contractual risk-transfer situation may include a "crossover." This example of a noninsurance or contractual risk transfer occurs in many emergency departments. Often, physicians staffing emergency departments are contract physicians and not hospital employees. Traditionally, in a noninsurance or contractual risk transfer, the contractor assumes liability. However, because the physicians are providing direct care to patients of the hospital, some percentage of the liability is transferred back to the facility due to vicarious liability—hence the term "crossover." In most states, "vicarious liability" laws impute professional liability to the healthcare entity even though the individual providing the care is not a direct employee of the entity. The entity has a duty to protect the patients, visitors, and employees from harm or injury. This issue can become very complex, and a thorough understanding of laws and regulations dealing with such issues is necessary. A close review of insurance policies and contracts is essential, since there is no margin for error when questioning exposure and coverage in these situations. Further, this issue has not yet been settled in the managed care arena, specifically for independent practice associations (IPAs). It is critical that close attention be given to precedents now being established in this area.

Segregation of Risk Exposures

A third element of risk transfer involves the segregation of risk exposures. With this technique, risks are identified and are divided into separate areas or entities. An example is the separation of one entity into two distinct entities or corporations. Each entity or corporation is then responsible for its respective liabilities. This technique is frequently seen with acquisitions and mergers.

Risk Retention

A third type of loss control is risk retention. Risk retention is accomplished through establishment of self-insured retention (SIR). The majority of large medical centers are self-insured to a certain level and then transfer a portion of the risk to the insurance carrier in an umbrella coverage plan. The management of this type of fund provides much more autonomy and role independence for the risk manager.

Claims Management

One of the primary objectives in a claims management program is to reduce the overall number and cost of claims. Like the risk management program, a claims management program should be a formalized process. Development of policies and procedures will define processes, delineate actions, and assign individual responsibility.

Most important is the identification of the incidents and information that should be reported. A general guideline should be that any event that has the potential to result in injury or any event that results in an injury to a patient, visitor, or staff member should be reported. Sentinel events must be reported to the Joint Commission. These incidents are referred to as "sentinel events" because they "signal" immediate review and feedback. Joint Commission defines a sentinel event as an "unexpected occurrence involving death or serious physical or psychological injury, or the risk thereof. Serious injury specifically includes loss of limb or function. The phrase 'or the risk thereof' includes any process variation for which a recurrence would carry a significant chance of a serious adverse outcome" (The Joint Commission, 2008). According to the Joint Commission, the goals of their sentinel event policy include the following:

- Preventing sentinel events by way of improved patient care, treatment, and services
- Assisting an organization who has had a sentinel event to uncover the root cause of the event, modify processes, and prevent the incidence of recurrence
- Increasing awareness of sentinel event causes and strategies for prevention
- Maintaining public and organizational confidence in the accreditation process (The Joint Commission, 2008)

Examples of reportable events include

- Suicides
- Any type of unexpected deaths (non-CPR or suicide)
- Birth-related injuries, including maternal or fetal death, low APGAR scores at 5 and 10 min, infant resuscitations, shoulder dystocias, fractures, dislocations, or decreased movements of any infant extremity after birth
- Any anesthesia-related injuries
- Unanticipated neurological or sensory deficits, such as brain damage, permanent paralysis including paraplegia and quadriplegia, and partial or complete loss of sight or hearing functions
- Unanticipated body-system failures, such as renal failure; or unexplained disease processes, such as coagulopathies or sepsis
- Burns from electrical, chemical, thermal, or radiological sources
- Any iatrogenic injuries to internal organs or major blood vessels
- Retention of a foreign body
- In-hospital injuries that limit activities of daily living, such as sprains, fractures, amputation, or disfigurement
- In-hospital drug–drug or food–drug reactions or unexplained allergic reactions
- Medication errors
- Leaving without being seen or leaving against medical advice
- Wrong-site surgery
- Infant abduction
- Severe blood transfusion reaction
- Allegations of in-hospital sexual assault

The instances listed above constitute major events. It is important to mention that not all reportable events are sentinel events. The risk manager will determine if an incident will be reported to the Joint Commission. Reporting should also include minor events, such as slips, falls and injuries in elevators, pneumatic doors, or parking lots. Patient or staff injuries resulting from physical altercations are also reportable events. Staff injuries such as needle sticks or muscle strains should be reported. Employee injury reports assist Employee Health Services by providing the framework for workman's compensation claims. Both patient and employee safety is impacted by the reporting of these events. The organization may decide to purchase patient transfer devices in order to improve employee safety and reduce workman's compensation claims related to back injuries sustained while moving patients. Near miss data should not be overlooked as this information creates opportunities for improvement. Examples of near misses include wrong medication sent by pharmacy the but not given, no signage on a wet floor after mopping, and failure to place a patient identification band.

A format and process should be established for the reporting of events. The form for reporting may be known as an incident report, occurrence report, safety report, or quality monitoring report. Online reporting systems are now available with real-time notification of risk management as incidents occur. This helps to expedite the review and follow-up by all parties involved. Upon notification of an event either by form or online, a thorough investigation of the event and an evaluation as to its potential for a claim should take place. The LNC must stay current with legislative activity at both the local and national levels. Florida state law protections related to medical peer review sustained a severe blow with Amendment 7, the patient's right to know about adverse medical events (Florida statutes 2005). The passage of this amendment eliminated statutory discovery protection on peer-reviewed information (Fla. R. Civ. P. 1.280[b] [5]) (*Notami Hospital of Fla., Inc. v. Bowen*, 2008). This action threatens the peer-review process nationwide. Concerns exist regarding the underreporting of incidents and a collapse or weakening of the entire process.

When there is a concern that a claim will be filed, the risk manager should begin an investigation. Employees will need to be interviewed, charts reviewed, and chronologies developed. Hospital administration and hospital defense counsel should be notified about significant events. If the facility utilizes the services of an outside agency or third-party administrator (TPA) for some of its claims management, then that entity should be put on notice as well. Generally, a letter of assignment and any pertinent documents are forwarded to the defense counsel or outside claims investigator. Upon receipt, the defense counsel or outside investigator sends a letter of acknowledgment to the facility. The timely notification of the defense counsel is of utmost importance because it helps establish attorney–client privilege. In the investigation process, the risk manager generally functions as coordinator of all investigation activity, including arranging employee interviews and securing evidence. As organizational policies are reviewed, modified, or deleted, measures should be taken to archive old polices to assure availability upon request.

Upon completion of the investigation, the defense counsel or TPA provides a report of the statement of the events to date, as well as any recommendations for further investigation or disposition of the claim. If additional investigation is required, periodic reports of the investigation should be provided to the facility by the defense counsel or TPA until the investigation is deemed to be completed. Again, any written report must be protected from discoverability. Disposition of the claim may include either offering a settlement to the claimant or proceeding to trial. In the event of a settlement, a settlement authority should be defined in the risk management plan.

The facility's insurance carrier should be included in the process of notification. In most instances, the initial indemnity reserve is established; however, the reserve amount should be adjusted periodically to reflect findings during the investigation or discovery process. Most insurance carriers have specific reporting requirements. These requirements may include an initial evaluation of the case as well as determination of liability, damages, and settlement value. Reporting timelines associated with the various types and levels of insurance coverage are also of great importance. Improper or inadequate reporting can have an adverse impact on the coverage provided. Reporting requirements are found in the policy language and should be reviewed accordingly. The claim or potential claim should be monitored carefully.

Monitoring of an incident or claim can be very time-consuming. The use of a form is helpful in this process. Sample forms are available in risk management text books and online. The key is to utilize a format that will capture the necessary information to monitor a claim across its life cycle.

Root Cause Analysis/Failure Mode Effects Analysis

The LNC must have a working knowledge of the Root Cause Analysis (RCA) and FMEA risk management tools. Hambleton writes, "that people make mistakes and systems fail" (Hambleton, 2005). Risk managers are moving away from the "what" and the "who" to understanding "why" an incident occurred. The RCA is a process designed to uncover how and why something happened and to identify ways to prevent it from happening again (Hambleton, 2005). The four-step process includes data collection, organization of contributing factors, identification of the root causes, and recommendations for corrective action.

FMEA is a proactive analysis to look at a particular process and look for ways that it might fail as opposed to a postevent evaluation. The Joint Commission has implemented new standards to address error reduction in hospitals and supports the FMEA technique. The first step is to define the process to be analyzed and find evidence-based data to support the analysis. Next, a multidisciplinary team will break the process into subprocesses and identify failure modes for each, followed by the assignment of risk priorities. An analysis of each failure mode will lead to recommendations for improvement and corrective action (Hambleton, 2005).

According to Morris et al., adverse events are the result of multiple system failures and frequently occur at the interface of systems or disciplines (Morris et al., 2003). For example, a patient receives an overdose of heparin. Upon investigation, it becomes clear that the nurse entered the weight as "200 lb." The computer (electronic medical record) defaulted to "200 kg" causing the pharmacy to prepare the wrong drip concentration (dose was ordered as mg/kg), the nurse failed to double check the admixture prior to medication administration. Electronic medication administration and documentation systems designed to improve the culture of safety within an organization present their own unique challenges. Nurses at the bedside are able to identify potential safety issues inherent with new technologies and clinical process changes. It is paramount that these same nurses are involved in the planning, education, and implementation of new patient-care initiatives.

Certification and Credentials for Risk Managers

The LNC interested in the role of risk manager should become well acquainted with licensing and certification requirements. Generally, the state board of insurance regulates licensing requirements for individuals functioning in the role of risk manager or risk management consultant. Qualification is usually obtained by examination. However, there is no consistency from state to state, and some states have no requirements for licensing or certification. Some states require an individual to be licensed as a consultant or adviser and, in some instances, as an insurance agent or broker. LNCs wishing to provide these services should become familiar with licensing requirements in the states in which they wish to consult.

Several avenues for certification in risk management are available. Some insurance carriers have programs that provide courses in risk management; however, these programs are not generally endorsed or recognized by any national risk management professional organization. The American Society for Health Care Risk Management of the American Hospital Association (ASHRM) offers a series of modules that, upon successful completion, provide the recipient with a certification that he or she has completed the course. Completion of the course can then be applied toward diplomat or fellow status (American Hospital Association, 2008). ASHRM also offers a certification program for risk management professionals who meet strict eligibility requirements. ASHRM confers the CPHRM (Certified Professional in Health Care Risk

Management) on risk management professionals who have met the eligibility criteria and successfully completed the qualifying examination (American Society for Healthcare Risk Management of the American Association, 2008). The Insurance Institute of America confers an Associate in Risk Management certification on students who successfully complete three required modules specific to risk assessment, control, and financing (Insurance Institute of America, 2008).

Risk Assessment Consultation

The LNC is an excellent choice to conduct a clinical risk assessment related to high-risk, problem-prone, and high-volume areas such as perioperative, perinatal, emergency, and behavioral health services. Examples include laproscopic procedures, shoulder dystocias, or management of the psychiatric patient in the emergency department. A clinical risk assessment is usually performed as part of an on-site visit.

The process includes

- One-on-one interview of key personnel
- Review existing policies and procedures compared with the professional organization's standards of care
- Review of documentation, including a sampling of charts
- Committee minutes
- Action plans that relate to performance improvement, patient safety, or risk management.
- A walk-through of the high-risk areas

It is prudent for LNCs to be aware of the laws governing discovery in the state in which they are working. Knowledge of restrictions, such as those established by the Health Insurance Portability and Accountability Act (HIPAA) of 1996 (Health Care Financing Administration, 2002), in the review of patient documents and the collection and use of data is imperative.

Risk assessments may intensely examine one department or service line. A risk assessment for "shoulder dystocia" would be very helpful in the obstetrical arena. The recommendations related to documentation following a shoulder dystocia case will provide the standards for practice and help strengthen the healthcare provider's defense in a malpractice claim. System analysis is another form of risk assessment. The assessment may be done on one or more systems, such as quality management, laboratory, or radiology reporting systems.

Many consulting firms and insurance companies have tools with which to conduct the assessment. Tools are constructed from knowledge of case law, accreditation and licensing standards, and professional standards. Opportunities exist for the LNC to create tools to be used in nontraditional settings, such as physician group practices, substance abuse centers, and mental health clinics.

Risk Education

Staff development and education are prime areas of opportunity for the LNC. Educational needs may be the result of an event, an identified need from a risk assessment, or part of the monitoring and evaluation process. Many healthcare entities have reduced costs by the elimination of attendance at outside seminars or, in some instances, elimination of an education department.

Qualitative Claims Analysis

Services that the LNC provides in the area of claims analysis vary depending on the needs of the client. One service is the review of claims for frequency, severity, and impact. Another service may be the investigation of the claim itself. This involves reviewing the medical records and interviewing all pertinent employees, visitors, patients, and family members. The decision for future management of the claim is determined after analysis of the findings. Total claims management service involves the management of a claim from the evaluation phase to final resolution of the case. This may involve communicating with the defense counsel and insurance carrier, monitoring expenses, establishing reserves, and monitoring the evolution of the case.

Report Preparation

Many consultative firms and insurance companies have specific guidelines for report-writing. Initially, the report should identify potential or actual areas for improvement, as well as areas that are being performed well. Recommendations or suggestions for implementing changes to improve performance are generally included as part of the process. Documentation or references that support recommendations or suggestions are required.

Reports should be as concise as possible, be completed in a timely manner, and not contain language unfamiliar to the reader. It is essential for the organization's risk management consultant to follow up on the incident within a reasonable time after the report is completed.

A report should always contain a caveat explaining the position of the individual preparing the report. Most caveats include a statement that releases the writer of any liability as a result of the report. If possible, reports should flow through the facility's legal counsel or be a component of the peer review or quality process to limit the potential for discovery of the document. An LNC in the role of outside consultant should work closely with the facility risk manager or legal counsel to determine the most appropriate method of communicating findings.

Summary

Many opportunities are available to the LNC interested in the area of risk management. By increasing one's body of knowledge related to the practice of legal nurse consulting, a career choice in healthcare risk management opens numerous possibilities to expand upon for professional growth and advancement. They can range from being an employee of the institution or organization to being an independent consultant within the healthcare risk management department. Regardless of the venue, the LNC can directly impact patient-care safety. Because the healthcare industry is in a state of constant change, the LNC should stay abreast of current trends in case law, professional standards, accreditation and licensing requirements, guidelines, and latest developments within the field.

References

Agency for Healthcare Research and Quality: The Patient Safety & Quality Act. http://www.ahcpr.gov
AHR Quality Indicators. (2006). Patient Safety Indicator Brochure (PSI). Retrieved July 25, 2008 from http://Quality Indicators; http://ahrq.gov./psi

American Hospital Association. (2008). Certified professional in healthcare risk management. Retrieved August 15, 2008 from http://www.aha.org/aha/CertificationCenter

American Society for Healthcare Risk Management of the American Association. (2008). Retrieved August 15, 2008 from http://www.hospitalconnect.com.ashrrn

ASHRM Task Force, Monograph. (2008). Tackling patient safety taxonomy. *Journal of Health Care Risk Management, 28*(1), 7–14.

Hambleton, M. (2005). Applying root cause analysis and failure mode and effect analysis to our compliance programs. *Journal of Health Care Compliance*, March–April, 5–12.

Health Care Financing Administration. (2002). *The Health Insurance Portability and Accountability Act of 1996 (HIPAA)*.

Rockville, MD: U.S. Department of Health and Human Services. http://cms.hhs.gov/hipaaInsurance Institute of America. (2008). Retrieved August 15, 2008 from http://www.aicpcu.org/flyers/arm.htm

Joint Commission on Accreditation of Healthcare Organizations. (2001). *Proposed revisions to Joint Commission Behavioral Health Care Standards in support of safety of individuals served and health care or service error reduction*. Oakbrook Terrace, IL: Joint Commission.

Kohn, L., Corrigan, J. M., & Donaldson, M. S. (2000). *To err is human: Building a safer health system*. Washington, DC: National Academies Press.

Levick, D. E. (2002). *Risk management and insurance audits techniques* (3rd ed.). Boston: Standard Publishing Corporation.

Manser, T., & Staender, S. (2005). Aftermath of an adverse event: Supporting health care professionals to meet patients expectations through open disclosure. *Acta Anaesthesiologica Scandinavica 49*(6), 728–34.

Morris, J. A., Jr., Carrillo, Y., Jenkins, J. M., Smith, P. W., Bledsoe, S., Pichert, J., & White, A. (2003). Surgical adverse events, risk management, and malpractice outcome: Morbidity and mortality review is not enough. *Annals of Surgery, 237* (6), 844–852. Retrieved August 8, 2008 from http://ovidsp.tx.ovid.com/spb/ovidweb.cgi

Notami Hospital of Fla., Inc. v. Bowen, No. SCO6-912 (Fla. 3-6-2008). Retrieved July 16, 2008 from http://caselaw.lp.findlaw.com/data2/floridastatecases/app

The Hospital and Healthsystem Association of Pennsylvania. (2008). Retrieved July 10, 2008 from http://www.Haponline.org/quality/infection/act52

The Joint Commission. (2008). Sentinel events. In *Comprehensive accreditation manual for hospitals: The official handbook* (SE-1). Retrieved August 12, 2008 from http://www.jointcommission.org

Additional Readings

Agency for Healthcare Research and Quality. (2001). *Making health care safer: A critical analysis of patient safety practices*. Rockville, MD: U.S. Department of Health and Human Services.

American Society for Healthcare Risk Management. (2001). *Perspectives on disclosure of unanticipated outcome information*. Chicago, IL: American Hospital Publishing.

Suggested Internet Sites

AIS Managed Care News: http://www.aishealth.com/AISManagedCare
Risk Management and Insurance Information Resource: http://www.irmi.com

Online Periodicals

American Association of Health Plans Online: http://www.aahp.org

Trade Journals

American Healthline: http://www.americanhealthline.com
American Hospital Association News: http://www.ahanews.com
Hospitals and Health Networks: http://www.hhnmag.com
Modern Health Care: http://www.modernhealthcare.com

Government and Regulatory Agencies

Agency for Healthcare Research and Quality: http://www.ahcpr.gov
Centers for Disease Control: http://www.cdc.gov
Centers for Medicare and Medicaid Services (formerly Health Care Financing Administration): http://cms.hhs.gov
Commission on Accreditation of Rehabilitation Facilities: http://www.carf.org
Food and Drug Administration: http://www.fda.gov
Health Resources and Services Administration: http://www.hrsa.gov/
National Center for Health Statistics: http://www.cdc.gov/nchs
National Clinical Guidelines Clearinghouse: http://www.guidelines.gov
National Institutes of Health: http://www.nih.gov
Office of the Inspector General: http://oig.hhs.gov
The Joint Commission: http://www.jointcommission.org
U.S. Department of Health and Human Services: http://www.hhs.gov

Professional Associations

American College of Health Care Administrators: http://www.achca.org
American College of Healthcare Executives: http://www.ache.org
American Hospital Association: http://www.aha.org/aha/about/index.html
American Medical Association: http://www.ama-assn.org
American Society for Healthcare Risk Management: http://www.ashrm.org/
Integrated Healthcare Association: http://www.iha.org
Risk and Insurance Management Society, Inc.: http://www.rims.org

Licensure, Certification, and Board Specialty

American Health Information Management Association: http://www.ahima.org/certification
American Society for Healthcare Risk Management: http://www.ashrm.org/

Test Questions

1. To have an effective and successful risk management program, which of the following is not necessary?
   A. Organizational commitment
   B. A "mindfulness" to a patient safety culture
   C. An interactive and visible risk manager
   D. An autocratic style risk management department

2. Which of the following positions has oversight of the facility wide safety program?
   A. Risk Manager
   B. Quality Improvement Manager
   C. CEO
   D. Patient Safety Officer

3. The evolution of enterprise risk management (ERM) can be described as which of the following?
   A. A risk-based approach to managing an enterprise integrating concepts of strategic planning, operations management, and internal management
   B. An activity to reduce or eliminate chance of loss or decrease the severity of loss
   C. An economic responsibility that assumes some or all of the risk of the organization
   D. A process that holds harmless a physician from professional liability

4. Which of the following is NOT a sentinel event reportable to the Joint Commission?
   A. Retention of a foreign body
   B. Wrong-site surgery
   C. Infant abduction
   D. Employee needle stick

5. Which statement best describes the FMEA process?
   A. FMEA is a proactive analysis to look at a particular process and look for ways that it might fail
   B. FMEA occurs after an incident has occurred and looks for what caused a particular event
   C. FMEA is designed to identify exactly "who" was responsible for the incident
   D. FMEA serves no purpose in the evaluation of healthcare processes

6. Which of the following is part of the RCA process?
   A. Data collection
   B. Organization of contributing factors
   C. Identification of the root causes
   D. Recommendations for corrective action
   E. All of the above

Answers: 1. D, 2. D, 3. A, 4. D, 5. A, 6. E

Chapter 7

The Legal Nurse Consultant as Case Manager

Valerie V. Parisi, RN, CRRN, CLCP and
Kathleen Ryan Kuntz, MSN, CRNP, CRRN, CLCP, RN-BC, MSCC

Second Edition
Doreen Casuto, MRA, BSN, RN, CCM, CRRN

Contents

Objectives

- To identify various arenas for case management services
- To describe the scope of practice and process of case management
- To identify the various roles and functions of the nurse case manager
- To recognize issues facing the nurse case manager
- To identify professional organizations and certifying bodies supporting the nurse case manager
- To recognize credentials of the nurse case manager

Introduction

Legal nurse consultants (LNCs) may diversify their practices to include case management activities, and case managers may incorporate legal nurse consulting as part of their role. The knowledge base and experience that each possess can be valuable assets in the various areas where case management is practiced.

The practice of case management requires a thorough understanding of the scope and role of the case manager, as well as an appreciation of the different arenas where these services are provided. Each area of practice has certain guidelines and restrictions that affect the way in which a case manager functions. Knowledge of these guidelines will improve the LNC/case manager's ability to fulfill the role, and enhance the impact they will have on the outcome of a case.

Definition of Case Management

The essential elements of case management involve collaboration, advocacy, timely coordination of healthcare services to meet an individual's specific needs, and efforts to assure quality services are provided in a cost-efficient manner, promoting a positive outcome. These services can occur in episodes or continuously, and are provided in various healthcare settings. While there are many descriptions of case management, the Case Management Society of America (CMSA, 2002) notes this definition to reflect such services in a dynamic healthcare environment:

> Case management is a collaborative process of assessment, planning, facilitation and advocacy for options and services to meet an individual's health needs through

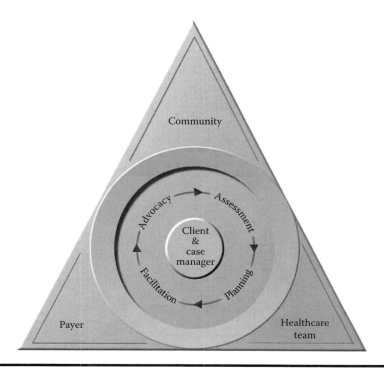

Figure 7.1   Case management model.

communication and available resources to promote quality cost-effective outcomes. (CMSA, 2002, p. 5)

The case manager facilitates communication with the client, provider, payer, and the community, coordinating services to minimize fragmentation, thereby potentiating the over-all benefit to the client. The case manager further educates the client, members of the health-care team, and the community, to facilitate informed decisions, problem-solving efforts, and appropriate use of healthcare resources. Figure 7.1 illustrates a model in which the client and case manager are partnered through the stages of assessment, planning, facilitation, and advo-cacy within an environment where, together, they interact with the healthcare team, payer, and community.

The philosophy of case management, as stated by CMSA (2002), identifies that all individu-als, particularly those with catastrophic injuries and/or chronic illnesses, should be evaluated for the need for case management services. Case management efforts foster care that is holistic, cli-ent-centered, and goal-directed, with an appropriate use of healthcare resources toward achieving health and maintaining wellness. The provision of case management, in collaboration with pro-viders, serves to identify care options that are acceptable to the client and family, thereby increas-ing adherence to the treatment plan and achievement of successful outcomes. Services provided by the professional case manager can enhance a client's safety, well-being, and quality of life while reducing total healthcare costs. Effective case management efforts, then, can collectively affect the social, ethical, and financial health of society and the general population (CMSA, 2002, pp. 6–7).

Standards of Practice and Professional Performance for Case Management

Competence of a case manager must be measured against accepted standards of care in the industry. As Mullahy (2004) notes, formal standards of care pertinent to nurse case managers have been developed by several professional organizations, including the CMSA, the Association of Rehabilitation Nurses (ARN), the International Association of Rehabilitation Professionals (IARP), the National Association of Professional Geriatric Care Managers (NAPGCM), and the American Nurses Association (ANA). Additionally, nurse practice acts promulgated into law by individual states for professional nurse licensure address nursing actions that are consistent with the role of case management.

Standards put forth by nursing organizations related to nursing practice identify the activities of the nurse to include assessment, diagnosis, outcome identification, planning, implementation (i.e., coordination of care, health teaching and health promotion, consultation, prescriptive authority/treatment), and evaluation (ANA, 2004; ARN, 2008). These professional organizations further identify standards of performance to include quality of care/practice, practice/performance appraisal, education, collegiality, ethics/advocacy, collaboration, research, resource utilization, and leadership. Those promoted by interdisciplinary case management organizations identify the activities of the case manager to include client identification/selection, problem identification, planning, monitoring, evaluating, and outcome identification, as illustrated in Figure 7.2. Performance indicators are further identified to include quality of care, qualifications, collaboration, regulatory and ethical practices, advocacy, resource management/stewardship, and research utilization (CMSA, 2002; NAPGCM, 2008a). These standards speak directly to the scope of practice and activities of the case manager within all associate disciplines. Representing the case

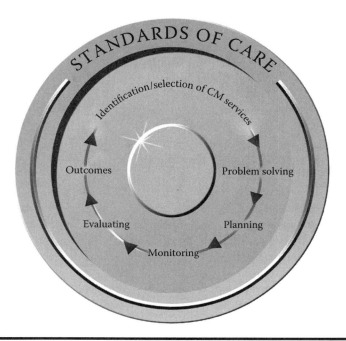

Figure 7.2 Standard of care.

management industry, an individual case manager is bound by these standards of practice, as well as the established professional code of ethics, whether or not they are members of the professional organization that promulgated them.

With advances in technology and the advent of telemedicine, the issue of interstate practice has come to the forefront. In the early part of this decade, a dilemma emerged as nurses were being tapped to provide telephonic case management for large firms with national and international centers. Questions arose as to whether these nurses were restricted in this practice by their state licensure, as case managers in other disciplines were not subject to the same regulations. In 1997, the National Council of State Boards of Nursing published a position paper noting some common functions of nursing practice and case management, but fell short of specifying any implications related to licensure. As a professional organization representing a large number of these professionals, the CMSA formally addressed this issue by incorporating a statement into the *Standards of Practice for Case Management* (CMSA, 2002), which notes as follows:

> The case manager practices in accordance with applicable local, state, and federal laws. The case manager has knowledge of applicable accreditation and regulatory statutes governing sponsoring agencies that specifically pertain to delivery of case management services. (CMSA, 2002, p. 18)

Despite these steps, discrepancies in practice continued, with inherent risks for liability. In 2004–2005, CMSA further addressed this issue by conducting a survey of all 50 State Boards of Nursing to determine if case management, as defined by the organization's standards, was viewed as the practice of nursing. When the role of the case manager was articulated, the nursing regulatory bodies universally identified it to represent the practice of nursing when performed by a registered nurse. Utilization management organizations, however, argued that these activities fell under the category of administrative oversight, and were *not* nursing practice. This issue has taken on less prominence as more states enter into the Nursing Licensure Compact, allowing multistate licensure based upon the practitioner's state of residence. However, it is important to recognize that the law which controls the relationship between the case manager and the client is that of the state where the client lives, not where the nurse or employer is located (Muller, 2006; Muller & Flarey, 2004).

Process of Case Management

The process of case management is similar to the nursing process. The CMSA (2002) identifies the process to include patient/client identification and selection of case management services, problem identification, planning, monitoring, evaluating, and outcome identification.

Patient/client identification and determination of necessary case management services are accomplished through health screening, application of evidence-based criteria, and provider assessment and referral. Clients may be selected to receive case management services based upon their identified potential for positive outcomes, or they may be mandated based upon disease state, age, payer, complexity of needs, or potential for high-intensity/high-cost services.

Problem identification is usually performed during an initial interview with the client. This can be done face-to-face or over the telephone, and should include the following activities:

■ Collecting updated information about the client's medical status including significant medical history

- Assessing functional status or ability to perform personal and instrumental activities of daily living
- Assessing psychosocial status including information about the client's social support system
- Assessing vocational status including a detailed work history (particularly in workers' compensation cases)

Consideration should be given to cultural factors and potential obstacles to recovery, such as preexisting and coexisting conditions, socioeconomic factors, and educational barriers. This information serves as a database from which an individualized case management plan can be formulated. The assessment phase includes contact with the physician and other healthcare providers, and in workers' compensation case management, also with the employer. After the client has signed a medical authorization, appropriate medical records should be obtained and a job description noting essential duties should be requested from the employer. When possible, an on-site job analysis by the case manager is an important aspect of this assessment process in a workers' compensation case.

The planning phase involves setting realistic and attainable short- and long-term goals with the client. These goals must be achievable and measurable, and the client must be involved in setting them. The treatment and rehabilitation team should be consulted prior to goal-setting. Meetings or contact with these providers should take place during the assessment phase, as should contact with the employer in workers' compensation cases. Strategies to meet these goals are developed by the case manager.

When initiating a case involving a workers' compensation or automobile accident, there is usually intense activity as a treatment plan is being formulated. The client may be in the hospital, and coordination is needed for either a transfer to an appropriate postacute facility or referral to home healthcare services. Durable medical equipment and supplies may also need to be ordered. The client may require referrals for a second opinion or specialty care. The case manager must be aware of available resources, both nationally and in the client's community. Included in this chapter is information regarding online resources that the case manager may find helpful when developing and implementing a plan of care.

Case managers must maintain open communication with the client and treatment providers so that effective coordination of care is achieved. Telephonic contact with the client is necessary in-between field visits to the home or provider's office. The case manager's role often involves providing client education. Information regarding medications and the disease process, as well as what signs and symptoms to report to the physician, are emphasized. Being aware of the usual course of recovery from an injury or illness enables the case manager to be proactive in preventing or minimizing the occurrence of complications. This is especially true in cases of catastrophic injury (i.e., spinal cord and traumatic brain injury). The case must continue to move forward toward resolution. Case management reports should be documented in a timely manner, reflecting the current case management plan and progress toward established goals, or changes that are required with the rationale for change.

Evaluation of the case management plan should be ongoing. Goals should evolve as the needs of the client are identified. The client and providers participate in this evaluation process to assure that steps continue toward an optimal outcome. It can be challenging for the case manager with long-term case management files to remain proactive, especially as the client might reach a plateau in recovery. Contact should be maintained to avoid a "crisis" situation should a complication arise. The case manager should demonstrate progress to the referral source, noting when goals are achieved, and any positive outcomes.

Key Issues in Case Management

Advocacy

According to the Commission for Case Management Certification *Code of Professional Conduct for Case Managers* (CMCC, 2005), advocacy is a process that promotes beneficence, justice, and autonomy with aims to promote client independence. The process involves education about rights, healthcare and human services, resources and benefits, and facilitates appropriate and informed decision making. Consideration is given to the client's values, beliefs, and interests. It is expected that case managers serve as advocates for their clients by performing comprehensive assessments of the client's needs, providing options for services, and access to resources. Case managers must be mindful that they are an advocate for the client, or injured individual, and not the funding or referral source.

Professional Conduct

The CMCC (2005) emphasizes the importance of maintaining client confidentiality. Case managers must be knowledgeable of, and act in accordance with federal, state, and local laws and procedures within their individual scope of practices regarding client consent, confidentiality, and the release of information. The case manager must also inform the client at the outset of the relationship that any information shared or discovered may be disclosed to third parties when they have a legal right to know. However, disclosure should be limited to what is necessary and relevant. The case manager must also reveal to appropriate authorities any information regarding a risk of the client causing harm to him/herself or others, as well as any knowledge related to the commission of criminal or fraudulent acts (Banja, 2008).

Another area of ethical concern is related to "dual relationships." Case managers can perceive that they have two "clients." There is the client who is in need of case management services through illness or injury, and the client who is the payer source. The case manager's duty is to the individual and not the payer source. Cost-effectiveness and resolution of a claim should never trump quality care as the prime concern of the case manager. Case managers who provide services at the request of a third party must disclose the nature of their dual relationship at the outset of the relationship by describing their roles and responsibilities to parties who have the right to know (CCMC, 2005).

A dual relationship exists when the client is a friend, relative, or coworker of the case manager. The case manager should not accept this assignment, but should refer the case to another case manager. Actual or potential conflicts of interest should also be disclosed to all parties involved. If any party raises an objection to the case manager's involvement, he/she should remove him/herself from the case.

A life care planner may also be asked to act as the client's case manager. During the course of a lawsuit, this would represent a conflict of interest. Once a case is resolved, a dual relationship no longer exists. In fact, at this point, the life care planner is in an ideal position to implement the life care plan, utilizing it as a road map for care toward the best possible case management outcomes.

Confidentiality/Privacy

Confidentiality of patient information is an issue that has a significant impact on case management practice. The Health Insurance Portability and Accountability Act of 1996 (HHS, 2003) has changed how healthcare organizations handle confidential information. Agencies have adopted policies and procedures to better protect the privacy of health information, and developed standards regarding electronic exchange of patient data.

Case Management Liability

All case managers, including those working in facilities, those working in the community, and those who work telephonically are at the same risk for liability as any professional when it comes to issues of negligence or breach of duty. Case managers can also create liability problems for their employer if they do not perform according to established standards of practice, or if they ignore inappropriate care or over-/underutilization of resources. Underutilization may result in poor patient outcomes, while overutilization may open the case manager to investigation of fraud and abuse. It is the case manager's responsibility to report such offenses according to the standards of practice (Case Management and Compliance, 2003).

Another source of liability is negligent referrals, or referrals made for unsafe or inappropriate resources. Case managers who abandon their role as patient advocate, and instead, serve the institution or funding source, are at risk for using inappropriate judgment when coordinating care for the client. For example, a worker's compensation carrier may focus upon cost containment; however, the case manager has an obligation to assure appropriate, cost-efficient care in order to reach a positive outcome.

Nondisclosure of information can also be an area of potential liability. Case managers are required to disclose their relationship to a third party, as well as their role and responsibilities at the outset of the relationship with the client. He/she is also required to inform the client that while disclosure of information will be limited to what is necessary and relevant, anything shared or discovered may be reported to third parties such as payers, service providers, and governmental agencies when they have a legal or ethical right or need to know. Situations can arise through the course of a case manager–client relationship, just as they do in a nurse–patient relationship, when the client wants to share something they ask to remain in confidence. At such a time, the case manager must remind the client of his or her legal and ethical obligations (Banja, 2008; CMCC, 2005).

Maldonado (2003) further identifies common causes of malpractice litigation in case management to be related to the following:

- ◾ Discourteous behavior
- ◾ Communication failures
- ◾ Lack of patient understanding
- ◾ Lack of information given to the patient and family

Case Example 7.1: Premature Discharge

An example of a situation with potential liability can be seen in the case involving a woman who had vascular surgery to her leg, followed by multiple complications. Her physician requested her length of stay be extended by 8 days; however, Medicaid approved only 4. After 4 days, the patient was discharged, and subsequently developed worsening complications, resulting in a need for amputation of the limb. The court ruled that third-party payers can be held accountable when medically inappropriate decisions result from defects in the design or implementation of cost containment mechanisms (Maldonado, 2003). Representatives of the health insurance entity (i.e., case manager, physician reviewer) are responsible for discussing all denials of care with the treating physician, and for providing information concerning appeals to the patient/subscriber.

Case Mix and Acuity

The number of cases that a case manager can effectively manage is dependent not only on numbers, but also on acuity. Some cases, such as those with catastrophic injuries, are complex and require more intense and/or long-term case management. According to a survey conducted by American Health Consultants (2001), the average caseload for a case manager was 16–30 cases, though telephonic case managers reported having as many as 75 cases. More current information from a representative sample of CMSA members (2008c) notes that 52% of case managers carry between 31 and 50 cases. Case managers are responsible for assuring that they can adequately manage their caseload, referring as needed so that quality standards can be maintained.

Professional Experience

Clinical experience is key for the case manager. It is recognized that lack of clinical experience can result in poor outcomes, or even unsafe conditions. A survey conducted by American Health Consultants (2001) found that 80% of case managers had 10 years nursing experience. However, more recent membership demographics presented by the CMSA (2008a) reveals that only 74% of case managers have this level of experience. It is further noted that this group reports that only 76% of case managers have more than 3 years of case management experience (2008b). Ideally, the case manager has achieved certification in case management, or another relevant area, and is experienced in case management before assuming independent responsibilities. This chapter later provides information regarding case management certifications. The CCMC (2005) dictates that case managers practice only within the boundaries of their competence, based on their education, training, appropriate professional experience, and other professional credentials.

Arenas of Practice/Case Manager Roles

Workers' Compensation

Workers' compensation is an arena where nursing case management is used extensively. "Workers' compensation" refers to medical and wage benefits that are provided when a worker is injured in the course of his or her employment. Each state has its own workers' compensation act that governs how the benefits are administered (Cunningham, 2008). These state programs are further regulated by the federal government.

DiBenedetto (2008) cites that the primary goals of workers' compensation are to "determine appropriate and effective medical care, coordinate timely delivery of that care, communicate goals to all stakeholders, and assist in the injured worker's return to work when possible" (DiBenedetto, 2008, p. 384). More globally, the case manager seeks to facilitate a plan that will maximize the client's functional recovery, while simultaneously assisting the injured worker, employer, and healthcare provider(s) to develop a return-to-work plan, including identification of modified-duty options during the recovery period, if available. Catastrophic work-related injuries, such as spinal cord or traumatic brain injuries, require long-term case management. This type of case management is often provided by field case managers who visit patients, providers, and employers on-site. They act as liaisons, providing a link among all involved parties.

Case Example 7.2: Traumatic Brain Injury

A 30-year-old male sustained a traumatic brain injury after a work-related fall from a forklift. The neurosurgeon who evaluated the patient at the hospital diagnosed a concussion, but was concerned about the amount of retrograde amnesia the patient was experiencing. Neuropsychological testing was done, and the patient continued with deficits in attention and concentration as well as dizziness and headaches. The carrier referred the case to medical case management. The nurse case manager referred the patient to a model brain injury setting for a series of evaluations, and a multidisciplinary rehabilitation program was established. The case manager evaluated the availability of modified duty with the employer and visited to perform a job analysis of this light-duty job. The patient returned to work in a part-time sedentary capacity with job coaching provided by the rehabilitation team. Positive outcomes were achieved by prompt referral to an effective rehabilitation program and return to modified employment.

Case Example 7.3: Carpal Tunnel Syndrome

A 38-year-old male factory worker was found to have right carpal tunnel syndrome on electromyogram. Carpal tunnel surgery was recommended. The carrier referred the patient for medical case management. The nurse case manager referred the patient to a specialist in hand surgery. Modified lifting restrictions were obtained on a temporary basis. The patient was given a celestone injection with relief and was able to return to full duty. The patient was able to avoid surgery by referral to the appropriate specialist.

In a workers' compensation case, the injured worker may settle the portion of the claim that compensates for lost wages, but may elect to keep it open for medical expenses. The case manager will then continue to work with the client, and may initiate a referral for vocational rehabilitation services. These cases involve permanent and often catastrophic injuries that require long-term case management to prevent and monitor complications. In the case of traumatic brain injury, the case manager may be attending team meetings, working closely with the family in determining which type of care facility is needed, especially when facing the impact of aging with a disability.

An LNC may become involved with a workers' compensation case by providing a Medicare Set-Aside report when the carrier and injured worker agree to settle both the indemnity and medical portion of the claim. All parties in a workers' compensation case have significant responsibilities under the Medicare Secondary Payer (MSP) statute to protect Medicare's interests in regard to future medical expenses. The recommended method to protect Medicare's interests is to prepare a Workers' Compensation Medicare Set-aside Arrangement (WCMSA), which reserves a portion of the settlement for future medical expenses. This portion takes into account medical expenses that are typically covered by Medicare, and is required when the injured worker has a reasonable expectation of receiving Medicare in a 30-month period (due to eligibility for social security disability benefits), and when the settlement is higher than $250,000.00. It is also required in settlements of a lower amount when the injured worker is already a Medicare recipient. LNCs who perform these services may obtain additional training and certification as a Medicare Set-aside Consultant Certified (MSCC). Additional information on Medicare Set Asides can be found in Chapter 11, "Medicare Set-Asides Arrangements."

Case Example 7.4: Traumatic Brain Injury

An injured worker sustains a traumatic brain injury in the course of his work setting up cones when he is hit by a car. He sustains severe cognitive deficits and requires long-term residential placement and continued medical care and therapies. He has been approved for social security disability income (SSDI) and will receive Medicare in 30 months. The case manager/LNC with MSCC certification has been asked to provide a Medicare Set Aside report for approval from Center for Medicare and Medicaid Services (CMS, 2008) after reviewing medical records and billing statements.

Accident and Health

Health insurers, especially managed care organizations, utilize nursing case management services to monitor the quality and cost of health care for the purpose of maintaining costs while optimizing outcomes. Often they can also be involved in the process of precertification of procedures and tests, as well as in concurrent utilization review (UR) of care being provided in the hospital and other healthcare settings. Group health plans can range from indemnity plans, preferred provider organizations (PPOs), to health maintenance organizations (HMOs). Government-sponsored plans, such as Medicare, Medicaid, and Tricare (insurance for military members and their families) may come into play (Cunningham, 2008). Case management in this arena is often telephonic and involves contact with clients and providers. Telephonic case managers may have many plan members to follow, leaving the role more limited than the field case manager, while still invaluable in the coordination of care. Telephonic case managers are responsible implementing the case management process, and for serving as advocates for their clients.

Coverage limits are dictated by the terms of the insurance contract for the plan purchased. This includes limits, caps, maximum coverage, coinsurance, copayment, and whether preexisting conditions or certain illnesses are excluded. In the case of accident insurance, a causal link must be established between the accident and the injury(ies) reported.

Employers that have purchased health insurance plans will selectively use on-site case managers in cases with catastrophic injury in which there is concern about the potential exposure, or risk of paying a large amount of money in claims or settlement payments. These cases usually involve clients who are young, or sustain complex injuries requiring case managers with specialized skills. In these cases, the case manager will be asked to perform an on-site assessment of the client, review the plan of treatment developed by the provider(s), and identify available resources in the local community that can be accessed to augment the plan's coverage.

Case Example 7.5: Brain Injury

An 11-year-old girl sustained a brain injury secondary to a playground accident. The carrier requested the services of a private case manager to assist in assessing the child, reviewing and critiquing the treatment team's plan of care, and providing recommendations. The case manager evaluated the child at the patient's rehabilitation center and evaluated the family home for accessibility issues, communicated with the school district, reviewed the status of referrals to state and governmental entitlement programs, and met with both the family and rehabilitation team. As a result, the case manager was able to assist the team and family in refocusing their outcomes necessary for discharge, initiate referrals to appropriate community providers, and identify and access additional benefits from the insurance company, which were not typically granted. The case manager's specialized rehabilitation skills and knowledge of legal issues ensured a more timely and effective result for the family and child.

Automobile/General Liability

As in the arena of workers' compensation insurance, the role of medical case management in cases of automobile accidents or general liability may depend on the state laws governing coverage for drivers. For example, in no-fault states such as New Jersey, which generally provides personal injury up to a capped amount, medical case management is used extensively to monitor the treatment plan for effectiveness from both a cost and quality standpoint. In states such as Pennsylvania, where drivers are required to carry a minimum $15,000.00 in medical coverage, the coverage is often exhausted before medical case management can be utilized, and referrals are made only in cases of catastrophic injury where extended medical benefits have been purchased.

Case managers can also be used in general liability cases to monitor for cost-effectiveness and accident-relatedness of care. The case manager can provide medical cost projections at the outset of the case for the purpose of setting reserves, or putting aside money for the client's potential medical expenses. Long-term case management may be required in these cases, which can involve such conditions as spinal cord injury, traumatic brain injury, amputations, orthopedic trauma, and chronic pain conditions (e.g., complex regional pain syndrome).

Case Example 7.6: Multiple Trauma

An 18-year-old was involved in a head-on collision. He sustained multiple orthopedic trauma with fractures of both femurs, the right ankle, and the left wrist. He also suffered from a renal contusion, and had an external fixation device on the right leg and a cast on the left leg. The patient was referred by the case manager to the appropriate rehabilitation facility. After discharge, he received home-care services for Lovenox injections and home physical therapy. He was eventually referred for outpatient physical therapy and was able to return to school. The medical case manager followed the case from hospitalization through the continuum of care and expedited appropriate referrals to the next level of care to enhance the patient's rehabilitation outcome and to preserve and stretch reserve dollars.

Case Example 7.7: Paraplegia

A 7-year-old boy is injured in a motor vehicle accident and sustained T-1 paraplegia. He has ongoing medical care and equipment and attendant care needs. The auto carrier has asked for a cost projection for the purpose of setting annual reserves to ensure that the child's needs are met. This cost projection is based on a home assessment of the child's needs, contact with the treatment team, and review of billing over the past year. Cost projections are typically updated on an annual basis.

Hospital-Based Case Management

Case management plays an important role in supporting the quality of care provided in both inpatient and outpatient settings. The American Hospital Association (AHA), the CMS, and The Joint Commission (formerly The Joint Commission on Accreditation of Healthcare Organizations) are only a few of the agencies who have mounted initiatives to improve the quality of care delivered by healthcare facilities in the United States (White, 2004). In many facilities, mandated functions of UR and discharge planning (DP) have evolved to comprise the role of the case manager in this setting. When limited in this manner, however, the balance of functions may tilt in favor of the fiscal interests of the facility (UR and reimbursement), rather than toward the needs of the client/ patient (DP and transition of care). The division of these functions fosters duplication of effort, and limits the case manager's ability to promote processes to streamline patient care and flow through the system. However, when the functions are combined, the workload of the case manager must be carefully considered so as not to limit the case manager's ability to affect the quality, access, and cost of care (Birmingham, 2007).

Over the last decade, a great deal of attention has been placed upon reducing costs and improving outcomes of hospital-based care. In response, Thomas (2008) evaluated the effect of the traditional model of case management (i.e., UR and DP) versus a full immersion model (i.e., defined role expectations, accountability to patient outcomes, and proactive communication between healthcare providers across the continuum). This study demonstrated a statistically significant reduction in length of stay and improvement in resource utilization with the implementation of a full immersion model.

Advances in the integration of evidence-based practice have also taken on a greater presence in hospital-based case management (Mitus, 2008). The use of statistically based decision support criteria to facilitate transition across the continuum of care helps to define care needs and support the delivery of quality, efficient care (i.e., those provided by InterQual, Milliman and Roberts, and Health Risk Management/Institute for Healthcare Quality).

Case Example 7.8: Bacterial Meningitis

A 14-year-old presents to the emergency department with fever, flu symptoms, and nuchal rigidity. A lumbar puncture is performed with elevated opening pressures indicating increased intracranial pressure, and cultures revealing a bacterial infection. Intravenous fluids and antibiotics are initiated, and he is admitted to an isolation room. As his condition improves over the next few days, he is noted to have muscle weakness with decreased mobility and function. Therapeutic services are provided, and a physiatry consult recommends that he transition to an acute rehabilitation facility for continued treatment. The inpatient case manager assesses his condition, assuring that criteria for an acute admission are met. This assessment and an initial treatment plan are communicated to the insurance company, with concurrent review provided each day. Considering the physiatry recommendation, a referral to an acute rehabilitation facility is made. At this facility, a referral coordinator/case manager reviews the medical and therapeutic documentation provided, meets with the patient and his family, and verifies a desire for transfer. A report is then prepared for the insurance carrier articulating the child's condition and specifying goals and expected outcomes with a proposed rehabilitation admission. Once approved by the carrier, the acute-care case manager makes arrangements to facilitate the transfer, including any necessary transportation. Upon admission to the rehabilitation facility, a rehabilitation case manager assesses the child's condition, and along with members of the interdisciplinary team, monitors his progress toward the goals set, periodically communicating this to the insurance company. This case manager collaborates with the patient and his family in planning for discharge throughout the admission. In preparation for discharge, further referrals for home-care and/or outpatient services are made. Case management responsibilities are then transferred to an independent case manager in the community, or to the primary-care provider.

Independent/Private Case Management

In addition to case management roles supported by the hospital or insurance carrier in the facility, clinic, or in the community, services of independent case managers are also available directly to individuals and their families. Irrespective of whom the case manager is paid by, they are bound by the standards of practice and codes of ethics defined by the profession, and as such, their role remains the same. Those hiring case managers seek individuals with experience and specialized knowledge related to their specific needs. They rely on the case manager to assess their needs, facilitate access to care, and identify available resources.

The independent case manager may be asked to provide a medical cost projection, especially in cases of catastrophic injury. The purpose of this medical cost projection is for the insurance company to set reserves for the client. This medical cost projection, unlike a life care plan, is a snapshot in time and is continually updated as client needs change. The medical cost projection includes such items as hospitalization, physician's fees, rehabilitation costs, home-care costs, durable medical equipment, and supplies. The case manager is in constant communication with facility case managers and treating providers to obtain updated information about the treatment plan, and may also make on-site visits to the hospital or rehabilitation facility to meet with the client, providers, and facility case manager or social worker.

Along with this, the case manager can promote appropriate use of insurance benefits, as well as governmental and philanthropic programs. It is important for the case manager to be knowledgeable of the legal rights of the client, and the responsibilities of insurance carriers and governmental agencies. The LNC as case manager, with experience in litigation processes, lends additional help in identifying actual or potential legal issues. This specialist is also able to facilitate access to legal services if necessary.

When a case manager is hired privately by an individual or their family, it is important that the role and responsibilities of the case manager be clearly understood by all parties, along with the desired outcome and duration of service requested, or required. To avoid misunderstandings, those involved in long-term case management need to involve the family with planning and coordination of future care, so that they can assume this role. Once the family has an understanding of the role, they can take on the responsibility themselves, or delegate it to others. Proper preparation will provide them with the knowledge needed, should the family relocate, or should the case manager no longer be available.

Case Example 7.9: Complications of Infection

An 18-month-old boy sustained a facial injury, which was treated, but misdiagnosed. As a result, the youngster developed a brain abscess, seizures, blindness, and a resultant right hemiparesis. Due to the increasing complexity of the child's medical needs during the trial, the life care planner was asked by the family to assume a case management immediately after the case ended. Having identified that the mother had the interest and necessary skills, the case manager worked with her to assume many of the roles and responsibilities ordinarily performed by the case manager. While maintaining responsibility for evaluation and planning, the case manager gave the mother education and support in assuming her new role. Frequently, this entailed preparing the mother for appointments, role modeling behaviors, and reviewing outcomes after appointments. The case manager gradually relinquished responsibility for attending meetings with providers. The mother initially called frequently to review issues and needs, but gradually gained more confidence in her skills. The case manager assisted her with identifying obstacles and reviewing strategies and techniques for advocating for her child's care needs. During the process, both the case manager and mother identified certain times when the mother did not feel that she could handle the responsibilities, requiring more assistance from the case manager. Such instances included preoperative evaluations, transition to home following a hospitalization, and meetings with school personnel.

A case manager may be retained to assist only with a specific activity that the family feels they cannot handle. It is important that the case manager understand the family's expectations; conflicts or differences of opinions should be discussed in advance. At times, the case manager may note that additional assistance or further consultation is needed, extending their involvement.

Case Example 7.10: Education Needs

A school-age child who sustained a traumatic brain injury requires the development of an individualized education program (IEP) upon his return to school. The family requests that the case manager attend the IEP meetings to assure that the plan provides for necessary and timely services from the school district. When appropriate and recommended services are discontinued, the case manager identifies the need for involvement of an attorney with specialized skill in dealing with education issues. After meeting with the family, the attorney and the case manager meet with school district officials to discuss the child's needs and the family's concerns. The case manager provides the necessary medical and therapeutic documentation to support the request, and the attorney applies his knowledge and experience with the Individuals with Disabilities Education Act (IDEA) to advocate for the child's care needs while in school.

Case Management in the Court System

Probate is the legal process of settling the estate of someone who has died, resolving all claims, and distributing property and other assets according to their will. It is necessary to probate the estate whenever an individual dies without a valid will, or when a property does not automatically pass to another by marriage or contract. When present, the probate court validates the will, promotes the wishes of the deceased, and protects the beneficiaries and executor, or administrator, of the will against claims.

The probate court also deals with issues such as conservatorship and guardianship. The court holds responsibility for making decisions to protect a minor or dependent adult's life and property, if deemed in jeopardy. The court protects minors and seniors, as well as individuals who are mentally ill or cognitively incapacitated, who were dependent upon the deceased person. A guardian (for a child younger than 18 years of age) or conservator (for an incapacitated adult) will be appointed by the court to assume responsibility for the health and well-being of their charge. Either the probate court or the guardian/conservator may enlist the services of a case manager to assist in evaluating and meeting the care needs of the dependent individual.

Legal proceedings related to medical malpractice or personal injury claims may result in the establishment of a trust fund for a dependent individual. Similar to situations of probate noted above, a trustee, or conservator, will be appointed to oversee distribution of funds to support the individual's health and well-being. In some instances, a discretionary supplemental needs trust (or special needs trust) allows the individual's inheritance to supplement government benefits, and is used to enrich the individual's life and make it more enjoyable. Again, the trust officer may seek the services of a case manager to assure that the use of funds is appropriate. In such cases, if a life care plan was developed as part of the suit, the services of a case manager may have been recommended. This individual can assist the court by providing support for expenses in an ongoing manner.

Case Example 7.11: Medical Foster Placement

A 5-year-old who suffered severe anoxia due to a birth injury was placed in a medical foster home as a young child when she demonstrated a failure to thrive. Her natural mother was a single parent who was pregnant with her second child. She acknowledged that she was unable to care for her daughter, and voluntarily placed her in foster care. Sequella from the birth injury included spastic quadriplegia with full dependence for care, cortical blindness, an inability to communicate, and respiratory compromise with the need for a tracheostomy, and gastrostomy tube feedings. A successful outcome to a lawsuit resulted in a structured settlement where a sum of money was invested, bearing interest, which funded a special needs trust. After the lawsuit, the natural mother gave up custody, allowing the medical foster parents to adopt the girl. The life care plan held a recommendation for a case manager, and the court appointed one as part of the settlement agreement. As the young girl grew, her medical needs persisted, and she required more and larger assistive devices. The adoptive parents sought to renovate their home to accommodate her needs, but did not have the money to accomplish this on their own. As home modifications were specified in the life care plan, the trust officer requested that the case manager assist the family in selecting and working with a contractor to make the necessary renovations. She was also instrumental in facilitating the development of a report explaining the need for the renovations for submission to the court with a petition to release the necessary funds. When the renovations were complete, she further submitted a report to the trust officer and the court indicating that the needs of the child were addressed with the alterations made.

"Legal issues affecting case management are interwoven in the complex matrix that is case management practice" (Muller, 2008a). Understanding the individual's rights, the provider's responsibilities, and the legal consequences of interactions can be a challenge for case managers (Muller, 2008b). When interfacing with the court system, an understanding of "power of attorney," "guardian," and "conservator" is important. A power of attorney is a document utilized to assign authority to another person to make decisions on their behalf. A guardian is an individual appointed by the court to assure proper care and financial management for an incapacitated person. A conservator is an individual appointed by the court to manage funds, and monitor their appropriate disbursement and use.

There are differences in the way each probate court functions, depending upon jurisdiction. The judge holds the responsibility of protecting the rights of the disabled individual, and supporting his/her needs. Many times judges are mindful of the needs of families for respite when caring for disabled dependents, yet are cognizant of budgetary constraints. While they feel that the individual should have appropriate care, services, and a reasonable quality of life, they also believe that a primary parenting responsibility remains, and so may restrict the use of funds for basic care needs, viewed as part of every parent's responsibility.

When acting as guardian or conservator, the court or fiduciary may request that a case manager be brought in to assist in the identification of needs and costs, and to determine whether funds have been appropriately spent. A case manager with legal nurse consulting experience, who is knowledgeable of the court system, is helpful in identifying the relevant issues, the medical needs, and the community resources available.

Elder Care/Geriatric Case Management

As the baby boomer generation reaches retirement age, this country will see an unprecedented number of elders requiring support. Accompanying this boom is the increased need for case managers in the community to address the needs of elders (Beeber, 2008; Schoenbeck, 2008). Schoenbeck (2008) notes geriatric case management is different from that for other patient populations. Numerous problems occur in this population, which are characterized by frequency, underrecognition and undertreatment, multiple causes, and tremendous impact upon the individual's ability to function independently.

The NAPGCM (2008b) notes that geriatric case managers specialize in assisting older people and their families to attain the highest quality of life given circumstances, which may, or may not, have occurred naturally. They conduct assessments, identify problems, arrange/monitor home care and other services, assist caregivers, review financial/legal/medical issues, and facilitate referrals. Additionally, they provide crisis intervention, act as liaison to remote family members, assist with transitions in care settings, provide consumer education and advocacy, and offer counseling and support.

Geriatric case managers may provide preventative services to individuals aged 65 and older by coordinating care of providers, increasing the quality of life of the elders, and promoting peace of mind of their adult children. However, it is usually initiated as the result of a crisis. Often the elders' adult children live a distance away, work full-time, or have responsibilities for small children, and cannot readily respond to their parents' needs. These case managers are often available 24 hr per day, 7 days per week, 365 days per year in order to be useful to the elders and their family. They respond to night-time calls related to falls or illness, and support the transition to home and home-care services following discharge from the hospital. Costs for this service are typically paid privately, or by a trust fund (Beeber, 2008; Cress, 2006).

Case Example 7.12: Hemorrhagic Stroke

After suffering a hemorrhagic stroke, an 82-year-old man was admitted to the intensive care unit. As his condition stabilized, he was transferred to the general nursing floor, and then to the inpatient rehabilitation unit. Due to his age and deconditioned status, however, he was not able to maintain the required level of therapeutic intervention (3 hr per day), and a transfer to a lower level of care was recommended. Considering that he would not likely receive sufficient attention in a subacute facility, and that he had the financial means, he and his family explored the possibility of returning home with private duty services to continue the rehabilitation process until he gained the endurance to be admitted to an acute rehabilitation facility for more aggressive treatment.

A private case manager was hired to coordinate a plan of care, which included 24-hr home-care services of a registered nurse and home health aide, in addition to private physical therapy to augment the home-care physical, occupational, and speech therapy services. Since family members lived a distance away, the case manager held the responsibility of coordinating staffing with the nursing agency, providing orientation to each new caregiver, updating the plan of care to integrate recommendations of therapists, facilitating transportation, and attending medical follow-up appointments. Additional consideration was given to maintaining open communication with concerned family members.

Over the subsequent months, he slowly regained the ability to stand briefly and assist with transfers, self-feed pureed foods with thickened fluids, and participate in toileting, hygiene, and grooming activities. Additionally, his spirits rose as his level of strength and endurance increased, allowing him to leave his home to visit friends, family, and attend holiday worship, each of which held great importance to him. After a 3-month period, he was accepted for admission to an acute rehabilitation facility, where he was able to withstand the rigorous regimen, and continued to demonstrate improvement in functional ability. Although he remained dependent upon the use of a wheelchair for community mobility, he regained the ability to ambulate household distances with a walker.

Upon discharge and returning home, the case manager assisted the client to privately hire a live-in caregiver to provide the level of assistance needed. As he continued to progress, the level of case management services was gradually reduced to continued "on-call" assistance with complex medical and insurance issues.

The case manager with experience as an LNC is an asset when assisting the elderly. Although the key elements of case management remain the same, elders have particular needs for assistance with eligibility, legal, and insurance issues. The knowledge to assess an elderly person's functional ability, support network, and available financial resources may mean the difference between their being able to stay in their own home, or needing to enter a residential facility. Meeting with all who comprise the "client system" will assist in identifying potential support and resources, as well as reveal individuals' motives for involvement. The ability to identify conflicting priorities may prevent potentially harmful situations (i.e., a caregiver who fosters a dependent relationship to assure continued employment). Although case managers may identify such an issue, their responsibility lies in assisting the elder to gain a full understanding so that they can make the ultimate decisions regarding their care.

The Role of LNC as Case Manager

Nursing case management is in many ways a natural role for LNCs, who have expertise in functioning in the legal and insurance arenas. LNCs bring to nursing case management expertise in reviewing medical records and bills as well as finely honed analytical skills. The American Association of Legal Nurse Consultants recognizes case management as a function of the LNC.

As described in the previous sections, nursing case management can take place in many arenas. Case managers can also work as independent contractors, just as LNCs do. Many LNCs also function as nurse case managers in their private practices.

The Case Manager in the Litigation Process

A case manager may be hired to assist the attorney and the client during the litigation process of a personal injury or medical malpractice case. During this phase, the case manager primarily coordinates evaluations, monitors care, identifies resources within the community, and plans and assists in the implementation of services. This role is important in facilitating the valuation of future care needs and the development of a life care plan. Having a nurse skilled in case management who knows about litigation helps the attorney to anticipate and identify issues that can affect the outcome of the case.

Workers' compensation cases often go into litigation when there is a dispute about the work-relatedness of the alleged injury. In most states, this involves a hearing in front of the workers' compensation commission or a judge. A worker who is permanently injured and unable to return to work may try to settle the lawsuit. Sometimes the injured worker may have a third-party suit if, for example, the injury was caused by a defective piece of equipment. Once the injured worker is represented by counsel, the case manager must work with the client through his attorney. Sometimes the client's attorney may prohibit direct contact with the client. In this case, the case manager can maintain contact with the treating providers and contact with the client through his attorney.

In both workers' compensation and automobile or general liability arenas, the case manager may be asked to set up an defense medical examination (DME). Choosing a physician for an DME is very much like choosing any other expert. This physician may well end up testifying in the case. The case manager is the appropriate person to know which specialty should be chosen and may help in locating a well-credentialed, objective physician for this evaluation. The case manager is often asked to send the medical records with a query letter including questions for the DME physician to answer, such as the relationship of the client's complaints to the alleged injury, appropriate treatment plan, further length of disability, and permanency of the client's injuries. The case manager may also be asked to attend the examination and can ask many of these questions. This is a distinctly different type of role from that of the LNC who is asked to attend an DME in order to observe the examination. In contrast to the role of the LNC, who will remain silent during the examination, the case manager takes an active role at the DME. The case manager will also review the report once it is received to ensure that the questions have been answered. Additional information regarding Defense Medical Exams can be found in Volume 1, Chapter 19, "Defense Medical Exams."

Nursing Case Management Credentials

An understanding of the credentials that nurse case managers can earn will help the LNC identify their background and accomplishments (web addresses identified as a resource for further information):

- ABDA—American Board of Disability Analysts (www.americandisability.org). Offers designation of Fellow and Diplomate; requires a minimum bachelor degree in an appropriate field and at least 4 years professional experience. Involves a peer-review process of work experience, work product, and professional references (*not a certification*). Designation continues while in good standing.
- A-CCC—Continuity of Care, Advanced (http://nbcc.net). Certification by examination; minimum requirement of a professional diploma/degree with 8 years experience providing continuity of care with verification of job responsibilities, or a bachelor degree (or higher) with 2 years qualifying experience within the preceding 5-year period. Recertification is required

every 5 years by points of credit for continuing education, formal education credit, and/or publication.

■ ACM—Accredited Case Manager (www.acmaweb.org). Certification by examination; minimum requirement of nursing diploma/degree or social work degree with unrestricted license and 2 years hospital case management experience. Recertification is required every 4 years by 40 hr approved continuing education credits, 30 hr of which must be specific to case management, or re-examination.

■ AOCNS—Advanced Oncology Certified Clinical Nurse Specialist.

■ AOCNP—Advanced Oncology Certified Nurse Practitioner (www.oncc.org). Certification by examination; minimum requirement of master of science in nursing degree from accredited clinical nurse specialist or nurse practitioner program including at least 500 hr supervised clinical practice in oncology. Recertification is required every 4 years by a combination of two of three elements: 1,000 practice hours in oncology setting, 125 continuing education credits, re-examination.

■ CCM—Certified Case Manager (www.ccmcertification.org). Certification by examination; minimum requirement of a completion of a postsecondary program of study leading to independent licensure with 24-month case management experience, or 12-month case management experience supervised by a CCM, or 12 months with responsibility for supervising case managers; job description meeting specific experiential requirements; demonstration of good moral character. Recertification is required every 5 years with 80 hr of acceptable continuing education or re-examination.

■ CDMS—Certified Disability Management Specialist (www.cdms.org). Certification by examination; minimum requirement of a completion of an associate degree in a related field and at least 40 hr documented experience in disability management, or a bachelors degree (or higher) in any field with 80 hr documented experience in disability management; 18 months work experience with at least 6 months under the supervision of a CCM, CDMS, or CRC; academic preparation in three domains (disability management, disability prevention and workplace intervention, and program development/management/evaluation). Recertification is required every 5 years with 80 hr of acceptable continuing education (including at least 4 hr related to ethics) or re-examination.

■ CLCP—Certified Life Care Planner (www.ichcc.org). Certification by examination; minimum requirement of undergraduate degree required for entry to healthcare profession; minimum 3 years rehabilitation experience in the preceding 5-year period; completion of a life care planning program of study earning at least 120 contact hours; peer review of a completed life care plan (through education program, supervision by CLCP, or submission with application). Recertification is required every 5 years with 80 hr of approved continuing education (including at least 8 hr related to ethics) or re-examination.

■ CMAC—Case Management Administrator Certification (www.cfcm.com). Certification by examination; requirement of baccalaureate degree or higher plus case management/case management administration experience (1–5 years), achievement of related certification, or faculty in case management program (two semesters). Recertification is required every 5 years by re-examination.

■ CMC—Case Management Certified (www.aiocm.com). Certification by examination; minimum requirement of sufficient points determined by application (education, general experience, professional experience); maintain membership in good standing in The American Institute of Outcomes Care Management. Recertification is required every 2 years by portfolio including continued membership, adherence to code of ethics, and combination of points for continuing education, publication, teaching, and peer review.

- CMC—Care Manager Certified (www.naccm.net). Certification by examination; minimum requirement of basic education in related profession (diploma/degree) with at least 2 years supervised care management experience (additional 2–4 years experience requirement with less than master's level degree). Recertification is required every 3 years with 1,500 hr practice and 45 hr continuing education in care management, as well as written verification of experience/education criteria being met.

- CNLCP—Certified Nurse Life Care Planner (www.aanlcp.org). Certification by examination; minimum requirement of unrestricted professional nurse licensure; minimum 5 years nursing experience with at least 2 years experience (4,000 hr) in case management; completion of a life care planning program of study earning at least 60 contact hours or 500 hr experience in life care planning within the preceding 2 years; peer review of a completed life care plan (through education program or submission with application). Recertification is required every 5 years with 60 points of credit comprised of acceptable continuing education, formal education, presentation, publication, association service, item development, or re-examination.

- COHN—Certified Occupational Health Nurse (www.abohn.org). Certification by examination; minimum requirement of diploma or associate degree in nursing, unrestricted professional nurse license, and 3,000 hr experience in field of occupational health within the preceding 5-year period or completion of a certificate program in occupational health for academic credit. Recertification is required every 5 years with evidence of 3,000 hr practice and 50 contact hours of continuing education related to occupational health nursing.

- COHN-S—Certified Occupational Health Nurse-Specialist (www.abohn.org). Certification by examination; minimum requirement of baccalaureate degree in nursing, unrestricted professional nurse license, and 3,000 hr experience in field of occupational health within the preceding 5-year period or completion of a certificate program/graduate program in occupational health for academic credit. Recertification is required every 5 years with evidence of 3,000 hr practice and 50 contact hours of continuing education related to occupational health nursing.

- COHN-CM—Certified Occupational Health Nurse-Case Manager (www.abohn.org). Certification by examination; minimum requirement of active certification as COHN or COHN-S, unrestricted professional nurse license and 10 contact hours continuing education related to case management within the preceding 5-year period. Recertification is required every 5 years with evidence of 3,000 hr practice and 50 contact hours of continuing education related to occupational health nursing, and 10 contact hours of continuing education specific to occupational health case management practice.

- CON—Certified Oncology Nurse (www.oncc.org). (See CPON for criteria.)

- CPON—Certified Pediatric Oncology Nurse (www.oncc.org). Certification by examination; minimum requirement of unrestricted professional nurse license with 12 months clinical experience within preceding 3 years, 1,000 hr practice in oncology setting, 10 contact hours approved continuing education credits related to oncology nursing. Recertification is required every 4 years by a combination of two of three elements: 1,000 practice hours in oncology setting, 100 continuing education credits; re-examination.

- CPHQ—Certified Professional in Healthcare Quality (www.cphq.org). Certification by examination without minimum education requirement, however, experience in healthcare quality is essential to successfully achieve certification. Recertification is required every 2 years with 30 continuing education credits in areas reviewed and specified by the Board on an annual basis.

- CRRN—Certified Rehabilitation Registered Nurse (www.rehabnurse.org). Certification by examination; minimum requirement of unrestricted professional nurse license with 2 years experience in rehabilitation nursing within the preceding 5-year period, or 1-year experience in rehabilitation nursing and 1-year advanced study in nursing beyond the baccalaureate level. Recertification is required every 5 years with 60 points of credit comprised of acceptable continuing education, formal education, presentation, publication, community service, or re-examination.
- CRRN-A—Certified Rehabilitation Registered Nurse (www.rehabnurse.org). Certification by examination; minimum requirement of CRRN credential and a master of science in nursing degree; administered 1997–2004.
- FIALCP—Fellow International Academy of Life Care Planners (www.rehabpro.org). Offers designation of Fellow; requires a minimum bachelor degree in an appropriate field; maintains necessary licensure and/or certification to practice in respective healthcare discipline; contributes to field through presentation, publication, research, mentoring activities. Involves peer-review process of work experience, work product, and professional references (*not a certification*). Designation continues while in good standing.
- CHCQM—Certified in Health Care Quality and Management (http://.abquarp.org). Certification by examination; minimum requirement of unrestricted professional license; 208 hr experience in healthcare quality and management (quality improvement, risk management, utilization management, case management/disease management, managed healthcare systems, or government) in preceding 5-year period, 20 approved continuing education credits in core content, and two professional recommendations. Recertification is required every 2 years with eight approved continuing education credits and continued membership in good standing of the American Institute for Healthcare Quality. Further certification in subspecialties available with requirement of 24 hr continuing education in the specified area.
- MSCC—Medicare Set-aside Consultant Certified (www.ichcc.org). Certification by examination; minimum requirement of undergraduate degree required for entry to healthcare profession; minimum 12 months experience in area of workers' compensation/liability insurance in preceding 3-year period; completion of a Medicare set-aside program of study earning at least 30 contact hours. Recertification is required every 3 years with 15 hr of approved continuing or re-examination.
- RN-C/RN-BC—Case Management Nurse (www.nursing world.org). Certification by examination; minimum requirement of unrestricted professional nurse license with 2 years nursing experience; 30 hr continuing education credit and 2,000 hr experience in nursing case management during the preceding 3-year period. Recertification is required every 5 years with points of credit comprised of acceptable continuing education, formal education, presentation, publication, or re-examination.

Professional Associations and Organizations

These professional organizations enhance the practices of nurse case managers by providing educational and networking opportunities:

- AANLCP—American Association of Nurse Life Care Planners (www.aanlcp.org)
- AAOHN—American Association of Occupational Health Nurses (www.aaohn.org)

- AIHQ—American Institute for Healthcare Quality (www.aihq.org)
- ARN—Association of Rehabilitation Nurses (www.rehabnurse.org)
- CMSA—Case Management Society of America (www.cmsa.org)
- IARP—International Association of Rehabilitation Professionals (www.rehabpro.org)
- IALCP—International Academy of Life Care Planners (www.rehabpro.org/ialcp)
- NAMSAP—National Association of Medicare Set-Aside Professionals (www.namsap.org)
- NAPGCM—National Association of Professional Geriatric Care Manager (www.napgcm.org)
- ONS—Oncology Nurses Society (www.ons.org)

Conclusions

The nurse case manager practices in many different arenas. The LNC as case manager has many different roles throughout the litigation process and has interaction with clients, physicians, other healthcare providers, insurance carriers, and attorneys. These multifaceted roles require the services of a nurse with a strong knowledge base, breadth of clinical experience, and appropriate qualifications/credentials. Both case management and legal nurse consulting demand similar skills including critical analysis, problem solving, and negotiation. The LNC and nurse case manager also must be self-motivating, and able to work both independently and collaboratively with others.

References

American Health Consultants. (2001). AHC/CMSA caseload survey. *Case Manager, 12*(4), 53.

ANA. (2004). *Nursing: Scope and standards of practice.* Silver Spring, MD: American Nurses Association.

ARN. (2008). *Standards and scope of rehabilitation nursing practice.* Glenview, IL: Association of Rehabilitation Nurses.

Banja, J. (2008). Ethical issues in case management practice. In S. Powell & H. Tahan (Eds.), *CMSA core curriculum for case management* (2nd ed., pp. 594–607). Philadelphia: Lippincott Williams & Wilkins.

Beeber, A. (2008). Luck and happenstance: How older adults enroll in a program of all-inclusive care for the elderly. *Professional Case Management, 13*(5), 277–283.

Birmingham, J. (2007). Case management: Two regulations with coexisting functions (utilization review + discharge planning = case management). *Professional Case Management, 12*(1), 16–24.

Case management and compliance: What every case manager needs to know. *Hospital Case Management, 11*(11), 161–163.

Center for Medicare and Medicaid Services (CMS). (2008, October). Worker's compensation Medicare set aside arrangements. Retrieved October 16, 2008, from http://www.cms.hhs.gov/workerscompagencyservices/04_wcsetaside.asp

CMCC. (2005). *Code of professional conduct for case managers.* Schaumburg, IL: Commission for Case Management Certification.

CMSA. (2002). *Standards of practice for case management.* Little Rock, AR: Case Management Society of America.

CMSA. (2008a). CMSA demographics: Years in clinical practice. Retrieved October 16, 2008, from http://www.cmsa.org/LinkClick.aspx?fileticket=UPlvu9KAZK0%3d&tabid=167&mid=717

CMSA. (2008b). CMSA demographics: Years in case management. Retrieved October 16, 2008, from http://www.cmsa.org/LinkClick.aspx?fileticket=1Q7qPAlJu8 k%3d&tabid=167&mid=717

CMSA. (2008c). CMSA demographics: Caseloads. Retrieved October 16, 2008, from http://www.cmsa.org/LinkClick.aspx?fileticket=Vu1rWjTUg5A%3d&tabid=167&mid=717

Cress, C. (2006). *Handbook of geriatric case management.* Sudbury, MA: Jones & Bartlett Publishers.

Cunningham, B. (2008). Health care insurance, benefits, and reimbursement systems. In S. Powell & H. Tahan (Eds.), *CMSA core curriculum for case management* (2nd ed., pp. 17–38). Philadelphia: Lippincott Williams & Wilkins.

DiBenedetto, D. (2008). Workers' compensation case management. In S. Powell & H. Tahan (Eds.), *CMSA core curriculum for case management* (2nd ed., pp. 364–399). Philadelphia: Lippincott Williams & Wilkins.

Health and Human Services. (2003, April). *Protecting the privacy of patients' health information.* Washington, DC: U.S. Department of Health and Human Services.

IARP. (2007). *IARP code of ethics, standards of practice, and competencies.* Glenview, IL: International Association of Rehabilitation Professionals.

Maldonado, D. (2003). *A case manager's study guide: Preparing for certification.* Sudbury, MA: Aspen Publishers.

Mitus, A. (2008). The birth of InterQual: Evidence-based decision support criteria that helped change healthcare. *Professional Case Management, 13*(4), 228–233.

Mullahy, C. (2004). *The case manager's handbook* (3rd ed.). Sudbury, MA: Jones & Bartlett Publishers.

Muller, L. (2006). CMSA supports compliance with multistate licensure law: Nursing compact states reach 20. *Lippincott's Case Management, 11*(3), 124–126.

Muller, L. (2008a). Legal issues in case management practice. In S. Powell & H. Tahan (Eds.), *CMSA core curriculum for case management* (2nd ed.). Philadelphia: Lippincott Williams & Wilkins.

Muller, L. (2008b). Power of attorney and guardianship: What we think we know. *Professional Case Management, 13*(3), 169–172.

Muller, L., & Flarey, D. (2004). Consent for case management: Using the CMSA standards of practice. *Lippincott's Case Management, 9*(6), 254–256.

NAPGCM. (2008a). *Standards of practice for professional geriatric care managers.* Tucson, AZ: National Association of Professional Care Managers.

NAPGCM. (2008b). Geriatric care manager. Retrieved October 16, 2008, from http://www.caremanager.org/displaycommon.cfm?an=1&subarticlenbr=20

Thomas, P. (2008). Case manager role definitions: Do they make an organizational impact? *Professional Case Management, 13*(2), 61–71.

White, A. (2004). Case management and the national quality agenda: Partnering to improve the quality of care. *Lippincott's Case Management, 9*(3), 132–140.

Additional Resources

ANA. (2001). *Code of ethics for nurses with interpretive statements.* Silver Spring, MD: ANA.

Balstad, A. (2006). Quantifying case management workloads: Development of the PACE tool. *Lippincott's Case Management, 11*(6), 291–302.

Banja, J. (2007). Case managers and ethics: Balancing advocacy with objective evaluation. *Professional Case Management, 12*(2), 68–69.

Cesta, T., Tahan, H., & Fink, L. (2002). *The case management survival guide: Winning strategies for clinical practice* (2nd ed.). St. Louis: C.V. Mosby.

Craig, K., & Huber, D. (2007). Acuity and case management: A healthy dose of outcomes, Part II. *Professional Case Management, 12*(4), 199–210.

DiBenedetto, D. (2003a). HIPAA privacy 101. *Lippincott's Case Management, 8*(1), 14–23.

DiBenedetto, D. (2003b). The HIPAA toolbox. *Lippincott's Case Management, 8*(1), 36–49.

Huber, D., & Craig, K. (2007a). Acuity and case management: A healthy dose of outcomes, Part I. *Professional Case Management, 12*(3), 132–144.

Huber, D., & Craig, K. (2007b). Acuity and case management: A healthy dose of outcomes, Part III. *Professional Case Management, 12*(5), 254–269.

Lambert, K. (2008). Important lessons learned. *Professional Case Management, 13*(2), 113–114.

McCollom, P. (2007). Paranoia or preparedness? *Lippincott's Case Management, 11*(2), 111–112.

Muller, L. (2003). HIPAA compliance: Implications for case managers. *Lippincott's Case Management, 8*(1), 30–35.

Muller, L. (2004). Interstate practice. *Lippincott's Case Management, 9*(3), 117–120.

Muller, L., & Flarey, D. (2004). Consent for case management: Using the CMSA standards of practice. *Lippincott's Case Management, 9*(6), 254–256.

Powell, S., & Tahan, H. (2008). *CMSA core curriculum for case management* (2nd ed.). Philadelphia: Lippincott Williams & Wilkins.

Shoenbeck, L. (2008). Geriatric case management. In S. Powell & H. Tahan (Eds.), *CMSA core curriculum for case management* (2nd ed., pp. 479–496). Philadelphia: Lippincott Williams & Wilkins.

Tahan, H. (2005a). Clarifying certification and its value for case managers. *Lippincott's Case Management, 10*(1), 14–21.

Tahan, H. (2005b). Essentials of advocacy in case management. *Lippincott's Case Management, 10*(3), 136–145.

Internet Resources for Case Management

1. Abledata (assistive technology resources): http://www.abledata.com
2. American Hospital Directory (medical costs and hospital data): http://www. ahd.com
3. Association of Rehabilitation Nurses: http://www.rehabnurse.org
4. Brain Injury Association of USA: http://www.biausa.org
5. Case Management Society of America: http://www.cmsa.org
6. Case Manager's Resource Guide: http://www.cmrg.com
7. Commission for Disability Management Specialists: http://www.cmds.org
8. MedMarket (medical supplies): http://www.medmarket.com
9. National Spinal Cord Injury Association: http://www.spinalcord.org
10. Oncolink: http://www.oncolink.upenn.edu
11. Commission for Health Care Certification: http:www.ichcc.org
12. American Association of Nurse Life Care Planners: http://www.aanlcp.com
13. National Guidelines Clearinghouse: http://www.guidelines.gov

Test Questions

1. Standards of practice for case management are
   A. Defined by the nursing process
   B. The same thing as outcomes
   C. Delineated by professional organizations
   D. Determined by each state's nurse practice act

2. Workers' compensation benefits
   A. Are the same nationwide
   B. Are specified by state law
   C. Provide for payment of medical care only
   D. Include tort action against the employer

3. The process for case management
   A. Includes assessment, planning, implementation, coordination, monitoring, and evaluation
   B. Should be implemented only by a certified case manager
   C. Determines the level of insurance reimbursement
   D. Is determined by the Case Management Society of America

4. A dual relationship exists when
   A. A case manager provides services to a friend, relative, or coworker
   B. A hospital case manager also works as a staff nurse for the employer
   C. A life care planner provides case management services after a case is settled
   D. A case manager provides vital case information to the physician and the insurance carrier

5. A case manager faces a potential for liability when
   A. Reimbursement is denied by the payer
   B. Inappropriate care or over-/underutilization of resources is disregarded
   C. Personal health information is conveyed to a provider in the continuum of care
   D. A and B

Answers: 1. C, 2. B, 3. A, 4. A, 5. B

Chapter 8

The Role of the Legal Nurse Consultant in the Insurance Industry

Deborah S. White, RN, BSN, LNCC

First Edition
Melanie Eve Longenhagen, MBA, MSN, RN, CCM

Second Edition
Patricia A. Jenkins-Barnard, RN; Melanie Eve Longenhagen, MBA, MSN, RN, CCM; and Melanie Osley, RN, MBA, CPHRM, FASHRM

Contents

Objectives

- Explain various types of automobile and liability insurance
- Describe and provide examples of the roles of a claims consultant/adjuster in evaluating injury claims

Types of Insurance

Automobile Insurance

An automobile insurance policy covers accidents and losses that arise out of the ownership or use of cars, trucks, and other motor vehicles. This type of insurance may be issued to a private person (personal) or to a business (commercial). Automobile coverage in part deals with property damage to the insured's vehicles and to other vehicles damaged in an accident. The remainder of the automobile policy (casualty) deals with damage or liability that results in bodily injury from the operation of an automobile.

Casualty insurance claims can be either "first party" or "third party" depending upon who is eligible for payment for an accident or loss. First-party claims refer to claims made by an insured or policyholder with their own insurance company. The insured has a contract with their insurance company that entitles them to payment in the event of an accident, depending upon the insurance coverage they purchased. In many states, first-party coverage follows the vehicle rather than the insured person; therefore, household members and passengers in an insured vehicle may also be eligible for benefits. Such first-party coverage for medical expense is limited to medical bills and applies regardless of whether the insured was at fault in the accident. Personal injury protection (PIP), also known as no-fault insurance, is another type of first-party coverage. In addition to medical bills, PIP may also cover wage loss and medical mileage.

Third-party claims refer to liability claims made against the insured by a third party. The third party, or claimant, does not have a contract with the insured's insurance company but may present a claim against the insured's policy in the event the insured is determined to have been at fault and liable for the accident. For instance, if the insured runs a red light and collides with another vehicle, resulting in injury to the driver or passenger in the other vehicle, that driver or passenger (claimant) may present a third-party claim (bodily injury claim) to the insured's insurance company. Bodily injury claims may include consideration of not only incurred medical bills, but future medical treatment, permanent impairment, wage loss, etc. (American Educational Institute, Inc., 1994).

Uninsured motorist (UM) or underinsured motorist (UIM) bodily injury coverage applies to losses incurred by the insured when the insured is involved in an accident with someone who carries no insurance of their own (UM) or has inadequate insurance coverage (UIM) to compensate for the injuries sustained by the insured.

General Liability Insurance

General liability policies cover accidents and losses that do not involve motor vehicles. Examples of events considered under general liability include injury of a bystander at a construction site, injury as a result of a slip and fall on a sidewalk or stairs, injury due to negligent security, food poisoning, and injury due to a defective manufactured product. A general liability policy can be issued to a private person (e.g., a homeowner's policy) or to a business (commercial general liability policy). When the insurance company's claims office receives a claim, it assigns it to an insurance adjuster, who evaluates all aspects of the claim, including the fault (liability) of the insured and the damages or injuries.

The Roles of the Legal Nurse Consultant

Claims Consultant/Adjuster

As a claims consultant/adjuster, the legal nurse consultant (LNC) utilizes a diverse nursing and business knowledge base for investigating, evaluating, and negotiating claims. The LNC may function as a technical analyst, consultant, or mediator and may be an employee of an insurance company, an employee of a vendor that offers consulting services, or an independent consultant. The process involves anticipating potential claims, reviewing actual claims, negotiating settlements directly with claimants or their attorneys, and participating in mediation on behalf of the insured.

The LNC's role as a claims consultant/adjuster is to investigate and evaluate claims to determine their worth or merit in relation to a specific illness or injury. Potential financial exposure of the insurance company must be anticipated so that an appropriate monetary reserve can be set aside. Depending on the state, the LNC claims consultant/adjuster may be required to pass an examination to obtain a license with periodic renewal and, in some states, may be subject to continuing education requirements to maintain standing. An LNC needs to be aware of which states do not allow an LNC to adjust claims without an adjuster license.

Evaluating damages is an area in which the LNC can have the most impact. Insurance adjusters may have a great deal of experience in assessing injuries and reading medical reports, but they rarely have any formal medical training or experience. The reading of medical records and interpretation of medical abbreviations and terminology can be challenging to adjusters, especially those less experienced. The LNC can provide practical support to the adjuster and to defense counsel in the following ways:

- Reviewing medical records to determine causal relationships, legitimacy of alleged injuries, preexisting and unrelated conditions, and potential medical outcomes
- Determining which medical records are missing and any additional records needed to complete a thorough review of the claim
- Evaluating whether treatment provided was appropriate or excessive
- Providing factual evidence for use in limiting damages
- Recommending appropriate medical experts, peer reviewers, etc.
- Researching unusual injuries, medical conditions, and complications that may impact recovery

The LNC is often called upon to help determine the relatedness of an accident to the claimed injury and to assist in evaluating the severity and permanency of the injury in preparation for settlement. To determine whether a plausible causal connection exists between the injury and the accident, the LNC may be asked to research the medical literature to answer such questions as

- Can new-onset diabetes occur as a result of abdominal trauma?
- Can trauma aggravate preexisting degenerative changes of the spine?
- Can a preexisting cardiac dysrhythmia worsen from steering wheel or airbag impact?
- Can first trimester pregnancy loss occur as a result of a slip and fall?

- Can posttraumatic stress disorder result from a car accident in which no party sustained serious physical injuries?
- Can a closed head injury occur as the result of a minor rear-end impact to a vehicle?

The LNC working for an insurance company participates in resolution of claims in a variety of ways. These include interpretation of medical terminology and abbreviations in medical records, joining roundtable discussions (committees) in the claims office, developing and delivering medical training sessions for adjusters, clarifying medical issues at arbitration or mediation, providing a thorough and objective analysis of current medical literature, and providing negotiation points for settlement.

Often LNCs work directly with defense counsel, in preparation of an appropriate settlement offer to be made to a claimant's attorney. In the event of pending litigation, an LNC may help locate medical experts in specific specialty areas and assist with development of pertinent deposition questions, chronologies of medical treatment, and trial exhibits. An LNC may also monitor case costs by tracking attorney activities to ensure payment amounts are not exceeded.

Example 8.1

An LNC employed as a claims consultant/adjuster for a major not-for-profit health insurance company has been asked to handle a claim. A 27-year-old male sustained second- and third-degree burns over 10% of his body, as a result of smoking in bed. The request for authorization of ambulance transport is the first indication of the accident. The injured party is treated and stabilized at a local hospital and then transported to a university-based hospital for further treatment. He is admitted to an intensive care burn unit and scheduled for a series of skin grafts. A family member is contacted to obtain consent to release his medical records and is informed that the LNC will be assisting in the processing of his bills.

Having obtained consent, the LNC contacts the attending plastic surgeon to determine the extent of injury and plan of care, and documents the conversation appropriately. According to corporate policy, the hospital case manager is contacted and informed of the situation. Together the LNC and case manager work to ensure that the client's care is medically appropriate and covered by the policy. The LNC verifies eligibility and documents this on the file. During the time of admission, the LNC identifies potential claims and notifies all appropriate parties, such as rating and underwriting members, so that appropriate reserves (money) can be set aside. After the client is discharged, the LNC obtains the bills for services rendered, reviews them for covered charges, and adjudicates or finalizes the claims for payment. Should any care rendered be noncontracted, the LNC will begin the process of determining medical appropriateness through the hospital case manager. Once the process is completed and services deemed medically appropriate, the LNC may negotiate rates for the services according to company policy, utilizing usual, customary, and reasonable (UCR) fee data or schedules for comparing charges. Once the claims are adjudicated, the LNC closes the file, maintaining the records for the time frame in accordance with company policy.

LNCs working in automobile or general liability insurance areas are well advised to become familiar with the processing and adjusting of such injury or casualty claims. This will allow the LNC to better meet the needs of the adjuster handling the claims and to understand the constraints under which adjusters operate; for example, policy limits, statutes of limitation, etc. Numerous factors are taken into account in arriving at a settlement offer; for example, severity of injury, extent of medical treatment (e.g., surgery vs. medical), medical bills, wage loss, duties under duress, future treatment, permanency, etc. Timely and fair settlement of claims is the goal. However, this can be subject to outside forces, for example, delays in receiving signed medical authorizations or requested medical records or bills, and necessitates cooperation and communication between the LNC and adjuster to achieve thorough review of claims issues and optimal claims resolution.

Also helpful is a basic familiarity with medical coding of diagnoses (*ICD-9—International Classification of Diseases, 9th Revision*) and procedures (*CPT—Current Procedural Terminology*) to allow interpretation of medical bills. Comparison of medical bills with the medical records helps ensure that all billed treatment is documented as having been done (e.g., multiple physical therapy modalities during a therapy session), charges are not duplicated or unbundled, and that procedure codes correlate with diagnosis or injury codes (e.g., while a complete blood count could be related to an injury, a lipid profile would likely not).

Insurance adjusters often need assistance in determining such issues as relatedness of injuries to the accident in question and investigating the appropriateness and necessity of medical treatment, severity and implications of injuries, and potential for permanency and future treatment. It is imperative that an LNC remain objective and support any recommendations with documentation from the medical records and from research of reliable medical literature so that adjusters feel confident in using those findings in their settlement negotiations.

LNCs evaluating auto or general liability claims should first attempt to establish the baseline of an injury. This allows the LNC to better evaluate whether the claim is logical and well grounded and to better grasp the subsequent course of treatment. This includes examining accident reports, claimant statements, adjusters' notes, ambulance records, emergency room records, and initial physician follow-up notes to determine the complaints and symptoms present from the outset or within a few days of an accident. Subsequent claims of injuries inconsistent with those documented initially may be questionable in terms of relatedness to the accident. LNCs have the ability to gather information from various sources and put it together in a total package, noting any inconsistencies that may exist.

Of particular value is an LNC's knowledge of the workings of the healthcare system and the processes that are common to most hospitals and providers. This allows an LNC to know what medical records to expect among the documentation provided in support of a claim. Any missing records can then be requested; for example, the emergency department (ED) physician's dictated note in addition to the ED forms completed in longhand. In another scenario, an adjuster may question the necessity of two sets of wrist x-rays done in the ED for a distal radius fracture. The LNC can explain that a second set of x-rays is routinely done after closed reduction of a fracture.

Preexisting medical conditions are pertinent to injury claims but do not preclude an injury to the same area of the body; for example, an acute lumbar strain in an individual with failed back syndrome and chronic low back pain. Obtaining prior medical records could be essential in determining the claimant's pain rating, medications and dosages, pattern of medical treatment, employability, etc. immediately before the accident as compared with postaccident. In the absence of disclosure of such a preexisting medical condition, a thorough review of medical records may suggest a relevant prior condition: for example, pain or anti-inflammatory medications being taken at the time of the accident, imaging studies compared with previous studies done at the same facility, and initial billing as an established patient with a spine surgeon.

After screening and initially evaluating a claim, an LNC may see the need for a peer review to better clarify certain medical issues. In that event, pertinent claim information (e.g., vehicle photos, accident report) and medical records are copied and submitted to a peer of the medical provider to obtain the peer's professional opinion on the claim presented. Some states have laws governing how such peer reviews are to be conducted; for example, reviewers may need to be certified insurance consultants. To ensure a fair and valid peer review, genuine attempts should be made to locate a peer reviewer of the same specialty as the provider; that is, a chiropractor reviewing a chiropractor, an orthopedic surgeon reviewing an orthopedic surgeon, etc. Such a peer review is often referred to as a "paper" review, in that the claimant is not seen or examined by the reviewer. This differs from an independent medical examination (IME), in which a physician interviews and examines the injured party and submits a report of their findings and professional opinion. In both peer reviews and IMEs, it is preferable to seek out physicians who are board-certified or board-eligible in their specialties, in active practice, and in good standing with their state boards.

Example 8.2

An LNC is employed by a casualty insurance company strictly in a consulting role, meaning in this case that the LNC has no authority to adjust or negotiate claims directly. The LNC is referred to a third-party bodily injury claim by an adjuster needing assistance evaluating a claim involving a rotator cuff tear. A demand package has been received from the claimant attorney. The claimant is a 53-year-old male who was the restrained driver of a small car that was rear-ended by the insured driving a mid-size car in stop and go traffic. As per property damage estimates in the claim file, both vehicles sustained less than $800 in property damage. As per the accident report, completed by the police officer at the scene, both vehicles sustained minimal damage and were driven from the scene. The claimant complained of neck pain at the scene but refused emergency medical services (EMS), and stated that he would seek medical treatment on his own. Upon review of the ED records, the claimant drove himself to the ED the next day for complaint of severe right shoulder pain, which he attributed to the motor vehicle accident (MVA). The claimant was taking Celebrex he had at home. The ED physician noted the absence of a contusion or muscle spasm and described an "unremarkable" shoulder exam. Shoulder x-rays revealed degenerative changes and findings consistent with a possible partial tear of the rotator cuff. The claimant was instructed to continue with the Celebrex and follow up with his regular doctor in 2–3 days. Pain medication was prescribed. In the meantime, he was to remain off work. The claimant was noted to be right-hand dominant and a self-employed drywall installer.

The only other medical records in the demand packet are office records from an orthopedic surgeon. The claimant was seen by the surgeon approximately 2 weeks after the accident for "follow-up partial supraspinatus tear with impingement." The surgeon briefly noted that injections and physical therapy had failed to relieve the claimant's symptoms and recommended proceeding to surgery. In the meantime, the claimant was to remain off work. The surgeon's progress note was copied to the claimant's regular doctor. Surgery remains pending. The bill for the office visit with the surgeon indicates the claimant was billed as an established patient. The claimant's attorney is demanding the insured's policy limits of $100,000 to cover the costs of medical bills and wage loss already incurred, future surgery, rehabilitation, permanent impairment, disability from work, etc. due to the MVA.

The LNC notes the following observations from a review of the above documentation:

- The police report and property damage estimates suggest a minor impact and minimal damage to the vehicles involved in the MVA.
- The claimant refused EMS at the scene for his complaint of neck pain. No complaint of shoulder pain at the scene was mentioned in the police report.
- The claimant was able to drive himself from the scene and then to the ED the next day. His complaint there differed from the scene. In the ED, there was no objective sign of acute injury despite the complaint of severe right shoulder pain and his examination was negative. No mechanism of shoulder injury in the MVA was documented. He was already on a prescription anti-inflammatory. Shoulder x-rays show degenerative changes in a 53-year-old male who works as a drywall installer and is right-hand dominant
- There is no documentation of the claimant's follow-up with his regular doctor as instructed in the ED.
- Two weeks after the MVA, the claimant was seen as an established patient by an orthopedic surgeon in follow-up for a previously diagnosed supraspinatus tear of the rotator cuff. The claimant was already noted to have been treated with injections and physical therapy,

neither of which had helped significantly. Surgery was proposed the same day. In the meantime, the claimant was to stay off work. The surgeon informed the claimant's regular doctor of his findings and recommendation.

The LNC recommends that the claimant's prior records from his regular doctor and from the orthopedic surgeon, including all x-rays and imaging studies, dating back 4 years before the MVA be requested from the claimant's attorney. Upon receipt and review of the prior records, it is determined that the claimant's regular doctor had been treating the claimant's increasing right shoulder pain with medication for a year before the MVA, with a shoulder magnetic resonance imaging (MRI) having been obtained 3 months before the accident. The MRI had revealed the rotator cuff tear and the claimant had been referred to the orthopedic surgeon for treatment. The surgeon's initial recommendations were physical therapy and steroid injections. The claimant had attended physical therapy for a week and had received two injections, but stated his pain was to the point where he could no longer work. At his last visit to the surgeon prior to the accident, the claimant had stated he wanted to proceed with surgery but had no health insurance and could not afford it. This information confirming the preexisting rotator cuff tear and active treatment for the same at the time of the MVA is submitted to the adjuster in a written report for the adjuster's use in negotiations with the claimant's attorney.

Professional Credentials and Certifications

American Educational Institute (AEI) offers several series of self-study courses in insurance coverage, claims law, and fraud. Successful completion of a program of courses can lead to such designations as AEI "Fraud Claim Law Specialist" or "Fraud Claim Law Associate."

National Insurance Crime Training Academy (NICTA) offers training and information for law enforcement, insurance adjusters, and the public through online courses. In states that require licensure, claims adjusters can earn continuing education credit. This antifraud training includes snapshots of such topics as common injuries, diagnostic testing, CPT coding, and different types of fraud. For more information, see www.nicta.org.

Chapter Summary

The LNC contributes a thorough and objective analysis of the medical records and medical information in order to help the insurance company pay first-party claims appropriately and reach fair and equitable settlements of third-party claims. This may involve denial or defense of claims with questionable or unsubstantiated injuries or undocumented treatment. Allowance and payment of questionable or fraudulent injury claims can increase insurance premium costs for all insureds.

Reference

American Educational Institute, Inc. (1994). *Fundamentals in coverage and claims law.*

Test Questions

1. Which of the following is true of a bodily injury claim?
   A. It is a first-party claim
   B. It applies regardless of fault in an accident
   C. It covers medical bills only
   D. It includes not only medical bills but future medical treatment, permanent impairment, wage loss, etc.

2. General liability insurance could apply to
   A. A slip and fall on stairs
   B. Food poisoning
   C. A manufacturer's defect
   D. All of the above

3. An LNC in the role of a claims consultant/adjuster reviews medical records to do all of the following *except*
   A. Determine causal relationships
   B. Assess legitimacy of alleged injuries
   C. Provide direct patient care
   D. Determine preexisting conditions

4. In evaluating auto or general liability claims, an LNC should *first* attempt to
   A. Establish the baseline of an injury
   B. Consider the potential for future medical treatment
   C. Identify missing medical records
   D. Obtain a peer review

5. In insurance terminology, a DME refers to an
   A. Defense mediation effort
   B. Defense medical examination
   C. Detailed medical equipment
   D. Defined medical event

Answers: 1. D, 2. D, 3. C, 4. A, 5. B

Chapter 9

Healthcare Claims Analysis

Heather M. Kennedy, MSN, MBA, RN, BC, LNCC

First Edition and Second Edition
Agnes Grogan, RN, BS

Contents

Objectives

Upon completion of this chapter, the reader will be able to:

- Describe the definition of a claim and the process of analysis
- Identify the components of a claim
- Discuss the process for reporting the legal nurse consultant's findings

- Describe areas with potential for fraudulent activity or abuse
- Identify two billing forms
- List resources and additional reading available to aid the legal nurse consultant
- Define the education and clinical experience incumbent to a legal nurse consultant, as well as applicable certifications

Introduction

Legal nurse consultants completing healthcare claim analysis today function in a variety of settings and are identified by various titles. While certain players, such as hospitals and workers compensation insurers, have long understood the value of employing nurses, others, such as large property-casualty carriers selling automobile or general liability insurance, may just be determining what a legal nurse consultant's presence on the team means to the bottom line. This chapter will discuss the legal nurse consultant, whether his/her role is of an auditor, analyst, causation reviewer, case manager or liability nurse, and the practice of healthcare claims analysis. Regardless of the title or practice setting, a legal nurse consultant in this role relies on a specialized skill set that meets a definite and broad need in the industry.

Healthcare Claims Analysis

A claim is an action taken by an insured or a defendant for benefits defined in a policy underwritten by an insurance company. Healthcare claims present in a variety of ways and are not limited to the healthcare setting. The word claim in and of itself intimates that the person filing has knowledge of an insurance policy in-force. Policies on which claims regarding health may be filed include but are not limited to the following:

- Healthcare insurance
- Dental insurance
- Vision insurance
- General liability insurance (similarly, professional or business)
- Automobile insurance [including First Party Medical (FPM) or Personal Injury Protection (PIP)]
- Workers compensation insurance
- Homeowners insurance

While each type of insurance is different in its coverage or benefits based on the company offering, the eligibility of the insured and the endorsements elected, all may provide either coverage for healthcare events or some form of reimbursement or settlement depending on the specifics of the claim.

Claim or file ownership frequently resides with a claims adjuster (also known as a representative). Adjusters work in both healthcare and nonhealthcare settings. Healthcare settings include hospitals, physician offices, long-term care centers, dental practices, and chiropractic offices. Nonhealthcare settings include insurance companies, law offices, insurance agencies, and/or brokerage firms and independent firms. Of the settings within the industry, generally they may be divided into dealing with accident and health insurance, property and casualty insurance or Medicare supplement, and long-term care insurance. Adjusters may or may not be licensed depending on the requirements of the state in which they work. In nonlitigated claims, adjusters, as owners of a claim, utilize the legal nurse consultant for analysis, which aids in refuting or mitigating the claim. In litigated claims, adjusters, defense and plaintiff counsels, and the healthcare provider may each utilize a legal nurse consultant in this capacity. Thus, the opportunity exists for the legal nurse consultant to work in many different settings on a variety of claims.

Claims analysis is the process by which a legal nurse consultant reviews a claim, determines its validity, and offers an opinion and/or recommendations. This involves addressing questions of causation, reviewing applicable records and billing, conducting research, educating the parties involved, opining on the merits of the claim, noting discrepancies, and identifying missing pieces needed for full review. An involved process, the legal nurse consultant must have a strategy for attack, which is grounded in his or her knowledge of claim anatomy and physiology.

Critical to claim analysis is the legal nurse consultant's working knowledge of a file (or claim). Each file has similar components, which are described as follows:

■ Demographic information including the name of all parties involved, date of loss or date the accident occurred, date notice received by the insurer, policy effective dates, date of service, and a brief description of the incident.

■ Reserves, or monies set aside to finance the claim, are most easily broken down into indemnity (or actual payout on the claim) and expense (or all other charges to the file). Expense reserves include attorney fees, medical record copying fees, travel expenses, cost of doing business, and any other associated costs.

■ Investigation includes such items as the statements (written or recorded) obtained by the adjuster or field staff of involved parties or witnesses, scene investigations, photographs, measurements, surveillance, and any other information obtained during the investigation.

■ Communication is the documentation on the file. This may include claim or file notes, letters sent to the involved parties, and tapes of interviews. All communication should be documented.

■ Medical records and billing make up the next component of the claim and may be voluminous. This can vary from notes from one physician visit or emergency department visit to 10 years of past medical history, which may be delivered to the legal nurse consultant for review and analysis.

■ Litigation, often maintained in its own separate file, will obviously not be a component of every file. In this section of the file, the legal nurse consultant will find the litigation strategy plan, interrogatories and answers, requests for production and accompanying material, and depositions. Each may provide important insight on the claim.

■ Policy. While not every file will have a copy of the policy attached, some will, especially if there is a question as to coverage and/or if reservation of rights has been extended. It is not the legal nurse consultant's responsibility to read and interpret the policy; however familiarity with general policies (such as a basic automobile, homeowners, or healthcare policy) is helpful, especially if the legal nurse consultant is reviewing many of the same types of claims. Also, it conveys a sense of commitment to the file owner and a willingness to further understand the claim on the product (i.e., policy) in question.

■ Expert reports, which give that person's review of the claim and opinions on things such as breaches in the standard of care or negligence. Typically, curriculum vitae will also be found here on experts. Review of this material will assist the legal nurse consultant in making recommendations on experts for their client's party to the claim.

Table 9.1   Role of the LNC

Role of the LNC in Healthcare Claims Analysis
Know your availability, communicate it to clients, and honor it. Contact information should be shared at the first meeting.
Interact in a timely and professional manner.
Set clear expectations with all clients.
Know when to decline an assignment.
Do not speculate—be factual and objective.
Produce a quality report.
Maintain meticulous records of time spent on the file.
Bill appropriately.
Have a portfolio with your curriculum vitae, letters of recommendation and a sample of your work.

The legal nurse consultant should review all information provided, as well as request anything relevant but missing from the claim file. Failure to be thorough may result in the nurse missing a key finding. For example, if the nurse reads only the medical records and the patient's subjective reporting to the physician, yet elects not to read the enclosed deposition, discrepancies in testimony may be overlooked which could impact the claim's outcome. For a description of the role of the LNC see Table 9.1.

Investigation

Frequently, legal nurse consultants are involved early on in the claims process, including during the investigation phase of the claim. During this phase the legal nurse consultant in conjunction with the principal investigators can utilize clinical knowledge to point out discrepancies (such as between mechanism of injury and alleged injury sustained) or items where further investigation is needed (for example, lab work and notice to local health agents in alleged food poisoning claims). The legal nurse consultant must also be able to identify areas for further investigation once review of the medical records and billing is complete. Noted prior illness or injury, previous treatment, or established patients and/or chronic conditions may point to a need for past medical records, perhaps from various sources other than the original one. Often, this is like putting together the pieces of a puzzle. The legal nurse consultant receives information, such as name, age, sex, date of birth, occupation, social security number, accident, injury, and initial medical records, and then must piece together, in partnership with the claim team, the whole picture.

Process and Technique

Each legal nurse consultant must determine the most comfortable claim analysis process for him/ herself. Various techniques may include reading the claim file first and writing the report last, writing the report while simultaneously reading, reading and taking notes, and then writing or any variation thereof. Certainly, discussions with the client (whether internal or external), research, and review with peers are also interjected. Some clients will be comfortable turning over their original file to the legal nurse consultant, whereas others will prefer to provide copies either in full or in piece. Regardless of the method, the legal nurse consultant must have a level of organization that supports an efficient process and effective outcome. Productivity combined with quality has a significant outcome on billing and either employment retention or future consultation, as well as reputation.

Two tools that may be beneficial to the legal nurse consultant and his or her client include a treatment calendar and a timeline. A treatment calendar may be generated using tables on a Word document with symbols to represent key events during treatment, such as attending physician visits, diagnostics, consulting specialist visits, emergency department visits, no-show dates, and release or return-to-work dates. The calendar can be as specific or as general as needed to convey a visual of care given across time.

Similarly, a timeline provides a visual representation of key events in the life of the claim; however, it need not be limited to treatment information only. The legal nurse consultant may choose to utilize the timeline to show overlap, additional accident or injury sustained dates, surveillance, and claims filed or suit dates. Not only do these tools aid the legal nurse consultant in putting the review into a chronological order, but it also provides an easy tool with which to educate the client as to the specifics of the claim. Examples of treatment and timeline documentation can be viewed in Table 9.2 and Figure 9.1.

Table 9.2 Treatment Calendar

AUGUST 2007						
SU	MO	TU	WE	TR	FR	SA
			1 ⊗	2 △	3 ◈	4
5	6 ○	7 ○	8 ○	9 ○	10 ○	11
12	13 ⊘	14 ○	15 ○	16 ○	17	18
19	20 ○	21 ○	22 ○	23	24 △	25
26	27	28 ○	29 ○	30	31	

SEPTEMBER 2007						
SU	MO	TU	WE	TR	FR	SA
						1
2	3	4	5	6	7	8
9	10	11	12	13	14	15
16	17	18 ⊘	19 ○	20	21 △	22
23 / 30	24	25 ☆	26 ○	27	28 ○	29

KEY	
Date of loss	⊗
Return to work date	☆
Attending MD visit	△
Chiro visit	○
Diagnostic performed	◈
No-show	⊘

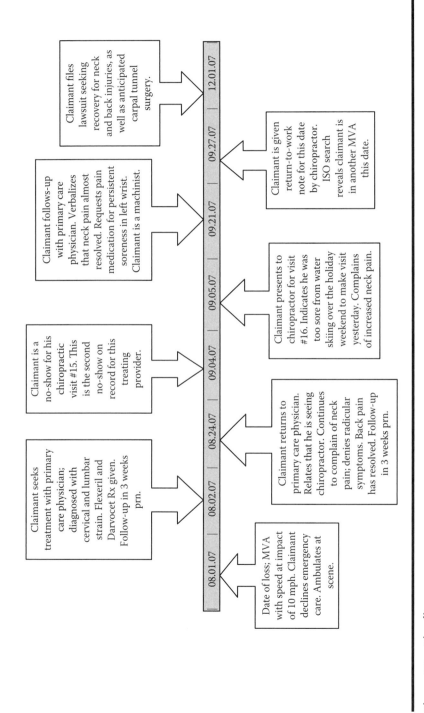

Figure 9.1 Timeline.

Partnership and Communication

In the healthcare setting, the legal nurse consultant will likely be called upon to interact with clinical and nonclinical staff, risk management, human resources, adjusters, employee health, the business office, executive and middle management, counsel, and experts. Similarly, in the nonhealthcare setting, the legal nurse consultant will interact with adjusters (which may include the assigned adjuster and members of the strategy or valuation team), coverage counsel, defense counsel, management, possibly defendant insureds and/or unrepresented claimants, investigators, case managers, providers, and/or insured account representatives. Each of these persons potentially has information known only to them. It is important, therefore, to establish good rapport and maintain open lines of communication. Speaking their language, whether it be clinical or claim, is important. All communication must, however, be balanced with privacy concerns and/or attorney/client privilege. Proprietary information, protected health information, strategy, valuation, etc. should not be discussed with all parties. With the exception of the file owner and/or counsel, a good rule of thumb is the need-to-know basis. Any information that needs to be further disseminated may be done by one of those two parties. Ultimately, the legal nurse consultant must be aware of and versed in HIPPA to ensure compliance.

If the claim is one the legal nurse consultant is going to work for an extended period of time, it is good practice to maintain a diary system. Such a system can be operated on an electronic calendar and should include important dates (i.e., depositions, mediations, due dates, etc.), as well as regularly scheduled dates for follow-up with involved parties. Such systems are routinely employed by file owners to track reserved adjustment dates, litigation dates, and follow-up with the claimant or insured. The legal nurse consultant can find similar use for these diary systems to maintain organization and ensure files are kept up to date.

Communication also encompasses written documentation. The legal nurse consultant should clarify upon acceptance of an assignment what the client wishes to have in writing versus what the client prefers to learn through discussions or verbally. Essentially, discoverability is at issue here and the legal nurse consultant must ensure reports are factual and able to be supported by research, grounded in evidenced-based practice, adherent with the standard of care, and based on policy, procedure, or protocol. Additionally, the legal nurse consultant should not allow his or her client's position to sway the message of the report. "Tell the truth, the whole truth and nothing but the truth. If a claim ... that (sic) should be paid is denied, appeal the denial and fight ... but do it honestly" (Kelly, 2008). Lack of or damage to one's credibility can be a career limiting or ending error. See communication examples in Table 9.3.

Bill Review

Many legal nurse consultants do not feel comfortable with bill review, also referred to as auditing, and frequently elect to outsource this component. In healthcare claim analysis, however, this is an area in which the legal nurse consultant should become educated, perhaps spending time shadowing the hospital coders, taking courses at a local community college, or learning through self-study programs. What most laypersons do not understand is that all clinical nurses, especially those in hospital settings, by and large have limited, if any, exposure to the intricacies of client billing, insurance reimbursement, Medicare and Medicaid payments, self-pay discounts, and other billing specifics. Certainly, personal experience offers some insight; however, this is not at the professional level needed, especially in identifying unrelated charges such as those specific to care obtained for

Table 9.3 Speaking the Language

	Claim versus Clinical	
Actual cash value	ACV versus CVA	Cerebral vascular accident
Date notice received	DNR	Do not resuscitate
Date of accident	DOA	Dead on arrival
Early tow	ETOW versus ETOH	Ethyl alcohol
Insured vehicle	IV	Intravenous
Location	LOC	Loss of consciousness; level of consciousness; level of care
Motor vehicle collision	MVC	Maximum voluntary contraction
Motor vehicle record; motor vehicle repair	MVR	Mitral valve replacement; minute volume of respiration
Other driver	OD	Overdose
Original equipment manufacturer	OEM	Occupational and environmental medicine; office of emergency management
Slip and fall	S&F versus SNF	Skilled nursing facility; skilled nursing floor
Uninsured motorist	UM	Unit manager; unaccompanied minor; utilization management
Vehicle identification number	VIN	Vulvar intraepithelial neoplasia

Note: The same abbreviations, as well as look-alike and sound-alike items, are found within the claim and clinical areas.

pre-existing conditions. If the legal nurse consultant decides to attempt/retain this piece of the analysis process, a good mentor, use of coding reference materials, and experience will help to facilitate understanding and knowledge.

Billing statements differ among provider types, health systems, and states due to differing office practices. An office that is part of a large, integrated healthcare system may use the same billing software as its partner hospital. Small, independent practices may have software much more limited in function and product; therefore, the forms have a different appearance. Furthermore, while some billing offices will happily generate standard forms for the claims professionals (such as a CMS-1500 or UB-04), others may produce variations ranging from a document indicating the total amount due only to an itemized statement. Certainly, if the legal nurse consultant feels additional documentation is needed for a thorough and accurate review, the consultant should communicate that request and rationale to the claim or file owner. For samples of billing forms, see Figures 9.2 and 9.3.

Once secured, the legal nurse consultant should review each piece of the billing statement and each item on the statement carefully, making comparisons and cross referencing, as appropriate. The legal nurse consultant should know which current state and/or federal regulations apply.

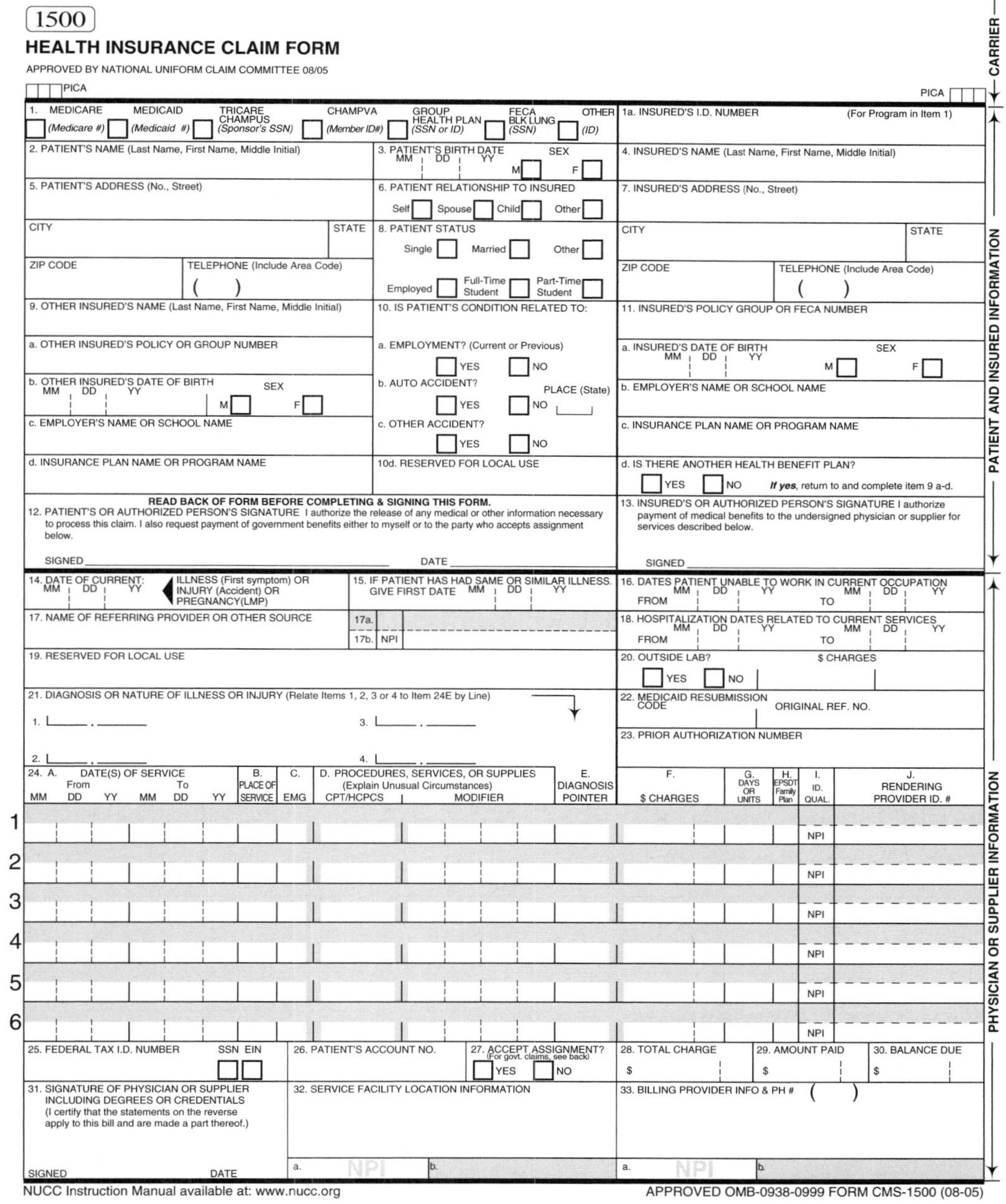
1500
HEALTH INSURANCE CLAIM FORM
APPROVED BY NATIONAL UNIFORM CLAIM COMMITTEE 08/05

PICA | PICA

1. MEDICARE (Medicare #) MEDICAID (Medicaid #) TRICARE CHAMPUS (Sponsor's SSN) CHAMPVA (Member ID#) GROUP HEALTH PLAN (SSN or ID) FECA BLK LUNG (SSN) OTHER (ID)
1a. INSURED'S I.D. NUMBER (For Program in Item 1)
2. PATIENT'S NAME (Last Name, First Name, Middle Initial)
3. PATIENT'S BIRTH DATE MM DD YY SEX M F
4. INSURED'S NAME (Last Name, First Name, Middle Initial)
5. PATIENT'S ADDRESS (No., Street)
6. PATIENT RELATIONSHIP TO INSURED Self Spouse Child Other
7. INSURED'S ADDRESS (No., Street)
CITY STATE
8. PATIENT STATUS Single Married Other
CITY STATE
ZIP CODE TELEPHONE (Include Area Code) ( )
Employed Full-Time Student Part-Time Student
ZIP CODE TELEPHONE (Include Area Code) ( )
9. OTHER INSURED'S NAME (Last Name, First Name, Middle Initial)
10. IS PATIENT'S CONDITION RELATED TO:
11. INSURED'S POLICY GROUP OR FECA NUMBER
a. OTHER INSURED'S POLICY OR GROUP NUMBER
a. EMPLOYMENT? (Current or Previous) YES NO
a. INSURED'S DATE OF BIRTH MM DD YY SEX M F
b. OTHER INSURED'S DATE OF BIRTH MM DD YY SEX M F
b. AUTO ACCIDENT? YES NO PLACE (State)
b. EMPLOYER'S NAME OR SCHOOL NAME
c. EMPLOYER'S NAME OR SCHOOL NAME
c. OTHER ACCIDENT? YES NO
c. INSURANCE PLAN NAME OR PROGRAM NAME
d. INSURANCE PLAN NAME OR PROGRAM NAME
10d. RESERVED FOR LOCAL USE
d. IS THERE ANOTHER HEALTH BENEFIT PLAN? YES NO *If yes*, return to and complete item 9 a-d.
READ BACK OF FORM BEFORE COMPLETING & SIGNING THIS FORM.
12. PATIENT'S OR AUTHORIZED PERSON'S SIGNATURE I authorize the release of any medical or other information necessary to process this claim. I also request payment of government benefits either to myself or to the party who accepts assignment below.
SIGNED DATE
13. INSURED'S OR AUTHORIZED PERSON'S SIGNATURE I authorize payment of medical benefits to the undersigned physician or supplier for services described below.
SIGNED
14. DATE OF CURRENT: MM DD YY ILLNESS (First symptom) OR INJURY (Accident) OR PREGNANCY(LMP)
15. IF PATIENT HAS HAD SAME OR SIMILAR ILLNESS. GIVE FIRST DATE MM DD YY
16. DATES PATIENT UNABLE TO WORK IN CURRENT OCCUPATION MM DD YY FROM TO
17. NAME OF REFERRING PROVIDER OR OTHER SOURCE
17a.
17b. NPI
18. HOSPITALIZATION DATES RELATED TO CURRENT SERVICES MM DD YY FROM TO
19. RESERVED FOR LOCAL USE
20. OUTSIDE LAB? YES NO $ CHARGES
21. DIAGNOSIS OR NATURE OF ILLNESS OR INJURY (Relate Items 1, 2, 3 or 4 to Item 24E by Line)
1. 3.
2. 4.
22. MEDICAID RESUBMISSION CODE ORIGINAL REF. NO.
23. PRIOR AUTHORIZATION NUMBER
24. A. DATE(S) OF SERVICE From MM DD YY To MM DD YY | B. PLACE OF SERVICE | C. EMG | D. PROCEDURES, SERVICES, OR SUPPLIES (Explain Unusual Circumstances) CPT/HCPCS MODIFIER | E. DIAGNOSIS POINTER | F. $ CHARGES | G. DAYS OR UNITS | H. EPSDT Family Plan | I. ID. QUAL. | J. RENDERING PROVIDER ID. #
1 NPI
2 NPI
3 NPI
4 NPI
5 NPI
6 NPI
25. FEDERAL TAX I.D. NUMBER SSN EIN
26. PATIENT'S ACCOUNT NO.
27. ACCEPT ASSIGNMENT? (For govt. claims, see back) YES NO
28. TOTAL CHARGE $
29. AMOUNT PAID $
30. BALANCE DUE $
31. SIGNATURE OF PHYSICIAN OR SUPPLIER INCLUDING DEGREES OR CREDENTIALS (I certify that the statements on the reverse apply to this bill and are made a part thereof.)
SIGNED DATE
32. SERVICE FACILITY LOCATION INFORMATION
a. NPI b.
33. BILLING PROVIDER INFO & PH # ( )
a. NPI b.
NUCC Instruction Manual available at: www.nucc.org
APPROVED OMB-0938-0999 FORM CMS-1500 (08-05)

Figure 9.2 CMS-1500.

Failure of the provider or carrier to comply may affect reimbursement up to and including nonpayment by the insurer, health plan, government agency, or others (Foehl, 2008). This may also affect third-party reimbursement in the event of settlement.

While bill review may be done manually, many legal nurse consultants are choosing to take advantage of available software programs specific to that purpose. For the independent legal nurse

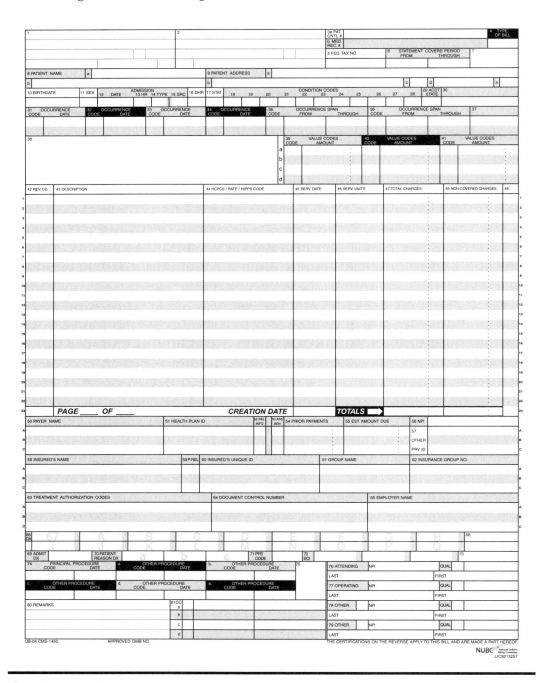

Figure 9.3   UB-04.

consultant in practice, this may be a purchase for the business to consider. Hospitals and integrated health systems likely will have these programs in place with their billing platforms. Larger entities, such as corporate insurance carriers, often have dedicated teams or offices for this purpose in support of the file owner and/or legal nurse consultant. While there may be some manual input required, electronically produced and/or standardized forms that may be scanned make this a much more efficient and error-reducing alternative. Certainly, the human element is not eliminated in its entirety. A knowledgeable reviewer with a keen set of eyes should always be considered a valuable part of the process.

Red Flags: Fraud

Fraud is the double-edged sword in claims analysis. While legal nurse consultants are almost always taught to never mention the word in their findings and reports, identifying and addressing fraud is critical to the outcome of a claim.

> ... the FBI estimates that healthcare fraud losses within the government (commercial sector excluded) total more than $100 billion annually ... a conservative estimate by the National Health Care Anti-fraud Association places fraud at a minimum of 3 percent of total commercial and Medicare and Medicaid healthcare expenditures. Other services report rates as high as 14 percent. (Lubao, 2008)

A legal nurse consultant who can identify fraud is valuable not only to the client and the claim in review but also to the industry as a whole. While the items discussed below do not in and of themselves indicate fraud, nor are they meant to insinuate that any provider or type of provider is fraudulent, attention to these types of items when reviewing claims may prove fruitful to the legal nurse consultant.

- Billing that is not consistent with the treatment identified in the medical records. This may include inappropriate codes [International Classification of Diseases (ICD-9), which numerically identify medical necessity, or Current Procedural Terminology (CPT), which numerically identify services and procedures] and Medicare Severity Diagnosis Related Groups (MS-DRGs), which identify disease-specific hospital admissions. Legal nurse consultants should be aware this could be as simple as an education need on behalf of the coder (for example, in a small physician's office, the physician's spouse may be the office manager but with limited coding experience) or as egregious as intentional miscoding in an attempt to secure higher payment.
- Provider activity that is curious include but are not limited to frequent office moves, listing of a post office versus street address, frequent telephone listing changes, providers who tend to rotate in and out of a practice at alarming rates, involvement or links to attorneys, and/or consistently repetitive referrals of patients to the same provider, especially when it does not appear to be warranted. Similarly, the legal nurse consultant should cautiously review care provided in offices where there seems to be a mix of providers and patients are referred within and often in a pattern (for example, an office that contains a medical doctor, chiropractor, pain management specialist, acupuncturist, and massage therapist with patients referred to each).
- Diagnostics ordered by a provider that are excessive or not accepted as the standard in the industry. This may include such things as diagnostic ultrasounds, whole body x-rays, surface electromyograms (EMGs), x-rays of numerous body parts on non-trauma patients, or x-rays on every patient seen. Likewise, the legal nurse consultant should question any diagnostic not read by a licensed provider and/or those read by a provider from a different

state, especially if there are local and competent resources that are not utilized. Any diagnostics that cannot be supported via formal reports of findings and/or copies of the diagnostics themselves upon request should be considered for nonpayment, reimbursement, etc.

■ Claimant activity that may be considered suspicious depending on the specifics of the claim includes late reporting of an accident or injury, directly reporting to a chiropractor with a moderate or severe injury (versus seeking emergency treatment), seeking treatment with a provider with whom the claimant is currently being actively treated for another condition, self-referral or family/friend referral to a specialist versus at the recommendation of the primary or attending physician, bypassing any steps in the normal care path, noncompliance including failure to show or gaps in treatment, and/or lack of cooperation with a case manager.

■ The appearance of excessive treatment, which may present as treatment for bilateral or symmetrical injuries, daily or every-other-day provider visits, use of more than the recommended or suggested modalities, and/or requiring the use of durable medical equipment that is not medically necessary or which may be purchased cheaper in a retail setting.

■ Primary or excessive adjunct treatment that falls outside mainstream Food and Drug Administration (FDA) approved care such as magnet therapy, dietary supplements, homeopathic medicines, and computerized or single-side range-of-motion measurements. While these and other treatments included under the umbrella of complementary and alternative medicines have their place in the individual's right to choose, caution must be exercised to ensure the patient is receiving the best care, as efficacy and long-term benefit of these alternative therapies have not been determined. Certainly, it is not in a business' best interest to financially dedicate more resources than are necessary to appropriately and fairly address the healthcare concern under consideration. Particular attention should be given to any provider requiring a medication or supplement that is only available for purchase in their office.

■ Doctor-shopping or provider-hopping especially if there is indication of drug-seeking behaviors. While more difficult to discover, the legal nurse consultant should in these situations be aware of patients who may seek care from more than one provider for the same injury without providers being aware of the services of others.

■ Ratings for impairments, disability, or other injuries that are given by a physician other than the primary or attending managing the patient's care should be questioned by the legal nurse consultant, as well as any ratings the patient may have for any and all prior injuries (California Department of Insurance, 2008).

If available to the legal nurse consultant, one of the best resources in identifying fraud results from partnering with the in-house or vendor investigative group. These professionals frequently have prior military and/or law enforcement background and have been formally trained with respect to investigation and potential criminal activity. In conjunction with the file owner, they are able to determine previous claims filed, any injuries sustained, payouts made, as well as authorize and/or conduct surveillance, record reviews, and other activities. Legal nurse consultants must know that not unlike a bedside nurse with a gut feeling that a patient is in imminent danger of decline, he/she, too, should trust intuition in these situations. If something is not "right" but it is not readily apparent why, continue to dig deeper, sharing concerns as appropriate. The end results may have significant impact on claim resolution, as evidenced by information from the Coalition Against Insurance Fraud found in Figure 9.4.

Nearly one of 10 Americans would commit insurance fraud if they knew they could get away with it. Nearly three of 10 Americans (29 percent) wouldn't report insurance scams committed by someone they know. *Progressive Insurance (2001).*

Nearly one of three physicians say it's necessary to game the health care system to provide high quality medical care. *Journal of the American Medical Association (2000).*

More than two of five property-casualty insurers have increased spending to fight fraud over the last three years. More than four of five insurers have formal anti-fraud programs. *Insurance Research Council-Insurance Services Office (2002).*

In 1996, Congress funded an added $548 million over seven years for health-care fraud enforcement. *FBI (2001).*

80 percent of healthcare fraud is by medical providers, 10 percent is by consumers and the balance is by other sources. *Health Insurance Association of America (1998).*

Without workers compensation anti-fraud laws, claims would have been 10.4 percent higher in 1997, the average claim would have been 7.3 percent larger and system costs per worker would have been 18.5 percent higher. *National Council on Compensation Insurance (1999).*

Figure 9.4   Fighting fraud: statistics.

Resources

There are a multitude of resources available to the legal nurse consultant easily categorized as software, internet, print, and community. Software packages available for purchase provide a platform for the independent legal nurse consultant working from home or an office. These packages provide report formats, templates, billing forms, and other forms for business management. Legal nurse consultants working in corporate settings may have these available for use; however, they may instead have home-grown documents, which may be electronic or hard. Other electronic resources available for the legal nurse consultant include databases of fee schedules, electronic ICD-9 or CPT tables, MS-DRG tables, usual reasonable and customary (UCR) pricing, and Medicare and Medicaid charges. This information can be found on free, for-purchase, and private sites. For example, some insurance companies will post their most frequent diagnoses and charges, while others trend and track their claims internally for employee education purposes only.

Internet sources for the legal nurse consultant are numerous and range from disease-specific information to establishing a consulting business to anatomy of a claim. Whatever the reason for seeking the information, the legal nurse consultant must take care to verify the website and evaluate its content. For the purpose of claims analysis, websites which may prove helpful include those from the state industrial commission or workers compensation bureau, Centers for Medicare/Medicaid, sites that offer information regarding evidenced-based practice such as schools of medicine, those with peer reviewed articles (e.g., eMedicine), a trustworthy pharmacy source, and government sites such as the National Institutes of Health. Certainly, access to a database such as CINAHL, EBSCOHost, or PubMed ensures readily accessible current research and literature.

While most information is now accessible via the Internet, print resources still have their place in the legal nurse consultant's repertoire. A good medical dictionary and anatomy book is handy both as a reference and when doing quick education. Likewise, current CPT, ICD-9 and MS-DRG manuals are useful, especially if learning billing/coding or if performing large amounts of bill review, as well as resources for questions regarding Healthcare Common Procedure Coding System (HCPCS) codes or DRG. The American Medical Association Guide to the Evaluation of Permanent Impairment textbook is critical if the venue of practice supports

Table 9.4   Opportunities

Opportunities for the Legal Nurse Consultant in Healthcare Claim Analysis

Case management companies

Defense and plaintiff law firms

Hospitals and healthcare systems

Independent practice

Insurance companies

Medical fraud investigation companies

Risk management firms

State and federal government agencies

---

disability ratings in nonworkers compensation cases. Likewise, Official Disability Guidelines (ODG) or a McMillan reference is particularly helpful with workers compensation claims. Lastly, pharmacy manuals for reference include a Physician Desk Reference (PDR) and the Drug Topics Red Book.

Finally, the community of professionals working as legal nurse consultants or in partnership, and the relationship with the same are important. Membership and attendance in a local legal nurse consultant chapter allows for development of a peer network, case review, continuing education, and other professional growth and development opportunities. Partnership with other professionals likewise is beneficial and includes such specialists as life care planners, economists, peer reviewers, independent medical examiners, and diagnostic reviewers who may be needed throughout the claim review process. For opportunities as an LNC, see Table 9.4.

Credentials: Education, Experience, and Certification

Nursing education of consultants varies from diploma, hospital-based program alumnae to nurses with doctorate degrees. Regardless of educational path, being a graduate of a nursing program at some level is mandatory, as is a current, unrestricted nursing license. Education to be or continuing education as a legal nurse consultant is available in many forms. Local community, technical, and vocational colleges offer legal nurse consulting programs, as increasingly do colleges and universities. Likewise, there are organizations and corporations which exist solely for the purpose of education legal nurse consultants and others who educate their legal nurse consultants themselves. Organizations also exist which provide certification. Many if not all of these options exist for continuing education as well. The legal nurse consultant must consider which route best suits his or her needs based on desired area of practice, employer preference, budget or tuition assistance, classroom versus home study, and time away from work and/or family.

With that in mind, experience then becomes the most important factor. Legal nurse consultants may choose to specialize in a certain area and then serve as an expert witness. An example would be an emergency department nurse certified as a Sexual Assault Nurse Examiner (SANE), caring for sexually assaulted victims, who then is able to work as a consulting expert in that area.

Likely this nurse would choose to continue practicing clinically, while additionally consulting. "This is a needed practice area that requires an astute, verbally competent registered nurse who is willing to maintain clinical competence while providing consulting services ... " (Meiner, 2005). Current experience in all nursing fields, regardless of specialty, enhances one's ability to function as an expert.

Nurses working as legal nurse consultants in other settings, for example full-time in the property casualty industry, are going to see a broad variation in injuries ranging from simple neck strains resulting from a motor vehicle accident to complex fractures due to a slip and fall in a place of business to repetitive motion injures in a workers compensation claim to burns sustained by a restaurant patron to total brain injury in a contractor falling off scaffolding while doing a home repair. Nurses in these settings who have strong medical-surgical backgrounds with additional experience in the emergency department, orthopedics, and/or rehabilitation are considered valuable. Regardless of the legal nurse consultant's preferred area of practice, it must be accompanied by experience.

Adjunct experience found in a well-developed clinical nurse wishing to consult includes committee experience. This translates to claim file review committee, strategy and valuation committees, those comprising adjusters, hospital or corporate management and counsel, and even covering mediation, deposition or trial situations. Likewise, nurses who have taken advantage of clinical ladders, where available to them in the clinical setting, will often (and as a result) have exposure to research, writing, and project work, skills that are much needed and transferable when partnering with file owners, counsel, etc. to resolve a claim over days to years.

Specific to nurses working in healthcare claims analysis is the opportunity to sit for and achieve licensure as an insurance adjuster. Depending on the state of practice, licensure may be available and may or may not require some formal coursework or self-study course prior to sitting for examination. Similarly, as is found with nursing licensure, continuing education requirements vary from state to state. While there is no compact act for insurance licensure as there is with nursing, some licensed states will honor licensure in another state and grant a dual licensure to the adjuster. Seeking licensure is not required of the legal nurse consultant; however, it provides basic claim education, as well as insight on the workings of the department of insurance. Additionally, those non-nurses in the insurance industry respect this commitment to their field.

Certification is the final credential and hallmark of the professional nurse. In the situation of the legal nurse consultant, it is two-fold. First is the nurse's certification to support their clinical specialty with a well-recognized certification body (such as the American Nurses Credentialing Center). This lends credibility and professionalism to the nurse. Second is the nurse's certification as a legal nurse consultant, which is attained with experience and shows dedication to the profession, as well as a commitment to the development of theory. Additional certifications may be attained specific to the legal nurse consultant's area of practice such as case management or risk management. Again, certification is an attribute of professionalism.

Additional Reading

American Association of Legal Nurse Consultants, *The Journal of Legal Nurse Consulting*
American Society for Healthcare Risk Management, Risk Management Handbooks
Business Insurance
Legal Eagle Eye Newsletter
Medical Malpractice Verdicts, Settlements & Experts
Modern Healthcare

References

California Department of Insurance. (2008). *Fraud: What is insurance fraud?* Retrieved August 2, 2008, from http://www.insurance.ca.gov/0300-fraud-division-overview/0100-what-is-insurance-fraud/

Coalition Against Insurance Fraud. (2008). *By the numbers: Fraud stats.* Retrieved August 2, 2008, from http://www.insurancefraud.org/stats.htm

Foehl, A. (2008, March 4). Insurer to reimburse mismanaged claims. The ASHA Leader, 13(3), 1, 7.

Kelly, G. (2008, February 1). Claim only the truth. EMS Magazine, February, 48.

Lubao, M. (2008). Claiming responsibility. *Health Management Technology*, (June), 16–18.

Meiner, S. (2005). The legal nurse consultant. *Geriatric Nursing, 26*(1), 34–36.

Test Questions

1. Claim analysis is best described as
   A. A focused review of billing to discover fraud and/or abuse
   B. A global review of claims within the organization for common threads
   C. A systematic review of all components of a claim, determines its validity, and offers recommendations for mitigation
   D. A data review to gather statistics for reporting purposes

2. A UB-04 is
   A. A form the LNC utilizes during claim analysis
   B. A form provided by the healthcare provider to the patient to obtain information
   C. A form mandated by the third party insurer prior to reimbursement
   D. A form utilized in the billing of healthcare services

3. In which of the following situations might partnership with investigative services prove useful?
   A. A provider who in an isolated situation utilizes an incorrect modifier.
   B. A provider who has incomplete medical records and consistently inappropriate billing.
   C. A provider who is utilizing a local tertiary care center for radiographic review services.
   D. A provider whose office is only open half-days on Thursdays

4. What is the most important thing to remember when utilizing electronic resources?
   A. Citing the date retrieved accurately
   B. Ensuring the authenticity of the site
   C. To share them with the client
   D. Providing feedback to the site owner

5. The credibility and reputation of the legal nurse consultant within the industry may be damaged if
   A. Billing is inappropriate and inaccurate
   B. Reports are timely and thorough
   C. Communication is professional and responsive
   D. Vendors are utilized appropriately

Answers: 1. C, 2. D, 3. B, 4. B, 5. A

Chapter 10

Administrative Health Law
Governing Health

Amy Heydlauff, RN, LNCC, MHSA

Contents

Objectives

The intent of this chapter is to assure that the legal nurse consultant can confidently manage activities and cases in which an understanding of bureaucratic agencies, regulations, codes, and laws is fundamental. The legal nurse consultant will be able to

- Provide a definition of administrative health law
- List the primary administrative agencies impacting healthcare
- Highlight auditing and quality initiatives and resulting opportunities for legal nurse consultants

Introduction

Modern American health care is a precarious balance between the private and public sectors. Many aspects of health care are a matter of public policy and largely funded through tax revenue. Federal, state, and local governments regulate the provision of health care and countless health-care-related private sector activities.

The purpose of healthcare laws and a variety of governmental, administrative agencies is to shield public health and government budgets through regulatory oversight of an industry, which currently is estimated to account for 16% of our gross domestic product (The Long Term Outlook for Health Care Spending: Introduction and Summary, 2008). Activities related to investigation and protection of the public and private sectors give rise to opportunities for professionals who have an understanding of clinical practice as well as government regulation and the resulting oversight.

Administrative Health Law

Administrative health law relates to the activities of administrative agencies of the government. Administrative agencies are bureaucratic institutions charged with interpreting, implementing, and enforcing laws passed by the legislature and signed by the Governor of a state or the President in the case of federal law. These new laws do not address the "how" of implementation; therefore, administrative agencies develop regulations and codify those regulations in order to direct implementation. The primary source of healthcare-related regulations is the Code of Federal Regulations (CFR, 2008), which contains thousands of regulations related to health care.

The responsibility of governing healthcare falls to many government agencies and the division of labor between agencies is complex. For instance, the Nursing Home Reform Act, passed by Congress in 1987, was gradually implemented by the Centers for Medicare and Medicaid (CMS). The CMS is the agency with primary oversight of nursing home care. All nursing homes receiving reimbursement from Medicare or Medicaid are subject to CMS inspections, as well as state inspections on behalf of CMS, through state surveying, licensing, and certification agencies. In addition, each state has its own regulations, which may or may not mirror, and sometimes conflict with, federal regulations. State regulations require additional inspections. Any or all of these agencies may inspect, investigate complaints, identify deficiencies, and take enforcement action (Walshe, 2001). Healthcare providers are held to the highest standard when more than one government agency holds regulatory oversight.

Administrative health law impacts all segments of the healthcare industry. The CMS have oversight of Medicare and Medicaid programs and the Department of Labor has oversight of Worker's Compensation. Drug and medical device research and development are regulated through the Food and Drug Administration (FDA). Healthcare fraud and abuse investigations may occur in state or federal jurisdictions and may be conducted by a state licensing bureau, Federal Bureau of Investigation (FBI), Office of the Inspector General (OIG), or the Government Accountability Office (GAO), among others. Some aspects of the health insurance industries are regulated through the Department of Health and Human Services (DHHS); others through the Department of Commerce. Homeland Security oversees healthcare organization's preparedness for disasters of all kinds.

Centers for Medicare and Medicaid

The CMS expends hundreds of billions of dollars on Medicare and Medicaid. These programs, plus State Children's Health Insurance Program (S-CHIP), follow the policies and regulations of the CMS.

Medicare

Medicare is a federal health insurance program for people 65 years of age or older and those under the age of 65 with a permanent disability. Those with permanent disability receive Social Security Disability Insurance (SSDI). The vast majority of citizens older than 65, regardless of medical history or income, and all SSDI beneficiaries are eligible for Part A Medicare Benefits. Part A covers inpatient hospitalization, skilled nursing care, home health, and hospice care, and accounts for approximately 40% of Medicare's expenditures. Medicare Part B is optional and covers outpatient services, including physician fees. Recipients with Part B coverage pay monthly premiums. Part C refers to Medicare's managed care program. Beneficiaries can enroll in healthcare plans managed by the private sector. Such plans might be a health maintenance organization, preferred physician organization, or fee for service plan offering combined coverage, inclusive of Parts A, B, and D. Part D is the outpatient prescription drug benefit. This benefit also requires the beneficiary to pay a monthly premium. Many citizens believe Medicare will cover the cost of their healthcare once they are eligible. They are surprised to discover coverage accounts for only about 45% of their total cost of inpatient care, outpatient services, and medications (Kaiser Family Foundation, 2007a).

The CMS contracts with private companies to act as fiscal intermediaries (FI) to reimburse healthcare providers for Parts A and B services delivered to Medicare beneficiaries. These FIs are simply conduits between the government and healthcare providers. Contracted FIs determine the amount of payment for claims and disburse U.S. government funds. Providers who believe FI decisions are erroneous are unable to file legal claims against the FI because the government of the United States is the actual party of interest in such claims. However, before the federal district courts will hear a claim against the government all administrative remedies must be exhausted. Administrative remedies generally start with a hearing before the FI and are followed by an appeal to the Provider Reimbursement Review Board (CFR, 42 U.S.C.§139500[a]).

In recent years, FIs have garnered increasing responsibility for determining the appropriateness of services provided to Medicare beneficiaries. This determination is called utilization review and is based on the FI's decision regarding the medical necessity of care provided. For instance, the Medicare definition of medical necessity for admission to an acute care hospital includes the expectation the patient will require overnight care (although the patient may not stay overnight for a variety of reasons), and is based on the complex medical judgment of the physician after considering a number of factors, according to Medicare. Definitions like this one leave a provider with little guidance, but also the ability to interpret the law broadly when undertaking an appeal of the FI decision. Utilization review of Parts A and B claims is generally undertaken to identify improper payment followed by a reduction in reimbursement to the providers. By 2011, contracts between FIs and the government are to be completely phased out in favor of Medicare Administrative Contractors (MACs). These new conduits will conduct the same claims management and utilization review activities as FIs.

Until 2002, Medicare contracted with Peer Review Organizations (PROs), generally on a state-by-state basis. PROs were developed to improve the effectiveness, efficiency, economy, and quality of medical care delivered to Medicare beneficiaries. Although review of medical care by "peers" called physician advisors was a primary purpose of the PROs, over time the focus of the PRO grew to include coding and billing as well as assessment of medical care.

In 2002, PROs were officially renamed Quality Improvement Organizations (QIOs). As noted, recent QIO focus is on quality and safety with economic concerns shifting to FIs and newly created MACs. Peer review continues to be a hallmark of the QIO, with assessment of the quality of care, safety of discharge plans, hospital requested reviews, Emergency Medical Treatment Active Labor Act case review, and accuracy of medical documentation being primary responsibilities of QIO physician advisors and the nurses who screen cases prior to physician advisor review. These contracted organizations also play an important role in submission of provider data to central data banks. The data are used to provide healthcare provider-related information to the public through public reporting sites like "Nursing Home Compare" (2008) and "Hospital Compare" (2008). QIOs are staffed by healthcare providers who work to assure and sometimes improve the health care available to Medicare beneficiaries.

Medicaid

Medicaid provides health insurance for low-income Americans. Medicaid covers most health care, including heavily regulated nursing home care, which accounts for 44% of the Medicaid expenditures. One in four children in the United States relies on Medicaid (Kaiser Family Foundation, 2007b). Other recipients include parents of dependent children, pregnant women, people with disabilities, and the elderly. To be eligible, the recipient's income must fall below a threshold determined by their state. Unlike Medicare, a program funded through employer contributions, payroll deductions, and beneficiary premiums, Medicaid is an entitlement program, funded through state and federal tax dollars. It is considered a safety net program. Nationally, the federal government covers 57% of Medicaid expenditures, although it varies by state, depending on the states' per capita income (Kaiser Family Foundation, 2007c). The remaining 43% of the expenditures come from the states' budgets.

The S-CHIP was created in 1997 and is Title XXI of the Social Security Act. This program is fully funded by the federal government and works with Medicaid to insure children. Since the inception of S-CHIP, millions of additional American children have become insured, although some children remain uninsured. Funding is intended to cover children in families who are not poor enough to meet Medicaid eligibility—generally families up to and sometimes above 200% of the federal poverty level. Each state determines how they will accomplish increased insurance for children. Some states expand their Medicaid programs, others develop separate S-CHIP programs, and others combine the two approaches.

Due to limited private health insurance access, the CMS must balance the need to insure ever greater number of Americans against the need to control public spending. Because Medicaid is funded jointly through state and federal coffers, both entities assume responsibility for auditing the medical necessity of care provided to Medicaid recipients.

The OIG is one federal agency engaged in protecting public funds spent on Medicaid programs and their use of data mining software is one tactic used by the OIG to analyze Medicaid claims data. They identify payment patterns like a sudden increase in the number of procedures by one provider or in one geographic area. Another enforcement activity is the Medicaid Integrity Program (MIP). The MIP is a federal oversight program but is also intended to support state efforts to reign in fraud and abuse. The contracted auditors are empowered to review billing and medical records of all healthcare providers who accept state and federal reimbursement for care provided to Medicaid recipients. Each state Medicaid agency is required to have a federally certified Medicaid Management Information System (MMIS). The MMIS purpose is to prevent inappropriate Medicaid payment. The program analyzes provider utilization to identify patterns of fraud, abuse, and inappropriate utilization. If an MMIS identifies suspected fraud or abuse, the case is referred to the State Medicaid Fraud Control Unit for prosecution.

Fraud and Abuse

The DHHS defines fraud as the intentional deception or misrepresentation that an individual knows, or should know, to be false, or does not believe to be true, and makes, knowing the deception could result in some unauthorized benefit to himself or some other person(s). Abuse is defined as a range of improper billing practices, misuse of codes, or improper cost allocation (Glossary inclusive of Fraud and Abuse, 2008). Generally, the CMS considers abuse to be mistakes and fraud to be intentional.

The FBI is the primary investigative agency for healthcare fraud, and has jurisdiction over both the federal and private insurance programs. The FBI leverages its resources in both the private and public arenas through investigative partnerships with agencies such as the DHHS-OIG, FDA, Drug Enforcement Agency (DEA), Defense Criminal Investigative Service, Office of Personnel Management, Internal Revenue Service (IRS), and various state and local agencies. On the private side, the FBI is actively involved with national groups, such as the National Health Care Anti-Fraud Association, the National Insurance Crime Bureau, the Blue Cross and Blue Shield Association, the American Association of Retired Persons, and the Coalition Against Insurance Fraud (FBI Fraud Investigation Partners, 2008). Common fraud schemes include billing for services not provided, billing for a higher level of service than provided, billing for medically unnecessary services, and fraudulent Internet pharmacies.

Penalties for fraud and abuse convictions may include imprisonment and civil monetary penalties. Of significant concern to providers is the mandatory exclusion from federal healthcare participation. Publicly funded healthcare program participation provides up to 50%, and sometimes more, of revenue to healthcare providers nationwide. Without government-funded reimbursement most participating providers could not remain open. This is particularly difficult in areas of the country with a high number of Medicaid recipients and therefore a larger percentage of marginal, federally funded reimbursement. The closure of physician offices, clinics, or hospitals due to exclusion from participation means elimination of access to care for recipients and a loss of jobs for those employed by the providers. The consequences of healthcare fraud and abuse conviction are severe and far-reaching.

Food and Drug Administration

The FDA is the primary regulator of biologics, devices, radiologic health, food, cosmetics, and veterinarian products. The FDA regulates drug development through Title XXI of the CFR. Drug companies are charged with assuring good clinical practice surrounding the protection of human subjects, investigation of new drugs, and application for new drug approval. Phase 2 drug trials involve human subjects in healthcare organizations around the world. Clinicians, including physicians, nurses, advance practices nurses, and physician assistants are among the clinicians protecting patients and measuring medication efficacy with sound scientific methods and regulations laid out in the CFR.

Beyond testing and approval of new pharmaceutical compounds is marketing and sales. Increased exposure of the public to a newly marketed drug is, essentially, the final trial of that new drug. Over time, the drug may be found to have a side-effect either the drug company or the FDA or both did not foresee, based on the science conducted prior to approval. The public may be notified of a serious side-effect by a *black box* warning on a drug's package insert; so named because the language of the warning is enclosed in a heavy black border. The black box warning is the strongest warning the FDA requires and may be added to the insert voluntarily or may be required by the FDA. Other protections come in the form of FDA recalls and individual and class action lawsuits against a pharmaceutical company.

Trends

As a result of the 2003 Medicare Prescription Drug, Improvement, and Modernization Act, the DHHS was directed to conduct a program to detect and correct improper Medicare payments. Every Medicare provider in the nation is subject to charge and medical record review by a revenue audit contractor (RAC) for nearly all services they provided dating back to October 1, 2007. Other legislation requires RACs to be permanent and nationwide no later than 2010. The nation has been divided into four regions with one RAC contracted for each region and auditing began in early 2009. The RACs are charged with detecting past improper payments and correcting those errors.

Revenue Audit Contractors

Prior to nationwide implementation of the project legislation required a 3-year demonstration project. Demonstration projects are the CMS way of determining if a new regulatory requirement is actually worthwhile. In this case, three states (California, Florida, and New York) were selected as demonstration states because they have the largest Medicare utilization. The demonstration project was successful, netting nearly $700 million for the Medicare trust fund, although this number does not include repayment to providers who launched successful appeals of the RAC decisions. For the first time in CMS history, the contractor payment method is a contingency fee, meaning a percentage of the dollars the RAC recovers on behalf of the CMS is paid to the contracted RAC.

As in the demonstration project, permanent RACs were selected through competitive bidding and audits take two forms. The first type of audit is an automated review, essentially based in data mining. The second type of review is labeled as a complex medical review and must be used if there is a probability but not certainty that overpayment occurred. A complex medical review requires review of the medical record. The DHHS requires these contractors to use qualified clinicians and coding staff to conduct medical record reviews. The RACs are also required to employ a physician as medical director.

Medicare Administrative Contractors and Comprehensive Error Rate Testing Contractors

MACs and their precedent FIs are also requesting and auditing medical records and provider charges. One MAC focus, reducing payment errors through pre- and postpayment utilization (medical necessity) audits, was the responsibility of the QIOs until 2008. According to Social Security Act, Title 18 § 1874A, other important MAC responsibilities include the following:

■ Determination of payment amounts and making payments to providers
■ Providing education, consultation, and outreach to Medicare beneficiaries
■ Acting as a liaison between DHHS and providers and suppliers
■ Providing education and technical assistance to providers (Responsibilities of MACs, 2008)

In 2008, the MACs began their inpatient provider audits with random medical reviews of selected claims. As the program progresses, the MACs will no longer conduct random audits but will concentrate on targeted claims with suspected improper payments.

Comprehensive Error Rate Testing Contractors (CERT) are also conducting medical record reviews. The purpose of a CERT audit is to measure payment error rates. The CERT contractors conduct medical reviews following payments, which are a second line audit designed to confirm MAC payment decisions and catch additional payment errors.

The RAC, MAC, and CERT audits overlap in many respects. One safeguard prohibits RACs from reviewing cases audited by any other federal agency or contractor, although the providers need to track audit requests themselves if they hope to avoid duplicate audits from more than one contractor. Additionally, it will be important for providers to understand the varying statutory requirements for each type of contractor. Table 10.1 provides a side-by-side comparison of QIOs, CERTs, and FI/MACs.

Savvy providers will also understand their appeal rights for each contracted auditor. A provider's ability to appeal is strengthened if they have carefully followed the Conditions of Participation requirement for a Utilization Review Plan and Committee (CMS Conditions of Participation, 2008). If these two requirements are solidly in place and a provider is convinced that it was medically necessary for a patient to receive the care or receive that specific level of care, the provider has appeal options. Appeal levels may consist of a written appeal to the QIO, a hearing before the FI or MAC, an independent contractor hearing, an administrative law judge determination, a federal appeals council review and a U.S. District Court review.

Quality

Institute of Medicine reports including *To Err is Human* in 1999 and *Crossing the Quality Chasm* in 2002 spurred development of many regulatory initiatives related to the safety and quality of health care. Initiatives include the Agency for Healthcare Research and Quality's Inpatient

Table 10.1 Comparison of Three Medicare Administrative Contractors

Issue	QIOs	CERT	FIs/MACs
Review selection	Random	Random	Targeted to claims with suspected improper payments. Initially there may be some random review
When the claim is selected for review	Postpayment: 3 months after discharge	Postpayment: medical record request letter sent 35 days after payment	Prepayment: shortly after the claim is submitted or postpayment—up to 4 years after payment
Credentials of reviewers	Qualified clinicians	Qualified clinicians	Qualified clinicians
Level of physician involvement in review process	Review all claims where nonphysician reviewer identifies a problem	As needed for complex cases	As needed for complex cases
Use of coding experts	Mandatory	Mandatory	Mandatory
Reimbursement for medical record copies	Yes	No	No
Where to file initial appeal	QIO	FI or MAC	FI or MAC

Source: Adapted from Inpatient Prospective Payment System Hospital and Long Term Care Hospital Review and Measurement Fact Sheet, pp. 3, 4; www.cms.hhs.gov/AcuteInpatientPPS/downloads/InpatientReviewFactSheet.pdf

Quality Indicators (http://qualityindicators.ahrq.gov/iqi), Prevention Quality Indicators (http://qualityindicators.ahrq.gov/pqi), Patient Safety Indicators (http://qualityindicators.ahrq.gov/psi), and Pediatric Quality Indicators (http://www.qualityindicators.ahrq.gov/pdi).

The Joint Commission (JC), a nongovernmental, accreditation body, also folded safety into their standards with the development of the National Patient Safety Goals, inclusive of standards addressing ambulatory care, assisted living, behavioral health, disease-specific goals, home care, inpatient care, laboratory, long-term care, and office-based surgery.

For an organization unable to uphold regulatory initiatives or accreditation standards, a variety of penalties have been developed. Accreditation is important to healthcare providers because under 42 U.S.C. §§ 1395bb(a), (b), a hospital that meets JC accreditation is deemed to meet the Medicare Conditions of Participation. Providers must meet the CMS Conditions of Participation in order to receive Medicare reimbursement (Impact of Non-Accreditation, 2008). Scores for specific initiatives are being reported publicly with a hope that public awareness will drive improvement in outcomes. A percentage of reimbursement is tied to overall quality and safety scores and providers may also receive reduced payment if individual patients experience a "never event."

Never events include surgery on the wrong site, objects left in during surgery, development of stage III and IV pressure ulcers, catheter-associated urinary tract infections, ventilator-associated pneumonia, and a growing list of other hospital-acquired conditions.

An increasing number of states require reporting of serious adverse events. Massachusetts Board of Medicine legislated responsibilities include oversight of adverse event reporting through the Patient Care Assessment program. Registered nurses, some carrying the designation of Legal Nurse Consultant, Certified, provide review of records and work with healthcare providers to ensure quality. Other states with similar initiatives include Minnesota, New Jersey, and Pennsylvania.

Roles and Practice Settings

In response to regulatory requirements, an entire healthcare industry segment of compliance and documentation specialists, medical record auditors, and consultants exists. The demand for nurses to audit medical records against screening criteria, national standard of care, quality, and safety indicators has increased within healthcare organizations, state and federal government agencies, and government and provider contracted companies. Utilization and Case Managers are taking on new responsibilities that include auditing for quality and safety outcomes. Compliance officers require a better understanding of clinical care, evidence-based medicine, and regulatory auditing. The lines between compliance, health information management, utilization, quality, and safety are now so blurred that many providers struggle to identify one or even two departments to respond to required audits, data collection, interpretation, and reporting.

Legal nurse consultants possess an unusual blend with an understanding of the law, regulations, the legal process, and clinical knowledge. No other nursing specialty enjoys the skill set necessary to step into compliance or auditing roles with an immediate understanding of how laws, courts, judges, physicians, and healthcare organizations work. Private sector consultants supporting providers will be invaluable as providers cope with the barrage of auditors, reimbursement recovery by the government, and subsequent appeals.

Government-contracted organizations are required by law to use qualified clinicians in the complex medical reviews, and legal nurse consultants are well qualified to step into these consulting and auditing roles. Some government contractors may require additional credentials, many of which are easily obtained by nurses with a background in healthcare law.

The provider arm of the healthcare industry is not generally familiar with the specialty of legal nurse consulting. The current environment is ripe for highly qualified legal nurse consultants to step into auditing, compliance, and consulting roles around the country.

Conclusion

Administrative health law is the governing of health care, and is a complicated and important part of the landscape of healthcare law in the United States. Many of our federal and state agencies play a role in governing the public's health and state and federal budgets. An awareness of the impact of these agencies on patients, providers, and healthcare law provides the legal nurse consultant with a foundational understanding of health care. Awareness also offers the potential to explore new areas of legal nurse consulting practice.

References

CMS Conditions of Participation. (2008). Retrieved October 27, 2008, from http://www.cms.hhs.gov/ CFCsAndCoPs/06_Hospitals.asp

Code of Federal Regulations (CFR). (2008). Retrieved September 4, 2008, from http://www.gpoaccess.gov/ CFR/INDEX.HTML

Code of Federal Regulations (CFR), 42 U.S.C.§ 139500(a).

FBI Fraud Investigation Partners. (2008). Retrieved October 5, 2008, from http://www.fbi.gov/publications/ financial/fcs

Glossary inclusive of Fraud and Abuse. (2008). Retrieved October 5, 2008, from http://www.cms.hhs.gov/ apps/glossary

Hospital Compare. (2008). Retrieved September 13, 2008, from http://www.hospitalcompare.hhs.gov

Impact of Non-Accreditation. (2008). Retrieved October 27, 2008, from http://www4.law.cornell.edu/ uscode/uscode42/usc_sec_42_00001395–bb000-.html

Kaiser Family Foundation. (2007a). Medicare at a Glance. *Fact sheet*, February 2007.

Kaiser Family Foundation. (2007b). Medicare and the uninsured. *Fact sheet*, March 2007.

Kaiser Family Foundation. (2007c). Medicaid and the uninsured. *Fact sheet*, March 2007.

Nursing Home Compare. (2008). Retrieved September 13, 2008, from http://www.medicare.gov/ NHCompare

Responsibilities of MACs. (2008). Retrieved October 11, 2008, from http://www.ssa.gov/OP_Home/ssact/ title18/1874A.htm

The Long Term Outlook for Health Care Spending: Introduction and Summary. (2008). Retrieved October 27, 2008, from http://www.cbo.gov/ftpdocs/87xx/doc8758/MainText.3.1.shtml

Walshe, K. (2001). Regulating U.S. nursing homes: Are we learning from experience? *Health Affairs, 20*(6), 130.

Resources

Agency for Healthcare Research and Quality. www.ahrq.gov

Code of Federal Regulations (CFR). http://www.gpoaccess.gov/CFR/INDEX.HTML

Joint Commission. www.jointcommission.org

Kaiser Family Foundation. www.kff.org

Weissert, C. S., & Weissert, W. G. (2006). *Governing health: The politics of health policy* (3rd ed.). Johns Hopkins University Press, Baltimore, MD.

Test Questions

1. Healthcare fraud or abuse may be investigated by
   A. FBI, OIG, and Office of Homeland Security
   B. FBI, Office of Homeland Security, and DEA
   C. FBI, DEA, and AHRQ
   D. FBI, DEA, and OIG

2. Quality Improvement Organizations are responsible for
   A. Peer review
   B. Medical necessity audits
   C. Measuring payment error rates
   D. Determining provider payment rates

3. Administrative health law provides opportunities for legal nurse consultants, including
   A. Auditing for quality, coding, and conducting root cause analysis
   B. Auditing for quality, safety, and screening for medical necessity
   C. Auditing for payment, coding, and conducting root cause analysis
   D. Auditing for quality, safety, and nursing process

Answers: 1. D, 2. A, 3. B

Chapter 11

Medicare Set-Asides Arrangements

Fran J. Provenzano, RN, BSN, CDMS, CCM, CLCP, MSCC

Contents

Objectives

- Discuss the financial impact of a Medicare set-aside (MSA) on the settlement
- Discuss how the injured workers current medical treatment will impact an MSA
- Identify the differences between Medicare and Medicaid
- Identify the components of an MSA
- Describe the type of injured worker who might require a formal MSA

Medicare Set-Aside Arrangements

The Medicare Secondary Payer (MSP) Statute was created with the passage of the Omnibus Reconciliation Act (OBRA) of 1981; however, it was not strongly enforced until 2001. Since 1981, there have been several amendments. MSP's goal is to prevent the shifting of financial responsibility of medical care from the primary or rightful payer to Medicare. Medicare's interest must be protected when settling for future medical needs in workers' compensation (WC), liability, medical malpractice, product liability, automobile settlements, nursing home abuse, or no-fault claims. An overview of WC, Medicare, and Social Security is included in the appendices of this chapter. In the MSP, Medicare has a dual role, that of subrogation interest to recover conditional payments or payments made in error as well as identification of future medical and prescription needs that are typically covered by Medicare. As Medicare Set-Asides (MSAs) are a relatively new field of practice, the requirements continue to evolve as CMS (Centers for Medicare & Medicaid Services) refines and revises its policies.

Liability MSA allocations are not addressed in CMS directives or in the memorandum. However, Medicare's interest must always be considered and protected when settling for future medical needs. Conditional/lien payments must also be repaid to Medicare when settling WC, liability, medical malpractice, product liability, automobile settlements, nursing home abuse, or no-fault claims.

The arrangement has three basic components: allocation amount, method of funding, and method of administration.

The allocation amount is determined by a comprehensive review of the medical records and pay-out history, physician recommendations (either a primary treating physician or a qualified examiner), and standards of care. There may be more than one treatment pathway, and the proposed allocation should be based on the last 2–3 years in which treatment and/or services were received.

The method of funding describes how the recommended allocation amount is to be funded. The options include a lump sum, annuity, or a combination of both. A lump sum is when the entire recommended allocation amount is paid into the account at the time of settlement. When a lump sum is paid, Medicare will not pay for any injury-related services until the entire lump sum amount is "properly" exhausted.

An annuity is a method of funding in which there are "seed monies" or initial funding of the MSA allocation account along with annual or periodic payments made into the account. The periodic or annuity payments must be sufficient to address the services projected within the MSA allocation. Should the MSA account be properly exhausted prior to the next funding cycle, Medicare will pay for Medicare-allowable injury-related services until the next funding cycle replenishes the account. The CFR (Code of Federal Regulations) does not mandate if the account is to be professionally administered or self-administered. However, it does state that the WCMSA must be placed in a separate interest-bearing account. A WCMSA must be administered by a competent administrator. This administrator may be the injured person, or if appropriate a court-appointed designee or a professional administrator. If the account is to be self-administered, the injured person must submit to the CMS an annual self-attestation form stating that monies have been exhausted properly.

> In professional administrative situations, the administrator of the MSA arrangement must forward annual accounting summaries concerning the expenditures of the arrangement to the CMS Medicare contractor responsible for monitoring the individual's case. Additionally, the Medicare contractor is responsible for verifying that no payments from Medicare are made for medical expenses related to the injury or illness/disease until the WCMSA is exhausted.

The administrator of the MSA and full contact information must be included within the submitted MSA document.

Medicare will not pay for those services for which payment has been made or can reasonably be expected to be paid in a prompt manner, in areas of WC for which treatment/services were received, treatment/services for injuries received as a result of an auto accident, areas of no-fault liability, or where medical health insurance would be considered the primary payer or a Medicare eligible individual who has health insurance.

The goal of the MSP, 42 USC 1395y, is to prevent shifting of the responsibility for medical treatment related to the injury, and covered by Medicare, from a primary payer or insurance carrier to Medicare.

When is an MSA Allocation Required?

Although not given this formal title, within the MSA industry, the injured person is often referred to as Class 1 or Class 2 beneficiary.

A Class 1 Medicare beneficiary is a person who is receiving Medicare at the time of settlement, regardless of the amount of settlement.

A Class 2 Medicare beneficiary is an injured person who has a reasonable expectation of receiving Medicare benefits within the next 30 months. The person may have applied for and been denied benefits, but anticipates reapplying, or may be an individual who is aged 62 years and 6 months or an individual with end-stage renal disease (ESRD), *and* the total settlement amount is $250,000.00 or more. The total settlement amount includes, but is not limited to, any previously settled portion of the settlement, future medical needs, fees, indemnity, attorney fees, annuity payouts (total payout value), and repayment of any conditional/lien payments.

Review Threshold

Review thresholds are completely different from the total amount of the settlement. On April 25, 2006, CMS released the updated review threshold memo of "... proposals for Medicare beneficiaries where the total settlement amount is greater than $25,000.00." CMS stated that this is a *workload review* threshold and not a substantive dollar or "safe harbor" threshold. Medicare beneficiaries must still consider Medicare's interests in all WC cases and ensure that Medicare is secondary to WC in such cases. Note that the computation of the total settlement amount includes, but is not limited to, wages, attorney fees, all future medical expenses (including prescription drugs), and repayment of any Medicare conditional payments. Any previously settled portion of the WC claim must be included in computing the total settlement amount payout, and totals for the annuity are to be projected for total payout value rather than cost or present value of the annuity. Also any previously settled portion of the WC claim must be included in computing the total settlement amount.

Changes in policy and procedure compel those involved in the MSA process to remain updated on the most current memorandums regarding MSA arrangements.

Historical Perspective: Legislation

In July 2001, CMS issued preliminary guidelines to regional offices in a memorandum titled "Workers' Compensation: Commutation of Future Benefits." CMS has attempted to address, with release of follow-up memos and FAQs, further clarification of issues.

The full text of these CMS memos may be found on the CMS website:

- July 23, 2001, "Workers Compensation: Commutation of Future Benefits."
- April 21, 2003, "Medicare Secondary Payer-Workers' Compensation (WC) Frequently Asked Question. Medicare Secondary Payer Regional Office WC contacts listed … Detailed list of documents necessary to complete a review of a settlement that includes a Medicare set-aside arrangement for future medical benefits."
- May 23, 2003, "Medicare Secondary Payer-Workers' Compensation, Additional Frequently Asked Questions."
- May 7, 2004, Use of administrative fees in WC cases.
- October 15, 2004, New and updated Workers' Compensation (WC) Frequently Asked Questions.
- July 11, 2005, New and updated Workers' Compensation (WC) Frequently Asked Questions.
- December 30, 2005, Part D and Workers' Compensation Medicare Set-Aside Arrangement (WCMSAs) Questions and Answer—Superseded by the July 24, 2006 memorandum.
- April 26, 2006, The Workers' Compensation Medicare Set-Aside Arrangement (WCMSAs) and the revision of the low dollar threshold for Medicare beneficiaries.
- July 24, 2006, Part D and Workers' Compensation Medicare Set-Aside Arrangement (WCMSAs) Questions and Answers.
- May 20, 2008, Use of life tables within a Medicare Set-Aside Arrangement (WCMSAs). Clarification to the May 20, 2008 Memorandum, the use of rated and actual ages remain acceptable.
- CMS has issued an Alert, regarding Section 111 of the Medicare, Medicaid and SCHIP Extension Act of 2007 (PL 110-173). The alert amends the Medicare Secondary Payer (MSP) provisions of the Social Security Act [Section 1862(b) of the Social Security Act; 42 U.S.C. 1395y (b)] to provide for a mandatory report for group health plan arrangement, liability insurance (including self-insurance), no-fault insurance, and workers' compensation. The provision will be implemented on January 1, 2009 for information about group health plan arrangement, and on July 1, 2009 for information about liability insurance, no-fault insurance, and workers' compensation.
- August 25, 2008, Implantable Devices, Termination of WCMSA Account, Life Expectancy.
- April 3, 2009, Methodology of pricing future prescription cost.

The OBRA has been amended twice. The first amendment (1984) allowed the government the right of recovery against primary payers for Medicare overpayments. The second, in 1986, extended the right of recovery to private entities (such as providers) against primary payers (such as insurance companies) for payments made by Medicare that were the responsibility of third-party payers.

As a part of MSP regulations, a specified portion of a settlement is to be set aside for payment of future medical expenses. The purpose of an MSA is to prevent the responsibility for the payment of future medical expenses from shifting from an individual's primary payer to Medicare. If a primary payer agrees to a settlement that includes future medical expenses, monies associated with the Medicare-allowable expenses must be set aside to cover those costs, and CMS approval of the amount reserved for future medical needs may be required.

The "set-aside amount" may be funded by a lump sum, structured annuity, or a combination of both. Should the lump sum set aside be properly exhausted, Medicare will agree to pay primary for those services covered by Medicare relating to the specific injury. In a situation where the MSA is funded by a structured annuity, if there is a proper depletion of funds prior to the next funding cycle, Medicare will pay for those services related to the work injury, typically covered by Medicare until the next funding cycle.

An MSA arrangement/allocation is a specified portion of the settlement that has been identified, and must be placed in a separate interest-bearing account, to pay for those services related to the work injury that would otherwise be covered by Medicare.

Medicare Beneficiaries and Settlement Amount

Federal guidelines specify that Medicare's interests must always be considered when settling the future medical needs of a Medicare beneficiary.

Those who are *not* receiving Medicare benefits may need to establish an MSA allocation if they meet both the following criteria:

- Have a "reasonable expectation" of Medicare enrollment within 30 months of the settlement date
- Anticipate receiving a settlement of more than $250,000.00

Two terms in the MSA criteria may require additional explanation:

Reasonable expectation: An individual is believed to be reasonably expected to become a Medicare beneficiary within 30 months if he or she satisfies the following criteria:

- Is between the ages of 62.5 and 65
- Has applied for, been approved for, or is receiving social security disability income (SSDI) benefits
- Has been denied SSDI benefits but expects to appeal the decision
- Has ESRD), but does not yet qualify for Medicare based on ESRD
- Is 62 years and 6 months old, as he or she may be eligible for Medicare based on his or her age within 30 months

Total settlement amount: This includes all funding for future medical expenses, indemnity, rehabilitation expenses, attorney fees, any past settlement amounts and all other costs associated with the case.

The Set-Aside Process

Through an MSA, future medical needs and associated costs for those services typically covered by Medicare are identified. are identified. Arrangement recommendations along with all the required submission documents are submitted to the Coordination of Benefits Contractor (COBC) of CMS. Once the proposal is reviewed, recommendations are sent to one of 8 regional CMS offices for approval.

To begin the set-aside process, the consultant will need to review

- Medical records of the last 2–3 years of treatment
- The individual's medical expense payment history of the last 2–3 years of treatment

- Physician recommendations
- Recognized standards of care in the healthcare fields

When submitting an allocation for CMS review, Medicare-covered expenses are identified, and related costs are indicated according to the payment schedule of that state, either usual and customary (U&C) schedule or fee schedule. The schedule is determined by the state in which the individual was injured, not necessarily the State where the individual is receiving medical care.

A "lien/conditional payment inquiry" must be initiated prior to finalizing the settlement. Research will identify if Medicare has paid for any services related to the injury being settled, for which they should not have been the primary payer. This conditional payment must be repaid to CMS, prior to settlement. Conditional payments may occur when the primary payer did not authorize a treatment, the primary payer did not pay for a service in a timely manner, or the beneficiary failed to file a proper claim or may occur in disputed or denied claims for which Medicare has may been billed incorrectly by the provider. All WC services that involve a Medicare beneficiary should be reported to the COBC.

There will be no lien/conditional payments for the non-Medicare injured worker, as Medicare would not have paid for any injury-related services.

When contacting the COBC to report a new WC occurrence by phone or by mail, the following information is required:

- Client's name
- Client's address
- Client's Medicare Health Insurance Claim Number (HICN) or Social Security Number (SSN)
- Date of Birth
- Date of incident
- Nature of illness/injury (ICD-9)
- Name and address of the WC insurance carrier
- Name and address of the legal representatives
- Name of the insured and policy/claim number

Upon receipt, the COBC will open a file (CWF—common working file) and apply it to the claimant's Medicare record, assign the case to a Medicare contractor to begin conditional payment research. All parties will be informed of the applicability of the MSP program and Medicare's recovery rights. Medicare's interests will not be determined until the claimant's record has been annotated with the specifics of the WC injury.

Once the settlement monies are received, the "set-aside" portion must be placed in a separate interest-bearing account and used *exclusively* for injury-related medical expenses, which would typically be covered by Medicare.

Consequences of Noncompliance

All parties involved in the settlement—insurance carrier, claimant, and their attorneys—remain exposed, even *after* settlement, should CMS deem Medicare's interest has not been protected. The claimant risks the denial of future Medicare benefits.

If the parties do not consider Medicare's interests when settling claims, noncompliance may lead to the following:

■ Medicare may deny primary payer status/payment for a claimant until *all* settlement funds designated for treatment of the work injury have been spent on future medical care.

■ Medicare may designate its own allocation if the settlement agreement does not make an allocation for future medical expenses, or if Medicare believes the allocation is unreasonable.

■ Medicare may allocate most or all of the settlement to future medical expenses if a proper allocation is not made at the time of settlement.

■ Medicare may deny responsibility for the payment of future medical expenses for a work-related condition if the claimant waives the right to future medical expenses, or if the settling parties try to maximize the claimant's benefits by releasing the carrier from liability for future medical expenses that are clearly work-related.

■ Medicare may take legal action with the claimant, the claimant's attorney, and/or the insurance carrier for payment of the claim. In a suit against an insurance carrier to recover its MSP claim, Medicare can seek double damages.

■ Any payments that Medicare may make for the claimant's work-related medical expenses after settlement can result in an MSP claim, leaving the claimant, the claimant's attorney, and the carrier vulnerable to potential future liability.

■ If Medicare refuses to recognize a settlement, the carrier may be instructed to notify the injured person that they should seek a reopening of the WC case.

Life Care Planning and MSA Arrangements

While similar to a life care plan, an MSA is much *narrower* in scope and identifies only the injury-related expenses that would ordinarily be *covered* by *Medicare*. Further, most MSA cost projections do not involve an on-site clinical interview with the individual and his or her family but derive patient-specific information only from a review of records, of the past 2–3 years. An MSA reflects only the medical expenses that ordinarily would be covered by Medicare. Further, in an MSA, the associated costs are based on the fee or U&C schedule in the individual's state of jurisdiction. An MSA is not intended to be a life care plan.

A life care plan is a projection of the future needs and services required for an individual, regardless of the payer source. In a life care plan, there is generally an on-site visit with the injured person and his or her family members as well as contact with the treating providers. A life care plan should not be confused with an MSA cost projection.

The MSA allocator may be provided with a copy of an LCP for the injured party. CMS has written that an LCP is required in catastrophic cases only, and the LCP would then be included within the MSA proposal forwarded to CMS.

Although they are similar, a life care plan is comprehensive and incorporates all of a patient's long-term needs, regardless of the payer source.

Commutations and Compromise

CMS defines commutation as WC settlements that are intended to compensate the claimant for *future* medical expenses. Compromise settlements are intended to compensate the claimant for *current* or *past* medical expenses.

Medicare's interests must be considered when the settlement involves *future* medical needs. A settlement is considered a commutation regardless of whether the parties admit or deny liability.

When is the Claimant Not Yet Eligible for Medicare

Not all WC settlements must be submitted to the CMS for review. If the injured party does not meet the two-pronged criteria, CMS review of the settlement *may* not be required. Although not given this formal title, within the MSA industry, the injured person is often referred to as Class 1 or Class 2.

A Class 1 Medicare beneficiary is a person who is receiving Medicare at the time of settlement, regardless of the amount of settlement.

A Class 2 Medicare beneficiary is an injured person who has a reasonable expectation of receiving Medicare benefits within the next 30 months. This person may have applied for benefits and been denied, but anticipates reapplying, or may be an individual who is aged 62 years and 6 months or an individual with ESRD, *and* the total settlement amount is $250,000.00 or more. The total settlement amount includes, but is not limited to, any previously settled portion of the settlement, future medical needs, fees, indemnity, attorney fees, annuity payouts, and repayment of any conditional/lien payments.

Review Threshold

CMS does not review every MSA allocation/arrangement, as it is not in their best interest. When a settlement leaves the medical aspect of the claim open, or the *total* settlement amount for the Medicare beneficiary is less than $25,000.00, or the injured person has applied for and/or if there is a reasonable expectation the injured party will be a Medicare beneficiary within the next 30 months, and the total amount of the MSA is less than $250,000.00, a review of the MSA proposal *may* not be required.

Conditional/lien payments may thrust an MSA, which is initially below the review threshold to that of one that requires review.

The CMS RO will generally not provide a written confirmation when the settlement is below the review threshold amount.

Although an MSA may not require CMS review, the settling parties must always consider Medicare's interest, when settling for future medical needs.

MSA Trusts

CMS refers MSA trust as Set-Aside Arrangements.

Regional Offices

There are 8 CMS Regional Offices (ROs). The role of each RO is to provide final approval of the amounts in the set-aside arrangement and issuance of written confirmation as to whether Medicare's interest has been protected. To assist the RO in its review of the proposed MSA, it is recommended that all required and supporting documentation be included within the proposed document. This will not only assist the reviewer, but will also allow for a faster response time to your proposal from the RO.

Criteria

CMS provides suggested guidelines, not a formal format, for required documentation within the proposal, as well as required documentation within the cover letter, that is to be a part of the submission document. Refer to the CMS website for specific information. Currently, these criteria are as follows: (1) date of Medicare entitlement, (2) basis for Medicare entitlement, (3) type and severity of injury or illness, (4) beneficiary's age, rated age, and life expectancy, (5) WC classification of the beneficiary as permanently or partially disabled, (6) prior medical expenses since the claimant reached maximum medical improvement, (7) amount of settlement and allocations to indemnity and future medical expenses, (8) whether commutation is for the claimant's lifetime or a specific time period, (9) the beneficiary's living arrangements, and (10) whether expected future medical expenses are appropriate based on the medical and payout records as well as the claimant's condition.

Set-aside arrangements must be funded based on the claimant's life expectancy and use of the CDC life tables, as directed by CMS, in the May 20, 2008 Memo, unless state WC law allows a shorter time period.

The proposed MSA dollar amount will be based on the State of Venue, using either a WC fee schedule or a U&C schedule. When monies are utilized from the MSA account, they must be based on the same Medicare criteria, relating to the specific injury. This will ensure proper exhaustion of the MSA monies.

Medicare will not make any payments for injury-related medical expenses after settlement until the amount of settlement allocated to those expenses has been properly exhausted. CMS has developed an electronic system that allows the contractor monitoring WC claimants to keep and maintain a "CWF" to determine when Medicare claims for a particular disabled worker should be denied. If the administrator of a set-aside arrangement denies payment of a claim when it is determined the claim was for non-injury-related services, and the contractor and the RO determine that Medicare will not pay the claim, Medicare's administrative appeal process will be available as for other claim denials.

CMS Review of the MSA Allocation/Arrangement

As of November 2009, there are two conditions that require *submission* to a CMS RO for review of proposed set-aside funds.

- If the claimant is currently a Medicare beneficiary and the total settlement amount exceeds $25,000.00, then a submission and review must be completed.
- If the claimant is eligible for Medicare or has a "reasonable expectation" of Medicare within 30 months and the future medical expenses and indemnity being offered in the settlement exceed $250,000.00, then a submission and review must be completed.

Under the MSP, the main goal is to protect Medicare's interests when resolving WC case's for *future medical expenses*. As per CMS, "the recommended method to protect Medicare's interests is a Workers' Compensation Medicare Set-aside Arrangement (WCMSA), which allocates a portion of the WC settlement for future medical expenses." The amount set aside is determined on a case-by-case basis and should be reviewed by CMS, when appropriate. Once the CMS-approved set-aside amount is properly exhausted, then Medicare will be the primary prayer for future Medicare-covered expenses related to the WC injury.

CMS has stated that they will not allow an injured individuals permanent waiver of their right to certain specific future medical needs and services related to the WC settlement. CMS has stated the injured person could change their mind and this would thrust CMS into the role of primary payer. CMS has responded with the following:

> … the ROs cannot approve settlements that promise not to bill Medicare for certain services in lieu of including those services in a Medicare set-aside arrangement. This is true even if the claimant/beneficiary offers to execute an affidavit or other legal document promising that Medicare will not be billed for certain services if those services are not included in the Medicare set-aside arrangement.

Medicare's interests must still be considered, and an MSA arrangement is recommended, regardless of whether or not the case must be submitted to CMS for approval.

Third-Party Liability

In a third-party liability settlement, a liability insurance carrier may have a lien against the WC carrier. When the case settles, the lien by the compensation carrier against the liability insurer may be waived. The future medicals are often "cashed out" without a separate set-aside. The beneficiary is no longer entitled to receive future medical care from the compensation carrier.

In the liability settlement, the beneficiary/injured worker has received a sum of money for the future skilled medical care that was "offset" against the compensation carrier's lien.

When a third-party liability settlement relieves a WC carrier of the responsibility for the beneficiary's future medical expenses, a Medicare Set-Aside must be considered unless the following hold:

- The future medical care under the WC portion of the settlement remains open and the WC continues to be primary in responsibility for those services once the liability settlement is exhausted
- Documentation may be produced that the beneficiary does not require any further WC-related medical services

When is a Set-Aside Unnecessary?

A Medicare Set-Aside is not required if:

- The settlement is only for past services already provided
- Written documentation is provided that states the beneficiary will no long require Medicare services
- The settlement is not attempting to shift responsibility for future medicals to Medicare

What is Necessary to Secure Medicare's Approval?

The review thresholds are subject to change; however, Medicare has been quite clear in that their interest must be considered in all cases when settling for future medical needs.

To secure CMS approval, the settling parties should first contact the COBC in New York. Once a CWF has been established and the MSA documentation has been received, the COBC forwards all submission materials to the Workers' Compensation Review Center (WCRC). When their review is completed, the recommendations are then sent to the appropriate CMS RO.

Currently, the COBC office for submission of WCMSAs is located in Detroit, Michigan. CMS has focused on standardizing the submission process by directing all MSA proposals through this central office, and then distributing documents to the appropriate RO.

What Supporting Documentation is Required?

As per CMS guidelines, the Medicare set-aside submission document must include a cover letter, a rated age if the proposal was developed using a rated age (the rated ages must be on the letterhead of the life company that provided the information), signed and dated releases, a life care plan (if appropriate), a settlement agreement, set-aside allocation, medical and payout records from the previous 2–3 years of treatment, name and contact information of the structured broker (if appropriate), name and contact information of the MSA administrator (if appropriate), copy of the Medicare card (if appropriate), and any additional supporting documentation one wishes to bring to the attention of CMS.

Administration of the MSA

The Federal Code of Regulations does not mandate what particular type of administration should be used for the MSA account. It may be administered by a professional administrator or self-administered, unless the claimant may be assigned a representative payee by the Social Security Administration (SSA). The duties and obligations of the administrator are the same for either professional administration or self-administration.

Generally, the carrier/account determines the method of administration for the MSA account and the medical custodial account.

Funding of the MSA Account

The funds for the MSA account must be placed in a separate interest-bearing account. The administrator of the MSA account must forward annual accounting summaries concerning the expenditures of the arrangement to the contractor responsible for monitoring the individual's case.

If professionally administered, the monitor of the individual's account is then responsible for ensuring/verifying that the funds allocated to the set-aside arrangement were exhausted on Medicare-allowable medical services, identified within the MSA allocation and related to the injury (work, liability, or other), for which this account has been developed.

CMS requires that annual accounting be submitted to the RO for approval. If the MSA account is not properly exhausted, CMS will not allow distribution of the MSA funds. CMS allows self-administration, however it cautions that a self-administered set-aside will be held to the same standards as that which is professionally administered. When self-administration of the MSA is determined, the claimant must be advised on proper administration of the set-aside.

Fees for the professional administration may *not* be charged back to the MSA account.

The treating providers must agree to continue accepting fee reimbursement per WC fee schedule or U&C schedule, on which the MSA was developed.

Appeals

At this time, there is no appeals process regarding a denial of a proposed MSA allocation amount or the "counter-higher" of the proposed amount, demanded by CMS.

Review Threshold for MSA Allocations

Not all WC settlements must be submitted to the CMS RO for review. The current CMS review threshold for Class I is a total settlement of $25,000.00, inclusive of all cost related to the file. When a Class II is involved, an individual has applied and been denied SSI, but anticipates reapplying for SSI, the threshold raises to $250,000.00. To determine whether an injured worker is within 30 months of Medicare enrollment, note that Medicare eligibility is based on one of two methods: attainment of age 65 or receipt of 24 months of SSDI regardless of age.

If the MSA allocation meets the review threshold, a CMS RO will issue a written opinion on the adequacy of the MSA allocation and settlement. Written confirmation from the CMS RO allows the carrier a full release, and once the funds in the MSA Trust or the other approved set-aside arrangement are properly exhausted on injury-related medical expenses, the worker is eligible for Medicare coverage for future medical expenses.

Compromised Settlement

Lump sum compromise settlements represent an agreement between the WC carrier and the injured worker to accept less than the injured worker would have received if they had obtained full reimbursement for lost wages and lifelong medical treatment for the injury or illness. In a typical lump sum compromise case between a WC carrier and an injured worker, the WC carrier disputes liability and generally will not have paid for all the medical bills relating to the accident.

Commutation Settlement

Commutation settlements are intended to compensate workers for future medical expenses required because of a work-related injury or disease.

A commutation settlement must allocate an amount for future medical expenses that considers Medicare interests. If settlement is for a "lump sum," Medicare will not pay for any future medical expenses related to work injury until the lump sum settlement amount projected for future medical needs is properly exhausted, as per 42 CFR 411.46.

A single WC lump sum settlement agreement may comprise both a WC compromise aspect and a commutation aspect. Single lump sum settlement agreements can apportion part of a settlement for an injured worker's future medical expenses and simultaneously designate another part of the settlement for all of the injured worker's medical expenses up to the date of settlement.

A commutation settlement may possess a compromise aspect to it when a settlement agreement also stipulates paying for all medical expenses up to the date of settlement.

In the settlement documents, failure to designate an amount allocated toward medical expenses being paid for past medical expenses will result in CMS withholding payment of future medical expenses up to the amount of such allocation. If no allocation is designated, CMS will designate what portion will be attributed toward "future medicals," and has the power to treat the entire lump sum amount as a payment toward future medicals.

Liability stipulations are not exempt from the MSP Act. Clarification within the settlement document must delineate what portion of the settlement is for future medical needs. A lump sum compromise settlement may be deemed to be a compensation payment for Medicare purposes, even if it is stipulated that there is no liability.

A proposed settlement may be apportioned as follows:

- Indemnity/wage replacement: $22,000.00 lump sum
- Future medical expenses of the type not normally covered by Medicare: $5,000.00 lump sum
- Additional future medical expenses and medications of the type normally covered by Medicare (MSA): $40,000.00 lump sum
- Attorney fees: $5,000.00
- Total: $135,000.00

Consideration of Medicare's Interest

All WC, liability, and auto settlements must consider Medicare's interest when settling for future medical needs. There is no mandate as to what type of arrangement must be used to set aside funds for Medicare.

The funds allocated to a set-aside allocation must reflect the fee schedule or the U&C schedule charge of the State of Venue (where the injury occurred, and not necessarily where the person is receiving treatment).

The MSA allocation must document the amount allocated to future medical expenses and how it was calculated, based on the State of Venue. Once the CMS RO has reviewed and approved the sufficiency of the arrangement based on the WC medical fee schedule, the medical providers will be paid based on what would normally be payable under the WC plan (i.e., under the WC medical fee schedule).

Settlement Agreement

The settlement agreement must address the provider's agreement to abide by the WC fee schedule or the U&C schedule reimbursement level. The providers are to be paid at the schedule delineated within the set-aside allocation. CMS requires a breakdown of how the monies are being addressed. They include payment for past medical, future medical, indemnity, attorney fees, and other. The projected medical needs of both the Medicare-covered and noncovered medical services must be addressed. The future medical expenses that would not otherwise be covered by Medicare may not be allocated to the set-aside arrangement as long as they are listed in the settlement agreement.

After the set-aside funds are depleted, there must be a complete accounting to the Medicare contractor to ensure that the funds were properly exhausted for medical services that would have been reimbursable by Medicare. Upon confirmation from Medicare that the MSA account was properly exhausted, Medicare can be billed for future medical services.

CMS will evaluate the allocation to determine whether it is sufficient to consider Medicare's interest. The allocation must be developed using Standards of Care along with the physicians' recommended treatment plan. An exception may be a court ruling on a physician's treatment plan or treatment recommendation outside all Standards of Care.

A treating provider's report, IME, AME, or other evaluation may provide clarification of the diagnosis, prognosis, frequency, and duration of future care, mechanism of injury (how it occurred), injured worker's history, and, if necessary, a life care plan. Other documents required by CMS to determine "reasonableness" include a copy of the settlement agreement, rated age, and letters from providers establishing the need and the agreement to the WC fee schedule reimbursement for future medical care.

The primary goal of the MSP is to ensure that there is no shifting of the responsibility for payment from the primary payer of medical services to Medicare. All submitted proposed settlements are reviewed on a case-by-case basis in order to determine whether Medicare has an obligation to provide services after the settlement. The criteria needed within a submission document include date of Medicare entitlement, basis for Medicare entitlement, type and severity of injury or illness, beneficiary's age, rated age, and life expectancy, WC classification of the beneficiary as permanently or partially disabled, prior medical expenses, amount of settlement and allocations to indemnity and future medical expenses with an explanation of the basis for the amounts of projected expenses for Medicare-covered services and services not covered by Medicare, confirmation if commutation is for the worker's lifetime or a specific timeframe, beneficiary's living arrangements, and whether expected future medical expenses are adequate for the worker's condition.

Although not required nor requested on all MSAs, in catastrophic cases a life care plan with a cost analysis of future medical needs is recommended, allocating appropriate funds for recommended future medical services.

WC Settlements with MSA Arrangements: Conditional/Lien Payment Issues

There are instances in which an MSP claim may develop due to erroneous billing to Medicare for services related to the claim being settled. Medicare addresses these errors as "overpayments" and will establish an MSP claim in any settlement arrangement. While a claim is being investigated and disputed, an individual who is without additional health insurance benefits may be impacted in their ability to receive medical care. This impact was never the intention of Medicare. When this occurs, Medicare will make "conditional payments" until a decision on compensability is reached.

Components of an MSA Arrangement

The primary components of an MSA are the *allocation amount*, the *method of funding the account*, and the *method of administering* the account.

Recall that the purpose of an MSA is to prevent shifting of the responsibility for payment of future medical expenses from an individual's primary payer to Medicare. If a primary payer agrees to a settlement that includes future medical expenses, an amount for Medicare-allowable expenses must be set aside to cover those costs.

Allocators developing a cost projection must identify all future medical needs, medical and prescription drugs, allowable under Medicare and, if applicable, the circumstances under which certain expenses are allowable. Researching allowable expenses can be a time-consuming process. The CMS website provides a searchable database of allowable items that may be of use to professionals (http://www.cms.hhs.gov/mcd/overview.asp).

WC Fee Schedule

The MSA must document whether the projection was based on a fee schedule or a U&C rate, Medicare-allowable expenses.

The MSA must also document that medications were priced at the Average Wholesale Price (AWP) and document the National Drug Classification Code of NDC. The arrangement is to be based on the state where the injury occurred (State of Venue), not necessarily where the injured party is receiving treatment. *There are a very few states in which the "State of Venue" will not apply.* Refer to the CMS website for additional information.

Allocation Amount

The allocation amount is the total number of dollars to be set aside at the time of settlement for future medical expenses related to an individual's injury. Again, this figure reflects the sum of all costs associated with an individual's injury that would be typically covered by Medicare.

The allocation amount is determined by

- Performing a comprehensive review of all medical records related to the injury
- Performing a comprehensive review of the medical payment history related to the injury
- Physician recommendations
- Standards of Care
- Life expectancy based on either standard age or rated/reduced age life expectancy

Review of Medical Records

A comprehensive review of all medical records related to the injury involves a careful notation of all assessments by qualified professionals, including physicians, specialists, therapists, and psychologists. Also note the type and frequency of services received to date. This will serve as a baseline for future needs. Primary consideration should be given to the services and results of evaluations completed poststabilization. Note the alternative treatment pathways that exist.

Review of the Medical Payment History

Compare the payments with the medical records received. This careful cross check of payments to records will identify any missing records. Establishing the total cost of care related to the injury over the past 2 to 3 year period allows the allocator to establish the baseline for future medical needs and expenses.

Physician Recommendations

Specifically identify any physician recommendations regarding the individual's future care and/or therapeutic intervention. If no such recommendations exist (with written permission of the patient), you may request this information. When there are recommendations from several physicians, the primary treating physician's opinion typically is regarded as more significant than that of a one-time independent medical examination or second opinion.

Standards of Care

Standards of Care in an industry or practice area are based on research, patient outcomes, longitudinal studies, and similar evidence-based methodology. Manufacturers' recommendations for cost projections related to equipment replacement schedules may be included. All supporting documentation should accompany the arrangement submitted to a CMS RO.

Life Expectancy

CMS will accept a standard life expectancy, if appropriate, using Table 1. Life table for total population; United States, 2004 of the National Vital Statistic Reports, Vol. 56, No. 9, December 28, 2007. If a rated age is used to project the life expectancy within the MSA, a median rated age *must* be used. The rated ages obtained must be on the letterhead of the life company, and given to CMS within the submission.

It is also recommended that you include the following statement: As per the *CMS directive, all rated ages obtained on the claimant have been included.*

Method of Funding

The two basic methods of funding an MSA account are lump sum payment and annuity.

Lump Sum Payment

The entire amount of the set-aside allocation is paid into the account at the time of settlement (lump sum). Medicare will not assume responsibility for payment of injury-related care until the entire lump sum amount has been properly exhausted.

Annuity

An annuity is a method of funding an MSA account that has been established with an initial deposit or "seed monies"; then payments are made according to a predetermined schedule. The annuity structure must be approved by CMS and found to adequately account for all allocated expenses. Medicare will become the primary payer during any year in which the account is properly exhausted, until the next scheduled annuity payment is made.

Method of Administering

The Code of Federal Regulations allows for either: self-administration or professional administration.

Self-Administration

If the account is self-administered, individuals must be made fully aware of their responsibilities in overseeing it and the consequences of noncompliance with all regulations.

Professional Administration

As of May 7, 2004, the Director of the Center for Medicare Management announced that fees associated with professional administration can no longer be deducted from an MSA account. The memorandum reads, in part:

> Administrative fees/expenses for administration of the Medicare Set-Aside arrangement and/or attorney costs specifically associated with establishing the Medicare Set-Aside arrangement cannot be charged to the set-aside arrangement. The CMS will no longer be evaluating the reasonableness of any of these costs because the payment of these costs must come from some other payment source that is completely separate from the Medicare Set-Aside arrangement funds.

Distribution of Funds

Regardless of whether the funds are professionally administered or self-administered, CMS requires that all funds be placed in a separate interest-bearing account used *exclusively* for those future medical needs identified in the MSA. Only injury-related Medicare-allowable expenses may be paid from the account until the individual becomes eligible for Medicare benefits. Funds must be paid according to the fee schedule of the State of Venue.

If payments from the set-aside account are used to pay for items or services that are not covered by Medicare or related to the injury, Medicare will not pay for injury-related claims until the funds have been restored to the account and properly exhausted.

Annual Account Summary and Administrative Requirements

The administrator of the MSA account, whether self-administered or professionally administered, is responsible for keeping records of all payments from the MSA account. Whether professionally administered or self-administered, both must comply with all CMS regulations. As per the CMS memo, "WCMSA should be placed in an interest-bearing account. WCMSAs should also be administered by a competent administrator (the representative payee, appointment guardian/conservator, or has otherwise been declared incompetent by a court) and the settling parties must include that information in their Medicare set-aside arrangement proposal to CMS."

If professionally administered, the administrator must forward annual accounting summaries concerning the expenditures of the arrangement to the CMS Medicare contractor that is responsible for monitoring the individual's case. Additionally, the Medicare contractor is responsible for verifying that no payments from Medicare are made for medical expenses related to the injury or illness/disease until the WCMSA is exhausted.

Fraudulent use of set-aside funds may result in severe penalties, including loss of all future Medicare benefits.

Annual accounting summaries of all transactions and the account status must be submitted to the case's assigned Medicare contractor. For each transaction, the annual accounting must include the following:

- Date of service
- Procedure(s) performed

- Diagnosis
- Paid receipt or canceled check

The COBC consolidates the activities that support the collection, management, and reporting of other insurance coverage for Medicare beneficiaries. By law, when Medicare beneficiaries have some private insurance, other insurers should pay first. The COBC collects information on the proper order of payers and ensures that Medicare makes primary payment only for those claims where it has primary responsibility. When mistaken Medicare primary payments are identified, recovery actions from other insurers are undertaken.

Medicare is the secondary payer to WC and has a priority right of recovery over that of any other entity to the proceeds of any settlement of an individual's claim and a subrogation right.

WC Data Sharing Agreements

CMS is currently working with states to provide WC data to match with the CMS Medicare eligible database. CMS's goal is to identify those beneficiaries that may have had claims paid mistakenly by Medicare when WC or another entity should have been responsible for the claim payment. This data sharing also identifies those specific ICD-9 codes related to the injury being settled.

Proposal Format

CMS does not have a required format for MSA proposals or submission documents.

MSA Cost Projection Report Guidelines

WCMSA submissions are mailed to CMS at c/o Coordination of Benefits Contractor, PO Box 33849, Detroit, MI 48232-5849. From Detroit, the submission is forwarded to the Workers Compensation Review Center (WCRC), to ascertain the sufficiency of the proposal. The WCRC provides an opinion, on the sufficiency of the submission, to the appropriate RO. The RO then reviews the proposal for appropriateness and provides a written opinion to the submitter, as to the sufficiency of the submitted allocation.

Submission Materials

Components of the MSA will be evaluated according to the guidelines provided in the "Medicare Set-Aside Proposal Requirements Checklist." CMS emphasizes the importance of submitting complete proposals to avoid delays in processing and approving the document. CMS has provided a sample submission, which may be found at http://www.cms.hhs.gov/WorkersCompAgencyServices/Downloads/samplesubmission.pdf

Case Example of an MSA Cost Projection Report

This example is meant to be used as a guideline only. The case example provides readers with a general framework when conceptualizing a suitable MSA proposal. In no manner, should it be interpreted as inclusive of all codes or that cost are accurate, but rather this is a sample MSA Allocation Report. Refer to the CMS guidelines for the most current format prescribed by the CMS checklist.

Sample MSA Cost Allocation Report

Date of Report: November 30, 2009

First Insurance
Attention: Mr. Charles Boat
2473 Claims Road
Settles, CA 99999
Re: Mary Smith
Claim Number: 123-4567

Identifying Information:

Claimant: Mary Smith

Address: 317 Main Road
Gain, CA 99999
Phone: 811-111-1111
SSN: 111-11-1111
HICN: 111-11-1111 A
DOB: 12-12-59
DOI: 9-25-2001
State of Jurisdiction: California

Claimant Attorney: Edward Plaintiff

Address: 50 Front Avenue
Noon, CA 99999

Employer: Lum Foods
1 Tom Avenue
Story, CA 99991

Carrier/Defense Attorney: Joann Defense
Address: 3321 Rain Road
Ment, CA 99999

Introduction

This file was referred to *We Are MSA* by Mr. Charles Boat of First Insurance for the development of an MSA Cost Projection. After review of the documentation provided by First Insurance, including medical records and payment history as well as National Clinical Guidelines, *We Are MSA* developed proposed MSA allocation.

Entitlement and COBC Contact Information

After signed consent was obtained from Ms Smith. The SSA was contacted to determine Social Security and Medicare benefit information. It was determined that Ms Smith is receiving Social Security disability benefits with an entitlement date 2-2008. She is also receiving Medicare Part

A and Part B with an entitlement date of 2-2008. Ms Smith is not receiving Medicaid or SSI benefits.

Confirmation has been obtained in writing that there have been $0.00 conditional payments made by CMS regarding this work injury.

Diagnosis: ICD-9 Related to the Industrial Injury

726.2 Impingement syndrome, bilateral shoulders

726.0 Subacromial bursitis, bilateral shoulders

718.1 Internal derangement right shoulder

Diagnoses not related to the industrial injury:
Sleep disorder, arthrosis bilateral knees, COPD, hypertension and chronic lumbar strain

Life Expectancy Issues

Ms Smith is a 49-year-old female with a median rated age of 56 and a life expectancy of 26 additional years. This information was obtained from the *National Vital Statistics Reports*, Vol. 56, No. 9, December 28, 2007, for the total population; United States, 2004, p. 8, which was used to determine the life expectancy. Rated ages were obtained from the following life companies of 54-ABC, 58-DEF, 56-GHI. Per CMS Directive, all rated ages obtained are included in this MSA.

Description of Injury and Initial Treatment

Description of Injury

Ms. Smith was employed by Lum Foods as a Maintenance/Machine Cleaner, when on 9/25/01 she was lifting pallets from the ground and experienced pain in her shoulders.

Key Medical Treatment Events

According to Mr Charles Boat of First Insurance, the diagnoses of chronic lumbar strain/sprain, prior arthroscopic knee surgery, and tricompartmental arthrosis bilateral knees are not accepted as compensable injuries by the insurance carrier. This MSA allocation addresses only the bilateral shoulder injury.

Initial care and treatment following the 9/25/01 injury included conservative treatment in the form of medication, physical therapy, and modified duty. An MRI of the right shoulder revealed a rupture of the long head of the biceps tendon as well as partial tear of the supraspinatus tendon. A Qualified Medical Evaluation (QME) was performed by orthopedic surgeon Dr. Albert Jones on 10/23/06. Dr. Jones diagnosed impingement syndrome of the bilateral shoulder joints with subacromial bursitis and a rupture of the long head of the biceps tendon as well as partial tear of the supraspinatus tendon. Of note are the additional diagnoses of chronic lumbar strain/sprain, prior arthroscopic knee surgery, and tricompartmental arthrosis bilateral knees, which were not accepted as compensable injuries by the insurance carrier.

Future care recommendations regarding the bilateral shoulder diagnoses included the possibility of surgical repair of both shoulders, diagnostic studies, short courses of physical therapy for flare-ups, injections, and medications. The following physical restrictions were recommended: avoid heavy lifting, heavy or repetitive pushing or pulling, as well as any above shoulder-level activity.

Diagnoses:

1. Impingement syndrome of the bilateral shoulder joints with subacromial bursitis
2. Rupture of the long head of the biceps tendon with partial tear of the supraspinatus tendon of the right shoulder as per MRI
3. Chronic lumbosacral sprain/strain superimposed upon lumbar spondylosis with 5 mm disc herniation at L4–5 as per MRI
4. Status postarthroscopic surgery of the bilateral knee joints
5. Tricompartmental arthrosis of the bilateral knees

Dr. Sun placed Ms Smith at permanent and stationary/maximum medical improvement on 10/23/2006.

Present Status and Current Treatment

As per the review of medical records, Ms Smith's height is 5'9" and her weight is 232 lb. Currently, Ms Smith requires no assistance with ambulation. Ms Smith does require some assistance with reaching items overhead and washing her hair. Current medication is Darvocent-N-100, taken for pain. Ms Smith's condition is currently stable.

Future Medical Needs Typically Covered by Medicare

The future medical treatment projected for the claimant is based on the treating physician's opinion, Ms Smith's medical evaluations, review of medical and financial records, and usual standard of care treatment guidelines.

It is anticipated that Ms Smith will remain stable based on the medicals and projected future medical treatment plan. The treatment plan includes future medical care for Ms Mary Smith. As there are life changes, Ms Smith may experience exacerbations.

Medicare-Covered Items

Physician Visits

Physician office visits (99213) 1 per year at $56.93 × 26 years = *$1,480.18*
Physician office visits for exacerbations (99213) at $56.93 × 15—per life expectancy = *$853.95*

Laboratory

Complete blood count (CBC) CPT 85025 and complete metabolic profile (CMP) CPT 80053, at $34.36 1 × yearly × 26 years = $896.36.

Diagnostic Studies

Shoulder MRI, one on the right, one on the left pre-op, and an additional MRI for each shoulder for LE for a total of four shoulder MRI (73222), at $696.00 each in 26 years = $2,784.00.

X-rays, shoulder (73030), 10 at $79.06, during 26 years = $790.60.

Physical Therapy

24 visits after each shoulder repair (97110) at $74.00 each × 2 surgeries = $3,552.00.
  40 visits projected for exacerbations, during 26 years = $2,960.00.

Surgery

Arthroscopy of each shoulder (29822) at $2,525.22, one × each shoulder during 26 years = $5,044.00.

Medications

Prescription Medications/Part D Formulary Coverage

The following medications were prescribed for the claimant:

Propoxyphene Napsylate and Acetamin (generic Naprosyn-n/100) NDC 24486032610 at
  $1.84 per pill, × 30 pills per month, × 26 years = $17,222.40.
Total lifetime costs of prescriptions: $17,222.40.
Total amount of Medicare-covered items: $18,278.09.
Total amount of MSA Allocation: $35,500.49.

Future Medical Needs Typically Not Covered by Medicare

Projected medical care typically *not covered* by Medicare would include
  Total amount of non-Medicare-covered items: $10,725.12.

Complications

It is anticipated that Ms Smith will remain stable with the treatment provided. No complications are foreseen.

Proposed Consideration of Medicare's Interests

In accordance with the foregoing, we propose that Medicare's interests be reasonably and sufficiently considered in this WC settlement by virtue of an MSA allocation of $35,500.49.

These funds are being designated exclusively for Ms Smith's future medical needs of the type typically allowable by Medicare.

Ms Smith has elected to self-administer the MSA funds. CMS states that Ms Smith must place the set-aside funds in an interest-bearing account that is separate from her personal checking and savings accounts. Ms Smith is to use the MSA funds only to pay for medical services related to the work injury that would normally be paid by Medicare.

Ms Smith will be responsible for keeping records of payments made from the account and forwarding annual account summaries of fund transactions along with the status of the account to the assigned Medicare contractor, MSPRC. These summaries are to include the date of each service, procedure performed, diagnosis, and paid receipt or canceled check.

Our recommended allocation amount is based on the WC fee schedule in the state of jurisdiction, in this case California. All payments to providers from the MSA funds are to be adjusted accordingly.

Submission of MSA Allocation to CMS for Approval

When the MSA allocation proposal is submitted to CMS for review, additional documents and documentation are required: a copy of the proposed MSA allocation along with a cost projection, a copy of the settlement document (which must address a breakdown of the settlement dollars as indemnity, future medical needs that are Medicare allowable, future medical needs that are not allowable by Medicare, past medical expenses, if appropriate, attorney fees, and any additional costs related to the settlement), a copy of the medical records and payout history for the past 2–3 years, signed and dated Medicare release, rated ages (on the letterhead of the life company that has provided the information), a life care plan (if required), an annuity proposal (with the name of the settlement company and complete contact information), a copy of the Medicare card or confirmation from SSA of dates of entitlement and all supporting documentation.

CMS has recommended that the most efficient method of submission is on a CD-ROM. The most recent recommendations from CMS regarding the submission packet whether being submitted electronically or paper, include the following:

Section 05 (Cover Letter). Mandatory information. Include all pertinent names, addresses, phone and fax numbers; all demographic information about the claimant; and all summary numbers and other data for the settlement and the WCMSA. Reference attachments only after summarizing the important information on them.

Section 10 (Consent Form). Mandatory information. Include the signed consent, plus any applicable court papers if the consent is signed by someone other than the claimant (for example, guardian, power of attorney, etc.) Do not include unsigned consents or consents to obtain medical records from a provider.

Section 15 (Rated Ages). Optional information. Include a stand-alone statement indicating whether all rated ages obtained on the claimant are included. Also include all rated ages obtained on the claimant, even those that appear to have expired or appear not to be independent. Make sure they are on letterhead (which includes company name and address) of the insurance company or companies that made the rating or the settlement broker that obtained them from the insurance companies. Do not include actuarial charts or life expectancy charts from the CDC or elsewhere, or statements that there are no rated ages. If actual age is used, leave this section blank.

Section 20 (Life Care/Future Treatment Plan). Optional information, except for drug and dosage lists which must be included. Include all pricing charts, cost projections, pricing information, drug and dosage lists, and explanatory narratives and analyses.

Section 25 (Court/WC Board Documents). Optional information upon submission, but final settlement documents are required to complete case. Include only official documents, such as WC petitions, mediation documents, prior awards and settlements, court orders, draft and final settlement agreements, and annuity rate sheets.

Section 30 (WCMSA Administration Agreement). Optional information. Include any official stand-alone agreement that provides the name and address of the administrator of the WCMSA.

Section 35 (Medical Records). Mandatory information. Include first report of injury, medical records of major surgeries, and medical records for the last two years of treatment, no matter how long ago those last two years were or who paid for the services. Also include depositions from medical providers. Do not include insurance billing forms (except C-4 forms in New York), subpoena forms, or correspondence seeking records.

Section 40 (Payment Information). Mandatory information. Include payment histories (indemnity, medical, and expenses) from all carriers, third party administrators ("TPAs"), employers, pharmacies, and prescription drug suppliers. Also include any signed statements from carriers or their attorneys with payment information or the last date of treatment. Include billing information, where paid claims information is not available. Do not include unsigned statements from carriers or their attorneys.

Section 50 (Supplemental/Additional Information). Optional information. Include copy of official birth certificate and driver's license where date of birth is unclear, copy of state law that submitter discusses elsewhere, and Social Security or Medicare card or correspondence if needed to verify Social Security or Medicare number or entitlement. Do not include submitter resume or copies of documents sent by CMS to the WCMSA submitter.

Once CMS/COBC receives one's proposal, it will be assigned a case control number, which will be sent to one along with the required information. The case control number is one's initial confirmation that one's submission document has been received. The case control number will be required on additional information that may be required in the review of the submission. If contacting the WCRC for a status of one's proposal, this case control number is required to obtain information.

Upon approval of an MSA, a copy of the final settlement agreement signed by the beneficiary and other representatives *must* be submitted to the CMS RO handling the case in order to finalize the arrangement.

There are training programs available, both in the private sector and through the National Alliance of Medicare Set-Aside Professionals (NAMSAP). These training sessions are geared to both the new practitioner and those seeking advanced training.

Additional information on Medicare, Social Security, CDC, and the National Alliance of Medicare Set-Aside Professionals (NAMSAP) may be found at the following.

Medicare

The CMS homepage of http://cms.hhs.gov/ will provide the link to articles, general information, frequently asked questions, and information for both the laymen and professionals. This will be the starting point in the research of Medicare issues, as they relate to an MSA.

Medicare Coverage Database

Go to the *Medicare Coverage* homepage (http://www.cms.hhs.gov/mcd/overview.asp?from2= overview.asp&). From the homepage, you may link to the *Medicare Coverage Database* that lets you access the *National Coverage Determinations* and *National Coverage Analyses* indices. Go to http://www.cms.hhs.gov/WorkersCompAgencyServices/05_wcmsasubmission.asp to view the checklist provided as a PDF through the CMS website.

Medicare Guidelines

20 FR §404.408(d); 42 USC §1395y(b)(2)(A)(ii); 42 CFR §411.20–411.52; Medicare Carrier's Manual, §§2370.7 and 2370.8. http://cms.hhs.gov/manuals/14_car/3b2336.asp; Medicare Intermediary.

MSA Sample Submission as per CMS

CMS has also provided a sample submission document titled Sample Submission (PDF, 135 KB) that can be found under the heading *Download* at http://www.cms.hhs.gov/WorkersCompAgency Services/05_wcmsasubmission.asp#TopOfPage.

MSA Submission Checklist

CMS published the "Medicare Set-Aside Proposal Requirements Checklist" that specifies all of the necessary information to be included in each MSA proposal. Click here (http://www.cms.hhs.gov/WorkersCompAgencyServices/05_wcmsasubmission.asp) to find the *WC Submission Checklist* under *Downloads* (toward the bottom of the page). The Checklist is now used by all ROs to review the submitted documentation.

Social Security Website

The most current information may be found on the Social Security Website of http://www.socialsecurity.gov/pubs/11000.html#part2

SSA publishes a booklet for physicians and other health professionals titled *Disability Evaluation Under Social Security* (No. 64-039). Referred to as "The Blue Book," it lists the medical criteria that SSA uses to determine disability.

Provisions and work exclusions may be found in *The Red Book on Work Incentives*: http://www.socialsecurity.gov/redbook/eng/main.htm

CDC Life Table

This is the current site to locate the life expectancy chart that will be used in the projection of the life expectancy: http://www.cdc.gov/nchs/data/nvsr/nvsr56/nvsr56_09.pdf

Medicare Regulations

Additional information on the MSP Statute may be found at the following sites:

http://www.cms.hhs.gov/manuals/downloads/msp105c07.pdf
http://www.cms.hhs.gov/manuals/downloads/msp105c01.pdf
http://www.cms.hhs.gov/MMAUpdate/downloads/PL108-173summary.pdf
http://ecfr.gpoaccess.gov/cgi/t/text/text-idx?c=ecfr&rgn=div5&view=text&node=42:2.0.1.2.1
    1&idno=42

Source of Additional Information

National Alliance of MSA Professionals

This nonprofit organization was formed in 2005 as a forum for addressing the unique issues and challenges of professionals working within the MSA arena. Click here (http://www.namsap.org) to learn more about the organization's educational programs, annual conference, and professional resources.

Test Questions

1. Medicare is a healthcare program administered by
   A. State
   B. Federal government
   C. Local municipality

2. Medicaid is based on financial needs
   A. True
   B. False

3. MSA are required for *all* injured person seeking a settlement
   A. True
   B. False

4. Formal MSA proposals are recommend in which of the following:
   A. Injured person is a Medicare beneficiary at the time of settlement
   B. Injured person has applied for and been denied and there is a reasonable expectation of reapplying for SS and the total amount of the settlement is $250,000.00 or greater
   C. Settlement is for $20,000.00 or greater
   D. A + B
   E. All of the above
   F. None of the above

5. Allocation projections are based on either the state fee schedule or the U&C schedule
   A. True
   B. False

6. Documents included within the MSA submission to CMS may include
   A. Medical records of the last 2–3 years of treatment
   B. Payout records of the last 2–3 years of treatment
   C. Releases
   D. Only independent medical evaluation reports
   E. All of the above
   F. A + B + C
   G. A + B + C + D

7. A "denied or disputed" case does not require an MSA allocation
   A. True
   B. False

8. Conditional payments may have been made by Medicare in which of the following instances:
   A. The primary payer does not pay in a prompt and timely manner
   B. Beneficiary failed to file a proper claim
   C. In disputed or denied claims
   D. Instances where the injured worker sought unauthorized treatment

    E. A + C + D

    F. All of the above

9. Settlement monies may be paid to the claimant by

    A. Lump sum

    B. Annuity

    C. Lump sum + annuity

    D. All of the above

    E. None of the above

Answers: 1. B, 2. A, 3. B, 4. D, 5. A, 6. F, 7. B, 8. F, 9. D

Appendix A: Overview of WC

This chapter will provide a brief overview of the WC System in the United States. As a result of the industrial age and the growing numbers of industrial injuries, laws were developed to protect workers injured on the job.

WC laws are state specific. Although governed by state statute, they are all focused on the overall goal: protection of the injured worker by providing medical care that will return him or her to the pre-injury status and do so in an expedient manner.

The injured worker is automatically entitled to receive certain benefits when he or she suffers an occupational disease or accidental personal injury arising out of the scope and course of employment. Benefits may include cash or wage-loss benefits, medical and vocational rehabilitation benefits, and, in case of the accidental death of an employee, benefits to dependents. Generally, independent contractors are not entitled to WC benefits, and in some states, domestic and agricultural workers are only partially covered or may be excluded from coverage.

Although a worker whose injury is covered by the WC System may not sue the employer, he or she may still sue a third party whose negligence contributed to the work injury. The WC System also compensates dependents of employees who are killed in work-related incidents.

Who is Eligible for WC Benefits

All employees of a business are protected by WC laws. Independent contractors, as well as others who may perform a service in an unconventional employer–employee relationship, may not be covered by WC.

WC is State-Specific in Statutes

As WC is state specific, so are the benefit coverage and reimbursement fees as well as the cost to employers.

Appendix B: Overview of Medicare

Introduction

Medicare is a Federal Health Program, which in 1965 was created by Congress for individuals of 65 years or older. The Medicare Program was expanded in 1972 to include some individuals under the age of 65 with specific disabilities and persons with ESRD. Medicare eligibility is *not* based on income or assets, unlike Medicaid. Medicare is administered by CMS, which is the nation's largest health insurance program.

The Medicare Program is divided into four parts: Medicare Part A, Medicare Part B, Medicare Part C, and Medicare Part D.

Medicare Part A is available at no charge for most individuals over the age of 65 who have worked at least 40 quarters of Medicare-covered employment.

Part A of Medicare generally covers inpatient hospital care, skilled nursing facility care, hospice care, and some skilled home health care. These services generally have limitations. There are deductibles and premiums, which historically increase yearly.

*2009 Part A premium is $244.00 per month for people having 30–39 quarters of Medicare-covered employment.

2009 *Part A premium is $443.00 per month for people who are not otherwise eligible for premium-free hospital insurance and have less than 30 quarters of Medicare-covered employment.

*Part B is purchased with a monthly premium and is based on a beneficiary's annual income, as required by the Medicare Modernization Act in 2007; $96.40 is the average monthly premium cost in 2009. Beneficiaries with higher incomes may have higher premiums. There is a yearly deductible of $135.50 associated with Part B. Part B coverage includes home health services, durable medical equipment, independent lab services, and physician's office lab services. Part B assists with payment for these covered services and supplies when they are deemed "medically necessary."

In 2009, the threshold amount was increased for disabled individuals. This amount may fluctuate yearly and will be used to determine if the individual's earnings are high enough to replace SSI and Medicaid benefits.

Medicare Eligibility and Coverage

Part A

Generally, Medicare Part A coverage is available on a national basis, and at no cost to individuals aged 65 or older (who have worked and paid Medicare taxes, or have a spouse who has done so for at least 10 years), younger people with disabilities, and patients withESRD.

Part A coverage is also available at no cost to those aged 65 or above who

- Are receiving retirement benefits from Social Security or the Railroad Retirement Board
- Have a record of Medicare-covered employment (or a spouse with such a record)

An individual who has not worked or paid Medicare taxes, is 65 or older, and is a citizen or permanent resident of the United States *may* be able to buy Part A. Those not receiving Social Security benefits 3 months before their 65th birthday will need to apply for Medicare. Individuals who apply close to their 65th birthday may avoid higher premiums.

Part A coverage may be available to people under age 65 without having to pay premiums if they are

- Entitled to Social Security or Railroad Retirement Board disability benefits for 24 months
- Diagnosed with amyotrophic lateral sclerosis (also known as Lou Gehrig's disease), becoming eligible to take advantage of Medicare benefits either at that time or at the first month they receive disability benefits, whichever is later
- Kidney dialysis or kidney transplant patients
- Receiving Social Security benefits (in which case the recipient may be automatically enrolled in Part B)

Medicare Part A (which may be referred to as "hospital insurance") helps cover inpatient hospital care, critical access hospitals (small facilities that give limited outpatient and inpatient services to people in rural areas), and skilled nursing facilities. It also covers hospice care and some home health care. Some guidelines regarding Part A coverage are listed below to provide an overview of reimbursable services (patient-specific information may influence the level of allowable coverage). A beneficiary may use any provider that accepts Medicare. *There are limitations associated with some of the coverage listed below.*

Hospital stays: Semiprivate rooms, meals, general nursing, and other hospital services and supplies are covered. This includes care received in critical access hospitals and inpatient mental health care, but does *not* include private duty nursing, a television, a telephone, or a private room unless medically necessary.

Skilled nursing facility care: A semiprivate room, meals, skilled nursing, and rehabilitative services. Other services and supplies are covered after a related 3-day hospital stay.

Home health care: This includes durable medical equipment (such as wheelchairs, hospital beds, oxygen, and walkers), home health aide services, medical supplies, medical social services, occupational therapy, part-time skilled nursing care, physical therapy, speech-language therapy, and other services.

Hospice care: Medical and support services from a Medicare-approved hospice are covered for patients with a terminal illness, including medications for symptom control and pain relief, and other services not otherwise covered by Medicare. Hospice care is given in the home. However, short-term hospital and inpatient respite care (care given to a hospice patient by another caregiver so that the usual caregiver can rest) may also be covered.

Blood: Transfusions at a hospital or skilled nursing facility during a covered stay are covered by Medicare.

Medicare Part B

The premium for Part B must be paid by the beneficiary if they elect to enroll in the program. The monthly premium is typically deducted from an individual's Social Security, railroad retirement, or civil service retirement check. For those who do not receive these retirement benefits, Part B premiums are paid every 3 months. There are deductibles required as well.

Medicare Part B assists with the coverage of certain aspects of physicians' services, outpatient hospital care, PT, OT, ST, certain diagnostic testing, DME, and some specific home health care as well as other medically necessary services that Part A does not cover. The following guidelines provide an overview of reimbursable services, however are subject to change. Therefore, maintaining an understanding of the current Medicare coverage is imperative. Individual-specific information may impact the level of allowable coverage.

Medical and other services: This covers doctors' services (but not routine physical exams), outpatient medical and surgical services and supplies, diagnostic tests, ambulatory surgery center facility fees for approved procedures, and durable medical equipment (such as wheelchairs, hospital beds, oxygen, and walkers). This may include second surgical opinions, outpatient mental health care, and outpatient physical and occupational therapy, including speech-language therapy.

Blood: Transfusions are covered during an outpatient visit or as part of another Part B service.

Clinical laboratory services: This includes blood tests, urinalysis, and other laboratory tests ordered by physicians.

Home health care: Coverage includes part-time *skilled* nursing care, physical therapy, occupational therapy, speech-language therapy, home health aide services, medical social services, durable medical equipment (such as wheelchairs, hospital beds, oxygen, and walkers), medical supplies, and other services.

Outpatient hospital services: Coverage includes a variety of physician-ordered hospital services and supplies for outpatients.

Examples of additional Medicare Part B coverage, with possible limitations, may include the following:

- Ambulance services when other transportation would endanger the patient's health
- Artificial eyes

- Braces for arms, legs, back, and neck
- Chiropractic services for manipulation of the spine to correct a subluxation (limited in duration)
- Emergency care
- Eyeglasses—one pair of standard frames after cataract surgery with an intraocular lens
- Immunosuppressive drug therapy for transplant patients covered by Medicare if the transplant was paid for by Medicare
- Kidney dialysis
- Treatment for macular degeneration of the eye ("wet" age-related) using ocular photodynamic therapy with verteporfin
- Medical nutrition therapy, with a doctor's referral, for patients with diabetes or kidney disease
- Medical supplies such as ostomy bags, surgical dressings, splints, casts, and some diabetic supplies
- Outpatient prescription drugs (very limited, e.g., some cancer medications)
- Preventive services–pap tests, pelvic exams, and clinical breast exams
- Prosthetic devices, including breast prosthesis after mastectomy
- Prosthetic limbs and replacement parts
- Second opinion by a doctor (in some cases)
- Services of practitioners such as clinical social workers, physician assistants, and nurse practitioners
- Telemedicine services in some rural areas
- Therapeutic shoes for people with diabetes (in some cases)
- Transplants of the heart, lung, kidney, pancreas, large/small intestine, bone marrow, cornea, and liver (under certain conditions when performed at approved facilities)
- X-rays, MRIs, CT scans, ECGs, and some other diagnostic tests

Medicare Part A and Part B: Nonallowable Items and Services

The original Medicare plan does not cover all treatments, items, and services that a Medicare beneficiary may require. Healthcare costs *typically not* covered by Medicare include the following:

- Acupuncture
- Deductibles, coinsurance, or copayments
- Dental care and dentures (in most cases)
- Cosmetic surgery
- Custodial care (help with bathing, dressing, toileting, and eating) at home or in a nursing home
- Health care received outside the United States (except in limited cases)
- Hearing aids and exams
- Orthopedic shoes
- Outpatient prescription drugs (with only a few exceptions)
- Routine foot care (with only a few exceptions)
- Routine eye care and most eyeglasses
- Routine physical exams
- Screening tests (except those for breast, cervical, vaginal, colorectal, and prostate cancer, and glaucoma, bone mass measurements, and diabetes monitoring)
- Vaccinations (except those for flu, pneumonia, and hepatitis B)

Medicare Part C

In 1997, Congress created an alternative to Parts A and B, with the development of Medicare Part C, also known as the Medicare Advantage Program. Part C offers a Medicare beneficiary an alternative to the traditional Medicare programs, often providing coverage options not typically found or covered by Medicare Parts A and B. Part C may be an Health Maintenance Organization (HMO), Preferred Provider Organization (PPO) or private fee-for-service program. While Medicare is a National Insurance Program, not all of the Part C alternative programs will be available across the nation. As Part C is generally provided by private companies, the coverage, premiums, copayments, and conditions may vary with not only the provider but also the geographic location. Traditionally, Medicare Choice (Part C) will enhance the standard benefits of Medicare, with a prescription drug plan, preventive care, some dental and vision services, and wellness programs. The beneficiary must be enrolled in Parts A and B and continue to maintain Part B payments. Typically, these providers assisting with coordinating represent a reduction in out-of-pocket expenses.

Medicaid–Medicare

Medic*aid* is an economic-based program that may aid a Medi*care* beneficiary with a low income and limited resources. For the individual who is eligible for full Medicare coverage, Medicaid may supplement Medicare coverage by providing services and/or supplies that are available under their state-specific Medicaid program. A Medicare beneficiary with limited income and resources may obtain limited assistance for out-of-pocket medical expenses from their State Medicaid program. Often, these services include nursing facility care beyond Medicare's 100-day limit, prescription drugs, eyeglasses, and hearing aids. When there is dual Medicaid and Medicare eligibility, Medicare may pay for covered services prior to Medicaid payment for the balance; however, this is limited to the maximum payment limit.

Individuals who were receiving Medicare due to disability, but have lost entitlement to Medicare benefits because they returned to work, may purchase Medicare Part A. If the individual has income below 200% of the FPL and resources at or below twice the standard allowed under the SSI program, and they are not otherwise eligible for Medicaid benefits, they may qualify to have Medicaid pay their monthly Medicare Part A premiums as Qualified Disabled and Working Individuals (QDWIs).

State Children's Health Insurance Program

The State Children's Health Insurance Program (SCHIP) is a program initiated by the Balanced Budget Act. In addition to letting states develop or expand existing insurance programs, SCHIP provides more federal funds for states to expand Medicaid eligibility to include more uninsured children. With certain exceptions, these are low-income children who would not qualify for Medicaid based on the plan that was in effect on April 15, 1997.

Funds from SCHIP also may be used to provide medical assistance to children during a presumptive eligibility period for Medicaid. This is one of several options from which states may select to provide healthcare coverage for more children, as prescribed in the Title XXI program of the Balanced Budget Act.

Appendix C: Overview of Social Security

On August 14, 1935, The Social Security Act was signed by President Franklin Roosevelt. Taxes supporting it were collected for the first time in January 1937, and the first one-time, lump sum payments were made that same month. Regular monthly benefits started in January 1940, and in 1956 disability benefits were added.

Three major programs administered by the SSA are general retirement benefits, SSI, and SSDI.

Eligibility for Retirement Benefits: 40 Credits

Anyone born in 1929 or later must accumulate 40 Social Security credits to be eligible for retirement benefits. Up to four credits may be earned each year, which means that individuals are required to be employed for at least 10 years, or 40 quarters, to receive retirement benefits. During an individual's working years, earnings covered by Social Security are posted to their Social Security record, and credits accrue based on those earnings. Each year, the amount of earnings needed for a credit rises as average earning levels rise. The actual earnings are adjusted or indexed to consider changes in average wages, since the year the earnings were received. The indexed monthly earnings are then calculated during the years in which the earnings were greatest.

For people who become disabled before the age of 62, the number of credits needed depends on their age at the onset of disability, with at least six credits required. Regardless of disability, no one can voluntarily contribute money to buy additional credits; they are accumulated only as a result of annual earnings.

Most people earn more credits than the minimum required to receive Social Security benefits; however, accumulating more than 40 does not increase an individual's benefit amount. It is the average earnings throughout the working years that determine the monthly payment.

Social Security bases its calculations on gross wages earned before any payroll deductions for income tax, Social Security tax, dues, insurance, or other deductions by the employer.

Exclusions in the calculation of gross wages include

- Earned interest
- Inheritance payments
- Investment income
- Individual Retirement Account distributions
- Pension payments

Credits and Earnings

While 40 credits of employment are needed to qualify for benefits, the amount of benefits is based on average earnings calculated through a formula set by law, not the number of credits. An individual may not be entitled to the maximum benefit simply because he or she accumulated 40 credits. Typically, the amount is calculated based on the average of a person's best 35 years of earnings. Younger workers may qualify with fewer credits, and family members who qualify for benefits based on a worker's record are not required to have earned work credits. There is no minimum age requirement, but individuals must have worked long enough and recently enough under Social Security to qualify for disability benefits.

Eligibility for Retirement Benefits: Age and Medicare

An individual may begin collecting Social Security retirement benefits at age 62, but Medicare benefits cannot be collected until age 65. Benefit amounts are reduced for those who receive them prior to full retirement age. Medical insurance coverage may continue through the employer or may need to be purchased from a private insurance company until the individual reaches age 65 when Medicare eligibility is obtained.

Full-Retirement Age

Full-retirement age was 65 for many years. However, beginning with individuals born in 1938, full-retirement age is gradually increasing until it reaches 67 for people born after 1959. The following chart shows the steps by which the age increases.

Year of Birth	Full-Retirement Age
1937 or earlier	65 years
1938	65 years and 2 months
1939	65 years and 4 months
1940	65 years and 6 months
1941	65 years and 8 months
1942	65 years and 10 months
1943–1954	66 years
1955	66 years and 2 months
1956	66 years and 4 months
1957	66 years and 6 months
1958	66 years and 8 months
1959	66 years and 10 months
1960 and later	67 years

Supplemental Security Income

SSA service programs that provide benefits to individuals based on *disability* are the SSI program and the SSDI program.

SSI represents benefits made by the SSA, which provide monthly income to people who are 65 years or older, are blind or disabled, and have limited income and financial resources. Disabled children under 18 years with limited income and resources may also be eligible. SSI payments are funded through general tax revenues and do not require the recipient to have a significant work history or to have made tax contributions to Social Security under FICA. *The goal is to provide a minimum income level for a disabled individual. SSI does not pay for medical care.*

Eligibility requires an individual to be a resident of the United States and a citizen or a noncitizen lawfully admitted for permanent residence. Also, some noncitizens granted special status by the Department of Homeland Security may be eligible.

Entitlement Programs:

- Medicare
- SSD

Eligibility is based on quarters worked (earned quarters) and level of disability.

Financial Need Programs:

- Medicaid
- SSI

Eligibility is based on *financial* needs and level of disability.

Definition of Disability

Disability as defined by Social Security includes the following: the individual must be unable to do *any* kind of substantial gainful work due to a physical or mental impairment (or a combination of impairments) expected to either last at least 12 months or end in death.

An individual who cannot do the work performed in the past due to a medical condition, age, education, and past work experience must be considered in determining reasonable vocational alternatives. Someone with transferable skills who can work in another field (even if the skills are different or the pay is less than that of his or her previous work) cannot be considered disabled for Social Security purposes.

Disability Determination

Disability determination is based on five basic criteria:

- *Ability to return to the same field of work:* If an individual's condition is severe but not as severe as impairments on SSA's list, the agency determines whether the condition prevents him or her from returning to work performed in the last 15 years. If he or she can resume previous employment, the claim is denied. If he or she cannot, SSA evaluates the claim further.
- *Ability to work in a different field:* For those who cannot return to work performed in the last 15 years, SSA evaluates whether they can do any other type of work. SSA considers an individual's education, past work experience, and transferable skills, and reviews the job demands of occupations as identified by the Department of Labor. If it is determined that an individual cannot perform any type of work, the application will typically be approved. If other work in a different field is possible, the claim will be denied.
- *Current employment status:* An individual who is working and earning a monthly average of more than the current threshold will typically be denied disability status.
- *Nature of the disability or condition:* SSA lists impairments that automatically qualify an individual as disabled. Other people are qualified if SSA considers their impairment as severe

as that of conditions on the list. If SSA determines that the disability or condition is not equal in severity, the individual's vocational circumstances are evaluated.

■ *Severity of the disability or condition:* If functional impairments affect the individual's ability to work, SSA will typically consider their disability claim.

5-Months Waiting Period

An individual with a disability expected to last at least 12 months may file a claim at the onset of the condition and begin receiving benefits after a 5-months waiting period. The intent is to help ensure that *only* individuals with long-term disabilities receive Social Security disability benefits, and to avoid duplicating payments by private disability plans and employer sick-pay plans during the early months of disability, as the timeframe is sufficient for most temporary disabilities to be corrected or for the individual to show signs of probable recovery within 12 months.

Disability Benefits and Medicare

SSA will automatically enroll individuals in Medicare after disability benefits have been collected for 2 years (beginning with the month of entitlement, *not* the month the first check was received). Medicare for patients with amyotrophic lateral sclerosis (Lou Gehrig's disease) begins with the month an individual becomes entitled to disability benefits.

Retirement and Disability Benefits

When a person reaches full retirement age, his or her benefits are called retirement benefits instead of disability benefits; however, no other change occurs.

Social Security Disability Insurance

Eligibility for SSI disability payments is based on financial need. Eligibility for SSDI benefits is based on prior work under Social Security. Under this program, payment is available to workers who are disabled, the child of an insured disabled worker, or the widow, widower, or surviving divorced spouse of an insured disabled worker.

Work Credits

To be insured, a worker must have earned at least 20 credits in the 10 years ending with the one in which he or she became disabled.

For people who become disabled prior to age 62, the number of credits needed depends on their age at the onset of disability, with a minimum of six credits required. The following general guidelines apply:

■ An individual under the age of 24 may qualify if six credits have been earned in the 3-year period ending with the onset of disability
■ An individual aged 24–30 may qualify if he or she has credit for having worked half the time between age 21 and becoming disabled
■ SSDI earnings analysis

The SSA uses the term "substantial gainful activity" (SGA) to determine if work is substantial enough to make a person ineligible for benefits. Monthly SGA earning limits are automatically adjusted annually based on increases in the national average wage index. The SSA evaluates the work activity of individuals claiming or receiving disability benefits in the SSDI program. Beginning January 1, 2009, an SSDI beneficiary who is not blind can earn up to $980.00 a month and remain eligible for benefits. For individuals who are blind, the monthly 2009 SGA amount was increased to $1,640.00.

Disability Benefits and WC

WC or other public disability payments may be impacted by Social Security benefits.

The Social Security disability payment will be reduced so that the combined amount of the Social Security benefit received by the individual (and family, where applicable) plus the WC payment (and/or public disability payment) does not exceed 80% of the recipient's average current earnings from any source.

Public disability payments may include civil service disability benefits, military disability benefits, state temporary disability benefits, and state or local government retirement benefits that are based on disability.

SSI:

- Funded by general tax revenues
- Eligibility *not* based on significant work history
- Eligibility and payment amount will be based on income and other resources (in 2009, the basic monthly payment was $674.00 for an individual and $1,011.00 for a couple)
- Needs based and only paid to a qualified individual
- No child/spouse benefits
- Savings and other assets impact eligibility
- State supplemented

SSDI:

- Based on prior work under Social Security (the individual must have earned a minimum of 20 credits within the past 10 years, ending in the year in which he or she became disabled. Younger workers requirements are different. Refer to the SSA site for specific information on the younger worker and SSDI)
- Child/spouse benefits
- An eligible beneficiary may include an injured worker, the child of an injured worker, the widow/widower of an injured worker, a divorced spouse, and individuals who are injured and remain working
- Funded by taxes paid by workers, employers, and self-employed persons
- In 2009, an individual could earn up to $980.00 per month and maintain eligibility (blind individuals could earn up to $1,640.00)
- No state supplement

These programs require the individual to be a resident of the United States, a legal citizen, or a noncitizen legally admitted for permanent residence. The goal of both programs is to assist individuals who are disabled or blind and have limited financial or income resources. In either program, the recipient must demonstrate inability to perform substantial gainful employment due to physical and/or mental impairment, which is anticipated to either last a minimum of 12 months or end in death. Refer to the SSA website for outlying information.

Chapter 12

Fraud
Government-Sponsored Health Plans and General Case Evaluations

Rebecca S. Busch, RN, MBA, CCM, CBM, CHS—III, CFE, FIALCP, FHFMA, CPC

Contents

Objectives

- Understand the mechanics of health care reimbursement
- Understand the elements of health care fraud
- Provide a case evaluation infrastructure for government sponsored health plans

Introduction

Fraud is defined as an intentional deception resulting in injury to another. Assessment of fraud within a government-sponsored health plan is complex by definition. This chapter will focus on distinguishing normal behavior patterns from those that are potentially fraudulent and which should trigger a more thorough review. Materials and data that are appropriate for such a review are discussed and applied to various scenarios. Appropriate guidelines for drawing conclusions from the information and materials reviewed are presented. After a review of this chapter, the legal nurse consultant will have a fundamental guide and standardized approach for the evaluation of cases involving potential fraud and/or abuse within a government-sponsored benefit plan.

Definition of Fraud

The elements of fraud are the following:

- Misrepresentation of a material fact
- Knowledge of the falsity of the misrepresentation or ignorance of its truth
- Intent
- A victim acting on the misrepresentation
- Damage to the victim

Another aspect of fraud that is important to understand is what is commonly referred to as the "Fraud Triangle" (Wells, 2001). The elements of the triangle include opportunity, pressure, and rationalization. Simply put, an individual faced with financial pressures finds an opportunity to initiate a fraud scheme and then rationalizes the behavior.

Review of the cases of potential fraud may be guided by the following checklist: (Please note that each question should be followed with "If so, determine who, what, where, why, when, and how?")

- Did any misrepresentation of a material fact occur?
- Did the perpetrator(s) have knowledge of the falsity of the misrepresentation or ignorance of its truth?
- Did the perpetrator(s) demonstrate intent?
- Did a victim act on the misrepresentation?
- What was the damage to the victim?
- In evaluating the perpetrator(s), how was the opportunity created? What pressures were involved? Finally, how was the behavior rationalized?

This model can be applied to any industry or issue in which fraud is the theme of the case review. When reviewing potential fraud cases in the healthcare environment, it is important to note that they typically take the following forms:

- Manipulating reimbursement and submitting a false claim
- Manipulating health information for advantageous gain or avoidance of liability
- Selling a fabricated, counterfeit product or service

The following section will provide applicable concepts that specifically impact the healthcare industry.

Overview of Legislation that Impacts Healthcare Fraud

The amendments to the Health Insurance Portability and Accountability Act (HIPAA) of 1996 further defined and established the scope of healthcare fraud via government-sponsored programs. The act defines a federal healthcare offense as "a violation of, or criminal conspiracy to violate" specific provisions of the U.S. Code, "if the violation or conspiracy relates to a health care benefit program" 18 U.S.C. 24 9(a). A healthcare benefit plan is "any public or private plan or contract, affecting commerce, under which any medical benefit, item or service is provided to any individual, and includes any individual or entity who is providing a medical benefit, item, or service which payment may be made under the plan or contract" 18 U.S.C. 24 (b). Finally, healthcare fraud is defined as knowingly and willfully executing a scheme to defraud a healthcare benefit program or obtaining, "by means of false or fraudulent pretenses, representations, or promises, any of the money or property owned by . . . any health care benefit program" 18 U.S.C 1347. HIPAA establishes specific criminal sanctions for offenses against both private and public health plans (Busch, 2007).

HIPAA federalized the crime of healthcare fraud by making it illegal for anyone to knowingly and willfully do the following:

- Defraud any healthcare benefit program or obtain by means of false representations any money or property of a healthcare benefit program
- Make "false statements" that criminalizes any false or fictitious statements "in any matter involving a healthcare benefit program"
- Embezzle, convert or steal any funds, property or assets of a healthcare benefit program
- Obstruct, delay, prevent, or mislead the investigation of federal healthcare offenses

Although many statutes address the issue of fraud, this chapter will focus on those that are most closely related to the healthcare industry. For example, a perpetrator could be prosecuted under the Mail Fraud Act for an offense that may be a healthcare fraud scheme. However, based on the evidence, the prosecution may choose statutes that are not directly defined within the health domain. Statutes for consideration within the scope of this chapter include

- Federal False Claims Act (FCA)
- Civil FCA
- State False Claims Statutes
- Medicaid False Claims Statutes
- HIPAA
- Stark I, II, and III

- Civil Monetary Penalties
- False Statements

The Federal FCA is governed by Title 18. This Act makes it illegal to present a claim upon or against the United States that the claimant knows to be "false, fictitious, or fraudulent." (18, U.S.C., § 287) (Note that this statute is distinct from the Civil FCA.) The original FCA dates back to the Civil War and was passed by Abraham Lincoln to counter widespread fraud by suppliers to the Union Army. In 1986, amendments were instituted making the following changes:

- Increasing penalties
- Clarifying standards and procedures for bringing fraud suits
- Providing new incentives for private citizens to report suspected frauds

This criminal statute applies to any federal government department or agency. In 1986, amendments were made to this Act mandating both fine and imprisonment for all convictions. The government must prove three elements to obtain a conviction for Medicare or Medicaid fraud under the FCA:

- The defendant presented a claim (demand for money or property) to the government seeking reimbursement for medical services or goods
- The claim was false, fictitious, or fraudulent
- The defendant had both knowledge of the claim's falsity and the intent to submit it

In addition to bringing a criminal action, the government may also bring a parallel civil action seeking relief (Busch, 2008b). The new law affords the government the opportunity to recover three times the amount of sustained damages. Civil penalties for each false claim range from $5,000 to $10,000. Criminal violations can incur fines of $250,000 for individuals and $500,000 for corporations. In addition, imprisonment can be up to 10 years. It is important to remember that the burden of proof in a civil case is by preponderance of the evidence. In a criminal case, the burden is beyond a reasonable doubt.

This Act affords the private citizen new incentives to report suspected frauds. It also gives *whistleblowers* extensive protection from harassment and retaliation from employers. Extensive protection is given to employees who sue their employers, including providing safety and preventing harassment, firing, demotion, suspension, or reprisals of any kind. The law provides "make whole" relief, including reinstatement with full security, back pay with interest, and compensation for any damages sustained as a result of discrimination.

The Civil FCA is governed by Title 31. The key points include the following:

- Any person who knowingly presents, or causes to be presented, to the U.S. government a false or fraudulent claim for payment or approval knowingly makes, uses, or causes to be made or used, a false record or statement to get a false or fraudulent claim paid or approved by the government or conspires to defraud the government by getting a false or fraudulent claim allowed or paid violated the Act.
- Those who violate the Act are liable to the government for a civil penalty of not less than $5,000 and not more than $10,000 for each false claim filed, plus treble damages sustained by the government. 31, U.S.C., §3729 (a).

Several states have followed suit and initiated a similar legislation via State False Claims Statutes that provide remedies for false claims and other frauds against state healthcare programs.

California adopted the first one in 1987. Other states include Illinois (720 ILL. Comp. Stat. 5/46–5), Florida (FLA.STAT.ANN. §68.081 through 78.092), and Louisiana (LA.Rev.Stat.Ann. §46.437.1 through 46.440.4). Contacting an individual state's Insurance Department is helpful in determining if statutes address both Medicaid programs and private insurers.

The Medicaid False Claims Statute addresses the following actions:

- Making false statements
- Representations made in connection with any applications for claim of benefits or payment
- Disposal of assets under a federal healthcare program
- The government must prove four elements to sustain a conviction under this statute:
  - The defendant made, or caused to be made, a statement of material fact in an application for payment or benefits under a federal healthcare program
  - The statement or representation was false
  - The defendant knowingly and willfully made the statement
  - The defendant knew the statement to be false

Significant enforcement activity occurs via the state law as well and ranges from provisions to general larceny. Statutes specifically intended to fight healthcare fraud have been adopted. Additional legislation includes the state FCA, anti-kickback laws, and self-referral statutes. In addition, many states have established Medicaid Fraud Control Units and others have specific agencies focused only on healthcare fraud. The insurance fraud division of an individual state is an excellent resource for determining that particular state's legislative activity regarding fraud.

Stark Laws

Stark I was enacted as part of the Omnibus Budget Reconciliation Act of 1989 (H.R. 3299, Section 6204). The focus of this statute is to prevent inappropriate financial influences over physicians' decisions about the best care for their patients. The overall market problem that resulted from this statute is that in practice, the prohibitions have caused uncertainty among providers as they struggle to respond to various market forces on cost constraints. The self-referral law, as enacted in 1989, prohibited a physician from referring a patient to a clinical laboratory with which he or she (or an immediate family member) has a financial relationship.

- Stark I initiated the rule that a physician or immediate family member may not have a financial interest with certain entities providing clinical laboratory services, and in cases in which they did, they may not bill Medicare or Medicaid.
- Stark II provided additional amendments and expanded the referral and billing prohibitions to additional "designated health services."

The Phase III Stark Final Rule (CMS-1810-F) is officially titled "Medicare Program; Physicians' Referrals to Health Care Entities with Which They Have Financial Relationships (Phase III)." This is commonly called Stark III, as it is an extension of Stark I and Stark II, which sets limits on self-dealing and kickbacks with respect to treatment of Medicare and Medicaid patients. The effective date of Stark III was December 4, 2007. The provisions include modifications such as

- Additional physician recruitment restrictions
- More flexibility in complying with nonmonetary compensation limits

- Reduction of the administrative burden of complying with some exceptions to the Stark limitations
- Clarification of Centers for Medicare and Medicaid Services' (CMS) interpretation of existing regulations

Elements of the offense include several attributes. To establish a Stark violation, the government must show:

- A financial relationship between a healthcare entity and physician; a financial relationship includes an ownership or investment interest in an entity by a physician or an immediate family member, or a compensation arrangement between a physician or his immediate family member and the entity. The prohibited compensation arrangements include direct or indirect remunerations that are made in cash or kind.
- A referral by the physician to the entity for designated health services.
- A referral includes a request for any designated health service payable under Medicare or Medicaid. It is important to note that because Stark II does not have an intent requirement, strict liability is imposed for referrals whenever a financial relationship exists.
- The submission of a claim for the services and an entity receiving a prohibited referral may not make a Medicare claim. Such an entity is also forbidden from billing any individual, third-party payer, or other entity for any designated health services for which the physician made the referral.
- The absence of an exception or safe harbor provisions. The Stark amendments contain several exceptions for certain financial arrangements. These exceptions fall into three categories:
  i. Exceptions that are applicable to both physician ownership or investment interests and compensation arrangements.
  ii. Exceptions for ownership or investment interests only.
  iii. Exceptions for compensation arrangements only.

In 1995, the Congress extended the law to prohibit a physician from referring patients to providers of 10 other categories of healthcare services if the physician or an immediate family member has a financial relationship with the service provider. The 10 affected services are: physical therapy (PT) services; occupational therapy (OT) services; radiology services and supplies; radiation therapy services and supplies; durable medical equipment (DME) and supplies; parenteral and enteral nutrients, equipment, and supplies; prosthetics, orthotics, and prosthetic devices and supplies; home health services; outpatient prescription drugs; and inpatient and outpatient hospital services. The law also prohibits an entity from billing for services provided as the result of a prohibited referral.

Overview of Healthcare Expenditures and Reimbursement Methodologies

One of the most complicated factors within the healthcare market is the complexity of reimbursement methodologies. This complexity co-exists in both the private and public markets. Medicare is a health insurance program for

- People aged 65 or older
- People under age 65 with certain disabilities

- People of all ages with end-stage renal disease (ESRD) (permanent kidney failure requiring dialysis or a kidney transplant)

It is important to note that within Medicare, patients are referred to as beneficiaries, while in the Medicaid program, they are referred to as recipients.

Medicare coverage incorporates Parts A, B, and D. Medicare Part A (Hospital Insurance) helps cover inpatient care in hospitals, including critical access hospitals (CAHs), and skilled nursing facilities, but not custodial or long-term care. It also helps cover hospice care and some home health care. Beneficiaries must meet certain conditions to get these benefits. Most people do not pay a premium for Part A because they or a spouse already paid for it through their payroll taxes while working.

Medicare Part B (Medical Insurance) helps cover doctors' services and outpatient care. It also covers some other medical services that Part A does not cover, such as some of the services of physical and occupational therapists, and some home health care. Part B helps pay for these covered services and supplies when they are medically necessary. Most people pay a monthly premium for Part B.

Medicare Part D was introduced in January 2006 as a voluntary outpatient drug benefit program, with private companies providing the coverage. Beneficiaries choose the drug plan and pay a monthly premium. Like any other insurance, if a beneficiary decides not to enroll in a drug plan when they are first eligible, they may pay a penalty if they choose to join later (http://www.cms.hhs.gov/MedicareGenInfo/). Medicare Part D includes stand-alone prescription programs (PDPs), Medicare advantage (MA), and prescription drug plans (MA-PDs). For the legal nurse consultant reviewing cases involving this complex program, the terms of the administration of the plan will need to be reviewed. From a patient perspective, it is also important to look at the current year offering by plan option. This information is available through www.cms.hhs.gov by searching Medicare Part D.

This section will introduce the methodologies that are currently utilized by Medicare to reimburse Medicare-approved services. Table 12.1 represents a list of payment systems utilized within government-sponsored programs. The detailed formulas may be found at the CMS website (http://www.cms.hhs.gov/home/medicare.asp).

CMS has a payment methodology for each of the services noted below. In evaluating a case it is important to identify which payment methodology may be involved. Obtaining the details will then provide the information that needs to be collected from the parties identified in the case that you are reviewing. Please note that any audit, review, or case analysis would in essence be about making sure that the rules of the reimbursement model were being followed.

- *Oxygen and oxygen equipment payment system:* Medicare may use data from the Federal Employee Health Plan to set a specific fee schedule for these types of items. They are published on the internet for CMS. The goal for DME is for the government program to enter into a competitive bidding process with suppliers.
- *Skilled nursing facility services payment system:* Skilled nursing reimbursement is based on a prospective payment system. Each Skilled Nursing Facility (SNF) has a base rate and is computed with factors such as an adjustment for geographic factors, hospital wage index, adjusted for case mix, multiplied by a Resource Utilization Group (RUG) weight which is impacted by patient characteristics. This process results in a payment determination. RUGs currently have 53 possible groupings.

Table 12.1 Overview of Payment Systems

Oxygen and oxygen equipment payment system

Skilled nursing facility services payment system

Physician services payment system

Psychiatric hospital services payment system

Rehabilitation facilities (inpatient) payment system

Outpatient therapy services payment system

MA program payment system

Outpatient dialysis services payment system

Outpatient hospital services payment system

Home healthcare services payment system

Hospice services payment system

Hospital acute inpatient services payment system

Long-term care hospitals payment system

Clinical laboratory services payment system

CAHs payment system

DME payment system

Ambulatory surgical centers payment system

- *Physician services payment system:* The physician payment system or professional services is driven by a variety of factors. They include provider characteristics, geographic designation, and so forth. Medicare uses a formula that is updated each year called the sustainable growth rate (SGR) system. The objective of this system is to keep spending on growth consistent with the economy. However, the Congress has been known to set a rate outside this formula. Physicians submit service information utilizing Healthcare Common Procedure Coding System (HCPCS) codes. The payment fee schedule is set by weights referred to as relative value units (RVUs). The weight determination is driven by several different factors and typically updated each year.
- *Psychiatric hospital services payment system:* Reimbursement is under a prospective per diem payment system. The inpatient psychiatric facility rate involves the computation of several factors: Inpatient Psychiatric Facility (IPF) per diem rate, geographic adjustment factors, hospital wage index, adjusted for facility and patient characteristics, DRG group, adjustments for daily costs, ER admission, and outlier adjustments.
- *Rehabilitation facilities (inpatient) payment system:* Reimbursement is under a prospective payment system. Inpatient rehabilitation facilities (IRFs) may be freestanding hospitals or specialized units that are hospital based. The PPS system is based on 92 intensive rehabilitation categories referred to as case-mix groups (CMGs). Patients are typically assigned based on the primary reason for the admission; for example, recovery from stroke. Once the

appropriate CMG group is selected, the calculation is processed through the facility's IRF base rate with adjustments based on geographic factors; hospital wage index; case mix index; patient characteristics such as age, comorbidities, cognitive and functional status; and the diagnosis requiring rehabilitation. Adjustments may be made for qualifying facilities and may be based on location or length of stay (LOS).

■ *Outpatient therapy services payment system:* This program pays for therapy services including PT, OT, and speech-language pathology (SLP). Reimbursement is driven by the HCPCS. Reimbursement rates are driven by a fee schedule based on RVUs. The weights are adjusted for such factors as geographic indicators, liability insurance, and complexity of service. These factors are then multiplied against any applicable modifiers for a final payment rate.

■ *MA program payment system:* The MA Program allows beneficiaries the option of receiving their benefits from private plans. Also, the beneficiary may pay additional premiums for expanded benefits. The reimbursement methodology needs to be evaluated by the specific plan chosen by the beneficiary. CMS will send out RFPs by geographic region for the private plan coverage. The calculation of rates is a blend of the RFP and other CMS factors.

■ *Outpatient dialysis services payment system:* This payment plan is focused on patients with ESRD. In 1972, the Social Security Act extended Medicare Part A and Part B benefits to individuals with ESRD. Reimbursement is calculated and determined from two potential starting points. The first is a freestanding composite rate; the second is for services rendered at a hospital which would be referred to as the hospital composite rate. These rates are adjusted for hospital wage index, geographic factors, drug add on, case mix budget neutrality factor, and adjusted case mix based on patient characteristics such as age, body mass index, and body surface area for a final payment.

■ *Outpatient hospital services payment system:* Reimbursement is driven by outpatient prospective payment system (OPPS). The services are classified using the healthcare common procedural terminology. The services are categorized into one of the ambulatory payment classifications (APCs). The services within one APC have the same payment rate. The base rate is then processed through a series of adjustments that include conversion factors, geographic factors, hospital wage index, complexity of service adjustments, policy adjustments for hospitals that qualify, such as rural facilities; the final payment determination may be further adjusted if the patient triggers a high cost outlier for an excessive LOS.

■ *Home healthcare services payment system:* These patients are generally restricted to their homes. Medicare will reimburse them on behalf of their beneficiaries' services that fall into the categories of skilled nursing care; physical, occupational, and speech therapy; medical social work; and home health-aide services. The reimbursement is typically based on 60 day (window) episodes. The patient may be designated into one of 153 home health resource groups (HHRGs) based on clinical and functional status and service use. These measurements are based on a system referred to as "Outcome and Assessment Information Sets (OASIS)." This system is divided into three categories. The first category is clinical factors; the second category is functional factors; and the third category is service utilization. A score is computed within each category. The compilation of the three scores will generate the correct HHRG designation. The actual reimbursed rate is impacted by traditional factors such as geographic index, hospital wage index, adjusted case mix, patient characteristics, and other adjustments for extraordinary outlier costs.

■ *Hospice services payment system:* Medicare will provide palliative treatment services for beneficiaries who forgo curative treatment regimens. CMS provides a list of services that are updated annually. They may include facility or home-based support and services. The reimbursement rate is a calculated daily rate. The categories of payments include routine home care (RHC), continuous home care (CHC), inpatient respite care (IRC), and general inpatient care (GIC). The actual rates are adjusted by the category, hospital wage index, and geographic location.

■ *Hospital acute inpatient services payment system:* Reimbursement is based on Medicare's acute inpatient prospective payments system (IPPS). Reimbursement is a very detailed, comprehensive, and complicated process. Additional information and literature research must be conducted and is a requirement in order to understand and comprehend the complexity of compliance. The facility reimbursement is driven initially by two important factors. The first is the patient's condition and treatment strategy. The second is the market value and condition of the facility's location. On discharge, patients are assigned a diagnosis related group (DRG). The process groups patients with similar conditions and clinical treatment regimens with the understanding that the patients in each DRG group will most likely have utilized similar resources. Currently, 743 severity-adjusted DRG groups exist. The process involves identifying a principal diagnosis, which is the condition after evaluation, along with up to eight secondary diagnoses. These secondary diagnoses may include comorbidities (conditions present on admission) and complications (issues developed during the hospital stay). The treatment or strategy used to manage the patient is defined by recording up to six procedure codes. These are CMS–DRGs. Currently, Medicare is evaluating the introduction of Medicare Severity (MS) DRGs. These new groupings and reimbursement structures are going to focus on the complications, comorbidity, and major complications. Once again the calculation rate for a specific DRG group will be impacted by geographic factors, hospital wage index, adjustments for case mix, and patient characteristics for a final payment determination.

Hospitals may receive additional payments beyond the per discharge calculation under certain circumstances. In the case of debt resulting from nonpayment by beneficiaries of deductibles and copayments, hospitals may receive additional reimbursement after reasonable efforts have been made to collect by the provider. Certain hospitals may receive additional operating and capital payments noted under "policy adjustments." Teaching hospitals may receive add-on payments to reflect care provided by medical residents or other physicians-in-training. Hospitals that treat a disproportionate share (DSH) of low-income patients may receive additional reimbursement for operating and capital payments to offset the financial impact of treating these patients. In addition, rural hospitals may receive additional payments through the sole community hospital (SCH) program. Other designations may impact reimbursement, including critical access hospital (CAH) and Medicare Dependent Hospital (MDH). It is important to note that private payers are never involved in the supplemental reimbursement that occurs. The final impact is that CMS ultimately may be paying more per patient versus the private sector due to their nonparticipation in adjustment factors that result in additional reimbursement to the hospital.

■ *Long-term care hospitals payment system:* Long term care hospitals (LTCHs) service clinically complex patients with multiple acute and/or chronic conditions. The average LOS exceeds 25 days in these settings. Services rendered are part of a prospective payment system referred to as long term diagnosis related groups (LTC-DRGs). Again, the grouping includes principal diagnosis, up to eight secondary diagnoses, up to six procedures, age, sex, and discharge status. Medicare has been shifting towards MS LTC-DRGs, which includes the base rates that are further subdivided into three potential severity levels. The actual payment will be adjusted by taking the LTCH base rate and multiplying geographic factors, hospital wage index, case mix, as well as patient characteristics such as principal and secondary diagnoses, procedures, age, sex, discharge status, and LOS.

■ *Clinical laboratory services payment system:* It provides coverage under Medicare Part B for medically necessary diagnostic and monitoring laboratory services. Medicare sets rates for at least 1100 HCPCS codes. Medicare sets fees via National Limitation Amounts (NLA). This is driven by paying for the lesser amount of the Provider Charge, the National Carrier Fee Amount, and or the NLA amount that is calculated at 74% of the medium fee schedule amount. The NLA is based on the pricing data of 56 carrier fee schedules. CMS is in the process of initiating studies on how to base the rates for laboratory tests into the future.

■ *CAHs payment system:* CAHs are small facilities limited to 25 beds. In addition, they may have up to 10 psychiatric beds, 10 rehabilitation unit beds, and home health agencies. It is estimated that about 1300 hospitals have CAH designation. They tend to be in rural areas and are not paid on the Medicare DRG prospective payment system. They are paid at 101% of the hospital's reported costs. The reimbursement is driven based on the completion of the Medicare Cost Report.

■ *DME payment system:* It provides coverage for equipment needed in the home environment. For example, in order to provide coverage for wheelchairs and respirators, the following criteria must be present: "withstand repeated use," "primarily serve a medical purpose," and "generally not be useful to a person without an illness or injury." Medicare also provides for prosthetics, orthotics, and some medications under the DME program. With respect to medication, these may include Heparin or Albuterol associated with a nebulizer. Medicare also provides coverage for additional items that can fall into 2000 categories. These categories can include: "inexpensive or routinely purchased equipment"; "items requiring frequent and substantial servicing"; "prosthetic and orthotic devices"; "capped rental items"; and "oxygen and oxygen equipment." Reimbursement rates are determined by fee schedules noted by the HCPC code. Exceptions include customized equipment and medication. These rates are determined by the regional carrier. Prices for most medications are based on the average sales price (ASP) at a factor of 106%. Drugs requiring delivery via infusion pumps are typically set at 95% of the average whole price (AWP). Another exception is home-based oxygen, which is based on pricing data from the Federal Employee Benefit Plan Price list. Again, as with any of the fee types listed, it is important to review for updated policy changes at CMS. The vendors that provide this coverage go through a bidding process. This bidding process will select 10 metropolitan statistical areas (MSAs) and eventually expand to 80 groups.

■ *Ambulatory surgical centers (ASCs) payment system:* Medicare provides coverage for free standing and hospital-based ASCs. Reimbursement is driven by surgical procedures that are classified into an APC. Please note that the payment groups are the same as the OPPS services. As with OPPS, Medicare will pay separately for the following items:
  – Corneal tissue acquisition
  – Brachytherapy sources
  – Certain radiology services
  – Many drugs
  – Implantable items

The reimbursement rate will be driven by the APC payment group that is impacted by the ASC conversion factor followed by adjustments for geographic factors, hospital wage index, complexity of service, and APC weight resulting in final payment calculation.

Case Evaluation Methodology

Methodology is "a set or system of methods, principles, and rules for regulating a given discipline, as in the arts or sciences" (Methodology, n.d.). Methodology is the cornerstone of the efficacy of your work, whether you are involved in a support role or as a potential testifying expert. The U.S. Supreme Court's decisions in *Daubert v. Merrell DowPharmaceuticals, Inc.* 509 U.S. 579 (1993) and *Kumho Tire* et al. *v. Carmichael*, et al. No. 97-1709 (1999) require that expert testimony meets the general tests of reliability and relevancy. The importance of "ensuring that an expert's testimony rests on a reliable foundation and is relevant to the task at hand" (*Daubert*) was noted. The Court provides flexible guidelines for determining the admissibility of expert evidence, noting that scientific evidence must be "grounded in the methods and procedure of science." The expert must employ the same level of intellectual rigor as he or she would outside the courtroom when working in the relevant discipline (Busch, 2006). As a result, the following case evaluation global methodology is offered (Busch, 2006):

- Step 1: Define scope of audit and case review
- Step 2: Define data necessary for evaluation
- Step 3: Define parties to be interviewed
- Step 4: Audit review and data analysis
- Step 5: Market comparison, research, analysis, and final report

In applying this methodology, three additional concepts will be introduced to initiate the steps listed. These concepts include the primary and secondary healthcare continuums along with the information continuum (IC). The following table represents the primary healthcare continuum (P-HCC, Figure 12.1) (Busch, 2008a). Please note that one episode of care will impact multiple parties within this continuum. Initially in the review of a case, it is important to identify the parties that are involved. Next, it is important to list the reimbursement methodology involved in that transaction. For example, does the case involve a dialysis patient versus an outpatient surgical patient? This chart illustrates the dynamics as well with respect to patients and plan sponsors. For example, the patient may be insured and have both Medicare and secondary private insurance. The healthcare record file may have both home-care records and hospital-based records. The key concept to understand is that the P-HCC represents direct and indirect participants in the delivery of a healthcare episode (Figure 12.1).

The implications of the P-HCC include the following sample questions:

- What type of patient is involved in the alleged scheme? Is it a Medicare recipient or a Medicaid recipient? Do they have private insurance? If yes, is it through their employer or is it individually purchased?
- What type of provider is involved? Is it a professional such as an MD, DDS, DC, or DO? Are facilities such as an acute hospital or nursing home involved?
- Are any third parties involved, for example the DME company, pharmaceutical, case manager, and/or a billing agent?
- What type of plan administrator or insurance company is involved? For example, is it the third party administrator (TPA) BCBS or United Health?
- Who is the plan sponsor? Is it a self-insured employer, government plan, or both?
- With respect to organized crime, are there any "store front" operations that are involved?

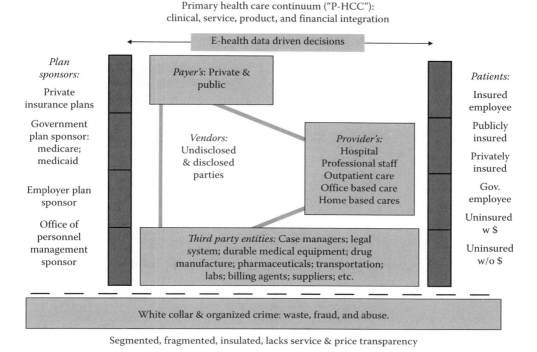

Primary health care continuum ("P-HCC"):
clinical, service, product, and financial integration

Figure 12.1. Primary healthcare continuum ("P-HCC"): clinical, service, product, and financial integration. (Copyright 2007. E-Heath Audit Guidebook, John Wiley & Sons, MBA Inc. 2007–2008. With permission.)

Organized crime is defined by the Oxford English Dictionary as "of or pertaining to a coordinated criminal organization directing operations on a large or widespread scale especially, 'organized crime (Table 12.2).'" Their features can be categorized as "activity," "organization," and "system." Health care is vulnerable. In particular, opportunities exist for illegal use of protected health information, which may generate significant revenue streams for criminal organizations that use and access both legal and illegal systems to perpetuate their criminal activity. Simply put, health care is a high-volume, cash-rich environment. Opportunities are boundless throughout our globalized economy (Busch, 2008b).

White collar crime is "a crime committed by a person of respectability and high social status in the course of his occupation" (Sutherland, 2008). Table 12.3 illustrates attributes of white collar crime (Busch, 2008a).

In the context of fraud, the concept of predication is important. Predication exists when all of the evidence and circumstances of a case "would lead a reasonable, professionally trained, and prudent individual to believe a fraud has occurred, is occurring, and/or will occur. Predication is the basis upon which an examination is commenced. Fraud examinations should not be conducted without proper predication" (Busch, 2008b). In addition, the anatomy of a fraud investigation may be noted in the following reference:

> Investigation of fraud consists of the multitude of steps necessary to resolve allegations
> of fraud—interviewing witnesses, assembling evidence, writing reports, and dealing

Table 12.2 Attributes of Organized Crime

Key Feature	Characterization of Organized Crime	Modern Technology
Activity	Organized crime = provision of illegal goods and services	Examples: Sale of new identities. Sale of medically unnecessary *legitimate* medications, health products, and procedures. Sale of *counterfeit* medications, health products, and procedures. Illegal and unethical marketing and recruitment schemes. Stealing resources and money from government programs, provider delivery systems, payer systems, and vendor systems. Intrastate or international theft of all of the above activity. Various schemes include: rent-a-patient, pill mill, and drop box
Organization	Organized crime = complex	Organization—complex layered, multidisciplined, multiprofessional, and highly skilled
System	Organized crime = integration of legal and illegal structures	Banking systems, industry specific vendors, employers, health care and payer systems, electronic mediums, and laws and regulations by country

Source: Busch, R. (2008a). *Electronic health records An audit and internal control guide.* Hoboken: Wiley & Sons. With permission.

Table 12.3 Characteristics of Organized Crime

Key Feature	Characterization of White Collar Crime	Modern Technology
Activity	Crimes committed by the affluent or individuals in position of influence in the normal course of business. They tend to be self-dealing in nature	Embezzlement; misappropriation of resources; collusion, price-fixing, and false advertising; illegal pollution; false financials; substandard products; illegal tax avoidance; illegal sale of unsafe products; illegal unsafe working conditions; misrepresentation of professionals, product, and service; false research; sale of unnecessary medical services; kickbacks; undisclosed commissions; other financial misrepresentations and/or falsifications
Organization	Individual or collective on behalf of the organization	Organization—complex layered, multi-disciplined, multiprofessional, and highly skilled
System	Crime = intermingle with legitimate business activity–transparent	Banking systems, executive office, licensed professionals, industry specific vendors, employers, health care and payer systems, electronic mediums, and laws and regulations by country

Source: Busch, R. (2008a). *Electronic health records an audit and internal control guide.* Hoboken: Wiley & Sons. With permission.

with prosecutors and the courts. The investigation of fraud, because it deals with the individual rights of others, must be conducted only with adequate cause of predication. (*Fraud Examiners Manual*)

In the context of data collection, it is important to appreciate the secondary healthcare continuum (S-HCC) which represents the components of secondary users of health information. The primary purpose in this chapter is to understand that health information generated by the P-HCC can be found among the S-HCC users of information. This channel of data may be important to appreciate during the discovery or investigation of an issue (Busch, 2008a).

The P-HCC continuum could be used as a guideline to identify nontraditional parties that may have relevant data to be collected. The S-HCC takes the process to a slightly different level. Based on the issues relevant to your case, this continuum may offer other opportunities to collect relevant data for your analysis. For example, the P-HCC generates data as a result of indirect or direct patient care activity. The S-HCC members are often users of that information. They in turn developed additional data or findings that could be utilized. The S-HCC "public health" may have studies based on a particular toxin. Public policy may have studies on identified market issues. Reports on organized or white collar crime activity may identify prior methodology utilized. When evaluating the S-HCC, ask yourself the following questions: "Of the list of entities or individuals previously identified within the P-HCC, do they interact with members of the S-HCC? How so? What type of data flow occurs between the two continuums?" The identification of additional information or parties should be added to your discovery list (Figure 12.2).

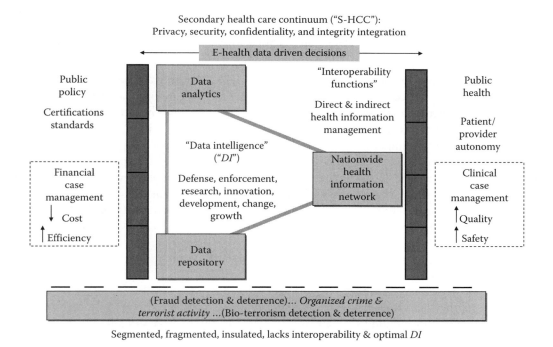

Figure 12.2. Secondary healthcare continuum ("P-HCC"): privacy, security, confidentiality, and integrity integration. (Copyright 2007. E-Heath Audit Guidebook, John Wiley & Sons, MBA Inc. 2007–2008. With permission.)

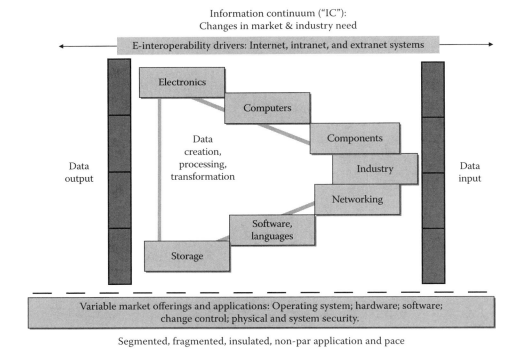

Figure 12.3. Information continuum ("IC"): change in market and industry needs. (Copyright 2007. *E-Health Audit Guidebook*, John Wiley & Sons, MBA Inc. 2007–2008. With permission.)

The third concept in gathering data is to appreciate the IC. As the market progresses into a true electronic environment, collecting information on the infrastructure in which your evidence or documents are generated and contained may impact your evaluation. The next table identifies the components of that infrastructure that should be identified (Figure 12.3).

The components are important to understand in the context of discovery. For example, there was one review in which a copy of a specific medical record was required. The paper record was lost. The ICU had an electronic record system. During the retrieval of a second copy of the record it was learned that due to budgetary reasons the ICU only purchased enough memory for three months of patient records. Upon reaching the limit, the ICU would just purge the records. No backup system was created. The following checklist of items is important with respect to the IC continuum:

- What electronic systems are utilized to generate data?
- How many and which type of computers are utilized?
- Who manages these systems?
- How are they networked?
- What are the current industry standards to maintain and manage systems?
- What software languages are utilized?
- What is the current storage capacity and technology utilized?

Another concept to understand is the use of metadata. Metadata is simply defined as "data about data" (McLean, 2008). It is the computer's record of any manipulations within a document.

The implications for discovery will be the need for the appropriate skill set for retrieval and analysis of the information. The market's movement from paper records to electronic medical records (EMR) will impact the e-discovery process. The implication in litigation will be the process in which metadata will be used to authenticate the EMR production.

Applications

(Received from http://www.oig.hhs.gov/fraud/enforcement/administrative/cmp/cmpitems.html#3.)

This section provides examples on how to apply the review model presented in this chapter. They will also illustrate that the scheme occurring may be relevant regardless of whether the patient is a Medicare beneficiary or a Medicaid recipient. In the first example, "patient dumping" is an issue regardless of the plan sponsor.

2007 Enforcement Action: Patient Dumping

Brackenridge Hospital (Brackenridge), Texas, agreed to pay $25,000 to resolve allegations stating that it failed to provide stabilizing treatment to an adult male who presented to its emergency department (ED) with complaints of having a severe headache for 4 days. A CT scan revealed a subarachnoid hemorrhage. Brackenridge's ED physician determined that the patient needed to be seen by a neurosurgeon. The ED physician called its on-call neurosurgeon. The on-call neurosurgeon refused to go to the ED to examine or treat the patient, stating that she would only see pediatric patients. The patient was transferred to a hospital nearly 66 miles away and was hospitalized for 3 days.

- Step 1: Define scope of audit and review:
  - Review the allegation of patient dumping
- Step 2: Define the data necessary for evaluation:
  - P-HCC—medical records, hospital policy and procedure, relevant claims data, and reimbursement rules on inpatient prospective payment rules on DRG's
  - S-HCC—any ED reporting data to the respective state, any relevant statistics from the CDC regarding the diagnosis involved
  - IC—identify the sources and systems of the data, the manner in which they are contained and stored
- Step 3: Define parties to be interviewed:
  - The patient, the provider facility, and professional staff
- Step 4: Audit review and data analysis
  - Organize the data for analysis and review
  - Utilize the nursing process of data, opinions, actions and procedures, evaluations, and follow-up data collection
- Step 5: Market comparison, analysis, and final report

The next example is government-specific. Although submitting a false claim is universal regardless of a private or public plan sponsor, the self-reporting guidelines and civil monetary penalties are typically discussed in the context of government programs. This next example is an interesting case. The submission of a false claim is often discussed from a provider perspective. In essence, the provider submits a claim for reimbursement that includes misrepresentation of service. This example involves a TPA actually altering the claim submitted by the provider. In the context of the statutes discussed earlier, the submission of a false claim by a provider that is paid by a benefit plan sponsor is the negligent or criminal act. Likewise, the submission or processing of an altered claim by the TPA on behalf of the plan sponsor is also considered as a negligent or criminal act.

2007 Enforcement Action: False and Fraudulent Claims

America's Health Choice, Inc. (AHC), Florida, agreed to pay $100,000 for allegedly violating the Civil Monetary Penalties Law. The OIG alleged that AHC misrepresented or falsified information furnished to the Secretary of HHS. Specifically, AHC submitted documents to the Secretary that misrepresented the academic credentials of an AHC employee. Submitted effectuation notices to the CHDR contained falsified dates of submission in an attempt to appear to be in compliance with CHDR's request for claims data.

- Step 1: Define the scope of audit and review:
  - Review the allegation of false claims processing
- Step 2: Define data necessary for evaluation
  - P-HCC—credential documents, policy and procedures, claims data, adjudication procedures, management reports, TPA contracts, and performance incentives. Collect sample claims information from target patients and providers. All reimbursement schedules would apply since these are processing claims collectively for all types of facilities and providers
  - S-HCC—documents submitted to the Department of Health and Human Service, market data on claims processing standards – Department of Labor
  - IC—identify the sources and systems of the data, the manner in which they are contained and stored. Claims processing software, EDI processing, and clearing house information
- Step 3: Define parties to be interviewed:
  - The operational staff, the payer management, and claims staff
  - Selected patient and provider interviews
- Step 4: Audit review and data analysis:
  - Organize the data for analysis and review
  - Reconcile data from patient, provider, and claim file
  - Utilize the nursing process of data, opinions, actions and procedures, evaluations, and follow-up data collection
- Step 5: Market comparison, analysis, and final report

The Americhoice case is a great example illustrating the concept one of episode of care being impacted by multiple parties and systems. In this case, information received by the patient can be reconciled with information maintained by the provider, the payer, and the plan sponsor. The multiple sources provide an opportunity to identify any anomalies.

The next example involves DME. This is a vulnerable area within the market. One of several rules includes covered DME payment to be authorized by an appropriate physician. Specifically in this case, it is important to have the referring physician to meet the criteria for reimbursement. In addition, another pattern that is often found is that the patient never actually received the DME item.

2007 Enforcement Action: False and Fraudulent Claims

Kay Medical Services Corporation, Florida, agreed to pay $440,949 and agreed to be permanently excluded from participating in all federal healthcare programs for allegedly violating the Civil Monetary Penalties Law. The OIG alleged that Kay submitted claims that listed physicians as the referring physician for certain DME services that were not provided as claimed and were false and fraudulent.

- Step 1: Define the scope of audit and review:
    - Review the allegation of false and fraudulent DME claims
- Step 2: Define the data necessary for evaluation:
    - P-HCC—the patient claim file, corresponding medical records, and physician listing for follow-up verification
    - S-HCC—product information and market use, demographic information on diagnosis associated with the DME product provided
    - IC—identify software utilized and retention policies for the retrieval of data for analysis
- Step 3: Define parties to be interviewed:
    - The provider, the patient, and the DME representative
- Step 4: Audit review and data analysis:
    - Organize the data for analysis and review
    - Utilize the nursing process of data, opinions, actions and procedures, evaluations, and follow-up data collection
- Step 5: Market comparison, analysis, and final report

   DME activity benefits from data mining tools. The data mining algorithms should reconcile the content of claims data, for example, the NPI number for the physician, the diagnosis codes, and the actual equipment. Compare the data elements identified such as NPI and product information with the recurring charges of quantity supplied and the duration of the products life span. The next example explores the contractual relationships among providers. The purpose of Stark is to avoid patient care decisions that have a financial basis. In this example, a clear direct financial arrangement was executed, which was in direct violation of the kickback and self-referral statutes.

2007 Enforcement Action: Kickback and Physician Self Referral

Advanced Neuromodulation Systems, Inc. (ANS), Texas, agreed to pay $2,950,000 and to enter into a 3-year corporate integrity agreement to resolve its liability for allegedly violating the Civil Monetary Penalties Law. The OIG alleged that ANS offered and paid remuneration to potential and existing referral sources in exchange for referrals to ANS for the purchasing, leasing, ordering, arranging for, or furnishing of medical devices, which were manufactured by ANS and were payable by a federal healthcare program. Other ANS practices raising kickback concerns included educational grants and fellowships, conferences held at resort locations, free dinners and gifts, and expenses paid to physicians under consulting agreements.

- Step 1: Define the scope of audit and review:
    - Review the allegation of kickback and physician self-referral

- ■ Step 2: Define the data necessary for evaluation:
  - – P-HCC—identify all contracted parties, obtain claims data, medical records data, and all contracts signed between the parties
  - – S-HCC—obtain market information of in-kind services or consulting arrangements
  - – IC—obtain marketing infrastructures
- ■ Step 3: Define parties to be interviewed:
  - – The contracted parties, representatives from educational grants and/or conference organizers
- ■ Step 4: Audit review and data analysis:
  - – Organize the data for analysis and review
  - – Utilize the nursing process of data, opinions, actions and procedures, evaluations, and follow-up data collection
- ■ Step 5: Market comparison, analysis, and final report

In the last example, it is important to understand the marketing relationship in which the contracts were "sold." The next example addresses pricing issues. The physician had accepted the terms in accepting Medicare Assignment. He circumvented this process by initiating an "association" program to collect additional compensation.

2007 Enforcement Action: Overcharging Beneficiaries

Lee R. Rocamora, MD, North Carolina, agreed to pay $106,600 to resolve his liability for allegedly violating the Civil Monetary Penalties Law. The OIG alleged that the practitioner requested payments from Medicare beneficiaries in violation of his assignment agreement. Specifically, the practitioner allegedly asked his patients to enter into a membership agreement for his patient care program, under which the patients paid an annual fee. In exchange for the fee, the membership agreement specified that the practitioner would provide members with (1) an annual comprehensive physical examination; (2) same day or next day appointments; (3) support personnel dedicated exclusively to members; (4) 24 hr a day and 7 days a week physician availability; (5) prescription facilitation; (6) coordination of referrals and expedited referrals, if medically necessary; and (7) other service amenities as determined by the practitioner.

- ■ Step 1: Define the scope of audit and review:
  - – Review the allegation of overcharging beneficiaries
- ■ Step 2: Define the data necessary for evaluation:
  - – P-HCC—collect patient contracts, marketing materials, and association materials. Obtain claim file information from Medicare and the provider. Obtain any information on third party support such as a billing agent
  - – S-HCC—research data available on prior billing practices and/or offenses by the provider
  - – IC—obtain systems for schedules, banking information, and invoicing process
- ■ Step 3: Define parties to be interviewed:
  - – The patient, the provider, and any other third party member
- ■ Step 4: Audit review and data analysis:
  - – Organize the data for analysis and review
  - – Utilize the nursing process of data, opinions, actions and procedures, evaluations, and follow-up data collection
- ■ Step 5: Market comparison, analysis, and final report

This type of behavior is difficult to measure among the entire population. It is dependent on patients being educated to report such offerings from their providers.

Conclusions

This chapter provided an introduction to fraud assessment of government-sponsored health plans. The critical components of fraud and its definition were reviewed. Key legislation highlighting potentially fraudulent behavior was presented. Historically, market behavior that initially materialize as abuse eventually becomes exposed and legislated as fraudulent activity. Monitoring the literature for behaviors that are being studied as abuse can be an indicator of future legislation. The section on healthcare reimbursement highlighted 18 different models for reimbursement of healthcare services. If a case involves a specific type of model, the legal nurse consultant should review specific updated information within the Medicare Manual that is available online at www.cms.hhs.gov. The case evaluation methodology presented here was structured to meet the standard of Daubert and collectively target the review to the relevant data types which would address most types of cases encountered. Finally, the application section helped to collectively apply them.

References

Busch, R. (2006). *Discussion on MBA methodology healthcare expense analysis scientific methodology healthcare reimbursement: usual & customary; medicare set aside.* Westmont: Medical Business Associates, Inc.

Busch, R. (2007). *Healthcare fraud auditing and detection guide.* Hoboken: Wiley.

Busch, R. (2008a). *Electronic health records an audit and internal control guide.* Hoboken: Wiley.

Busch, R. (2008b). Healthcare Fraud Course (Revised) (Association of Certified Fraud Examiners, 2008). *Fraud Examiners Manual.* Association of Certified Fraud Examiners.

McLean, B. (2008). *Electronic medical record metadata: uses and liability.* American College of Surgeons.

Methodology. (n.d.). *Dictionary.com Unabridged (v 1.1).* Retrieved June 13, 2008, from http://dictionary.reference.com/browse/methodology

Retrieved from http://www.cms.hhs.gov/MedicareGenInfo/

Retrieved from http://www.cms.hhs.gov/home/medicare.asp

Retrieved from http://www.oig.hhs.gov/fraud/enforcement/administrative/cmp/cmpitems.html#3

Sutherland, E. (2008). *White collar crime the uncut version.* New Haven: Yale University Press.

Wells, J. (2001). Why employees commit fraud. *Journal of Accountancy.* Retrieved 2008 from http://www.acfe.com/fraud/view.asp?ArticleID=41

Test Questions

1. Which of the following elements is required by the law for the allegation of fraud to exist?
    A. Overinflated billing cycles
    B. Victim acting on inaccurate information
    C. Lost or missing medical documents
    D. Gaps in service provided

2. Which of the following protections is available for "whistleblowers"?
    A. Protection from harassment and retaliation of employers
    B. Some protection for promotions and retirement
    C. Unpaid leave during suspension from work
    D. Protection from gossip in the workplace

3. Which of the following would an LNC expect to do in any fraud investigation? **Choose all that apply.**
    A. Interviewing witnesses
    B. Writing reports
    C. Defending victims
    D. Negotiating settlements

4. Which of the following is most important for the LNC working in a fraud unit?
    A. Intimate knowledge of the local marketplace
    B. Experience in the courtroom setting
    C. Monitoring the literature for behaviors which suggest abuse
    D. Previous experience in case management

5. Which of the following represents fraudulent activities? **Choose all that apply.**
    A. Deceased physicians billing for services
    B. Medically necessary services
    C. Billing for services after patient discharges
    D. Providing services under a contract agreement

Answers: 1. B; 2. A; 3. A, B; 4. C; 5. A, C

Chapter 13

The Life Care Planning Expert

Nancy LaGasse, RN, MS, CDMS, CCM, CLCP, LHRM, ARM, MSCC and Helen "Heather" McDaniel, RN, LNCC, CNOR, CNLCP

First Edition and Second Edition
Mona Yudkoff, BSN, MA, RN, MPH, CRRN, CCM, CLCP

Contents

Objectives

After reading this chapter, the legal nurse consultant will be able

- To evaluate the utilization of a life care plan in assessment of damages in a case
- To identify facts involved in choosing a life care planner
- To discuss the steps required to complete a life care plan
- To analyze the steps of litigation as they apply to life care planners

Introduction

According to the International Academy of Life Care Planners (IALCP), "Life Care Planning is an advanced practice which is collaborative in nature and includes the patient, family, care providers and all parties concerned in coordinating, accessing, evaluating and monitoring necessary services" (http://www.rehabpro.org/ialcp/about-ialcp/scope). At the 2000 Life Care Planning Summit, more than 100 professionals who were experienced in preparing life care plans met to discuss the life care planning process. A consensus was reached that stated a life care plan should be individualized to reflect the specific needs and promote optimal health, function, and autonomy. It needs to be written in an objective and consistent manner, in addition to being comprehensive, based on multidisciplinary data and adaptive to change. An accepted definition of a life care plan was established during the 2000 Life Care Planning Summit, and adopted by the IALCP in 2003:

> The life care plan is a dynamic document based upon published standards of practice, comprehensive assessment, data analysis, and research, which provides an organized, concise plan for current and future needs with associated costs for individuals who have experienced catastrophic injury or have chronic health care needs. (LexisNexis eCommerce)

Today, life care planning is performed by a wide array of health professionals, and several professional organizations have included life care planners among their membership. These include the aforementioned IALCP, the American Association of Legal Nurse Consultants (AALNC), the Association of Rehabilitation Nurses (ARN), the International Association of Rehabilitation Professionals (IARP), the American Association of Nurse Life Care Planners (AANLCP), and the Case Management Society of America (CMSA). While many groups believe life care planners are multidisciplinary providers, one group, AANLCP, was founded for Registered Nurses (RNs) with an interest in life care planning and with the goal of establishing nurse life care planning as a nursing practice role, based on the nurses' scope and standards of practice and the nursing process (AANLCP, 1998).

Today, life care planners are utilized in litigation to present future medical damages in cases involving catastrophic injuries or illnesses. The life care plan can serve multiple purposes, both in litigation and in the financing aspects of a nonlitigated injury or illness. It can also be used as a financial planning document for individuals establishing trust accounts, or insurers setting reserves on catastrophic cases. Case managers often utilize life care plans to assist in determining costs and time frames for equipment and service needs for clients. It is important for legal nurse consultants (LNCs) to understand all of the practical aspects of life care planning and the varied parties who incorporate it into their businesses in order to be knowledgeable of the damages side of the litigation process.

Understanding the Value of a Life Care Plan

The unspoken question foremost in civil litigation is "How much is this case worth?" In personal injury cases, including medical malpractice and product liability, damages are directly related to the injuries suffered by the plaintiff. These injuries may include bodily harm, psychological damage, loss of future earnings, and pain and suffering. A quantifiable estimate of future costs to the plaintiff resulting from the injury is critical to the assessment of the case's value. In civil litigation, a life care plan relates specifically to disability subsequent to the catastrophic illness or injury alleged to have been caused by the defendant. The preexisting medical conditions are often acknowledged in the plan, but any costs related to preexisting conditions should not be projected as a part of the plan unless those preexisting costs are exacerbated by the injury or illness of the subject in the life care plan.

The purpose of a life care plan for an insurance carrier might be other than for settlement, as they must be sure that their cases are not underinsured in order for them to remain solvent. They are often required by agreement with a reinsurance carrier to report and/or place a value on a case for purposes of reinsurance funding in order to alert the reinsurance carrier to their potential exposure. Often life care planning is used for the identification and management of categories of claims. Some cases may initially appear to have a relatively small value, but upon re-evaluation are found to have the potential to be catastrophic from a claims standpoint. On the other hand, injuries consisting of multiple traumas are often considered to be catastrophic in nature upon notification by the nonmedical person, but can heal with either minimal or no permanent impairment. An example of this would be injuries involving multiple simple fractures and/or soft tissue injuries, which are resolved with proper treatment over a relatively short period of time. The LNC plays a role in educating the attorney or carrier regarding the potential need for a life care plan.

Insurance carriers also use life care planning as a tool in discerning those cases that are advantageous for them to settle and to establish a projected value. They can also use it as a means of outlining the plan for case management. The case manger is dedicated to the coordination of claims requiring medical monitoring in order to avoid the development of complications.

When a life care planner is involved, this professional educates the parties concerned about the impact of the disability on the individual's life expectancy. A detailed analysis of the injured person's medical, psychosocial, educational, and vocational needs presents a clear picture of dollar costs.

In cases that go to trial, the plaintiff attorney often presents a life care plan. The life care planner in this role assists the trier-of-fact (bench judge or jury) in understanding the necessity of the damages involved in the case, and its impact on the plaintiff's life.

Defense attorneys are responsible for mitigating damages if they fail to disprove liability. Life care planners are frequently retained by the defense to evaluate the validity of the plaintiff's damages proposal. The defense attorney will determine based on trial strategy whether or not the life care planner will testify at trial. The life care planner may be retained by the defense counsel to review the life care plan of the opposing side and develop strategies for cross-examination of the plaintiff's expert or to present an alternative strategy for meeting the injured party's needs in a reasonable and economical manner (Deutch, 1990).

Choosing an Appropriate and Qualified Life Care Planner

In most ways, choosing a life care plan expert is similar to choosing any testifying expert. The Federal Rules of Evidence (Article VII, Opinions and Expert Testimony, Rules 701–706) governs all testifying experts and how they form their opinions.

Rule 702. Testimony by Experts:

> If scientific, technical, or other specialized knowledge will assist the trier-of-fact to understand the evidence or to determine a fact in issue, a witness qualified as and expert by knowledge, skill, experience, training, or education, may testify thereto in the form of an opinion or otherwise, if (1) the testimony is based upon sufficient facts or data, (2) the testimony is the product of reliable principles and methods, and (3) the witness has applied the principles and methods reliably to the facts of the case.
>
> (As amended April 17, 2000, eff. December 1, 2000) (Federal Rules of Evidence, 2004; SKAPP)

In June of 1993, the U.S. Supreme Court issued an opinion relating to how federal judges should decide when and whether to allow expert testimony in the courtroom. Prior to this, most federal and state judges considered two standards: relevance to a fact at issue, and whether it would be useful to the jury. They also looked to a 1923 ruling known as *Frye*, which held that conclusions must be generally accepted within the expert community.

In *Daubert v. Merrell Dow Pharmaceuticals, Inc.*, the U.S. Supreme Court sought to clarify these standards, by directing the judges to act as "gatekeepers" in the courtroom, to examine the scientific method underlying expert evidence, and to admit it only if determined to be both "relevant and reliable." Two later cases, *General Electric v. Joiner* and *Kumho Tire Co. v. Carmichael*, expanded upon this opinion.

When the U.S. Supreme Court issued its opinion in *Daubert*, it gave four primary criteria for determining admissibility:

1. Is the evidence based on testable theory or technique?
2. Has the theory or technique been peer reviewed?
3. In the case of a particular technique, does it have a known error rate and standards controlling the technique's operation?
4. Is the underlying science generally accepted? (SKAPP)

During a jury trial, any challenge to an expert's testimony will typically be decided prior to or outside the jury's hearing of their opinions; therefore, it is vital that the life care planner be able to address these issues knowledgeably and confidently with the attorney in the initial interview. According to FRE, Rule 702, it is imperative that the life care planner can articulate the principles and methods used in preparation of the life care plan, and the reliability of such standards and methods as they are applied to the specific case for which the life care planner is retained.

One way for the LNC to assess the life care planner's knowledge is through review of the potential expert's education, experience, training, and skill as well as recognized credentials. Significant experience in the care of persons with chronic and catastrophic deficits would likely be seen as a major advantage for any life care planner. Additionally, the life care planner who has case management experience, a role that includes coordination of services to the catastrophically ill or injured, could also be determined as beneficial. Familiarity with vendors and healthcare providers, as well as the ability to find these sources in various locales, is essential. It is preferable that the expert should have a professional background and experience that are relevant to the diagnosis, age, and medical needs of the injured or ill individual. Finally, the life care planner should have excellent communication skills and a professional appearance.

Given that life care plans are completed by professionals from varied backgrounds, each professional will possess differing credentials, licensures, and certifications. This will require the attorney or LNC to have an understanding of the various educational programs and certifications relevant to life care planning in order to determine the most appropriate person for the case. Advanced academic preparation shows an enriched knowledge base with commitment to professionalism. Membership in professional associations, attendance at professional meetings, conferences, and continuing-education courses all demonstrate ongoing acquisition of current skills and knowledge. These activities are an important component in the assessment process for the LNC.

Requesting a sample life care plan may provide information such as writing style, past recommendations, and formatting. In general, this will provide information helpful to the LNC in understanding the plan's interventions, and the underlying methodology utilized by the life care planner.

Credentials

Many life care planners hold certifications in life care planning beyond those usually seen in the general healthcare field in which the professional practices. Valid certifications are offered by professional organizations, and awarded by a third-party, standard-setting organization, which should be independent of special interests. Knowing the difference between a "certificate" and a "certification" should be part of the LNCs knowledge base when interviewing experts. The AALNC (http://www.AALNC.org) has information on its website to educate individuals in the difference between certificate and certification.

The following is a list of credentials that are often held by life care planners:

■ CRRN (Certified Rehabilitation Registered Nurse): This certification program is administered by the Rehabilitation Nursing Certification Board (RNCB), an autonomous component of the ARN. The CRRN program is accredited by the American Board of Nursing Specialties (ABNS). Rehabilitation nurses help individuals affected by chronic illness or physical disability to adapt to their disabilities, achieve their greatest potential, and work toward productive, independent lives. They take a holistic approach to medical, vocational, educational, environmental, and spiritual needs (ARN).
■ CCM (Certified Case Manager): This is a multidisciplinary case management specialty practice certification within the health and human services profession. The certification program is administered by the Commission for Case Manager Certification (CCMC), an autonomous component of the CMSA. The CCM program is accredited by the National Commission for Certifying Agencies (NCCA). Case management is a collaborative process that assesses, plans, implements, coordinates, monitors, and evaluates the options and

services required to meet the client's health and human service needs. Each discipline would be held to its own scope of practice (CMSA).

■ CDMS (Certified Disability Management Specialist): This is a multidisciplinary specialty that includes individuals with Bachelor's, Master's, or Doctorate degrees related to disability management, as well as RNs with a current state license, active and in good standing. The CDMS program is managed by the Certification of Disability Management Specialists Commission (CDMSC). The CDMS program is accredited by the NCCA. Disability management specialists analyze, prevent, and mitigate the human and economic impact of disability for employees and employers. The practice behaviors may include (1) disability case management; (2) disability prevention and workplace intervention; (3) program development, management, and evaluation. Each discipline would be held to its own scope of practice (Certification of Disability Management Specialists).

■ CRC (Certified Rehabilitation Counselor): This is a certification program developed and administered by the Commission on Rehabilitation Counselor Certification (CRCC). The CRC program is accredited by the NCCA. There are several categories in rehabilitation counseling and counseling offered to meet the criteria for eligibility (Commission on Rehabilitation Counselor Certification).

■ CLCP (Certified Life Care Planner): This is a multidisciplinary life care planning specialty practice certification program for qualified healthcare practitioners, administered by a corporation, the Commission on Healthcare Certification, Inc. (CHCC) also known as the International Commission on Healthcare Certification (ICHCC). The CHCC/ICHCC announced that an application for accreditation by the NCCA was submitted in September of 2007, and at that time the 3rd edition publication was working toward approval (Commission on Healthcare Certification, Inc).

■ CNLCP (Certified Nurse Life Care Planner): This is a certification program administered by the American Association of Nurse Life Care Planners Certification Board (AANLCPCB), an autonomous component of the AANLCP. An application for accreditation by the ABNS was submitted in August of 2007, and at that time the 3rd edition publication was working toward approval. The nurse life care planner utilizes the nursing process to assess, identify issues, and plan for appropriate interventions, implementation, and evaluation in the nurse life care planning process (AANLCP, 1998).

■ LNCC (Legal Nurse Consultant Certified): This certification program is administered by the American Legal Nurse Consultant Certification Board (ALNCCB), an autonomous component of the AALNC. The LNCC is accredited by the ABNS. Legal nurse consulting is a nursing specialty in which the primary role of the LNC is to evaluate, analyze, and render informed opinions on the delivery of healthcare and its outcomes (AALNC).

There are other healthcare provider's credentials that have not been included in the above list (e.g., occupational therapists and physical therapists) but would be important for the LNC to investigate if and when necessary. Although holding a current accredited certification is an important indicator for the evaluating LNC, inclusion of the above certifications in this chapter does not imply validation by the AALNC. The retaining attorney or the firm's LNC must evaluate the validity of certifications presented by a life care planner as well as the appropriateness of their role in the case.

Data Collection and Analysis

Life care planners must obtain the data needed to analyze the injured or ill individual's past and present health status. Additionally, the life care planner must begin to form a basis for research into future care needs. In the initial stages of data collection, the life care planner may have medical records, employment records, school records, and other documents to review which of them provide history and direction. Frequently, the life care planner will also collaborate with other healthcare providers to collect supplemental information and data for the life care plan. A brief listing of those providers follows:

- The physiatrist: A physiatrist is a physician who specializes in the field of physical medicine and rehabilitation in "... the process of helping a person to reach the fullest physical, psychological, social, vocational, avocational and educational potential consistent with his or her physiologic or anatomic impairment, environmental limitations, desires and life plans" (DeLisa & Gans, 1998). The physiatrist is often chosen as a testifying expert, when catastrophic injuries cause major musculoskeletal and neurological problems.
- The medical case manager: When working for an insurance carrier, the medical case manager coordinates the medical care and needs of the injured individual with his physician, insurance carrier, and/or attorneys. They provide ongoing monitoring of the injured person's medical and psychological status, in addition to their medical needs. There are also independent medical case managers. In certain instances, the case manager can be a resource for the life care planner to be assured that all of the individual's medical and psychological needs have been included in planning for the future.
- The certified rehabilitation counselor: The CRC, who may also be a vocational counselor, provides an evaluation of the injured individual's ability to perform certain jobs within the physical, emotional, and cognitive abilities, as outlined by a treating physician's restrictions. The CRC also researches, and provides job leads, in addition to providing assistance in interviewing and recommending job modifications and obtaining employment. The CRC may also provide assistance with job retraining. In conjunction with life care planning, the CRC can also be utilized to evaluate and project lost wages to include loss of long-term benefits.
- Economist: An economist by nature of their education and training provides a financial analysis of present and future inflationary rates for the products and services recommended in the life care plan. This professional may also provide wage loss information and in some instances reduce the life care plan to the present dollar value.

Certainly, there will be other collaborative disciplines depending on the specific injuries and needs unique to the injured person. A few examples might include treating physicians, occupational therapists, physical therapists, prosthetists, neuropsychologists, psychologists or psychiatrists, home modification experts, and special education consultants. The list can be extensive and must be unique to the individual life care plan. A Special Needs Trust specialist might also be involved if the injured party is a minor or has other special circumstances requiring that a Special Needs Trust be implemented.

Steps Required for Developing a Life Care Plan

Assessment

The life care planner collects comprehensive data pertinent to the injured or ill individual's health status and need for ongoing medical, psychosocial, educational, and vocational needs. Often the life care planner begins this process with a comprehensive review of all available medical records. An on-site assessment of the injured or ill person's current status is completed by the life care planner whenever possible. When an on-site visit is not possible, and after documentation of such a request by the life care planner, the assessment may need to be performed on a record review basis. All available records relevant to damages should be reviewed. The LNC can play a valuable role in collaborating with the life care planner to obtain as complete a medical record or document list as possible. It may be necessary to request ongoing treatment records and additional assessments to build an adequate foundation for the opinions of the life care plan. A literature search may be needed to define the expected course and treatment of a particular diagnosis. The life care planner will rely on evidence-based literature for opinions included in the life care plan.

A face-to-face meeting with the injured person is almost always beneficial. The injured person's home is usually the most productive environment for the gathering of information, given the ability to view equipment, medications, and needs for modification in the individual's usual residential setting. The assessment/life care planning interview should include the primary caregiver(s) whenever possible. When the injured person has sustained cognitive injuries, is unable to communicate, or is a minor child, the caregiver may be the primary source of information regarding daily care.

The injured person's healthcare providers are often solicited for input into future care when appropriate. When future care is not discussed in the records, it is generally appropriate to seek additional information directly from the physician or other providers with appropriate legal permission. In litigation, the life care planner would discuss this option with the referring attorney prior to any contact with current or past treatment providers. Due to the enactment of Health Information Portability and Accountability Act (HIPAA) in 1996, it is necessary to obtain signed medical release authorization forms from the injured or ill person or their responsible party prior to contacting treating medical professionals. This is often handled by the referring attorney. Generally, when working with defense counsel, it is more difficult or impossible to be in contact with medical providers. It may also be impossible to meet with the injured or ill individual from a defense perspective. A request should be made through the defense attorney for access to an on-site meeting with the injured or ill individual and contact with treatment providers as the life care planner deems appropriate. In some cases, the life care planner will discuss future care needs with the experts retained by the defense counsel when a meeting with the injured or ill individual or their medical providers is unavailable.

Determining the Issues and Needs

Each recommendation in the life care plan must be supported by medical records, input from healthcare professionals, the assessment of the life care planner and/or evidence-based literature as appropriate. Services and products must be available in reasonable proximity to the injured party's residence. The plan should provide the reader with a clear rationale for the relationship between recommended services and the injury or illness. It is critical to evaluate duration and frequency of recommended services and products, as well as to delineate changes in frequency, which could be due to growth, disease process, complications, aging, or other factors.

Creating the Plan

Although life care planners use a variety of formats, basic writing principles for expert reports apply. The ultimate goal is a clear picture of the injured person's needs, as well as the relationship of these needs to the sustained injuries. The life care plan should reflect the desired outcomes being rehabilitative, restorative, and supportive of the injured or ill individual's ongoing needs. Clarity and brevity are essential. A well-prepared life care plan projects future care in a defensible and organized report. Each plan is unique and comprehensive in nature. In the preparation of a life care plan, collaboration with other healthcare professionals, vendors, and specialists for the exchange of knowledge and ideas about how to best deliver health care maximizes the quality and credibility of the finished product. Recognition of the expertise of others outside one's profession is often necessary and appropriate. In the end, regardless of its collaborative nature, the life care plan contains the opinions and conclusions of its author.

Determining Costs

Costs in the life care plan are typically presented in today's dollars. The completed life care plan may be forwarded to an economist by the attorney to compute the present value of future costs set forth in the life care plan; and if the plan is not well structured, it can pose difficulties for the economist to analyze (Weed, 2004). It is for this reason that the life care planner includes start and stop dates as well as frequency and duration for all equipments, products, and services within the life care plan. The attorney usually retains an economist to interpret the numbers, incorporate inflation, interest rates, and other economic factors, since these calculations are beyond the scope of expertise of most life care planners. The economist must ensure that the final cost projection conforms to local jurisdiction rulings. The life care planner must include costs for usual and customary rates in the geographic area proximate to the injured person's home.

It is helpful for the life care planner to be knowledgeable of Current Procedural Terminology (CPT) codes, current edition of International Classification of Diseases (ICD) codes, Diagnostic Related Groups (DRGs), and Healthcare Common Procedural Coding System (HCPCS) when obtaining costs. If the injured person is not currently receiving the recommended services, a representative sample of appropriate providers should be referenced. The life care planner will determine the methodology for estimating costs. Some life care planners use the middle range of costs as a reasonable estimate of the cost within a particular future item; others show the entire range of costs to cover a broader spectrum of future provider accessibility.

The life care plan must portray a fair and comprehensive picture of the injured or ill individual's needs, relative to the catastrophic injury or chronic illness. Components of a life care plan may include medical care, skilled nursing care, attendant care, household services, therapeutic assessments, therapeutic modalities, monitoring by physicians, orthotics/prosthetics, orthopedics, preventive health care, equipments, supplies, medications, diagnostic testing, hospital care, accessibility (housing), transportation, psychological support, case management, and educational and vocational needs. The goal of the life care plan is to allow the injured or ill individual to approximate as closely as possible the levels of independent function and quality of life that could have reasonably been expected if the injury or illness had not occurred.

Medical care projections should incorporate costs of care by physicians, allied health professionals, and therapeutic modalities, as well as costs associated with diagnostic testing and anticipated hospitalizations and procedures. Surveillance or preventive care should be included to avoid or retard further complications. A comprehensive plan may include the services of a case manager to direct future care and implementation of the plan.

Costs of durable equipment should include replacement costs, length of expected service, and annual maintenance charges. Both unit cost and frequency of use should be described in lists of costs for medications and supplies.

When housing modifications are needed to improve accessibility, the life care planner should provide a detailed assessment of the current or future home and specific modifications recommended.

When modifications are extensive and outside the scope of one's practice, these costs can be obtained in collaboration with an appropriate professional.

In many life care plans, the costs of medications, attendant care, and/or respite services are the most expensive items. It is important to be able to justify the medical necessity of the level of home-care personnel recommended (RN, LPN/LVN, CNA, unskilled attendant, or other in-home supportive services). The frequency of service should also be clearly explained. Services should not be duplicated. If services are provided to prevent complications, then the cost of those complications typically should not be included unless there is a reasonable likelihood of the complications occurring despite the recommended interventions.

Cost projections in the life care plan should be categorized and organized in a logical manner and often separated into the years in which the service will be required and/or changing. A summary table significantly facilitates the economist's work and also allows the jury to understand that the planner has taken into account any changes that the injured person is likely to undergo over the course of a lifetime.

Life Care Plan Reviews

In litigation, the life care planner may be retained by either a plaintiff or a defense attorney to provide commentary on the life care plan presented by the opposing counsel. In performing this type of review, each issue should be evaluated for appropriateness to the injury or illness, relevance to the litigated damage, reasonableness of costs, absence of duplication in services, and availability of goods and services geographically close to the individual with the illness or injury. The attorney may be particularly interested in potential sources of investigation to delineate any preexisting medical issues that would impact the current claim. For example, examination of school records or work history may show premorbid cognitive deficits that mitigate some of the alleged damages.

The attorney may request an oral report before receiving any of the life care planner's written opinions. In some cases, the defense attorney may request a complete life care plan, independent of the plaintiff's submission.

A review of any collateral sources, such as government or private agencies, which may provide services and equipments, is often a request of the defense attorney. The life care planner will educate the attorney regarding collateral sources. Life care planners may be judicious or refrain from guaranteeing funding from collateral sources, understanding that approval of equipment and services is often based on legislative and budgetary criteria and not guaranteed from year to year. The admissibility of such collateral sources also depends upon the local rules of evidence. Use of collateral funding sources as an offset for projected costs depends on the local jurisdiction of the case, and this should be clarified with the hiring attorney.

Life Expectancy

Opinions on life expectancy or economic considerations related to the life care plan, but not within the expert's scope of practice, should be carefully considered. The life care planner is sometimes requested to obtain a life expectancy by the retaining attorney. At the attorney's request, the life care planner may be asked to participate in determining life expectancy. In some cases, the life care planner may work with a structured settlement company or insurance underwriter to obtain a rated age for life expectancy. A rated age is the medical age of the injured party, which is then used to determine a life expectancy found in the CDC (Center for Disease Control and Prevention) life tables. Most nonphysician life care planners do not project life expectancy, outside of use of the CDC tables.

Preparing for Deposition as a Life Care Planner

File Review

Careful file review precedes the deposition. The deposition request usually includes a call for the expert's entire file. The opposing attorney is entitled to review all notes, drafts, resources, and records in the file. File maintenance should be a priority throughout all stages of consulting. The expert should bring an updated curriculum vitae to the deposition. Before the deposition, the life care planner should review any current medical records that have been generated between completion of the report and date of deposition. An addendum to the life care plan is often considered appropriate and is provided to both sides prior to testimony. The plaintiff's expert should contact the plaintiff or caregiver for an update if the deposition takes place several months (or more) after the completion of the report. The defense expert should request an update on the plaintiff's condition through the defense attorney's office. Depositions and reports of fact witnesses and other expert witnesses should be made available for review by the life care planner.

Preparation with the Attorney

The deposition is essentially a dress rehearsal for trial testimony and basically a discovery opportunity for opposing counsel to learn an expert's opinions, explore qualifications, evaluate credibility, explore the methods the expert used in arriving at their opinions, probe for bias or pecuniary interest, and/or to intimidate or lock down the expert. Before the deposition, it is wise for the attorney who has retained the expert to review all areas of anticipated questioning, as well as any perceived potential weaknesses of the case, with the life care planner.

If a trial is to be held in Federal Court, there are some specific expert disclosures required, contained in the *Federal Rules of Civil Procedure v. Depositions and Discovery*. If the life care planner is unaware of these provisions, these requirements should be clarified. Basically, as with any expert, the life care planner will need to do as follows:

> Provide a written report that is prepared and signed by the expert. The report shall contain a complete statement of all opinions to be expressed and the basis and reasons therefore; the data or other information considered by the witness in forming the opinions; any exhibits to be used as a summary of or support for the opinions; the qualifications of the witness, including a list of all publications authored by the witness within the preceding ten years; the compensation to be paid for the study and testimony; and a listing of any other cases in which the witness has testified as an expert at trial or deposition within the preceding four years. (Federal Rules of Civil Procedure)

Deposition Testimony

Deposition testimony differs from trial testimony in that the questioning begins with the opposing attorney. Most of the deposition time is allotted to the opposing attorney. The retaining attorney may elect to ask questions at the end of the deposition in order to get certain facts on the record before trial or to interject corrections into the testimony for the written record. Successful testimony in damage cases is dependent on consistency, credibility, and clarity, just as in all expert witness testimony. In some cases, the deposition may be videotaped and used at trial in place of live testimony from the expert or to demonstrate appearance, demeanor, or factors that might be seen as unfavorable by the opposing counsel.

The Trial Process

File Review

File review and update is the first step in preparing for trial testimony. With many months or years between preparation of the report and the trial date, an update of the file is required, even if no changes are made. In most cases, if more than 6 months have passed, it is advisable to contact the attorney for recent medical information, followed by updating of the life care plan if found necessary. Updated medical records and new relevant depositions must be obtained and reviewed. When able, it may be helpful to speak with physicians, therapists, home health nurses, and vendors. When possible, the plaintiff or the plaintiff's caregiver should be contacted, and a new assessment interview is often appropriate for evaluation and reassessment. The expert should have a well-organized file for easy reference if necessary. The life care planner should also have a knowledgeable and comfortable grasp of case details during testimony. Demonstrating knowledge of the plaintiff's condition without constant referral to the files is most convincing. Careful review of deposition testimony of the plaintiff, caregivers, other damage experts, and defendants provides critical information about the opposing attorney's theories in the case as well as the attorney's style of cross-examination. It is helpful to review one's own deposition testimony. The opposing attorney may seek to elicit contradictions in prior testimony, while in front of the jury, by reading sections of the deposition. Having knowledge of one's deposition allows for clarification and augmentation of information deleted by the opposing attorney. Explanations for any changes in opinions between deposition and trial should be carefully considered and discussed with the hiring attorney prior to trial.

Preparation with the Attorney Prior to Trial Testimony

A pretrial meeting or at least a conference call should occur before trial. The retaining attorney should carefully review all aspects of trial testimony with the life care planner. Some attorneys prefer to rehearse direct examination, while others prefer more general discussions of the point to be covered. Preparation is most critical in regard to cross-examination questions. The attorney and life care planner must anticipate the strategy of the opposing attorney and consider concise answers to expected areas of attack. Expert testimony involving damages is usually presented toward the end of trial, which provides the opportunity to discuss previous testimony. It is helpful for the life care planner to know what the jury has already heard. The life care planner should be very familiar with his/her own deposition testimony as the opposing attorney will look to it as a means of impeachment. Familiarity with the details will help the expert recall the context of the statements made. Similarly, the expert might be confronted with what may seem to be a contradictory statement from a previous case since the opposing counsel has access to all previous depositions and testimony of the life care planner in other cases to look for inconsistencies. All of this should be discussed prior to trial.

Trial Testimony

Testimony focuses initially on the expert's qualifications. The witness must be able to present background information and credentials in a clear, confident, and impressive manner. The trier-of-fact must regard the witness's testimony as credible and important to the verdict. Recent legal decisions have affected the process of qualifying experts. Some jurisdictions demand more rigorous standards of proof of expertise.

The life care planner will be asked about remuneration, in the attempt to assign "hired-gun" status to testimony. The opposing counsel may ask if the life care planner were paid prior to their testimony and what was the amount of those charges. It must be clear that the expert is objective and that fees are not related to the outcome of the case. The life care planner is being paid for their time and not their opinions. It is usually helpful if the expert has testified in prior cases on behalf of both plaintiffs and defendants. They will often be asked to provide information regarding those cases in which they previously provided testimony, the percentage of plaintiff and defense cases, and the dates and location of the testimony.

During direct examination, the opinions expressed by the life care planner are presented. The attorney usually leads up to specific recommendations with an introduction to the life care planning process itself. The opposing attorney attempts to prove that the life care planner's opinions are invalid. A well-written, defensible life care plan is the best preparation for cross-examination.

Conclusion

Every trial has two sides, plaintiff and defense. Every trial also has two parts, liability and damage. Damage experts are required to place monetary values before the jury or tier of fact for successful resolution of each case. The life care planner is in a unique role to demonstrate future care needs based on sound methodology and evidence-based practices. Appendix A contains a sample narrative report and Appendix B contains sample life care plan tables.

References

American Association of Legal Nurse Consultants (AALNC). www.aalnc.org

American Association of Nurse Life Care Planners (AANLCP). (1998). www.aanlcp.org

Association of Rehabilitation Nurses (ARN). www.rehabnurse.org

Case Management Society of America (CMSA). www.cmsa.org

Certification of Disability Management Specialists (CDMS). www.cdms.org

Commission on Healthcare Certification, Inc. (CHCC). www.ichcc.org

Commission on Rehabilitation Counselor Certification (CRCC). www.crccertification.com

DeLisa, J. A., & Gans, B. M. (1998). *Rehabilitation medicine principles and practice.* (3rd ed., p. 3). Philadelphia: Lippencott-Raven.

Federal Rules of Civil Procedure v. Depositions and Discovery. Rule 26. General Provisions Governing Discovery; Duty of Disclosure: (2) Disclosure of Expert Testimony. (A), (B), (C).

Federal Rules of Evidence. (2004, December). 108th Congress, 2nd Session, Committee Print No. 8 (p. 13). U.S. Government Printing Office, Washington.

SKAPP. *Daubert: The most influential Supreme Court ruling you've never heard of* (p. 4). A publication of the Project on Scientific Knowledge and Public Policy (SKAPP), coordinated by the Tellus Institute.

Weed, R. O. (2004). The role of the economist in life care planning. In E. Dillman (Ed.), *Life care planning and case management handbook* (Chap. 11, p. 265). Boca Raton, FL: CRC Press.

Additional Readings

Barker, E. (1999). Life care planning. *Registered Nurse, 62*(3), 58.

Casuto, D., & McCollum, P. (2000). Life care planning. In M. O'Keefe (Ed.), *Nursing practice and the law* (Chap. 23). Philadelphia: F. A. Davis.

Deutsch, P. (1990). *A guide to rehabilitation testimony: The expert's role as an educator*. Orlando, FL: PMD Press.

Deutsch, P. (1994). Life care planning: Into the future. *National Association of Rehabilitation Professionals Private Sector Journal, 9*, 79.

Deutsch, P., & Sawyer, H. (1999). *Guide to rehabilitation*. Purchase, NY: Ahab Press.

Elliot, T. (1994). The plaintiff's view of the life care plan for the catastrophic case. *National Association of Rehabilitation Professionals Private Sector Journal, 9*, 69.

Field, T. F., Stein, D. B. (2002). *Scientific vs. non-scientific and related issues of admissibility of testimony by rehabilitation consultant*. Athens, GA: Elliott & Fitzpatrick, Inc.

Gunn, L. D., IV. (1994). Life care planning: A defense perspective. *National Association of Rehabilitation Professionals Private Sector Journal, 9*, 63.

Holakiewicz, L. (2008). Lessons from the Stand. *AANLCP Journal of Nurse Life Care Planning, 8*(3), 10–15.

McCollum, P. (1997). Life care planning. In K. Johnson (Ed.), *Advanced nursing practice in rehabilitation: A core curriculum* (pp. 251–255). Glenview, IL: ARN.

Powers, A. S. (1994). Life care planning: The role of the legal nurse. *National Association Rehabilitation Professionals Private Sector Journal, 9*, 51.

Weed, R. (2004). *Life care planning and case management handbook*. Boca Raton, FL: CRC Press.

Yudkoff, M., & Iyer, P. (2001). The life care plan expert. In P. Iyer (Ed.), *Nursing malpractice* (2nd ed., p. 652). Tucson, AZ: Lawyers and Judges Publishing Company.

Test Questions

1. A life care planner's role in damages includes which of the following? (**Choose all that apply**)
   A. Reviewing extensive medical records and testifying to the standard of nursing care
   B. Reviewing pertinent medical documents, school or employment records
   C. Recommending resources that meet future care needs of an individual
   D. Educating attorneys, jurors and judges regarding disability issues

2. The life care plan may be utilized for which of the following? (**Choose all that apply**)
   A. Portrayal of damages at trial
   B. For insurance reserve setting
   C. Within a special needs trust for resource allocation
   D. As a case management tool in Workers' Compensation claims

3. Which of the following exemplifies the underlying premise of Life Care Planning?
   A. A certified life care planner is the best qualified person to do all life care plans
   B. A life care plan is a dynamic document that will be updated periodically as appropriate
   C. Case Managers rely on the life care plan to manage care in Workers' Comp cases
   D. Life Care Plans are used to litigate liability in medical malpractice cases

4. Which of the following would a life care planner working for the defense weigh carefully for exclusion in the review process?
   A. General needs of the plaintiff related to preexisting medical diagnoses
   B. Accuracy of the costs projected
   C. Relation of the recommendations to the injuries alleged in the action
   D. Appropriateness of the recommendations

5. Which of the following would the life care planner expect to testify to at trial? (**Choose all that apply**)
   A. Information clearly within the limits of their professional expertise
   B. Information regarding objective assessment of the needs related to the injuries in the action
   C. Information that is advantageous to the referral source (plaintiff or defense)
   D. Information that is well supported by appropriate professional foundation

Answers: 1. B, C, D; 2. A, B, C, D; 3. B; 4. A; 5. A, B, D

Appendix A

October 14, 2008

Dear:

Thank you for the opportunity to provide a life care plan for Jose Smith. A life care plan is a dynamic document that outlines the future medical, psychosocial, educational and vocational needs for an individual who has experienced a catastrophic illness or injury. In preparation of this life care plan the following records were reviewed:

1. List of Records reviewed would appear here.

History

Mr. Smith is a 30-year-old Hispanic male who experience a work related accident on August 15, 2006. Reportedly while working for XYZ Company, Mr. Smith was working with a concrete hose which "got loose" and hit him in the back of the head. Mr. Smith fell into the wet concrete and was unable to move due to paralysis. He was taken by ground ambulance to Medical Center in ABC city where a diagnosis of C4 burst fracture and spinal cord injury was made. Mr. Smith was identified as a quadriplegic with no feeling below the nipple line. Intravenous steroids were started and he was transferred to the University Trauma Unit for surgical repair of the cervical fractures.

Upon admission to the University Trauma Unit, Mr. Smith received decompression of the C4 burst fracture and a 360 degree cervical fusion from C3 through C5 with bone harvested from the iliac crest. He developed complications with diabetes insipidus and hyponatremia. Mr. Smith also developed a deep vein thrombosis (DVT) in his calf and required a Greenfield filter placement in the inferior vena cava. He was stabilized medically and transferred to an acute rehabilitation setting at CDE Rehabilitation Hospital (CDER) on October 2, 2006, where he stayed until November 9, 2006. At the time of admission to CDER Mr. Smith was alert, but a bit depressed. His upper extremity strength was 0/5 and he had a slight shoulder shrug. Both lower extremities had edema and he had a healed pressure ulcer in the sacral area.

Mr. Smith received physical and occupational therapies at CDER and made good progress. He developed one urinary tract infection during his rehab stay that required antibiotic treatment and a two-day hospitalization at Local Hospital Medical Center. During this rehab stay Mr. Smith developed skin breakdown on his right lower extremity. It was treated with duoderm and healed. Mr. Smith also experienced pain from his injuries and was treated with MS Contin, oxycodone and Neurontin for pain management. Spasticity was treated with Baclofen and Valium.

Upon discharge, Mr. Smith was using a power wheelchair with a hand control for the left hand. He could propel the wheelchair greater than 200 feet with minimal assistance. He required maximal assistance with bed mobility 25% of the time, and was dependent for ambulation. Mr. Smith needed a moderate assist for feeding 50% of the time, maximal assistance with grooming, moderate assistance for bathing, and was dependent for dressing, toileting, and transfers.

Following discharge from CDER, Mr. Smith was followed for case management at the Resource Center, from November 2006 through January 2007. Continued progress was noted. The focus of rehabilitation was re-entry to the community with Mr. Smith's sisters as his primary caregivers.

Mr. Smith attended a day program at CDER for the month of April 2007. During this time an occupational therapist worked with Mr. Smith on upper extremity and lower extremity strengthening.

Mr. Smith began physical therapy sessions with Dynamo Physical Therapy in September 2007. According to the records reviewed, Mr. Smith attended therapy sessions as prescribed and made good progress with physical therapy and occupational therapy. At the time of discharge from therapy, in June 2007, Mr. Smith was able to use adaptive equipment to feed himself, required supervisory assistance and assistive devices for upper and lower body dressing, and required maximal assistance with toileting. Assistive devices included a long handled shoe horn and reacher device. Mr. Smith could walk up to 500 feet with a rolling walker, use a treadmill and stair stepper. Mr. Smith was discharged from occupational therapy because all goals were met and he reached a plateau in progress. Physical therapy discharged Mr. Smith with some goals only partially met. The therapist comments that Mr. Smith will use a home exercise program to see if he can maintain his strength and gains at home. Further evaluation was suggested to determine whether continued progress outside a formal therapy program was effective for Mr. Smith. No further therapy records are available for review.

Mr. Smith has been followed primarily by three physicians. Dr. Dean has monitored Mr. Smith's physical progress from an orthopedic standpoint, Dr. Clover provides Botox injections for decreased spasticity, and Dr. Greene follows Mr. Smith for urology issues. In addition a defense medical exam has taken place on two separate occasions, one in 2007 and another in 2008. From the physician examinations it is clear Mr. Smith is totally disabled from working and has suffered permanent impairment from his injuries of August 15, 2006.

Current Status

A rehabilitation evaluation was completed on September 22, 2008 in the office of Dr. Dean. Present at the time of the evaluation was Dr. Dean, Mr. Smith, Cathleen Smythe, interpreter, and a male family caregiver. Dr. Dean did a physical assessment of Mr. Smith, whose chief complaint was that his legs can't move and his ankles can't move. The examination by Dr. Dean revealed minimal active motion in both lower extremities with the left greater than right. Mr. Smith could invert both feet, but had no dorsiflexion capability. There is no sign of the ability to actively use the right upper extremity, with a weak shoulder shrug, minimal elbow mobility and no active wrist mobility. Some discomfort was noted with passive flexion of the right wrist and movement of the right leg.

The left shoulder is weak, with moderate weakness in wrist extension, only minimal finger extension and a weak grasp of the left hand. The left foot can abduct to 90 degrees. Dr. Dean provided Mr. Smith with a prescription for a resting hand splint and hydrotherapy sessions to reduce spasm. Mr. Smith will need assistance in obtaining services in his local area. A functional review was completed as follows:

- **Mobility:** Mr. Smith reports in his last therapy session he was walking 200 to 300 feet, but is no longer able to do that because his leg starts to spasm when he uses his walker. He can walk short distances with his rolling walker, but cannot accomplish inclines. Mr. Smith uses a manual wheelchair while out in the community. He has a power wheelchair at home but has no transportation that will accommodate the wheelchair. He is unable to use the power wheelchair within his home as the home is too small to accommodate the turning radius of the chair and doorways are too narrow.
- **Elimination:** Mr. Smith performs self catheterization with a #14 French catheter, under sterile technique every 2 to 3 hours. He reports his urine volume is good and he drinks lots

of fluids to maintain good urine output. He reports he has had 3 to 4 urinary tract infections in the past year or so, and is seeing Dr. Greene for follow-up every 1–2 months. Since he went to sterile one use catheters, Mr. Smith reports his urinary tract infections have decreased. Bowel elimination is handled by use of a suppository and digital stimulation as needed. He occasionally has an incontinent episode, and wears depends while out of the home and at night.

- **Sexual Evaluation**: Mr. Smith reports he has not been able to engage in any sexual relations since his accident. He is not reporting any erections or ejaculations.
- **Medications**: Mr. Smith reports he takes Ultracet for pain, especially in damp or cold times. He uses about 2 per day, but not everyday. Additionally he receives Baclofen for spasm, uses Ducolax for his bowel routine, and receives Botox injections from Dr. Clover every 3 months to reduce spasticity. At times of urinary tract infection, Mr. Smith will take oral antibiotics as prescribed by Dr. Greene. There are no known drug allergies.
- **Nutrition**: Mr. Smith has gained almost 50 pounds since his accident. He reports he has no appetite but eats regular meals. He denied snacking. He would benefit from ongoing nutritional evaluations.
- **Residential Setting**: Mr. Smith lives with his sister who is his primary caregiver. There have been some family issues with who will care for Mr. Smith. He currently resides in a 2-story home with the full bathroom on the upper floor. There is a powder room on the lower floor to which Mr. Smith has access. In order to bath, Mr. Smith does so outside at night with a hose. There are two steps to enter and exit the home, and Mr. Smith reports he can do the steps with assistance.
- **Community Access**: Mr. Smith cannot get into the vehicles available to him for transportation. He must be lifted into the vehicle and has no access to a vehicle that would enable him to be transported in his wheelchair. Mr. Smith has a rolling walker which he can use for short distances in his home, but fatigue and pain prevent him from using it for community access. Mr. Smith is not a licensed driver, but his sister and family friends are able to drive him to appointments.
- **Psychosocial**: Mr. Smith reports he has good days and bad days depending on the weather. He is in more pain with damp cold weather. There have been some family issues and currently one sister is no longer providing care for Mr. Smith. He has changed homes because of this care giving relationship which places him in a non-accessible home. Mr. Smith reports he will do whatever he can to continue to improve. He is interested in some formal exercise program and in discussion with Dr. Dean, aqua therapy is recommended, as well as a fitness center. Mr. Smith speaks little English and is hampered in his ability to access services independently. He will require ongoing case management services to coordinate and supervise care.
- **General Health**: Mr. Smith reports his health prior to the accident was very good. Currently he suffers from headaches and dizziness, burning of his eyes and blurring of vision. His overall health remains good and he only suffers the usual amount of colds or flu, which he reports don't last long.
- **Spasticity**: Mr. Smith has spasticity in his arms and legs. He visits Dr. Clover to receive Botox injections every 3 months with improvement in reducing spasticity. A resting hand splint was ordered by Dr. Dean to decrease contracture of the right hand. In the future, Mr. Smith may need AFOs to reduce foot drop as well.

Summary

In reviewing the medical records for Mr. Smith, it is clear he suffered a catastrophic injury on August 15, 2006. He remains totally unable to return to work and is challenged with physical disabilities that require ongoing medical interventions. The following pages provide the services currently predicted to meet Mr. Smith's needs specific to his injury of August 15, 2006. Services are projected to a reasonable degree of rehabilitation probability given the information available at the time of the report. Should additional information become available, it may require adjustments to the Life Care Plan.

Respectfully submitted,
Sue Smith, MSN, RN, CRRN, CLCP
Nurse Consultant

Appendix B

Table B1 Life Care Plan: Projected Evaluations

Evaluation	Age/Year Initiated		Age/Year Suspended		Frequency	Base Cost per Year	Growth Trend	Recommended by
Physical therapy	30	2008	Life expectancy		One time per year	$100–$125 per year	To be determined by the economist	Sue Smith, MSN, RN, CRRN after review of available records
Life skills assessment	30	2008	Life expectancy		Annual evaluation (three times only)	$176–$440 per year	To be determined by economist	Sue Smith, MSN, RN, CRRN after review of available records
Recreational therapy evaluation	30	2008	30	2008	One time only evaluation	$150–$185 per year	To be determined by economist	Sue Smith, MSN, RN, CRRN after review of available records
Nutritionist	30	2008	Life expectancy		Two times per year at $65–$90 per evaluation	$130–$180 per year	To be determined by economist	Sue Smith, MSN, RN, CRRN after review of available records

Table B2 Life Care Plan: Projected Therapeutic Modalities

Evaluation	Age/Year Initiated		Age/Year Suspended		Frequency	Base Cost per Year	Growth Trend	Recommended By
Physical therapy	30	2008	Life expectancy		2–3 times per week for 12 weeks × 4 sessions at cost of $50–$200 per week	$1,200–$7,200 (four times only through life expectancy)	To be determined by the economist	Sue Smith, MSN, RN, CRRN after review of available records
Life skills training	30	2008	30	2009	4–6 hr per week at rate of $40–$50 per hour	$8,000–$15,000	To be determined by the economist	Sue Smith, MSN, RN, CRRN after review of available records
Rehabilitation case management	30	2008	Life expectancy		6–10 hr per month for 6 months, then 6–10 hr per quarter for 5 years; then 2–4 hr per quarter for life expectancy at rate of $75–$105 per hour	$3,600–$10,000 for 1 year, then $1,800–$5,000 year 2–6, then $600–$2,000 per year to life expectancy	To be determined by the economist	Sue Smith, MSN, RN, CRRN after review of available records
Interpreter	30	2008	Life expectancy		2–6 hr per month for life expectancy at cost of $35–$50 per hour plus $.25 per mile (estimated to be 500 miles per year)	$840–$3,600 per year plus $125 for mileage per year for life expectancy	To be determined by the economist	Sue Smith, MSN, RN, CRRN after review of available records
Recreational therapy	30	2008	30	2009	Weekly for 6–8 weeks at cost of $135–$160 per session (one time only)	$810–$1,300 for 1 year only	To be determined by economist	Sue Smith, MSN, RN, CRRN after review of available records

Table B3 Life Care Plan: Transportation

Equipment	Age When Purchased		Replacement Schedule	Equipment Purpose	Base Cost	Growth Trend	Catalog/Supplier
Adapted van with raised roof, lifts and tie downs	30	2008	Once every 8–10 years while in home-care setting	Facilitate transportation	$38,000.00–$48,000.00	To be determined by economist	Local vendors
Cellular telephone	30	2008	One time every 3 years	Emergency assistance access	$50.00 to $100.00 per replacement and $20.00 to $30.00 monthly access fee for basic service	To be determined by economist	Local vendors

Table B4 Wheelchair Needs

Evaluation	Age When Purchased		Replacement Schedule	Equipment Purpose	Base Cost	Growth Trend	Catalog/Supplier
Power wheelchair	34	2012	Every 7–10 years	Mobility within the environment	$8,500–$10,500	To be determined by the economist	Local vendor
Quickie two manual wheelchair	30	2008	Every 5 years	Mobility within the environment	$1,850–$2,200	To be determined by the economist	Local vendor
Seating system for power chair (includes J-2 cushions	30	2008	Every 2–3 years at cost of $500–$1,050 per replacement	Positioning in wheelchair	$1,000–$2,100	To be determined by the economist	Local vendor

Table B5 Life Care Plan: Wheelchair Accessories and Maintenance

Evaluation	Age When Purchased		Replacement Schedule	Equipment Purpose	Base Cost	Growth Trend	Catalog/Supplier
Lap tray for wheelchair	30	2008	Every 3–5 years	Facilitate activities at waist level	$230–$250 every 3–5 years	To be determined by economist	Local vendor
Back pack for wheelchair	30	2008	Yearly	Provide ability to carry equipments or supplies	$25–$50 per year	To be determined by economist	Local vendor
Wheelchair maintenance contracts	30	2008	Annual renewal	Maintenance of manual wheelchairs	$200–$305 per year	To be determined by economist	Local vendor
Batteries for power wheelchair	30	2008	Annual replacement	Facilitate power	$350.00 to $400.00 per year	To be determined by economist	Local vendor

Table B6 Life Care Plan: Home Furnishings and Accessories

Evaluation	Age When Purchased		Replacement Schedule	Equipment Purpose	Base Cost	Growth Trend	Catalog/Supplier
Shower transfer chair[a]	30	2008	Every 3–5 years	Safety and support for bathing	$175–$200	To be determined by economist	Local vendor
Hand held shower[a]	30	2008	Every 2–3 years	Facilitate bathing independence	$40–$50	To be determined by economist	Local vendor
Portable ramping	30	2008	Every 3–5 years	Mobility access in home and community	$150–$350	To be determined by economist	Local vendor
Transfer Board[a]	40	2018	Every 5–7 years	Facilitate transfers	$75–$100	To be determined by economist	Local vendor
Electric hospital bed[a]	30	2008	Every 8–10 years with mattress replacement every 3–5 years	Facilitate positioning and independence	$1,230–$1,500 for bed package every 8–10 years; Mattress replacement every 3–5 years at $550–$650 per replacement	To be determined by economist	Local vendor

[a] Costs may be included in residential setting costs, but would be required for home modification should the home-care option be chosen.

Table B7 Life Care Plan: Orthodics/Prosthetics

Evaluation	Age When Purchased		Replacement Schedule	Equipment Purpose	Base Cost	Growth Trend	Catalog/Supplier
Molded hand splint	30	2008	Every 1–2 years	Positioning and support for right hand	$200–$300 every 1–2 years	To be determined by economist	Local vendor
AFO	30	2008	Annual replacement due to increased tone	Positioning and support for left foot	$750–$900 every year	To be determined by economist	Local vendor
Rolling walker	30	2008	Every 3–5 years	Promote balance in ambulation or transfers	$150–$170	To be determined by economist	Local vendor

Table B8 Orthopedic Equipment Needs

Evaluation	Age When Purchased	Replacement Schedule	Equipment Purpose	Base Cost	Growth Trend	Catalog/Supplier
No needs identified in this area at this time						

Table B9   Life Care Plan: Aggressive Treatment Modalities

Evaluation	Age/Year Initiated	Age/Year Suspended	Frequency	Base Cost per Year	Growth Trend	Recommended By
Botox injections	30	2008	Life expectancy	Four times per year at cost of $500–$900 per session	$2,000–$3,600	To be determined by the economist	Sue Smith, MSN, RN, CRRN after review of available records

Table B10   Home/Facility Care

Facility Option	Home-Care Option	Age/Year Initiated	Age/Year Suspended	Hours/Shifts/Days	Base Cost per Year	Growth Trends
Option #1: Residential setting assisted living facility placement		30 2008	Life expectancy	24 hr per day at rate of $150–$200 per day	$54,750.00–$73,000.00	To be determined by economist
	Option #2A: Home health aide services for 2–4 hr per day	30 2008	Life expectancy	14–30 hr per week at rate of $19.00–$24.00 per hour	$13,832–$34,944	To be determined by economist
	Option #2B: Respite care services to relieve sister of care giving responsibility	30 2008	Life expectancy	24 hr per day for 3–5 days per month at cost of $19.00–$24.00 per hour	$16,416–$34,560	To be determined by economist

Table B11 Life Care Plan: Drug and Supply Needs

Supply Description	Drugs	Purpose	Per unit Cost	Per year Costs	Growth Trend	Catalog/Supplier
	Baclofen 20 mg twice daily	Reduce spasticity	$1.45–$1.75 per dose	$1,058.50–$1,307.50	To be determined by economist	Local pharmacy
	Ducolax suppository	Bowel regimen	$.50–$.75 per suppository (use of approximately 400 per year)	$200.00–$300.00	To be determined by economist	Local pharmacy
	Ultracet 1–2 tablets every 4 hr as needed for pain	Pain management	$1.50–$1.75 per dose (use of approximately 500 per year)	$750.00–$875.00	To be determined by economist	Local pharmacy
Disposable diapers and underpads		Elimination management	$70.00–$75.00 per month	$840.00–$900.00	To be determined by economist	Local supplier
Sterile #14 French intermittent catheters		Drain bladder	$1.45–$1.89 per catheter use of 6–8 per day	$3,175.50–$5,518.80	To be determined by economist	Local supplier
Gloves and lubricant		Bowel and bladder program 6–8 pairs per day and 2 tubes of lubricant per month	Gloves $.05–$.08 per glove lubricant $4.00–$5.00 per tube	$315.00–$530.20	To be determined by economist	Local supplier

Table B12 Life Care Plan: Future Medical Care-Routine

Medical Care	Frequency of Visits	Purpose	Cost per Visit	Cost per Year	Growth Trend	Recommended By
Physiatrist	3–4 times per year	Medical management of disability; Botox injection	$250–$290 per visit	$250–$580 per year	To be determined by economist	Sue Smith, MSN, RN, CRRN after review of available records
Orthopedist	1–2 times per year	Monitoring of orthopedic conditions	$250–$290 per visit	$250–$580 per year	To be determined by economist	Sue Smith, MSN, RN, CRRN after review of available records
Internist	2–4 times per year	Routine health maintenance	2–3 visits per year in excess of expected routine care included in LCP (other visits not associated with disability) at cost of $65–$75 per visit	$130–$225 per year	To be determined by economist	Sue Smith, MSN, RN, CRRN after review of available records
Dentist	4 times per year	Routine dental care	Two visits per year in excess of routine care (other visits not associated disability) at cost of $100–$150 per visit	$200–$300 per year	To be determined by economist	Sue Smith, MSN, RN, CRRN after review of available records
Podiatrist	12 times per year	Routine care of toenails	$75–$125 per visit	$900–$1,500 per year	To be determined by economist	Sue Smith, MSN, RN, CRRN after review of available records
Urologist	Four times per year	Management of neurogenic bladder	$250–$300 per visit	$1,000–$1,200 per year	To be determined by economist	Sue Smith, MSN, RN, CRRN after review of available records

Table B13 Leisure Time/Therapeutic Recreational Equipment

Description	Age/Year Initiated		Age/Year Suspended	Replacement Schedule	Base Cost	Growth Trend	Catalog/Supplier
Gym membership (aqua therapy)	30	2008	Life expectancy	Annual membership at $45–$55 per month	$540–$660 per year	To be determined by economist	Local vendors

Table B14 Educational/Vocational

Recommendation	Age/Year Initiated	Age/Year Suspended	Frequency	Per Year Cost	Growth Trend	Recommended By
No needs determined in this area						

Table B15 Life Care Plan: Aids for Independent Function

Equipment	Age/Year Purchased		Replacement Schedule	Equipment Purpose	Base Cost	Growth Trend	Catalog/Supplier
Overhead reacher	30	2008	One time every 1–2 years	Increase independence	$20–$100	To be determined by economist	Local provider
Extended shoe horn	30	2008	One time every 1–2 years	Increase independence	$15–$25	To be determined by economist	Local provider
Adapted feeding equipment	30	2008	One time every 1–2 years	Increase independence	$50–$75	To be determined by economist	Local provider

Table B16 Life Care Plan: Diagnostic Testing

Recommendation	Age/Year Initiated		Age/Year Suspended	Frequency	Base Cost	Growth Trend	Recommended By
Orthopedic x-rays	30	2008	Life expectancy	Every 3–5 years	$100–$200 per event	To be determined by economist	Sue Smith, MSN, RN, CRRN after review of available records
Urinalysis	30	2008	Life expectancy	$15–$25 per test with estimate of 4–6 tests per year	$60–$150 per year	To be determined by economist	Sue Smith, MSN, RN, CRRN after review of available records
Urine culture	30	2008	Life expectancy	$18–$22 per test with estimate of 2–4 tests per year	$36–$88 per year	To be determined by economist	Sue Smith, MSN, RN, CRRN after review of available records

Table B17 Life Care Plan: Potential Complications (For Information Only)

Complication	Estimated Costs
Contractures	May require splinting and increased physical therapy costs; untreated or resistant contractures could require hospitalization and surgical repair
Skin breakdown	Costs would include protective seating systems, enhanced skin care routine, home nursing visits, medications or possible surgery
Urosepsis	Costs would include IV antibiotics, hospital admission

Table B18 Life Care Plan: Architectural Renovations

Accessibility Needs		Accessibility Needs		Costs
Ramping	x	Bathroom		Costs would be one time for life expectancy and are dependent on home chosen for retrofitting
		Sink	x	
Light/environmental controls				New construction costs would increase 20–30% to incorporate accessibility features
		Cabinets	x	
Floor coverings	x			Retrofitting existing structures can cost between $50,000 and $150,000 depending on age, number of stories, and amount of accessibility options required
		Roll-in-shower		
Hallways	x			
		Temperature control guards		
Doorways	x			
		Heater		
Covered parking	x			
		Fixtures		
Kitchen				
Sinks/fixtures	x	Door handles	x	
Cabinets	x	Additional electric outlets	x	
Appliances	x	Central air/heat	x	
Windows	x	Therapy/equipment storage	x	
Electric safety doors		Attendant bedroom		
Fire alarm	x	Other		
Smoke detector	x			
Intercom system	x			

Chapter 14

Pediatric Case Evaluation

Paula Deaun Jackson, RN, MSN, CRNP, LNC and
Christine Revzin Merritt, MSN, RN, LNCC

Contents

Objectives

- ■ To discuss differences found in the pediatric population versus the adult population
- ■ To describe at least two standards of care specific to pediatrics
- ■ To describe the types of medical misadventures found in pediatric malpractice cases
- ■ To recognize the concept of emancipated minor and how it applies to pediatric case evaluation
- ■ To identify pediatric-specific resources

The work of childhood is play. Children are not little adults. The authors of this chapter have had the privilege of working with the pediatric population for many years. During clinical experiences and interactions with the child and family, the professional nurse learns that the above sayings are guiding principles for pediatric nursing. When caring for children and families, the nurse must rely on psychosocial skills as well as technical knowledge. Whether a child was born with a condition or disease that requires lifelong care and supervision, or the child was an otherwise healthy individual before becoming sick or injured, the nurse knows that the care delivered is specialized. Differences in pediatric care and case evaluation go beyond the difference in equipment and accepted ranges for vital signs compared to that of the adult. It is equally important for the legal nurse consultant (LNC) to remember this principle when reviewing pediatric records.

In negligence claims over the past 20 years, pediatric cases account for approximately 3% of all claims, ranking it 10th among the 28 specialties in the terms of closed claims. According to data from Physician Insurers Association of America (PIAA), the five most common diagnoses involved in pediatric malpractice claims are brain-injured infants, meningitis, routine infant/child health check, respiratory problems in the newborn, and appendicitis.

A medical misadventure is a descriptive phrase used to identify an alleged departure from accepted medical practice. Errors in misdiagnosis are the most prevalent medical misadventure, with meningitis being the most common diagnosis in this category. The second most prevalent pediatric claim involves issues where a newborn is found to have a brachial plexus injury that occurred during delivery. The claim may have several defendant breaches in the cumulative care of the patient resulted in injury. Failure to supervise or monitor the care of a patient has the highest indemnity payment rate. Examples of this type of case include brain-injured infants, children with respiratory problems, as well as children with meningitis. The fifth most prevalent medical misadventure is medication errors, which in pediatric patients can be associated with asthma care, routine well child checks, bronchiolitis, and seizure management. The claim in these types of cases is often a delay in performance, with the provider deferring testing or treatment of the patient, resulting in a bad outcome.

Demographics

The National Practitioner Data Bank (NPDB) began collecting patient age information for malpractice payees in 2004. Since that time (through March 31, 2008), a total of 60,801 malpractice payment reports submitted to the NPDB have contained patient age information. A total of 8,031 payments (13.2%) were for 18-year-old or younger claimants and 52,770 payments (86.8%) were for 19-year-old or older claimants. In terms of dollar amounts paid, a total of $3,354,093,627 was paid out for 18-year-old or younger claimants (median payment = $200,000; mean = $417,643.34). The median is a more accurate measure of the "average" or typical payment since the means are skewed by a few very large payments. (Robert E. Oshel, PhD, Associate Director for Research and Disputes, Division of Practitioner Data Banks, 2008.)

What Makes Pediatric Cases Different, and What is the LNC Role?

As children grow, they learn about their environment daily. Their ability to understand and assimilate information about their world depends on their chronological age as well as their level of cognitive development. Younger children tend to be concrete thinkers who interpret the term "draw your blood" literally, and expect the caregiver to draw a picture of the blood in their body. The preschooler who can be uncooperative with care tasks in the hospital or clinic setting needs to be reassured that when the provider is "taking their temperature" that they are not going to lose something on their body and that personal possessions will not be taken from them.

Children's ability to understand the role of healthcare providers depends upon their previous experience with healthcare delivery and providers, as well as the influence of their family, friends, and society. The child is part of a family, both traditional and nontraditional in nature. The caregivers of the child become part of the nurse's patient load in terms of responsibilities of care. The nurse must disseminate and explain information, empower the caregiver to assist with care tasks, teach the caregiver skills to provide care for the child at home, provide emotional support, and advocate for the child and family (Aiken & Catalano, 1994).

Growth and Development

The work of Erik Erikson, one of the leading psychologists who developed theories on psychosocial development throughout the human lifespan, can be an informative guide to the LNC reviewing pediatric cases. Using Erikson's stages as a reference, the LNC can familiarize himself or herself with the emotional issues a child is encountering at a particular stage in the child's life. The LNC will then be able to analyze records and determine if age-appropriate care was rendered during any phase of the healthcare delivery process (School Nurse Emergency Medical Services for Children [SNEMS-C] Program, 2001).

Consider the following example of age-appropriate care documented in the medical record by a healthcare provider: Susie Brown is a 3-year-old female with a 4-day history of signs and symptoms of an upper respiratory tract infection with temperature to 102°, not subsiding with antipyretics. After administering Tylenol suspension p.o. for age and weight, the nurse offered Susie a picture book and plastic baby doll to accompany her to radiology for a chest x-ray to rule out pneumonia. The child was transported to radiology while being held in her mother's arms. Because Susie is in the toddler stage, during which she would be learning what she can or cannot control in her environment, these care interventions are appropriate. By taking familiar items with her for exams and procedures, she is able to exert some control in the unfamiliar hospital environment in a potentially frightening situation.

Healthcare providers who have a working knowledge of normal childhood growth and development and milestones that children reach at different ages will be able to deliver and document developmentally appropriate care to the child and his or her family. The LNC can consult numerous resources to assist in learning this information for case review. The LNC should consult credible websites and authoritative references for guidance, such as those in the appendix, which lists professional pediatric organizations and government regulatory agencies as resources for the review of pediatric cases.

Multidisciplinary Team Approach

The LNC will find that pediatric cases often involve professionals from a variety of backgrounds, including child life specialists, social workers, nutritionists, physical therapists, speech therapists, occupational therapists, respiratory therapists, home health agencies, school nurses, public health nurses, hospital and clinic nurses, and physicians and surgeons.

Because each of these disciplines may have documented interventions delivered to the child at some point, the LNC will need to find the information from these disciplines and identify any missing records that should be obtained from these other professions (i.e., prenatal and birth records, pediatrician records, school records).

Each of these professionals can play an integral role in the care of a child with an injury or illness. The LNC needs to consider these individuals as resources because they may be valuable as expert witnesses to support or refute a claim.

Family-Centered Care

Another major difference in pediatric cases is the focus on family-centered care, in which the healthcare providers consider the whole family and not just the child in healthcare delivery along a wellness continuum. The importance of including the child's family in care cannot be overstated. A child's major social experience is within his own family, and it is within this relationship that the child learns behaviors, traditions, and values. This includes the child's response to injury and illness and interactions with providers in the healthcare system.

Provider documentation should include the family members who present with the child during care for injury and illness, as well as those with whom the child spends most of his or her time, to provide a snapshot into the child's regular routines and activity. Medical records should reflect that the family members present were afforded the opportunity to be involved in the child's care as much or as little as they desired. All teaching and instruction given to the family members by various staff (doctors, nurses, physical therapists, etc.) should be available for review in the records. Some important questions to ponder during pediatric case evaluation include the following:

- What was the disposition of the child?
- Were the parents or guardians involved in the patient's care?
- Were they notified of changes in the patient's condition?
- Were they notified of medication errors and outcomes?
- Were they involved in the informed consent process?
- Is there documentation in the chart or records to show evidence of discharge teaching and after care instructions and that the parents understood them?

Appropriate Treatment

One of the key questions for the LNC to keep in mind during pediatric case review is whether the child received appropriate care. Was the treatment safe and in accordance with nationally recognized guidelines? Did the provider follow a treatment plan that would be reasonable and accepted by other providers of the same specialty? Appropriate care will depend on growth and development, as well as on medical facts.

Expert Witnesses

The LNC may need to recommend an expert witness who would be of value in providing testimony on a case, giving recommendations for the type of specialist needed. There are a host of pediatric subspecialists, which the LNC should consider. In some cases, the pediatric specialist may be relied upon for outside record review and testimony, as the specialist would be in the best position to render an opinion on a particular pediatric case.

Future Losses

Yet another difference in pediatric cases is the potential for future losses. Babies and young children do not have occupation-related issues such as wage loss to consider. However, potential future losses secondary to childhood injury or illness as a result of professional negligence or bodily injury should be considered as a consequence of the injury. The LNC needs to review the case for damages that the child suffered. A pediatric lifecare planner may be required to establish a formal list of damages and coexisting present and future costs associated with the case. An economist may be required to establish loss of future-earning capacity. The LNC will initially review the case, looking for damages, and will want to recommend to the attorney appropriate referrals and additional sources of information. Some questions to consider include

- Was the child hurt, and if so, in what way?
- What was the mechanism of injury?
- What evaluation and assessment was noted in the records?
- What was the diagnosis or clinical impressions that directed the recommended treatment plan?
- What body system(s) were affected?
- Did the child treat with medical providers? What type of providers? How long was the child in treatment?
- Were there complications related to the medical treatment?
- Is there evidence of follow up care?
- What is the current health status of the child?
- Did the child sustain permanent injury?
- Are there cognitive issues to consider, as may be the case for a traumatic brain injury?

Missing Documents

The LNC needs to identify records that are missing from the file that may be crucial for analysis. If the case involves an injury during birth, it is necessary to request and obtain fetal monitoring strips, which are not always part of the medical record. LNCs will be wise to develop a list of case-specific questions to consider in determining where to search for discoverable documents. A sample of this type of questions might include

- Was there prenatal care?
- Would the prenatal records provide insight into issues of relatedness of prenatal exposure and birth defects?
- What documentation exists for the infant's first 24–48 hr of life?
- Was follow-up care documented?
- Are there well child checks including immunization records and developmental information to review?
- Would school records or report cards shed light on a child's cognitive status prior to and after a motor vehicle accident with posttraumatic brain injury?
- If there are preexisting conditions including the use of medications for any conditions, is there evidence of this in the records?
- Are there missing records from specialists, such as psychologists or neurologists?
- Did the child sustain permanent injury?
- Are there cognitive issues to consider, as may be the case for a traumatic brain injury?

Screening for Abuse and Neglect

Pediatric admissions often include a screening for abuse and neglect. The LNC will be reviewing this documentation. An important issue to keep in mind is that healthcare professionals are mandated reporters, and have a legal responsibility to notify authorities if they suspect the child is a victim of abuse or neglect.

Restraints

Pediatric clients often require restraints for medical procedures. The LNC will need to consider: Was the use of restraints (mechanical or chemical) documented according to facility policy? For example, a pediatric patient with a peripheral IV line in the arm, hand, wrist, ankle, or other site, likely has an arm board, which limits or prohibits the use of the area with the IV to avoid accidental or intentional removal of the IV. Most facility policies address the condition of the skin and site being routinely monitored and documented. In the intensive care units, pediatric clients may require chemical restraints. Chemical restraint in the intubated child in an intensive care unit setting should be clearly documented by drug name, dose, and route. The child's response to the use of these restraints should be documented by the provider as well.

Transfer

Children often need to be transferred to another unit or facility for higher level acuity needs. The documentation should support the need for transfer (i.e., diminished ability to maintain the airway or a change in cardiac status). The child's condition during such transfer should be evidenced by documentation in the records.

Pain

The LNC should research the records for documentation that reflects assessment of the "fifth vital sign" or pain. An appropriate pain scale for a child aged three and older is the FACES Pain Rating Scale developed by Wong and Baker. The tool is made up of six drawings of cartoon faces that represent levels of pain in terms the child can understand (e.g., "No hurt" to "Hurts worst" for maximum level of pain) (Figure 14.1).

| 0
No hurt | 1
Hurts
little bit | 2
Hurts
little more | 3
Hurts
even more | 4
Hurts
whole lot | 5
Hurts
worst |

Figure 14.1 FACES Pain Rating Scale. [From Hockenberry, M. J., Wilson, D., & Winkelstein, M. L. (2005). *Wong's essentials of pediatric nursing* (7th ed., p. 1259). St. Louis: Copyright Mosby. With permission.]

Wong–Baker FACES Pain Rating Scale is the standard of care for reporting pediatric pain levels. The LNC should expect to find assessments, reassessments, and interventions that meet the facility policy and procedure for documentation of pain.

Patient Education

Any teaching done with the patient and family by all healthcare providers should be clearly documented. The learning needs should be identified, whether it was the disease process, medications, plan of care, or discharge instruction. The type of teaching done should be noted, including verbal, verbal and handouts, materials provided, demonstration and return demonstration, etc. The response of the learner (child and/or caregiver) should be noted as well, including verbalization of instructions, concepts, and/or a return demonstration of teaching.

Battered Child Syndrome

The "battered child syndrome" *if accepted by the court*, facilitates proof of child abuse in appropriate cases. Evidence of the syndrome is accepted more readily in civil than in criminal cases, but often plays a role in the latter.

Case law example #1: Two-year-old C was admitted to the hospital and placed in intensive care, where she had to be fed intravenously for 2 weeks. She was covered with bruises and abrasions, including an open lesion of the size of a nickel under her left eye. She was severely dehydrated and had internal abdominal injuries that were later diagnosed as a fractured spleen, pancreatitis, and liver dysfunction. The injury had occurred approximately 1 week before C arrived at the hospital. C's medical history, as given by F to the physicians, was inconsistent with C's injuries. F and M were tried for injury to a child and convicted. They appealed, claiming that the trial court erred in admitting evidence of battered child syndrome. On appeal the court upheld, "Expert testimony is permitted, in the court's discretion, if the witness has a special skill or knowledge, beyond the ken of the average juror, that, as properly applied, would be helpful to the determination of an ultimate issue. Battered child syndrome had become a well-established medical diagnosis. Expert medical witness, therefore, may appropriately explain the syndrome to the jury and express his opinion that the victim suffers from it." (*State v. Dumlao*, 3 Conn.App. 607, A.2d 404, 1985.)

Case law example #2: M was convicted of the murder of her infant daughter, C. M had called the police and asked for an ambulance. C appeared to be unconscious. The emergency technicians discovered multiple bruises on C's face, neck, chest, and abdomen, and a patch of skin was missing from her neck. One side of C's head was (mushy?) due to blood and fluid under the skin. M said that the child had fallen out of her hands and struck the floor. An autopsy revealed other injuries, including a broken arm and an injured liver. According to a forensic pathologist, these injuries were consistent with battered child syndrome. A clinical psychologist constructed a profile of the typical abusive parent. The profile fit M's character. M was convicted. The issue on appeal was whether the testimony as to battered child syndrome should have been admitted. (Result: Testimony should not have been admitted. "[U]nless a defendant has placed her character in issue or has raised some defense which the battering parent syndrome is relevant to rebut, the state may not introduce evidence of the syndrome, nor may the state introduce character evidence showing a defendant's personality traits and personal history as its foundation for demonstrating that the defendant has the characteristics of a typical battering parent." However, the court went on to find that the error was harmless due to the overwhelming evidence of M's guilt, and it affirmed the judgment.) (*Sanders v. State*, 251 Ga.70, 303 S.E.2d 13, 1983.)

Types of Issues

Statute of Limitations

There are many issues the LNC can consider during pediatric case evaluation. In most states, laws give special consideration to children because they lack the legal capacity to sue. Some states postpone applying the statute of limitations to an injured child until he/she reaches the age of majority. The age of majority may be 18 or 21 depending on the state.

The statute of limitations for injury cases is different for minors, and the law varies from state to state. For example, in Utah the statute of limitations for medical malpractice is 2 years with the discovery rule (1 year from the act), but never more than 4 years from occurrence. Actions against healthcare providers must be filed within 2 years of the malpractice or within 2 years from the date the injury was or could/should have been discovered. "In no event may a person file a medical malpractice action more than four years from the date of the act giving rise to the injury. These time limitations also apply to minors under 18." (From http://www.statutes-of-limitations.com/state/utah retrieved online August 28, 2008.) In Vermont, a medical malpractice suit may not be filed more than 7 years from the date of malpractice. The above examples underline the need for the LNC to be knowledgeable of the statue of limitations in the jurisdiction in which the litigation is filed.

Retention of Records

The retention of records for minors is typically until they reach adulthood or 18 years of age. If the LNC reviewing a case identifies missing records or the need for prior records, longer limits on retention of records for minors may allow these to be found more readily (Association for Sport and Physical Education, 1995).

According to the American Health Information Management Association Practice Brief on the Retention of Health Information (2002), "If the patient was a minor, the provider should retain health information until the patient reaches the age of majority (as defined by state law) plus the period of the statute of limitations, unless otherwise provided by state law. A longer retention period is prudent, since the statute may not begin until the potential plaintiff learns of the causal relationship between an injury and the care received" (Maternal and Child Health Bureau, 1999).

Minors and Consent

In general, parent(s) must consent to any medical treatment given their minor child, except in an emergency. When a child requires medical treatment and the parents deny such treatment, the juvenile court may appoint a guardian for the child and direct that guardian to consent to necessary treatment.

Case law: A child was diagnosed as having a type of leukemia. The child's parents refused to consent to chemotherapy.

Court ruling:

> Natural parents do not have the authority of life and death over their children. The parents' right to control the child's nurture is akin to a trust, subject to a correlative duty to care for *and* protect the child. That right is terminable by the parents' failure to discharge their obligations. Although the parents were loving and devoted in all other

respects, their refusal to continue with chemotherapy for their child amounted to an unwillingness to provide necessary medical care and warranted an order removing legal custody from them. (*Custody of a Minor*, 375 Mass. 733, 379 N.E.2d 1052, 1978).

The LNC should be aware of several issues regarding minors and consent. The doctrine of "informed consent" has limited *direct* application in pediatrics. This is due to a child's limited decision-making capacity and legal empowerment. Therefore, only a child with decision-making capacity and legal empowerment can give their informed consent. In all other situations, parents or a surrogate provide informed permission for all medical treatment with the assent of the child whenever possible (Lee et al., 2006). The pediatric patient, whenever reasonable, should participate in the decision-making process commensurate with their developmental level. The LNC should review the medical documents for an indication of the child's assent to care.

Mature Minors

A mature minor is a nonemancipated minor in their mid- to late teens who shows clear signs of emotional and intellectual maturity. A mature minor may be able to exercise certain adult rights; however, this is state dependent.

Emancipated Minors

Special consideration in pediatric record review is the emancipated minor. A person may be considered an emancipated minor if the state in which he lives recognizes this status and he meets the criteria. The LNC should be aware that not all 50 states recognize or allow emancipation. A person under the age of 18 is considered a minor, but may be emancipated if he marries or joins the armed forces, or if he is able to show he is capable of living independently and managing his own finances. The emancipated minor is able to make decisions regarding his own health, education, living arrangements, and is able to initiate a lawsuit as well as being sued himself.

The following are examples of situations involving minors and consent that are state specific. The LNC should familiarize themselves with their jurisdictional specifics:

Nonemancipated minors

Mature, nonemancipated minors

Emancipated minors

Parental or guardian disagreement

Minors needing emergency treatment

Minors and abortion

Minors and contraception

Minors and communicable disease treatment

Minors and drug abuse treatment

Minors and mental health treatment

Minors' treatment and religious belief conflicts

Case law: At the age of 16½, a *child* refused to enter an in-patient facility for psychiatric evaluation. The *father* locked her out the home and refused to support her. The *child* maintained herself with a part-time job and the help of friends and neighbors. The child petitioned the court for support from the *father*.

Result: The court ruled in favor of the *child*. A *parents'* obligation does not cease simply because the child has disobeyed instructions or is at odds with the parents.

> The *child's* part-time position was not enough to sustain her and did not result in her emancipation.
>
> Inasmuch as the *father* refused to allow the *child* to return to the home "there is no injustice in having him provide for her support elsewhere." (*Jennifer S v. Marvin S.*, 150 Misc2d 300, 568 N.Y.S.2d 515, 1991)

Minors with a Legal Right to Consent for Specific Treatment

Various states have enacted statutes granting minors the ability to give legal consent to a variety of medical procedures, particularly those involving drugs, alcoholism, and sexual behaviors. The U.S. Supreme Court's concern with minor's right to abortion has facilitated new inroads in this area.

Abortion

The U.S. Supreme Court has held that a "mature" minor may obtain an abortion without parental consent or notification if she establishes her "maturity" in an appropriate "bypass procedure." The court has not set a fixed age for "maturity" or provided a clear definition of "maturity." What is a judicial bypass? A judicial bypass is an order from a judge that allows a minor to have an abortion without telling or receiving consent from her parent or legal guardian. To get a judicial bypass, a judge must decide that the minor meets at least one of the following "grounds" (reasons):

- The minor is mature and sufficiently well informed about her pregnancy options to make the decision without a parent or legal guardian being involved
- It is not in the minor's best interest for the parent or legal guardian to be notified
- Notification of a parent or legal guardian could lead to physical, sexual, or emotional abuse of the minor

Case law: The first example of the Supreme Court's initiative in an abortion is viewed in the case of a Missouri abortion issue. The Missouri statute required the parents' written consent to an abortion requested by an unmarried woman under 18, unless a licensed physician certified that abortion was necessary to preserve the mother's life. On appeal the U.S. Supreme Court held the blanket parental consent requirement unconstitutional. No significant state interests, whether to safeguard family unity or parental authority or otherwise, were found to justify conditioning abortion on parental consent. (*Planned Parenthood of Central Missouri v. Danforth*, 428 U.S. 52, 96 S. Ct. 2831, 49 L.Ed.2d 788, 1976.)

A second case presents a slightly different view of informed consent in minors requesting abortions. A Pennsylvania statute required a minor wishing to obtain an abortion to obtain the informed consent of one of her parents. A judicial "bypass" procedure was available. On appeal the Supreme Court held the one-parent consent requirement is constitutional. "Except in a medical emergency, an unemancipated young woman under 18 may not obtain an abortion unless she and one of her parents (or guardian) provides informed consent ... If neither parent nor guardian provides consent, a court may authorize the performance of an abortion upon a determination that the young woman is mature and capable of giving informed consent, or that an abortion would be in her best interests. ... Our cases establish, and we reaffirm today, that a State may require a minor seeking an abortion to obtain the consent of a parent or guardian, if there is an adequate judicial bypass procedure. Under these precedents, in our view, the one-parent consent requirement and judicial bypass procedure are constitutional." (*Planned Parenthood v. Casey*, 505 U.S. 833 112 S.Ct 2791, 120 .Ed.2d. 674, 1992a.) The Supreme Court balances the parents' right to control health-care decisions of teens with the child's right to access reproductive services. Similar statutes exist for protection of younger children.

Legal Concerns and Young Children

Child Health and Safety

A majority of young children are enrolled in out-of-home child-care programs. Both high-quality early education and child care for young children improve their health and promotes their development and learning. Licensing is the first line of protection for children in out-of-family child-care settings in the United States. In general, licensing intends to insure that the care provided is adequate to prevent harm to children; inferring that the building is safe and sanitary, and appropriate adult supervision exists in the program. Some of the most common injuries that children in child care are at risk for include choking, strangulation, suffocation, entrapment, poisoning, sudden infant death syndrome (SIDS), human biting, and transportation accidents.

Child Injury Statistics

More than 200,000 children aged 14 and younger are treated in emergency rooms each year due to a playground-related injury (CDC, 2004). Nearly half of the injuries sustained are considered severe and include fractures, concussions, dislocations, and amputations (Tinsworth & McDonald, 2001). For children under 6, playground-related injuries number about 90,000 each year and account for more visits to the emergency room than any other child-care-related injury (Tinsworth & McDonald, 2001). Most injuries occur when a child falls from the playground equipment onto the ground. In a study conducted in 1999, it was found that 24% of the child-care settings did not have safe playground surfacing, and 27% of the child-care settings did not keep the playground surfacing well maintained (Tinsworth & McDonald, 2001).

Approximately 15 children die each year from playground-related injuries, and three children have died on playgrounds at child-care settings since 1990 (Tinsworth & McDonald, 2001).

CFOC Standards for Maintaining a Safe Playground

In a cooperative effort, the American Academy of Pediatrics, American Public Health Association, and National Resource Center for Health and Safety in Child Care and Early Education developed a comprehensive source, *Caring for Our Children: National Health and Safety Performance*

Standards: Guidelines for Out-of-Home Child Care Programs: Second Edition, that lists over 700 health and safety practices in the following areas:

- Staffing
- Program activities (child development)
- Health promotion and protection
- Nutrition
- Facilities, supplies, equipment, and transportation
- Infectious diseases
- Children eligible for services under Individuals with Disabilities Education Act (IDEA)
- Administration

While Caring for Our Children (CFOC) is a comprehensive resource, the LNC should note that all licensed child-care facilities must first comply with state regulations. The LNC can familiarize his or herself with the standards in Stepping Stones, a group of 234 standards from *Caring for Our Children*, which have been determined to have the greatest impact in reducing disease, disability, and death in child care. Another good source on policies is Pennsylvania AAP's *Model Child Care Health Policies, 4th edition*. In relation to playgrounds, the *CFOC* standards suggest daily and monthly checks by the child-care provider to both examine deterioration of structures and initiate correction or removal of hazards (5. 194, 5.196, 5.197, CFOC). In addition to these important daily and monthly checks, a child-care facility should have an independent inspection conducted by a trained playground safety professional at least annually.

Day Care Setting

The LNC reviewing day care center cases will want to consider the following:

Child-to-staff ratio and group size: Child-to-staff ratios and smaller group sizes are associated with improved quality in child-care centers in a number of studies.

Staff turnover: Staff turnover rates are quite high in child-care centers—roughly three times more than the rates of school teachers. Turnover has a clear connection to the quality of programs.

Staff education and training: Staff education and specific training in child-related fields (the general education level and number of years of schooling) and specific training in child-related fields are both related to quality of programs. Compensation, turnover, and education are all interrelated.

Director competency: There are specific educational requirements that are essential for the position of program director. Refer to each state's regulating agency for the specific requirements. The ability of the program director to provide leadership in program functioning at the administrative level predicts program quality.

Maintenance: Safe and sanitary design and maintenance of the physical environment are necessary. Research has clearly demonstrated the value of requiring hygienic practices, particularly stressing the value of hand washing in the reduction of the spread of infectious diseases in child-care facilities. The LNC should look for training and policies that address procedures of hygiene.

Relationships and activities: It is more difficult to regulate aspects of programs that have a significant impact on children and child care, such as continuity of child relationships with adults, child participation in representational play, and positive relationships between parents and staff. In additional to early childcare, there are many standards and much regulation of school age children. As the child grows from day care to the school setting, a different set of regulations apply.

School Health

In general, there are many resources for the LNC to look to in addressing pediatric health services. For more information, see the resource section in the appendix to this chapter. In the area of school health services, two excellent resources are *The American Academy of Pediatrics, Council on School Health and the National Association of School Nurses* (NASN). *Occupational Safety and Health Administration* (OSHA), the *Clinical Laboratory Improvement Amendment of 1998* (CLIA), the *Family Education Rights and Privacy Act* (FERPA), and *Health Insurance Portability and Accountability Act* (HIPAA) are laws that have a significant influence on school health service policy development and implementation. When looking for information regarding qualifications, the LCN should refer to state mandates. Within these mandates, the LNC can expect to find a definition of the qualifications for school health professionals, guidelines that dictate communication between the school and student, mandated health screenings, and immunization requirements. State health laws address specifics of service sites, the range of services, and what level of professionals can provide those services in schools.

Cases involving school health nursing may include negligence claims. Nursing negligence is conduct that is unreasonable and fails to meet the nursing standards of care (Aiken & Catalano, 1994, p. 285). Negligence cases against school nurses tend to involve the following:

- Injuries, particularly involving physical education and sports
- Inactions or actions of guidance counselors (failure to report abuse)
- Failure to prevent sexual assault by personnel or students
- Failure to meet the needs of students with disabilities

A Look at a Legal Case Study

An 18-year-old Louisiana student died of an asthma attack at a senior high school in New Orleans Parish after school officials delayed calling 9-1-1 as had been requested. The school was trying to contact the mother to see if she would pay for the ambulance. In a negligence action brought by the family, a state district judge found the school principal, a guidance counselor, and the school board negligent in the student's death for the following reasons:

- The principal had "shirked his duty to protect the child from harm"
- The counselor "had abandoned common sense and placed rigid rules before a dying child's needs"
- The school board had failed to provide adequate training for its employees or to have a clear policy on medical emergencies

The family was awarded $1.6 million. The principal's and counselor's insurance company paid $1.4 million. The school board was responsible for the additional $200,000 (Declovet v. Orleans Parish School Board, 1998). The defendant was deemed responsible for the plaintiff's injuries (death).

Issues for the LNC Found in Pediatric Cases

The remainder of the chapter focuses on a sampling of specific issues that can be discovered during pediatric case analysis.

Apparent Life-Threatening Event

An apparent life-threatening event (ALTE) is characterized by some combination of apnea, color change, marked change in muscle tone, choking and gagging. ALTE occurred in approximately 10 per 1,000 live births. The median age of presentation in infants with an ALTE ranges between 7 and 8 weeks of age. Premature birth places an infant at increased risk. The LNC should look for documentation of the following:

- A detailed history and description of the infant at the time of the event
- Circumstances and characteristics of the event
- Thorough physical examination (including abnormalities that may account for the infant's symptoms)

The differential diagnosis should consider gastroesophageal reflux, neurological causes, lower respiratory tract infections, cardiac arrhythmias, urinary tract infections, and neoplastic causes among others (AAP, 2003).

Asthma Management

Asthma is a chronic inflammation of the airways with reversible episodes of obstruction caused by an increased reaction of the airways to various stimuli. Asthma breathing problems usually happen in "episodes" or attacks, but the inflammation underlying asthma is continuous.

- Asthma is the most common chronic disorder in childhood, currently affecting an estimated 6.8 million children under 18 years; of whom 4.1 million suffered from an asthma attack or episode in 2006.
- An asthma episode is a series of events that results in narrowed airways. These include swelling of the lining, tightening of the muscle, and increased secretion of mucus in the airway. The narrowed airway is responsible for the difficulty in breathing with the familiar "wheeze."
- Asthma is characterized by excessive sensitivity of the lungs to various stimuli. Triggers range from viral infections to allergies and to irritating gases and particles in the air. Each child reacts differently to the factors that may trigger asthma.
- Secondhand smoke can cause serious harm to children. An estimated 400,000 to one million asthmatic children have their condition worsened by exposure to secondhand smoke.
- Asthma can be a life-threatening disease if not properly managed. In 2004, 3,816 deaths were attributed to asthma. However, deaths due to asthma are rare among children. The number of deaths increases with age. In 2004, 141 children under 15 died from asthma compared to 684 adults over 85.
- Asthma is the third leading cause of hospitalization among children under the age of 15. Approximately 32.6% of all asthma hospital discharges in 2005 were children under 15; however, only 27.8% of the U.S. population was less than 15 years old.
- In 2005, approximately 679,000 emergency room visits were due to asthma in those under 15. (The National Heart, Lung, and Blood Institute [NHLBI], 2007.)

The long-term goal of asthma therapy is asthma control (reduction of risk and impairment). The LNC should look for several key clinical activities. The LNC should confirm that an asthma diagnosis has been established by the provider as evidenced by medical history and physical examination to determine whether symptoms of recurrent airflow obstruction are present. The documentation should support that the following four components of asthma care were addressed:

- Assessment and monitoring
- Education
- Control of environmental factors and comorbid conditions
- Medications (The National Heart, Lung, and Blood Institute [NHLBI], 2007.)

The National Asthma Education and Prevention Program Expert Panel Report 3: *Guidelines for the Diagnosis and Management of Asthma* provides an excellent resource for the LNC reviewing cases involving asthma.

Cancers in Childhood

Some of the solid tumors seen in children include Wilm's tumor, neuroblastoma, and retinoblastoma. Malignant tumors that arise in bone but may occur in soft tissues include osteosarcoma and non-Hodgkin lymphoma. The LNCs should be able to find thorough and accurate documentation of the child's risk factors and signs and symptoms. Documentation should indicate that the treating provider considered and ruled out differential diagnoses/possibilities. The diagnostic approach and treatment should clearly follow recognized standards of care, such as those developed by the AAP or the National Cancer Institute. See the appendix for resources.

Fever of Unknown Origin

Fever of unknown origin is defined as 2 weeks of daily temperatures >38.3°C (101°F) without a cause determined by simple diagnostic tests. The etiology of most cases of fever of unknown origin is common pediatric illnesses that are either self-limited or treatable. Infectious illness accounts for the majority of FUO in children. Careful documentation of fever is necessary before diagnosing FUO. "Day of fever" is defined as a 24-hr period in which a temperature >38.3°C (101°F) occurs at least once. Circumstances that may affect body temperature must be recorded, including

- All medications taken
- Activities in which the child has participated
- Environmental temperature

The LNC should look for indicators of a thorough and accurate history and diagnostic testing. There should also be indicators that the treating provider considered other infections and processes in their differential diagnosis. The AAP has a comprehensive guideline to use as a reference for LNCs.

Injury Prevention

Injury is the most significant health problem of childhood and adolescence. They cause a majority of deaths of children and adolescents aged 1–19 years. Injuries are classified as intentional or unintentional. Strategies that prevent unintentional injuries may also prevent some intentional injuries, such as locking up firearms or turning down the water heater temperature. For most types of injury, boys are at greater risk than girls. Therefore, there should be evidence of increased vigilance for higher risk groups.

Unintentional Injury

One of the many responsibilities of pediatric healthcare providers is the identification of, discussion about, and treatment of unintentional childhood injuries. From infancy through adolescence, the child is continuously learning about his environment and absorbing new information about how the world works. This learning process can contribute to accidents and childhood injury (a well-researched topic that the LNC can review in the analysis of cases involving children).

The LNC should look at the records for indications that the child's family or caregivers were given anticipatory guidance during routine health visits, such as reviewing age-appropriate safety. This might include documentation of handouts given to the parents of a toddler regarding the need to keep pans turned inward on the stovetop to prevent burns, or keeping the water heater temperature set at 120° to avoid scalding, or to keep firearms unloaded and locked in a safe place where the child cannot reach them.

The natural curiosity of an infant combined with mechanical factors, including the infant's smaller airway and inability to chew thoroughly, can lead to choking on food and small objects such as beads or buttons. Airway obstruction, including suffocation, choking and strangulation, "is the leading cause of unintentional injury-related death among infants under age 1 ... more than 16,000 children in this age group needed hospital emergency room treatment for airway obstruction injuries in 2001 alone." (Consumer Product Safety Commission (CPSC) Child Safety Protection Act of 1994. p. 12). As a result, the U.S. Consumer Product Safety Commission (CPSC) enforces the Child Safety Protection Act passed in 1994, which "bans any toy intended for use by children under age 3 that possess a choking, aspiration or ingestion hazard and requires choking hazard warning labels on packaging for these items when intended for use by children ages 3 to 6." (Consumer Product Safety Commission (CPSC) Child Safety Protection Act of 1994. p. 12).

While statistics will vary somewhat from year to year, there are some consistencies in the type and frequency of unintentional childhood injury. The Centers for Disease Control and Prevention and U.S. SafeKids Campaign have been monitoring the trends for childhood injury, both fatal and nonfatal. The U.S. SafeKids Campaign document can be accessed at www.usa.safekids.org/content_documents/nskw03_report.pdf. The LNC can utilize these resources for performing statistics searches to assist in understanding the trends and to educate the attorney client on published findings.

Medication Errors

Medication error is believed to be the most common type of medical error. It is a significant cause of preventable adverse events. Medication dosing errors in pediatrics are more common because of weight-based dosing calculations, fractional dosing (e.g., mg vs. Gm), and the need for decimal points. According to the Joint Commission, the potential for pediatric medication errors is three times higher than in the adult population (JCAHO, 2008).

Children are more prone to medication errors and resulting harm because of the following:

■ Most medications used in the care of children are formulated and packaged primarily for adults. Therefore, medications often must be prepared in different volumes or concentrations within the healthcare setting before being administered to children.

- Most healthcare settings are primarily built around the needs of adults.
- Children—especially young, small, and sick children—are usually less able to physiologically tolerate a medication error due to still developing renal, immune, and hepatic functions.
- Many children, especially very young children, cannot communicate effectively to providers regarding any adverse effects that medications may be causing.

Additional risk factors that lead to medication errors are similarities in trade names of drugs, illegible prescriptions and medical orders, look-alike drugs, calculation errors, etc. (Diav-Citrin et al., 2000).

LNC should therefore look for indications of the following:

- A system of checks and balances to offset the increased risk from using a series of pediatric-specific calculations and tasks.
- Training that is directed to providing developmentally appropriate care to the pediatric population, pediatric care protocols, and pediatric reference materials.
- Assessment tools and procedures that are designed to address the special needs of the pediatric population.

Case example: Ten-year-old Julie is a terminally ill child with relapsed acute lymphoblastic leukemia (ALL). Her family is given instruction on a prescription for oral morphine solution for home use. Due to an error in pharmacy labeling, her parents give her twice the recommended dose for her age and weight. When Julie's parents discover her to be lethargic and nonresponsive, they phone emergency medical services who transport her to the hospital for evaluation and treatment of respiratory depression due to an overdose of morphine.

The LNC reviewing the records would check for teaching instructions given by the prescribing physician and/or the outpatient clinic nurses and compare this with the pharmacy records and the parents' report of the incident for discrepancies to determine where the duty was breached and whether Julie's parents received adequate instruction based on this documentation.

Meningitis

Meningitis is most often caused by an infectious agent. It is caused less commonly by medication or cancer. Early diagnosis and treatment of bacterial meningitis is essential because this infection is often quickly fatal. The terms viral meningitis and aseptic meningitis are often used interchangeably although they are not synonymous. Aseptic meningitis refers to inflammation of the meninges without the presence of visible organisms on routine gram staining. Neonatal meningitis is considered separately because the responsible organisms are unique. Fever is usually present in bacterial meningitis. The absence of fever, however, does not preclude the diagnosis. The inflammation of the meninges can be characterized by (but not limited to) irritability, anorexia, headache, vomiting, nuchal rigidity, and photophobia. The Kernig and Brudzinski signs are utilized to demonstrate meningeal inflammation. The assessment should be thorough and guide the provider to the next steps of diagnostic testing and treatment. The clinical situation should influence the amount of data required before a clinical decision is made. The LNC should be able to see indication of the distinction between bacterial and other types of meningitis, as treatment for bacterial meningitis must be started promptly. Laboratory and radiological testing should follow recognized practice standards. The *Red Book* is a reference for the manifestations, etiology, epidemiology, diagnosis, and treatment of some 200 childhood infectious diseases. The *2009 Red Book* is in its 28th printing, and it is a proven resource for the LNC to utilize when reviewing meningitis cases.

Postoperative Care

Routinely performed outpatient surgical procedures include general surgery, ophthalmologic surgery, genitourinary surgery, orthopedic surgery, and otorhinolaryngeal surgery. Serious post-operative complication in healthy children undergoing outpatient surgery are, for the most part, low, but some minor postoperative complications occur commonly. Postoperative nausea and vomiting (PONV) is the most frequent complication of general anesthesia. Other complications include emergence phenomena. Emergence from general anesthesia in healthy patients is often accompanied by transient symmetrical neurologic changes such as

- Sustained and nonsustained ankle clonus
- Bilateral hyperreflexia
- Babinski reflex
- Decerebrate posturing

These reflexes can often be detected within minutes of discontinuing the general anesthetic and may persist for hours. The discovery of *focal* neurologic deficits in a postoperative patient is never normal. Such neurologic deficits should point to a possible central or peripheral nervous system injury and require further investigation.

Intubation Complications

Intubation-related complications include reports of sore throat upon awakening. The causes of this complication stem from endotracheal intubation and airway manipulation or instrumentation (laryngeal mask airway). Postintubation croup is also known as postextubation subglottic edema. Children are more prone than adults to develop croup after intubation because of differences in their airway anatomy.

Postoperative Complications

Early Postoperative Complications

Postoperative complications are grouped as early or late complications. Early postoperative surgical problems include the following:

Fever: Postoperative fever is generally caused by the four Ws. These include wind (lungs)—atelectasis, wound (operative site)—infection, water (urinary tract)—urinary tract infection, and walker (legs)—deep vein thrombosis (AAP, 2008).

Wound infection: As a general rule, the earlier the onset of wound sepsis, the more destructive and life-threatening the infection will be. Most wound infections do not usually become apparent until the 5th to 10th postoperative day.

Postoperative bleeding: Persistent bleeding is defined as either bleeding and bloody ooze that continue for more than 6–8 hr after the operation, or the need to change a blood-soaked wound dressing more than twice in the first 6–8 hr after surgery. It almost always indicates inadequate hemostasis. It is usually due to a superficial skin arterial bleeding site. However, coagulopathy might also be responsible.

Posttonsillectomy hemorrhage: The incidence is estimated to be 5–10%. A small number of patients who have tonsillectomies require additional operations. Either early or late bleeding may occur after a tonsillectomy. Early bleeding occurs in the first 24 hr, usually after hospital discharge. Late bleeding occurs 5–14 days after surgery. It results from dislodgement of the scab from the operative bed. The bleeding may be severe and life-threatening.

Late Postoperative Complications

Wound infection: Pyrexia 48 hr or more after outpatient surgery is unusual and may indicate a serious wound infection. In patients who develop fevers more than 5 days after a surgical procedure, either an anaerobic infection or a mixed (symbiotic) infection of anaerobic and gram-negative rods should be suspected.

Wound infection is most commonly caused by gram-positive organisms. Wound infections caused by *Staphylococcus aureus* or *Staphylococcus epidermidis* are usually characterized by a milky white, purulent drainage. They usually occur 3–5 days after surgery and produce high, spiking fevers (temperatures of 102.2–104°F [39–40°C]). Leukocytosis with a white blood cell count of >12,000 mm^{-3} will be present. Enteric, encapsulated, gram-negative organisms such as *Escherichia coli* are usually associated with erythema, tenderness, and purulent discharge. These infections usually occur more than 5 days after surgery. An anaerobic infection or a mixed (symbiotic) infection of anaerobic and gram-negative rods caused by gram-positive cocci of *Clostridium perfringens*; infection causes exquisite pain, brown discoloration, a wound that is crepitant to palpation, gas may be seen in the subcutaneous tissues on a plain radiograph.

Gram-negative rods of the *Bacteroides* species (usually *Bacteroides fragilis*) infections are usually purulent and malodorous. Both of these anaerobic infections are life-threatening.

Conclusions

The LNC's review and analysis of pediatric records can prove invaluable to an attorney. Delivery of optimum care to pediatric patients and support of their caregivers is a great responsibility for the pediatric healthcare provider. Analysis of the care given includes identification of potential issues and concerns that can differ from the adult population. Evaluation of pediatric cases can be rewarding both personally and professionally, as the LNC develops the skills necessary to perform a thorough review of pediatric cases.

References

Aiken, T. D., & Catalano, J. T. (1994). *Legal, ethical and political issues in nursing.* Philadelphia: F.A. Davis Company.

American Public Health Association. (1992). *Caring for our children* (pp. 161–162). Elk Grove Village, IL: American Academy of Pediatrics.

Association for Sport and Physical Education. (1995). *National standards for athletic coaches.* Dubuque, IA: National Association for Sport and Physical Education.

Hockenberry, M.J., Wilson, D., & Winkelstein, M.L. (2005). *Wong's essentials of pediatric nursing* (7th ed., p. 1259). St. Louis: Copyright Mosby.

Maternal and Child Health Bureau. (1999). *Basic emergency lifesaving skills (BELS): A framework for teaching emergency lifesaving skills to children and adolescents.* Newton, MA: Children's Safety Network, Education Development Center, Inc. www.nmchc.org

Sanders v. the State. (1983). 251 Ga. 70, 303 S.E. 2.d 13

School Nurse Emergency Medical Services for Children (SNEMS-C) Program. (2001). University of Connecticut, College of Continuing Studies website. Available at http://www.ce.uconn.edu/CPD-SNEM.html (accessed January 3, 2001).

Test Questions

1. Documentation in pediatric medical records should include all of the following except
   A. Informed consent
   B. The child's birth place
   C. Screening for abuse or neglect
   D. Patient and family education
   E. Assessment of pain
   F. All of the above
   G. A, C, D, and E

2. Three reasons identified by the U.S. Supreme Court as to why children are treated differently than adults under the U.S. Constitution:
   A. The vulnerability of children
   B. The inability to make critical decisions in an informed manner
   C. The importance of the parental role in childbearing
   D. The decreased earning potential of children
   E. All of the above
   F. A, B, and C

3. An example of an age-appropriate pain scale for children over the age of 3 years is the FACES pain scale. (True/False)

4. Children present special challenges in the drug dosing and delivery area. The most significant cause of medication errors in pediatrics is
   A. Rapid and dramatic changes in weight over time
   B. Stock solutions of medicines are often available only at adult concentrations and must be diluted for use in children
   C. Children may be more prone to adverse drug events than adults because they have less physiologic reserve with which to buffer errors such as overdoses
   D. Drug dosages must be calculated individually, leading to increased opportunities for error

5. You have been asked to review the chart of a 10-year-old with moderate persistent asthma, who is neurologically devastated as a result of an asthma attack. His past medical history is significant for two inpatient hospitalizations for asthma. The child was diagnosed at his primary-care provider's office, prescribed Albuterol MDI 2 puffs every 4–6 hr for wheezing, and is followed by the office for asthma-related concerns three times a year. As the LNC reviewing the records:
   A. What standards of care would be appropriate to reference?
   B. Were there any deviations from the standard of care?
   C. If so, list the deviations from the standard of care.
   D. Can you distinguish what actions are considered the standard of care versus best practice?

Answers

1. G
2. E
3. True
4. B
5. A. The National Asthma Education and Prevention Program—Expert Panel Report 3: *Guidelines for the Diagnosis and Management of Asthma.*

   B. Yes

   C. Records do not reflect a prescription for a medication such as inhaled steroids for daily management; the frequency of follow-up visits was inadequate given the severity of the condition and prior inpatient hospitalizations; documentation does not support referral to any specialist(s).

   D. Standard of care would include more frequent follow-up for management of the condition and a daily medication for symptom control. Best practice could include referral to a specialist, such as an allergist/immunologist or pulmonologist.

Appendix

Standards of Care

American Academy of Pediatrics. (2006). In L. K. Pickering, C. J. Baker, & S. S. Long (Eds.), *Red book 2006: Report of the Committee on* Infectious Diseases (27th ed.). Elk Grove Village, IL: American Academy of Pediatrics.

American Academy of Pediatrics, Committee of Fetus and Newborn. (2003). Apnea, sudden death syndrome, and home monitoring. *Pediatrics, 111*(4 Pt 1), 914–917.

American Academy of Pediatrics, Section on Hematology/Oncology. (2004). Guidelines for pediatric cancer centers. *Pediatrics, 113*(6), 1833–1835.

American Cancer Society. National Cancer Institute. http://www.cancer.gov/

Committee on the Future of Emergency Healthcare in the United States. (2008). The Institute of Medicine, Emergency Care for Children: *Growing Pains*. Available for purchase online: http://www.nap.edu/catalog/11655.html (accessed November 4, 2008).

Expert Panel Report 3 (EPR3). Guidelines for the Diagnosis and Management of Asthma. http://www.nhlbi.nih.gov/guidelines/asthma/asthgdln.htm

Preventing pediatric medication errors. http://www.jointcommission.org/SentinelEvents/SentinelEventAlert/sea_39.htm

Sáez-Llorens, X., & McCracken, G. H., Jr. (2003). Bacterial meningitis in children. *Lancet, 361*, 2139–2148.

Tunkel, A. R., Harlman, B. J., Kaplan, S. L., Kaufman, B. A., Roos, K. L., Scheld, W. M., & Whitely, R. (2004). Practice guidelines for the management of bacterial meningitis. *Clin Infect. Dis., 39*, 1267–1284.

Yogev, R., & Guzman-Cottrill, J. III. (2005). Bacterial meningitis in children: Critical review of current concepts. *Drugs, 65*, 1097–1112.

Informed Consent

Baston, J. (2008). Healthcare decisions: A review of children's Involvement. *Paediatric Nursing, 20*, 3.

Eder, M., Yamokoski, A., Wittmann, P., & Kodish, E. (2007). Improving informed consent: Suggestions from parents of children with leukemia. *Pediatrics*, 119, e849–e859.

Kimberly, M., Hoehn, K., Feudtner, C., Nelson, R., & Schreiner, M. (2006). Variation in standards of research compensation and child assent practices: A comparison of 69 Institutional Review Board-approved informed permission and assent forms for 3 multicenter pediatric clinical trials. *Pediatrics, 117*, 1706–1711.

Medication Errors

American Academy of Pediatrics: Committee on Drugs and Committee on Hospital Care. (2003). Prevention of medication errors in the pediatric inpatient setting. *Pediatrics, 112*, 431–436.

Fortescue, E., Kaushal, R., Landrigan, C., McKenna, K., Clapp, M., Federico, F. et al. (2003). Prioritizing strategies for preventing medication errors and adverse drug events in pediatric inpatients. *Pediatrics, 111*, 722–729.

Hagan, J. F., Shaw, J. S., & Duncan, P. M. (Eds.). (2008). *Bright futures: Guidelines for health supervision of infants, children, and adolescents* (3rd ed.). Elk Grove Village, IL: American Academy of Pediatrics.

Stebbing, C., Kaushal, R., & Bates, D. (2006). Pediatric medication safety and the media: What does the public see? *Pediatrics, 117*, 1907–1914.

The Joint Commission: Sentinel Event Alert Issue 39—April 11, 2008: Preventing pediatric medication errors. http://www.jointcommission.org/SentinelEvents/SentinelEventAlert/sea_39.htm

Walsh, K., Adams, W., Bauchner, H., Vinci, R., Chessare, J., Cooper, M. et al. (2006). Medication errors related to computerized order entry for children. *Pediatrics, 118*, 1872–1879.

Child Care

American Academy of Family Physicians. (2001). Patient *Education in Your Practice: A Handbook for the Office Setting*. Leawood, KS: American Academy of Family Physicians.

American Academy of Pediatrics. (2008). *Guidelines for Health Supervision III* (3rd ed.). Elk Grove Village, IL: American Academy of Pedriatics.

Azer, S., & Morgan, G. (1998). *Trends in child care licensing and regulation*. Boston: The Center for Career Development in Early Care and Education.

Azer, S., & Morgan, G. (2001a). *2001 state child care licensing regulations at a glance*. Boston: Wheelock College Institute for Leadership and Career Initiatives.

Azer, S., & Morgan, G. (2001b). *Trends in child care licensing and regulation*. Boston: Wheelock College Institute for Leadership and Career Initiatives.

Black, R., Dykes, A., Anderson, K., Wells, J., Sinclair, S., Gary, G. et al. (1981). Handwashing to prevent diarrhea in day care centers. *American Journal of Epidemiology, 113*(4), 445–451.

Brazelton, T. B., & Nugent, J. K. (1995). *Neonatal behavioral assessment scale*. London: Mac Keith Press.

Burchinal, M. R., Cryer, D., Clifford, R. M., & Howes, C. (in press). Caregiver training and classroom quality in child care centers. *Applied Developmental Sciences*. 6(1), 2–11.

CPSC 2008 public playground safety handbook. http://www.cpsc.gov/CPSCPUB/PUBS/325.pdf-630.4KB

Fletcher, D. M., & Rhodes, H. B. (1999, June). *Practice brief: Retention of health information* (updated June 2002). Chicago, IL: American Health Information Management Association.

Green, M., & Palfrey, J. S. (Eds.). (2008). *Bright futures: Guidelines for health supervision of infants, children, and adolescents* (3rd ed.). Arlington, VA: National Center for Education in Maternal and Child Health.

Green, M., Palfrey, J. S., Clark, E. M., & Anastasi, J. M. (Eds.). (2000). *Bright futures: Guidelines for health supervision of infants, children, and adolescents—Second edition: Pocket guide*. Arlington, VA: National Center for Education in Maternal and Child Health.

Hockenberry, M., Wilson, D., Winkelstein, M., & Kline, N. (Eds.). (2003). *Wong's nursing care of infants and children* (7th ed.). Mosby, Inc.

Iyer, P. W. (2003). *Legal nurse consulting: Principles and practice* (2nd ed.). Boca Raton, FL: American Association of Legal Nurse Consultants.

JCAHO tort resolution and injury prevention—Healthcare at the crossroads guide (52pp.). http://www.jointcommission.org/PublicPolicy/tort.htm

Korn, A. Press releases—President Bush signs Landmark Product Safety Legislation. H.R. 4040, Consumer Product Safety Improvement Act of 2008. (Information retrieved online August 17, 2008).

Langely, G. T., Nolan, K. M., Nolan, T. W., Norman, C. L., & Provost, L. L. (1996). *The improvement guide: A practical approach to enhancing organizational performance*. San Francisco, CA: Jossey-Bass.

McKenry, P. C., & Price, S. J. (Eds.). (2000). *Families and change: Coping with stressful events and transitions*. Thousand Oaks, CA: Sage Publications, Inc.

National Association of Pediatric Nurse Practitioners (NAPNAP). (2008a). NAPNAP Position Statement on the prevention of unintentional injuries in children. *Journal of Pediatric Health Care, 22*, 27A–28A.

National Association of Pediatric Nurse Practitioners (NAPNAP). (2008b). *Pediatric Nursing: Scope and Standards of Practice*. Cherry Hill, NJ: National Association of Pediatric Nurse Practitioners.

Olson, R. E. (2000). *Procedural utilization facts: Chiropractic and physical therapy treatment standards, a reference guide* (6th ed.). Kennesaw, GA: Data Management Ventures, Inc.

Parker, S., & Zuckerman, B. S. (2004). *Behavioral and developmental pediatrics: A handbook for primary care*. New York, NY: Little Brown & Co.

Schnitzer, P. G. (2006). Prevention of unintentional childhood injuries. *American Family Physician, 74*(11), 1864–1870.

Slosberg, E. J., & Smith, C. G., Jr., Esquire. (2007). The importance of disclaimers: Distinction between optimal care and standard of care. *Pediatrics, 120* (2), 453–455. www.pediatrics.org (accessed August 6, 2008).

The Children's Foundation. (2001a). *The 2001 child care center licensing study*. Washington, DC: Author.

Wallis, A. L., Cody, B. E., & Mickalide, A.D. (2003). *Report to the nation: Trends in unintentional childhood injury mortality, 1987–2000*. Washington, DC: National SAFEKIDS Campaign.

www.cdc.gov/mmwr/preview
www.cdc.gov/ncipc/fact_book/factbook.htm
www.cdc.gov/ncipc/factsheets
www.cdc.gov/ncipc/wisqars
www.nhtsa.dot.gov
www.safekids.org
www.statutes-of-limitations.com/
www.usa.safekids.org/content_documents/nskw03_report.pdf
www.usa.safekids.org/tier3_cd.cfm?content_item_id=26171&folder_id=300

Pediatric Practice References

- Office for Human Research Protections. http://www.hhs.gov/ohrp/
- OHRP Guidance Topics by Subject. http://www.hhs.gov/ohrp/policy/topics.html
- U.S. Food and Drug Administration. http://www.fda.gov
- National Bioethics Advisory Commission. http://www.georgetown.edu/research/nrcbl/nbac
- President's Council on Bioethics. http://www.bioethics.gov
- NIH Office of Human Subjects Research. http://ohsr.od.nih.gov
- NIH Infosheets, Forms, Checklists. http://ohsr.od.nih.gov/info
- NIH Office of Extramural Research. http://grants.nih.gov/grants/oer.htm
- Bioethics Resources on the Web. http://www.nih.gov/sigs/bioethics
- Melissa's Living Legacy Foundation: Teens Living with Cancer. www.teenslivingwithcancer.org/about/mllf.asp
- Curesearch, a component of the Children's Oncology Group. www.curesearch.org/
- National Library of Medicine Bibliography—Ethical Issues in Research Involving Human Participants. http://www.nlm.nih.gov/pubs/cbm/hum_exp.html
- ABA Center on Children and the Law, Selected early childhood online resources. http://www.abanet.org/child/baby-links.shtml
- Information about NIH/NCI cancer research studies. http://cancertrials.nci.nih.gov
- Standards of care and clinical guidelines applicable to your cases. www.medmalrx.com
- Full Disclosure Consulting—medical legal consulting. www.fulldisclosureconsulting.com
- Children's Hospitals listings. www.childrenshospitals.net
- American Association Legal Nurse Consultant. www.aalnc.org
- American Bar Association. www.abanet.org
- American Academy of Pediatrics. www.aap.org; www.aap.org/topics.html
- Association of Asthma Educators. www.asthmaeducators.org
- Bureau of Health Professions. http://bhpr.hrsa.gov/dqa/
- Children's Defense Fund. www.childrensdefense.org/
- Children's Hospital of Philadelphia. www.chop.edu (or your local children's hospital)
- The Center for Disease Control, National Center for Health Statistics. http://www.cdc.gov/nchs/nhcs.htm
- The Center for Disease Control, National Center for Health Statistics, Child Health. http://www.cdc.gov/nchs/fastats/children.htm
- The National Guideline Clearinghouse. http://www.guideline.gov/
- Healthy Childcare America. www.healthychildcare.org/
- The Joint Commission. www.jointcommission.org/PatientSafety/
- Kids Health. www.kidshealth.org/

- The Mayo Clinic. www.mayoclinic.com/health/childrens-health/CC99999
- The Maternal Child Health Bureau. www.mchb.hrsa.gov/
- American Urologic Association's—Urology Health. www.urologyhealth.org
- Medline Plus—Children's Health. www.nlm.nih.gov/medlineplus/childrenshealth.html
- The National Center for State Courts. http://www.ncsconline.org/
- U.S. Courts. http://www.uscourts.gov/
- www.findlaw.com
- www.cornell.edu
- www.Law.com

Selected Early Childhood Online Resources

- Administration for Children and Families: National Child Care Information Center. http://nccic.org/index.html
- Administration for Children and Families: Office of Head Start. www.headstartinfo.org
- Administration for Children and Families: Head Start Information & Publication Center. http://eclkc.ohs.acf.hhs.gov/hslc (Early Childhood Learning and Knowledge Center)
- Agency for Healthcare Research and Quality: Children with Special Health Care Needs or Chronic Conditions. www.ahrq.gov/child/Findings/cdshcncc.htm
- Alliance for Health Reform: Health Insurance. www.allhealth.org/issues.asp?wi=2
- American Academy of Child and Adolescent Psychiatry. www.aacap.org/
- American Academy of Pediatrics. www.aap.org
- American Heart Association: Children and Nutrition. www.americanheart.org/
- Association of Maternal and Child Health Programs: Early Childhood and Early Intervention Services. www.amchp.org/
- Bright Futures. www.brightfutures.org/
- Center for Children with Special Needs. www.cshcn.org/index.cfm
- Center on the Social and Emotional Foundations of Early Learning. www.vanderbilt.edu/csefel/
- Child Care Law Center. www.childcarelaw.org/
- Child Trends: Early Childhood Measures Profiles. http://aspe.hhs.gov/hsp/ECMeasures04/report.pdf
- Child Welfare League of America: Child Care & Development. www.cwla.org/programs/daycare/default.htm
- Children's Defense Fund: Improving Children's Health. www.childrensdefense.org
- Children's Dental Health Project. www.cdhp.org
- Commonwealth Fund: EPSDT (Early Periodic Screening, Diagnosis, and Treatment program—child health component of Medicaid) and Commonwealth Fund: Study Tracking Early Childhood Development. www.cmwf.org
- The Data Resource Center (DRC) for Child and Adolescent Health. www.childhealthdata.org
- Developmental and Behavioral Pediatrics Online. www.dbpeds.org/
- Early Head Start National Resource Center. www.ehsnrc.org/
- Georgetown University Center for Child and Human Development. www.gucchd.georgetown.edu/
- Health Resources and Services Administration: EPSDT. www.hrsa.gov/epsdt/
- National Alliance on Mental Illness: Child and Adolescent Action Center. www.nami.org

- National Association for the Education of Young Children. www.naeyc.org/ece/
- National Center for Education in Maternal and Child Health. www.ncemch.org
- National Child Traumatic Stress Network. www.nctsnet.org
- National Head Start Association. www.nhsa.org/
- National Health Law Program: EPSDT. www.healthlaw.org
- National Maternal and Child Oral Health Resource Center. www.mchoralhealth.org/
- National Resource Center for Health and Safety in Child Care and Early Education. http://nrc.uchsc.edu/
- Ounce of Prevention: At-Risk Infants, Toddlers, Preschoolers. www.ounceofprevention.org/
- Zero to Three: National Center for Infants, Toddlers and Families. www.zerotothree.org/

Chapter 15

Neonatal Nursing

Judith Romanow Guidash, RNC-NIC, BSN

Contents

Objectives

- Define neonate
- Identify the qualifications of a neonatal nurse
- Identify the practice setting of the neonatal nurse

- Identify the role of the Legal Nurse Consultant in litigation involving neonatal case evaluations
- Identify several common areas of litigation involving neonates
- Identify medical records commonly used in neonatal case evaluations

Introduction

Although on the surface, a medical malpractice claim involving a neonate or newborn may appear as any other medical malpractice case, care should be taken to realize the differences between neonatal and adult physiology, nursing care requirements, and liability. Neonates are not "little adults" nor should they be treated as such. From their first introduction to extrauterine life, rapid physiologic changes occur requiring a specialized nurse to care for this complex little human. The neonatal intensive care unit (NICU) patient includes a varied population of patients ranging from extremely low-birth-weight infants to large-for-gestational-age infants, each possessing unique problems and complex medical needs.

Define Neonate

Technically, an infant is considered a neonate from birth to 28 days. The first American NICU was opened in New Haven, Connecticut in 1965, and in 1975 the American Board of Pediatrics established a sub-board certification for neonatology. Neonatal nursing is a specialty that evolved from the increase in survival of preterm infants, technology, and complications occurring from labor and delivery. A neonatal nurse may work in neonatal intensive care units taking care of acutely ill neonates and premature infants or in mother–baby or newborn nurseries taking care of healthy newborns.

Differentiate Levels of NICUs

There are three levels of newborn nurseries, levels I, II, or III, in which a nurse may work as a bedside neonatal nurse or an advance practice nurse. These levels of care are set forth by the Perinatal Regionalization Model and are also described in the *Guidelines for Perinatal Care*, 4th ed., published by the American Academy of Pediatrics and the American College of Obstetrics and Gynecology, 1997, Elk Grove Village.

Generally, level I facilities offer neonatal care to healthy term newborns. Level II is an intermediate care or special care nursery where the baby may be born prematurely or may be suffering from an illness; these babies may need supplemental oxygen, intravenous therapy, specialized feedings, or more time to mature before discharge. The level III NICU admits all neonates who cannot be treated in either of the other two nursery levels. These babies may be small for their age, premature, or sick term infants who require high technology care, such as ventilators, special equipment or incubators, or surgery. The level III units may be in a large general hospital or part of a children's hospital. Neonatal nurses provide direct patient care to these infants.

In addition, level II facilities have two subgroups: level II A and level II B. A level II A nursery provides care for preterm neonates greater than 32 weeks gestation, and weighing more than 500 g and level II B nurseries offer short-term mechanical ventilation for infants with respiratory distress syndrome. Finally, level III facilities are capable of handling very preterm infants and infants needing ventilatory support for a long period of time, high-frequency ventilatory oscillation or nitric oxide inhalation. Infants of all gestational ages with severe malformations or morbidities requiring surgical management should also be referred to level III maternity units (EPIPAGE, 2006).

Qualifications, Certifications and Experience Required for NICU Nurse

NRP, CPR, PALS, RNC

Entry-level requirements for neonatal nurses vary from institution to institution. There is no special program for neonatal nursing in basic registered nurse (RN) education, but some nursing programs may have an elective course in neonatal nursing. The advanced practice nurse (APN) requires advanced education in the field of neonatal nursing. The APN includes the neonatal nurse practitioner and the clinical nurse specialist.

Requirements for working as a neonatal nurse are established by the institution. Competency checklists may be utilized to assess a nurse's ability in using medications, math calculations, intravenous lines, cardiopulmonary resuscitation, and other knowledge needed for direct patient care. Continuing education requirements are mandated by the state or a certifying body. The state board of nursing sets the number of hours, if any, required during a 2-to-3 year period (depending on the time of license renewal) to maintain the RN license. As a staff or an APN, one may also hold national certification in neonatal nursing, validating one's specialized knowledge in the field of neonatal nursing (http://www.nursesource.org/neonatal.html).

The facility in which a nurse is employed may require training in CPR, NRP, and/or PALS. CPR is Cardiopulmonary Resuscitation developed by the American Heart Association (AHA). NRP is the Neonatal Resuscitation Program developed by the American Academy of Pediatrics (AAP). According to the AAP, the NRP is an educational program that introduces the concepts and basic skills of neonatal resuscitation. Completion of the program does not imply that an individual has the competence to perform neonatal resuscitation (http://www.aap.org/nrp/nrpmain.html).

PALS is the Pediatric Advanced Life Support program developed by the AHA. The goal of the PALS course is to aid the pediatric healthcare provider in developing the knowledge and skills necessary to efficiently and effectively manage critically ill infants and children, resulting in improved outcomes (http://www.americanheart.org/presenter.jhtml?identifier=3012001).

Certifications that may be obtained by a nurse working in the neonatal intensive care setting include those from the National Certification Corporation (NCC) and the American Association of Critical Care Nurses (AACN).

The NCC offers certification for RNs who have current licensure as an RN in the United States or Canada, 24 months specialty experience as a U.S. or Canadian RN comprising a minimum of 2,000 hours and employment in the specialty sometime in the last 24 months. They offer both a low-risk neonatal examination and a neonatal intensive care nursing examination. The designation of an RN who has achieved this certification would include the privilege of having the letters RNC-LRN and RNC-NIC after her signature (http://www.nccnet.org/public/pages/index.cfm?pageid=111).

The AACN Certification Corporation administers certification and recertification programs for nurses to proudly demonstrate the specialized knowledge, skills, and abilities necessary for safe and effective acute and critical care nursing practice. Applicants must hold current, unencumbered RN licensure in the United States. Critical care practice as an RN is required for 1,750 hours in direct bedside care of (adult, neonatal, or pediatric) acutely or critically ill patients during the 2-year period preceding the date of application, with 875 of those hours accrued in the most recent year preceding the application. All 1,750 hours must be in the care of the same patient population (http://www.aacn.org/WD/Certifications/Content/ccrn.pcms?menu=Certifications#Eligibility).

Role of Legal Nurse Consultant with Neonatal Experience in Litigation

An RN with neonatal nursing experience is an invaluable member of the litigation team involving medical malpractice claims. This RN may serve as a fact witness to educate the jury on the topic of dispute. The RN may serve as an expert witness to assist the plaintiff or defense, testifying to relevant standards of care and any deviation that may have occurred, or if the nurse was acting within her scope of practice as determined by the state Nurse Practice Act. This RN may also serve as a consulting expert assisting an attorney to determine if indeed standards of care were not met, or if a particular case has merit. Any of these roles can be satisfied while working as an in-house LNC or on a consultative basis, but most likely it will be on a consultative basis.

In reviewing cases of medical negligence, nursing negligence, or malpractice, the nurse consultant will need to determine if the four elements of negligence have in fact been met, thus determining that a case for negligence exists. The four elements of negligence include duty, breach, causation/proximate cause, and damages. Analyzing a case for negligence involves asking questions to determine if each element of negligence has been satisfied. If even one element is not satisfied, then negligence has not occurred.

Duty is established by the standard of care. In a neonatal case, the standards are set by either a professional organization such as the National Association of Neonatal Nurses (NANN) and the Association of Women's Health, Obstetric and Neonatal Nurses (AWHONN), the state practice act, and/or the institution itself. The medical practice standards are drawn from the customs and behaviors of the members of the profession. Hence, the subspecialty of neonatal nursing has developed documents that reflect the consensus on how the profession should be practiced. These documents will set the standard for judging individual transgressions. The policies and procedures created by the institution would be a worthwhile document to obtain when reviewing a case. A literature search identifying evidence-based practices may also be beneficial in determining standards of care, remembering to use journals, books, and publications that were published prior to the event in question.

In reviewing a case, the LNC will determine if there was a breach in the standard of care. As an expert, the LNC will determine if the breach in the standard of care is evident and describe the precise nature of the violation. When reviewing the medical records, one needs to focus on the event in question and pay close attention to the events leading to the alleged event. Note any conflicting or supporting data. It is often helpful to read the narrative notes first in order to get an idea of the events and the situation. Look specifically at the documentation of the assessments/findings, intervention, and the patient's response to see if they were documented. Create a chronology of the medical records to organize the data, which may include a timeline of events, graphs, or charts.

As an expert, one may be required to attend depositions as well as a trial. One will need to allow time for literature review, document review, and report preparation. As an expert, one will also need to investigate standards of care. One will need to investigate the certification criteria set by the institution and/or state for employment as a neonatal nurse, as well as the nurse's academic preparation required by the state. One will also need to review the hospital policy and procedures.

In addition to reviewing medical records and standards, the LNC will need to review the depositions of those involved looking for contradictions and inaccuracies between individuals and what is documented in the medical records.

A written report documenting one's findings should be submitted only when requested. The report should include an overview of the patient's clinical condition and the nurses' actions, compared with the appropriate standards of care. If a breach in the standard of care has occurred, a detailed account should be provided, along with a description of any resultant harm (Foster, 1998).

The Neonatal Nursing Experience/Common Areas of Litigation

Neonatal Resuscitation

The transition from fetus to newborn requires intervention by a skilled individual or team in approximately 10% of all deliveries. Approximately 1% of newborns require extensive resuscitative measures. Perinatal asphyxia and extreme prematurity are the two complications of pregnancy that most frequently require a complete resuscitation by skilled personnel. Only 60% of asphyxiated newborns can be predicted antepartum. The remaining newborns are not identified until the time of birth. Approximately 80% of low-birthweight infants require resuscitation and stabilization at delivery (Bissinger, 2006).

The AAP and the AHA collaborated to develop the NRP in the late 1980s. This program was developed for the purpose of providing consistency at a teaching hospital and affiliated outlying hospitals in the care of the newborn at delivery. The AAP and the AHA published guidelines regarding neonatal resuscitation in 2000. These were reviewed most recently in 2006. Typical guidelines state that one person at every delivery should have the primary responsibility of caring for the newborn. This person should be capable of initiating resuscitation, including administration of positive pressure ventilation and chest compressions. Either that person or someone who is immediately available should have the skills required to perform a complete resuscitation, including endotracheal intubation and administration of medication.

When evaluating a neonatal case involving resuscitation, it is imperative that the LNC be cognizant of the applicable guidelines at the time of the alleged injury. She/he should be familiar with the procedures involved in resuscitation and the guidelines set forth by the AAP and the AHA.

The initial steps of resuscitation are to provide warmth and position the head in a "sniffing" position to open the airway. The airway should then be cleared of mucus and the baby dried to stimulate breathing. After immediate postbirth assessment and administration of initial steps, further resuscitative efforts should be guided by simultaneous assessment of respirations, heart rate, and color. The Apgar score is a standardized assessment for infants after delivery. The Apgar score assesses the infant's heart rate, color, muscle tone, respirations, and reflex irritability. The infant is generally scored at 1 and 5 minutes post-delivery. The assignment of a score should not cause delay in providing necessary resuscitative measures if warranted. If the need for resuscitation is required before a score can be assigned, the score can be used as an assessment of the results of the resuscitative interventions. Because the Apgar score contains subjective components and is affected by gestational age, maternal medications, resuscitation, and cardiorespiratory and neurological conditions, the score should not be used to determine the degree of neurological outcome of the infant. As stated in the AAP guidelines, the Apgar score alone cannot be considered as evidence or a consequence of asphyxia (http://aappolicy.aappublications.org/cgi/content/abstract/pediatrics;117/4/1444).

When reviewing a case involving neonatal resuscitation, resuscitation flow sheets in the medical records should be compared to the neonatal flow algorithm. The responsibility of the nurse should be compared to the hospital policy regarding neonatal resuscitation. One must also review the Nurse Practice Act of the state. Because many cases involving resuscitation of the newborn involve prenatal events as well, it may be prudent to investigate the hospital policies involving physicians and resuscitation as well as the qualifications of the physician who performs resuscitation (Figure 15.1).

Neonatal transition is a gradual process and even healthy infants born at term may take greater than 10 minutes to achieve an oxygen saturation greater than 95% and nearly 1 hour to achieve postductal saturation greater than 95% (Circulation, 2005).

Once a delivery is classified as high-risk with the possibility that advanced resuscitation efforts may be required, it is recommended that at least two persons be present to manage the neonate, one with complete resuscitation skills and another to assist with the resuscitation efforts. Table 15.1 includes the equipment recommended to be available at a high-risk delivery for resuscitation.

The textbook of neonatal resuscitation, fifth edition, is available through the AAP.

Whether working for the plaintiff or defense, issues regarding neonatal resuscitation may include the following:

- Failure to provide appropriate neonatal resuscitation
- Failure to provide timely intervention
- Failure to document
- Failure to initiate chest compressions in a timely manner
- Failure to use and/or maintain appropriate and necessary resuscitation equipment
- Failure to possess proper knowledge and competency

Hypoglycemia

McGowan and Perlman (2006) define hypoglycemia as "a blood glucose concentration at which the glucose supply to the brain is less than the demand for substrate created by the rate of brain energy metabolism. Most practitioners consider blood glucose of 35–40 mg/dL to be the minimum in a full term infant. However, the minimum blood glucose level for a preterm, septic, or asphyxiated infant may be much higher."

In term infants, symptomatic hypoglycemia may be associated with developmental delay or seizure (McGowan & Perlman, 2006).

The incidence of hypoglycemia in preterm infants is three times greater than in full-term newborn infants. The compensatory mechanisms responsible for protecting the brain are not entirely in place. Severe hypoglycemia is known to cause neurological death and subsequent neurodevelopmental abnormalities. However, the level at which hypoglycemia becomes clinically important and intervention is warranted is ill-defined.

During transition, the newborn's circulating glucose concentration decreases to one-third of the maternal concentration (40–60 mg/dL) by 2–4 hours of age. In late preterm infants, the concentration may be as low as 30–40 mg/dL. Blood glucose stabilizes at 12–24 hours after birth to 60–80 mg/dL.

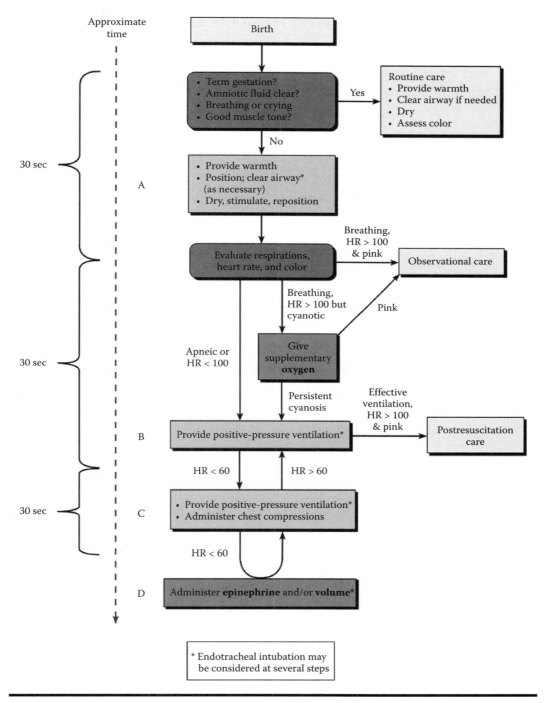

Figure 15.1. Neonatal flow algorithm. [http://circ.ahajournals.org/content/vol112/24_suppl/images/large/25FF1.jpeg Circulation. (2005). *American Heart Association Journals, 112*, IV-188, IV-195. With permission.]

Table 15.1 Equipment for Neonatal Resuscitation

Respiration

- Oxygen supply
- Assorted masks
  - Neonatal bag and tubing to connect to an oxygen source
  - Manometer
  - Endotracheal tubes (2.5–4)
  - Tape and scissors
  - Laryngoscope (0 and 1 sized blades)
  - Extra bulbs and batteries

Suction

- Bulb syringe
- Regulated mechanical suction
  - Suction catheters (6F, 8F, 10F)
  - Suction tubing
  - Suction canister
  - Replogle or Salem pump (10F catheter)
  - Feeding tube (8F catheter)
  - Syringe, catheter tipped, 20 mL
  - Meconium aspirator

Fluids

- IV catheters (22 g) tape and sterile dressing material
- D10W
- Isotonic saline solution
- T-connectors
- Syringes, assorted (1–20 mL)

Drugs

- Epinephrine (1:10,000)
- Sodium bicarbonate (0.5 mEq/mL)

Procedures

- Umbilical catheters (2.5F, 5F)
- Chest tube (10F catheter)
- Sterile procedure trays (e.g., scalpels, hemostats, forceps)

Source: Data from Bissinger, R. L. (2006). *Neonatal resuscitation*. Retrieved June 24, 2008, from http://www.emedicine.com/ped/TOPIC2598.HTM

As noted by Devaskar and Garg (2006), signs and symptoms of hypoglycemia include:

- Change in the level of consciousness, irritability, excessive crying, lethargy, or stupor
- Apnea episodes, cyanosis
- Feeding poorly
- Tachypnea, tachycardia, grunting
- Hypothermia
- Hypotonia, limpness
- Tremors, seizures, jitteriness

As shown in Table 15.2, The AAP has identified risk factors that may compromise an infant's ability to adapt to the metabolic demands of extrauterine life for which they recommend routine monitoring. The table identifies infants at risk based on those risk factors.

Armed with the knowledge of at-risk infants and signs and symptoms of hypoglycemia, the medical team has an obligation to use these tools to assess, monitor, and provide the appropriate intervention when necessary. The LNC reviewing a case involving neonatal hypoglycemia will need to review medical records including nursing flow sheets, lab reports, physical assessments, and physicians' orders. Careful attention should be paid to the narrative notes of the nurse specifically regarding assessment, documentation, intervention, and re-evaluation. Of particular importance is

Table 15.2   Neonates at Risk for Developing Hypoglycemia

A. Those born to mothers with altered metabolism due to

    1. Intrapartum administration of glucose

    2. Drug treatment

        a. Terbutaline, ritodrine, propranolol

        b. Oral hypoglycemic agents

    3. Diabetes in pregnancy/infant of diabetic mother

B. Those born with neonatal problems:

    1. Perinatal hypoxia-ischemia

    2. Infection

    3. Hypothermia

    4. Hyperviscosity

    5. Erythroblastosis fetalis, fetal hydrops

C. Those born with metabolic disorders:

    1. Hyperinsulinism

    2. Endocrine disorders

    3. Inborn errors of metabolism

Source: Data from Aynsley-Green, A., Cornblath, M., Hawdon, J., Kalhan, S., Schwartz, R., Ward-Platt, M., Williams, A. (2000). Controversies regarding definition of neonatal hypoglycemia: Suggested operational thresholds [Electronic version]. *Pediatrics 105*, 1141–1145.

obtaining the institution's Nursing Practice Guidelines or Clinical Practice Guidelines or Policy and Procedures regarding hypoglycemia relevant to the infant's at-risk status.

Areas of potential litigation may include the following:

- Failure to monitor for hypoglycemia (both prior to treatment and after treatment). (Keeping in mind the fact that glucose level depends on the status of the infant i.e., preterm, high-risk septic infant, infant of a diabetic mother.)
- Failure to initiate treatment in a timely manner. (Also keep in mind that the nurse has the responsibility to notify the APN or the physician of hypoglycemia in order to administer a glucose bolus.)
- Failure to reassess the infant after intervention.
- Failure to document intervention and assessment.
- Failure to administer the correct dose. (Glucose bolus should be 2–2.5 mL/kg of D10W IV)

Hyperbilirubinemia

Hyperbilirubinemia is a condition which is characterized by an excessive level of serum bilirubin. If left untreated and levels continue to increase, a condition called kernicterus develops which is a disabling disease process as well as potentially fatal. Kernicterus, or bilirubin encephalopathy, is a condition caused by bilirubin toxicity to the basal ganglia and various brainstem nuclei. In the acute phase, severely jaundiced infants become lethargic, hypotonic, and suck poorly. If the hyperbilirubinemia is not treated, the infant becomes hypertonic and may develop fever and a high-pitched cry. Surviving infants usually develop a severe form of athetoid cerebral palsy, hearing loss, dental dysplasia, palsy of upward gaze, and intellectual and other handicaps. Kernicterus is highly preventable but according to the AAP and the Joint Commission of Hospital Accreditation, cases of kernicterus continue to increase each year (JCAHO, 2001).

When evaluating a case involving sequelae associated with kernicterus or hyperbilirubinemia, it would be beneficial to review the clinical practice guidelines regarding neonatal jaundice published by the AAP. In 2004, the AAP revised the clinical practice guidelines for neonatal jaundice and kernicterus. The new guidelines can be found on the AAP website at http://aappolicy.aappublications.org/. These guidelines were developed using the evidence-based approach to guideline development. The guidelines encourage the use of the term "acute bilirubin encephalopathy" to describe the acute manifestations of bilirubin toxicity seen in the first weeks after birth. It also encourages the use of the term "kernicterus" to be reserved for the chronic and permanent clinical sequelae in bilirubin toxicity. The hope in the development of the guidelines is that by following the recommendations, kernicterus would be largely preventable. The guidelines emphasize the importance of a systematic assessment and prompt intervention. These guidelines are pertinent to infants of more than 35 weeks gestation.

AAP has created an algorithm for the assessment of newborns and the management of jaundice.

Generally speaking, phototherapy should be initiated whenever there is indication that the total serum bilirubin (TSB) level is increasing or approaching a level that requires an exchange transfusion. The guidelines recommend a universal standard for determining a level. Although phototherapy is virtually risk free when used appropriately, rare complications can occur. There is no standard for the discontinuation of phototherapy. Cessation depends on the age of the infant at commencement and the cause of the hyperbilirubinemia.

The AAP also provides recommendations for levels regarding exchange transfusions. Levels are based on the gestational age and hours of life. An exchange transfusion is a process in which the infant's circulating blood is replaced with donor blood. In the event of severe hyperbilirubinemia, it is used to prevent the negative effects caused by increased circulating bilirubin. The process of an exchange transfusion ideally requires the placement of an umbilical arterial and umbilical venous catheter (UVC). Because exchange transfusions are not without high risks, prompt and appropriate phototherapy is recommended initially to prevent the need for an exchange transfusion.

Risk factors for developing hyperbilirubinemia include race, age, and genetics. Males are at a greater risk than females but African-American males are less affected than white males. The risk of developing neonatal jaundice is inversely proportionate with gestational age. Infants with a sibling who required treatment of hyperbilirubinemia are more likely to develop jaundice. In addition, a maternal history of illness such as viral or other infection, drug intake or birth trauma also predisposes an infant to developing jaundice (Hansen, 2007). A prudent nurse should be aware of such risk factors, which would then prompt for early monitoring and continued assessment of neonatal jaundice.

In 2003, the NANN published Position Statement #3040 Prevention of Bilirubin Encephalopathy and Kernicterus in Newborns validating neonatal nursing's commitment to educating parents as well as commitment to their profession considering the risks associated with untreated hyperbilirubinemia. NANN sets the standards for neonatal nursing. Nurses need to update policies and procedures to enhance the process of diagnosis and management of hyperbilirubinemia.

Appropriate nursing care of a neonate includes educating parents of high-risk infants about the signs and symptoms of hyperbilirubinemia including icteric sclera, hypotonia, poor feeding and decreased urinary output. Documentation of teaching is paramount in reducing liability.

Being aware of the AAP guidelines allows the LNC reviewing a case for possible negligence or personal injury involving hyperbilirubinemia to list the areas of neglect. These areas may include:

- Failure to assess the infant at ongoing intervals or at discharge
- Failure to test for Coombs, blood type for Rh-mom
- Failure to notify the physician of a change in condition that is, increased transcutaneous bilirubin, TSB, or physical assessment
- Failure to follow up in a timely manner after discharge
- Failure to recognize the risk factors associated with hyperbilirubinemia
- Failure to initiate therapy in a timely manner
- Failure to document assessment/lab values/teaching
- Failure to identify at-risk infants

Records that may be beneficial to the LNC for reviewing a case involving hyperbilirubinemia/kernicterus are the following:

- *Nursing flow sheet:* Review nursing notes looking particularly for the ongoing assessment of (phototherapy) light level to determine efficacy of the treatment, documentation of the initiation of treatment/phototherapy, and observation of signs and symptoms of hyperbilirubinemia. Look for documentation for adequate intake and temperature homeostasis, output, and monitoring of transcutaneous bilirubinometry (TSB or TcB).
- *Physician assessment:* Carefully review the discharge summary of at-risk infants for a hyperbilirubinemia assessment, noting any differential diagnoses. Assessments should include

physical assessment for color, tone, alertness, urine output, feeding intake, and possibly specific gravity.

■ *Nomogram:* Identify if a nomogram was used to plot TSB levels. A nomogram is a graph used to predict if a child is at risk and determine the level of risk the infant may have for developing hyperbilirubinemia.

■ *Hospital policy and procedure for assessment of jaundice:* Although the AAP has set the standard, the physician and nurse may be required to follow the institutional policy. The assessment should recommend no less than every 8–12 hours.

Umbilical Venous Catheter

Indwelling umbilical catheters are currently considered to be a standard technology in the NICU. The umbilical vein is relatively easy to cannulate, and provides a readily accessible and reliable route to administer emergency medications and volume boluses. UVCs are used to obtain central blood samples to monitor organ and system function. Additionally, UVCs provide a route to perform exchange transfusions for hyperbilirubinemia. The use of a UVC provides reliable vascular access for the administration of hydration and nutritional fluids. Because UVCs are centrally located they can be used to administer both medications and hyperosmolar solutions, which may otherwise cause endothelial damage and irritation to peripheral blood vessels resulting in infiltration.

It is important for all caregivers to understand umbilical vein anatomy, which is the basis for key complications arising from UVC use. The UVC tip should be placed in the inferior vena cava just below the junction of the vena cava and right atrium. Accurate positioning is critical to prevent cardiac complications, which occur if the catheter is too high, and hepatic and portal venous complications, which occur if the catheter is too low. At a minimum, radiographic confirmation of all UVC placements should be obtained.

Despite the multiple advantages of accurately placing an UVC, there are many areas of potential complications lending itself to potential areas of litigation. Commencing with the line placement, it is a nursing responsibility to assess, obtain, and document baseline vital signs and continue to monitor the infant's vital signs during and after the catheter placement. Responsibilities also include restraining the infant properly to prevent contamination, anticipating thermoregulation needs, assisting with maintenance of the sterile field, securing the catheter, labeling the catheter correctly, verifying that the stopcocks are not open to air, and maintaining Luer-locks on all connections.

After placement of the catheter, validation of proper placement should be obtained prior to line usage. Standardized documentation should be used to promote communication between caregivers, such as recording the centimeter marking on the catheter at the umbilical stump at the time of the radiograph and insertion.

Ongoing assessments of the infant should include assessment of the integrity of the tubing and catheter, signs and symptoms of infection, maintaining aseptic technique with medication administration, tubing changes, and obtaining blood specimens.

Even careful insertion may lead to complications; thus the nurse should beware of the potential complications and perform focused assessment for complications associated with malposition and discontinuation, particularly thrombus formation, introduction of air embolus, hepatic injury, and omphalitis.

Potential areas of litigation involving umbilical catheters include:

■ Failure to document placement, vital signs, assessments
■ Failure to monitor

- Failure to assess
- Failure to maintain sterile field and prevent dislodgement
- Failure to perform aseptic technique
- Failure to inform proper medical personnel about change in assessment

Medical records that may be beneficial to obtain for the LNC reviewing a case involving umbilical catheters are nursing flow sheets for vital signs, centimeter markings on the catheter indicating correct placement at the umbilical stump, physical assessment of the infant prior to and during line placement, ongoing assessment of the infant post placement, assessment that the catheter is secure and stable, and assessment of the umbilical stump, in addition to the physician's procedure notes, the physician's orders and x-ray verifying the placement.

Sepsis

Sepsis is the body's response to an infection somewhere in the body. The infection can originate in any system of the body and can be bacterial, viral, or fungal. Premature infants are especially susceptible to infections due to their low birth weight, immature immune systems, immature skin, and immature respiratory systems. The diagnosis of sepsis seems to be a magnet for litigation because sepsis can often be fatal or have debilitating effects on the youngest of patients.

While the common symptoms of infection in a healthy term newborn may include tachycardia, tachypnea, and increased temperature, the symptoms of infection in a premature infant or an already compromised infant may manifest itself much less obviously. For example, the nurse may notice that after several days of successful oral feeding, the infant may now be requiring oxygen to maintain his oxygen saturation during feeds. The nurse may notice that after providing routine nursing care that the infant may experience more frequent desaturations or that his recovery time is increased compared with days earlier. The parents may comment to the nurse that their infant has been asleep during their entire visit. Although these observations may have simple explanations, it is the unexplainable observations with which the nurse needs to be concerned. These observations, especially if accompanied by vital sign changes and oxygen requirements, need to be relayed to the physician and the causes need to be investigated.

The following table includes signs and symptoms that an infant may exhibit if developing infection, or if it has already developed infection. Alternatively, many of these symptoms may be exhibited in the absence of infection as well and be related to alternative diagnoses (Table 15.3).

Knowledge of these vague signs may lead to early detection, intervention, and prompt diagnosis and treatment. Unfortunately, despite early detection and prompt intervention, devastating consequences of infection may be unavoidable.

Potential areas of litigation involving sepsis and infection include the following:

- Failure of the hospital to perform an accurate and thorough assessment
- Failure of the hospital staff to document changes in the physical assessment
- Failure to communicate changes in the assessment to the physician
- Failure to treat suspected/diagnosed infection
- Failure to treat changes in assessment
- Failure to order appropriate tests for diagnosis-suspected infection
- Failure to reevaluate and document changes in treatment related to infection

Table 15.3   Subtle Signs of Infection as Manifested in the Preterm Infant

Signs	Manifestation
Temperature change	Increased heater output by isolette or radiant warmer
	Multiple blankets needed to maintain temperature in open crib after period of temperature stability
	Decrease in temperature
Change in heart rate	Heart rate greater than 160 or any sustained increase in heart rate over the patient's normal resting heart rate
	Increased number of bradycardic episodes
Change in breathing rate	Respiratory rate is greater than 60 breaths per minute or any sustained increase over the patient's normal resting breathing rate
	Increased apneic episodes
	Increased work of breathing (i.e., retractions, grunting)
Change in oxygen demands	Increased oxygen requirement (may be seen at rest, during feeds or during activity)
	Unexplained oxygen desaturations
	Change in ventilatory support (i.e., room air to nasal cannula, nasal cannula to CPAP or increased ventilator settings)
Change in activity	Increased duration of sleeping with no alert times
	Irritability
	Sleeping during care (i.e., during diaper changes, not interested in feeding)
	Decrease in activity or movement (i.e., no spontaneous change in position)
	Decrease in strength of grasp
	Decrease in strength of suck
	Poor muscle tone
Change in feeding pattern/tolerance	Increased residual feeding noted in infant who is gavage fed
	No interest in bottle feeding/breast feeding in infant who previously fed orally
	Increased reflux
	Increase in number and frequency of stools or change in appearance of stool

Near-Term Infant

The topic of late preterm infants or near-term infants has grown increasingly popular in the last decade, with the realization of the special needs of this often overlooked population of newborns. These infants are born at 34 weeks to 36⁶/₇ weeks gestation. They are both physiologically and metabolically immature and thus are at an increased risk for developing medical complications. They are at a greater risk for developing hyperbilirubinemia, respiratory distress, hypoglycemia, hypothermia, and dehydration secondary to feeding difficulties. These infants are often placed in a level I nursery.

According to the clinical report by Engle, Tomashek, Wallman, and the Committee on Fetus and Newborn (2007), this population may warrant special discharge instructions and closer follow-up after discharge. Because this population of patients has not been widely studied, there are few practice guidelines to review. The importance of documentation regarding parent education, assessments, interventions, and reevaluations are critical to the legal nurse consultant reviewing a case involving this population.

Conclusion

There are numerous topics involving the neonatal population that have the potential for litigation in addition to the topics mentioned such as hypothermia, medication administration errors, and brachial plexus injury. Regardless of the topic of interest, it is imperative for the LNC to research the available Clinical Practice Guidelines, Nursing Practice Guidelines, and the institutional policies and procedures for the topic in question. Remember to thoroughly review the pertinent medical records and research the topic for information pertinent for the time period during which the event occurred.

Case Scenario

You are hired by an attorney to review a case for merit. The following is the information that she/he is able to provide to you.

A baby boy was born after delivery by an emergency cesarean section. He received Apgar scores of 4, 7, and 8. He required resuscitation in the delivery room including supplemental oxygen, suctioning, and bag-mask ventilation. Meconium was noted to be present at delivery and the infant's nasal and oropharynx were suctioned for thick meconium. Laryngoscopy was performed and revealed there is no meconium below the cords. Umbilical cord blood gas results revealed a pH of 6.85, CO_2 of 80 and base excess of −17.3.

According to the nurse's notes, she received the infant at 11:00 a.m. He was placed on the radiant warmer bed, vital signs were obtained (including heart rate, respiratory rate, and blood pressure, all of which were within normal limits) and an initial physical assessment was performed. Peripheral intravenous (PIV) access was attempted and achieved immediately upon admission by the doctor.

Upon further evaluation, the nurse noted that the infant experienced periods of apnea. She attempted to stimulate him and maintain his airway with bag-mask ventilation. Narcan was given twice to reverse the effects of Stadol that had been given in the delivery room. Upon placement of a PIV in the left hand, a normal saline bolus was given.

After completion of the normal saline bolus, labs were drawn by the doctor, including an arterial blood gas. The infant was placed on nasal continuous positive airway pressure (NCPAP) of 5. Sodium bicarbonate was administered. Respiratory support was increased to NCPAP of 7, and an umbilical arterial catheter was established. An x-ray of the chest and abdomen was performed and a second bolus of normal saline was administered as ordered.

The infant was intubated and suctioned for thick meconium, and ventilator support was initiated at 1:00 p.m. A second PIV was established in the left foot, a second dose of sodium bicarbonate was administered through the left foot PIV and a third dose of normal saline was also administered via the left hand PIV. An arterial blood gas was drawn upon completion of the normal saline bolus and ventilator settings were increased. At 1:45 p.m. it was discovered that the medication tubing was not connected in the left hand PIV.

1. What medical records would you recommend obtaining from the plaintiff?
2. Based on the information presented, was the element of duty satisfied in this example?
3. Can you predict areas of possible breach of this duty?
4. Can you anticipate what damages may occur if a breach in the duty to the patient occurred?

References

American Academy of Pediatrics (AAP). (2004). Management of hyperbilirubinemia in the newborn infant 35 or more weeks of gestation. *Practice Guideline [Electronic version]. Pediatrics, 114,* 297–316.

Aynsley-Green, A., Cornblath, M., Hawdon, J., Kalhan, S., Schwartz, R., Ward-Platt, M., & Williams, A. (2000). Controversies regarding definition of neonatal hypoglycemia: Suggested operational thresholds [Electronic version]. *Pediatrics, 105,* 1141–1145.

Bissinger, R. L. (2006). Neonatal resuscitation. Retrieved June 24, 2008 from http://www.emedicine.com/ped/TOPIC2598.HTM

Circulation. (2005). Part 13. Neonatal resuscitation guidelines [Electronic version]. *American Heart Association Journals, 112,* IV-188, IV-195.

Devaskar, S., & Garg, M. (2006). Glucose metabolism in the late preterm infant [Electronic version]. *Clinics in Perinatology, 33,* 803–810.

Engle, W. A., Tomashek, K. M., Wallman, C. and the Committee on Fetus and Newborn. (2007). "Late-preterm" infants: A population at risk. *Pediatrics, 120,* 1390–1401.

EPIPAGE Study Group. (2006). Improving regionalization by predicting neonatal intensive requirements of pre-term infants: an EPIPAGE-based cohort study [Electronic version]. *Pediatrics, 118,* 84–90.

Foster, J. (1998). The liability nurse expert witness. In J. Bogart (Ed.), *Legal nurse consulting principles and practice* (pp. 643–656). Boca Raton: CRC Press.

Hansen, TWR. (2007). Jaundice, neonatal. Retrieved June 24, 2008, from http://www.emedicine.com/ped/TOPIC1061.HTM, http://www.aacn.org/WD/Certifications/Content/ccrn.pcms?menu=Certifications#Eligibility, http://www.aap.org/nrp/nrpmain.html, http://www.nccnet.org/public/pages/index.cfm?pageid=111, http://www.nursesource.org/neonatal.html,

Joint Commission on Accreditation of Healthcare Organizations. (JCAHO). (2001). Sentinel event alert 18: Kernicterus threatens healthy newborns. Retrieved June 24, 2008, from http://www.jcaho.org/about+us/news+letters/sentinel+event+alert/sea_18.htm

McGowan, J. E., & Perlman, J. M. (2006). Glucose management during and after intensive delivery room resuscitation. *Clinical in Perinatology, 33,* 183–196.

National Association of Neonatal Nurses. (NANN). Position statement #3040, prevention of bilirubin encephalopathy and kernicterus in newborns. Retrieved June 24, 2008, from http://www.nann.org/i4a/pages/index.cfm?pageid=790

Test Questions

1. Standards of care for neonatal nursing are set by
   A. ANA
   B. NANN
   C. AWHONN
   D. AAP

2. Common areas of litigation involving neonates include all the following except:
   A. Sepsis
   B. Medication errors
   C. Resuscitation
   D. Falls

3. Requirements for working as a neonatal nurse are established by
   A. The institution
   B. The state board of nursing
   C. NANN
   D. AAP

4. When evaluating a malpractice case for negligence involving a newborn or neonate, it is imperative to have a background in neonatal nursing because
   A. Only neonatal nurses with special certifications are permitted to review such cases by law
   B. Neonates undergo a complex transition to the extrauterine environment best understood by a nurse with neonatal nursing training and experience
   C. It is not imperative to have neonatal experience because neonates behave physiologically as "little adults" and thus their treatments are similar to that of adults

5. A neonate requiring extended mechanical ventilatory support should be cared for in which level of NICU:
   A. I
   B. II
   C. III
   D. It does not really matter as long as there is 1:1, nurse/patient ratio.

Answers: 1. B,C, 2. D, 3. A, 4. B, 5. C

Chapter 16

Advanced Practice Nursing

Wendy Bonnar, RN, WHNP-BC, MSN

Contents

Objectives

- Discuss the range of services nurse practitioners can provide
- Discuss the various education requirements and certifications required for nurse practitioners
- Discuss the advantages of having guidelines/standardized procedures in place for the nurse practitioner
- What is primary liability?
- List at least four different ways the nurse practitioner may establish a relationship with their patient
- Explain the common areas of liability for the nurse practitioner

Introduction

Under California state law, a nurse practitioner (NP) is defined as "registered nurse who possesses additional preparation and skills in physical diagnosis, psychosocial assessment and management of health-illness needs in primary health care and who has been prepared in a program conforming to board standards as specified in section 1484" (Ac. Code Regs. tit. 16, S 1480 [a]) (Bupert, 2004, p. 2).

Other titles given to NPs include Physician Extender, Mid-level Provider or Practitioner, and Advanced Practice Nurse (APN). NPs practice in many specialties including pediatrics, oncology, internal medicine, family practice, gynecology, obstetrics, psychiatry, dermatology, geriatrics, and adult medicine to name a few. NP's responsibilities and duties are many and can vary with state Nurse Practice Acts. In some states, the Nurse Practice Act is very broad and NPs may perform any service agreed upon by the NP and collaborating physician. In general, NPs may provide the following services:

- Perform physical examinations and obtain medical histories
- Diagnose and treat health problems
- Order and interpret laboratory tests and x-rays
- Prescribe medications and other treatments such as physical therapy
- Provide well-child care and immunizations
- Education and counseling in many areas
- Case management and coordination of care
- Take after hours call
- Make hospital visits and follow hospital care of established patients
- Perform suturing if necessary

NP's scope of practice in the gynecologic/obstetric arena may also include the following:

- Provide prenatal care and family planning services
- Perform gynecological examinations and pap smears
- Perform various invasive procedures, including biopsies and colposcopy
- Prescribe drugs and devices used for birth control and drugs and devices for postmenopausal women:
  - These would include pessarys, diaphrams, vaginal contraceptive rings, vaginal rings, and patches for use as hormone therapy

A Brief History of Nurse Practitioners in the United States

The history of the NP stretches over decades and has evolved into an important specialty in nursing and a necessity for the healthcare industry. Economic and societal needs over the past 30 years have significantly affected the healthcare delivery system, resulting in changes for all healthcare provider roles, especially the NP.

In the 1960s, Dr. Henry Silver and Loretta Ford, PhD (a nurse educator) at the University of Colorado created a program to educate nurses to respond to the need for primary-care providers in rural areas. Dr. Silver and Dr. Ford established a pediatric practitioner program based on the nursing model. This was the first of the NP programs that educated nurses to make medical diagnoses while providing care in a nursing model. The idea was revolutionary and initially not well accepted by the academic nursing profession. The first graduates began to practice in the late 1960s. The program was at the master's level, requiring a nursing license and experience in patient care for admission. In subsequent years, several programs moved away from the master's degree model to certificate programs but, more recently, the trend has again shifted back to master's education.

The nursing profession initially expressed skepticism with the educational process and the new identity of the NP. Education that incorporated a medical model to create a physician "extender" was threatening to nursing's roots and to its exclusive orientation to care. It was only as the NP profession evolved and the academic and training programs were clarified that the profession embraced the new roles for nurses.

In 2000, NPs were legally enabled to practice in every state and the District of Columbia. Practice varied considerably across states with different statutory and regulatory limitations on prescriptive authority, direct reimbursement, and the required legal relationship with physicians. NPs were generally regulated by state Boards of Nursing, but in some states, Boards of Medicine were directly involved in regulation of the profession. In some states, agencies other than the Department of Health were involved in professional oversight activities for NPs. In 2000, NPs were not title protected in every state. In 49 states and the District of Columbia, NPs were provided with some form of prescriptive authority, which varied from the ability to prescribe only legend drugs to full prescriptive authority including controlled substances. The educational requirements to obtain prescriptive authority varied widely across states (retrieved August 10, 2008, from http://bhpr.hrsa.gov/healthworkforce/reports/scope/scope1-2.htm#2).

Demographics

According to the Pearson Report (Pearson, 2009), there are 147, 295 NPs in the United States as of February 2008. The top three states with the most NPs are California with 15,320, New York with 14,272, and Florida with 10,277. North Dakota and South Dakota have the least number of NPs with 343 and 372, respectively. Wyoming is a close third with 435.

Education and Certification

In the 1990s, some obstetric and gynecologic (Ob/Gyn) NP programs offered certificate programs. Many of these programs were offered by Planned Parenthood. Certificate programs were a one-year program of study at the master's level and concentrated on advanced physical assessment, clinical practice, pharmacology, and interpretation of laboratory results. Some states "grand-fathered" in NPs with certificates after passing laws requiring new graduates of NP programs to have master's degrees. For example, as of January 2008, California requires new applicant NPs to have master's degrees.

All states except New York require NPs to have master's degrees, graduate degrees, or masters in nursing to practice (Pearson, 2008). An excellent resource for information on NP practice in all states can be found at www.webnp.net. This is a free access to the Pearson Report as written in *The American Journal of Nurse Practitioners*. Linda J. Pearson has summarized NP legislation, recapping the latest information from each state's Nurse Practice Act and rules and regulations, along with presenting pertinent government, policy, and reimbursement information on NP practice issues.

National certification has become the standard for NPs in all specialties. All but seven states required national certification from a certifying body in order to qualify for licensure or registration as an NP. These states are California, Colorado, Indiana, Kansas, New York, North Dakota, and Oregon. (Pearson, 2008).

Examinations qualifying NPs for national certification are provided by the American Academy of Nurse Practitioners Certification Program (AANPCP), the American Nurse Credentialing Center (ANCC), the American Board for Pediatric Nurse Practitioners (PNCB), and the National Certification Corporation for the Obstetrical, Gynecologic, and Neonatal Nursing Specialties (NCC). When an NP is certified in women's health, she may use the title Women's Health Nurse Practitioner (WHNP). She may also add a B.C., meaning Board Certified. For more detailed information, go to http://www.nccnet.org/public/pages/index.cfm?pageid=1.

The American Academy of Nurse Practitioners also has added a new practice bulletin. The bulletin is titled *Standards for NP Practice in Retail Based Clinics*. The full position statement may be found at http://www.aanp.org/AANPCMS2/Publications/PositionStatementsPapers/.

In some states, NPs may start their own practice. Generally, an independent practice requires a physician to be available for consultation (not necessarily on premises), and in some states there is no requirement for Medical Doctor (MD) involvement; the NP may practice completely independently.

Claims Allegations

NPs practicing in outpatient clinics are just as vulnerable to claims liability as NPs who work in a hospital setting. Data from the Nurse Practitioners Claims Study (CNA Financial Corporation, 2005) reveal that approximately one-half of all NPs provide primary care in family or adult-care specialties. The remaining NPs deliver healthcare services in other clinical specialties such as emergency medicine, psychiatry, gerontology, pediatrics, and women's health.

The NPs specified scope of practice is critical with respect to any theory of liability or potential allegations that may be asserted in malpractice litigation. It also forms the context within which a court will determine whether negligent conduct occurred and whether the NP acted within the scope of practice (CNA Financial Corporation, 2005). See also Figure 16.1.

Nurses Service Organization ([NSO], 2005), an insurer of nurses and NPs, has identified three main reasons why litigation is increasing against NPs; they are (1) increased collaboration and autonomy and less direct supervision, (2) increased prescriptive authority, and (3) recognition of NPs by insurance companies as primary-care providers.

A CNA study of claims against NPs from 1994 to 2004 showed 75% of claims were in the specialty areas of family practice and adult/geriatric practice. About 8.5% of claims were in

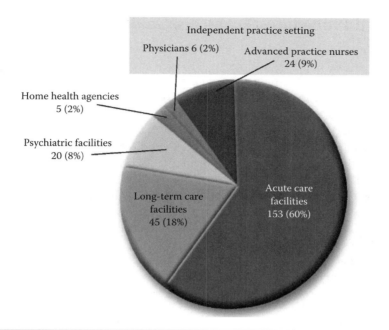

Figure 16.1. **Incidence of nursing negligence allegations by setting, 1995–2001. Total number of complaints = 253; percentages are rounded to the nearest 1%; resulting in a total of 99%. [From Croke, E.M., (2003).** *The American Journal of Nursing, 103*(9), 54–63. With permission.]**

obstetrics and gynecology. While NPs provide prenatal and postpartum care, they are typically not involved in the actual labor and delivery. The data pertaining to the obstetrics/gynecology specialty presented in this study support this practice pattern. It should be noted, however, that NPs in the clinical setting frequently read nonstress tests (NSTs); and this is a frequent area of litigation in regard to the care of pregnant women. The NP who reads NSTs should be trained to do so. Policies of an institution should clarify competencies and provide guidelines for assessment and documentation.

Miller (2007) reports 81.6% (*n* = 523) of the claim allegations against NPs fell into three categories: diagnosis, treatment, and medication occurrences. Miller further reports that these identical categories representing 82% (*n* = 368) of payment reports are supported by a 14-year study by the National Practitioner Data Bank (NPDB). For more information, see Table 16.6.

Swenson (2006) discusses other common themes amid claims against NPs. These include the following:

■ Failure to diagnose: the majority of these cases involved female cancers of the reproductive system
■ Negligent treatment: one-third was medication related
■ Failure to consult or refer to an MD when there was a change in a patient's condition
■ Delay in treatment

Communication breakdown and failure to give informed consent can also be troublesome areas for NP practice.

Standardized Procedures/Protocols/Guidelines

An important issue in regard to clinical practice is the development of standardized procedures (SPs). SPs (protocols) are written guidelines under which an NP may practice. Laws governing the formality of these protocols vary by state. In those states that require APNs to work under a collaborative agreement, it is important the physician be identified and cosign the protocol. The protocol should also describe the situations requiring physician referral or consultation (James, 1999). Protocols should be reviewed on an annual basis to ensure they are in compliance with current practice and community standards. It is the NP's responsibility to make certain the guidelines are in compliance with state statutes. It is not the responsibility of the facility or the collaborating physician (James, 1999).

Protocols may be very specific or general, depending on the institution or type of practice. Guidelines and protocols help health professionals offer the best possible care for their patients by recommending treatment based on scientific evidence and expert clinical opinion and by ensuring consistency of care from provider to provider.

Even though collaborative practice results in the best patient care, other healthcare providers may not cooperate when it comes to defending themselves against allegations of malpractice.

> Since the nurse practitioner has the ability to examine, diagnose, and establish treatment plans for patients, friction may develop among the various healthcare professionals. Should these professionals become co-defendants in professional liability litigation, an adversarial situation may result. In some jurisdictions, physicians may carry lower limits of professional liability coverage than a nurse practitioner. In such cases, the nurse practitioner may become the focus of the defendant's claim in order to attach additional liability insurance coverage. (CNA Financial Corporation, 2005, p. 4)

In *Sermchief v. Gonzalez* "the court recognized that NPs who function in an advanced practice role must be aware of the limits of their knowledge and the limits contained in the written standing orders and protocols" (Henry, 2001, p. 480).

The above is an example of the importance of SPs and a collaborative relationship with physicians and other healthcare providers. Even if there is no state requirement for written protocols the NP should develop their own for use in practice. Clinicians increasingly use practice guidelines and protocols to standardize patient care. These practice guidelines should be based on evidence-based practice, current NP credentialing organization guidelines, current medical practice and other relevant guidelines, and the clinician's experience (Table 16.1). As a specialist in women's health, the WHNP should develop and utilize protocols based on guidelines promulgated by the American College of Obstetrics and Gynecologist (ACOG), the Association of Women's Health Obstetric and Neonatal Nurses (AWHONN), evidence-based practice, state Nurse Practice Acts, and other professional resources.

Accountability/Liability

Accountability is an integral part of professional practice (Iankova, 2006). NPs are responsible for their own actions irrespective of the specific language of the state Nurse Practice Act and clinical protocols. This is known as direct or primary liability. They will be held accountable for the standard of care as it applies to their specific practice.

Table 16.1   Current NP Credentialing Organizations

Program Clinical Focus	National Credentialing Body
Family	American Nurses Association (ANA)
	American Academy of Nurse Practitioners
Adult	ANA[a]
	American Academy of Nurse Practitioners[a]
Gerontology	ANA[a]
Women's health care	National Certification Cooperation for the Gynecological/ Obstetrics and Neonatal Nursing Specialities
Pediatric	ANA[a]
	National Certification Board of Pediatric Nurse Practitioners and Nurses[a]

Source: Current nurse practitioner credentialing organizations. Retrieved August 31, 2008, from http://www.ispub.com/ostia/index.php?xmlFilePath=journals/ijanp/vol1n2/scope.xml.

[a] Reporting using the "Advanced Nurse Practitioner" category began on March 5, 2002. The "Advanced Nurse Practitioner" category was changed to "Clinical Nurse Specialist" on September 9, 2002. Prior to March 5, 2002, these nurses were included in the "RN (Professional Nurse)" category.

In nursing malpractice cases, legal accountability is established by the expert witness. Simpson and Chez (2001, p. 29) state "Courts recognize nurses as professionals who poses the specialized knowledge and skills required to act interdependently as a collaborative member of a team of caregivers."

Legal accountability can be established by the following:

■ Nurse Practice Acts
■ Parameters of professional practice established by professional organizations
■ Legislative changes
■ Institutional standards
■ Expert witness

Maintaining accountability in one's practice can be assured by the following:

■ Ethical decision-making
■ Using evidence-based practice
■ Keeping current in competencies that reflects current nursing practice and by continuing education
■ Knowing institutional or clinical policies and procedures
■ Keeping current with technical skills: computer, PDA
■ Accurate and thorough and legible documentation of care provided
■ Peer evaluation, "which fosters the refinement of knowledge, skills and decision making at all levels and in all areas of clinical practice" (American Nurses Association [ANA], 2004)

- Self-regulation by the profession of nursing
- Collaboration with colleagues, patients, family, and others

NPs are in a unique position in that they are licensed to perform medical as well as nursing functions. Therefore, the NPs license gives them accountability for general oversight of all patient care, and face dual legal liability. APNs should always clarify their independent role as well as their relationship with the collaborating physician. For example, in *Hernicz v. State of Florida, Dept. of Professional Regulation* (1980), a nurse was held liable for failure to inform a patient of the expanded role and that the NP was not a physician (James, 1999).

Clinical Practice

Many publications about clinical practice guidelines and recommendations come from professional organizations. These may include disclaimers that the recommendations are guidelines rather than standards of care. However, in claims involving malpractice the plaintiff and defense frequently will offer these professional publications as standards of care in support of their case. Even though these publications are offered to present guidelines based on evidence-based and current practice, publications from American College of Obstetrics and Gynecology (ACOG), the Association of Women's Health, Obstetrics, and Neonatal Nursing (AWHONN), the American College of Nurse Midwives (ACNM), American Academy of Pediatrics (AAP), and the American Society of Anesthesiologists (ASA), these do become standards of care "for all practical purposes in legal proceedings" (Simpson, 2008, p. 3).

The Nurse Practitioner Data Bank (NPDB)

NPDB is a "repository for damage award data from professional liability insurance companies on behalf of their clients to injured parties for successful malpractice claims" (Bupert, 2008, p. 259). It is under the responsibility of the U.S. Department of Health and Human Services.

Under the law, any insurer who pays any amount to a plaintiff on behalf of an NP or MD in a malpractice claim must report the amount to the NPDB. If a payment is made directly to the plaintiff by the NP or MD, the claim does not have to be reported. The insurance company must report damage rewards to state licensing agencies. In addition, state licensing agencies are required to report adverse license actions, and hospitals are required to report adverse clinical privilege actions. Table 16.6 shows malpractice payments by malpractice reason. This table includes only disclosable reports in the NPDB as of the end of the current year. Voided reports have been excluded. Medical malpractice payment reports, which are missing data necessary to determine the malpractice reason (eight reports for RNs), are excluded.

Risk Management

The NP's relationship with a patient starts under many different circumstances; for instance, when a patient sees the NP in the office, in the hospital, or a home visit. Relationships can be established in other ways:

- Over the telephone
- By email

- Voicemail messages
- Text messages
- At social gatherings
- Giving sample medications
- Giving advise to family and friends
- Assuming care of another providers patient
- In consultation with another provider in regard to patient care

As an example, an NP is at lunch with a few people from the office. One of the receptionists says that her mother has been sick with a sinus infection and a bad cold for weeks. She asks the NP if she would mind calling in a prescription for azythromycin for her mother. Her mother feels awful and does not want to get out of bed to see her provider. Azythromycin has always worked in the past and she has no drug allergies. If the NP calls in the prescription for the antibiotic, the receptionists' mother then becomes her patient whether she has seen the NP or not.

In another example, NP Smith receives a telephone message from a patient she has not seen in several years. The patient is asking for a refill for her birth control pills. In reviewing the patient chart you see she has had several abnormal pap smears and has not had any recent follow up. Should NP Smith refill the patients' birth control pills? The answer is no. The patient has a possibility of a continuing abnormal pap smear and could possibly have developed a precancerous condition. If NP Smith refills the birth control pills without proper evaluation, NP Smith could be liable if the patient ultimately develops cervical cancer. This is a prudent response to a potential liability.

These examples may seem elementary; however, the NP needs to be aware that no matter how innocuous a situation may seem they should not provide care that does not involve the normal evaluation process. It is wise to remember that the NP ultimately has responsibility to any health-care advice given to anyone.

Common Areas of Liability

Practicing Beyond Scope of Practice

Scope of practice determines who an NP can see and treat, determines reimbursement for medical care, determines limits and privileges of an NPs license, and determines the ability to be covered under malpractice insurance. Klein (2005) states, "according to Nurses Service Organization (NSO) claims data in 2004, practicing beyond scope accounted for 6% of all claims filed. Scope also determines the 'minimum standard' of competency for a provider with like knowledge and training in a given specialty; 32% of NSO claims in the same report pertained to failure to meet minimum standards."

Klein also discusses collaboration and delegation. Below are some main points concerning these two areas:

- According to the Federation of State Medical Boards, The American Medical Association does not have an official definition of collaboration.
- The terms "independent," "collaboration," and "supervision" vary widely in interpretation and regulatory definition. The Joint Commission on Accreditation of Healthcare Organizations (JCAHO) defines an LIP, or Licensed Independent Provider, as "any individual permitted by law and by the organization to provide care and services, without direction or supervision, within the scope of the individual's license and consistent with individually granted clinical privileges." Recent acknowledgment by JCAHO in their *Medical Staff Handbook* of the LIP role of the NP offers support for hospital privileges based

upon the NP's individual credentials, training, competency, and scope, rather than using the proxy of supervision as the primary eligibility requirement (JCAHO, 2004).

■ The state of California Nurse Practice Act states the following in regard to collaboration: "Standardized Procedures are authorized in the Business and Profession Code, Nursing Practice Act (NPA) Section 2725 and further clarified in California Code of Regulation (CCR 1480). Standardized procedures are the legal mechanism for registered nurses, nurse practitioners to perform functions which would otherwise be considered the practice of medicine. Standardized procedures must be developed *collaboratively* by nursing, medicine, and administration in the organized health care system where they will be utilized. Because of this interdisciplinary *collaboration* for the development and approval of standardized procedures, there is accountability on several levels" (California State Board of Registered Nursing, 2008).

■ According to the Federation of State Medical Boards: "Delegated services must be ones that a reasonable and prudent physician using sound medical judgment would find appropriate to delegate and must be within the defined scope of practice both of the physician and the non-physician practitioner" (Klein, 2005).

Having a physician supervise, co-sign, or otherwise endorse a practice or task that is not within the legal and professional scope does not make it within the realm of practice. See Table 16.2 also.

Telephone Triage

Triage was developed during World War I as a method to determine treatment priorities. Mahlmeister and Van Mullem (2000) describe the steps of triage as rapid assessment of the patient or client, identification of problem(s), determination of acuity, and deployment of personnel and equipment to meet needs.

In-person triage and telephone triage occur in all ambulatory and acute-care settings. The risks associated with obstetric and gynecologic triage are considerable and the triage must conform to national evidence-based standards. Clinical protocols must be based on current practice from accepted organizations such as ACOG, AWHONN, and other professional groups.

In-hospital triage of perinatal patients in the United States is regulated by federal law, the Emergency Medical Treatment and Active Labor Act (EMTLA). In the ambulatory clinic setting this law does not apply. Therefore, in some instances, telephone triage is done by unlicensed personnel such as medical assistants and people who answer the telephone. This practice is unacceptable, unsafe, and below the standard of care. Any healthcare provider or institution that allows this practice is held accountable for adverse events resulting from advice given by these unlicensed personnel. It should be noted also that many states only allow RNs to perform this function. RNs who perform triage must be qualified to do so and protocols need to be in place outlining specific qualifications upon which the institution, NPs, and MDs have agreed. Safe and effective triage requires a high degree of clinical expertise and sound clinical judgment.

Mahlmeister and Van Mullem (2000) state that the most common areas of claims regarding telephone triage in the outpatient setting are a failure to perform a systematic assessment of the client's problem, failure to identify the nature and acuity of the problem, failure to make proper disposition of the patient (delay between calling and seeing patient), delay in returning phone calls, and negligent advice. Other areas of concern are failure to document patient complaints, advice given and follow-up, failure to have the complaint reviewed by a healthcare provider, failure to have protocols in place for triage advice, and failure to advise the patient to seek inpatient evaluation and treatment.

Table 16.2   Scope of Practice: Domains and Questions

Domain: Knowledge

Did I complete a program that prepared me to see this population (family, adult, pediatric) of patients?

Did this program include supervised clinical and didactic training focusing on this population?

Did I complete a program that prepared me for subspecialization (acute care, geriatric, neonatal)? If so, is the patient in question in that category?

Do I have the knowledge to differentially diagnose and manage the conditions for which I am seeing this patient?

Domain: Role Validation

Am I licensed to practice in this role?

Is additional licensure or certification required to do this skill on an ongoing or specialized basis?

Do professional organizations define this role through specialty scope statements and criteria or standards of practice?

Do professional standards support or validate what I am doing?

How do I "hold myself out" (define my role) with the public? Do my qualifications, training, and licensure match this?

Is the information regarding my training easily accessible and can it be validated to the public, healthcare credentialing staff, facilities, and other interested parties?

Domain: Competence and Skill

What are the clinical competence/skills required to treat this condition?

Have I been trained to differentially diagnosis this type of patient?

Did this training include clinical and didactic training?

How have I achieved and demonstrated competence?

How have I maintained competence?

What is the standard of a practitioner in this field and do I meet it? Do I meet these standards on a limited or broad basis?

Have I completed a specialty preceptorship, fellowship, or internship that qualifies me beyond my basic educational training?

Domain: Environment

Does the environment that I work in support this scope or practice through structures such as staffing, consultation, policies and procedures, protocols, and community standards?

Am I an expert, novice, or midlevel provider in this field? Do my credentialing to the public and my consultative network match this?

Is access to care an issue? Will I be facilitating or impeding access to the best trained professional?

continued

Table 16.2 (Continued) Scope of Practice: Domains and Questions

Domain: Ethics

What are the potential consequences of accepting treatment responsibility for this patient?

Am I prepared to accept and manage the consequences of my diagnosis and treatment, or do I have a formally established relationship with a provider who is so trained and immediately available?

If I am not the primary-care provider, will my provision of care be shared with this person?

Is the safety of the patient at acute risk if I do not act?

Will the safety of the patient be compromised if I do act?

Is there a personal or formal relationship with this patient that would potentially affect my ability to provide or deny care?

Source: Klein, T. A. (2005). *Topics in Advanced Practice Nursing eJournal*. Retrieved September 13, 2008, from http://www.medscape.com/viewprogram/41d88_pnt

An Indiana malpractice case outlines the risks of telephone triage in the outpatient setting. A woman who was ten weeks pregnant called her obstetrician's office complaining of a sore throat, swollen glands, and a low grade fever. The call was taken by a Licensed Practical Nurse (LPN) who diagnosed the woman's problem as a cold, and without consulting the MD, advised the woman to gargle with salt water and take over the counter medications to relieve her symptoms. Six days later, the woman called again and stated she still felt ill and had swollen glands. Again the LPN did not consult with the physician and advised the patient to keep her scheduled prenatal appointment, which was in five days. The woman called back later that same day to report she was now vomiting. For a third time, the LPN failed to speak with the physician, telling the woman to call back if the vomiting persisted. Three hours later, the woman called back stating she was still vomiting. The LPN did consult with the physician and a prescription for an antiemetic medication was called in to a pharmacy and the patient was given an appointment the same day. When she arrived in the office the woman's condition was deteriorating rapidly and she was sent directly to the hospital. She died 6 hours later from group B *Streptococcus pyogenes* sepsis (Mahlmeister & Van Mullem, 2000). This case illustrates the importance of having trained, experienced personnel who perform telephone triage.

The American Academy of Ambulatory Care Nursing has practice standards for telephone triage: *Telephone Nursing Practice Administration and Practice Standards* (4th ed., [2007]; this edition may be purchased on line at http://www.aaacn.org/cgi-bin/WebObjects/AAACNMain). Several other sources for telephone triage guidelines are *Telephone Triage for Obstetrics and Gynecology* (2004) by Vicki E. Long and Patricia C. McMullen (Lippincott, Williams & Wilkins) and *Telephone Triage for the Obstetric Patient: a Nursing Guide* (2003) by Deborah E. Swenson (W.B. Saunders).

Decreased Fetal Movement

Decreased fetal movement is a common complaint of pregnant women (see Table 16.3). Fetal movement may be perceived by some women as early as 16–17 weeks gestation, or if nulliparous not until after 20 weeks. Fetal movement generally does not become regular until the age of 26–28 weeks gestation. Any woman complaining of decreased fetal movement must be taken seriously and evaluated promptly. If the gestational age is before 30 weeks, it may be hard to establish a reactive NST; therefore, the woman should be brought into the clinic and a hand-held fetal

Table 16.3   Factors Associated with Decreased Fetal Movement

Fatigue	Alcohol Use
Busy mother	Intrauterine growth restriction
Fetal sleep	Cortiosteroids
Hypoxia	Neurological abnormality
Poly-or-oligohydramnious	Sedative use
Hypothyroidism	Motor vehicle accident
Other maternal trauma (domestic violence)	Fetal anemia

ultrasound doppler can be used to auscultate fetal heart tones. If needed, a biophysical profile can be performed. All women who are greater than 28–30 weeks need to have an evaluation by NST. This gives reassurance to the woman and assures fetal well-being. All care must be appropriately documented in the prenatal record.

The recording of fetal movements as perceived by a pregnant woman is one of the oldest methods to assure fetal well-being. Fetal movement is an indirect measure of fetal central nervous system integrity and function (Christensen, Olson, & Rayburn, 2003). The teaching of daily fetal movement charting is practiced by many obstetrical healthcare providers. Charting of fetal movements can be done any time or anywhere without expensive monitoring equipment. There are several methods of fetal movement counting (FMC) techniques; no one method has been shown to be better than the other. ACOG (1999) states numerous counting protocols have been in use; however, neither the optimal number of movements nor the ideal duration for counting movements has been defined.

The literature reports several counting techniques that are frequently employed. Olesen and Svare (2004) report the count-to-ten technique. The pregnant woman is asked to register, once daily, how many minutes it takes to feel ten distinct movements. The movements should be counted when the fetus is usually active. The number of minutes it takes may be recorded in a fetal movement record. Kicks, stretches, or rollovers are counted, but not hiccups. The patient is asked to call in if more than 1 hours is needed to feel ten movements. ACOG (1999) reports a perception of ten distinct movements in a period of up to two hours is considered reassuring.

Moore and Piacquadio as reported by Olesen and Svare (2004) have shown that the count-to-ten method of fetal movement is effective in reducing the intrauterine death rate in low-risk pregnancies.

"Fetal movement is an indirect measure of fetal central nervous system integrity and function. Perceived inactivity has long been recognized as a sign of jeopardy" (Christensen et al., 2003). FMC is beneficial in providing reassurance of fetal well-being.

Vaginal Bleeding

Vaginal bleeding is a common complaint addressed by the APN, especially in the first trimester. Vaginal bleeding in the first trimester is not always an ominous sign. There are many innocuous things that can cause first trimester bleeding; one such thing is vaginal intercourse.

Bowers et al. (2008) report about one in five pregnancies will have bleeding. The incidence and cause can vary by trimester. About half the bleeding episodes in pregnancy have unknown causes; however, vaginal bleeding in any trimester needs prompt evaluation. Of utmost importance, if first trimester bleeding occurs, is ruling out ectopic pregnancy.

Ectopic Pregnancy

In the United States, ectopic pregnancy is the leading cause of pregnancy-related death during the first trimester (AGOG, 1998). The Centers for Disease Control and Prevention (formally the Centers for Disease Control [CDC]) first began collecting data on ectopic pregnancies in 1970. At that time, the rate was 4.5 per 1,000 reported pregnancies (AGOG, 1998). In 1992, about 9% of pregnancy-related deaths were due to ectopic pregnancy. Today, data on ectopic pregnancy are hard to estimate because many ectopic pregnancies are treated in the outpatient setting.

The most important risk factor in ectopic pregnancy is prior pelvic inflammatory disease (PID). PID is commonly caused by *Chalmydia trachomatis*. Other risk factors include previous ectopic pregnancy, cigarette smoking, prior tubal surgery, diethylstilbestrol (DES) exposure, and increasing age (AGOG, 1998). Seeber and Barnhart (2008) report other risk factors for ectopic pregnancy are tubal ligation, use of intrauterine device, infertility, multiple sexual partners, vaginal douching, and first intercourse before the age of 18.

The classic signs and symptoms of ectopic pregnancy include abdominal or pelvic pain and vaginal spotting or bleeding with a positive pregnancy test. These symptoms, however, can range from mild to severe. They are neither sensitive nor specific for ectopic pregnancy (Seeber & Barnhart, 2006, 2008). The most common signs are found on pelvic examination. Abdominal tenderness is found in 90% of patients and rebound tenderness in 70% (Seeber & Barnhart, 2006, 2008). Cervical motion tenderness is present in about two-third of patients, while adnexal mass and tenderness is present in 10–50%. Pain radiating to the shoulder, syncope, and shock are indications of probable rupture of the fallopian tube and require immediate surgical intervention. It should be noted that in some cases of ectopic pregnancy there are no symptoms.

Sheehy (2000) reports a case of missed ectopic pregnancy in the emergency room (ER). While visiting a friend, 26–year-old women fainted and hit her head. Her friend called 911. When the paramedics arrived the woman was awake and alert. She stated she experienced a sharp pain in her abdomen before passing out. Her vital signs were stable and she was transferred to the ER for evaluation. The patient was evaluated by the RN and vital signs continued to be stable. The RN asked questions regarding the syncopal episode and the events surrounding it. Other information obtained from the patient included a history of sexual activity and her menstrual period was eight days in duration, beginning again one day before the episode. The ER MD evaluated the woman and found a negative exam with the exception of a small amount of blood in the vagina. A urine sample was sent to the lab for a pregnancy test. She was discharged with a diagnosis of gastroenteritis and sent home with the instructions that she would be notified if the results of the pregnancy test were positive. Before leaving, the patient gave the ER nurse the address and telephone number of the place she was staying.

Later, the results of the pregnancy test in the ER were returned positive. At this point what happened regarding the attempts to contact the patient is not known. Four weeks after her ER visit, the patient called the hospital's administration office to inform them that she had recently been discharged from another hospital three and a half weeks earlier where she had been admitted with ruptured ectopic pregnancy and hypovolemic shock. The patient demanded a monetary settlement or threatened to sue.

The hospital's risk manager along with the ER's nurse manager reviewed the woman's record. No documentation was found of any attempts to contact the patient. Also, no proof was found that a letter was sent to the address where the patient was staying. The ER nurse was interviewed and said she had made a number of attempts to contact the patient by telephone but could not reach her. She did not document these attempts. She stated she did not attempt to send a letter and did not know if anyone else had tried to do so.

Given the lack of documentation, the hospital determined it could not defend the case and negotiated a settlement of six figures. This case illustrates many classic signs of ectopic pregnancy, abdominal pain, vaginal spotting, and syncope. It is clear the patient should not have been discharged without the ER staff knowing results of the pregnancy test.

Diagnosis of ectopic pregnancy can be determined by serial quantitative levels of the beta subunit of human chorionic gonadotropin (B-hCG) in combination with transvaginal ultrasound. The minimal rise in B-hCG levels for a viable pregnancy has been reported in the literature to be 53% in two days. The minimal decline of a spontaneous abortion is about 21–35% in two days but this depends on the initial level of hCG. A rise and fall that is slower than this is suggestive of an ectopic pregnancy (Seeber & Barnhart, 2006). The diagnosis and management of suspected ectopic pregnancy should be decided by the "discriminatory cutoff" of B-hCG. According to Seeber and Barnhardt (2006), "This cutoff is defined as that level of B-hCG at which a normal intrauterine pregnancy can be visualized by ultrasonography with sensitivity approaching 100%." This cutoff is usually defined as 1,500–2,500 IU/L. A normal intrauterine pregnancy should be visualized at these levels depending on the equipment used and the operator of the equipment. These levels are not universal, and each institution should indentify their own thresholds.

If there is no visualized intrauterine pregnancy, no fetal heart tone can be visualized in the adnexa, and the hCG levels are above the "discriminatory cutoff," there are several ways to confirm diagnosis.

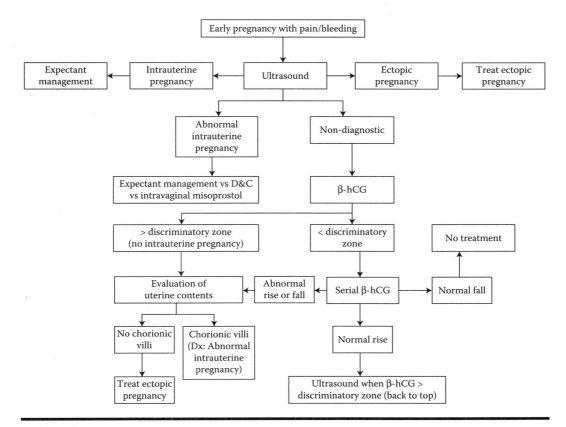

Figure 16.2. **Diagnostic algorithms for ectopic pregnancy. [From Seeber, B.E., & Barnhart, K.T., (2006). *Obstetrics and Gynecolology, 107*(2, pt. 1), 300–413. With permission.]**

One is to do a uterine curettage. If there is no presence of chorionic villa on histological exam, then the diagnosis of failed intrauterine pregnancy or ectopic pregnancy can be made. If a histological exam is not possible, "B-hCG determinations are further employed for diagnosis after uterine curette. If h-CG levels do not decline after 12–24 hr from a level drawn immediately before surgery, the pregnancy is presumed ectopic and treatment should be initiated" (Seeber & Barnhart, 2008).

Treatment for ectopic pregnancy can be managed medically in many cases. Methotrexate therapy has been used successfully in treating ectopic pregnancy for decades. Methotrexate belongs to a class of drugs called folic acid antagonists (Seeber & Barnhart, 2006). Methotrexate can be administered orally, intramuscularly (IM), and by infusion. The most common way is to administer by IM injection. There are many regimens for treatment. One of the most common is to base a single injection dose on the patient's weight and height (50 mg/m^2). Additional information regarding use of methotrexate including drug calculations information can be found at http://www.halls.md/body-surface-area/bsa.htm.

The regimen that is preferred by the institution should be put in the NP protocol book along with other blood testing that needs to be done before administering methotrexate. Common blood tests would include complete blood count, liver function tests, and serum creatinine. ACOG has stated absolute contraindications to methotrexate therapy, which can be found in Table 16.4.

Follow-up for methotrexate should incorporate serial B-hCG levels as previously discussed. Levels may plateau or rise before decreasing. Signs of treatment failure include significantly worsening abdominal pain regardless of change in h-CG levels, hemodynamic instability, B-hCG levels that do not decline by at least 15% between day 4 and 7 postinjection, and B-hCG levels increasing or plateauing after the first week of injection (ACOG, 1998). Any doubt about methotrexate failure requires the NP to consult with the MD as what to do for subsequent treatment.

Second- and Third-Trimester Bleeding

Vaginal bleeding after mid-pregnancy is associated with maternal and fetal risks. One common cause of bleeding is placenta previa. Other causes are placental abruption, vasa previa, and severe

Table 16.4   Absolute Contraindications to Medical Therapy with Methotrexate

Breastfeeding

Overt or laboratory evidence of immunodeficiency

Alcoholism, alcoholic liver disease, or other chronic liver disease

Preexisting blood dyscrasias, such as bone marrow hypoplasia, leucopenia, thrombocytopenia, or significant anemia

Known sensitivity to methotrexate

Active pulmonary disease

Peptic ulcer disease

Hepatic, renal, or hematologic dysfunction

Source: Adapted from ACOG Practice Bulletin. (1998, December). *Medical Management of Tubal Pregnancy*, No. 3.

trauma. Vasa previa is an uncommon condition in which the velamentous insertion of the umbilical cord into the membranes in the lower uterine segment resulting in the presence of fetal vessels between the cervix and the presenting part (Sakornbut, Leeman, & Fontaine, 2007). Vaginal bleeding in later pregnancy requires prompt evaluation. Evaluation of bleeding should include ultrasonography. Transvaginal ultrasound is more accurate in evaluation of placenta previa than transabdominal ultrasound because the placental edge and cervical os is often obscured by shadows from the symphysis or the fetus (Sakornbut et al., 2007).

The NP should refer the patient to labor and delivery (L&D) for evaluation, or consult with an MD. If referring to L&D, the on-call MD should be notified as well as the charge nurse in the L&D unit. The prenatal records should be faxed to the hospital for staff reference. See Table 16.5 for risk factors of bleeding in late pregnancy.

Table 16.5 Risk Factors for Major Causes of Bleeding in Late Pregnancy

Placenta Previa

Chronic hypertension

Multiparity

Multiple gestations

Older age

Previous cesarean delivery

Tobacco use

Uterine curette

Placental Abruption

Chronic hypertension

Multiparity

Pre-eclampsia

Previous abruption

Short umbilical cord

Thrombophillias

Tobacco, cocaine, or methamphetamine use

Trauma: blunt abdominal or sudden deceleration

Uterine fibroids

Vasa Previa

In vitro fertilization

Low-lying and second trimester placenta previa

Marginal cord insertion

Multiple gestation

Succenturiate-lobed and bilobed placentas

Source: From Sakornbut, E., Leeman, L., & Fontaine, P. (2007). *American Family Physician, 75*(8), 1199–1206. With permission.

Table 16.6 Number of Medical Malpractice Payment Reports by Malpractice Reason—Professional Nurses (Registered Nurses, Nurse Anesthetists, Nurse Midwives, Nurse Practitioners, and Advanced Practice Nurses/Clinical Nurse Specialists)

Malpractice Reason	RN (Professional) Nurse[a]	Nurse Anesthetist	Nurse Midwife	Nurse Practitioner	Advanced Practice Nurse/Clinical Nurse Specialist[b]	Total
Anesthesia related	137	973	1	10	1	1,122
Behavioral health related[c]	6	1	0	1	1	9
Diagnosis related	253	17	43	267	2	582
Equipment or product related	60	6	0	6	0	72
IV or blood product related	172	14	0	2	0	188
Medication related	605	31	4	73	1	714
Monitoring related	776	21	19	29	0	845
Obstetrics related	482	7	483	32	1	951
Surgery related	399	69	9	13	1	491
Treatment related	761	36	36	148	6	987
Miscellaneous	227	6	1	13	0	247
All reasons	3,824	1,181	596	594	13	6,208

Source: From The National Practitioner Data Bank. Retrieved December 28, 2008 from http://www.npdb-hipdb.com/pubs/stats/2006_NPDB_Annual_Report.pdf

a A Professional Nurse is an individual who has received approved nursing education and training who holds a BSN degree (or equivalent), an ADN degree (or equivalent), or a hospital program diploma, and who holds a state license as a Registered Nurse. This definition includes RNs who have advanced training as Nurse Midwives, Nurse Anesthetists, APNs, etc.

b Reporting using the "Advanced Nurse Practitioner" category began on March 5, 2002. The "Advanced Nurse Practitioner" category was changed to "Clinical Nurse Specialist" on September 9, 2002. Prior to March 5, 2002, these nurses were included in the "RN (Professional Nurse)" category.

c The "Behavioral Health" category was added on January 31, 2004. Reports involving behavioral health issues filed before January 31, 2004 used other reporting categories. Cumulative data in this category include only reports filed after January 31, 2004.

Nonobstetrical Abdominal Pain

Many nonobstetric conditions can cause abdominal pain in pregnancy. Angelini (2003) reports approximately 1 in 500 pregnancies is complicated by a nonobstetric condition. The most common causes of this pain are appendicitis, cholecystitis, pancreatitis, and bowel obstruction. These conditions can mimic many conditions related to pregnancy; for instance, appendicitis can be missed during the first trimester of pregnancy as the symptoms are similar to hyperemesis. For these conditions, it is not wise to try to diagnose over the phone or in the office setting. If any nonobstetrical surgical condition is suspected, the patient should be referred to the ER where diagnosis can be confirmed.

Conclusions

The role of the NP has evolved into an important specialty in nursing and a necessity for the health care industry. NPs have an obligation to keep current in their practice, know the laws for practice in their state, develop practice guidelines, and assume responsibility for their own practice. In meeting these obligations the NP will reduce the risk of professional liability and assure safe competent practice.

References

ACOG Practice Bulletin. (1998, December). *Medical Management of Tubal Pregnancy*, No. 3.

ACOG Practice Bulletin. (1999, October). *Antepartum Fetal Surveillance*, No. 9.

American Nurses Association. (2004). *Nursing scope and standards of practice*. Maryland: Nursebooks.org.

Angelini, D. J. (2003). Obstetric triage revisited: Update on non-obstetric surgical conditions in pregnancy. *Journal of Midwifery and Women's Health, 48*(2), 111–118.

Bowers, N. A., Curan, C. A., Freda, M. C., Kreening, C. F., Poole, J. H., Slocum, J. et al. (2008). High risk pregnancy. In K. R. Simpson & P. A. Creehan (Eds.), *AWHONN perinatal nursing* (3rd ed., pp. 125–299). Philadelphia, PA: Lippincott, Williams & Wilkins.

Bupert, C. (2004). *Nurse practitioner's business practice and legal guide* (2nd ed.). Sudbury, MA: Jones and Bartlett Publishers.

Bupert, C. (2008). *Nurse practitioners business and legal guide* (3rd ed.). Sudbury, MA: Jones and Bartlett.

California State Board of Registered Nursing. (2008). An explanation of standardized procedure requirements for nurse practitioner practice. Retrieved September 13, 2008, from http://www.rn.ca.gov/pdfs/regulations/npr-b-20.pdf.

Christensen, F. C., Olson, K., Rayburn, W. F. (2003). Cross-over trial comparing maternal acceptance of two fetal movement charts. *The Journal of Maternal–Fetal and Neonatal Medicine, 14*(2), 118–122.

CNA Financial Corporation (2005, September). The nurse practitioner's claims study. Retrieved September 1, 2008, from http://www.cna.com/cnaeportal/vcm_content/CNA/internet/Static%20File%20for%20Download/Risk%20Control/Medical%20Services/NursePractitionerClaimsStudy.pdf.

Croke, E. M. (2003). Incidence of nursing negligence allegations by setting, *The American Journal of Nursing, 103*(9), 54–63.

Henry, P. J. (2001). The nurse in advanced practice. In N. J. Brent (Ed.), *Nurses and the law: A guide to principles and applications* (2nd ed., pp. 459–487). Philadelphia, PA: Lippincott.

Iankova, A. (2006). The accountability of emergency nurse practitioners. *Emergency Nurse, 14*(6), 20–25.

James, T. D. (1999). Advanced practice nursing. In D. M. Rostant & R. F. Cady (Eds.), *Liability issues in perinatal nursing* (2nd ed., pp. 300–302). Philadelphia, PA: Lippincott.

Joint Commission on Accreditation of Healthcare Organizations. (2004). *The medical staff handbook: A guide to Joint Commission standards*. (2nd ed.). Oakbrook Terrace, IL: JCR.

Klein, T. A. (2005). Scope of practice and the nurse practitioner: Regulation, competency, expansion, and evolution. *Topics in Advanced Practice Nursing eJournal.* Retrieved September 13, 2008, from http://www.medscape.com/viewprogram/41d88_pnt.

Mahlmeister, L., & Van Mullem, C. (2000). The process of triage in perinatal settings: Clinical and legal issues. *The Journal of Perinatal and Neonatal Nursing, 13*(4), 13–30.

Miller, K. P. (2007). Feeling the heat: Nurse practitioners and malpractice liability. *The Journal for Nurse Practitioners, 3*(1), 24–26.

NSO. (2005). NSO risk advisor. *NSO, 13*(1–2), 7.

Olesen, A. G., & Svare, J. A. (2004). Decreased fetal movements: Background, assessment, and clinical management. *Acta Obstetrica et Gynecologia Scandinavia, 83*, 818–826.

Pearson, L. J. (2008). The Pearson report. *The American Journal for Nurse Practitioners, 12*(2), 9–16.

Pearson, L. J. (2009). The Pearson Report. *The American Journal for Nurse Practitioners, 13*(2), 4–82.

Sakornbut, E., Leeman, L., & Fontaine, P. (2007). Late pregnancy bleeding. *American Family Physician, 75*(8), 1199–206.

Seeber, B. E., & Barnhart, K. T. (2006). Suspected ectopic pregnancy. *Obstetrics and Gynecology, 107*(2, pt 1), 300–413.

Seeber, B. E., & Barnhart, K. T. (2008). Ectopic pregnancy. In R. S. Gibbs, B. Y. Karlan, A. F. Haney, & I. E. Nygaard (Eds.), *Danforth's obstetrics and gynecology* (10th ed., pp. 71–87). Philadelphia, PA: Lippincott Williams & Wilkins.

Sheehy, S. B. (2000). Law and the emergency nurse. A duty to follow up on laboratory reports. *Journal of Emergency Nursing, 26*(1), 56–57.

Simpson, K. R. (2008). Perinatal safety and professional liability issues. In K. R. Simpson & P. A. Creehan (Eds.), *AWHONN perinatal nursing* (3rd ed., pp. 3–5). Philadelphia: Lippincott Williams & Wilkins.

Simpson, K. R., & Chez, B. F. (2001). Professional and legal issues. In K. R. Simpson & P. A. Creehan (Eds.), *AWHONN perinatal nursing* (2nd ed., pp. 29–31, 51). Philadelphia: Lippincott.

Swenson, D. E. (2006). Advanced registered nurse practitioners: Standards of care and the law. *Journal of Legal Nurse Consulting, 17*(4), 3–6.

The National Practitioner Data Bank. Retrieved December 28, 2008 from http://www.npdb-hipdb.com/pubs/stats/2006_NPDB_Annual_Report.pdf

Chapter 17

Critical Care Case Evaluations

Rachel Cartwright-Vanzant, RN, MS, CNS, LHRM, FNC, LNCC;
Michelle Myers-Glower, RN MSN; and Ellen Plummer,
DL, MJ, RN, BSN, CCRN

Contents

Critical Care

This chapter covers evaluation of high acuity cases most seen in, but not limited, to the critical care setting. In reviewing a critical care case, it is important for the Legal Nurse Consultant (LNC) to have relevant clinical experience or the ability to consult with a nurse who can provide insight into this unique arena.

LNCs must be able to tell a story from the medical records. This requires the LNCs to organize and review the records as if they were writing a book. Identifying the deviation from the standard of care is the focus. Working within the legal arena requires the LNC to keep in mind the dates of the critical care stay and correlate this time frame to the time frame that corresponds with the appropriate hospital policy, rules, and regulations.

The American Association of Critical Care Nurses (AACN) sets standards for critical care nursing. These standards set parameters for clinical practice which are cutting-edge and evidence based to encourage the highest quality care being available for patients and their families. The cases presented in this chapter are actual cases that demonstrate how the LNC identified the deviations in the standards. For additional information regarding critical care standards, see www.aacn.org.

Critical care nurses in the United States are predominately *registered nurses* (RNs). Licensed practical nurses (LPNs) or licensed vocational nurses (LVNs) may be employed in some critical care units as auxiliary staff, but due to the unstable nature of the patient populations, LPNs/LVNs are rarely utilized in a primary care role. In reviewing critical care charts, it will be important for the LNC to review the hospital's policy and the State Nurse Practice Act to determine what role an RN versus an LPN/LVN can play in direct patient care. Critical care and specialty certifications with specific patient populations are not required to work in an intensive care unit (ICU), but these are encouraged by employers. The certification, while difficult to obtain, is looked upon by many in the field as demonstrating expertise in the area of critical care nursing. It also demonstrates the individual nurse's desire to advance their knowledge base and skill set, thereby allowing them to better care for their patients.

Critical care is the sophisticated medical and nursing care provided to patients facing life-threatening illness or injury. Many hospitals have designated intensive care areas for certain specialties of medicine as dictated by the needs and available resources of each hospital. The naming of these units is not rigidly standardized. Critical care units or beds are occupied by patients with a wide range of clinical conditions, but all have dysfunction or failure of one or more organs, often the respiratory and cardiovascular systems. Patients usually require intense monitoring and most need some form of mechanical or pharmacological support, such as mechanical ventilation, renal replacement therapy, or vasoactive drugs. As patients are admitted from every department in the hospital, intensive care staff need to have a broad range of clinical experience and a holistic approach to patient care.

Nurses working in this area are expected to complete yearly skill competencies as defined by the units in which they work. Typically, the competency may be for equipment/procedures that are low volume, high risk, or on the most frequently used high-technology equipment. Patients requiring a higher level of care would be placed or transferred in a unit as described above. The LNC will want to review operational procedures, including the criteria for admitting and discharging patients in the unit. An often asked question is, was the patient discharged too soon? Operational procedures also should govern decisions made regarding the transfer of patients from one facility to another. These operational procedures may also include various safety practices used during the provision of direct patient care at the bedside and elsewhere.

Safe patient care is directly and positively linked to the quality of staff nurses' work environments. Healthy work environments are empirically linked to patients' satisfaction and to retention, reduced turnover, job satisfaction, and lower degree of job stress and burnout among nurses. Increasingly, professional organizations and state and national commissions are challenging nurses, hospital administrators, and healthcare organizations to improve the practice environment for staff nurses in order to reap the benefits, particularly patients' safety and nurses' job satisfaction and retention (Ballard, 2003).

Components of the Critical Care Environment

Equipment common to critical care environments includes artificial airways and mechanical ventilatory support systems, a web of intravenous lines, feeding tubes, nasogastric tubes, suction pumps, drains and catheters, and a wide array of *drugs* to treat the main condition, induce sedation, reduce pain, and prevent secondary infections. Hemodynamic and cardiac monitoring systems, *intra-aortic balloon pumps* (IABP), *ventricular assist devices* (VADs), *continuous renal replacement* therapy (CRRT), *extracorporeal membrane oxygenation* circuits (ECMO), and many other advanced life support (ALS) devices reside in the critical care environment. Generally, the training for the use of this equipment is provided through a network of hospital-based in-services, manufacturer training, and many hours of education time with experienced operators. It is important for the LNC reviewing any case involving equipment to determine how the nurse was trained in the specialty equipment and how updated credentialing of nurses is handled in the unit. Continuing education units (CEUs) may be required by the state of licensure for the critical care nurse. Identifying courses taken by the nurse as part of a continuing education session is helpful for the LNC in identifying training and competencies for critical care staff. The LNC may also need to check online for the nurse's licensure history to be aware of any restrictions or revocations of nursing licensure.

Nurses working in the critical care arena are often part of a specialized unit. Subspecialties of critical care nursing include areas such as neonatal intensive care unit (NICU), pediatric intensive care unit (PICU), cardiac care unit (CCU), and adult intensive care unit (ICU). The patient population of these units is generally based on the age or medical diagnosis of the patient. Caring for a patient in any of the subspecialties requires critical care nurses to acquire additional education and training in the particular age or category of medical diagnosis in the unit.

Provision of excellent critical care services requires a continuous commitment to self-examination and improvement. Hospitals that make a commitment to provide critical care units must designate the type and level of unit they will provide for patients and be prepared to staff the units appropriately. The LNC reviewing medical records from a critical care unit will need to identify if the patient was in the right facility for his care and whether any lapse existed in the care needed by the patient. During the LNC's review, assessment falls into three categories:

1. Assessment of what level of critical care the hospital is able to provide
2. Assessment of the hospital's resources and the referral systems (Regional Referral Networks) required to properly care for critically ill patients
3. Assessment of the hospital's continuous monitoring of resources and outcomes as part of ongoing improvement and quality efforts

Hospitals are generally required to adhere to established protocols for patient care management if they are accredited by an outside accrediting body. Protocol compliance is a nationwide expectation and public knowledge. Protocols should include a measure to monitor compliance with protocols and an area the LNC should assess in a record review. The Joint Commission (TJC) (http://www.jointcommission.org/) is one reference for these standards. Reviewing the hospitals past survey results may also assist the LNC with understanding any compliance issues.

Critical thinking and precise care delivery are necessary to ensure optimal patient outcomes for those patients that warrant intensive care monitoring following surgery. Nurses must be alert to subtle changes that may warrant further assessment, intervention, and/or communication with the appropriate healthcare provider. When subtle changes are missed or simply not recognized by the nurse, a chain reaction of events can occur. This chain of events can lead to further compromise of the patient including lifelong debilitating conditions and, in some cases, unexpected death.

Reviewing surgical critical care cases is challenging. The first and most important aspect of a timely case review is to assure that the medical records are in a logical order. Chronological order, from admission through discharge, is often the most efficient way to organize the records. Chronological order facilitates reading about care as it unfolds. Customized hospital tabs can be ordered from medical supply companies to assist with organization of the medical records. Use of a three-ring binder is recommended once the records are organized with tabs. Multiple pages of flow sheets should be clustered and stapled together in order by date. Cases with operative or invasive procedures should have documents pertaining to those procedures clustered together.

In the surgical critical care case, these might include informed consent, anesthesia consent, preoperative checklists, holding area documentation, intraoperative nursing records, anesthesia records, and postanesthesia care records. Once the medical records are in order and clustered appropriately, the LNC can begin to read the record like a book. It is recommended that the LNC avoids reading the discharge summary or the autopsy report until an opinion regarding the care depicted according to the medical records is formulated. This prevents the LNC's opinion from being biased. Often the LNC will find the medical records portraying a different course of care than the discharge summary or the autopsy reports reflect.

Cardiac/Medical Intensive Care

The LNC not familiar with cardiothoracic or pulmonary cases will find these cases particularly challenging to review. These cases frequently require knowledge of special assessment techniques, diagnostic studies, and advanced hemodynamic monitoring systems. Arterial lines, pulmonary artery catheters, end-tidal CO_2 monitoring, intra-aortic counterpulsation, ventilator management, and surgical complications such as bleeding and dysrhythmias are the key components of most cardiothoracic or pulmonary care cases. In addition, vital to the quality of the review is the LNC's knowledge of the pathologic conditions common to this area of critical care. Pathophysiologic processes may include the following: acute ischemic heart disease, congestive heart failure, shock, hypertension, multiple organ failure, coagulopathies, acute renal failure, acute respiratory failure, acute respiratory distress syndrome (ARDS), pneumonia, and pulmonary embolism. Knowledge of the special skills sets required to care for a higher-acuity patient is essential. The facts of cardio-thoracic/pulmonary cases can become very detailed. There are typically numerous healthcare providers that have rendered care. The care delivered by each healthcare provider will need to be evaluated individually and collectively, as these represent the continuity of care the patient had a right to receive. Often individual nurses will be named as defendants in a particular case. Some plaintiff attorneys will request the LNC's involvement in determining which parties should be named as defendants in the law suit. To assist the attorney, the LNC will want to recognize the care rendered according to the standards of practice as well as recognizing care provided that did not meet the standards of practice. The LNC will be educating the attorney as to how nurses should have managed the complex needs of a patient in the critical care setting.

Particularly in cardiothoracic or pulmonary cases, it may be necessary to create a timeline of each and every patient's blood pressure, pulse, central venous pressure (CVP) reading, and pulmonary artery pressure to demonstrate trends in patient condition. In addition to identifying data in the medical documents, this type of review can be very useful when the time comes to educate the jury, should the case go to trial. Enlarged graphs of the patient's trends may be used by the law firm to make complex information easier for jurors. A picture can speak a thousand words when the vital signs of a patient drifting downward before an acute incident occurred are demonstrated on an enlarged graph. The plaintiff's attorney, using these data, can theorize that the acute incident could have been prevented if the subtle change in the patient's condition were recognized earlier and immediate action were taken by the nurses. The defense attorney using these data can support or challenge testimony rendered by defendants and/or experts. Nurses in critical care areas have been known to have greater autonomy than those nurses in noncritical care settings when managing the care of their patients. The LNC may need to determine the level of autonomy allowed to the critical care nurse in order to appropriately review the standard of care. By reading the care as it unfolds as suggested by the use of a chronological format, the LNC will be less likely to miss subtle changes in the patient's condition. This also allows the LNC to observe the patient as the critical care nurse saw the patient at the bedside.

Organ Donation and Transplantation

Legal concerns associated with transplantation of tissue and organs include consent and/or authorization to donate. Concerns also exist with the determination of death when organ procurement from a cadaveric donor is intended. The Joint Commission on Accreditation of Healthcare Organizations requires hospitals to have protocols in place for approaching families for organ donation (The Joint Commission, 2008). The Uniform Anatomical Gift Act (UAGA) provides the legal foundation and mechanisms for organ and tissue donations. The UAGA authorizes persons or their families to make an "anatomical gift" of all or part of his or her body to take effect upon death. A person has the legal right to direct the disposition of his/her own remains after death. An anatomical part includes organs, tissues, eyes, bones, arteries, blood, other fluids, and other portions of the human body. Legal requirements for transplantation by a living donor include consent of the donor for organ procurement. Competent adults should give voluntary consent after being informed of potential risks, benefits, and alternatives (Hawke, Kraft, & Smith, 1990).

Donors must be screened in order to determine their suitability for donation. The medical record of the donor must be reviewed and correlated with the physical examination. Documentation of specific laboratory tests, as minimal acceptable standards for an independent organ procurement agency, is required by the United Network of Organ Sharing (UNOS).

The National Organ Transplant Act (NOTA) was enacted in 1984, and from this organization the Organ Procurement and Transplantation Network (OPTN) was created to match prospective donors to prospective recipients and prohibit the sale of organs. The OPTN created a system to facilitate a fair and equitable allocation of organs throughout the United States. They accomplished this by facilitating regional independent organ procurement agencies (IOPAs). The UNOS is a not-for-profit entity overseeing the OPTN. Federal oversight of the UNOS is provided by the Division of Organ Transplantation under the Health Resources and Services Administration within the Public Health Service and the Department of Health and Human Services.

During the postoperative period, there is always a concern of transmission of disease from an organ or tissue donation. One of the most common clinically significant infections in transplant recipients is cytomegalovirus (CMV). Other serious diseases that can affect transplant recipients are cancer and infections with human immunodeficiency virus (HIV), hepatitis B, tuberculosis, toxoplasmosis, and Jakob–Creutzfeldt disease (Durie, 2006). Inadequate screening of donor organs can lead to litigation. Negligent liability could result if the disease or defect is discovered by standard medical practices. For example: the failure to test for HIV antibody would be a breach in the standard of practice in cases of heart transplantation, but it would result in liability only if the recipient subsequently developed an HIV infection.

Trauma

Traumatic injury is not planned and by its very nature is inherently linked to the need for specialized care, often taxing already stretched resources of care and personnel. Some people intuitively think that injured patients should be taken to the nearest hospital, but historically this behavior had disastrous results if the nearest hospital had neither the resources nor the specially trained personnel to care for these victims. A far greater conflict arises when a hospital that has limited resources to provide care for some injuries accepts, for fiscal reasons, patients with injuries far beyond its capabilities to manage (Ledgerwood, Lucas, & Lucas, 2004). The Emergency Medical Treatment and Active Labor Act (EMTALA) defines a trauma center's obligation to provide treatment independent of fiscal resources by the patient (42 U.S.C., 2002).

The existence of trauma centers and trauma protocols can serve as guidelines for treating specific injuries, but not treatment standards. These guidelines are aids to treatment choices, but each patient may present with a slightly different variation of an injury resulting in care choices that may be in conflict with written guidelines (Ledgerwood et al., 2004).

Complications of Traumatic Injury

Hospitalization in a critical care unit may be necessary for trauma patients due to the severity of injuries. The ability to resuscitate patients with injuries that would have previously been fatal is vastly improved; however, there are still numerous opportunities for severely injured patients to develop and ultimately succumb to significant but preventable complications. Those preventable complications include bleeding and coagulopathies, cardiovascular or pulmonary failure, acute renal failure, secondary brain injury caused by cerebral edema and increased intracranial pressure, multiple organ dysfunction, and sepsis.

Hemorrhage is a leading cause of death after injury and is a priority in trauma care (Fakry & Michetti, 2004). Inadequate cardiovascular and/or pulmonary performance that leads to hypoperfusion of the heart and lungs are well documented determinants that can lead to organ failure and death in critically injured patients (Fink, Puyana, & Lisbon, 2004). Acute renal failure following injury is often associated with increased morbidity and mortality because of its effect on all other organ systems (Chandler, Blinman, & Cryer, 2004). The complex immune response to traumatic injury can easily become deranged following subsequent ischemic episodes, resulting in a cumulative impact and ultimately overwhelming sepsis, particularly in those patients who spend long periods of time in critical care environments. Multiple organ failure remains the leading cause of late postinjury deaths in ICUs today (Moore & Moore, 2004).

Primary brain injury occurs when a mechanical force impacts the head. Because there is currently no direct treatment for primary brain injury, the only prevention that remains is effective intervention. Not all brain injury occurs immediately at the time of initial impact. Within seconds, hours, or days, a pathologic biochemical cascade of events is initiated within the injured or ischemic cells, leading to further cell death and secondary brain injury. Injury, hypoxia, and ischemia are the fundamental initiators of the cascade that results in secondary brain injury (McQuillan & Thurman, 2008).

Any systemic or neurologic complication that compromises adequate oxygen and nutrient delivery to the brain's cells, causing hypoxia or ischemia, can cause or exacerbate the cascade of events that leads to secondary brain injury. These include hypotension, hypoxia, hypercapnia, hypocapnia, hyperthermia, anemia, fluid and electrolyte imbalance, acid–base alternations, systemic inflammatory disorders, hypoglycemia, and hyperglycemia (Chi et al., 2006; Henzler et al., 2007; Jeremitsky et al., 2003; McQuillan & Thurman, 2008; Sanchez-Olmedo et al., 2005). If systemic hypotension occurs in the prehospital resuscitation or critical care phase of care after a brain injury, mortality and morbidity rise significantly (Barton et al., 2005; Jones et al., 1994; McHugh et al., 2007). Ischemia may be the single most important secondary event affecting outcomes after severe brain injury. Brain ischemia in the acute phase following injury is associated with poor outcomes (Coles, 2004).

Trauma Center Designation

Traumatic injury creates many variables that compromise the idealistic concept that skillful and specially trained trauma teams can fully return an injured patient to his or her preinjury condition, even when care is excellent. Legislative designation of a hospital as a trauma center implies that specific published patient care criteria have been met. Such a designation has far-reaching legal implications. The hospital administration, nurses, and physicians must be available to initiate treatment to the level defined by the designation process or to resuscitate and prepare for transport to a facility with greater resources than they can provide (Ledgerwood et al., 2004). Any delay in implementing a transfer to a higher level of care creates a potentially litigious situation, as has been historically noted in *Nevarez v. New York City Health and Hospitals Corporation* (*Nevarez v. New York*, 1997). In this case, a pregnant mother was delayed 7 hr in being transferred to a higher level of care for her premature labor. The infant was born with hypoxia, blindness, and cerebral palsy. A jury determined the delay in transfer by the hospital was below the standard of care.

The designation of trauma facilities is a geopolitical process, through which empowered entities, government or otherwise, are authorized to act. The American College of Surgeons (ACS) does not designate trauma centers; instead, it verifies the presence of the resources listed in *Resources for Optimal Care of the Injured Patient* (Resources, 2006). This document outlines the resources necessary for optimal emergent patient care and is used as a guide for the development of trauma centers throughout the United States. It is also the document by which trauma centers are reviewed by the ACS approved site surveyors (Resources, 2006).

The ACS's long history of activities directed toward the improvement of trauma care was enhanced substantially in 1987 with the creation of the Consultation/Verification Program. This program validates the resources for trauma care at trauma centers. The program is administered by the Consultation/Verification Ad Hoc Committee of the ACS's Committee on Trauma (COT), commonly referred to as the Verification Review Committee (VCR) (Resources, 2006).

Trauma center verification is the process by which the ACS confirms that the hospital is performing as a trauma center and meets the criteria contained in the *Resources for Optimal Care of the Injured Patient* document (Resources, 2006). If, during a verification review, a hospital is found to have criterion deficiencies, it must demonstrate that they have been corrected before a certificate is issued. If the deficiencies are significant, an on-site focus review may be necessary (Resources, 2006). An on-site review requires approximately 6–8 hr and all trauma care areas of the hospital may be visited. Emphasis is placed on evaluating medical records of trauma patients and correlating patient care with the performance improvement program. The VCR receives a report of the site visit and determines the presence or absence of deficiencies and whether a hospital can be verified (Resources, 2006).

Level I, Level II, Level III, and Level IV Trauma Centers

The Level I trauma facility is a regional resource trauma center that is a tertiary care facility central to the trauma care system. All patients who require the resources of the Level I center should have access to it. This facility must have the capability of providing leadership and total care for every aspect of injury, from prevention through rehabilitation, and it must have adequate depth of resources and personnel (Resources, 2006).

The Level II trauma center is a hospital that also is expected to provide initial definitive trauma care, regardless of the severity of the injury. Depending on geographical location, patient volume, personnel, and resources, the Level II trauma center may not be able to provide the same comprehensive care as a Level I trauma center can. Patients with more complex injuries may have to be transferred to a Level I center (Resources, 2006).

The Level III trauma center serves communities that do not have immediate access to a Level I or II institution. Level III trauma centers can provide prompt assessment, resuscitation, emergency operations, and stabilization, and can also arrange for possible transfer to a facility that can provide definitive trauma care. General surgeons are required in a Level III facility. Planning for care of injured patients in these hospitals requires transfer agreements and standardized treatment protocols. Level III trauma centers are generally not appropriate in an urban or suburban area with adequate Level I and/or Level II resources (Resources, 2006).

Level IV trauma facilities provide advanced trauma life support before patient transfer in remote areas where no higher level of care is available. Such a facility may be a clinic rather than a hospital and may or may not have a physician available. As with Level III trauma centers, treatment protocols for resuscitation, transfer protocols, data reporting, and participation in system performance improvements are essential and must have a good working relationship with the nearest Level I, II, or III trauma center (Resources, 2006).

Air-Medical Transportation of the Injured Patient

Helicopter evacuation and transport of trauma patients have been debated numerous times and has resulted in controversy surrounding its use in terms of improvements in patient outcomes. Helicopter transport seems to be beneficial predominantly in rural areas. Some studies have shown a benefit of using air transportation; others have shown little to no benefit. There is, however, little controversy that the transport of critically injured patients from a rural facility with limited resources to a major trauma center is beneficial to the patient. Minimally, helicopters are universally equipped as ALS units (Salomone & Frame, 2004).

Ground/Ambulance Transportation of the Injured Patient

Ground Emergency Medical Services (EMS) units may possess transport capabilities or they may operate as a "quick response" unit that contains only personnel and equipment, but otherwise requires an ambulance to transport the patient to the hospital. These quick response units are more common in rural areas. All ambulances must conform to size and performance specializations and possess the required equipment to be fully functional. The specialization requirements are generally outlined by a governmental agency. Minimal staffing for a Basic Life Support (BLS) unit is two Emergency Medical Technician (EMT)-Basics with ALS backup available when needed (Salomone & Frame, 2004). An ALS unit must consist of at least one team member possessing training beyond the EMT-Basic level. Additional equipment and supplies are generally available on an ALS unit to support the defined scope of practice (Salomone & Frame, 2004).

Review of Medical Records of Trauma Care

A review of trauma care cases can be very challenging and complex and will require the LNC to have a comprehensive knowledge of the current trauma standards of care as well as critical injury and illness standards of care. In addition, knowledge of the trauma system in place for the region of the case is beneficial, particularly when there are questions of triage to a local facility or a trauma center, or the availability of a tertiary care center that is able to care for trauma patients.

Trauma cases frequently involve either failure to diagnose an injury, failure to timely treat an injury, or failure to consider a transfer of the patient to a higher level of care. Therefore, the LNC should have a specific knowledge of trauma, mechanisms of injury, and critical care of the injured patient, as well as criteria for necessitating a transfer of a patient to a higher level of care.

As with many other case reviews, it may be necessary to create a timeline or chronology of events that may show a failure to diagnose or, more importantly, a failure to timely treat a particular injury, such as a vascular injury resulting from an orthopedic fracture or a worsening level of consciousness from a seemingly minor head injury in an intoxicated patient. Additionally, it would also be beneficial for the reviewer to have knowledge of the various age groups and populations that sustain specific types of injuries as well as how those various age groups respond to traumatic injury. The geriatric patient responds very differently to, and can have very different outcomes from, even a less severe injury compared with a younger patient with the same injury.

The LNC reviewing the case should have some specific knowledge of the overwhelming complications that are inherent in traumatic injury. Some have been generalized above; most can impose a substantial burden on the care of the patient and can be an important cause of patient morbidity and mortality. It should be noted however, that any trauma care guidelines or protocols for trauma critical care must take into account the individual and sometimes complex practices that exist in a given unit. For example, guidelines that govern infections from central lines or ventilators must consider the line usage type or ventilator protocols as well as the nursing management practices that are used (Mackersie, Pittet, & Dicker, 2008).

The LNC should be cognizant of the expertise of both the physician group and the nursing group. Trauma care is considered a specialty for both groups and requires additional training and experience gained from other specialties. Some emergency department physicians and nurses may not have specialty training in trauma care if their emergency department typically does not care for a high volume of trauma patients. Conversely, those physicians and nurses who work in emergency departments of Level 1 or 2 Trauma Centers should be competent in trauma care, as those facilities typically treat a higher volume of traumatic injuries and should recognize and be able to appropriately treat the patients. The emergency department is required to know and be able to provide initial life-saving interventions such as an artificial airway, mechanical ventilation, intravenous access, and fluid resuscitation. In those centers that treat low volumes of trauma cases, it would be incumbent upon the physicians to be aware of when they cannot provide adequate care for a trauma patient and initiate a transfer to a tertiary or higher level of care center that can provide the necessary care. The attorney and/or the LNC should request the medical records from all facilities that cared for the patient, as well as any prehospital records of treatment for a thorough review.

Extremes of Ages: Pediatric and Geriatric Critical Care

There are a multitude of similarities and differences between critically ill or injured children and critically ill or injured geriatric patients. Nurses often have the primary responsibility for not only recognizing any subtle changes in either a child's or adult's condition, but also for understanding the normal growth and development of children as well as the aging process of older adults. Small variations in either age group can cause a significant change in their condition. It is imperative that these subtle variations or changes in condition in either age group be recognized and action be taken immediately.

Pediatric Critical Care: Evaluation and Treatment Considerations

By most accounts, it is recognized that children are resilient to illness and injury. Pediatric care, particularly critical care, is a body of knowledge that addresses the special needs and characteristics of children who are ill or injured. Children are not small adults. This difference is overwhelmingly obvious in comparison with outcomes of children and adults. Both the etiologies of illness and the epidemiology of injury in this population are vastly different and ultimately affect the therapies and treatments for them.

The anatomy of children renders them especially vulnerable to injury. The head of a child is disproportionately larger in relation to body mass compared with these proportions in an adult. Head injury is the most common cause of traumatic death in children (Moloney-Harmon, 2008). Injury alone is the leading cause of death in children under 14 years of age (National Center for Injury Prevention and Control, 2005). Child abuse and neglect are on the rise in the United States (Zenel & Goldstein, 2002). Nurses caring for these young victims of abuse or neglect have the responsibility to detect abuse and to report it to a child protective service agency.

The priorities of care for a critically ill or injured pediatric patient depend on the patient's response to treatment. A thorough history should be obtained in order to determine any incidents, illnesses, or issues that precipitated the child's present illness or injury. The Emergency Nurses Association (ENA) recommends taking a CIAMPEDS history (Emergency Nurses Association, 2004):

- C = Chief complaint
- I = Immunizations
- A = Allergies
- M = Medications
- P = Past medical history
- E = Events surrounding the illness or injury
- D = Diet
- S = Symptoms associated with the illness or injury

The physical examination of a child should include vital signs and a head to toe assessment, including an assessment of the neurological, cardiac, pulmonary, abdominal, genitourinary, musculoskeletal systems, and skin integrity. Hypothermia is a significant problem in an injured infant or child and can have disastrous effects on survivability.

Pulses should be obtained at the radial, brachial, and carotid or femoral arteries and should be counted for a full minute. Blood pressures should be obtained using a cuff that is not less than half and not more than two-thirds the length of the upper arm. If a pediatric cuff is not available, an adult cuff can be used on the child's thigh. The normal systolic blood pressure for individuals from 1 to 21 years of age is 90 plus two times the age in years. The diastolic pressure should be approximately two-thirds the normal systolic blood pressure (Moloney-Harmon, 2008).

There are both similarities and differences in the management of a pediatric patient when compared with that of an adult or geriatric patient. For example, the management of a pediatric patient with a head injury is similar to that of an adult. However, the methods and protocols for caring for intracranial pressure monitoring devices are standardized in many institutions for both populations. Children have increased energy requirements and greater energy needs than adults do. Children also have a higher risk than adults for the development of protein calorie malnutrition in the critical care stage of care (Moloney-Harmon, 2008).

Pain is often referred to as the fifth vital sign and is an unfortunate part of being a patient in a critical care environment. Pain medication should never be withheld from a child or an adult if it seems to be the only effective means of pain relief.

Electrolyte imbalances are more likely to occur in children than in adults. Serum glucose, calcium, and potassium levels should be monitored closely in children. Infants can become intolerant of low glucose levels, particularly during stress from illness or injury (Moloney-Harmon, 2008). Fluid administration should be closely monitored in children to avoid overhydration.

Shock in a pediatric patient is quite different from shock in an adult patient. The pediatric trauma patient is in shock most often because of blood loss. Children rarely have diseases that predispose them to the development of shock. Hypotension in a pediatric patient, therefore, usually indicates a significant degree of blood loss (Moloney-Harmon, 2008).

Critical care management of the pediatric patient generally requires a multidisciplinary approach. This management should include monitoring of hemodynamic parameters, support of the respiratory and cardiovascular system, neurological monitoring, and monitoring for impending complications of immobility such as pneumonia or sepsis.

Healthcare providers who are charged with caring for pediatric patients must be well trained and the facilities must be well equipped to handle a child. It is imperative that appropriate supplies and equipment be readily available to care for this population.

Review of Medical Records for Pediatric Cases

As with any other medical records review, pediatric case records review should involve a timeline or chronology of events leading up to the complaint. Effective care of the pediatric patient requires special knowledge, precise management, and scrupulous attention to details of the unique needs of this population. Therefore, when reviewing the medical records of a pediatric case, the LNC should be knowledgeable in all aspects of pediatric care and treatments. If the LNC is not comfortable or knowledgeable in this specialty, it would be more appropriate to request the attorney to have the records reviewed by a nurse or physician who specializes in this population or one with particular experience in pediatric critical care.

Pediatrics

ICU staff are confronted on an almost daily basis by difficult and emotional ethical issues, but perhaps none more so than when a child is involved. In all ethical situations, decision making is very subjective and dependent, among other factors, on individual experience and beliefs, and cultural and religious backgrounds. Although there is now considerable literature on end-of-life decisionmaking in the adult ICU population, much less has been written about pediatric patients, although many deaths in pediatric ICUs are now preceded by a decision to forgo or limit life-sustaining therapy. In the case of a child with a short life expectancy who experiences an iatrogenic episode that leads to irreversible anoxic encephalopathy, many questions come into play, in particular, those related to differences in opinion between staff and parents regarding the value of continuing active care. The hospitalization may have a complicated course resulting in respiratory and cardiac arrest. With no hopes of recovery, the healthcare team may conclude that continuing therapy would be futile and that discontinuation of active treatment should be presented to the parents as the best option. The parents may request continuation of care indefinitely. This poses an ethical dilemma with regard to continuation of treatment. The ICU staff expresses concerns with respect to continuing care. They acknowledged that the child may eventually progress to skilled nursing care and would never be back to baseline in the sense that the family desired.

The team may feel that continued care represented the prolongation of futile therapy for a child whose brain has been lost from severe postanoxic brain damage and would prevent any substantial long-term neurological recovery. Furthermore, if any more invasive procedures were needed and were done, this could possibly be seen as battery because the risks clearly exceeded the benefits.

At issue in this case are fundamental questions about clinical decisionmaking at the end of life when interested parties disagree as to the best course of action. Are patients or doctors in the best position to determine the course of treatment? The physician's goals should be to sustain life and relieve suffering. When these goals become mutually exclusive, the wishes of the patient should prevail. In general, the principle of patient autonomy remains paramount. However, physicians are not obliged to deliver medical care that, in their best professional judgment, does not have a reasonable chance of benefiting their patients. Disagreements regarding goals of therapy affect patient care, family satisfaction, and the healthcare team's ability to function.

A review of interdisciplinary communications and consultations as contained in the medical records may be beneficial for the LNC in determining the approach to the ethical issues in the case. Although responsibility for addressing ethical issues varies from institution to institution, social workers or the Pastoral Care department are often the professionals working with staff and families on these issues. Look for a consult in the chart that reflects what the parents might consider futile care for their child and what therapies were discussed as within acceptable limits for the healthcare team. It is not necessary, and indeed it is unlikely, to have absolute certainty of outcome before withdrawal of life-sustaining medical therapy.

The Neonatal Workgroup of the International Liaison Committee on Resuscitation recently made available their rigorous review of the scientific evidence base for selected neonatal resuscitation issues. The Neonatal Resuscitation Program guidelines have been recently revised based on that review and is published as the *Textbook of Neonatal Resuscitation*, 5th ed. This text highlights pertinent changes in recommendations, including revisions in oxygen use; CO_2 detectors for confirmation of intubation; management of the infant born through meconium-stained amniotic fluid; initial ventilation devices and strategies; thermal protection of very small preterm infants; medications, including doses and routes of delivery; and postresuscitation therapies for consideration and ethical issues in initiation and discontinuation of resuscitation.

The TJC now requires all accredited hospitals to have a mechanism in place that identifies where staff can turn to in situations when there is a conflict between families and healthcare providers on end-of-life issues. Finally, if the parents maintain their decision to continue life sustaining medical therapy and the healthcare team feels morally unable to provide it, then a transfer to another institution or healthcare provider (with the family's and accepting institution's approval) may be sought. Failure to offer this option to families may result in a failure to honor patient autonomy, in the case of a minor, the family's decisions.

Geriatric Critical Care: Evaluation and Treatment Considerations

Normal aging is a gradual process. To date there is no universal definition of when a person becomes "old." Multiple age ranges exist in the literature to define the elderly and include the ranges of 55, 60, 65, 70, 75, and even 80 years of age.

Those over the age of 65 account for 42–52% of ICU admissions and for almost 60% of all ICU days (Angus, Kelley, Schmitz, et al., 2000).

Various illnesses and injuries can result in a critical care admission for an elderly person. The elderly may have the presence of comorbidities or preexisting illnesses or injuries that may affect standard treatment plans or ultimately affect the outcome of illness or injury. As with the younger trauma population, assessment and resuscitation of the elderly patient should be rapid and efficient. However, a rapid and thorough assessment of the elderly patient may be more difficult, particularly if unfounded or inaccurate assumptions are made of their preexisting conditions or comorbidities. While the presence of any one chronic illness has not been a direct predictor of mortality in elderly patients with critical illness or injuries from trauma, comorbid conditions have been associated with increased mortality varying with the type and number of conditions (Kauder, Schwab, & Shapiro, 2004).

Cardiovascular disease is one of the most common medical problems in elderly patients and often leads to death in this population. Age is a major risk factor for cardiovascular disease, which accounts for over 40% of the deaths in those older than 65 years of age (Lakatta, 2002). Elderly patients may be unaware of any cardiac dysfunction or may have few, if any, symptoms until the time of a traumatic injury or stresses from illness.

As is true for all elderly patients, initial measurements of blood pressure are likely to be misleading because of compensation or prior dysfunction. The presence of "normal" vital signs may mask severe physiologic compromise, particularly in cardiac conditions or situations where hypovolemia or dehydration is suspected. Hypertension is one of the more common preexisting conditions in the elderly population. Some elderly people may be taking medications to treat the hypertension. Both the hypertensive state and the medications can alter physiologic compensatory mechanisms and often obscure signs of various conditions, such as shock or cardiac failure. An elderly patient taking a prescription beta blocker for treatment of hypertension may not have the ability to increase the heart rate in response to trauma, hypovolemia, or metabolic derangement.

Elderly patients may also be taking medications that could lead to further bleeding or other complications of a traumatic injury. Many elderly people are on anticoagulant therapy. Warfarin (coumadin) is the fourth most prescribed cardiovascular agent and the 11th most prescribed drug in the United States (Horton & Bushwick, 1999; National Prescription Audit, 1998). The use of warfarin anticoagulation therapy in the elderly population is typically for the treatment of atrial fibrillation, cardiac valve replacement, venous thrombosis, and pulmonary embolism. Elderly patients taking warfarin or coumadin require a thorough evaluation and close monitoring, as these patients with head injuries, orthopedic injuries, or internal injuries may exhibit increased bleeding.

The lasting impact of a critical illness or injury on lifestyle in the elderly patients remains poorly defined. Although the majority of elderly patients do survive a serious illness or injury, and some survivors achieve independent living, long-term follow-up indicates significant residual disability in quality of life (Inaba, Goecke, Sharkey, et al., 2003). Previous outcomes research has shown a higher mortality and complication rate with longer periods of hospital stay and disproportionately higher use of hospital resources in this age group, particularly when the patient is injured, when compared with younger injured or critically ill patients (McGwin et al., 2000).

Review of Medical Records for Geriatric Cases

Similar to the pediatric case review, reviewing the records involved in geriatric cases would require specialized knowledge of the aging process, chronic conditions, and the sequelae of preexisting illnesses, as well as common injury patterns associated with the geriatric population.

The LNC should evaluate the records for specific causes of the complaint as well as any associated situations or problems that may have led to the causative agent. For example, if the complaint involves an elderly patient's fall, it would be important to look for causative agents independent of safety issues. These may include medication administration combinations and reactions, or untreated or unrecognized electrolyte imbalances. Additionally, mental status changes that occur only at night, or any previously untreated falls, might be considered as the reason for frequent falls in the elderly patients. It may be necessary to request any available medical records from the patient's primary care physician or other care providers for review.

The LNC and Critical Care Record Review: Key Issues in Critical Care Nursing

Duty to Protect

Nurses are obligated to respect the privacy and confidentiality of their patients. The Health Insurance Portability and Accountability Act (HIPAA) of 1996 incorporates written standards protecting the confidentiality, integrity, and availability of data. Provisions of the Act also include protecting appropriate disclosures of identifiable health information and patient rights protection. Computerized medical records are more vulnerable to access by unauthorized individuals; therefore, the healthcare facility must have in place safeguards to protect the patient's health information from being breached by unauthorized parties.

Patients in a critical care setting are frequently unable to assert their rights as they would if they were in a less acute setting. The overall goal of a patient's advocate is to protect his/her patient's rights. The nurse as an advocate should inform patients about their rights and provide information to them as needed to assist in making informed decisions regarding their care. Patients have the right to expect a nurse–patient relationship that is based on shared respect and trust. Collaboratively, the nurse will assist the patient in problem solving related to health and healthcare needs, always considering their values and feelings. The nurse should have a relationship with patients which involves providing care according to acceptable standards of care.

Duty to Provide Competent Care

Competent practice is a major legal safeguard for nurses. The care nurses provide must fall within the legal boundaries of their practice and within the boundaries of their facility's policies and procedures. Each nurse is responsible for being familiar with his/her own facility's policies and procedures. Educational experiences must be adequate to provide safe care delineated in their job description. Competency also involves care that protects the patient from harm. Anticipating sources of potential injury or harm is part of the assessment process. Educating the patient on measures implemented to prevent injury is also important. Application of the nursing process is essential to demonstrate safe and effective patient care. All assessments must be documented accurately and appropriate communication regarding patient status can also protect the nurse from negligence claims (Joint Commission, 2008).

Failure to Rescue

The problem of patients developing complications during hospitalization and suffering morbidity and mortality as a consequence has always been present. But recently, intense attention has been focused on this phenomenon, as it is the primary cause of preventable hospital mortality.

"Failure to rescue" is a term used to refer to a caregiver who fails to appropriately notice or respond when a patient is dying of preventable complications in a hospital (Kremsdorf, 2005). It is not whether you get all the 15 min vitals written down on a post-op patient; it is how much time does it take for the nurse to pick up on the trend that the patient is deteriorating and take action to attempt to turn the situation around? The basics of assessment are breathing, circulation, and bleeding. In a critical care setting, the medical records will demonstrate the tight timeline of action and inaction.

Some reasons for failure to rescue may be closely related to errors of omission: the results of a diagnostic test, the rate change of an intravenous anticoagulant agent, vital signs not available when initially evaluating the patient for comparison, fevers not recorded, and a treatment delay for an evolving septicemia. The LNC will want to evaluate any situation where a code was called for the patient. The LNC should begin evaluating the code and work backward to determine if there was a precipitating factor causing the sudden change in patient condition. If a single causative agent is not determined, the LNC should begin to evaluate the continuity of care from shift to shift. Frequently, the previous shift documentation provides significant information when compared with the current situation. Failure of the critical care nurse to compare available data and intervene is often the basis of a failure to rescue law suit.

Patient care staffing, nursing experience, and skill levels are being looked at as contributing factors. Furthermore, the issue has acquired an official name, "Failure to Rescue from Complications," and a precise definition from the Agency for Healthcare Research and Quality (see AHRQ's *Guide to Patient Safety Indicators* at www.qualityindicators.ahrq.gov). The Health Grades Quality Study, *Patient Safety in American Hospitals* (July, 2004), highlights the frequency of patients dying from complications that develop while in hospitals. Failure to rescue, according to the 3-year study, accounts for 60,000 deaths each year in Medicare patients under the age of 75. The LNC will want to determine if there is any protocol within the organization that would trigger a medical emergency team (often called a rapid response team) to evaluate the patient. Comparing the policy with the actual documentation in the medical record may shed light on whether or not the standard of care was upheld in the case. AACN has developed a web-based system of Practice Alerts to assist critical care nurses in bringing evidence-based nursing interventions to the bedside. These can be found at http://www.aacn.org/WD/Practice/Content/practicealerts.pcms?pid=1&&menu=Practice.

Clinical Competency Validation

Determining the competency of nurses is challenging. As an LNC you can assist the attorney in identifying the documents necessary to evaluate competency. Some documents the attorney can use to assess the competency of nurses include the job description, orientation checklists, competency evaluation tools, annual competency validation tools, performance evaluations, and licensure. Often attorneys will ask the LNC to assist in preparing a list of documents to include in a Request for Production process. Certainly, the paper trail is just one aspect of competency validation. The nurse's documentation in the medical record adds another component to evaluate critical thinking. Critical thinking can be impacted by many factors including familiarity with the unit or facility, experience in the nursing field, and patient staff ratios.

Lack of knowledge of proper process and/or procedures may be an additional factor when dealing with per diem facility staff or contract agency personnel. In critical care settings, many policies and procedures are different between facilities, and per diem or contract staff may not be well versed in the policies for the respective facility.

Critical Care Staffing

Needleman, Buerhaus, Mattke, Stewart, and Zelevinsky (2002) looked for evidence about the relationship between nurse staffing ratios and failure to rescue in five life-threatening conditions: pneumonia, shock or cardiac arrest, upper gastrointestinal bleeding, sepsis, and deep vein thrombosis. This was the first large-scale study with a sample of more than 6 million patients from

799 hospitals. Their findings are as follows: lower rates of failure to rescue were associated with a higher proportion of hours of care by RNs. More recently, Aiken, Clarke, Sloane, Lake, & Chaney (2008) confirmed those findings, pointing out that when staffing falls below safe levels, nurses are too busy to notice and act on the often-subtle clues that signal the onset of a complication. In reviewing a critical care case involving failure to rescue, the LNC will want to request information regarding the hours per patient day (HPPD).

Errors and Omissions

Determining the cause of hospital errors that lead to harm has already been under study. One such study, *To Err Is Human*, the landmark Institute of Medicine report released in 1999, successfully highlighted the enormous problem of patient safety. This report emphasized blatant errors that had been carefully documented in published studies. Many of the errors noted in this report included errors of omission.

Errors of omission, on the other hand, are errors that occur as a result of a step not taken or when an appropriate step is left out from a process. The traditional use of the phrase has referred to the omission of a diagnostic test, such as blood cultures in the septic patient, or failure to administer a form of prophylaxis or therapy, such as giving aspirin to a patient with a strong indication based on cardiac assessments. Yet, other deficiencies in care also represent errors of omission. Consider this scenario: a doctor making rounds cannot find the clipboard with the vital signs and as a result, does not know that the patient had a fever the night before. That night an even higher fever spike occurs. The infection has now been untreated for another day and the patient develops septic shock that might have been avoided if the patient had received prompt therapy.

In reviewing for errors of omission, the LNC will need to review times in the records that dictate when the patient became symptomatic and the time appropriate interventions were started.

Age-Related Considerations

Many elderly patients have a limited ability to respond to hospital-acquired infections that occur in critical care settings. Two of the most common and ultimately the most expensive and difficult ones to manage are ventilator-assisted pneumonia (VAP) and central line sepsis. Endotracheal intubation is considered a risk factor for VAP because of the bacterial growth that occurs in contaminated fluids that lie near the top of the tube and in the oropharynx; these bacteria eventually make their way into the pulmonary system where they can result in pneumonia (Mackersie et al., 2008; Porzecanski & Bowton, 2006).

Another care management issue that typically affects either the pediatric or geriatric population of critical care patients is unplanned extubations. The reported incidence for the pediatric population is between 0.6% and 13.3% (Ream et al., 2007; Scott et al., 1985). The reported incidence of unplanned extubations for the adult population is between 1% and 14% (Boulain, 1998; Krinsley & Barone, 2005). Unplanned extubations have been linked to inadequate sedation or inadequate restraint use in agitated patients. The mortality for unplanned extubations is approximately 2%, making it an important cause of preventable death (Mackersie et al., 2008).

Emerging Topics in Critical Care

As with all areas of law, case law lags behind clinical practice. With the advent of ever-changing technology, increased nursing shortages, and a recessive economy, new areas of litigation will most likely emerge. A review of the AACN (www.aacn.org) website indicates topics such as ICU overflow patient management, mandated staffing ratio legislation, public safety expectations, clinical quality measures, cost and the futility of care, sentinel events, electronic medical records and medication administration systems, high-alert drugs, and many other topics, which in the future, may be the subject of litigation in this high volume, high-tech patient care area.

Conclusion

Critical care units by their nature house some of the sicker patients within the healthcare arena. Specialized protocols, increased autonomy, and staffing shortages impact the effective delivery of nursing care within these units. The LNC desiring to review critical care medical records may find these records difficult to interpret at best. A solid background in critical care nursing or access to a consulting peer is the key to successful record review by the LNC.

References

42 U.S.C. §1395 dd(a) (2002a). EMTALA.

42 U.S.C. §1395 dd(b) (2002b). EMTALA.

Aiken, L. H., Clarke, S. P., Sloane, D. M., Lake, E. T., & Cheney, T. (2008). Effects of hospital care environments on patient mortality and nurse outcomes. *Journal of Nursing Administration (JONA)*, *38*(5), 220–226.

Angus, D. C., Kelley, M. A., Schmitz, R. J., White, A., & Popovich, J. (2000). Caring for the critically ill patient: Current and projected workforce requirements for care of the critically ill and patients with pulmonary disease. Can we meet the requirements of an aging population? *JAMA*, *284*, 2762–2770.

Ballard, K. (2003). Patient safety: A shared responsibility. *Online Journal of Issues in Nursing*, *8*(3), Manuscript 4. Available at www.nursingworld.org/MainMenuCategories/ANAMarketplace/ANAPeriodicals/OJIN/Tableofontents/Volume82003/No3Sept2003/PatientSafety.aspx.

Barton, C. W., Hemphill, J. C., & Morabito, D. (2005). A novel method of evaluating the impact of secondary brain insults on functional outcomes in traumatic brain injured patients. *Academic Emergency Medicine*, *12*, 1–6.

Boulain, T. (1998). Unplanned extubations in the adult intensive care unit: A prospective multicenter study. *American Journal of Respiratory and Critical Care Medicine*, *157*, 1131–1134.

Chandler, C. F., Blinman, T., & Cryer, H. G. (2004). Acute renal failure. In E. E. Moore, D. V. Feliciano, & K. L. Mattox (Eds.), *Trauma* (5th ed., pp. 1323–1350). New York: McGraw-Hill.

Chi, J. H., Knudson, M. M., Vassar, M. J., McCarthy, M. C., Shapiro, M. B., Mallet, S., Holcroft, J. J., Moncrief, H., Noble, J., Wisner, D., Kaups, L., Bennick, L. D., & Manley, G. (2006). Pre-hospital hypoxia affects outcome in patients with traumatic brain injury: A prospective multicenter study. *The Journal of Trauma*, *61*, 1134–1141.

Coles, J. P. (2004). Regional ischemia after head injury. *Current Opinion in Critical Care*, 10, 120–125.

Durie, C. (2006). Organ donation: Process and standards leading to transplant. *Journal of Legal Nurse Consulting*, *17*(4), 12–18.

Emergency Nurses Association (2004). *Emergency nursing pediatric course: Provider manual.* (3rd ed.). Des Plaines, IL: Emergency Nurses Association.

Fakry, S. M., & Michetti, C. P. (2004). Bleeding and coagulation complications. In E. E. Moore, D. V. Feliciano, & K. L. Mattox (Eds.), *Trauma* (5th ed., pp. 1251–1273). New York: McGraw-Hill.

Fink, M. P., Puyana, J. C., & Lisbon, A. (2004). Cardiovascular failure. In E. E. Moore, D. V. Feliciano, & K. L. Mattox (Eds.), *Trauma* (5th ed., pp. 1275–1294). New York: McGraw-Hill.

Hawke, D., Kraft, J., & Smith, S. (1990). Tissue and organ donation and recovery. In S. Smith (Ed.), *Tissue and organ transplantation* (pp. 83–102). St. Louis, MO: Mosby.

Health Insurance Portability and Accountability Act (HIPAA). (1996). Available at www.hipaa.org.

Henzler, D., Cooper, D. L., Tremayne, A. B., Rossaint, R., & Higgins, A. (2007). Early modifiable factors associated with fatal outcome in patients with severe traumatic brain injury: A case control study. *Critical Care Medicine, 35*, 1027–1031.

Horton, J. D., & Bushwick, B. M. (1999). Warfarin therapy: Evolving strategies in anticoagulation. *American Family Physician, 59*(3), 635–646.

Inaba, K., Goecke, M., Sharkey, P., & Brenneman, F. (2003). Long-term outcomes after injury in the elderly. *The Journal of Trauma, 54*(3), 486–491.

Needleman, J., Buerhaus, P., Mattke, S., Stewart, M., & Zelevinsky, K. (2002). Nurse-staffing levels and the quality of care in hospitals. *New England Journal of Medicine, 346*(22), 1715–1722.

Jeremitsky, E., Omert, L., Dunham, C. M., Protetch, J., & Rodriguez, A. (2003). Harbingers of poor outcome the day after severe brain injury: Hyperthermia, hypoxia, and hypoperfusion. *The Journal of Trauma, 54*, 312–319.

Joint Commission on Accreditation of Healthcare Organizations Hospital Accreditation Standards. (2008). (pp. 286–288, 351–352). Oakbrook Terrace, IL: Joint Commission Resources, Inc.

Jones, P. A., Andrews, P. J., Midgley, S., Anderson, S. I., Piper, I. R., Tocher, J. L., Housley, A. M., Corrie, J. A., Slattery, J., & Dearden, N. M. (1994). Measuring the burden of secondary insults in head injured patients during intensive care. *Journal of Neurosurgical Anesthesiology, 6*, 4–14.

Kauder, D. R., Schwab, C. W., & Shapiro, M. B. (2004). Geriatric trauma: Patterns, care, and outcomes. In E. E. Moore, D. V. Feliciano, & K. L. Mattox (Eds.), *Trauma* (5th ed., pp. 1041–1058). New York: McGraw-Hill.

Kremsdorf, R. (2005, July/August). Failure to rescue and errors of omission. *Patient Safety & Quality Healthcare.* Retrieved July 7, 2008, from http://www.psqh.com/julaug05/ails.html.

Krinsley, J. S., & Barone, J. E. (2005). The drive to survive: Unplanned extubation in the *ICU. Chest, 128*, 560–567.

Lakatta, E. G. (2002). Age associated cardiovascular changes in health: Impact on cardiovascular disease in older persons. *Heart Failure Review, 7*, 29–49.

Ledgerwood, A. M., Lucas, K. A., & Lucas, C. E. (2004). The convergence of trauma, medicine, and the law. In E. E. Moore, D. V. Feliciano, & K. L. Mattox (Eds.), *Trauma* (5th ed., pp. 1427–1440). New York: McGraw-Hill.

Mackersie, R. C., Pittet, J. F., Dicker, R. A. (2008). Principles of critical care. In D. V. Feliciano, K. L. Mattox, & E. E. Moore (Eds.), *Trauma* (6th ed., pp. 1195–1222). New York: McGraw-Hill.

McGwin, G., Melton, S. M., May, A. K., & Rue, L. W. (2000). Long-term survival in the elderly after trauma. *The Journal of Trauma, 49*, 470–476.

McHugh, G. A., Engel, D. C., Butcher, I., Lu, J., Steyerberg, E. W., Hernandez, A. V., Mushkudiani, N., Mass, A. I., Marmarou, A., & Murray, G. D. (2007). Prognostic value of secondary insults in traumatic brain injury: Results from the IMPACT study. *Journal of Neurotrauma, 24*, 287–293.

McQuillan, K. A., & Thurman, P. A. (2008). Traumatic brain injury. In K. A. McQuillan, M. B. Makic, & E. Whalen (Eds.), *Trauma nursing, from resuscitation through rehabilitation* (4th ed., pp. 448–518). St. Louis: Saunders Elsevier.

Moloney-Harmon, P. A. (2008). Pediatric trauma. In K. A. McQuillan, M. B. Makic, & E. Whalen (Eds.), *Trauma nursing, from resuscitation through rehabilitation* (4th ed., pp. 810–834). St. Louis: Saunders Elsevier.

Moore, F. A., & Moore, E. E. (2004). Post-injury multiple organ failure. In E. E. Moore, D. V. Feliciano, & K. L. Mattox (Eds.), *Trauma* (5th ed., pp. 1397–1424). New York: McGraw-Hill.

National Council of State Boards of Nursing (NCSBN). (2008). Available at www.ncsbn.org.

National Center for Injury Prevention and Control, Centers for Disease Control and Prevention. (2005). Available at http://www.ced.gov.

National Prescription Audit. (1998). *Physician specialty report*, Dispensed Data, Plymouth Meeting. PA: IMS America.

Nevarez v. New York City Health and Hospitals Corp., 670 N.Y.S. 2d 486 (N.Y. App. Div. 1st Dept. 1997).

Organ Procurement and Transplant Network (OPTN). (2008). Available at www.optn.org.

Porzecanski, I., & Bowton, D. L. (2006). Diagnosis and treatment of ventilator-associated pneumonia. *Chest, 130*, 597–604.

Ream, R. S., Mackey, K., Leet, T., Green, M. C., Andreone, T. L., Loftis, L. L., & Lynch, R. E. (2007). Association of nursing workload and unplanned extubations in a pediatric intensive care unit. *Pediatric Critical Care Medicine, 8*(4), 366–371.

Resources for Optimal Care of the Injured Patient. (2006). American College of Surgeons, Committee on Trauma. 1–2 and 135–137.

Salomone, J. P., & Frame, S. B. (2004). Prehospital care. In E. E. Moore, D. V. Feliciano, & K. L. Mattox (Eds.), *Trauma* (5th ed., pp. 105–125). New York: McGraw-Hill.

Sanchez-Olmedo, J. I., Flores-Cordero, J. M., Rincon-Ferrari, M. D., Perez-Ale, M., Munoz-Sanchez, M., Dominguez-Roldan, J., & Murillo-Cabezas, F. (2005). Brain death after severe traumatic brain injury: The role of systemic secondary brain results. *Transplantation Proceedings, 37*, 1990–1992.

Scott, P. H., Eigen, H., Moye, L. A., et al. (1985). Predictability and consequences of spontaneous extubation in a pediatric intensive care unit. *Critical Care Medicine, 13*, 228–232.

United Networks for Organ Sharing (UNOS). Available at www.unos.org.

Zenel, J., & Goldstein, B. (2002). Child abuse in the pediatric intensive care unit. *Critical Care Medicine, 30*, S512–S523.

Appendix A: American Heart Association "Chain of Survival"

Lethal arrhythmias can occur in any setting. A person's chances of surviving a sudden death episode with neurological and cardiac function intact increase, when emergency measures are employed rapidly and in an organized fashion. Reviewing the code blue sheets for times is crucial. Compare the code teams response time. Was the code called and implemented in a timely manner based on the patient's symptomatology? The American Heart Association, based on years of research into the causes and management of sudden cardiac death episodes, has identified a specific sequence of events that has been found to improve survival and outcomes following cardiac arrest. These events have been grouped together in a conceptual model referred to as the "Chain of Survival."

Early Access

The first link in the Chain of Survival concept is early access. In simple terms, early access means that a cardiac arrest patient receives help as soon as possible. Two actions are critical: recognition of the emergency and activation of the emergency medical system. Again, this will be found in the records of the code blue flow sheets.

Early Defibrillation

It has been shown that early initiation of CPR is most effective when it has been followed rapidly by defibrillation. Did the team follow ACLS guidelines in the resuscitation efforts?

Ethical Decisions and Futile Attempts: The Big Debate

Futile care issues take on a special significance at the end of life, both from a caregiver perspective and that of the legal system.

1. The interests of the patient may be perceived as greatly diminished at this time and clinicians may be more likely to consider the needs of the family. Consider, for example, the question of whether to initiate chronic ventilation for a severely demented elderly patient who is primarily cared for by his family. A documented DNR order in the medical records for this patient may be confusing for many healthcare providers. As an LNC, the definition of DNR has many different meanings from one organization to another. Know the defined terms and the intent for the patient. It needs to be spelled out specifically in the orders. Similar issues arise with the use of sedatives at the end of life. If the nurse administers a dose of morphine outside the range of recommended dosages, then it may be construed as something more serious that ends in litigation.

    Consider a patient who is near death and having agonal respirations. The Family may find this very distressing, despite reassurances from the clinicians that the patient is unconscious and not experiencing any suffering. They may push for more medication. Should the physician administer additional opioids to the patient, with the intention of making the patient appear more peaceful for the benefit of the family? This can be viewed as expediting death.

2. Both of these examples present relatively common dilemmas that are not well addressed by the standard principles and paradigms that currently exist in bioethics.

   Critical care units are, frequently, the settings for the delivery of end-of-life care. A case study describing pain management for a terminally ill woman in an ICU is used to illustrate conflicts that may be experienced by critical care nurses. Pain management is considered the fifth vital sign and is used frequently in reviews of the medical record.

3. Zalon ML, Constantino RE, and Andrews KL describe the application of standards of professional organizations and regulatory bodies, as well as the ethical principles of autonomy, veracity, beneficence, and nonmalfeasance.

   - The Ethics Committee of the Society of Critical Care Medicine. Recommendations for end-of-life care in the ICU: Robert D. Truog, MD; Alexandra F. M. Cist, MD; Sharon E. Brackett, RN, BSN; Jeffrey P. Burns, MD; Martha A. Q. Curley, RN, PhD, CCNS, FAAN; Marion Danis, MD; Michael A. DeVita, MD; Stanley H. Rosenbaum, MD; David M. Rothenberg, MD; Charles L. Sprung, MD; Sally A. Webb, MD; Ginger S. Wlody, RN, EdD, FCCM; William E. Hurford, MD.
   - *Crit Care.* 2004; 8(4): 213–218. Published online 2004 June 30. doi: 10.1186/cc2909. Roundtable debate: Child with severe brain damage and an underlying brain tumor. Scott Gunn, Satoru Hashimoto, Michael Karakozov, Thomas Marx, Ian K. S. Tan, Dan R. Thompson, and Jean-Louis Vincent.

4. *Dimens Crit Care Nursing.* 2008 May–June; *27*(3):93–101

Appendix B: Vascular Procedures Case Study

Angiography has been considered relevant in cardiovascular case management; however, it is not without risk and is an expensive procedure. When reviewing postprocedure care, variations may exist in size and amount of pressure applied and methods used to secure pressure dressings. Variations in technique to effect relative immobilization of the access site will also be seen and may include (a) use of sandbags over the accessed site (groin) or along the involved limb to prevent movement; (b) use of sheets secured over the knee on the side of the accessed artery and tucked firmly beneath the mattress to prevent flexion of the involved leg; and (c) use of soft restraints near the ankle of the involved limb to prevent the flexion of hip or knee. Similar restraint devices are used for brachial access sites. Occasionally, the nurse may encounter a commercial pressure device such as FemoStop plus Femoral Compression System (Radi Medical Systems), which used to apply pressure directly over the artery puncture site. These devices should be used only for brief periods in order to bring about hemostasis and usually require specific training in application, usage, and removal. These devices are usually applied immediately following withdrawal of the catheter and are removed prior to the return of the patient to the nursing unit. When reviewing a procedural case, such as an angiogram, the LNC will want to look for pressure device policies for determination of length of time to be applied and what was actually done.

Some key concepts to look for when assessing for deviations in the standards of care of a patient's postoperative angiogram cases include

- Deviations in baseline vital signs (necessary to determine changes in the patient's condition).
- Notation regarding the presence or absence of characteristics and symmetry of peripheral pulses, particularly the brachials, radials, femorals, and dorsalis pedis and posterior tibial pulses. (Baseline pulse determinations are imperative for postprocedure comparisons.)

- Determination and utilization of baseline renal function tests (blood–urea–nitrogen [BUN] and creatinine) prior to the study. (Use of radiopaque contrast agents may be nephrotoxic, particularly to a client with existing, impaired kidney function, and special attention to hydration is a priority for clients with impaired renal function.)
- Documentation of the color and temperature of the client's extremities, pre- and postprocedure.
- Documentation of the condition of the dressing at the insertion site and any weights or pressure applied.

There are several questions for the LNC to consider when reviewing cases involving angiography. Some questions to consider may include

- Was the pressure dressing too tight as to impede arterial flow and caused diminished pulses downstream?
- Was the pressure dressings too loose, permitting "oozing" of blood from the artery into tissues and subsequent hematoma formation?
- If the dressing is found to be too tight, was their release of pressure documented?
- Was there notification to the physician or qualified practitioner for confirmed absent or diminished pulse?
- If the site is oozing or bleeding, was their documentation noted that reapplication of direct pressure (manual) and reapplication of pressure dressing was done?
- Was the patient given water, following the procedure, to decrease the risk of complications, especially renal?
- Were there any dysrhythmias that occurred? If so, did they need treatment? Many patients undergoing angiography have underlying cardiac conditions. Attention should be placed on medications that may not have been taken while the client was NPO prior to the procedure. Some ectopic beats may occur. The procedure nurse needs to be alert for life-threatening arrhythmias and know proper protocol to follow.
- Did the patient void prior to the angiography? A vasovagal reaction, consisting of nausea, hypotension, and bradycardia, may be precipitated by a distended bladder. If this should occur, were the proper interventions in place, including trendelenburg positioning and cardiac medications.

The following case scenario represents a post-procedure patient who was symptomatic, and has a notable assessment, plan, and intervention documented. Not all complications from procedures lead to bad outcomes. Early intervention is the key to preventing long-term complications. Documentation is the key to identifying the appropriate standard of care.

Case

Anna May, a 76-year-old female, returned to the nursing unit following an aortogram and bilateral femoral angiogram. Her blood pressure was noted to be 94/58 on admission to the unit; all pulses were average upon palpation and her limbs were slightly cool but blanch with pressure and refill in less than 2 sec. She admitted "some" discomfort at the right femoral arterial access site. The dressing was dry and intact and the femoral pulse was average upon palpation. She had a patent IV reservoir in her left forearm. She reported nausea and refused any oral fluids. One hour following the return to the unit, all findings were unchanged except her blood pressure, which was then 88/54. The nurse suspected that the hypotension might be caused by relative hypovolemia as the patient gave a history of little intake in 24 hr and had received a contrast agent during the angiographic procedure. The patient took only sips of water and reports on nausea remained. The nurse phoned the physician with a report of the client's condition. After obtaining an order, the nurse administered 1 L of normal saline, and then continued an infusion of normal saline at approximately 100 cc/hr. The nurse medicated the client for nausea and monitored the intake and output. The client improved and no long-term complications developed. A successful outcome was put into place by the nurse's actions. This may not be the case when trauma is the issue at hand.

Chapter 18

Ambulatory Care Settings

Cynthia Lacker, RN, MS, LNCC and Karen L. Rollo, RN, MSN

Contents

Objectives

Upon reading this chapter, the legal nurse consultant will be able to:

- Review the legal nurse consultant's focus related to demonstrative evidence and presentation
- Describe the role of the legal nurse consultant in preparation and presentation of demonstrative evidence
- Discuss preparation of digital exhibits and successful presentation of case issues
- Review the admissibility and use of technical demonstrative evidence in the courts

Evaluating Emergency Department Cases

As healthcare organizations, accrediting bodies, and committees focus attention on the occurrence of errors in hospital practice, the emergency department (ED) does not escape this scrutiny. This section will provide an overview of legal risks to ED personnel and to the ED in general. Included are selected areas of risk faced by ED doctors and nurses, specific behaviors that increase risk, suggestions for the legal nurse consultant (LNC) to consider when evaluating ED cases, and ways that ED physicians and nurses can protect themselves against potential litigation.

The ED is a practice setting fraught with areas of vulnerability to litigation, and is "a natural laboratory for the study of error" (Glatter, Martin, & Lex, 2008, p. 1). Emergency medicine is considered a high-risk specialty. According to Hubler and Brown (American College of Legal Medicine, 2007), emergency physicians are named in 53% of lawsuits. Research conducted by the Institute of Medicine Kohn et al. (2000) confirms that number. Often the ED is the first portal of entry to healthcare for many members of the population here in the United States. ED visits in the United States are estimated at 115.5 million yearly according to the most recent data published in 2005, and are increasing each year (Nawar, Niska, & Xu, 2007). As a result, emergency caregivers are vulnerable to involvement in a lawsuit at some point in their careers.

Why Are EDs Susceptible to Medical-Legal Risk?

The reasons that EDs are error-prone are not surprising to any emergency physician or nurse. Emergency physicians do not enjoy the benefit of an established relationship with their patients, as do primary care physicians. ED patients are strangers to ED physicians and nurses. Emergency physicians manage multiple patients with a variety of chief complaints simultaneously, requiring them to process and retain large volumes of data related to their many patients. Patients present with acute changes in their health status, requiring emergency physicians and nurses to make assessments and care decisions within a narrow window of time (Kohen et al., 2000). Patients may present with symptomatology atypical of the thousands of diagnoses seen in the ED.

Patients may or may not know their complete medical history, the details of medications they take, or what specific reactions they may have had in the past to documented allergies. The patient may present to the ED unable to communicate verbally and family members are often unavailable or unable to assist with giving a history of the current problem or details about past medical history. In addition, ED physicians may not have immediate access to the patient's medical records, especially if the patient has no previous admissions at the treating hospital. Therefore, treatment decisions must often be made with incomplete, sparse data, and the emergency physician has little or no time for reflection—fast action may be necessary to save a life.

Today, due to situations of ED overcrowding, patients remain in the ED for longer periods of time waiting admission or transfer, sometimes requiring definitive, higher levels of care by other medical or surgical specialties. Any delay in treatment poses increased risk not only for the patient but also for the emergency physicians and nurses (American College of Legal Medicine, 2007). The LNC should take into consideration factors particular to this practice environment, and at the same time be aware of certain areas of risk and vulnerability particular to the fields of emergency medicine and emergency nursing. Finally, privacy is at a premium in the chaotic environment of the hospital environment, so that accurate and confidential communication between the physicians, nurses, and patients can be easily compromised.

Emergency Medicine and Emergency Nursing Defined

Emergency medicine is defined as "the medical specialty dedicated to the diagnosis and treatment of unforeseen illness or injury. It encompasses a unique body of knowledge as set forth in the Model of the Clinical Practice of Emergency Medicine (ACEP, 2007a). The practice of emergency medicine includes the initial evaluation, diagnosis, treatment, and disposition of any patient requiring expeditious medical, surgical, or psychiatric care. Emergency medicine may be practiced in a hospital-based or freestanding emergency department (ED), in an urgent care clinic, in an emergency medical response vehicle or at a disaster site" (ACEP, 2007b). The American College of Emergency Physicians (ACEP) is the governing organization for the specialty of emergency medicine, and provides policy and standards, position statements, recommendations for treatment protocols, as well as resources for ED physicians and residents to utilize in managing risk reduction.

Trimble describes emergency nursing as "a nursing specialty in which nurses care for patients in the emergency or critical phase of their illness or injury" (Trimble, 2008). Emergency nursing encompasses the care of individuals of all ages, ethnicity, and socioeconomic levels. The difference between emergency nurses and nurses practicing in other specialties caring for patients experiencing acute changes in health related to illness or injury is that in the ED the patient's diagnosis and the cause of the problem are usually unknown while care is taking place.

The Emergency Nurses' Association (ENA) is the governing body for the specialty of emergency nursing in conjunction with the American Nurses Association, and with requirements set forth by the Joint Commission. ENA has published many position statements and resources related to specific areas of emergency nursing practice, which are available through the organization's website. ENA also establishes the scope and standards of practice for emergency nursing (ENA, 1999). In its mission and value statements, ENA promotes excellence in emergency nursing care, respect for the diversity of the patient population as well as that of emergency care colleagues, collaborative practice, dedication to research and the development of an evidence-based body of knowledge, focus on prevention of illness and injury, and commitment to continuing education and professional development of nurses in this specialty practice (ENA, 1999). The LNC can visit the sites of these organizations and find a wealth of resources related to standards of care within these practice specialties.

Major Areas of Risk in Emergency Medicine

Emergency physician members of the ACEP have identified 10 areas of vulnerability of which emergency attending and resident physicians should be aware (ACEP, 2007b). When evaluating an ED case, the LNC should look for the following potential problems in the emergency records.

Knowledge Deficit

Did the treating physician recognize the emergency medical condition (EMC) in the patient's signs and symptoms? The LNC should be aware that even board-certified emergency physicians might not have encountered the myriad of ways that a patient with serious illness may present. For instance, an elderly patient with an aortic dissection may present with flank pain, or low back pain, without associated symptoms, rather than the more frequently seen abdominal pain, syncope, and shock (Weinstock, Longstreth, & Henry, 2006).

What education and training has the physician had related to the specialty of emergency medicine? Is the physician a board-certified emergency physician, meaning that he or she completed a residency in emergency medicine and passed both the written and oral examination administered by the American Board of Emergency Medicine (ABEM, 2008). It is possible that some emergency care centers, such as the freestanding ED or urgent care center, may not be staffed with physicians educated and trained in the specialty of emergency medicine. Physicians in other specialties who sometimes "moonlight" in EDs and may have limited training and experience in the specialty of emergency medicine. The LNC evaluating an ED case should always investigate the physician's credentials and training.

Failure to Take a Complete Patient History

Neglecting to take an adequate patient history is risky in any medical specialty; however, the ED practitioner must be attentive and assure that all the key components of the history are documented in the patient's chart. Essential pieces of the history should include the "history of the present illness, risk factors, past medical history, family history, and personal/social history" (ACEP, 2007b). Documentation of risk factors is an area frequently missing or lacking in adequate recording of cases resulting in claims of malpractice, according to ACEP (2007b). For example, it is standard to ask the patient experiencing chest pain about risk factors such as smoking, hypertension, family members who died as a result of cardiac disease and at what age, cholesterol levels, and past cardiac events. While the physician most likely did ask the questions, if these risk factors are not documented, potential jurors may conclude that the physician took an incomplete history in a case involving a patient who sustains permanent disability or dies as a result of acute coronary syndrome. Although the LNC cannot opine or testify on physician standard of care, the LNC can assist with locating an emergency physician expert who may be able to explain the potential defendant physician's actions in a courtroom setting.

Failure to Perform an Adequate Examination

When patients present to the ED, they expect that the physician is going to perform a thorough physical examination. When reviewing the record, the LNC should look for all parts of the examination to be documented thoroughly. The absence of documentation of any element of the examination conveys the perception that a complete examination was not performed. For example, an ED physician treating the complaint of pediatric fever should be meticulous about documenting the child's mental status, the appearance of the skin and presence of any rashes, and the presence of any meningeal signs such as rigidity of the neck and spine, especially when meningitis is a consideration in the differential diagnosis (Newberry & Criddle, 2005).

Failure to Consider Differential Diagnoses

ACEP (2007b) considers it prudent for the ED physician to include documentation of all differential diagnoses considered in order to explain the practitioner's reasoning for treatment rendered. When reviewing ED records, the LNC should note whether any discussion of diagnoses that were ruled out appears in the record. Documentation of possible differential diagnoses validates the LNC's perception that a thorough examination took place.

Failure to Order/Interpret Diagnostic Tests

When patients present to the ED with a complaint, they generally expect that the ED physician will order certain tests in order to diagnose their problem. When a bad outcome occurs, the failure to order diagnostic studies will likely be an important part of the plaintiff case. For example, patients presenting with a complaint of chest pain expect to have an electrocardiogram and laboratory tests performed to rule out an acute myocardial infarction. The patient with a complaint of the "worst headache of my life" may expect to undergo a computed tomography scan (CT scan) of the brain. For the female patient of child-bearing age with a complaint of acute abdominal pain and subsequent ruptured ectopic pregnancy, the LNC should determine if a pregnancy test was performed. Not only should the physician order the appropriate tests, but also, exercising diligence in interpreting and acting on abnormal results is critical. This "failure" may result in a delay of treatment and subsequent potentially adverse outcomes.

In a survey study investigating physicians at high risk of malpractice, 126 emergency physicians respondents reported having ordered imaging studies such as magnetic resonance imaging (MRI), CT scan, or x-rays, (63% of physicians), cardiac workups (12%), and "other tests" (11%), as the "most recent act of defensive medicine" they had performed at the time of this study (Studdert et al., 2005, p. 2613). The term "defensive medicine" refers to physician practices such as ordering extensive diagnostic tests, which are implemented specifically for the purpose of avoiding legal liability, whether or not they are medically necessary for the patient at the time of treatment. In addition, emergency physicians and nurses may document assessments or observations with an eye on the courtroom, taking care to remain detailed but objective in written documentation and avoid putting assumptions in writing. For example, when ED personnel suspect a patient may be malingering, it is prudent to provide the same consistent level of care and examination, and remain objective when charting rather than documenting doubts about the veracity of a patient's complaint.

Failure to Diagnose

Glatter et al. (2008) maintain that diagnostic error "is the most important source of adverse events in the ED, where there is a discrepancy between clinical diagnosis and postmortem findings 20–40 percent of the time" (p. 3). The LNC should ask: does documentation of the patient's history, examination findings, and diagnostic test results support the diagnosis in the chart? The LNC should consider whether other "failures" may exist, since allegations of negligence may be accompanied by charges of other "failures." The ED physician may not be able to arrive at a definitive diagnosis in every case; however, at the time of the patient's disposition, the chart should reflect the physician's clinical impression and tentative diagnosis based on a thorough examination and appropriate diagnostic workup (ACEP, 2007).

Failure to Treat

Failure to treat does not usually mean that the physician refused to treat a patient, resulting in an adverse outcome. Failure to treat most often refers to circumstances that result in delays in treatment where treatment is time sensitive, or the absence of treatment that is appropriate and standard to specific diagnoses. For example, the patient with suspected sepsis should receive intravenous (IV) antibiotics within a certain window of time (Dellinger et al., 2008). Defense of this allegation might include ED overcrowding and subsequent delays in treatment, nurse staffing shortages, unavailability of necessary diagnostic equipment, such as a CT scan, or errors in triage.

Failure to Consult

The ED physician is a specialist in emergency medicine. Therefore, the ED physician should consult other physician specialists for patients who require definitive treatment care for any problem that falls outside of the ED physician's specialized scope of practice. For example, a cardiologist should be consulted for the patient with a myoscardial infarction, a pediatrician for a child in need of admission, or a neurosurgeon for a patient diagnosed with a subarachnoid hemorrhage. "When a physician would be reasonably expected to consult a specialist and does not, and there is a bad outcome, the outcome can be used as proof of the need for consultation" (ACEP, 2007, p. 3).

Failure to Admit

When the patient is discharged from the ED and his condition becomes worse, or he suffers complications, this "failure" comes into play, and may be coupled with failure to diagnose" (ACEP, 2007, p. 3). The LNC evaluating a case of failure to admit should review the discharge instructions thoroughly, with these questions in mind: did the discharge instructions list the name of the follow-up physician, when the follow-up should take place, what the patient should expect in terms of symptoms, and detailed reasons that the patient should return to the ED? Is there documentation beyond the patient's signature on the discharge, such as a note stating the patient's verbal understanding of the instructions?

Failure to Communicate

Physicians who generate patient complaints may put themselves at higher risk of legal action according to Hickson et al. (2002). In a study that examined the relationship between patient complaints and initiation of risk management action ranging from the opening of a risk management file to lawsuit, Hickson et al. (2002) studied several complaint categories. These categories included communication, care and treatment, humaneness, access, and billing. They found a significant positive correlation between physician clinical activity, the presence of a risk management file and action, and complaints lodged in the above variable categories. This study did not include emergency physicians, due to the authors' statement that patient satisfaction surveys do not consistently identify specific ED physicians. However, the ED is a prime clinical environment where training for staff in the acquisition of patient satisfaction and service recovery skills is beneficial and may result in quantifiable decreases in patient complaints (Mayer & Zimmerman, 1999). During the course of evaluating allegations of negligence or other "failures," the LNC may discover that the perception of lack of empathetic treatment by ED personnel facilitated the patient's and the patient's family's decision to bring a claim of malpractice. ED physicians and nurses should strive to care for patients with the same level of care they would want to receive as a patient, in order to "achieve optimal patient satisfaction" (ACEP, 2007). Listening and informing the patient of the "who, what, when, where and why of the workup" (ACEP, 2007, p. 4) may go a long way toward pre-empting a lawsuit.

Role of the Emergency Nurse

ED physicians are not the only emergency practitioners susceptible to allegations of malpractice. Nurses share accountability for the care of the ED patient and can be held liable for breaches of duty that occur during the patient's ED stay. The modern RN fulfills a complex role in patient care, especially in the ED, and is not merely a recorder of events. The ED RN, like other nurses, functions in a collaborative relationship with ED physicians. The ED RN performs physical assessments and obtains detailed histories. Often the nurse is considered the "eyes and ears" of the ED physician, who, as previously mentioned, is responsible for managing large volumes of patients simultaneously, especially in a large ED. ED physicians may rely heavily on the ED RN to appreciate and report even subtle changes in the patient's condition. Missed or inaccurate nursing assessments leading to delays in treatments pose significant risk to patient welfare and increased likelihood that the nurse may face malpractice charges (O'Keefe, 2001).

Nursing Standards of Care

"Standards of care" are authoritative statements by which the nursing profession describes the responsibilities, skills, and activities, such as comprehensive patient assessment, for which nurses are held accountable. Furthermore, for legal purposes, standards of care also describe "what is reasonable and prudent for someone with the same or similar knowledge and skills to do in the same or similar circumstance" (O'Keefe, 2001, p. 44). Nursing standards reflect the values and principles of the nursing profession that are derived from a body of research in nursing and other disciplines, and provide direction for practice guidelines that are reasonable and result in measurable outcomes. Although various hospital systems across the United States may develop nursing policies and protocols for specific complaints that vary slightly from region to region, registered nurses are all held to the minimum standard of having to pass a national nursing licensure examination, the National Council Licensure Examination, or NCLEX. ENA describes the "competent level" emergency nurse as one who attains the following:

> Basic Life Support provider status ... Advanced Cardiac Life Support provider status and/or Pediatric Life Advanced Life Support status, as appropriate, attains Certification in Emergency Nursing (CEN), attains Trauma Nursing Core Course (TNCC) provider status (minimum level of education for emergency nurses caring for trauma patients), and attains Emergency Nursing Core Course (ENPC) status (minimal level of education for emergency nurses caring for pediatric patients. (ENA, 1999, p. 36)

ENA has published standards of emergency nursing practice that are aligned with those published by the American Nurses' Association (ANA) (ENA, 1999). The nurse with CEN designation provides competent care that is measured in accordance with skills and knowledge identified as minimally standard to this nursing specialty (O'Keefe, 2001). Aside from standards put forth by professional organizations, the LNC can search for standards of care from several other resources. These include state and local statutes, position statements, Nurse Practice Acts, national and institutional nursing practice guidelines, peer-reviewed journals and textbooks, equipment and policy manuals, job descriptions, treatment pathways when used in the ED as basis for treatment and standing orders, court decisions, case law, federal law such as the Consolidated Omnibus Budget Reconciliation Act of 1985 (COBRA), and standards mandated by the Joint Commission (Gorombei, Oldham, & Bausch, 2006). The hospital's role in implementing these types of practice guidelines and policies is to assure that its nurses are licensed according to NCLEX and individual state Nurse Practice Acts, and that organizational practice policies are in line with national guidelines and other authoritative resources such as those listed above. Nurses are therefore faced with the challenge of following federal, state, local, and organizational standards, while delivering quality, skilled, and empathetic patient care and acting as a patient advocate at all times.

Major Areas of Risk for Emergency Nurses

The potential for legal risk increases when EDs pull nurses from other disciplines to provide staffing coverage in times of shortages. Utilizing unqualified nurses in the ED, who may not have the necessary education, training, and certifications that are standard in emergency care is legally hazardous. When evaluating a case involving an emergency nurse, it is important for the LNC to request a curriculum vitae/resume of the nurse involved in order to validate the nurses' qualifications, or lack thereof, to provide care in an ED. EDs that utilize nurses from other specialties to fill staffing needs should be prudent and place those nurses in assignments where patient acuity meets their education, training, and experience. Nurses who do not meet standards of care specified by hospital policy or the professional organization governing the scope and standard of practice of emergency nursing care face the possibility of being held liable in the event of a lawsuit (O'Keefe, 2001).

Nurses have a legal obligation to uphold several "duties" of care in the ED. Emergency nurses have a daunting job; they must uphold hospital policy, procedure, nurse practice standards, state and federal laws, and follow physicians' orders (O'Keefe, 2001).

Duty to Obey Physician Orders

The emergency nurse is no different from nurses in other specialties with regard to following physician orders. One characteristic of emergency nursing that attracts nurses to the specialty is the autonomy they experience in their practice. However, while ED nurses are able to function relatively independently in the ED, the nurse must remember that writing and executing medical orders for patient care remains the domain of the emergency physician. Failing to follow prescribed orders or initiating treatment without a physician order can lead to allegations of practicing medicine without a license. Consider the following case:

> In *Toth v. Community Hospital at Glen Cove*, nurses were held negligent when they failed to follow the physician's orders for delivery of oxygen to a set of twins. The physician had ordered oxygen to be administered at the rate of 6 liters per minute for the first 12 hours and then 4 liters per minute thereafter. The nurses were held negligent when they delivered 6 liters per minute continuously over several weeks, creating blindness in one twin and severe damage to one eye in the other twin. (O'Keefe, 2001, p. 378)

Although this is not an ED case, it illustrates the legal liability faced by nurses who disregard physician orders.

Duty to Report Negligent Physicians

If a nurse recognizes that the physician is not acting in the best interest of the patient or has committed an act that may be detrimental to the patient's outcome, the nurse has a duty to report suspected physician negligence (O'Keefe, 2001). The LNC evaluating a malpractice case involving alleged physician negligence should facilitate the investigation into whether nurses involved in the patient's care were aware of the physician's negligent actions and reported them.

Case Example

Two ED nurses were assigned to the trauma bays in a Level 1 trauma center when paramedics called in requesting a trauma code, reporting that they were enroute with a male truck driver in his 40s who was severely injured. While on the shoulder of the interstate checking a malfunction in his truck, the truck driver had been struck by another vehicle and pinned to the front of his truck. He sustained an "open-book" pelvic fracture and a femur fracture. On arrival to the ED, the patient was awake, in excruciating pain, tachycardic and hypotensive but oriented to person, place, and time, and was cooperative. His heart rate was 140+, and his blood pressure dropped to 60 systolic within the first 15 min of arrival. His airway was patent, breath sounds equal, but he was pale, diaphoretic, with a distended abdomen, an unstable pelvis, and signs of hypovolemic shock. Fluid resuscitation was instituted in the field with crystalloid solution and continued in the trauma room. Despite aggressive fluid resuscitation with crystalloids, he remained hypotensive—he needed blood and was transferred to the operating room. The nurses asked the chief resident in charge of the trauma to order uncrossed blood until type-specific blood became available from the hospital's blood bank. For unknown reasons, the resident refused the nurses urging to order blood. After several unsuccessful requests that blood be ordered, the nurses notified the ED-attending physician. The ED-attending physician arrived, ordered the blood, and called the trauma-attending physician, who arrived in the trauma bay immediately, assumed care, and dismissed the resident from the patient's care. Had the nurses not recognized the importance of reporting this resident's actions, the patient may have likely suffered an adverse outcome, and the nurses possibly could be held liable for failure to report presumed negligent actions by the resident physician negligence (Anonymous, personal communication, 2000).

Failure to Question Patient Discharge

If the nurse believes that a patient scheduled for discharge is in danger of suffering complications or a deterioration in condition if he/she is discharged, it is the nurse's duty to question the discharge (O'Keefe, 2001).

Case Example

A nursing home patient transferred to the ED was examined by a physician, who wrote an order to discharge the patient back to the nursing home. The oncoming midnight shift nurse received the report that the patient was waiting for an ambulance transfer and that "the doctor didn't find anything." The ED nurse questioned the lack of testing done on the patient while in the ED and reviewed the nursing home chart and interagency form for documentation of the reason for transfer. Unable to find a nursing note, the ED nurse called the nursing home and spoke to the nurse who had cared for the patient to learn that the reason for transfer to the ED was that the patient had fallen and struck her head. The nursing home records revealed the patient was on Coumadin. The ED nurse found no documentation of a CT scan of the brain while the patient was in the ED, approached the physician to relay what she had learned about the reason for transfer to the ED, and questioned the discharge. Fortunately the physician listened, cancelled the discharge, and ordered the CT scan. The physician had not taken an adequate history as the patient was unable to verbally communicate what had happened to her. A prudent action would have been to call the nursing home and inquire about the history of current event and reason for transfer. The patient suffered a small intracerebral bleed and was admitted with a neurosurgical consult (Anonymous, personal communication, 2007).

This example has several potential problems that were averted by the ED nurse's astute actions. Allegations of negligence could have included failure to take an adequate history, failure to diagnose, failure to treat, and failure to order the appropriate tests. By questioning the discharge, the ED nurse in this case prevented the patient from further harm, and prevented the physician from potentially being sued for malpractice.

Failure to Report Patient Changes

Nurses in all specialties have a duty to report changes in patient condition to the physician (O'Keefe, 2001), and in the ED the patient's condition can change rapidly, requiring close monitoring. If the physician is unresponsive to the nurses' reports of patient deterioration, nurses have a duty to contact hospital administration and follow the chain of command in advocating for the patient.

Case Example

Darling v. Charleston Community Memorial Hospital is a 1965 case that illustrates the result of failure to advocate for the patient and continue reporting an acute change in patient status. The patient was a young man casted for a broken leg who developed pain disproportionate to the injury, accompanied by extreme swelling and darkening of his toes, decreased sensation, and a cold, darkened extremity that emitted a foul odor. The patient was admitted. Although the nurses did assess, document, and report these neurovascular changes, the physician took no action for several days. Three days later the attending physician split the cast, causing bleeding, drainage, and odor to be emitted from inside the cast, evidence of necrosis of the leg. The patient remained in Charleston Hospital for 14 more days before being transferred and placed under the care of another orthopedic surgeon, who discovered considerable amount of dead tissue in the patient's leg. The patient had to undergo a below the knee amputation because of the extremity. The hospital corporation was held liable for the nurses' failure to advocate and report the change in the patient's condition through the hospital's organizational hierarchy when the physician was negligent in responding. The patient's condition began as compartment syndrome, a very treatable condition if identified early. A condition not uncommon to ED physicians and nurses, missed cases of compartment syndrome are a common reason for medical malpractice lawsuits (Gulli & Templeman, 1994). Two "failures" occurred in *Darling*: the failure to report changes and the failure to report physician negligence.

Other Legal Concerns in the ED

The Emergency Medical Treatment and Active Labor Act

One facet of emergency medicine is that patients must often be transferred to another healthcare facility for a higher level of care than the original facility can provide, such as the availability of neurosurgical services. The Emergency Medical Treatment and Active Labor Act (EMTALA) is federal legislation that governs interfacility patient transfers. EMTALA falls under the larger legislative umbrella of the COBRA, enacted in 1986 (Lee, 2001; Strickler, 2006). The intent of EMTALA is to prevent hospitals from "dumping" unstable patients who are poor or uninsured. Media accounts in the 1980s told of patients being turned away or transferred out from emergency departments because of "negative wallet biopsies" (Lee, 2000, 2001).

> EMTALA mandates that any individual who arrives at the ED seeking emergency care or is in active labor is entitled to receive a medical screening examination (MSE), within the hospital's capability, to determine whether an emergency medical condition (EMC) exists. (Lee, 2001, p. 138)

For EMTALA to apply, an individual must enter the ED or the hospital, not necessarily through ED doors, must request to be seen by a doctor, have a request made on his/her behalf, be in active labor (not seeking routine obstetrical care), and must receive an appropriate medical screening. The appropriateness of a medical screening is subject to interpretation, but should involve a physician screening, or a screening performed by a physician extender or nurse practitioner as designated by hospital policy, rather than a nursing assessment or triage assessment only. Screening must occur prior to asking the patient to produce any financial forms or insurance information. The screening should also include whatever diagnostic resources are available to the physician in order to determine if an EMC exists that may result in serious consequences to the patient, and that the patient is stabilized prior to transfer (Lee, 2000, 2001; Strickler, 2006).

One question an LNC may ask is, what is the minimum standard that constitutes an MSE? What is "appropriate"? The answer is that there is no uniform legal standard defining the components of an MSE; an MSE is measured against the institution itself, and what the hospital's capability is to provide the examination, including "whether it was applied equally to patients with similar symptoms, not whether an accurate diagnosis of the patient's illness occurred" (Lee, 2001, p. 142). This was the ruling of the 5th Circuit in the case of *Marshall v. East Carroll Parrish* (1998), in the case of a 15-year-old minor who was presented to the ED with a complaint of "failure to communicate." The patient was seen, discharged, transferred to another ED the same day, and received a diagnosis of cerebrovascular accident (CVA) caused by a left middle cerebral artery infarction. The allegations included an EMTALA violation stating that the patient did not receive an appropriate MSE at the first ED.

An EMC is defined by law as "acute symptoms of sufficient severity, including severe pain, such that the absence of immediate medical attention would reasonably result in serious jeopardy to the health of the individual, serious impairment of bodily functions, or serious dysfunction of any bodily organ or part" (CMS, 2006). EMTALA is most often viewed as "the antidumping law" but in fact it is a mandated standard of practice for the care of any patient arriving in the ED and requiring subsequent transfer (Stricker, 2006). The nurse's responsibility is to assure that the patient understands the benefits and risks of transfer as explained by the physician, verifies that the patient agrees to the transfer, and prepares copies of the record and any test results to accompany the patient to the receiving hospital.

EMTALA's reach extends to hospitals that receive funding from Medicare; therefore, privately owned emergency care centers that do not receive federal funding may be exempt from EMTALA. Hospitals that violate EMTALA are subject to fines and termination of their Medicare agreements. EMTALA allegations may be attached to a case in which other allegations of negligence occur, particularly in cases where the patient sustained an adverse outcome (Lee, 2001).

Case Example

In the case of *Cleland v. Bronson Health Care Group, Inc.*, the parents of a 15-year-old son brought suit under EMTALA in an effort to recover for the death of their son who was incorrectly diagnosed as having influenza. They took him to the ED with complaints of abdominal cramps and nausea. In fact, the boy was suffering from intussusception. He was discharged from the ED, and died within 24 hr. The Clelands alleged that under EMTALA, the ED failed to provide an appropriate medical screening and discharged their son without stabilizing his condition. The court found that there was no violation of EMTALA. At the time of discharge, the Clelands' son was stable and experiencing no acute change in his medical condition. The ED evaluation was found to be appropriate. Decision was for the defendant hospital. Unfortunately for the Clelands, the case did not also attach claims of other "failures" (*Cleland v. Bronson Health Care Group, Inc.*, 1990).

The Health Insurance Portability and Accountability Act

The ED environment is noisy and chaotic place, where patient privacy is very difficult to maintain. ED physicians and nurses must ask sensitive questions and obtain personal information from the patient, often when other patients, family members, and staff are in proximity. The Health Insurance Portability and Accountability Act (HIPAA) was enacted in 1996, for the purpose of addressing and publishing the rules governing the use, disclosure, and exchange of "protected health information" (PHI) (U.S. Department of Health and Human Services, 2003). Violations of (HIPAA) frequently occur unintentionally in EDs due to the nature of the environment. It is difficult, but not impossible, to assess a patient at triage during times of overcrowding, without someone else overhearing at least some of the conversation.

In a case involving claims of HIPAA, the LNC should assess the environment, whenever possible, to gain information as to department policies regarding managing private, sensitive information, how charts are stored, who has access to ED records, and what mechanisms are in place to protect patient confidentiality. In addition, the LNC must show that PHI was released. The components of PHI include patient identifiers such as the patient's name, social security number, or birth date, and these identifiers must be directly linked to the patient's diagnosis, for there is a HIPAA violation to incur (U.S. Department of Health and Human Services, 2003).

One example of a HIPAA violation common in the ED involves the police officer who arrives in the ED to follow up on, or interview, a patient suspected of driving under the influence (DUI). It is not uncommon for an officer to ask an ED nurse if an alcohol level was obtained, and ask what the level was. For a patient who is not under arrest or in custody of the police, under HIPAA, the police are not entitled to the hospital's laboratory results without a warrant or subpoena, and a doctor or nurse who volunteers the information from the patient's chart as a matter of "professional courtesy" is violating HIPAA. This author's experience is that many ED nurses are unaware that releasing the patient's alcohol level constitutes a HIPAA violation and that they put themselves at legal risk when doing so. The LNC evaluating a case of DUI when the driver was taken to the ED must be aware of state and local laws governing the rights of law enforcement versus the patient's rights under HIPAA.

Issues Surrounding Consent

The issue of consent in the ED is not as straightforward as in other medical environments. ED physicians must know about several types of consent and apply that knowledge appropriately. When a patient enters the ED and is registered, he or she signs a general consent form to treat in most cases. This consent allows the ED physician to assess and treat the patient for their complaint. However, this consent is not a substitute for consent forms specific to invasive procedures performed in the ED.

For invasive and even life-saving procedures, one of four types of consent may come into play:

1. *Express consent:* This type may be verbal or written, and is voluntary on the part of the patient seeking medical treatment; the amount of information required to be provided to the patient about the diagnosis, purpose of the procedure, risks and benefits, and alternative treatments varies according to state laws (ENA, 2000; Lee, 2001).
2. *Informed consent:* When applied, informed consent dictates that the physician satisfies three elements: the procedure is fully explained to the patient, alternative treatments if any exist, are explained to the patient, and the physician explains all known risks and benefits, as well as any disclosures, and the patient must have ample opportunity to ask questions (ENA, 2000; Lee, 2001).
3. *Implied consent:* This type of consent is generally applied when a patient is unable to provide express or informed consent, such as when a patient is confused, unconsciousness, unresponsive, hemodynamically unstable, or if next of kin is unavailable. Implied consent is self-explanatory; it presumes that the patient would consent to the procedure if able to do so (ENA, 2000; Lee, 2001).
4. *Emergency exceptions consent:* This is similar to implied consent and is used in cases requiring life-saving interventions when a patient is unable to provide consent and the family is not present to ask. In this case a physician will sign a consent form verifying that the procedure was necessary to save a life (Lee, 2001).

Minors

The age of consent in terms of receiving emergency care varies from state to state. When evaluating an ED case, the LNC must research the age of consent in the state where the case took place. The age of majority in all but two states is 18; in Alabama and Nebraska it is 19 (Lee, 2001). The conditions under which a minor can consent vary widely from state to state. For example, in the State of Delaware, the age of majority is 18, and the conditions of a minor's ability to consent include being at least 18 years of age, if the minor less than 18 but is married, or is a minor unmarried parent (in which case the minor can consent for their child's treatment but may require a guardian or parent to provide consent for the minor's treatment).

However, under Delaware law as of 1995, a minor aged 12 can consent to receive treatment for pregnancy, sexual assault examination, and communicable disease, or in cases of "life or health threatening trauma after reasonable attempts to contact a parent are unsuccessful" (Lee, 2001, p. 44). In some circumstances, such as runaways, or homelessness, some state laws allow a minors under the age of 18 to consent for emergency treatment when parental consent is not available (Lee, 2001). Tsai et al. (1993) provide a thorough review and algorithms for the treatment of minors and describe three categories ranging from no express consent necessary to consent required for parental caregivers, in their reference on the evaluation and treatment of minors.

Leaving without Treatment and against Medical Advice

One way that patients refuse consent for treatment is by leaving the ED without completing treatment (LWT) or leaving without being seen (LWBS). Both acronyms may be found in the ED documentation when this happens. Patients may or may not alert the staff that they are leaving. A common reason a patient might LWBS is the long wait at triage. When assisting in the representation of a patient who left without treatment, the LNC should ask the patient why, as long waits may contribute to delays in treatment that result in a patient sustaining complications of their illness or injury. If the patient notifies the nurse that he or she is leaving, the prudent nurse attempts service recovery, reassesses the patient's condition, tries to convince the patient to remain and complete treatment, and seeks to expedite care whenever possible. When those efforts are unsuccessful and the patient insists on leaving, the doctor should still try to provide the patient with verbal and written discharge instructions, or request that they sign an "against medical advice" (AMA) form advising them of the risks of leaving and document this interaction clearly in the chart (Lee, 2001).

Leaving AMA, however, is not as simple as signing a form. The physician must first verify that the patient has the mental capacity to make this decision to leave. Examples of types of patients where capacity to decide may be an issue include those mentally challenged, under the influence of alcohol or drugs, and psychiatric patients. If the patient is unable to understand the risks and benefits of leaving versus staying to complete treatment, and leaving will seriously endanger the patient, every effort must be made to keep the patient in the ED, even if an order for restraints is needed. Detailed documentation is critical in these cases. An LNC evaluating a case in which a patient left AMA and sustained further complications will ask if all the risks, including death, were explained to the patient before they left. Was there clear and specific documentation of the risks and of the conversation with the patient? Was there a mental status exam performed and documented prior to the patient leaving? Is there documentation of the patient's behavior? All are important components that should be validated before the patient is allowed to leave, whenever possible.

Triage

The role of triage nurse is a high-risk function for the ED nurse, as the triage nurse is often the first to assess patients and must bear the burden of determining the extent of the patient's emergency. Triage has evolved in the United States over the last 40 years as healthcare delivery has changed. Once staffed by a nonnursing employee who served as merely a traffic director, EDs today that experience daily overcrowding should employ a comprehensive triage system. Comprehensive triage refers to an advanced system of triage in which the ED nurse ideally performs a rapid assessment and decision regarding treatment within two minutes of the patient's arrival. This system requires a skill set that ED nurses usually acquire after several years of experience, which is emergency nursing and is supported by the ENA Standards of Emergency Nursing Practice:

> The emergency nurse triages each patient and determines the priority of care based on physical, developmental and psychosocial needs as well as factors influencing access to health care and patient flow through the emergency care system. Triage is to be performed by an experienced nurse who had demonstrated competency in the triage role. The goal is to rapidly gather "sufficient" information to determine triage acuity. (ENA, 1999, p. 23)

Triage means "to sort," in that the triage nurse must be able to perform a rapid assessment, sometimes called a "thumbnail" assessment, of the presenting patient, assign an acuity level according to established triage criteria, and decide if the patient must be treated immediately or is safe to wait. ENA promotes a five-level triage system, called Emergency Severity Index (ESI) that assists the triage nurse to make decisions based on patient assessment data and an algorithm that takes the triage nurse through several decision points. Patients are assigned an acuity level from one to five, with five being the least urgent acuity category. Such data include vital signs, responsiveness, pain levels, associated comorbidities, age, and the number of resources the patient will need (Gilboy, Tanabe, Travers, Eitel, & Wuerz, 2003).

EDs across the United States experience overcrowding situations almost daily. Factors contributing to overcrowding and subsequent delays and backups at triage include the closing of EDs across the country, making access more difficult for patients, longer length of stay in the ED, an aging population, and inability to move admitted patients into beds within the hospital because of reduced numbers of available beds. Many EDs are now faced with caring not only for their ED population, as the ED doors never close, but must also maintain the standard of care for "ED boarders"—those admitted waiting for an available inpatient bed (Gilboy et al., 2003). Care of ED boarders places additional stress on the ED and its nursing staff, as inpatient standards of care must be maintained regardless of the patient's location within the hospital. Compounded with the nursing shortage, overcrowding can make triage a legal minefield of risk for patients, physicians, and nurses alike.

The LNC evaluating a case involving issues at triage must research what the conditions in the ED were at the time of the event. The LNC should question the experience and training of the triage nurse, identify how patients are tracked, identify staffing patterns that may contribute to sentinel events at triage, and determine what degree of treatment and subsequent monitoring of the patient occurred after treatment in the triage area. Did the treatment and reassessment of the patient in the triage area meet established department, hospital, and state and federal standards regardless of staffing patterns? "The triage process is delegated to nurses who must demonstrate extraordinary skills, while receiving little legal support for errors in clinical judgment" (O'Keefe,

2001, p. 390). The LNC who is evaluating a case involving potential errors at triage should investigate what ED and hospital-wide procedures are in place to manage patient flow and minimize legal risk in this volatile patient care area.

For example, the LNC can inquire about the existence of ED observation units or alternative treatment areas that can serve triage patients. Many hospital systems today utilize "express admission units" to relieve ED overcrowding. These are inpatient units separate from the ED environment that serve patients needing admission and further evaluation in the interim period until the appropriate type of inpatient bed is available for the patient. Another solution is the development of "clinical decision units" (CDU), which are generally 23 hr admission units. Patients must meet certain admission or exclusion diagnostic criteria to be admitted to a CDU and possibly bypass a long wait in the ED. According to one CDU Nurse Manager who has visited other units of this type nationally, three diagnoses frequently seen in a CDU include chest pain, syncope, and atrial fibrillation (Kara Streets, RN, MS, CEN, personal communication, 2008). Finally, the LNC can inquire as to the priority a hospital system places on decompressing an overcrowded ED so that patient flow at triage is improved, and what specific policies are in place to support those priorities.

Bouncebacks

Patients who have been recently discharged from the ED only to return and receive a different diagnosis from that on the first admission are referred to as "bouncebacks." Weinstock et al. (2006) have compiled 30 cases of patients who bounced back to the ED after originally being discharged. Many of the patients presented with very common complaints such as chest pain, abdominal pain, fever, back pain, and headache. Some of these patients had seen their primary care doctor before going to the ED in the first place. Once they returned, their dispositions varied from being discharged once again, to arresting shortly after readmission. The authors outline each case, providing detailed information about history and physical, diagnostics ordered, documentation, consults, and they provide an evaluation of the case based on thoroughness of patient evaluation, documentation, risk of serious illness being missed, and a risk management legal rating. In the interest of patient safety, a discussion about the diagnosis, including key issues in the case and teaching points, follows each case presentation. This text is a valuable resource for LNCs evaluating ED cases involving patients who bounced back as it also includes a section written by defense attorneys titled "So You Want to Be Sued for Malpractice—Top 10 Ways to Maximize Your Risk" (Weinstock et al., 2006). Triage nurses should be mindful of bounceback patients and err on the side of safety by assigning a higher acuity level than the one assigned on the original visit, since the patient who returns may be more seriously ill the second time they present.

Do Not Resuscitate

Do not resuscitate or DNR orders are a written, legal reflection of the patient's wish to withdraw or refuse consent in the event of a cardiopulmonary arrest. The attending physician can write a DNR order in the event that a patient is unconscious or incompetent, and will usually make every attempt to discuss and verify the patient's wishes with the next of kin.

An example of a situation in which orders to discontinue resuscitation efforts may occur without family consent includes the implementation of standing orders utilized by paramedics and supported by the ED medical control physician. In out-of-hospital situations, paramedics may discontinue life-saving efforts, or pronounce a patient dead in the field, if the patient has signs or injuries that are incompatible with life. Extensive levidity or severe traumatic injury in a pulseless, apneic patient is one example. Typically the paramedics would call the hospital, provide a detailed report of the deceased patient's status, what actions were taken to that point, and the medical control physician would concur and order any resuscitation efforts stopped, or approve pronouncing the patient dead. Family may or may not be present in these circumstances.

Caring for the patient with DNR orders in the ED can sometimes place the ED professional in a precarious legal position and may be situation or patient specific. For instance, a patient who arrives via paramedics may have DNR orders, yet paramedics and ED physicians and nurses may be forced to implement advanced life-saving interventions if documentation of the DNR status is not available or does not accompany the patient to the hospital (Lee, 2001). The patient may make last-minute requests just before losing consciousness regarding withholding life-saving interventions, without benefit of a witness (O'Keefe, 2001). If the ED staff resuscitates this patient, evidence may support a lawsuit.

Another example is the hospice patient who is facing imminent death, and the family panics, despite hospice staff instructions not to call 911 and have the patient transported to the hospital. Family members may not be able to cope with the clinical characteristics of end of life, or may change their mind and change the DNR order as the patient is dying. Resuscitation of a DNR patient can incur liability, just as failure to resuscitate can result in liability. These situations present ethical dilemmas for the ED staff. Therefore, the key for ED personnel to best avoid liability with respect to the patient with DNR orders is to perform a rapid assessment of the situation, decide the best approach, and act according to known state statutes and standards of care and ED/hospital policy (Lee, 2001).

Selected High-Risk Chief Complaints

Many patients treated in the ED report complaints that are considered high in terms of both medical and legal risk. When discussing how ED physicians think, Glatter et al. (2008) describe a phenomenon referred to as the "signal-to-noise ratio" in the ED. They state that ED physicians must learn to recognize patterns in their cognition and impediments to sound reasoning amid the chaotic environment of the ED, where decisions must be made rapidly and in a context of sparse or ambiguous data. For example, a "low" signal-to-noise ratio exists when the diagnosis and treatment path is fairly straightforward, such as with a wrist fracture or laceration. Complaints that generate a "high" signal-to-noise ratio are those that offer atypical or vague presentation of symptoms and may not always present with classic features ... "may be missing in the 'noise', resulting in a low signal" (Glatter et al., 1998, p. 4). The following are examples of complaints that may have a high signal-to-noise ratio and therefore raise the stakes in terms of legal risk. A more comprehensive list of high-risk chief complaints appears in Appendix A.

Chest Pain

Chest pain is one of the most common chief complaints of patients seeking emergency care. Patients entering the ED with a complaint of chest pain must be taken seriously and assigned a high acuity level (ESI 2), until a serious condition is ruled out and the acuity level can be downgraded (Gilboy et al., 2003). Chest pain can be a manifestation of a nonserious condition, such as costochondritis, or it may be a manifestation of a life-threatening condition. Life-threatening conditions in the differential diagnosis of chest pain, which prompts the patient to seek emergency care, include acute myocardial infarction, unstable angina, pulmonary embolus, dissecting aortic aneurysm, pneumothorax, and esophageal pathology (Newberry & Criddle, 2005).

The LNC evaluating a case involving the patient with chest pain who suffered an adverse outcome should consider several questions. Was an electrocardiogram (EKG) performed? An EKG is a quick, simple, noninvasive test to perform and should be completed promptly for a patient complaining of chest pain. Absence of an EKG would be critical (Quinn, 2005). What was the door to EKG time, and the interval from time of arrival to treatment time (when a physician performs an evaluation)? Were there any delays in treatment? What is the ED standard with regard to assessment and treatment of chest pain? Many EDs have established treatment pathways for a number of complaints, including chest pain—was a pathway implemented? Other considerations to investigate within the ED record are specific diagnostics, such as chest x-ray, or cardiac markers, whether a complete history was performed, including documentation of associated symptoms, such as dizziness, shortness of breath, radiation and quality of the pain, diaphoresis, nausea and vomiting, and risk factors. Was there a consult placed to cardiology, and what treatment did the ED initiate such as oxygen, aspirin, nitrate therapy, and β-blockers when appropriate (Quinn, 2005)? Is there a cardiac catheterization laboratory on-site with a team on call, and if so, what was the response time? How is the team mobilized? If there is no cardiac catheterization laboratory on-site, what was done to stabilize the patient and what procedures and services, such as a transport team, are in place to transport the patient to a hospital that can provide definitive cardiac care?

Abdominal Pain

Abdominal pain is another frequent complaint of patients who are presented to the ED for care. Patients with abdominal pain may be experiencing a minor illness, such as cramps associated with a viral syndrome, or may be experiencing a life-threatening event. Potential life-threatening events associated with abdominal pain include dissecting or ruptured AAA, appendicitis, ruptured ectopic pregnancy, ruptured peptic ulcer, or other source of gastrointestinal bleeding, abdominal injury due to trauma, such as ruptured spleen, intestinal obstruction, perforated bowel, and mesenteric ischemia (should be considered especially in the elderly) (Newberry, 2005; Quinn, 2005). The LNC should examine the ED record to determine if a complete examination was performed, including "guiac of stool for occult blood, auscultation of the abdomen for bruits, and evaluation of the iliac/femoral pulses to rule out aortic aneurysm?"(Quinn, 2005, p. 60). The examination should also include a thorough history inclusive of data related to changes in bowel habits, weight loss, dietary habits, and past menstrual history. For women experiencing abdominal pain who are of child-bearing age, ask if a pregnancy test was performed. What laboratory tests and diagnostics were ordered?—the LNC should look for imaging studies such as abdominal or pelvic ultrasounds, CT scan of the abdomen, and x-rays of the chest and abdomen (Quinn, 2005). In cases involving abdominal trauma, was focused assessment sonography in trauma (FAST) examination available, and performed? This rapid, inexpensive, bedside noninvasive study "is used primarily to detect the presence of hemoperitoneum in patients primarily with abdominal trauma" (ENA, 2007, p. 159). Finally, the LNC should determine if a surgical consult was necessary and whether one was requested, and if the patient was discharged, did the patient receive detailed appropriate discharge instructions including instructions to return if the pain persisted or came back.

Pediatric Fever

Parents arriving to the ED, carrying a febrile child is a frequent occurrence. Causes of fever in children are many, the most common being viral illness or infection, but fever can be symptomatic of dehydration, poisoning, heat exposure, metabolic disorders, or connective tissue diseases (Newberry & Criddle, 2005). Life-threatening conditions manifesting in fever, among other signs and symptoms, include bacterial meningitis and epiglottitis.

A complete examination of any infant or child with a fever is required and should include a mental status assessment, documentation of history of lethargy, oral intake, the presence of any suspicious rashes, headache, and evaluation for the presence of rigidity of the neck and spine, which would signal meningeal signs. ED staff assessing possible epiglottitis would expect parents to report sudden onset of symptoms, excessive drooling, fever, pallor, stridorous respirations, and the child's need to sit in such a position as to maximize air exchange, since a hallmark of epiglottitis is narrowing of the trachea due to swelling and inflammation. Epiglottitis is usually seen in children ages 2–5 years old who have not received the *Haemophilus influenzae* type B vaccination. Epiglottis may require emergency intubation under controlled circumstances such as in the operation room (Newberry & Criddle, 2005).

The LNC investigating a suspected case of missed meningitis should determine what laboratory tests were ordered, such as a complete blood count (CBC). Was a chest x-ray performed? Was the cause of the fever determined and were all potential sources of fever identified and the appropriate tests ordered? Were IV fluids and antibiotics started prophylactically or were antibiotic administration delayed until a diagnosis was made? Did the ED physician have sufficient education, training, and experience to treat a seriously ill infant or child? A fever of unknown origin in an infant under 3 months old demands a septic workup, which includes blood and urine cultures, and a lumbar puncture to evaluate cerebrospinal fluid for the presence of infection (Newberry & Criddle, 2005).

The Impaired Patient and the "Frequent Flier"

Patients often arrive in the ED in a state of altered consciousness due to illness, alcohol intoxication, or impairment as a result of substance abuse. Sometimes patients are well known to the ED staff and may be referred to as "frequent fliers"—those who visit the ED frequently, or may "hop" from one ED to another. They may exhibit drug-seeking behavior and complain of an ailment often associated with pain for which they wish to be treated (medicated with narcotics). Frequent flier patients may visit the ED as a result of other psychosocial circumstances. It is extremely important that ED staff address these patients with the same level of care as any other patient making the same complaint.

Assessments and reassessments of impaired patients, particularly, must be documented frequently, especially when their ability to verbally communicate is compromised. The ED physician or nurse who performs a cursory examination and leaves the impaired patient to "sleep it off" is inviting legal risk. Standards of care should not be violated or abbreviated because a patient is viewed as a bother, or is viewed as a disenfranchised member of society. For instance, the alcoholic who is "found down" may have sustained a head injury resulting in subdural hematoma, or a spinal injury and may not present with textbook symptomatology. Thus, frequent assessments may identify missed injuries or conditions in the unresponsive or semiconscious patient.

Carriere and Ellsworth (1998) discusses the case of a 58-year-old patient who was "found down" as a result of an overdose. The patient had an altered level of consciousness and had lain on the floor of her home for an unspecified amount of time before being found and transported to the ED. Her diagnoses included renal failure and rhabdomyolysis, but she persisted in complaining about leg pain, although there was no history or evidence of trauma. Only through listening to the patient and performing frequent assessments was the diagnosis of compartment syndrome also made and the patient required a fasciotomy. Carriere (1998) points out "the key teaching point in this case is the importance of reassessing patients in the emergency department ... in this case, reassessment of a patient with an altered level of consciousness led to the identification of compartment syndrome, rhabdomyolysis, and renal failure" (p. 217).

Likewise, the "frequent flier" who is arriving by ambulance for the fourth time in a month complaining of chest pain might be having an acute myocardial infarction that fourth time. In their book *Bouncebacks*, Weinstock et al. (2006) include a section titled "So You Want to Be Sued for Malpractice—The Top 10 Ways to Maximize Your Risk." In this section, the authors describe 10 ways that ED physicians can place themselves at legal risk. One way to maximize risk facetiously states "Assume that frequent fliers are not acutely ill" (p. 456). The advice given sums up the legal threat that may accompany shoddy care of the frequent flier patient:

> Here's a great tip. Keep a list of your frequent fliers and when they come in, pass them through a quick exam and GET THEM OUT! That way you can bill for your services and move on to a real patient. As a bonus, a malpractice suit may follow! And if that happens, your frequent flier list can be used to prove that the patient got the care he deserved!" (Weinstock, et al., 2006, p. 456)

The LNC should investigate whether the examination was thorough, were nursing assessments documented with the same frequency as they would be with any other patient with the same complaint, was the workup appropriate to the complaint, and did it meet established standards of care? Ask if a frequent flier list exists and make and request to recover it, as it may be discoverable.

The Adult Psychiatric Patient

Behavioral or psychiatric emergencies account for about 6% of all ED visits in the United States annually. Behavioral problems can range from the suicidal patient, acute psychosis, manic episodes, major depressive episodes, and substance abuse. Many behavioral emergencies involve a dual diagnosis of psychiatric disorder and substance abuse, and patients can also present with coexisting psychiatric and medical disorders (Lukens et al., 2006). ACEP has published a clinical policy regarding the treatment of psychiatric patients in the ED. ED physicians are frequently called upon to make the first assessment of a psychiatric emergency, since these patients may not be admitted to a psychiatric facility until "medical clearance" has been confirmed and documented. This means that the patient must be shown, through examination and diagnostics, to be free of an EMC that may manifest as psychiatric symptoms, before admission to a psychiatric facility can occur. In addition, for the psychiatric patient who is under the influence of alcohol or drugs, the ED physician must establish that the patient's cognitive abilities are not impaired so as to prevent a psychiatric evaluation. In order to accomplish this, ACEP has made recommendations about decision points in the treatment of a psychiatric patient, such as when a urine drug screen, alcohol level, or medical workup is warranted. In terms of the alcohol level, that the level alone should not be enough to prevent recommended admission if the patient is able to walk independently and communicate effectively, and is otherwise medically stable (Lukens et al., 2006).

Suicidal patients can heighten risk not only to themselves, but to ED staff as well, and their presence can increase legal risk to the ED staff. Suicidal patients are unpredictable, and it is imperative that departmental policies address their civil rights while protecting their safety, that of other patients, and the safety of the ED staff. The LNC evaluating a case of a patient who attempts or succeeds in committing suicide while in the ED must determine what safety mechanisms were in place to prevent the act. Questions to consider include the following: based on the patient's presentation and evaluation, were suicide precautions ordered, instituted, and what specific components are included in suicide precautions? Does the institution have a patient safety checklist and was it completed? Did suicide precautions include 1:1 observation and how frequently were checks of the patient made and documented? Where was the patient's location in the department—was the patient visible to staff? Were all objects that could be potential instruments of death removed from the suicidal patient's room? Was the patient fully undressed and belongings secured by nursing, or hospital security? Was the patient restrained, and were restraint orders written, and executed in compliance with hospital policy? Were the patient's behavior and affect documented, and were patient statements documented in quotations? Was a psychiatric consult ordered, and what was the time from the order until an evaluation took place? These questions are important considerations in the determination of liability when an adverse event befalls the suicidal patient in the ED. Additionally, staff who were harmed when caring for a psychiatric patient may hold the hospital liable if mechanisms and policies are not in place for the protection of ED staff.

Reviewing ED Records

Throughout this chapter, the author has referred to important parts of the ED record that the LNC should review. An ED registration clerk who records demographic, insurance, and billing data generates ED records. The first piece of information that should be collected, however, before any insurance and billing data are obtained is found at the triage desk and should include the chief complaint, the rapid assessment, and the assignment of an acuity level by an ED nurse. At this point, an ED triage nurse makes a decision whether the patient should be taken directly to treatment or can wait.

The ED record should also contain a nursing assessment form, including chief complaint, physical assessment, past medical history, medications taken at home, and allergies. Other pertinent data would include the date of the patient's last tetanus vaccine, a domestic violence screening, and last menstrual period in the case of female patients, treatment rendered prior to arrival, and the documentation related to the initiation of any ED treatment protocols or standing orders. ED nurses who follow a consistent assessment format such as the "OPQRST" approach of evaluating the patient's chief complaint and signs and symptoms are less likely to miss serious problems in the initial physical assessment (Gorembei et al., 2006). OPQRST is a mnemonic used by nurses and physicians; the letters represent prompts for healthcare practitioners to ask questions about the history and presentation of the current symptoms as follows: "O" equals onset, "P" equals provocation, "Q" equals quality, "R" equals radiation, "S" equals severity, and "T" equals time. Similarly, ED nurses who are certified as TNCC providers should employ the "A-I" approach to assessing trauma patients, so as not to miss potential serious injury. "A-I" encompasses both the primary and secondary surveys, incorporating assessments from the airway to inspecting the patient's back, and is a consistent established method of trauma assessment (ENA, 2007).

The ED physician's chart forms include the physician's documentation of the history of present illness; a systems review of examination findings; the doctor's order sheet containing orders for diagnostic tests, medications, and treatments; and the physician's documentation of procedures he or she performed, such as the application of a cast or the placement of a chest tube. Both nursing and physician documentation should also include the patient's response to interventions (Quinn, 2005). Other important pieces of information gleaned from the ED record are patient demographics, billing information such as next of kin, insured, and responsible party, a signed consent to treat, mode of arrival, the presence of family members (potential future witnesses), time of arrival, time of treatment (when first seen by a nurse or doctor), time of discharge, medications given, laboratory reports, imaging reports, EKG findings, preliminary diagnosis and treatment plan, discharge instructions, and admission transfer forms (Quinn, 2005).

Questions for the LNC to consider when reviewing the ED record include the following: who was the first person to see the patient, was it an ED nurse, and did that person record the patient's chief complaint? Did the triage nurse document the complaint in the patient's own words (subjective assessment)? Are there any words in the patient complaint that lend a pejorative impression of the patient's truthfulness—words such as "patient alleges or patient claims." What was the interval between the event and the patient's arrival to the ED, and if there was a delay, what was the reason for the delay? Are there any patient language barriers—if so, what procedures are in place to obtain interpreters for the patient? Was the patient ambulatory on arrival or did the patient use any assistive devices, such as a cane or walker? Was spinal immobilization of the patient necessary in the field, indicating the possibility of more severe injury? These and other questions relevant to the contents of the ED record appropriate to the LNC's inquiry are outlined in Quinn (2005).

Selected Concerns in ED Documentation

When evaluating ED records, the LNC may see documentation that appears different in format and content from other hospital record documentation. For instance, during a trauma resuscitation case, the chart may reflect a nurse recorder whose single role in the patient's care was to document rapid interventions and assessments as they occurred, in order to provide a complete, chronological, and real-time record of the trauma team's care (ENA, 2000).

ED documentation should reflect that prior medical records for the patient were ordered, if the patient had previously been admitted to that hospital. All communications should be documented and available, including nurse to physician communication, calls made to consultants, administrators, and supervisors, and any calls reflecting the nurse's efforts to follow the chain of command for the benefit of the patient. Some forms of communication may be found in the ED record, others in a clerical log, and still others, such as unusual events or occurrences, may be found in incident reports.

All forms and consents for procedures performed in the ED should be included in the ED record. In addition, documentation of the care of critically ill ED patients, admitted or not, should demonstrate evidence of intensive nursing care in the form of frequency of vital signs and assessments. Finally, if a serious problem is discovered during the patient assessment and interventions to correct the problem are implemented, the resolution of the problem and the patient's response should also be documented (ENA, 2000). For example, if the physician identifies respiratory distress and emergently intubates the patient, the patient's response to intubation, such as the presence of bilateral breath sounds, pulse oximetry, end-title carbon dioxide reading, and rise and fall of the chest, should be documented.

Evaluating Physician Office-Based Cases

Physician office-based care is not limited to primary care physicians. Indeed, it encompasses care from specialists in many areas such as urology, endocrinology, gynecology, obstetrics, gastroenterologists, and podiatrists, among others. As more and more patient visits are conducted in physician offices, the number of claims against office-based physicians continues to rise. In 2005, annual physician office visits reached 964 million in the United States, according to the National Center for Health Statistics. Claims analysis data (Schafer, 2000) suggest that diagnosis-related claims (wrong diagnosis, failure to diagnose, and delay in diagnosis), especially those involving cancer, are a major source of loss via insurance payout for physician practices. In addition, claims involving medication errors, administrative issues such as telephone protocols, communication and tracking issues, credentialing, and office-based procedures (surgery and anesthesia) are prevalent. LNCs who find themselves involved in office-based litigation can expect to see any or all of these types of allegations against office-based physicians and their practices. Each of these areas is discussed below.

Physician Office Standards of Care

Physician office standards of care arise from a variety of sources. Clinical standards and guidelines are issued by the American Medical Association (AMA), as well as the professional organizations for specialty care such as American Academy of Family Physicians, which issues family practice standards and guidelines, the American Academy of Pediatrics, the American Board of Internal Medicine, and the American College of Cardiology, to name just a few.

In addition to clinical guidelines and standards, however, office-based practice management guidelines are also relevant and are issued by select professional groups. Perhaps most well known is the Medical Group Management Association (MGMA), founded in 1926. With over 21,000 members affiliated with nearly 270,000 physicians, the MGMA's mission is to continually improve the performance of medical group practice professionals. MGMA has a variety of tools available for practice management assessment including surveys and benchmark tools, and resources for billing and collections, coding, electronic health records, integrated delivery systems, risk management, operations, and patient safety, among others. Many of their tools are available to the public. MGMA is affiliated with the American College of Medical Practice Executives and the MGMA Center for Research. Certification is available for group practice executives (Certified Medical Practice Executive). MGMA, in conjunction with the Health Research and Educational Trust and the Institute for Safe Medication Practices, has developed a multipart Physician Practice Patient Safety Assessment, which can be used to appraise safety and quality processes in physician practice settings. This tool is particularly helpful when analyzing physician office claims, from either the plaintiff or defense perspective.

Another source for practice management standards is the Accreditation Association for Ambulatory Care (AAAC). AAAC issues a handbook for accreditation that contains a wealth of standard and scope of practice information. Core standards include rights of patients, governance, administration, quality of care provided, quality management and improvement, clinical records and health information, and facilities and environment. In addition to the core standards, ambulatory care centers must meet adjunct standards depending upon their type of facility. For instance, there are adjunct standards for office-based surgery, multispecialty group practice, and hospital-sponsored ambulatory healthcare programs. Other sources of standards and ambulatory care resources are listed in Appendix B.

LNCs may need to access both clinical and office-based practice management standards, depending upon the type of alleged negligence. For example, a failure to diagnose cervical cancer claim could be traced both to substandard care—cervical dysplasia which required a 6-month follow-up but was not performed for over 2 years—as well as office practice management issues—the laboratory result was misfiled in another patient's record.

Major Areas of Risk

Diagnosis-Related Claims

Diagnosis-related claims represent approximately 40% of all office-based claims with 44% of all claims involving failure to diagnose, or a delay in the diagnosis of cancer. The most frequently cited cancer claim is breast cancer, followed by colon cancer (National Center for Healthcare Statistics). Other claims include delays in ordering appropriate diagnostic tests, narrow diagnostic focus, and lack of follow-up.

Case Examples

Example 18.1: Diagnostic Delay

A 39-year-old woman suffered a 10-month delay in the treatment of her breast cancer after doctors failed to accurately diagnose the condition when she presented with a lump in her breast. The patient presented to her gynecologist with a lump in her breast and family history of cancer. The doctor palpated the lump, but the mammogram and ultrasound did not indicate a tumor. The patient was eventually sent to a surgeon for biopsy 10 months later which confirmed the presence of a cancerous tumor that had metastasized, requiring bilateral mastectomies, chemotherapy, radiation, and removal of both ovaries. The treatment resulted in cardiac damage, and due to the 10-month delay in diagnosis, a 50% chance of cancer recurrence. The jury returned an 825,000 dollar award for the Plaintiff (*Storm v. Pike*, 2003).

Example 18.2: Misdiagnosis

A 49-year-old woman suffered worsening of her rectal cancer after a doctor misdiagnosed rectal cancer as internal hemorrhoids. The patient presented to the gastroenterologist complaining of rectal bleeding and the doctor diagnosed hemorrhoids based upon a digital rectal examination, an endoscopy, and an anoscopy. Two years later, the patient presented to an emergency room with profuse rectal bleeding. The same doctor examined her and again diagnosed hemorrhoids, concluding that the condition was aggravated by medications she was taking. The doctor prescribed suppositories. A year later, the patient visited a colorectal surgeon who diagnosed a rectal lesion. After biopsy, stage III rectal carcinoma was diagnosed, requiring extensive surgery, radiation, chemotherapy, and a permanent colostomy. The jury found the initial gastroenterologist, who had treated her in the office and in the emergency room, liable and awarded the patient 1,750,000 dollars (*Knight v. Reed*, 2005).

Example 18.3: Lack of Follow-Up/Diagnostic Delay

A 31-year-old male suffered a 5-month delay in the diagnosis and treatment of testicular cancer due to the failure of the doctor to communicate the results of an abnormal ultrasound to him. The patient reported testicular pain to his family physician, who referred the patient to the urologist. An ultrasound was ordered and performed at a local hospital. The hospital mailed the results of the ultrasound to both the urologist and family practice physician, neither of whom contacted the patient. The patient returned to the urologist 5 months later with severe pain and a palpable testicular lump, which proved to be cancerous. Extensive surgery with removal of lymph nodes and chemotherapy were required, which caused additional complications. The patient sued the hospital, the urologist, and the family practice physician, claiming that the 5-month delay resulted in the need for aggressive therapy and high risk for cancer recurrence. The jury found the hospital 20% responsible and the urologist 80% responsible. The jury awarded the patient 375,000 dollars in damages (*Berzonski v. Defendants*, 2004).

As these examples indicate, diagnostic error can contribute significantly to office-based malpractice litigation and delays in ordering appropriate tests can lead to aggravated injury, illness, and death. LNCs working on physician office-based cases need to research standards and guidelines related to the diagnosis and treatment of many different office-based medical conditions. Additionally, compensation may be warranted for the loss of a reasonable chance of recovery due to the delayed diagnosis.

Improper Medication Management

Another type of claim associated with physician practices is improper medication management. Often, this type of claim may arise from failure to prescribe and treat, prescribing the wrong medication, or the wrong dose, failure to educate and warn the patient of medication side effects, and/ or failure to assess drug therapy efficacy.

Example 18.4: Duty to Warn/Improper Medication Management

A 43-year-old male suffered permanent sexual impotence as a result of a side effect of an antidepressant, Desyrel, prescribed for him by his treating physician. The patient woke with a painful erection after taking the medication for 10 days. The advisory letter provided by the drug store included information that a painful erection was an unlikely side effect, but did not advise prompt medical attention. Neither the prescribing physician nor the pharmacist warned the patient about this serious side effect and after 24 hr, the patient presented to the emergency room, facing a urologic emergency that required immediate surgery to insert a shunt. The patient was left with permanent sexual impotency. The case settled for 1,025,000 dollars, with partial negligence assigned to the physician and the pharmacy for failure to warn (*McDonald v. Thrift Drug, Inc.*, 2000).

Additional medication risk areas include failure to identify patients' medications (with subsequent dangerous drug interactions), failure to communicate drug therapies to other treating physicians, and failure to monitor therapeutic levels for medications such as Digoxin, Synthroid, Insulin, and others. Physicians in office-based practices must also monitor and control the use of drug samples, and maintain standardized procedures for verbal orders and prescriptions.

Administrative Issues

Administrative risks are associated with office staff and operations generally involving telephone triage and advisement, communication and tracking issues, and credentialing issues. These risks are sometimes referred to as "indirect risks," because in and of themselves they rarely cause patient harm. However, when administrative procedures are ineffective, they can contribute to patient injury, or they can trigger a claim when the medical outcome is undesirable.

Telephone Triage

Telephone advice and telephone triage present a challenge for physician practices. A common malpractice risk situation exists when non-clinical personnel assess medical conditions or provide medical advice to patients over the phone. Job-specific duties for clinical and nonclinical personnel should be clearly delineated. Office-based nurses should use guidelines developed for telephone triage of patients available from the American Academy of Ambulatory Care Nursing (AAACN), or the Tele-health Nursing Practice Administration and Practice Standards (AAACN, 2007). Office-based practices should develop telephone triage protocols taking the following into account.

- Clinical input in all telephone advice policies and procedures is essential
- Policies and procedures are compliant with professional practice laws
- Adequate and appropriate staff training is provided regarding the telephone triage protocols

In addition to clarifying who can give advice over the telephone, practices should consider using advice protocols.

Example 18.5: Telephone Advice in an Office-Based Practice

The mother of a new baby called the physician office 2 days after birth to report that the baby was not eating well. The medical assistant advised the mother to try formula instead of breast milk. The next day the mother called again stating that the baby still was not eating and had diarrhea. The medical assistant advised her to continue formula for another day. By the third day, the baby was listless with a fever. After a third call to the office, the baby was rushed to the hospital, where he was found to be very ill. He suffered permanent brain damage and paraplegia. During litigation, it was found that the telephone calls had not been documented. The medical assistant remembered only one call. Advice protocols may have prevented the above illustrated patient injury.

Communication and Tracking Issues

Communication and tracking issues are just as important as good clinical care in physician offices. Patient well-being hinges on multiple systems that have been developed to ensure timely documentation of diagnostic findings, tests, referrals, and other important health-related information. Communication and tracking risks include the following:

- Problems communicating lab results (incorrectly filed, physician not informed of results, or patients not informed of results) contributing to delayed or missed diagnoses
- Failure to follow up on missed appointments resulting in treatment delay
- Failure to follow up on recommended treatment or therapies (no system to track referrals to specialists or other providers)
- Failure to communicate with other healthcare providers regarding medications, treatment, and other issues

Credentialing

Liability for improper credentialing and privileging in physician offices has been established in most states. Most physician offices are required by state law to have a defined credentialing and recredentialing process. Other entities may require credentialing, too. For example, the Joint Commission accredits physician-hospital organizations, and office-based surgery practices. Primary source verification of physician licensure, education, training, experience, and current competence is expected.

Related to credentialing is the exclusion of providers from federally funded programs for a variety of reasons including program-related fraud and patient abuse, licensing board actions, and default on health education assistance loans. The Office of the Inspector General (OIG) maintains a list of excluded individuals and entities from federal healthcare payments. Excluded entities and individuals may not receive funds from any federal program including Medicare and Medicaid. The list is frequently updated and may be accessed at http://oig.hhs.gov/fraud/exclusions.html. Physician practices must cross-reference partners, covering physicians, and all employees with this database to ensure compliance with OIG regulations.

Office-Based Surgical Procedures

A substantial area of risk in physician office-based practices is surgeries. As noninvasive surgery for many conditions becomes technologically possible and increasingly more popular, more and more surgeries are being performed outside of hospital and surgical centers. In fact, according to the Joint Commission, the physician office is the fastest growing venue for delivery of surgery in the United States, performing 8.3 million surgical procedures in 41,000 physician offices in 2000 (Joint Commission, 2001), which included cosmetic surgery including liposuction, abdomino-plasty, breast augmentation, and reduction, pregnancy termination, colonoscopy, endoscopy, knee arthroscopy, and microlaparoscopy.

As a surgical setting, the physician offices are vastly different from hospital-based surgical suites or ambulatory surgical centers and tend to be wholly unregulated entities [National Center for Health Statistics (NCHS)]. In the early 1990s, several sensational reports of patients dying in physician offices were reported after procedures like liposuction, which prompted some regulatory and legislative [state] review of physician office-based surgery. California was the first state to enact regulatory controls over physician office-based surgery in 1996, followed by New Jersey (1998), and Florida (2000). The New York State Department of Health issued office-based surgical guidelines in 2001. Medical specialty groups for anesthesia, surgery, dermatology, and plastic surgery enacted or updated guidelines for office-based surgery. Because regulation of office-based surgeries is new and evolving, LNCs should research state regulatory authority on each claim. See Appendix C for standards and guidelines that may apply to physician office-based surgery.

Intraoperative and Postoperative Care

All operative procedures involve inherent risk, especially when combined with sedative or anesthetic agents. What is not known is whether procedures performed in physician office practices carry a greater injury risk than those same procedures performed in a hospital or ambulatory surgical center. However, claims data and review of anecdotal reports of experiences with physician office-based surgery does reveal specific areas of risk. For example, one report described a patient who was left alone in a physician office overnight to recover from a liposuction procedure. She awoke in pain and crawled outside to seek help where she lay on the sidewalk for hours before being found. She was transferred to a local hospital where she required 5 days to recover.

In another report, a patient spent the night in a physician office under the care of a private agency nurse. When the nurse realized that the patient's oxygen tank was empty and that the patient was in respiratory distress, she contacted the agency for guidance. The nurse called paramedics 30 min later, and the patient was pronounced dead on arrival at the hospital (LaMendola, 1998).

Generally, the lack of risk management structures typically found in hospitals and ambulatory surgical centers place patients at heightened risk. Many physician offices lack the ability to effectively respond to intraoperative or postoperative complications. With appropriate postoperative care, the patient injury and death in the above examples could have been avoided. Patients should never be left alone to recover in a physician office.

Anesthesia

Anesthesia presents a unique set of problems in the physician office-based surgical setting. In 2001, anesthesia-related claims revealed that claims arising from office-based anesthesia were of higher severity than claims arising from ambulatory surgical centers (Domino, 2001). The claims reviewers believed that better patient monitoring would have prevented most of the adverse incidents. All of the preventable office-based anesthesia claims were related to adverse respiratory events in the postoperative period including airway obstruction, bronchospasm, inadequate oxygenation, poor ventilation, and esophageal injury. One-half of the claims were related to care that the reviewers deemed substandard. Additionally, drug-related events such as wrong dose, wrong drug, and malignant hyperthermia and drug allergies were noted on the anesthesia claims.

Professional Guidelines and Standards for Office-Based Anesthesia

Several organizations have standards or guidelines for office-based anesthesia (American Association of Nurse Anesthetists, 2005; American Academy of Dermatology Association, 2005; American College of Surgeons, 2004; American Society of Anesthesiologists, 2004). Some of the components of these guidelines/standards are as follows:

- The operating surgeon is certified by the American Board of Plastic Surgery.
- The office-based surgical facility is accredited by a nationally or state-recognized accrediting agency, or is state licensed or Medicare certified. Nationally recognized accrediting agencies include the American Association for Accreditation of Ambulatory Surgery Facilities (AAAASF), the Joint Commission, and the Accreditation Association for Ambulatory Health Care (AAAHC).
- The surgeon has privileges at an accredited acute care hospital for the specific procedure being performed.
- Patients undergoing procedures that involve sedation are appropriately monitored by registered nursing personnel. If general anesthesia is used, it is administered by a board-certified anesthesiologist or certified registered nurse anesthetist.
- The emergency equipment and anesthesia monitoring devices in the surgical facilities are equivalent to those that would be necessary for the same surgical procedure performed in a hospital or freestanding ambulatory surgery center.
- Provisions are made for hospital admission in the event of unforeseen complications.
- There is a separate recovery area with monitoring equipment equivalent to that which would be necessary for the same procedure performed in a hospital or ambulatory surgery facility.
- Until the patient is fully recovered, a physician is at the site, in addition to a registered nurse.
- Discharge from the facility is always determined by the responsible surgeon.

Patient Selection and Consent

Candidates best suited to office-based surgery are those who are relatively healthy, without chronic or serious medical conditions. Some patients should never be candidates for office-based surgery.

Those with serious comorbid conditions, chronic health problems, or even psychiatric or personality disorders may be denied surgical intervention in the office setting. Elective cosmetic surgical candidates require careful screening to rule out unrealistic surgical or life expectations. Courts have held that physicians may have a duty to refer certain patients to mental health professionals, or to seek out mental health consultation before performing elective cosmetic surgery (*Lynn, G. v. Hugh,* 2000). Proper patient consent must be carefully evaluated when reviewing these claims.

Physicians have a duty to inform patients of the benefits and risks of any particular procedure and about alternatives to the procedure (including doing nothing) and their related benefits and risks. Patients acknowledge this information, and their opportunity to ask questions and receive information by signing a surgical consent form, just as in any hospital or ambulatory surgical center. Anesthesia consent should be provided separately. There is, perhaps, a heightened sense of well-being by the patient, when a procedure is performed in a physician office. Office-based procedures are perceived as "minor" in nature and so adverse events are all the more unexpected. Full disclosure via informed consent is absolutely necessary in this environment.

Reviewing Office-Based Surgical Procedure Claims

In analyzing claims arising from office-based surgical procedures, many areas must be considered:

- Physician credentialing. Did the physician who performed the procedure operate within the scope of practice and clinical privileges?
- Are there state or Federal laws that govern the operation of the physician office-based surgery?
- Is the physician office accredited? If so, did they meet all of the accrediting body's standards and guidelines?
- Was appropriate intraoperative and postoperative oversight, including both medical and nursing oversight, provided?
- Did all of the anesthesiologists, nurse anesthetists, and surgeons have Advanced Cardiac Life Support certification?
- Was informed consent given? Were there separate surgical and anesthesia consent forms? Was the patient informed of the risks and benefits of the procedures?

Claims can be cross-referenced to the appropriate standards and guidelines. LNCs are obligated to investigate diverse areas of regulatory oversight and clinical competence when analyzing office-based physician practice claims. The LNC should request complete medical records from physician practices including the history and physical, progress notes, medications, laboratory, radiology and EKG, insurance/correspondence, and consultation/hospitalizations. Billing records can also be requested.

Home Health Care

Introduction to Home Healthcare Risk Management

As our population continues to age, the use of home healthcare services continues to expand. Home healthcare services are delivered to patients recovering from illness or injury in hospitals or skilled nursing facilities, the disabled, the frail elderly, and the chronically ill or terminally ill patient in need of nursing, medical, or therapeutic treatment, as well as assistance with the activities of daily living.

Many home health agencies are Medicare certified, meaning they may bill Medicare for home care services provided to patients in their homes. There are, in fact, over 9,000 Medicare-certified home healthcare agencies throughout the United States. In 2006, over 3 million patients were served, and nearly 104 million visits were made (CMS, 2005). There are also many private duty home health agencies providing services to individuals who pay privately for their care.

Home health care is a covered Part A Medicare benefit, and it is also covered by some of the national insurance companies. It consists of part time, medically necessary, intermittent skilled visits. Skilled visits are those performed by nurses, and occupational, physical, or speech therapists. If patients are eligible for "skilled" visits, they may also be eligible for nonskilled services such as assistance from a home health aide for personal care needs. Patients must be considered "home-bound" (leaving the home is a major effort, patients are normally unable to leave the home unassisted, and patients normally leave for medical care, or for short, infrequent nonmedical reasons) in order to receive services, which are delivered in the patient's home. Medicare oversees certified home healthcare agencies via the Conditions of Participation (42 CFR 484), regulatory criteria that cover topics such as patient rights, personnel qualifications, release of identifiable Outcomes and Assessment Information Set (OASIS) information, compliance with laws and regulations, acceptance of patients, plans of care and medical supervision, reporting OASIS information, skilled services, clinical records, and comprehensive assessment of patients (CMS, 2006).

In 2000, the federal government began requiring that each Medicare-certified home health agency collect and submit quality data via the OASIS. These data are available on their website at http://www.cms.hhs.gov/OASIS/09a_hhareports.asp#TopOfPage. In 2005, a private, not for profit agency, the National Quality Forum (NQF) reviewed the data collected via the OASIS forms, and developed 10 measures that would be used for public reporting. Those measures are as follows:

- Improvement in ambulation/locomotion
- Improvement in bathing
- Improvement in transferring
- Improvement in management of oral medication
- Improvement in pain interfering with activity
- Acute care hospitalization
- Emergent care
- Discharge to community
- Improvement in dyspnea
- Improvement in urinary continence

These data help the Centers for Medicare and Medicaid implement quality initiatives and calculate Medicare payments for discrete episodes of care. The public can access these data to determine the quality of agencies, and the Federal government uses it to develop focused medical reviews of home care agencies.

While OASIS is the primary tool used for quality improvement in the home healthcare arena, there are many other regulations, standards, and guidelines that govern or offer guidance in the provision of care in the home setting listed in Appendix D. The National Association for Home Care and Hospice (NAHC) is the professional association organization, and publishes industry news, trends, and guidelines that are available to members. NAHC also provides a certification program for qualified home care administrators.

Home care agencies must comply with mandated statutes and regulations from entities such as the Safe Medical Device Act (SMDA), the Americans with Disabilities Act (ADA), and the

Occupational Safety and Health Administration (OSHA). Additionally, there are fraud and abuse statutes, physician referral regulations (Stark II), Operation Restore Trust, antitrust legislation, and price discrimination laws that govern home health care, discussed later.

Theories of Liability on Home Care

According to a 2003 study (Croke, 2003), there was a 2% rate of malpractice litigation in the home healthcare setting where nurses were defendants in civil lawsuits as a result of unintentional action. One can reasonably expect to see this percentage increase as more care is shifted to the home environment. General negligence and malpractice are the two most likely legal allegations arising from clinical care in the home setting. Clinical personnel in the home are required to assess, treat, and intervene appropriately without the oversight normally found in the acute care setting. Care management and communication with off-site providers are important. For example, a diabetic patient could allege negligence in the care of a diabetic ulcer that required eventual amputation if the treating nurse failed to appreciate signs of infection and failed to report the worsening condition to the treating physician.

Major Areas of Risk

In home health care, patient care and nursing interventions center on an autonomous patient. The nurse and all of the professionals involved in the patient care must communicate goals, interventions, and progress clearly and in a timely fashion. Legal liability is often based upon failure to follow standards of care, failure to document care, failure to monitor and communicate patient status, and failure to use equipment responsibly.

Failure to Follow Standards of Care

There are many organizations that have developed standards for the provision of home care services. Examples include the Center for Medicare and Medicaid Services (CMS), the Joint Commission, the AMA, the American Academy of Home Care Physicians, and the Home Health Nurses Association, to name a few (Appendix D). As in other practice settings, the home care practitioner (whether nurse, physical therapist, or other licensed provider) must comply with accepted professional clinical standards of care, and must act as other reasonable practitioners would act in a similar situation within their legal scope of practice.

Using the above diabetic wound example, a nurse would likely prevail in a lawsuit even if the wound deteriorated, if professional assessment and treatment standards were met. Was the wound assessed? Was wound deterioration and lack of progression reported promptly? Were recommendations made to change the wound care treatment when lack of progress was documented? Was the patient educated regarding wound infection? Was all care including education documented? It is possible to have a poor medical outcome even when practitioners follow all reasonable standards of care for several reasons including the uncontrolled environment, poor patient compliance with the treatment regimen, or because the patient's physiological systems are too compromised for treatment success.

Example 18.6: Uncontrolled Home Environment

A 35-year-old male was receiving cancer treatment in the home with chemotherapy being administered through a central venous catheter. The patient's cat chewed through the IV line and he was admitted to the hospital, where the central line was removed. He later developed a fever and blood cultures revealed infection with *Pasteurella multocida*, a common organism found in human bite wounds from cats and dogs (Majeed, Verghese, & Rivera, 1995).

This case illustrates that even with optimal care the uncontrolled home care environment can present insurmountable difficulties. Practitioners rendering care in the home must assess the home environment, document safety hazards, and educate the patient and family regarding safety issues in the home. Ideally, the home safety assessment is begun prior to admission, completed in the home during the initial home care visit, and continually monitored.

Failure to Document Care

Abiding by clinical standards of care can be shown through comprehensive documentation. Care providers in the home healthcare arena should thoroughly document their patient assessments, interventions and treatments, patient and family education, and communication with physicians and ancillary care providers. Unlike the acute care setting, where physicians and other nurses are available for immediate consultation, and medical charts are available for immediate review, home care providers rely almost exclusively on the quality of the medical record to plan and implement patient care activities.

The home care admission is an important event and an area of potential liability in home health care. Nurses must be careful to assess each admission for appropriateness for home care services. Upon admission, the agency incurs a legal duty to provide care safely for that patient, and must have adequate resources and technical expertise to provide care for each patient.

Home care agencies should have admission criteria and communicate these to all referral sources. Some important areas that should be addressed in an agency's admission criteria include area of service, adaptability of the home to the patient's needs, telephone availability, the presence of a responsible caregiver in the home, a demonstrated ability on the part of the patient and/or family members to follow instructions and perform procedures, and family availability to care for the patient in the home environment. Preserving the legal right to refuse admission to inappropriate patients, even when contracted under a managed care organization, is important (Aspen, 1995).

Once a patient is admitted to service, all home care practitioners have a duty to document care rendered. Care must be provided via a "plan of care" developed in consultation with the physician that covers all pertinent diagnoses, and other information including mental status, types of services and equipment required, frequency of visits, prognosis, rehabilitation potential, functional limitations, activities permitted, nutritional requirements, medications and treatments, safety measures to protect against injury, instructions for timely discharge or referral, and any other appropriate items (42 CFR 484.18, 2006).

Areas that can be problematic include documentation of a full and thorough admission assessment, all physician orders and all communication with the physician, interdisciplinary communication (a required element of the Home Health Care Conditions of Participation), and all patient and family education. Additionally, correct and complete OASIS documentation is a mandated requirement for Medicare-certified home health agencies (42 CFR 484.20, 2007).

Failure to Assess, Monitor, and Communicate Patient Status

In the home care arena, litigation can stem from the nurse's failure to communicate patient changes in status to the physician in a timely manner, resulting in missed diagnoses, or delayed diagnosis and treatment. Because physician involvement is interdependent with nurse communication, physicians can be insulated from allegations of negligence when the home care staff fails to communicate accurately and in a timely manner.

Wound care is a particular area of risk in home care. Agencies should have wound care admitting criteria and wound care policies that govern how wounds are assessed and treated. Because the frail elderly and chronically ill patients are even more susceptible to skin wounds and ulcers, it is important that agencies have clearly defined care parameters. Appropriate timely reporting of changes in wound size, signs, and symptoms of infection, necrotic tissue, or development of a new wound area is essential. Compliance with agency wound care policy and procedure can help defend against allegations of negligence and/or malpractice.

With other disease processes, nurses must communicate altered patient status such as changes in vital signs signaling infection, worsening cardiovascular or respiratory status, or other indications of patient deterioration. Nurses are responsible for interpreting these signs and symptoms, implementing or revising the nursing plan of care, and notifying the physician of all important changes in the patient status. While nurses can teach the patient and family to perform some basic care techniques such as dressing changes, the nurse may never delegate nursing assessment to patients, family members, or to unskilled caregivers.

Failure to Use Equipment in a Responsible Manner

As the acuity of home care patients becomes more severe, home treatments and procedures may require the use of ancillary equipment. Treating newborn jaundice with bilirubin lights, administering chemotherapy through central lines, and caring for ventilator-dependent patients all require a mastery of specific medical equipment. All nurses should undergo annual skills verification, as mandated by the Joint Commission and Medicare. Agencies have a legal duty to accept only those patients for whom the agency can safely provide care and must have a mechanism to document mastery of skills and techniques. This can be done through annual verification of skills testing, through a preceptor program where hands-on training is provided, or through direct supervision of staff when new equipment is being introduced. Occasionally, outside vendors will supply specialized equipment directly to the home and may also teach the patient how to manage the equipment. Vendor teaching does not absolve the home healthcare practitioner of the duty to use equipment in a responsible manner. The home healthcare nurse is still responsible for equipment safety and should contact the vendor if either the nurse or patient needs additional instruction regarding safe use.

Failure to Act as a Patient Advocate

Liability can be incurred through inappropriate discharge of a home healthcare patient, especially if the patient required further services and was not provided adequate notice or sufficient time to find another service provider. If reasonable notice was not given, the home healthcare company could be held liable for any damages arising from patient abandonment. Home healthcare agencies should have policies and procedures related to appropriate discharge of the home care patient. During the admission procedure, all patients should be educated regarding the policies and procedures for discontinuing services, and the circumstances under which this may occur, which may include the following:

- Patient is not homebound (a Medicare Condition of Participation requirement)
- Patient noncompliance with medical care

- Patient verbal or physical abusiveness
- Unsafe home environment (presence of illegal drugs, unsafe weapons, etc.)
- Nonpayment of agreed upon fees (Medicare patients must have been notified orally and in writing of the fees required before services were initiated)

Patient and caregiver personality conflict is not an adequate cause for termination of services. If the patient and care provider cannot resolve a personality conflict, another caregiver should be assigned to the case.

If a patient was terminated from services, the LNC can assess whether the following steps were taken:

- There was sufficient documentation of the problem in the medical records (noncompliance with physician treatment orders; unsafe home environment) and the steps taken to rectify the situation were documented.
- The physician was notified of the problem and kept informed of the need to discharge the patient.
- The patient was directed to another home healthcare provider if services were still needed.
- The patient was notified in writing of the termination of service in advance of the event. If the agency has a policy and procedure regarding termination of services, these should be reviewed to determine if the policy was followed. Agencies may not specify a time limit on advance termination of services as the need to terminate is case specific. For example, if an agency employee is in danger due to an unsafe home environment, such as weapons in the home, the need to terminate services is much more urgent compared with provider termination due to patient noncompliance.
- Reasonable steps were taken to ensure continuity of care.
- A copy of the patient's medical record was forwarded to the new agency.
- Careful admission screening and selection should minimize the risk of liability related to patient abandonment.

Corporate Liability

Corporate liability in the home healthcare arena is serious and covers a wide range of topics. LNCs working on home healthcare cases may find themselves researching antitrust issues, Stark Amendments, Operation Restore Trust guidelines, or even researching criminal statutes. Examples of corporate liability issues are presented here.

Fraud and Abuse

Fraud and abuse regulations prohibit offering or receiving any payment, including kickbacks, bribes, or rebates directly or indirectly in return for referring an individual to a person or entity where Medicare/Medicaid will pay for all or any part of the services supplied, and purchasing, leasing, or ordering any facility, service, or item where Medicare/Medicaid will pay for any part of said facility, service, or item.

Fraud and abuse is classified as a felony and punishable by fines of up to 25,000 dollars and imprisonment for up to 5 years. Civil sanctions include suspension from participating in Medicare/Medicaid programs. Other statutes make it a crime to submit false or fraudulent claims to a government agency; to conspire to defraud the United States Government; to make false statements; or to commit mail fraud related to submitting false statements for payment.

Example 18.7: False Claims

In 2005, the U.S. government sued Registered Nurse Lourdes Perez for violation of the False Claims Act. According to the government, Ms Perez, who operated two home healthcare agencies, billed Medicare for approximately 40 million dollars, most of which had been illegally embezzled by submitting hundreds of falsified documents. The government sought return of all illegally embezzled funds. The parties settled and nearly 34 million dollars was recovered. The Defendant Perez was expected to receive 46 months in prison for her role in the theft (*United States and state of California ex rel, Marietta Diaz v. Lourdes Perez*, No. CV 033074).

Physician Referral Regulations

"Stark" laws regulate physician self-referral to entities where they have a financial interest. In 1989 Congress passed "Stark I," a statute prohibiting a physician from referring Medicare patients to an entity for clinical laboratory services if the physician (or an immediate family member of the physician) had a financial relationship with that entity. In the Omnibus Reconciliation Act of 1993, Congress enacted "Stark II," which expanded the federal self-referral ban to include certain designated health services provided to Medicare patients. Stark II also extended the referral prohibition to the Medicaid program by denying federal financial participation for certain Medicaid services provided pursuant to a tainted referral. The designated health services identified in Stark II are as follows:

- ■ Clinical laboratory services
- ■ Physical therapy services
- ■ Occupational therapy services
- ■ Radiology services, including ultrasound, MRI, and CT scans
- ■ Radiation therapy services
- ■ Durable medical equipment
- ■ Parenteral and enteral nutrients, equipment, and supplies
- ■ Prosthetics, orthotics and prosthetic devices, and supplies
- ■ Home health care services
- ■ Outpatient prescription drugs
- ■ Inpatient and outpatient hospital services

To avoid potential fraud and abuse allegations, home healthcare agencies must guard against making any payment, or providing any special benefit to a referral source based upon volume of service. Remuneration in return for a referral is the link that triggers a criminal penalty. LNCs may be asked to analyze referral patterns to determine compliance with Stark regulations.

Abuse

All 50 states and the District of Columbia prohibit the abuse and neglect of the elderly in both private homes and in institutions. Most state laws mandate suspected abuse or neglect of dependent older persons be reported. Every state has enacted mandatory reporting of child neglect or abuse and healthcare providers have a legal duty to report suspected cases of child abuse or neglect.

Healthcare providers should be trained to recognize signs of child and elder abuse and neglect. If a wrongful death claim is brought against a home healthcare agency that is associated with neglect or abuse, individual practitioners could be liable for failing to report the abuse or neglect to the appropriate authorities.

In many states, it is a criminal offense for a paid healthcare provider to intentionally injure a patient. In Pennsylvania, for example, state law can hold direct caregivers, as well as owners, operators, and managers of home care facilities criminally liable for patient abuse.

LNC Role in Home Healthcare Litigation

Home healthcare liability can be very broad. In addition to general negligence and malpractice issues related to home healthcare staff, liability can stem from one of several Federal and state regulations related to corporate liability. LNCs who are familiar with the basic premise of this wide range of legal issues related to home healthcare services are likely to provide strong analysis of the home healthcare claim, whether working for the defense of the agency and its practitioners, or working for the plaintiff attorney on behalf of an injured patient.

Summary

As the length of stay in hospitals has become the domain of insurance companies and the cost of hospitalization rises, much patient care transpires in ambulatory care settings. As segments of care move into the outpatient or ambulatory care arena, so also does increased legal risk to healthcare practitioners in these settings. Ambulatory care settings encompass several practice areas, including physician offices, both primary care and specialists, home health care, and EDs (hospital based, freestanding, or urgent care centers).

Practice standards for physicians practicing in ambulatory care settings are derived from the AMA, as well as physician specialty organizations that establish mission statements, position statements related to specific treatment decision points, set minimum standards for Board certification, provide oversight of the specialty, provide current information regarding healthcare legislation, and benchmark-specific performance indicators. Examples of these organizations include but are not limited to the AAAC, MGMA, ACEP, and ENA.

Doctors and nurses practicing in specialties under the umbrella of ambulatory care face legal risks every day. Major areas of risk are those cases that result in misdiagnosis, delays in diagnosis or treatment, failure to follow up with the patient, failure to report diagnostic findings, communication issues, medication errors, and errors in treatment. Areas of legal vulnerability in ambulatory care can involve the lack of proper education, training and experience, and the failure to maintain competency in practice. These constitute important reasons for the LNC to thoroughly investigate the credentials of all parties named in a malpractice claim.

An emerging trend as more and more procedures are performed outside the traditional hospital operating room is the development of freestanding or office-based surgical centers. Any operative procedure incurs inherent risks. However, those functioning outside the auspices of hospitals must have definitive policies and procedures in place regarding patients receiving anesthesia, including protocols for the administration of anesthetic agents, consent and patient selection guidelines, the monitoring of the patient receiving anesthesia, provisions for transport and hospitalization of the patient who experiences adverse reactions to anesthesia, minimum standards for equipment, and staffing guidelines.

Home healthcare risk management issues stem primarily from the unintentional actions of nurses. As care shifts from the hospital to the home environment, home healthcare risks may rise. Major areas of risk in the home healthcare setting include failure to follow standards of care, failure to document care, failure to assess, monitor and communicate patient status, failure to use equipment in a responsible manner, failure to act as a patient advocate, corporate liability, fraud, and abuse. Abuse of the elder or vulnerable patient in the home care setting has come to the forefront in recent years. The LNC evaluating cases involving home healthcare liability should have a broad knowledge base and range of experience with patients in order to provide solid case analysis.

EDs are also ambulatory care facilities, as the majority of ED patients are discharged after treatment. A significant difference in the physician–patient relationship in the ED as opposed to that in the primary care physician office or home healthcare setting is that the ED physician generally has no prior relationship with his/her patients and may not have access to patient records. In a setting where treatment decisions are sometimes life and death and must be made rapidly, the risk of error and liability is high. ED nurses and doctors alike face high levels of risk in this chaotic, noisy, often crowded setting.

The types of allegations made against ED physicians, however, are similar to those made in other ambulatory care settings. Claims may be made regarding failure to perform an adequate examination, failure to consider differential diagnoses, failure to diagnose, failure to treat, failure to consult, failure to communicate, knowledge deficit, failure to order/interpret and report diagnostic results, and failure to admit. ED nurses are not exempt from liability and claims may be made regarding failure to report patient changes, failure to follow orders (nurses), failure to report physician negligence, and duty to question patient discharge.

Legal risk in the ED can come from other sources such as violations of privacy under HIPAA, dilemmas regarding the execution of DNR orders, errors in triage, and issues surrounding consent, just to name a few. The LNC evaluating ED cases must have keen investigative abilities, as the large numbers of patient situations in the ED that can result in legal action are broad.

Finally, the ED record is a rich forensic resource for the LNC, containing innumerable pieces of information that can facilitate a multitude of questions regarding a patient's ED stay. The LNC evaluating cases in ambulatory care settings has a daunting task due to the large number of resources that may require investigation. Experience, attention to detail, and an inquisitive nature are key to the LNC's success within this practice area.

References

42 CFR 484.18. (2006). *Condition of participation: Acceptance of patients, plan of care and medical supervision.* Available at http://edocket.access.gpo.gov/cfr_2004/octqtr/42cfr484.18.htm. Accessed on July 8, 2008.

42 CFR 484.20. (2007). *Condition of participation: Reporting OASIS information.* Available at http://edocket.access.gpo.gov/cfr_2004/octqtr/42cfr484.20.htm. Accessed on Jul 8, 2008.

American Academy of Ambulatory Care Nursing (AAACN). (2007). *Telehealth nursing practice administration and practice standards.* New Jersey: Pitman, NJ.

American Academy of Dermatology Association. (2005). *Guidelines of care for office surgical facilities.* Available at http://www.aad.org/pm/management/index.html. Accessed on September 16, 2008.

American Association of Nurse Anesthetists. (2005). *Standards for office-based anesthesia practice.* Available at http://www.aana.com/uploadedFiles/Resources/Practice_Documents/stds_officebasedanesth.pdf. Accessed on September 16, 2008.

American Board of Emergency Medicine (ABEM). (2000). *General information.* Accessed September 12, 2008, from http://www.abem.org

American College of Emergency Physicians (ACEP). (2007a). *Model of the clinical practice of emergency medicine [policy statement].* Accessed July 24, 2008, from http://www.acep.org/practres.aspx?id=29580.

American College of Emergency Physicians. (2007b). *Risk management outline and resources.* Accessed July 24, 2008, from http://www.acep.org

American College of Legal Medicine. (2007). *The Medical Malpractice Survival Handbook.* Philadelphia: Mosby Elsevier.

American College of Surgeons. (2004). [ST-46] *Statement on patient safety principles for office-based surgery utilizing moderate sedation/analgesia, deep sedation/analgesia, or general anesthesia.* Available at http://www.facs.org/fellows_info/statements/st-46.html . Accessed on September 16, 2008.

American Society of Anesthesiologists. (2004). *Guidelines for office based anesthesia.* Available at http://www.asahq.org/publicationsAndServices/sgstoc.htm. Accessed on Jul 1, 2008.

Aspen. (1995). *Preparing for capitation in home health care.* Gaithersburg, MD: Aspen Publishers, Inc.

Berzonski v. Defendants, Case No. 112 Civil (2004) (September 2005).

Carriere, S. R., & Elsworth, T. (1998). Found down: Compartment syndrome, rhabdomyolysis, and renal failure. *Journal of Emergency Nursing, 24*(3), 214–217.

Centers for Medicare and Medicaid Services (CMS). (2005). *Home health quality initiatives.* Available at http://www.cms.hhs.gov/HomeHealthQualityInits/. Accessed on Jul 3, 2008.

Centers for Medicaid and Medicare Services. (2006). *Special responsibilities of Medicare Hospitals in emergency cases.* 42 CFR CH. IV Section 489.24. Accessed September 10, 2008, from http://www.cms.hhs.gov/EMTALA

Cleland v. Bronson Health Care Group, Inc., C.A.6 (Mich.) (1990). F.2d 266.

Croke, I. (2003). Nurse, negligence and malpractice. *American Journal of Nursing, 103*(9), 54–64.

Dellinger, R. P., Levy, M. M., Carlet, J. M., Bion, J., Parker, M. M., Jaeschke, R., Reinhart, K., Angus, D. C., Brun-Buisson, C., Beale, R., Calandra, T., Dhainaut, J., Gerlach, H., Harvey, M., Marini, J., Marshall, J., Ranieri, M., Ramsay, G., Sevransky, J., Thompson, B. T., Townsend, S., Vender, J. S., Zimmerman, J. L., & Vincent, J. (2008). Surviving sepsis campaign: International guidelines for management of severe sepsis and septic shock: 2008. *Critical Care Medicine, 36*(1), 296–327. Accessed September 30, 2008, from http://www.medscape.com/viewarticle/568518_print

Darlington v. Charleston Community Hospital. 33 Ill. 2d. 326; 211 N.E. 2d 253 (1965).

Domino, K. B. (2001). Office-based anesthesia: Lessons learned from the closed claims project. *American Society of Anesthesiologists Newsletter, 65*(6), 9–11.

Emergency Nurses' Association (ENA). (1999). *Standards of emergency nursing practice* (4th ed.). DesPlaines, IL: ENA.

Emergency Nurses' Association. (2007). *Trauma nursing core course, provider manual* (6th ed.). DesPlaines, IL: ENA.

Glatter, R. D., Martin, R. E., & Lex, J. (2008). How emergency physicians think. *Medscape Emergency Medicine.* Accessed July 22, 2008, from: http://www.medscape.com/viewarticle/575739_print

Gilboy, N., Tanabe, P., Travers, D. A., Eitel, D. R., & Wuerz, R. C. (2003). *The emergency severity index handbook: A five level triage system.* DesPlaines: Emergency Nurses' Association.

Gorembei, D. A., Oldham, R. M., & Baulch, M. N. (2006). Legal issues in transport. In D. Y. Clark, J. Stocking, & J. Johnson (Eds.), *Flight and ground transport nursing core curriculum.* Denver, CO: Air & Surface Transport Nurses Association.

Healthcare Standards Official Directory 2004. ECRI (2004).

Hickson, G. B., Federspiel, C. F., Pichert, J. W., Miller, C. S., Gauld-Jaeger, J., & Bost, P. (2002). Patient complaints and malpractice risk. *JAMA, 287*(22), 2951–2957.

Institute of Medicine. (2000). *To err is human.* Washington, DC: National Academy Press.

Iserson, K. V., Sanders, A. B., & Mathieu, D. (1986). *Ethics in emergency medicine* (2nd ed.). Tucson: Galen Press, Ltd.

Joint Commission on Accreditation of Health Care Organizations. (2001). Joint commission presents first office based surgery accreditation award (press release) [cited July 1, 2008]. Available at www.jcaho.org

Knight v. Reed, Case No. 03-GD-010449 (June 9, 2005).

Kohn, L. T., Corrigan, J. M., & Donaldson, M. S. (Eds.). (2000). *To err is human: Building a safer health system.* Washington, DC: National Academy Press.

LaMendola, B. (1998). *Cosmetic surgery: The hidden dangers.* Available at Sun-Sentinal.com. Accessed on July 2008.

Lee, G. (2000). Legal issues. In *Emergency nursing core curriculum* (5th ed.) Emergency Nurses Association (ENA). Philadelphia: W.B. Saunders Co.

Lee, N. G. (2001). *Legal issues in emergency care.* Philadelphia: W.B. Saunders Co.

Lukens, T. W., Wolf, S. J., Edlow, J. A., Shahabuddin, S., Allen, M. H., Currier, G. W., & Jagoda, A. S. (2006). Clinical policy: Critical issues in the diagnosis and management of the adult psychiatric patient in the emergency department. *Annals of Emergency Medicine, 47*(1), 79–99.

Lynn, G. v. Hugh, 710 N.Y. 2d (A.D. 1st Dept., 2000).

Majeed, H., Verghese, A., & Rivera, R. R. (1995). The cat and the catheter [Letter]. *The New England Journal of Medicine, 332*(5), 338.

Marshall v. East Carroll Parrish, 1998 FED App. 30592 (5th Cir. 1998).

Mayer, T. A., & Zimmerman, P. G. (1999). ED customer satisfaction survival skills: One hospital's experience. *Journal of Emergency Nursing, 25*(3), 187–191.

McDonald v. Thrift Drug, Inc., Case No. 1907 (September 21, 2000).

National Center for Health Statistics, 2008. Available at http://www.cdc.gov/nchs/fastats/docvisit.htm. Accessed on July 1, 2008.

Nawar, E. W., Riska, R. W., & Xu, J. (2007). *National hospital ambulatory medical care survey: Emergency department summary* (Abstract). U.S. Department of Health and Human Services, Centers for Disease Control and Prevention. Accessed September 15, 2008, from http://scholar.google.com/scholar?hl= en&rls=com.microsoft:*:IE-SearchBox&rlz=1I7SUNA&q=author:%22Nawar%22+intitle:%22National+ Hospital+Ambulatory+Medical+Care+Survey:+2005+...%22+&um=1&ie=UTF-8&oi=scholarr

Newberry, L., & Criddle, L., (Eds.). (2005). *Sheehy's manual of emergency care* (6th ed.). St. Louis: Elsevier Mosby.

O'Keefe, M. E. (2001). *Nursing practice and the law: Avoiding malpractice and other legal risks.* Philadelphia: F.A. Davis.

Quinn, C. (2005). *The medical record as a forensic resource.* Sudbury: Jones and Bartlett Publishers.

Schaefer, M. A. (2000). CRICO office-based malpractice cases: 1989–1998. *Forum, 20*(2), 1–5.

Storm v. Pike, Case No. 5259 GN 2003 (August 18, 2006).

Strickler, J. (2006). EMTALA: The basics. *Journal of Nursing Administration's Healthcare Law, Ethics, and Regulation, 3*(8), 77–80.

Studdert, D. M., Mello, M. M., Sage, W.M., DesRoches, C. M., Peugh, J., Zapert, K., & Brennan, T. A. (2005). Defensive medicine among high-risk specialist physicians in a volatile malpractice environment. *JAMA,* 293(21), 2609–2616.

Tsai, A. K., Schafermeyer, R. W., Kalifon, D., Barkin, R. M., Lumpkin, J. R., & Smith, E. E. (1993). Evaluation and treatment of minors: Reference on consent. *Annals of Emergency Medicine, 22*(7), 1211–1216.

Trimble, T. (2008). Definition of emergency nursing. *Emergency Nursing World.* Accessed September 12, 2008, from http://ENW.org

U.S. Department of Health and Human Services: Office of Civil Rights. (2003). *Summary of the HIPAA privacy rule.* Accessed September 15, 2008, from http://www.hhs.gov/ocr/hipaa

Weinstock, M. B., Longstreth, R., & Henry, G. (2006). *Bouncebacks! Emergency department cases: ED returns.* Columbus: Anadem Publishing.

Appendix A: High-Risk Patient Categories, Complaints, and Conditions in the ED as outlined by the ACEP

Chest pain	Meningitis
Acute coronary syndrome	Airway problems
Pulmonary embolism	Trauma
Thoracic aorta dissection	Head injury
Abdominal pain	Spinal injury
Abdominal aortic aneurysm (AAA)	Wounds
Appendicitis	Fractures
Headache	Testicular torsion
Subarachnoid hemorrhage	Ectopic pregnancy
Stroke	Sepsis
Pediatric fever	

Source: ACEP (2007a, 2007b).

Appendix B: Standards and Resources for Ambulatory Care

Organization	*Contact Information*
Accreditation Association for Ambulatory Health Care	Accreditation Association for Ambulatory Healthcare, Inc., Suite 300, 3201 Old Glenview Road, Wilmette, IL 60091-2992, (847)853-6060
Medical Group Management Association	104 Inverness Terrace E, Englewood, CO 80112-5306, 877-275-6462, http://www.mgma.org
American Academy of Ambulatory Care Nursing	PO Box 56, E holly Ave, Pitman, NJ 08071, 856-256-2350, http://www.aaacn.org
American Health Information Management Association	Suite 2150, 233 N Michigan Ave, Chicago, IL 60601-5800, 312-233-1100, http://www.ahima.org
American Association of Office Nurses	109 Kinderkamack Road, Montvale, NJ 07645, 800-457-7504, http://www.aaon.org
American Medical Association	515 N State Street, Chicago, IL 60610, 800-621-8335, http://www.ama-assn.org
Joint Commission	One Renaissance Boulevard, Oakbrook Terrace, IL 60181, 630-792-5600, http://www.jcaho.org

continued

Organization	Contact Information
American College of Medical Practice Executives	104 Inverness Terrace E, Englewood, CO 80112-5306, 877-275-6462, http://www.mgma.org/acmpe
National Committee for Quality Assurance	Suite 500, 2000 L Street NW, Washington, DC 20036, 202-955-3500, http://www.ncqa.org
Office of the Inspector General	Office of Public Affairs, Department of Health and Human Services, Room 5541 Cohen Building, 330 Independence Avenue SW, Washington, D.C. 20201, 202-619-1343, http://www.oig.hhs.gov

Appendix C: Standards and Resources for Office-Based Surgical Procedures

Organization	Contact Information
Accreditation Association for Ambulatory Health Care	Accreditation Association for Ambulatory Healthcare, Inc., Suite 300, 3201 Old Glenview Road, Wilmette, IL 60091-2992, (847)853-6060
American Association for Accreditation of Ambulatory Surgery Facilities	1202 Allanson Road, Mundelein, IL 60060, 847-949-6058, http://ww.aaaasf.org
American Academy of Dermatology	930 N Meacham Road, PO Box 4014, Schaumberg, IL 60168-4014, 847-330-0230, http://www.aad.org
American College of Surgeons	633 N St. Clair Street, Chicago, IL 60611-3211, 312-202-5000, http://www.facs.org
American Gastroenterology Association	7910 Woodmont Ave, Bethesda, MD 20814, 301-654-2055, http://www.gastro.org
American Society of Anesthesiologists	520 N Northwest Highway, Park Ridge, IL 60068-2573, 847-825-5586, http://www.asahq.org
American Society of Plastic Surgeons	444 E Algonquin Road, Arlington Heights, IL 6005-4664, http://www.plasticsurgery.org
Anesthesia Patient Safety Foundation	4246 Colonial Park Drive, Pittsburgh, PA 15227-2621, 421-882-8040, http://www.apsf.org

Appendix D: Standards and Resources for Home Health Care

Organization	Contact Information
Centers for Medicare and Medicaid services	Conditions of Participation: Home Health Agencies. 42 CFR 484 at http://www.access.gpo.gov/nara/cfr/waisidx_06/42cfr484_06.html
American Medical Association	Geriatric Health Department, 515 North State Street, Chicago, IL 60610, 312-464-5085
Joint Commission	One Renaissance Boulevard, Oakbrook Terrace, IL 60181, 630-792-5600, http://www.jcaho.org
American Nurses Association	8600 Maryland Ave SW, Suite 100 W, Washington, DC 20024, 202-651-7000
National Association for Home Care	228 Seventh Street, SE, Washington, DC 20003, Phone: (202) 547-7424, www.nahc.org
Community Health Accreditation Program	1300 19th Street, Suite 150, Washington, DC 20036, 202.862.3413, www.chapinc.org

Chapter 19

The Role of the Legal Nurse Consultant in the Preparation of Technical Demonstrative Evidence

Donna Miller, BSN, LNCC and Nancy Angelo Finzar, RN, MN

Second Edition
Rosie Oldham, BS, RN, LNCC

Contents

Objectives

Upon reading this chapter, the legal nurse consultant (LNC) will be able

- To review the LNC's focus related to demonstrative evidence and presentation
- To describe the role of the LNC in preparation and presentation of demonstrative evidence
- To discuss preparation of digital exhibits and successful presentation of case issues
- To review the admissibility and use of technical demonstrative evidence in the courts

Introduction

Today's technology makes it easy for more than 100 federal courtrooms to be prewired for paperless trials. However, many trial lawyers remain hampered because they do not possess specialized technological skills to be able to present demonstrative evidence in these courtrooms. Trial lawyers still present demonstrative evidence by holding up exhibits, handing documents to jurors, and using foam board blow-ups and easels that the jurors cannot see with ease. Demonstrative evidence needs to be presented clearly and precisely to the jurors to convey the intended message. Choosing the most fitting avenue to convey this message is as important as encompassing the bullet points that founded the complaints in the case. People learn and remember information in many different ways. Visual images are more effective than verbal scenarios in most instances.

Legal nurse consultants (LNCs) possessing technical skills and legal nurse consulting experience can provide a winning edge to their attorney clients through the technical presentation of evidence. The LNC would be an invaluable asset to the attorney client by keeping current with technological advances. Educational opportunities are abundant in learning about computer software and technical hardware functionalities. Online education programs such as www.eLearners.com, www.hp. com, and many universities offer computer technology courses online to help the novice as well as keeping the expert current in computer science and technology. Locally, computer science and computer technology courses are available at most community colleges and colleges that offer adult education provider courses. To learn about presentation format, investigate courses specific to adult education where part of most curriculums provide education on how to troubleshoot and maintain presentation hardware. The best way to present evidence, particularly in document-intensive cases, is to use readily available software such as Microsoft Office, equipment such as a laptop computer, and a portable projector. If they fail to operate consistently, self-written and/or infrequently utilized software can create testifying difficulties causing distraction from the intended and clearly implied message. The jury is made up of everyday citizens, a "jury of your peers." They are also acclimating to the computerized Internet world, so consider software familiar to a typical jury pool.

The next section of this chapter discusses the skill requirements and the equipment that LNCs need to incorporate into their practices. This information is critical to presenting evidence at conferences and trial by electronic methods.

Skill Requirements for the LNC

Advanced Technical Skills and Use of Software, Hardware, and Equipment

A "technical nurse consultant" is an LNC who has advanced expertise in the use of technical equipment and assists the attorney client in presenting the demonstrative evidence. It is essential for technical nurse consultants to be very familiar with hardware and software integration, aware of potential conflicts that may exist in coordinating the resources of the computer to match or exceed the software requirements, and able to troubleshoot these systems independently.

The LNC must be able to problem-solve, remove, or replace hardware and software components that may stop functioning during a presentation. A local backup technician should be identified and prepared in advance to repair or replace the equipment on-site if the LNC is not able to do so. It is recommended that additional equipment be available on-site to use as an alternative plan in case the LNC is unable to restore the malfunctioning system. Backup equipment is a virtual necessity because postponement of the presentation during a trial will likely frustrate everyone in the courtroom, the attorney, client, judge, and jurors. This may well compromise the relationship between the LNC and the attorney client. The LNC should arrive early to insure that equipment and programs are up and functional. Equipment difficulties reflect unpreparedness, something the LNC should try to avoid. Know where the light switches are before the presentation. Decide where the best place is to stand to avoid becoming a distraction. *Always* have a backup plan in case the facility's capabilities are incompatible with the computer software being used to present the demonstrative evidence of the case.

The equipment needed for technical presentation of a case minimally includes a laptop computer (with dual monitor capability), appropriate trial presentation and graphics software, and a projector. A desktop computer can be used if a laptop computer is not available. The main drawback to the desktop computer is its size and weight, which make it cumbersome to move.

Presentation software costs and functionality have a broad range. Software programs such as Microsoft PowerPoint® are basic and easy to use, and expand to programs designed to organize thousands of courtroom exhibits such as documents, graphs, illustrations, videotapes and audiotapes, video depositions, and photographs. The American Bar Association has a Legal Technology Resource Center that compares various software products available with contacts to the vendors. Individual software programs need to be closely analyzed for functionality in the specific environment. This is critically important where the operating systems between the software and hardware are involved.

Exploring a program requires time to evaluate its trial version (the test version) before deciding to purchase. If the maker does not offer a trial version, then an in-depth brochure about the software should be available, although it is difficult to determine a program's applicability from only a description.

The software purchase creates a foundation for other computer purchasing decisions. Software requirements dictate how much memory and disk space the laptop computer requires. The hard drive must have the capacity (20–60 gigabytes) to accommodate large volumes of digitized documents; no size is too big. Some Internet sites that can help the LNC begin investigating equipment and software are http://www.indatacorp.com, http://www.trialvis.com, http://www.projectorcentral.com, http://www.microsoft.com, and http://www.projectus.com. Their mention here is not to be construed as an endorsement of any particular product. A simple search engine, such as http://www.google.com, is beneficial in locating current Internet sites for medical graphics software. Google Scholar is an invaluable resource. It can be accessed it from the main Google page under "Google Scholar" or www.scholar.google.com.

The projector's quality is measured in lumens and resolution. The choice of projector depends on where the presentation will take place. Larger rooms require higher lumens. It is recommended that the native resolution of the projector match the screen resolution the computer uses. Wireless routers are available to interface the projector and the laptop. *Computer Hardware, Inc* and *Infocus* are examples of online hardware pricing websites.

A projector stand, a screen, sound equipment, and a surge protector are also probable needs. A surge protector is recommended because the building's electrical system may have variances that can cause damage to the equipment. Some manufacturers of surge protectors provide insurance for the equipment if the surge protector fails to protect it. The technical nurse consultant should consider purchasing additional insurance on the equipment to cover theft, damage, and loss. Always bring a long extension cord in case outlets are far away.

A digital video camera can also be set up on a tripod and connected to the projector to project three-dimensional exhibits onto the screen, allowing everyone to see the exhibits simultaneously. This method is used primarily with three-dimensional exhibits that have not been digitized (scanned) previously or that will be handled in the courtroom.

Technical presentations can be complex, and attorneys may have difficulty understanding the labor-intensive process of developing demonstrative evidence. It is practical to give attorney clients a terms-of-engagement document that outlines issues related to use of technology in the courtroom. A good business attorney can assist in the development of this document.

Presentation Style

The LNC who chooses to enter the realm of technical nurse consulting or expert fact witnessing (many provide both services) must possess excellent skills to evaluate, analyze, and present information in a visual manner that enables jurors and judges to understand the case issues. A minimum of 2 years' experience as an LNC is crucial because reviewing and analyzing medical records prepare the nurse to develop technical presentation skills based on knowledge of case facts. Effective skills in public speaking are critical to insure that voice tone and nonverbal gestures are in sync. The LNC must focus on the judge and jury's ability to visualize and be able to simplify the complexity of the information being presented so that everyone in the courtroom can understand it.

The LNC should possess highly sophisticated technical skills to assist the attorney with presenting the case by utilizing graphics that clearly reflect relevant issues. The LNC must pay attention to scale, color, and contrast. Taking a basic art class may assist the LNC in developing these creative skills. Colors are especially meaningful, and the judicious use of color in demonstrative evidence can communicate ideas beyond printed words. High contrast at a distance improves readability. For example, blue text on a green background would distract from the intended message.

Not only must the LNC's dress and demeanor be professional, but his or her ability to appear calm and confident is vital. Taking a speech class or joining a *Toastmasters International* group can assist the LNC with building confidence in making presentations. Attending classes that provide preparation for using software during a mock presentation can be very helpful.

Knowledge of Resources, Utilization of Graphics and Anatomical Exhibits, and Digitization of Exhibits

Authoritative Internet sites, textbooks, and journals can be used as resources for preparation of information to be used as demonstrative evidence. Exhibits can be purchased from any medical organization with a website that is considered to be an authoritative body, or from standard-of-care resources (e.g., http://www.americanheart.org). Some sites may require subscription activation to access information and exhibits. Authoritative textbooks and journals are mainstay resources for potential exhibits.

Graphics and anatomical exhibits can be obtained by outsourcing to a medical exhibit company such as http://www.doereport.com or http://www.vesalius.com. The exhibits can be scanned from authoritative medical textbooks, with adherence to the appropriate copyright regulations. Most often the price of exhibits purchased from medical exhibit companies includes the copyright fee, and the companies give instructions on how their copyright restrictions apply.

Advantages of digitizing (scanning) exhibits and using an electronic presentation method include the following:

- This technology provides easy on-screen annotation during presentation, including zooming in on and enlarging a particular portion of the exhibit.
- Annotated exhibits can be saved for later use without having to take an actual exhibit out of the courtroom for copying.
- Video depositions and other video files can be played onto the projector from the computer.
- Videos can be displayed side by side with the synchronized transcript.
- Using special deposition software, other exhibits can be displayed simultaneously on the screen to correlate to the video segment. The exhibit can be "attached" to a certain segment of the transcript in advance in order to appear automatically in the open field on the screen, and the video can be paused while the exhibit is discussed.
- Significant segments of the audio or video can be made into clips and instantly retrieved and played at just the critical moment.
- Computer-animated accident re-enactments can easily be presented.
- Poor-quality audio or video can be enhanced for clarity by linking with the transcript of a particular tape, such as a "911" audiotape that may be difficult to hear.
- A simultaneous transcript can be cued for synchronous play to allow visual clarity of the content.

Trial-presentation programs can often support multimedia file formats such as RealAudio™ and RealVideo™, and tools such as Microsoft PowerPoint, Adobe Acrobat™, Internet Explorer™, Microsoft Word™, and QuickTime Player™.

File formats supported often include, but are not limited to, AVI, WAV, MPEG (Babitsky & Mangraviti, 2002), Word, ASCII, PowerPoint, HTML, PDF, JPG, TIFF, and BMP.

Digital exhibits can be prepared in a thumbnail format (minimized picture of the image) in a trial notebook for easy reference, with an associated bar code next to the thumbnail image for retrieval and display.

Digital exhibits can be sent over the Internet to facilitate discussion by the legal team of the applicability of the particular exhibit for a particular witness or segment of the trial. Graphics and presentations can be uploaded to a password-secured website for viewing by the trial team. Digital exhibits make it possible to have all demonstrative evidence on hand in the courtroom. Case documents and other exhibits are digitized and stored on CD-ROM discs. Digitization for a large number of exhibits is best outsourced to a production company that has equipment to scan and digitize large numbers of exhibits quickly. The production company scans each exhibit and assigns a file name and Bates number or bar code to each document. The original exhibits are returned along with one or more CD-ROMs on which the digitized documents are stored. The software program will dictate the file format for the exhibits. If fewer than 10–20 exhibits are to be used, they can be digitized with an office scanner.

A digital exhibit file can be located by various methods, the simplest method being the bar code that was assigned to that document. The bar code technology is extremely beneficial for long trials in which document retrieval is often time-consuming. Other methods of file retrieval are dependent upon the particular presentation software that is used.

Example 19.1

Use of technical demonstrative evidence helped result in an $18 million verdict in *Guerrero v. Republic Silver State Disposal*, Department 19, District Court of Las Vegas, NV in November 2001. Graphics showing evidence of the defendant's liability (the driver of the disposal truck) were reflected by using a "scrolling" timeline depicting multiple safety citations. Accident photos in which sections were enlarged while projected on the screen showed the damage to the plaintiff's crushed car. Pictures of the plaintiff before and after the accident were critical in showing the damage to the client. The use of the technology enhanced the jurors' understanding of the brain damage that the plaintiff had incurred in the accident.

Role of the LNC

Identify Critical Time Frames and Coordinate Evidence with Facts

As part of a legal team, the LNC uses clinical expertise to assist attorneys with the medical records review and analysis of case evidence where law and medicine are intertwined. The LNC may work as a technical nurse consultant or expert fact witness with the legal team on cases in the arenas of medical malpractice, product liability, personal injury, and other medical issues. Through clinical experience, education, and research, the LNC identifies significant medical facts of the case and educates the legal team about the healthcare issues and what evidence would best be presented in the courtroom. The LNC's goal is to "tell the story" of the event through the use of the factual data correlating with clinical experience, education, and research.

Through the review of relevant medical records, the LNC is able to develop an analysis of case evidence. The LNC must summarize and analyze pertinent medical information and correlate this with the allegations relevant to each case. Providing literature research, the LNC identifies pertinent standards of care, guidelines, and regulatory requirements. The LNC may be needed to define and identify issues of liability, negligence, or inconsistencies in deposition testimony, and interpret complex information in the medical records. Simplifying complex information in a graphic chart will help the judge and jurors understand the issue presented. For example, in a case in which unexpected post-operative bleeding is indicated by abnormal vital signs as seen in the anesthesia record, a graphic of the vital signs can be produced that indicates the approximate time the bleeding began. If the bleeding was recognized, the anesthesiologist may have documented this on the record. The vital sign graphic and the digitized record by the anesthesiologist can be presented side by side to assist the jurors with understanding the proximity of vital sign changes in the patient to the actual time the bleeding began.

It is important during production of evidence to identify critical time frames and their correlation with the facts of the case. Once these issues are identified, collaboration with the LNC allows the litigation team to focus on the key points.

Issue and Focal Point Identification

Evidence obtained through the LNC's review of medical records and other relevant documents is frequently used as demonstrative evidence. This evidence, which is usually gathered during the discovery phase of a case, can be illustrated through the use of technology. Technologically generated images can emphasize key points in the legal team's arguments. As part of the litigation team, the LNC must understand the key points of the case and determine how the attorneys want those points presented to the jury. Communication between the LNC and the legal team is critical to a successful strategy for presenting the demonstrative evidence. It is critical to the LNC's credit-ability that a document that clearly lists any and all relevant references be kept. Prepare any and all documents to be placed into evidence and reviewed in detail.

Conference with the Legal Team to Develop Case Strategy

Demonstrative evidence is a powerful tool and one that needs to be fine-tuned. Brainstorming sessions help in the development of powerful and cost-effective courtroom graphics, animations, and illustrations. The brainstorming process reduces cost by fine-tuning what will actually be use-ful in the presentation of the evidence. The ideal situation allows the LNC to plan ahead 3–5 months before trial. The initial meeting focuses only on the technical strategies of demonstrative evidence and how it will be illustrated, generated, and presented to the jury. It is important that all members of the litigation team be present.

The brainstorming process begins with the development of ideas. This leads to the details for each idea and an evaluation to determine which are relevant. For example, in a case in which a lung was perforated by placement of a nasogastric tube, the details of the graphics included an animation of the tube being advanced correctly into the stomach. A second presentation for this case included animation of the tube placement through the lung with the addition of blood at the site of perforation. During the planning process, the LNC needs to assess who will use the graphic in testimony or whether it will be a part of the opening statement or closing argument. It is impor-tant that the source of the evidence or data be documented and disclosed to the court.

Final Review

Once the litigation team has decided on the demonstrative evidence and how it will be presented, a step back must be taken to ensure the illustration's merit to the case. The LNC should evaluate the flow and quality of the evidence. It is imperative after completion of the project to have a last review of the evidence with the litigation team and others important to the final presentation of the evidence (Babitsky & Mangraviti, 2007; Krehel, 2000).

The LNC is responsible for determining which exhibits should be digitized. The attorney gives final authorization that is based on consideration of costs and deadlines. Adherence to deadlines prior to trial or settlement conferences is mandatory.

Preparation of Demonstrative Evidence

Legal Team Review of Admissibility of Evidence in Presentation Format and Rules of Procedure

Countless hours can be spent generating demonstrative evidence that the technical nurse consultant or fact witness will present. It is the attorney's responsibility to obtain the court's approval of the use of the technical nurse consultant or expert fact witness. The technical nurse consultant and the expert fact witness roles may be intertwined but also may be separate. The technical nurse consultant may present the information in the courtroom using a laptop computer without ever taking the witness stand. The expert fact witness may never utilize a computer, but present testimony with or without demonstrative aids. Attorneys are recognizing the value of the expert fact witness capable of presenting information from the medical record using demonstrative evidence.

The attorney must follow certain preliminary steps, such as authentication and accuracy. This is known as "laying the foundation" and is mandatory whenever any scientific expertise is forthcoming. Foundational requirements (other than those dealing with the expertise of the person) usually involve the following:

- Authentication: The demonstrative evidence should convey what it is meant to convey.
- Representational accuracy: The demonstrative evidence should depict the scale, dimensions, and contours of the underlying evidence fairly.
- Identification: The demonstrative evidence must be an exact match to the underlying evidence or the testimony illustrated (Connor, 2001).

The U.S. Supreme Court decided in *Daubert v. Merrell Dow Pharmaceuticals* (1993) that the role of the judge is to be the gatekeeper who evaluates the methodology, reliability, and relevance of expert opinions. If the judge decides that expert opinions are not founded on valid scientific methodology, then the expert's opinions are not admitted into evidence for consideration by the jury (Oldknow, 2001). The LNC needs to be aware of the principles of the Daubert decision and the impact that decision has made on the admissibility of evidence. The sources used for the presentation must reflect scientific knowledge and accuracy. Several of the Federal Rules of Evidence (FRE) were amended on the basis of the Daubert case. It is important for the LNC to understand these rules and to be aware of state requirements regarding evidence admissibility.

FRE 104 refers to the preliminary questions. This rule states as follows:

(a) Preliminary questions concerning the qualification of a person to be a witness, the existence of a privilege, or the admissibility of evidence shall be determined by the court, subject to the provisions of subdivision (b). In making its determination, it is not bound by the rules of evidence except those with respect to privileges.
(b) When the relevancy of evidence depends upon the fulfillment of a condition of fact, the court shall admit it upon, or subject to, the introduction of evidence sufficient to support a finding of the fulfillment of the condition.

LNCs must be prepared to answer questions regarding nursing education and clinical experiences. A copy of the LNC's curriculum vitae should have already been provided to the attorney. Be prepared to discuss any updates to the curriculum vitae between the time that it was sent to your attorney and the trial. It is advisable to submit one's current vitae to one's attorney shortly before the trial date and discuss updates with them before entering the courtroom. Bring a copy along to depositions and trials.

FRE 401 refers to the definition of "relevant evidence." This rules states:

"Relevant evidence" means evidence having any tendency to make the existence of any fact that is of consequence to the determination of the action more probable or less probable than it would be without the evidence.

The evidence must correspond to the information in the medical records that is to be presented and must be pertinent to the facts of the case. The purpose of the evidence must be to help educate on the facts about the medical issues of the case.

FRE 402 refers to the admissibility of relevant evidence. This rule states as follows:

> All relevant evidence is admissible, except as otherwise provided by the Constitution of the United States, by Act of Congress, by these rules, or by other rules prescribed by the Supreme Court pursuant to statutory authority. Evidence which is not relevant is not admissible.

The LNC must make sure that all information presented refers to the specific medical issues of the case and keep the information clear and concise. It is important to stick to the facts of the case. It is also critical that the judge and/or jury understands the point being made. Use nonmedical words and phrases to explain the medical facts when possible and define the complex medical terminology if another word cannot be found.

FRE 403 refers to the exclusion of relevant evidence. This rule states as follows:

> Although relevant, evidence may be excluded if its probative value is substantially outweighed by the danger of unfair prejudice, confusion of the issues, or misleading the jury, or by considerations of undue delay, waste of time, or needless presentation of cumulative evidence.

Again, the judge might choose, on the basis of pretrial motions, to exclude some information that could be presented. The LNC must keep abreast of changes by communicating directly with the attorney and insisting on motion updates that may impact the presentation, and be ready to make changes as necessary. The attorney needs to be aware of this responsibility and to advise the LNC of changes.

FRE 611 refers to the mode and order of interrogation and presentation. This rule states as follows:

(a) The court shall exercise reasonable control over the mode and order of interrogating witnesses and presenting evidence so as to (1) make the interrogation and presentation effective for the ascertainment of the truth, (2) avoid needless consumption of time, and (3) protect witnesses from harassment or undue embarrassment.
(b) Cross-examination should be limited to the subject matter of the direct examination and matters affecting the credibility of the witness. The court may, in the exercise of discretion, permit inquiry into additional matters as if on direct examination.

The judge has the final say in permitting the presentation by the LNC expert fact witness.

FRE 701 refers to the opinion testimony by lay witnesses. This rule states as follows:

(a) If the witness is not testifying as an expert, the witness' testimony in the form of opinions or inferences is limited to those opinions or inferences which are (a) rationally based on the perception of the witness [and] (b) helpful to a clear understanding of the witness' testimony or the determination of a fact in issue . . .

The expert fact witness does not provide any opinions regarding the issues. The LNC is to provide an educational presentation regarding the medical facts of the case.

FRE 702 refers to the testimony by experts. This rule states as follows:

> If scientific, technical, or other specialized knowledge will assist the trier of fact to understand the evidence or to determine a fact in issue, a witness qualified as an expert by knowledge, skill, experience, training, or education, may testify thereto in the form of an opinion or otherwise, if (1) the testimony is based upon sufficient facts or data, (2) the testimony is the product of reliable principles and methods, and (3) the witness has applied the principles and methods reliably to the facts of the case.

The LNC must make sure that research is done from accurate and reliable sources. Anatomical pictures or diagrams must be from reliable, authoritative resources.

FRE 703 refers to the bases of opinion testimony by experts. This rule states as follows:

> The facts or data in the particular case upon which an expert bases an opinion or inference may be those perceived by or made known to the expert at or before the hearing. If of a type reasonably relied upon by experts in the particular field in forming opinions or inferences upon the subject, the facts or data need not be admissible in evidence in order for the opinion or inference to be admitted. Facts or data that are otherwise inadmissible shall not be disclosed to the jury by the proponent of the opinion or inference unless the court determines that their probative value in assisting the jury to evaluate the expert's opinion substantially outweighs their prejudicial effect.

The LNC must make sure that the information presented is accurate.

FRE 1006 refers to summaries. This rule states as follows:

> The contents of voluminous writings, recordings, or photographs which cannot conveniently be examined in court may be presented in the form of a chart, summary, or calculation. The originals, or duplicates, shall be made available for examination or copying, or both, by other parties at reasonable time and place. The court may order that they be produced in court.

Often the LNC may use graphs or charts to reveal the sequence of the medical facts of the case. These must be accurate, reliable, and relevant to the issues of the case.

FRE 1008 refers to the functions of court and jury. This rule states as follows:

> When the admissibility of other evidence of contents of writings, recordings, or photographs under these rules depends upon the fulfillment of a condition of fact, the question whether the condition has been fulfilled is ordinarily for the court to determine in accordance with the provisions of rule 104. However, when an issue is raised (a) whether the asserted writing ever existed, or (b) whether another writing, recording, or photograph produced at the trial is the original, or (c) whether other evidence of contents correctly reflects the contents, the issue is for the trier of fact to determine as in the case of other issues of fact.

The judge makes the final decision as to the admissibility of evidence. The attorney client working with the LNC will help the LNC understand the decisions. The LNC must expect that testimony will include a review of qualifications and nursing education because the LNC is presenting the demonstrative evidence as an expert fact witness. The LNC must be able to adapt smoothly to changes made during the legal proceedings.

Developing Evidence for Disclosure: Digitizing Medical Records and Pertinent Documents

Production companies usually take several days to a week to digitize trial exhibits. Once the LNC receives the files on disk, the LNC can organize the files into folders, that is, opening statement, witness folders, closing arguments, etc. The software also allows the organization of the documents into categories for quick and easy retrieval, such as medical records, graphics, depositions, video, digital video transcripts, and OLE files such as PowerPoint presentations, Adobe files, etc.

Often last-minute exhibits require digitization. Sending them to the production company as they come in is recommended. This saves time and money by avoiding last-minute in-house scanning. The typical cost to have documents and graphics digitized at the production house is approximately $.17–$.25 each. This is quite a savings over in-house scanning.

Exhibits that are frequently used throughout the development of the case include the following:

- Photographs
- Deposition testimony
- Policies and procedures
- Standards of care
- Research
- Regulatory-agency documents
- Diagnostic films
- Videos
- Audiotapes

Organization of these potential exhibits and authorization from the attorney client for their use and disclosure should ideally be planned well in advance of disclosure deadlines.

Many production companies also can convert video or audio into file formats such as MPEG and AVI. Synchronizing a transcript to the video will require a software program that supports the relevant file format and also converts the video and transcript into an editable format. Refer to http://www.indatacorp.com, http://www.trialpro.com, and http://www.trialtec.com for examples of such programs. This type of file is not easily produced at the LNC's office without extensive knowledge and an investment in highly specialized equipment. The typical rate for digitizing video- or audiotapes with a transcript is $150–$200 per hour of tape. To digitize only the video- or audiotape without a synchronized transcript costs approximately $100 per hour of tape.

Presentation Delivery at Settlements, Arbitration and Mediation Hearings, and Trial

The LNC must be well prepared for the presentation of the demonstrative evidence. By the time the case is ready for any settlement conferences, arbitration or mediation hearings, or trial, the LNC must know the case details intimately. The LNC must be comfortable relating the medical and nursing issues of the case to the legal representatives, such as attorneys, mediators, judges, and jurors. It is important for the LNC to have practiced the presentation in order to provide the highest quality presentation possible. The LNC must allow for plenty of time to arrive at the hearing destination and set up the equipment in preparation for the presentation. The clerk of the court or the bailiff can be very helpful in providing information about the courtroom. It is strongly suggested that the LNC set up a time prior to trial to do an "equipment layout" visit to the courtroom.

The LNC should prepare a checklist of items and equipment that are necessary for the presentation. It should include extras of items such as batteries and light bulbs. With good organization and preparation, the presentation will be seen as professional and will be well received.

Conclusion

The use of technology by the LNC in presenting demonstrative evidence can be very rewarding. A lot of preparation time is involved. A thorough knowledge of the technology and commitment to learning new software programs are absolute necessities. Only imagination limits the use of presentation methods today.

References

Babitsky, S., & Mangraviti, J. (2002). *Writing and defending your expert report: The step-by-step guide with models.* Falmouth, MA: SEAK, Inc.

Babitsky, S., & Mangraviti, J. (2007). *Depositions: The comprehensive guide for expert witnesses.* Falmouth, MA: SEAK, Inc.

Connor, T. (2001). Demonstrative evidence: MegaLinks in criminal justice. http://faculty.ncwc.edu/toconnor/.

Federal Judicial Center Advisory Committee. (2001). *Effective use of courtroom technology: A judge's guide to pretrial and trial* (pp. 14–15).Notre Dame, IN: National Institute for Trial Advocacy.

Krehel, G. (2000). Think first, draw second: planning better visuals. *Trial*, April, 58.

Oldknow, P. (2001). Daubert, the scientific method, and the legal nurse consultant. *Journal of Legal Nurse Consulting, 12*(4), p. 3.

Additional Readings

Beerman, J. N. (1998). The expert fact witness: Noneconomic damages testimony. In J. B. Bogart (Ed.), *Legal nurse consulting: Principles and practices* (pp. 687–693). Boca Raton, FL: CRC Press.

Federal Rules of Evidence. (2000).

Gudgell, K. (1998). Access to medical records. In J. B. Bogart (Ed.), *Legal nurse consulting: Principles and practices* (pp. 119–137). Boca Raton, FL: CRC Press.

Heninger, S. (2000). Persuasive proof. *Trial*, April, 55.

Joyce, M. (2000). Avoiding 10 pitfalls of demonstrative evidence. *Trial*, November, 94.

Perry, C. (1999). What evidence works. *Trial*, December, 66.

Rouda, R., & Bailey, R. (2000). Multiple benefits of multimedia. *Trial*, April, 53.

Watts, S. (2000). Technology creates winning visual evidence. *Trial*, September, 68.

Webopedia. http://www.pcwebopedia.com.

Woods, W. (2001, August). Electronic exhibits trump trial boards in cost, convenience. *Maricopa Lawyer.*

Test Questions

1. What court decision was instrumental in changing the ways that evidence was reviewed?
    A. Smith v. Jones
    B. Daubert v. Merrell Dow Pharmaceuticals
    C. Webster v. Merriam
    D. Darrell v. Clarke Enterprises

2. The main points to remember regarding the admissibility of evidence for legal proceedings are
    A. Length and subject
    B. Content and readability
    C. Reliability and relevancy
    D. Color and style

3. Which of the following is not an important aspect of the presentation style and use of graphics?
    A. Color
    B. Contrast
    C. Scale
    D. Age

4. Which of the following is the simplest way to locate a digital exhibit file while in the courtroom?
    A. Bar code
    B. Order from the exhibit company
    C. Obtain from Internet site
    D. Check out from library

5. Which of the following federal rules refers to the definition of "relevant evidence"?
    A. FRE 104
    B. FRE 611
    C. FRE 401
    D. FRE 1008

Answers: 1. B, 2. C, 3. D, 4. A, 5. C

Chapter 20

Employment Law and Occupational Health and Safety, the Role of the LNC

Kathleen P. Buckheit, MPH, BSN, RN, COHN-S/CM/SM, FAAOHN; Moniaree Parker Jones, RN, MSN, COHN-S, CCM; and Judith S. Ostendorf, MPH, RN, COHN-S, CCM, FAAOHN

Contents

Objectives

- Identify the major regulatory agency that addresses occupational health and safety issues
- Describe at least five major employment laws, standards, and regulations related to occupational health and safety
- Describe the role of the LNC in the area of occupational health and safety

Introduction

Understanding occupational health and safety is an important role for the legal nurse consultant (LNC). LNCs need to have an understanding of the many laws and regulations affecting this complex area of healthcare practice. Federal and state laws such as the Occupational Safety and Health Act (OSH Act) have been enacted to protect the health and safety of workers. Employers who are not in compliance may receive fines and citations depending on the severity of the violation. The role of the LNC can be enhanced by having knowledge about the scope of practice of the occupational and environmental health nurse (OEHN). Knowledge of what records may exist to assist in the investigation and support of a case involving occupational safety and health issues is helpful to the discovery process.

Employment Laws

Historically, individual states were responsible for enacting safety and health laws to protect workers. However, increasing numbers of deaths and disabling injuries as a result of work-related incidents demonstrated that in general, although a few states met their obligation in providing reasonable or adequate safety and health legislation, most states had inadequate safety and health standards, enforcement procedures, budgets, and staff. The increasingly high work-related injury/death toll in the 1960s (more than 2.2 million disabling injuries and 14,300 deaths annually) was considered unacceptable and the need for federal legislation was determined (Hagan, Montgomery, & O'Reilly, 2001).

Occupational Safety and Health Act

The most comprehensive occupational safety and health federal legislation today is the OSH Act, which was signed into law by President Richard M. Nixon on December 29, 1970. The major requirement of the OSH Act is as follows:

> to assure safe and healthful working conditions for working men and women; by authorizing enforcement of the standards developed under the Act; by assisting and encouraging the States in their efforts to assure safe and healthful working conditions; by providing for research, information, education, and training in the field of occupational safety and health; and for other purposes. (An Act, 1996, p. 1)

The OSH Act created three separate bodies: the Occupational Safety and Health Administration (OSHA), the National Institute for Occupational Safety and Health (NIOSH), and the Occupational Safety and Health Review Commission (OSHRC) to administer the major requirement of the act. All three are joined together by an Advisory Committee.

Occupational Safety and Health Administration

The OSHA, administered by the Assistant Secretary for Labor, is housed in the Department of Labor and has as its role "to assure the safety and health of America's workers by setting and enforcing standards; providing training, outreach, and education; establishing partnerships; and encouraging continual process improvement in workplace safety and health" (U.S. Department of Labor, Occupational Safety and Health Administration [U.S. DOL, OSHA], 2006, p. 3). OSHA provides assistance to employers and informational and training materials that focus on safety and health hazards in the workplace. Through these activities, workplace injury and illness rates have declined 40% and workplace fatalities have decreased more than 60% (U.S. DOL, OSHA, 2006).

The OSHA coverage includes private sector employers and their employees in all 50 states and certain territories and jurisdictions under federal authority, including the District of Columbia,

Puerto Rico, the Virgin Islands, American Samoa, Guam, Northern Mariana Islands, Wake Island, Johnston Island, and the Outer Continental Shelf (U.S. DOL, OSHA, 2006). The OSH Act covers employers and employees through one of two programs: either Federal OSHA or through OSHA-approved state programs. OSHA does not cover the self-employed; members of immediate family of farm employers who do not employ non-family workers; workers covered by safety and health requirements of other federal agencies, such as the military; and employees of state and local governments. The states that meet certain criteria and have OSHA-approved state programs are required to provide OSHA coverage for state and local government employees (U.S. DOL, OSHA, 2006). A listing of OSHA-approved state programs may be found on the OSHA website, www.osha.gov, by clicking on the State Partners link.

The National Institute for Occupational Safety and Health

The NIOSH was established by the OSH Act and is located in the Centers for Disease Control and Prevention (CDC), within the Department of Health and Human Services (DHHS). NIOSH is the federal agency responsible for conducting research, education, and training. Although NIOSH makes recommendations based on research findings, it is OSHA's responsibility to promulgate and enforce the regulatory standards.

NIOSH also is responsible for developing training and education programs in order to provide an adequate supply of qualified personnel to carry out the purpose of the OSH Act. This is accomplished by providing contracts and grants to colleges and universities to expand their curricula in areas such as occupational health nursing, occupational medicine, industrial hygiene, and occupational safety and ergonomics. The agency also publishes NIOSH Registry of Toxic Effects of Chemical Substances, an annual listing of all known toxic substances and the concentration at which toxicity is known to occur (Center for Disease Control and Prevention, National Institute for Occupational Safety and Health [CDC, NIOSH], n.d.).

Occupation Safety and Health Review Commission

The OSHRC is a quasi-judicial board of three members appointed by the president and confirmed by the Senate. OSHRC is not part of the DOL; it is an independent agency of the executive branch of the U.S. government created to decide contests of citations or penalties resulting from OSHA inspections of work sites. It functions as an administrative court with established procedures for conducting hearings, receiving evidence, and rendering decisions by its Administrative Law Judges (U.S. Occupational Safety and Health Review Commission [U.S. OSHRC], 2008).

National Advisory Committee on Occupational Safety and Health

The OSH Act established a 12-member National Advisory Committee on Occupational Safety and Health (NACOSH) that provides advice, consul, and recommendations to the Secretaries of Labor and Health and Human Services about the administration of the OSH Act. Eight members are designated by the Secretary of Labor, and four by the Secretary of Health and Human Services.

They are representatives from labor, management, occupational safety and health professionals, and the public.

Standards, Laws, and Regulations Applicable to Occupational Safety and Health

OSHA is responsible for promulgating, modifying, and revoking legally enforceable standards with which employers must comply. Generally OSHA standards require that employers maintain conditions and adopt practices reasonably necessary and appropriate to protect workers on the job; be familiar with and comply with standards applicable to their establishments; and ensure that employees have and use personal protective equipment (PPE) when required for safety and health. Standards are written for a wide variety of workplace hazards, including toxic substances, harmful physical agents, electrical hazards, fall hazards, trenching hazards, hazardous waste, infectious diseases, fire and explosion hazards, dangerous atmospheres, machine hazards, and confined spaces (U.S. DOL, OSHA, 2006). Where there is no specific OSHA standard, employers must comply with the OSH Act's "general duty clause." The general duty clause, Section 5(a)(1) states that each employer "furnish . . . a place of employment . . . free from, recognized hazards that are causing or are likely to cause death or serious physical harm to his employees" (U.S. DOL, OSHA, 2006, p. 10). A few of the standards that often involve the OEHN include the Bloodborne Pathogens Standard, Hazard Communication Standard, Recording and Reporting of Occupational Injuries and Illnesses Standard, Access to Medical and Exposure Records Standard, Occupational Noise Exposure Standard, and PPE Standard. All standards may be accessed at the OSHA website: www.osha.gov.

Bloodborne Pathogens Standard

The Bloodborne Pathogens Standard (29 CFR 1910.1030) was put into effect in 1991 in order to limit occupational exposure to blood, bodily fluids, and other potentially infectious materials. Occupational exposure means that it can be reasonably anticipated that skin, eye, mucous membrane, or parenteral contact with blood or other potentially infectious materials may occur during the performance of an employee's duties. This includes a wide variety of occupations, but are not limited to, physicians, dentists, dental employees, phlebotomists, nurses, morticians, paramedics, medical examiners, laboratory and blood bank technologists and technicians, housekeeping personnel, laundry workers, employees in long-term care facilities, home care workers, and depending on their work assignment, may include research laboratory workers and public safety personnel such as fire, police, rescue, correctional officers, etc. (U.S. DOL, OSHA, 1996). Other potentially infectious materials include the following: (1) *Human body fluids:* semen, vaginal secretions, cerebrospinal fluid, synovial fluid, pleural fluid, pericardial fluid, peritoneal fluid, amniotic fluid, saliva in dental procedures, any body fluid that is visibly contaminated with blood, all body fluids in situations where it is difficult or impossible to differentiate between body fluids; (2) Any unfixed tissue or organ (other than intact skin) from a human (living or dead); and (3) HIV-containing cell or tissue cultures, organ cultures, and HIV- or HBV-containing culture medium or other solutions as well as blood, organs, or other tissues from experimental animals infected with HIV or HBV (U.S. DOL, OSHA, 1996).

When employees with occupational exposure have been identified, the hazards must be communicated to them (U.S. DOL, OSHA, 1996). Training and information on occupational exposures must be provided at no cost to the employee, at the time of the initial assignment,

- How to obtain a copy of the regulatory text and an explanation of its contents
- Information on the epidemiology and symptoms of bloodborne diseases
- Ways in which bloodborne pathogens are transmitted
- Explanation of the exposure control plan and how to obtain a copy
- Information on how to recognize tasks that might result in occupational exposure
- Explanation of the use and limitations of work practice and engineering controls, and personal protective equipment
- Information on the types, selection, proper use, location, removal, handling, decontamination, and disposal of personal protective equipment
- Information on hepatitis B vaccination such as safety, benefits, efficacy, methods of administration, and availability
- Information on who to contact and what to do in an emergency
- Information on how to report an exposure incident and on the post-exposure evaluation and followup
- Information on warning labels and signs, where applicable, and color-coding
- Question and answer session on any aspect of the training

Figure 20.1   Bloodborne pathogen standard training elements. [Adapted from U.S. DOL, OSHA (1996, p. 3–4).]

during working hours, and, thereafter, at least annually. The person providing the training must be knowledgeable about the subject matter and the information provided must be appropriate in content and vocabulary to the educational level, literacy, and language of the audience. The box above lists the training elements required by the Bloodborne Pathogen Standard (Figure 20.1).

The Bloodborne Pathogens Standard identifies how to determine who has occupational exposure and how to reduce workplace exposure through developing an exposure control plan. The plan must be written and include the following:

- The exposure determination
- The procedures for evaluating the circumstances surrounding an exposure incident
- The schedule and method for implementing sections of the standard covering the methods of compliance, HIV and HBV research laboratories and production facilities, hepatitis B vaccination and post-exposure follow up, communication of hazards to employees, and recordkeeping (U.S. DOL, OSHA, 1996, p. 2).

The plan must be reviewed, updated at least annually or when new tasks and procedures affect occupational exposure, made accessible to employees, and made available to the Assistant Secretary for OSHA and to the director of NIOSH for examination and copying.

The Standard identifies preventive measures that employers must have in place, such as making the hepatitis B vaccine and vaccination series available free of charge to all employees who have occupational exposure, as well as providing a post-exposure evaluation and followup to all employees who experience an exposure incident. Employees who decline the vaccination must sign a declination form.

Methods of exposure control include equipment engineering, work practice controls, and PPE. Engineering controls are the preferred method of control because they either remove or isolate the hazard or isolate the worker from exposure. An example of an engineering control for the bloodborne pathogens standard is self-sheathing needles. Work practice controls alter the manner in which a task is performed. Work practice controls for the bloodborne pathogen standard might include restricting eating, drinking, smoking, applying cosmetics or lip balm, and handling contact lenses, prohibiting mouth pipetting, and preventing the storage of food or drink in refrigerators or other locations where blood or other potentially infectious materials are kept. The use of PPE might include, but is not limited to, gloves, gowns, laboratory coats, face shields or masks, and eye protection.

If an exposure incident occurs, the employee must receive an adequate evaluation according to the Standard's provision, which includes providing HBV and HIV serological testing, counseling, and safe and effective post-exposure prophylaxis following the current recommendations for the U.S. Public Health Service (U.S. DOL, OSHA, 1996).

Specific requirements for recordkeeping and confidentiality are identified in the Standard. For example, for each employee, an employer must preserve and maintain an accurate record of occupational exposure according to OSHA's standard governing access to employees' exposure and medical records, which will be discussed later in this chapter.

On November 6, 2000, The Needlestick Safety and Prevention Act was signed into law. Congress identified that occupational exposure to bloodborne pathogens from accidental sharps injuries in healthcare and other occupational settings was continuing to be a serious problem, so much so that an amendment to OSHA's Bloodborne Pathogens Standard was appropriate. The amendment was set forth in greater detail and made OSHA's requirement for employers to identify, evaluate, and implement safety-engineered sharp devices more specific. The Act also mandated additional requirements for maintaining a sharps injury log and for the involvement of non-managerial healthcare workers in evaluating and choosing devices (U.S. DOL, OSHA, 2001b).

Hazard Communication Standard

The Hazard Communication Standard (29 CFR 1910.1200) was implemented in 1983 and covers all workers exposed to hazardous chemicals in all industrial sectors. The purpose of the Standard is to prevent workplace illness and injury by providing information to employees about the chemical hazards. A comprehensive, detailed, and documented Hazard Communication Program includes appropriate labels on chemical containers, material safety data sheets (MSDSs), and employee training as requirements of the Standard. The hazards of all chemicals are evaluated and the information is communicated to employers and employees by the manufacturer through container labeling and documentation on MSDSs. MSDSs provide valuable information about the chemicals including a brief summary of the hazards and PPE that must be used when working with the chemicals. Employee training ensures that workers know how and where to readily access the MSDSs, what PPE procedures to follow, what emergency medical treatment is required for exposure, and be able to understand the information on the labels and MSDSs. Training must be done when employees are first assigned to an operation that exposes them to hazardous chemicals and again whenever a new hazard is introduced into the work area or the chemicals change.

Recording and Reporting of Occupational Injuries and Illnesses Standard

The original Recording and Reporting of Occupational Injuries and Illnesses Standard (29 CFR 1904) was enacted in 1971 and amended in 2002 (29 CFR 1904.7). This Standard allows the identification of high hazard industries and the notification to employees of their employer's safety record. The actual recordkeeping system is maintained by the Bureau of Labor Statistics within the U.S. Department of Labor.

Basically, the employer must decide if an injury or illness meets the OSHA recording criteria. It is considered a recordable case if the injury or illness results in any of the following: death, days away from work, restricted work or transfer to another job, medical treatment beyond first aid, or loss of consciousness. A case also meets OSHA recording criteria if it involves a significant injury or illness diagnosed by a physician or other licensed healthcare professional, even if it does not result in death, days away from work, restricted work or job transfer, medical treatment beyond first aid, or loss of consciousness. The Standard provides an algorithm to assist in determining if an injury or illness is considered occupational in nature and includes a detailed list of first aid definitions. An example of a non-recordable first aid case is when the injury is determined to be work-related, and the employee visits a doctor or healthcare professional for evaluation, but no treatment is administered or medication prescribed. An example of a recordable injury is when the injury is determined to be work-related, the employee visits the healthcare provider, and is given a prescription for medication or physical therapy, and requires restricted work activities.

Access to Medical and Exposure Records Standard

OSHA's Access to Medical and Exposure Records Standard (29 CFR 1910.1020) gives an employee who has had a possible exposure to or uses toxic substances or harmful physical agents in the workplace the right to access relevant medical and exposure records. This knowledge may help the employee detect, prevent, and seek treatment for occupational disease (U.S. DOL, OSHA, 2001a). The Standard identifies who has the right to access the medical and exposure records, describes types of exposures that may be included, and defines access, employee exposure records, and employee medical records.

The records may be accessed by the following:

■ A current or former employee who is or may have been exposed to toxic substances or harmful physical agents
■ An employee who was assigned or transferred to work involving toxic substances or harmful physical agents
■ The legal representative of a deceased or legally incapacitated employee who was or may have been exposed to toxic substances or harmful physical agents (U.S. DOL, OSHA, 2001a)

The toxic substances and harmful physical agents may include the following:

■ Metals and dusts, such as lead, cadmium, and silica
■ Biological agents, such as bacteria, viruses, and fungi
■ Physical stress, such as noise, heat, cold, vibration, repetitive motion, and ionizing and non-ionizing radiation (U.S. DOL, OSHA, 2001a)

Access is defined in the Standard as the right to examine and copy medical and exposure records. Employee exposure records include monitoring results of workplace air or measurements of toxic substances or harmful physical agents in the workplace, biological monitoring results, such as blood and urine test results, and MSDSs containing information about a substance's hazards to human health.

Employee medical records include medical and employment questionnaires or histories, results of medical examinations and laboratory tests, medical opinion, diagnoses, progress notes, recommendations, first-aid records, descriptions of treatments and prescriptions, and employee medical complaints. Medical records must be maintained for the duration of the employee's employment plus 30 years and exposure records for 30 years.

Occupational Noise Exposure Standard

The purpose of the Occupational Noise Exposure Standard, 29 CFR 1910.95, is "to protect workers with significant occupational noise exposures from hearing impairment even if they are subject to such noise exposures over their entire working lifetimes" (U.S. DOL, OSHA, 2002, p. 1). The Standard requires that employees exposed to noise at or above 85 decibels (dB) averaged over 8 working hours, or an 8-hr time-weighted average (TWA), are included in the company hearing conservation program. A hearing conservation program is required to include five components: sound exposure monitoring, noise controls, education and motivation, hearing protection, and audiometric monitoring. Sound exposure monitoring must be conducted during a typical work situation and include all continuous, intermittent, and impulsive noise within an 80–130 dB range (U.S. DOL, OSHA, 2002).

Engineering and administrative noise controls are OSHA's preferred method of abatement. Examples of engineering controls are to eliminate the noise source or redesign the process to reduce sound levels; however, this is not always possible. Administrative controls include work practices such as rotating workers to areas of lower noise levels. Efforts to implement engineering and administrative controls should be documented.

Education and motivation of workers are keys to the success of the program. Employees who understand the need to protect their hearing and the reasons for the hearing conservation program will be more motivated to wear their hearing protection. Employees must be trained at least annually, and the training must be documented.

When engineering and administrative noise controls are not possible, PPE is required to be provided. Hearing protection includes ear plugs, ear muffs, and canal caps. All employees must wear hearing protection if they are exposed to 8-hour TWA noise levels of 85 dB or above for 6 months and they have not had their baseline hearing test, if they have incurred a standard threshold shift, or if they are working in an area where noise levels are 90 dB or above.

Audiometric testing is used to monitor an employee's hearing during employment. Baseline audiograms are performed at time of hire or when transferred from a low-noise to a noise level work area requiring monitoring. Annual tests are performed and compared with the baseline for changes in hearing levels.

PPE Standard

The PPE Standard (29 CFR 1910.132) was promulgated to provide information on the types of protection available for employees where engineering and administrative controls were not available or effective in controlling occupational hazards. OSHA's preferred method of hazard abatement is always engineering controls, second is administrative or work practice controls, and if neither of these is feasible or do not provide sufficient protection, employers must provide PPE. The employer is responsible to assess the workplace for hazards, to provide and determine when to use PPE, and to provide PPE training and instruction in proper care and use of equipment.

Examples of PPE include, but are not limited to, hearing protection devices, gloves, foot protection, eye protection, hard hats, and respirators. The PPE must be appropriate protection for the type of hazards and must be the correct size for the employee to be effective. Specifically, fit testing is required for hearing protection and respirator use (U.S. DOL, OSHA, 2003).

Workers' Compensation

Workers' Compensation is a limited liability, no fault, state-specific legal system that is administered by each state. The first Workers' Compensation Law was passed in Wisconsin in 1911. Prior to 1911, injured workers and their families were forced to cope with lost wages and had to pay their own medical care and rehabilitation costs.

Today, occupational injuries and illnesses are compensable in all states. An injury is compensable if it is caused by an accident and arises out of and in the course of employment. The definition of occupational disease varies from state to state, but generally it must be caused by an exposure to a hazardous condition or substance during employment, which places the employee at an increased risk of developing the disease than members of the general public and must result in disability or death (Koron, 1999).

Workers' compensation has three common characteristics in all states. These common characteristics include the following:

■ Benefits formulas, which are prescribed by law and generally fully cover medical care and rehabilitation expenses. Lost wages are partially covered
■ Employers incur the cost of the benefits, which is their legal responsibility
■ A "No-fault" system, which means that injured workers do not need to prove that the injury was caused by employer's neglect

Equal Employment Opportunity Laws

The U.S. Equal Employment Opportunity Commission (EEOC) within the U.S. DOL makes and enforces policy concerning worker rights. Areas that the EEOC addresses include the following:

■ *Race, color, religion, sex, national origin:* Title VII of the Civil Rights Act of 1964 (amended) prohibits discrimination in employment areas, such as hiring, promotion, discharge, pay, fringe benefits, job training, classification, referral, and other aspects of employment, based on race, color, religion, sex, or national origin.
■ *Disability:* The Americans with Disabilities Act (ADA) of 1990 (amended) protects qualified applicants and employees with disabilities from discrimination in hiring, promotion, discharge, pay, job training, fringe benefits, classification, referral, and other aspects of employment based on disability. The law requires that employers who are covered entities provide qualified applicants and employees with disabilities with reasonable accommodations that do not impose undue hardship.
■ *Age discrimination:* The Age Discrimination in Employment Act of 1967 (amended) protects applicants and employees 40 years of age or older from discrimination based on age in hiring, promotion, discharge, compensation, terms, conditions or privileges of employment.

■ *Sex discrimination:* In addition to sex discrimination prohibited by Title VII of the Civil Rights Act of 1964 (amended) the Equal Pay Act of 1963 (amended) prohibits sex discrimination in payment of wages to women and men performing substantially equal work in the same establishment.

Retaliation against a person who files a charge of discrimination, participates in an investigation, or opposes an unlawful employment practice is prohibited by all of these Federal laws (U.S. Equal Employment Opportunity Commission [U.S. EEOC], 2005).

Rehabilitation Act of 1973

Rehabilitation Act of 1973 identifies that the purposes of this act are to empower individuals with disabilities, to maximize employment, economic self-sufficiency, independence, and inclusion and integration into society, and to ensure that the federal government plays a leadership role in promoting the employment of individuals with disabilities, especially individuals with significant disabilities, and in assisting States and providers of services in fulfilling the aspirations of such individuals with disabilities for meaningful and gainful employment and independent living (Boston University, 1997).

Section 504 of the Rehabilitation Act of 1973 protects *qualified* individuals from being discriminated against based on a disability. The nondiscrimination requirements apply to employers and organizations receiving financial assistance from any Federal department or agency, including the U.S. DHHS. These include many hospitals, nursing homes, mental health centers, and service programs. Under this law, *individuals with disabilities* are persons with a physical or mental impairment which substantially limits one or more major life activities. For purposes of employment, *qualified individuals with disabilities* are persons who with reasonable accommodation can perform the essential functions of the job. *Reasonable accommodation* requires that an employer must take reasonable steps to accommodate the disability unless it causes the employer undue hardship (U.S. Department of Health and Human Services [U.S. DHHS], Office for Civil Rights [OCR], n.d.). Federal employees and applicants began coverage by the Rehabilitation Act of 1973, instead of the Americans with Disabilities Act. The protections are mostly the same (U.S. Equal Employment Opportunity Commission, 2009).

Americans with Disabilities Act

The ADA is civil rights legislation that resulted from decades of advocacy to improve the lives of persons with disabilities. Since the 1970s, advocacy by persons with disabilities has increased. The emergence of the disability rights and independent living movements has been important in the development of state and federal disability policy leading up to the ADA of 1990. The ADA reaches farther than previous laws as it applies to private entities not linked to federal funds, and to places of public accommodation (such as restaurants, hotels, theaters, etc.).

The ADA is applicable in public and private sectors with more than 15 employees, which includes those not covered by Section 504 of the Rehabilitation Act. This includes a requirement that employers make reasonable accommodations, unless this would impose an undue hardship on the employer. Employers also are prohibited from discriminating against people who have an association with an individual with a disability, such as parents of a child with a disability.

The ADA expands on the requirement of Section 504 of the Rehabilitation Act, which requires state and local government programs that receive federal financial assistance to provide equal opportunity to individuals with disabilities to participate and benefit. Public services may not discriminate against individuals with disabilities. All government programs, services, facilities, and communications must be accessible, consistent with the requirements of Section 504 of the Rehabilitation Act. Three agencies that enforce or participate in assisting with ADA regulations, enacted by a formal complaint are: EEOC; Department of Justice (DOJ); and Office of Disability Employment Policy (ODEP). These are located within the U.S. DOL, which provides publications and other technical assistance on the basic requirements of the ADA, but does not enforce any part of the law. The Office for Civil Rights (OCR) within the U.S. DHHS has been designated enforcement responsibility under Title II of the ADA for state and local healthcare and human service agencies (U.S. DHHS, Office on Disability, 2005).

The Family and Medical Leave Act

The Family and Medical Leave Act (FMLA) is administered by the U.S. DOL, Employment Standards Administration (ESA). Covered employers must allow eligible employees up to a total of 12 work-weeks of unpaid leave during any 12-month period for any of the following reasons:

- The birth and care of the newborn child of the employee
- Placement of a child for adoption or foster care with the employee
- Care of immediate family member (spouse, child, or parent) with a serious health condition
- Medical leave of the employee with a serious health condition who is unable to work

An employer covered by FMLA is any person engaged in commerce or in any industry or activity affecting commerce, employing 50 or more employees in the current or preceding calendar year for each working day during each of 20 or more calendar work-weeks. Also covered by FMLA include employers acting, directly or indirectly, in the interest of a covered employer to any of the employees, any successor in the interest of a covered employer, and any public agency. Public agencies are covered employers without regard to the number of employees employed. Public and private elementary and secondary schools are also covered employers without regard to numbers employed (U.S. DOL, Employment Standards Administration [ESA], 2008b).

Health Insurance Portability and Accountability Act

The Health Insurance Portability and Accountability Act (HIPAA) of 1996, Public Law 104–191, was enacted on August 21, 1996. Sections 261 through 264 of HIPAA require the Secretary of DHHS to publicize standards for the electronic exchange, privacy, and security of health information. The *Standards for Privacy of Individually Identifiable Health Information* ("Privacy Rule") establishes national standards for the protection of certain health information. The DHHS issued the Privacy Rule to implement the requirement of the HIPAA. The Privacy Rule addresses the use and disclosure of an individuals' health information, called "protected health information" by those subject to the Privacy Rule, referred to as "covered entities." It also addresses individuals' privacy rights to assist individuals in understanding and controlling how their health information is used. The Privacy Rule calls this information "protected health information." The Privacy Rule and the Administrative Simplification rules apply to health plans, healthcare clearing houses, and to any healthcare provider who uses the electronic form to transmit health information. The Privacy Rule does not include employment records that a covered entity maintains in its capacity as an employer and education and certain other records subject to, or defined in, the Family Educational Rights and Privacy Act, 20 U.S.C. §1232 g as protected health information.

The Privacy Rule protects all individually identifiable health information held or transmitted by a covered entity or its business associate, in any form or media, whether electronic, paper, or oral. Individually identifiable health information is information, including demographic data that relates to the following:

- The individual's past, present or future physical or mental health or condition
- The provision of health care to the individual
- The past, present, or future payment for the provision of health care to the individual
- Information that identifies the individual or for which there is a reasonable basis to believe it can be used to identify the individual

Individually identifiable health information also includes many common identifiers, such as name, address, birth date, and Social Security Number.

A major goal of the Privacy Rule is to assure that individuals' health information is properly protected while allowing the flow of health information needed to provide and promote high quality health care and to protect the public's health and well being. Within DHHS, the OCR is responsible for implementing and enforcing the Privacy Rule with respect to voluntary compliance activities and civil money penalties. Covered entities may disclose protected health information as authorized by, and to comply with, workers' compensation laws and other similar programs providing benefits for work-related injuries or illnesses. Otherwise, a covered entity must obtain the individual's written authorization for any use or disclosure of protected health information that is not for treatment, payment or healthcare operations or otherwise permitted or required by the Privacy Rule (U.S. DHHS, Office for Civil Rights-HIPAA, 2006).

Department of Transportation

The Department of Transportation (DOT) regulations generally cover employers and employees involved with safety-sensitive transportation and enforce regulations governing transit. This involves medical clearance to perform safety sensitive jobs and includes alcohol and drug testing of employees in those positions.

Each DOT agency and the U.S. Coast Guard have specific drug and alcohol testing regulations that outline what employees are subject to their testing regulations. DOT agencies include: Federal Railroad Administration (FRA); Federal Motor Carrier Safety Administration (FMCSA); Federal Transportation Administration (FTA); Federal Aviation Administration (FAA); and Pipeline and Hazardous Safety Materials Safety (PHMSA) (U.S. Department of Transportation [U.S. DOT], Office of the Secretary, 2008).

Working Partners for an Alcohol and Drug-Free Workplace

Employers can protect their businesses from the adverse effects of substance abuse in the workplace by developing drug-free workplace programs designed to educate employees about the dangers of alcohol and drug abuse and encourage employees with related problems to seek help. The U.S. Department of Labor's (DOL) Working Partners for an Alcohol and Drug-Free Workplace website provides employers with free resources to help implement these programs in order to help protect the safety and health of workers. However, drug-free workplace programs are not required by any DOL laws or regulations, nor does the DOL administer the Drug-Free Workplace Act of 1988 (U.S. DOL, Office of Compliance Assistance Policy, 2008a).

Environmental Protection Agency Worker Protection Standard

In August 1992, the Environmental Protection Agency (EPA) revised the Worker Protection Standard (WPS) (40 CFR Part 170) for Agricultural Pesticides. The WPS is federal legislation that represents a major national effort to ensure the health of agricultural workers and pesticide handlers. The Standard is designed to protect employees on farms, forests, nurseries, and greenhouses from occupational exposures to agricultural pesticides. The WPS offers protection to approximately 2.5 million agricultural workers (production of agricultural plants) and pesticide handlers (mix, load, or apply pesticides) who work at over 600,000 agricultural establishments. Effective implementation of the WPS will substantially lower the risk of pesticide poisonings among agricultural workers and pesticide handlers (U.S. Environmental Protection Agency [U.S. EPA], 2007b).

Pesticides are regulated under several laws, primarily the Federal Insecticide, Fungicide, and Rodenticide Act (FIRFA), which authorizes EPA to oversee the registration, distribution, sale, and use of pesticides. The Act applies to all varieties of pesticides, including insecticides, herbicides, fungicides, rodenticides, and antimicrobials. EPA works to assure compliance with federal environmental laws. Individuals who apply pesticides must use them in a way consistent with federal and state laws and regulations. In general, states have primary authority for compliance monitoring and enforcement against the use of pesticides in violation of the labeling requirements. Also, the agency with responsibility for pesticides differs from state to state. Usually it is a responsibility of a state's department of agriculture, but it may be a state's environmental agency or other agency (U.S. EPA, 2007a) that is responsible.

Youth Health and Safety

There are specific rules on the wages that workers under 18 years may be paid, the occupations and industries in which they are allowed to work, and the hours they may work. All states also have child labor standards. When federal and state standards are different, the rules that provide the most protection to young workers apply. The child labor provisions of the Fair Labor Standards Act (FLSA) are administered and enforced by the U.S. DOL, Employment and Standards Administration's Wage and Hour Division (WHD). The WHD's "Youth Rules!" website (www.youthrules.dol.gov/) provides information and resources that help promote positive and safe work experiences for young workers. OSHA also offers assistance for young workers, their employers, and their parents to help keep them safe at work. These resources include e-tools on the safe employment of youth in restaurants and in agriculture (U.S. DOL, 2008b).

The DOL is the only federal agency that monitors child labor and enforces child labor laws. The federal law that restricts the employment and abuse of child workers is the FLSA. Child labor rules under FLSA are designed to protect the educational opportunities of youth and prohibit the employment of youth in jobs that are detrimental to their health and safety. FLSA restricts work hours for those under 16 years of age and identifies hazardous occupations that are considered too dangerous for young workers. The WHD of the DOL's ESA is responsible for the enforcement of the FLSA's child labor provisions. Twelve is usually the minimum age for agricultural work. At 16, the federal agricultural laws no longer apply (U.S. DOL, ESA, 2008a).

Whistleblower Protection Act

First enacted in 1989, the Whistleblower Protection Act (WPA) provides statutory protections for federal employees who engage in "whistleblowing," which means an employee who provides evidence of illegal or improper government activities. On March 9, 2007, the House Committee on Oversight and Government Reform reported H.R. 985 (110th Cong.) H. Rept. 110-42, the Whistleblower Protection Enhancement Act of 2007, which would amend the WPA by providing protections for certain national security, government contractor, and science-based agency whistleblowers, and by enhancing the existing whistleblower protections for all federal employees (U.S. DOL, OSHA, n.d.).

An employee may file a complaint with OSHA if the employer retaliates by taking unfavorable personnel action because the employee engaged in protected activity relating to workplace safety and health, commercial motor carrier safety, pipeline safety, air carrier safety, nuclear safety, the environment, asbestos in schools, corporate fraud, Securities Exchange Commission rules or regulations, railroad carrier safety or security, or public transportation agency safety or security. To help ensure that employees are, in fact, free to participate in safety and health activities, Section 11(c) of the Act prohibits any person from discharging or in any manner discriminating against any employee because the employee has exercised rights under the Act. These rights include complaining to OSHA and seeking an OSHA inspection, participating in an OSHA inspection, and participating or testifying in any proceeding related to an OSHA inspection (U.S. DOL, OSHA, n.d.).

Occupational and Environmental Health Nursing

Rogers (2003) defines occupational and environmental health nursing (OEHN) as follows:

> the specialty practice that focuses on the promotion, prevention, and restoration of health within the context of a safe and healthy environment. It includes the prevention of adverse health effects from occupational and environmental hazards. It provides for and delivers environmental health and safety services to workers, worker populations, and community groups. Occupational and environmental health nursing is an autonomous specialty and nurses make independent nursing judgments in providing healthcare services. Many companies have onsite occupational health services with occupational and environmental health nurses (OEHN) who may provide the following services for the employees: first aid and emergency response, primary care for occupational and non-occupational injuries and illnesses, workers' compensation and disability case management, return-to-work activities, worksite assessments, health promotion, wellness training, health fairs and screenings, health surveillance, and several types of reports, documentation, and recordkeeping. Those companies without onsite occupational health services usually rely on specified private practice, urgent care, or hospital health services to which employees are referred. They frequently provide pre-placement

and health surveillance physicals, first aid care and emergency treatment, and assessment for work accommodations and clearance to return-to-work and should be familiar with the workplace and company policies. (Rogers, 2003, p. 52)

"OEHNs have a combined knowledge of health and business that they blend with healthcare expertise to balance the requirement for a safe and healthful work environment with a 'healthy' bottom line" (American Association of Occupational Health Nurses [AAOHN], 2008, §7). Working in this specialty area, the practice not only focuses on the health and safety of the employee and workplace, but also requires an awareness of the laws, regulations, and guidelines that the employer must follow. Although paid by the employer, the OEHN is responsible understanding the workplace hazards and for should work to control worker exposure as an advocate for the employee.

Scope of Practice in Nursing

The Board of Nursing in each state is responsible for determining and enforcing an acceptable set of activities that constitute every nurse's scope of practice. The level of nursing education and preparation determines what that scope may be for that particular state. For example, a nurse practitioner, registered nurse, and licensed practical nurse all function in different capacities, as each state determines what variety of nursing activities are allowed under the Nurse Practice Act.

"Boards of Nursing are state governmental agencies that are responsible for the regulation of nursing practice in each respective state. Boards of Nursing are authorized to enforce the Nurse Practice Act and develop administrative rules/regulations and other responsibilities per the Nurse Practice Act" (National Council of State Boards of Nursing [NCSBN], n.d., §1). Boards establish the standards for safe nursing care and issue licenses to practice nursing. Once a license is issued, the board's job continues by monitoring licensees' compliance to state laws and taking action against the licenses of those nurses who have exhibited unsafe nursing practice. The boards in the 50 states, the District of Columbia, and four United States territories (Guam, Virgin Islands, American Samoa, and the Northern Mariana Islands) comprise the membership of the National Council of State Boards of Nursing (NCSBN).

The Nurse Licensure Compact (NLC) is the mutual recognition model of nurse licensure that allows a nurse to have one license (in his or her state of residence) and to practice in other states (both physically and electronically), subject to each state's practice law and regulation. Under mutual recognition, a nurse may practice across state lines unless otherwise restricted. As of July 2008, 23 states were part of the NLC (NCSBN, 2004).

Standards of Practice in Occupational and Environmental Health Nursing

Standards of Practice have been developed by the AAOHN for OEHN to define and advance practice and provide a framework for evaluation. These authoritative statements describe the accountability of the practitioner and reflect the values and priorities of the profession. "AAOHN has identified 11 professional practice standards that describe a competent level of performance with regard to the nursing process and professional roles of the occupational and environmental health nurse. Criteria developed for each standard are key indicators of competent practice and permit occupational and environmental health nurses to evaluate their practice relative to the

---

STANDARD I: ASSESSMENT
  The Occupational and Environmental Health Nurse systematically assesses the health status of the client(s).
STANDARD II: DIAGNOSIS
  The Occupational and Environmental Health Nurse analyzes assessment data to formulate diagnoses.
STANDARD III: OUTCOME IDENTIFICATION
  The Occupational and Environmental Health Nurse identifies outcomes specifically to the client(s).
STANDARD IV: PLANNING
  The Occupational and Environmental Health Nurse develops a goal-directed plan that is comprehensive and formulates interventions to attain expected outcomes.
STANDARD V: IMPLEMENTATION
  The Occupational and Environmental Health Nurse implements interventions to attain desired outcomes identified in the plan.
STANDARD VI: EVALUATION
  The Occupational and Environmental Health Nurse systematically and continuously evaluates responses to interventions and progress toward the achievement of desired outcomes.
STANDARD VII: RESOURCE MANAGEMENT
  The Occupational and Environmental Health Nurse secures and manages the resources that support occupational health and safety programs and services.
STANDARD VIII: PROFESSIONAL DEVELOPMENT
  The Occupational and Environmental Health Nurse assumes accountability for professional development to enhance professional growth and maintain competency.
STANDARD IX: COLLABORATION
  The Occupational and Environmental Health Nurse collaborates with clients for the promotion, prevention, and restoration of health within the context of a safe and healthy environment.
STANDARD X: RESEARCH
  The Occupational and Environmental Health Nurse uses research findings in practice and contributes to the scientific base in occupational and environmental health nursing to improve practice and advance the profession.
STANDARD XI: ETHICS
  The Occupational and Environmental Health Nurse uses an ethical framework as a guide for decision making in practice.

Figure 20.2   The AAOHN standards of occupational and environmental health practice. From American Association of Occupational Health Nurses, Inc. Copyright 2008. With permission.

standards" (AAOHN, 2004, p. 1). The AAOHN Standards of Occupational and Environmental Health Practice (2004) are listed in the box (Figure 20.2).

Maintaining Professional License and Skills

OEHNs must also maintain and increase competency through continuing professional development. This may occur through self-study, reading and researching professional literature, networking with peers and other professionals, and participating in conferences, seminars, and academic courses. Each state has its own continuing education requirements for nursing licensure renewal.

Certifications

The American Board for Occupational Health Nurses, Inc. (ABOHN) is the sole certifying body for OEHNs in the United States and awards four credentials: Certified Occupational Health

Nurse (COHN); Certified Occupational Health Nurse—Specialist (COHN-S); Case Management (CM); and Safety Management (SM). Accredited by The National Commission for Certifying Agencies (NCCA) and The American Board for Nursing Specialties (ABNS), ABOHN uses predetermined standards of nursing practice derived from AAOHN Core Curriculum, standards, competencies, etc., to validate an individual registered nurse's qualifications, knowledge, and practice in specific areas of occupational health nursing (American Board for Occupational Health Nursing [ABOHN], 2008).

Standing Orders

The professional OEHN is a licensed registered nurse working within his or her scope of practice that is set by the state's board of nursing, but also is guided by the scope and practice of occupational and environmental health nursing established by the professional society. The OEHN uses nursing judgment and follows acceptable clinical practice protocols as a treatment plan based on a nursing assessment. Protocols should be reviewed by the nurse and physician. Standing Orders or clinical guidelines, signed by a physician, provide a legal framework for the OEHN to use treatments outside the scope of practice, such as administering prescription medications. Standing Orders should be reviewed regularly by the healthcare providers, usually once a year. In the development and implementation of clinical protocols, individual state nurse practice acts must be followed (Rogers, 2003).

Documentation and Medical Records

As with any health record, the OEHN must maintain strict control over the health information to ensure confidentiality. However, most workplaces do not employ OEHNs and the medical records are maintained by Human Resources. The OEHN does not divulge personal health information to the employer, supervisor, or other workers. Rules for health record documentation apply to occupational health nursing as in any specialty's nursing notes.

Confidentiality

One of the reasons that nurses have a special relationship with the employees is the understanding that nurses are to be trusted in keeping patient health information confidentiality. The employee is the patient who is in the care of the nurse. As with the HIPAA laws, responsible and ethical nurses are also required by their scope of practice to maintain confidentiality of health information and therefore, the trust of the employees in the nurse is maintained. "Unauthorized release of health records could result in personal liability, suspension of license to practice nursing by the state agency responsible for regulating the practice of nursing, or termination of employment by the employer" (Knoblauch & Strausser, 2006, p. 96).

The ethical responsibility of keeping personal health information confidential is inherent in any area of nursing practice. However, according to AAOHN (2006), "Most legislation protecting health information is enacted at the individual state level. These protections, where they exist, are inconsistent from state to state, leading to disparities and complexities for individuals practicing in multiple states. Most states do not protect communication between occupational health professionals and their clients, since they are acting as agents of employers" (AAOHN, 2006, §3).

Standards of Care

The Standards of Care provided by the American Nurses Association (ANA) and other nursing specialty associations describe a competent level of nursing care. AAOHN has developed *the Core Curriculum in Occupational and Environmental Health Nursing*. Rogers states that "the *Core Curriculum* delineates concepts and principles to support the knowledge base of the specialty practice" (Rogers, 2003, p. 692). "AAOHN has developed *Competencies and Performance Criteria in Occupational and Environmental Health Nursing*, which includes nine competency categories delineated by three levels (competent, proficient, and expert) and performance criteria for each stated competency" (Rogers, 2003, p. 692). The levels of care are demonstrated through the nursing process, which is the foundation of clinical decision-making and includes actions taken by nurses in providing care.

Within each category, three levels of practice are identified. The competent level is considered the core for practice in the specialty. The other two levels are proficient and expert. Proficient implies increased ability based on experience to evaluate client situations and act on them appropriately. The expert level has extensive experience and knowledge, enabling the OEHN to assess a situation quickly and initiate appropriate action. The code of ethics, standards of practice, core curriculum, and competencies provide the basis for scope of practice, knowledge, skill, and the legal and ethical framework in occupational and environmental health nursing. Standards of care are important if a legal dispute arises over whether a nurse practiced appropriately in a particular case (AAOHN, 2007).

According to AAOHN Advisory, Managing Professional Risk (2007),

> Plaintiffs usually allege that the employer is liable for negligent actions of a nurse employee under the principle of respondeat superior so that the plaintiff can recover from the employer for the employee's negligence. This term is derived from the Latin "let the master answer" also known as vicarious or agency liability. This principle of law holds that when an employee or "agent" is found liable for the negligent actions, the employer or company must accept responsibility for their actions if the employee was acting within the scope of employment. The employer may use this as a defense if the employee was not acting within the scope of their employment. If OHNs act outside the scope of their employment/job responsibilities or provide inappropriate or unsafe care, the nurses will be accountable for their actions. (§9)

The AAOHN Advisory continues to state that

> Malpractice, or liability in professional practice, occurs with professional misconduct, improper discharge of professional responsibilities, and/or the professional's failure to meet the standard of care that results in harm to others. This is also known as a "breech of care" or "breech of standard of care." The standard of care is defined by standards of practice or "what's reasonable under the same circumstances by a similarly qualified professional." (AAOHN, 2007, §6)

The Role of the LNC in Occupational Health and Safety

Many LNCs have diverse backgrounds, such as in CM, insurance, or critical care and some have experience in occupational and environmental health nursing leading to a better understanding of the role of the OEHN. Occupational and environmental health nursing is a specialty field of registered nurses who independently observe and assess the worker's health status with respect to job tasks and hazards. OEHNs also recognize and prevent health effects from hazardous exposures and treat workers' injuries/illnesses (U.S. DOL, 2008a).

LNCs may interface with the OEHN during case witness interviews, investigations, depositions, record discovery, and expert testimony. The LNC, depending on the nature of the case, may work with the OEHN to compare facts in a case, identify possible witnesses, and determine additional sources of records. For example, the OEHN interface with the LNC working on a chemical exposure case can provide valuable information, because the OEHN is probably familiar with the workplace chemical and able to give important details about the exposure source, as well as treatment protocols for the industry. This information is helpful in identifying questions for the attorney to present during depositions and mediations. The LNC assists in the litigation process by educating attorneys on healthcare issues, seeking medical experts, drafting medical chronologies, obtaining job essential function descriptions, identifying subpoena needs, and performing other aspects of discovery.

Occupational Health Records

OSHA Recordkeeping for First Aid Visits, Injury and Illness Reports

First aid is emergency care provided for injury or sudden illness before emergency medical treatment is available. A workplace first-aid/injury program includes management and employee involvement, worksite analysis, hazard prevention and control, and safety and health training. The aim is to minimize the outcome of accidents or exposures. OSHA has certain requirements regarding first aid and injury reports in the workplace. As previously described, employers are required by OSHA standard 29 CFR Part 1904 and 1952 to abide by certain recordkeeping obligations. It is essential that data recorded by employers be uniform and accurate for validity and for statistical use by OSHA. Some employers may be subject to additional recordkeeping and reporting requirements not outlined in the above document such as record retention, exposure monitoring, inspections, or other activities relevant to occupational safety and health.

All employers must report to OSHA any workplace incident that results in a fatality or hospitalization of three or more employees. Injuries and illnesses meeting the OSHA definitions are required to be recorded on the OSHA 300 (Log), 300A (Summary) and 301 (Incident Report) forms. Welding flash burns and fractures are two examples of workplace illnesses and injuries needing to be recorded. Recording an injury or illness on an OSHA 300 Log does not necessarily indicate qualification for workers' compensation or benefits. The recording should show two things: (1) that an injury or illness has occurred, (2) that the employer has determined that the case is work-related using OSHA's definition. Many recorded cases are compensable under the State workers' compensation system while others are not. When an injury or illness occurs to an employee, the employer must take into consideration both OSHA recording rules and the requirements of the State workers' compensation system to decide if a case is recordable, compensable, or both. Not all cases are recordable by OSHA definition.

The aggravation of a pre-existing condition by a workplace event or exposure also makes a case work-related. The records are used by employers to implement safety and health programs with recognized importance in workplace tracking and problem solving (U.S. DOL, OSHA, 2008b). The LNC's job is to understand and relate the medical facts of a case in a format that is easily understandable to the attorney. A strong contribution to the litigation process can be made when the LNC is familiar with the OSHA recordkeeping rules for cases involving work-related injuries and illnesses. Knowledge of the rules allows the LNC to describe any red flags in the medical chronology as well as present the standards of care related to OSHA guidelines. Basic knowledge of the recordkeeping process is an added benefit to refining the medical and regulatory issues in work-related cases.

Accident Investigation Reports

Accidents occur throughout the United States every day. The failure of people, supplies, equipment, or surroundings to behave or react as expected is the cause of most accidents. Accident investigations determine how and why the failures occur (U.S. DOL, OSHA, 2008d). Information gained through an investigation may help prevent similar or perhaps more disastrous accidents as well as help determine cause and harm important to case investigation and best practices. The LNC's primary role in accident investigation reports is to determine if the report has been included in records from subpoena and the inclusion of the report in any medical chronology written on behalf of the attorney in fact finding. For example, the LNC might uncover from the reports that an unsafe act caused the accident, or that the employer failed to provide adequate safety equipment.

Workers' Compensation Claims

Workers' Compensation laws are designed to ensure that injured or disabled employees are compensated with designated monetary awards that will assist in eliminating the need for expensive litigation. The laws also provide certain benefits for the dependents of workers who are fatally injured due to work-related accidents or illnesses. State Workers' Compensation statutes establish the framework for most employment. Federal statutes are limited to federal employees or those workers employed in some significant type of interstate commerce. The Federal Employment Compensation Act provides compensation for non-military, federal employees. The Federal Employment Liability Act, while not a workers' compensation statute, provides that railroads engaged in interstate commerce are liable for injuries to their employees if negligent. The Black Lung Benefits Act provides compensation to miners suffering from "black lung disease" (U.S. DOL, ESA, 2008c). It is important for the LNC to be aware that these Federal laws exist in order to research and interpret work-related medical records appropriately for the attorney. Certain lung diseases for example, require B-Reader radiologists by federal law. The LNC using knowledge of these laws can determine if the standard of care has or has not been met.

In the United States most employees who are injured on the job have an absolute right to medical care for that injury or illness, and in many cases monetary payments to compensate for any resulting disabilities whether permanent or temporary. Most employers are required to have insurance for workers' compensation or face penalties. Most states have public uninsured employer funds for payment of benefits to workers employed by companies not participating in purchased insurance services. The vast majority of companies however, have workers' compensation insurance provided solely by private insurance companies.

It is illegal in most states for an employer to terminate an employee for reporting a work-related injury or illness or for filing a workers' compensation claim. Most states also prohibit employment refusal to candidates previously having filed a workers' compensation claim. Employers can consult commercial databases of claims data, however, making it difficult to prove that an employer discriminated against a job applicant. It is also illegal to falsely claim workers' compensation benefits. Employers sometimes hire private investigators to videotape claimants engaged in acts disproving claims. Since state laws differ, it is best to consult the regulating state agency or the U.S. Department of Labor ESA for any verification of wrongful termination laws. The LNC needs to be knowledgeable about all aspects of workers compensation claims such as analysis to determine if prompt and appropriate care was received, panel physicians were offered when indicated, compliance with the American Disability Act was carried out, and any other red flags. The LNC handling workers compensation claims must be familiar with the applicable statutes and laws specific to each case as well as become familiar with where and how to research them for the purpose of creating an accurate Critical Facts Summary to be used by the attorney. Critical Facts Summaries are attorney-client privileged medical chronologies, and contain information not to be shared outside of the litigation team. The value of the LNC's work in developing these summaries is often critical to the case and extremely valuable.

Exposure Monitoring Records

Understanding the basics of exposure records is important to the LNC who may need to prepare medical summaries, exposure charts or timelines related to a formal complaint. Lack of knowledge in how or where to research information could lead to inadequate reports. Exposure monitoring rules are found in 29 CFR1910.1020 Access to Employee Exposure and Medical Records. This ruling is often seen as a companion standard to the hazard communication rule. The Access to Exposure and Medical Records rule allows for the examination of the results of monitoring and any measured level of exposure to chemicals as well as any medical records that might provide information about health status and the relationship of the exposure. The access rule also includes exposure to biological hazards such as bacteria, viruses, fungi, and physical hazards such as radiation and vibration.

The standard defines a record as "any item, collection or grouping of information regardless of the form or process by which it is maintained (e.g., paper, x-ray, microfilm, or automated data)." The standard differentiates between medical records and exposure records. The medical record is defined as "a record concerning the health status of an employee which is made or maintained by a physician, nurse or other healthcare personnel or technician." Medical records include: questionnaires, histories, medical examination results, physicals, laboratory tests, biological monitoring records, medical opinions, progress notes, recommendations, first aid records, treatment, prescriptions, and employee medical complaints. Exposure records are defined as "employee exposure records" containing any of the following information: environmental workplace monitoring or measuring of a toxic substance or harmful agent, biological monitoring that directly assesses the absorption of a toxic substance or harmful physical agent, and MSDS that reveal the identity of a chemical or substance. Exposure to molds and ergonomic stresses are considered part of the employee exposure records. Other examples include exposure to ultraviolet light emitted from welding operations or exposure to radiofrequency energy at a transmitting antenna tower or microwave dish.

Records must be preserved and maintained for at least the duration of employment plus 30 years, unless a specific occupational safety and health standard provides a different period of time. The access rule has provisions for trade secrets. An employer can withhold trade secret information in an otherwise disclosable record provided that three conditions are met: the claim that information held is a trade secret can be supported, the employer informs the requesting party that the chemical is a trade secret, and all other available information on the properties and effects is disclosed. There is also an emergency provision for trade secret release if a physician or nurse determines that an emergency exists (Rekus, 2008).

The LNC may be involved in toxic tort cases, which are civil actions for recovery of damages related to exposure to a chemical, an emission, or to a substance which may have allegedly caused physical or psychological harm. This type of complex litigation often involves multiple contacts, different jurisdictions, and numerous witnesses. The LNC may be involved in interviewing industrial hygienists, safety officers, physicians, OEHNs, and other healthcare and safety team members regarding these types of cases. The LNC must be cognizant of the existence of exposure monitoring records and which members of the workplace may have access to these records. It is essential for the LNC involved in toxic tort litigation to have an understanding of federal and state rules affecting this type of litigation and knowledge of where to do research concerning exposure records.

Material Safety Data Sheets

An Material Safety Data Sheets (MSDS) is a document prepared by the manufacturer of a hazardous chemical which describes its physical and chemical properties, hazards for handling, storage and proper disposal. These informational sheets are extremely important to workers and emergency personnel since they contain the procedures for handling or working with that substance in a safe manner. MSDSs may be obtained by contacting the manufacturer. It is extremely important that these sheets be kept updated according to the standard and that they are accessible to all employees (U.S. DOL, OSHA, 2008c). The LNC should be familiar with the definition of an MSDS as well as where one might be obtained should there be a need for this information in a case. The information found on the MSDS can be important in this specialized area of litigation. The attorney may need to know the limits of exposure for example, and the MSDS would identify this information. The MSDS can be helpful in determining if adequate treatment was sought based on the manufacturer's written warnings for the product that would be of interest to the attorney in case fact finding.

Health/Medical Surveillance Documentation

Medical surveillance is a term used by the Occupational Safety and Health Administration (OSHA) to describe protocols for monitoring specific exposures that extend beyond medicine to include a type of health or medical surveillance. The purposes of surveillance examinations are to protect workers from adverse exposures, assure the employee's ability to perform the job activity, and to meet governmental requirements as outlined in certain federal standards such as asbestos and lead exposure (Burgel, 2006).

The LNC needs to be familiar with where to find OSHA protocols governing surveillance examinations and proper monitoring. For example, when reviewing records related to an employee involved in a vinyl chloride chemical exposure, the LNC would need to look at the appropriate OSHA standard for the medical surveillance section to determine if the standards were met. OSHA standards may include mandatory tests in a specified time frame for employees working in certain areas.

The Vinyl Chloride standard requires that an employee have liver function tests yearly for less than 10 years of service in an exposed area, and every 6 months for employees who have worked in an exposed area for greater than 10 years. Exposure to vinyl chloride from any previous industry must be included in the calculation of exposure time. This means that if an employee worked previously at a vinyl plant for 5 years, and now has now been employed at the current plant for 5 years, liver enzyme testing must be done every 6 months rather than yearly. Knowledge of these types of legal standards becomes important in the LNC's medical summaries, which may include assurance of proper record maintenance, company policies, employee performance tests and interpretation, maintenance of confidentiality of records, record retention, record storage, health education, and counseling or referral for conditions of exposure or possible exposure (Knoblauch & Strausser, 2006). Familiarity with the above helps determine confidentiality breach or lack of breach, as well as expected adherence or lack of adherence to protocols and standards.

Employee Training Records

Several standards from OSHA require the employer to train employees in the safety and health aspects of their jobs. Other standards require the employer to limit certain job assignments to employees who have been trained or certified as qualified for the job with the goal of safety in mind. One such example is the OSHA requirements found in the Highly Hazardous Chemicals standard (Title 29 Code of Federal Regulations Part 19.10.119), which contains several special requirements. The location of a written hazardous chemical training program must be communicated, readily accessible to all employees, and training records must be kept. There must be safe handling of hazardous chemicals with controls in place to protect workers. Labeling systems for hazardous chemicals must be in place, and training must be provided with emphasis on emergency procedures in the event of an exposure. Training must include contract workers and be maintained on a regular basis to include training for life-threatening emergencies (U.S. DOL, OSHA, 2008e).

Employee training records are of special interest to the LNC in order to determine company compliance and likelihood of injury. These records may hold answers to questions during investigation of harm such as: did the employee have the proper training, was the employee qualified to operate certain equipment, and who were the trainers and were they qualified?

Discovery

Legal and ethical issues frequently occur in the occupational setting. The LNC involved in cases related to the occupational health setting will need to be familiar with state and federal regulations. Malpractice involves negligence and a professional misconduct or unreasonable lack of skill. Negligence can include failure to take action, failure to communicate danger, delay in assistance, medication errors, and failure to obtain consent. The interpretation of laws, rules, and regulations may change as new cases decide common law and precedents are established (Knoblauch & Strausser, 2006). Knowing how to do an effective critical facts summary or medical chronology is important to the litigation process. The LNC who is familiar with the employment law and worker's compensation is valuable to case discovery. The LNC has the ethical obligation to inform the attorney of negative aspects in a case as well as any critical information that could impact the case either negatively or positively. The LNC must be knowledgeable in many areas and often act as a case manager, researcher, analyzer, risk assessor, and valuable member to the legal team (Jones, 2008).

References

American Association of Occupational Health Nurses. (2004). *Standards of Occupational and Environmental Health Nursing*. Atlanta: American Association of Occupational Health Nurses, Inc.

American Association of Occupational Health Nurses. (2006).Confidentiality of employee health information. Retrieved September 18, 2008, from http://www.aaohn.org/public_policy/aaohn_in_action/Conf/upload/Confidentiality-of-Employee-Health-Info-0806.pdf

American Association of Occupational Health Nurses. (2007). *Managing professional risk*. Retrieved September 18, 2008, from www.aaohn.org/practice/advisories/

American Association of Occupational Health Nurses. (2008). *AAOHN fact sheet*. Retrieved September 18, 2008, from http://www.aaohn.org/press_room/fact_sheets/aaohn.cfm

American Board for Occupational Health Nurses. (2008). *Who we are and what we do*. Retrieved September 18, 2008, from http://www.abohn.org/index.html

An Act. (1996). Public Law 91-596, 91st Congress, S. 2193, 29, 1970, as amended by Public Law 101-552, 3101, November 5, 1990. U.S. Government Printing Office.

Boston University. (1997). *The rehabilitation act of 1973*. Retrieved August 28, 2008, from http://www.bu.edu/cpr/reasaccom/whatlaws-rehaba.html

Burgel, B. (2006). Direct care in the occupational setting. In M. K. Salazar (Ed.), *Core curriculum for occupational & environmental health nursing* (3rd ed., pp. 313–323). St. Louis: W.B. Saunders.

Center for Disease Control and Prevention, National Institute for Occupational Safety and Health. (n.d.). About NIOSH. Retrieved June 30, 2008, from http://www.cdc.gov/niosh/about.html

Hagan, P. E., Montgomery, J. F., & O'Reilly, J.R. (Eds.). (2001). *Accident prevention manual for business and industry: Administration and programs*. (12th ed.). Chicago: The National Safety Council.

Jones, M. P. (2008). Strategies for an effective medical chronology. *Journal of Legal Nurse Consulting, 19(3)*, 7–11.

Knoblauch, D. & Strausser, P. (2006). Legal and ethical issues. In M.K. Salazar (Ed.), *Core curriculum for occupational & environmental health nursing* (3rd ed., pp. 72–73, 84–88, 96). St. Louis: W.B. Saunders.

Koron, S. R. (Ed.). (1999). *Workers' compensation handbook* (4th ed.). Durham: North Carolina Occupational Safety and Health Project.

National Council of State Boards of Nursing, Nurse Compact Administrators. (n.d.). Boards of nursing. Retrieved September 18, 2008, from https://www.ncsbn.org/boards.htm

National Council of State Boards of Nursing, Nurse Compact Administrators. (2004). Nurse licensure compact (NLC). Retrieved September 18, 2008, from https://www.ncsbn.org/nlc.htm

Rekus, J. (2008). OSHA's other recordkeeping standard: Access to employee exposure and medical records. *Occupational hazards*. Retrieved June 14, 2008, from http://www.occupationalhazards.com/Issue/Article/36711/OSHAs_Other_Recordkeeping

Rogers, B. (2003). *Occupational and environmental health nursing—Concepts and practice* (2nd ed.). Philadelphia: Saunders.

U.S. Department of Health and Human Services, Office for Civil Rights. (n.d.). Your rights under section 504 of the rehabilitation act, what is section 504? Retrieved September 10, 2008, from http://www.hhs.gov/ocr/504.html

U.S. Department of Health and Human Services, Office for Civil Rights-HIPAA. (2006). Medical privacy-national standards to protect the privacy of personal health information. Retrieved September 15, 2008, from http://www.hhs.gov/ocr/hipaa/finalreg.html

U.S. Department of Health and Human Services, Office on Disability. (2005). The Americans with Disabilities Act. Retrieved September 15, 2008, from http://www.hhs.gov/od/about/fact_sheets/ada-factsheet.html

U.S. Department of Labor, Employment Standards Administration. (2008a). Compliance assistance–Fair Labor Standards Act (FLSA). Retrieved September 19, 2008, from http://www.dol.gov/esa/whd/flsa/

U.S. Department of Labor, Employment Standards Administration. (2008b). Family and Medical Leave Act overview. Retrieved September 18, 2008, from http://www.dol.gov/esa/whd/fmla/index.htm

U.S. Department of Labor, Employment Standards Administration. (2008c). Office of Workers' Compensation Programs: About OWCP. Retrieved July 12, 2008, from http://www.dol.gov/esa/owcp/index.htm

U.S. Department of Labor, Occupational Safety and Health Administration. (n.d.). The whistleblower protection program. Retrieved September 18, 2008 from http://www.osha.gov/dep/ola/whistleblower/index.html

U.S. Department of Labor, Occupational Safety and Health Administration. (1996). Occupational exposure to bloodborne pathogens (OSHA Publication No. 3127). Washington, DC: Author.

U.S. Department of Labor, Occupational Safety and Health Administration. (2001a). Access to medical and exposure records (OSHA Publication No. 3110). Washington, DC: Author.

U.S. Department of Labor, Occupational Safety and Health Administration. (2001b). Standard interpretations: Needlestick Safety and Prevention Act amplifies the requirements to use safer needle device. Retrieved July 29, 2008, from http://www.osha.gov/pls/oshaweb/owadisp.show_document?p_table=INTERPRETATIONS&p_id=24012

U.S. Department of Labor, Occupational Safety and Health Administration. (2002). Hearing conservation (OSHA Publication No. 3074). Washington, DC: Author.

U.S. Department of Labor, Occupational Safety and Health Administration. (2003). Personal protective equipment (OSHA Publication No. 3151-12R). Washington, DC: Author.

U.S. Department of Labor, Occupational Safety and Health Administration. (2006). All about OSHA (OSHA Publication No. 3302-06N). Washington, DC: Author.

U. S. Department of Labor, Occupational Safety & Health Administration. (2008a). Nursing in occupational health. Retrieved July 19, 2008, from http://www.osha.gov/dts/oohn/ohn.html

U.S. Department of Labor, Occupational Safety & Health Administration. (2008b). OSHA recordkeeping handbook. Retrieved July 19, 2008, from http://www.osha.gov/recordkeeping/handbook/index.html

U.S. Department of Labor, Occupational Safety & Health Administration. (2008c). Recommended format for material safety data sheets (MSDSs). Retrieved June 14, 2008, from http://www.osha.gov/dsg/hazcom/msdsformat.html

U.S. Department of Labor, Occupational Safety & Health Administration. (2008d). Safety and health topics: Accident investigation. Retrieved July 12, 2008, from http://www.osha.gov/SLTC/accidentinvestigation/index.html

U.S. Department of Labor, Occupational Safety & Health Administration. (2008e). Training requirements in OSHA standards and training guidelines. Retrieved July 19, 2008, from http://www.osha.gov/dcsp/compliance_assistance/frequent_standards.html

U.S. Department of Labor, Office of Compliance Assistance Policy. (2008a). Safety and health in the workplace: Drug-free workplaces. Retrieved September 19, 2008, from http://www.dol.gov/compliance/topics/safety-health-working-partners.htm

U.S. Department of Labor, Office of Compliance Assistance Policy. (2008b). Youth in the workplace. Retrieved September 19, 2008, from http://www.dol.gov/compliance/audience/youth.htm

U.S. Department of Transportation, Office of the Secretary. (2008). What employers need to know about DOT drug and alcohol testing. Retrieved September 19, 2008, from http://www.dot.gov/ost/dapc/testingpubs/REVISED_EMPLOYER_GUIDELINES_AUGUST_25_2008.pdf

U.S. Environmental Protection Agency. (2007a). Overview of EPA authorities for natural resource managers developing aquatic invasive species rapid response and management plans: Federal Insecticide, Fungicide, and Rodenticide Act. Retrieved September 14, 2008, from http://www.epa.gov/owowwtr1/invasive_species/invasives_management/fifra.html

U.S. Environmental Protection Agency. (2007b). Part 170–Worker Protection Standard. Retrieved September 14, 2008, from http://www.epa.gov/pesticides/safety/workers/PART170.htm

U.S. Equal Employment Opportunity Commission. (2005). Employers and other entities covered by EEO laws. Retrieved September 5, 2008, from http://www.eeoc.gov/abouteeo/overview_coverage.html

U.S. Equal Employment Opportunity Commission. (2009). Disability Discrimination. Retrieved November 10, 2009, from http://www.eeoc.gov/laws/types/disability.cfm

U.S. Occupational Safety and Health Review Commission. (2008). About OSHRC. Retrieved July 25, 2008, from http://www.oshrc.gov/

Test Questions

1. What agency promulgates the standards that employers are required to follow?
   A. National Institute for Occupational Safety and Health (NIOSH)
   B. Environmental Protection Agency (EPA)
   C. Occupational Safety and Health Administration (OSHA)
   D. Department of Transportation (DOT)

2. OSHA requires mandatory reporting for any workplace incident that results in:
   A. Hospitalization of one employee
   B. Hospitalization of three or more employees or any fatality
   C. Fatalities only
   D. Within one week of a workplace injury

3. The LNC reviewing records for surveillance exams would find protocols in
   A. OSHA Standards
   B. The specific company policy manual
   C. WHO protocols for industry
   D. None of the above

4. The LNC handling workers' compensation claims must be familiar with the fact that
   A. Employee exposure records must be maintained for at least 30 years
   B. Record retention is left up to the particular industry standards
   C. Records must be preserved and maintained for at least 10 years
   D. Employee medical records must be maintained for at least the duration of employment plus 30 years

5. The Occupation and Environmental Health Nurse (OEHN) who works with employees in several different states must be licensed by the state in which
   A. The OEHN resides
   B. The OEHN provides care for the worker
   C. The employer has corporate headquarters
   D. The employee resides

Answers: 1. C; 2. B; 3. A; 4. A, D; 5. B

Chapter 21

Worker's Compensation Case Evaluation

Joan Hand, BSN, RN, CCM

Contents

Objectives

- To describe five underlying principles of the workers' compensation system
- To list the workers' compensation benefits provided to the employee or injured worker
- To discuss the role of the legal nurse consultant (LNC) in assisting with causation in workers' compensation claims
- To compare the workers' compensation LNC plaintiff and defense roles
- To describe the role of the LNC in catastrophic injury claims

Introduction

Legal nurse consulting has been underutilized both in the plaintiff and defense workers' compensation legal practice areas. Each state has its own workers' compensation laws or statutes. Because of the statutory differences between jurisdictions and ongoing legislation with changing statutes, attorneys must have expertise in the area of workers compensation in order to successfully represent their clients.

Defense law firms are more likely to hire a legal nurse consultant (LNC) than the plaintiff law firm. Plaintiff litigation in workers' compensation claims may be financially limited due to explicit state workers' compensation laws, which mandate the format for financial settlements for future medical and disability costs. Because workers' compensation benefits are provided regardless of fault ("no-fault" principle), there is no tort law allowing for recovery from damages against the employer. This sometimes can limit the financial exposure and need for services the LNC can provide in plaintiff workers' compensation litigation.

When the states' laws allow for settlement of future medical and disability needs for the injured worker, workers' compensation plaintiff attorneys help the injured worker obtain all of the benefits due in a worker's compensation claim. Sometimes, tort law will apply because of a third-party lawsuit. The plaintiff attorney usually handles both the worker's compensation litigation and third-party lawsuit on behalf of the injured worker. Examples of third-party lawsuits in a worker's compensation injury claim include injuries caused by another driver and injuries resulting from working with unsafe equipment (product liability). In third-party lawsuits, the LNC's contributions are the same as in other personal injury practice areas. The LNC provides the necessary medical expertise to assist with defining the financial medical exposure so that appropriate settlement can be made on behalf of the plaintiff who, in this case, also has a workers' compensation claim. In fact, many plaintiff attorneys do not confine their practice areas to workers' compensation, but include other areas such as personal injury and medical malpractice.

Since the largest single factor affecting the value of a worker's compensation claim is the strength of the medical evidence, some insurance companies have recognized the value of having a medical expert available to work side by side with the attorneys. It is more economically justifiable for large defense law firms specializing in workers' compensation litigation, to hire an LNC.

Law firms that provide staff counsel to large property and casualty insurance companies hire attorneys that specialize in defending personal and commercial injury claims or workers' compensation claims. Generally, the two practice areas are separated within the law firm because the expertise for workers' compensation litigation is complex.

What occurs in the insurance company's decision-making in regard to litigated personal injury, commercial injury, and workers' compensation claims is related to the financial exposure of the claim. Major insurance companies realize that their staff law firms provide a significant financial impact by successfully disputing and reducing inappropriate settlement amounts. In workers' compensation cases, defense strategies incorporate causation and medical necessity for future medical and disability expenses. The LNC makes a vital contribution in defining the medical issues.

History of Workers' Compensation

The history of workers' compensation is important for the LNC working in this practice area because the system is based on unique changes in determination of negligence and awarding damages. The workers' compensation system was developed after the Industrial Revolution in response to the dangerous working environment brought on by inventions of production machinery. The centralization of manufacturing in huge factories, as well as the mass movement of products by railroad and steamships, increased the demand for workers while at the same time placing them at greater risk for injuries. Machinery, with its exposed fast-moving parts and the crowded conditions in factories, made the work environment more dangerous. Catastrophic injuries and work-related deaths rapidly increased (Devenny & Morgan, 2008).

To recover damages, the injured workers had to prove that the accident was the fault of the employer. At this time in history, common law allowed the employer to use several defenses against the injured worker's claim of negligence, and the injured workers had to prove all of several elements related to employer negligence in order to recover for damages. Frequently, injured workers did not prevail and were never compensated for injuries received during the course of employment. With no compensation, the burden for the expense of medical treatment, as well as loss of wages, became the responsibility of the injured worker's family and friends.

The increased risk of injury to workers could have affected the rapid progress of the Industrial Revolution. As injuries to workers increased, workforce reduction slowed production. For example, when railroad injuries increased, transportation of goods was delayed placing a strain on several parts of the economic industrial chain. Likewise, when injuries to factory workers increased due to the development of machinery with exposed moving parts, factory production was reduced. The decrease in the number of factory workers in any one factory placed additional stress on the factory's ability to produce goods. The result was either a decline in production or an increase in injuries caused by placing greater demands on remaining workers until additional workers could be hired and trained.

In 1908, as a result of increasing railroad injuries, President Theodore Roosevelt pushed Congress to pass the Federal Employer's Liability Act (FELA). This act, which is still in existence today, created legislation allowing injured workers to sue the employer without the traditional common law employer defenses regarding proof of negligence (Devenny & Morgan, 2008).

Finally, in 1911, after the Triangle Shirtwaist Factory fire in New York City killed more than 100 workers including women and children, states began passing legislation providing benefits for the injured worker without regard to employer fault. By 1948, each state had adopted workers' compensation legislation giving the injured worker medical and wage replacement benefits

(Devenny & Morgan, 2008). All jurisdictions require either a state industrial board or an insurance commissioner to approve coverage contracts. Most states require insurance coverage, but there are a few states that allow employer self-insurance coverage for their employees.

Principles of the Workers' Compensation System

While states have individual statutes, there are certain basic principles of the workers' compensation system that provide underlying premises for all benefits provided by the system.

No-Fault System

The leading principle of the workers' compensation system is to eliminate fault as a basis of recovery for the injured worker. Under state's workers' compensation systems, the injured worker gives up the right to bring a tort claim against his employer, regardless of fault or negligence. In return, the injured worker is guaranteed medical and wage benefits by some method of insurance coverage. In the event of death, benefits are paid to the worker's dependents (Devenny & Morgan, 2008). The result of the no-fault principle is to avoid delay in medical treatment for the injured worker and allow the employer to avoid damages in a lawsuit.

Administration of Workers' Compensation Laws by the State

Generally, workers' compensation disputes are administered through a quasijudicial system. In all states, the courts serve as an appellate forum for workers' compensation claims. In a few states, the courts conduct the initial administration of workers' compensation claims.

When the state's administration of compensation laws is not under the court's system, it is usually placed under the control of an industrial accident commission or labor and industry board. For example, the state of Louisiana has an Office of Workers' Compensation Court within the Louisiana Department of Labor, which is a "statewide court having jurisdiction of claims for workers' compensation benefits, the controversion of entitlement to benefits, and other relief under the workers' compensation act" (Louisiana Government, 2008). Texas, on the other hand, eliminated its administrative commission known as the Texas Workers' Compensation Commission or TWCC and placed administrative function in a division under the Texas Department of Insurance. New rulings and administrative hearings were set up to provide easier access and its administration of the Texas workers' compensation acts (Texas Department of Insurance, 2008).

Workers' compensation acts provide for compensating an employee whose injury *arises out of and in the course of employment* (Jones, 1998). The labor boards or commission usually resolve disputes and their decisions are binding regarding statements of facts. Appeals are usually made to the courts when there is a question of law.

Prompt Payment of Benefits

The workers' compensation system provides protection for the right of every injured worker by administrating the statutory benefits for medical, wage replacement, and disability if the injured worker is unable to return to his former job because of injury (Jones, 1998). State statutes explain all time elements and access requirements for the attainment of medical treatment, payment for medical treatment, reimbursement for medical treatment, amount of wage replacement, length of time for wage replacement, and means of determining temporary and permanent impairment or disability (Jones, 1998).

Medical Benefits

Each state decides how the choice will be made for choosing a treating physician, use of second opinions, and determination of when to end medical benefits.

Some states, such as Texas, provide lifetime medical benefits for the injury (Texas Department of Insurance, 2008). Of course, there is, again, a trade-off that takes place with lifetime medical benefits. There is no ability to settle for future medical benefits; hence, there is no need for the injured worker to hire an attorney. This becomes a significant factor for the legal practices that specialize in workers' compensation since the effect of this statute is to limit or eliminate the need for attorney representation for the injured worker. The LNCs area of practice in regard to workers' compensation may be quite limited in certain states due to the differing statutes.

Indemnity for Time Lost from Work

Benefits for wage loss are usually calculated by a percentage (usually 66.67% or more) using an average weekly or monthly wage assessment (Jones, 1998). The waiting periods and retroactive payment of loss wages are provided by each individual state statute. Legal representation in many cases is sought when the injured worker is unable to obtain lost wages or the correct amount of lost wages. When this is the case, it is important to understand the laws of the particular state and learn how to calculate the average weekly wage as well as communicate waiting periods, retroactive payment of wages, and so on.

Vocational Benefits

Some states provide vocational benefits to ensure training in the event of the injured workers' inability to return to the same job activity. Other states do not have statutory vocational benefits for the injured worker. Statutes provide a means for payment for permanent impairment based on state-specific impairment and disability ratings. Lifetime benefits are decided with predetermined specificity regarding extent of injury, disability, impairment, or catastrophic losses including death (Jones, 1998).

Catastrophic Injuries and Death Benefits

Catastrophic injuries usually result in permanent impairment and disability. Usually, the injured worker does not return to former work activities because the injury is so severe that functional capacity in the same job may be limited. Some of the common catastrophic injuries for workers include spinal cord injuries resulting in paralysis, head injuries with cognitive and functional ability losses, amputation of upper extremities or lower extremities, and toxic exposures resulting in chronic respiratory problems and/or cancers decreasing life expectancy.

Workers' compensation coverage not only pays for all medical treatment related to the injury, but provides in-patient and out-patient rehabilitation and occupational services, durable medical equipment such as braces and electric wheelchairs, home modifications, vehicle modifications for driving, long-term residential placement, and caregiver services, if necessary. Benefits for catastrophic injuries can be very complex and expensive. Nurse case managers (NCMs) with the workers' compensation insurance carrier are usually assigned these types of cases in order to assist the claim handler. The LNC may be utilized, on either the plaintiff or defense side, to assist the injured worker with obtaining and retaining necessary medical benefits to help make recovery the best that it can be.

In the case of death, death benefits are paid according to each jurisdiction or state workers' compensation guidelines. Burial insurance and benefits are available to minor dependents according to most jurisdictions. It is good to be familiar with the death benefits in the state in which the LNC provides services in order to be able to console the family in a knowledgeable way in regard to available benefits.

Compensability: Injuries and Diseases Covered

Compensability is a principle in workers' compensation that refers to whether or not the injury is covered. Although workers' compensation is required by every state for injuries that occur in the workplace, not all injuries and diseases are covered and not all workers are covered. Compensability must be determined and accepted by the employer and the insurance carrier in order for the employee to receive workers' compensation benefits. Determining compensability may require analysis of how the injury or disease occurred, when it occurred, and the connection between both.

In workers' compensation, injury by accident and occupational disease are the two categories for which compensability is provided. Injury that occurs by accident, usually termed an "incident," has a defined time and place. There is usually a description of the mechanism of injury. Occupational diseases, on the other hand, cannot always be defined by a specific time of when the disease began nor a specific place where the disease occurred.

The term "accident" refers to an unanticipated or unexpected and unforeseeable event that occurs as a result of employment work duties during the time of employment. There are 34 states' workers' compensation acts that contain the phrase injury "by accident" or "accidental injury." Ten states have omitted the requirement that the injury be by accident in order to be compensable (Jones, 1998). There are several ways to determine cause of the injury besides interpretation of a strict accidental event; for instance, a man who bends over repetitively in the course of his job duties to pick up cases of soda may someday suffer a herniated disc. The herniation of a lumbar disc may be unforeseeable or accidental, but the activities of repetitive bending over to pick up a case of soda are not. Interpretation could be made that the employee's activities were not an "accident"; therefore, not compensable. That is why it is important to understand the state's statutes in the particular jurisdiction where the injury occurs.

Occupational diseases must meet certain criteria to be compensable. All states' workers' compensation acts determine compensability if the disease is the result of causes and conditions which are characteristic of and peculiar to a particular trade, occupation, or employment. Excluded are those diseases that are considered ordinary diseases of life to which the general public is equally exposed without regard to employment. In fact, most occupational diseases are scrutinized on the basis of whether or not they are distinguished from ordinary diseases of life (Jones, 1998).

Another way of determining occupational disease is to look at whether or not the job exposure to a disease or condition places the worker at greater risk than the general population. For example, a nurse who has never had the chicken-pox virus may be more susceptible to developing the disease by working in a pediatric clinic compared with the general population of the same nurses who work in specialty areas that do not have pediatric patients. Thus, the occupational disease does not result exclusively from the job, but does place the employee at a greater risk than the general population for exposure of developing the disease. However, there is room to analyze the relationship to exposure and make this distinction between ordinary diseases of life if the relationship is questionable.

The LNC may be asked to assist with the determination of occupational disease compensability based on factors that relate to length of exposure, incubation periods of diseases, and the date when the disease is presumed to occur. The date that the disease first occurs is extremely important because it determines who is responsible for providing workers' compensation coverage to the injured worker. Depending on the state's statute, the onset of an occupational disease may be determined by the date the disease first manifested, when the physician first made the employee aware of the diagnosis, or the date the employee first became disabled. The statute may define the onset even further by placing additional time parameters around the date the employee first knew of the occupational disease. The assistance of the LNC in analyzing the medical records, along with the statutory definitions, is critical to confirming compensability in occupational disease cases (Jones, 1998).

Some of the occupational diseases that have clearly been established as related to higher exposure risk are asbestosis, silicosis, lead poisoning, and mercury poisoning to name a few. Also, allergic reactions as a result of latex exposure can have a very clear work-related relationship, while other exposures will need to be thoroughly investigated for compensability.

Other occupational diseases may be classified due to the repetitive nature of the injury such as carpal tunnel syndrome. These are referred to as cumulative trauma or repetitive motion injuries. Obviously, these injuries must have a clearly established relationship to repetitive movements as seen in the injured worker's job activities. Repetitive grasping, twisting, flexing of the wrist, and other movements are common factors in the development of carpal tunnel syndrome.

Determining the onset of cumulative trauma can be difficult, as well. Date of onset is vital to determining if the current or previous employer is responsible for the disease or condition. Sometimes, the onset of cumulative trauma is determined by the last injurious exposure rule, which is defined as the last employment where activities of the job could have caused the disease or condition (Jones, 1998). For example, if a new employee is claiming a cumulative trauma injury and performed similar job activities in the previous employment, the current employer is responsible for providing workers' compensation benefits regardless of the fact that the cumulative activities began with the previous employer. This is because the new employee's current job activities provided the last exposure to the cumulative trauma injury.

Some state statutes define cumulative trauma as an occupational disease and determine onset similar to onset of other occupational diseases by the date the symptoms first appeared or the date the physician made the employee aware of the diagnosis. Obviously, the current employer would not be responsible for providing benefits in these situations. Again, each state defines cumulative trauma injury claims differently and the applicable jurisdictional statute should be applied.

Mental injury claims, stress claims, and hernia injuries have distinct compensability rules depending on the states' statutes, which can vary greatly from state to state. For example, California allows stress claims under more liberal interpretation than does Texas. Mental injury claims vary widely with some states requiring an associated physical injury with a mental injury and some states do not address mental injury at all (Jones, 1998).

Hernias generally have associated rules for interpretation of compensability that limit the occurrence to specific incidents such as lifting. These injuries are usually given other specific requirements such as pain at the time of lifting, no preexisting protrusion or rupture, and exertion. The length of time benefits will be applied is limited in some states to 6 weeks only.

Exclusive Remedy

The principle of workers' compensation coverage is that it provides the *exclusive remedy* for workers injured in the course of employment without consideration of fault or negligence (Jones, 1998).

Exclusive remedy provides the injured worker with prompt, immediate medical and wage replacement benefits. In return for prompt medical treatment and wage replacement benefits, the injured worker relinquishes his right to sue his employer for negligence. Thus, tort claims resulting in large monetary recovery for pain and suffering and punitive damages are eliminated under the exclusive remedy of workers compensation. On the other hand, if the injured worker is at fault for the injury, the no-fault rule applies, as well.

There are few exceptions to the no-fault exclusive remedy rule in workers' compensation. One is intentional tort actions such as assault and battery in the workplace. The other involves injuries that occur as a result of third parties such as a plumber injured in a motor vehicle collision by another vehicle while driving to his work site. The plumber will have a civil tort claim against the other vehicle's driver if the driver's negligence causes the collision. The plumber will also have a workers' compensation claim. Generally, the workers' compensation carrier will have a subrogation interest against the damage awards of the third-party tort claim. This prevents double recovery by the injured worker and properly places the cost of the accident on the third party.

The Role of the LNC in Determination of Compensability

The LNC's medical expertise is crucial when helping to determine compensability. Some of the factors that the LNC must understand are based on the principles of workers' compensation claims. Obviously, the claims adjuster and attorney have extensive knowledge and experience in these principles and their state workers' compensation statutes. The LNC brings medical expertise, analytical skills, application of the nursing process, and ability to communicate this information when assisting the defense or plaintiff team in determining compensability. A partnership between the LNC, attorney, and claims adjuster provides careful investigation of a workers' compensation claim so that it is accepted or denied based on several universal state statute compensability requirements.

The Employment Relationship

In order for the injury to be compensable, the injured worker must be an employee of the employer. This is a seemingly obvious principle, but is sometimes difficult to determine. As such, an employment relationship is defined by several criteria such as control, consent, and consideration or wage exchange for services. For example, an individual working as a volunteer for an organization may receive no consideration for work performed. He or she is volunteering services without regard to compensation and is not covered under workers' compensation. An independent contractor, who is not controlled in terms of how, when, and where the work is performed, is not a covered employee under workers' compensation when performing work for another business. Certain employees such as domestic workers and farm workers are exempted from workers' compensation depending on state law. Each state's laws or statutes specifically outline the employee–employer relationship with which the attorney and claim adjuster are familiar (Jones, 1998).

Causation

The LNC's role in a worker's compensation case may be to assist with the determination of causation. As with medical malpractice and personal injury, causation is an important element in determining if a case is going to be assessed for damages (Jones, 1998). In medical malpractice, if the damages are not caused by medical negligence, there is no need to pursue litigation. In a personal injury case, such as a slip and fall on an uneven sidewalk, if the condition or injury was not caused by the slip and fall, there are no damage considerations.

Arising Out of and In the Course of Employment

The terminology that is used in the workers' compensation statute is that the injury must *arise out of and in the course of employment* (Jones, 1998). The injury must occur during the course of the injured worker's employment and while the injured worker is engaged in employment work activities. For a worker's compensation claim to be accepted, it has to be the result of an accident that occurs within the employment relationship and caused by the duties within this relationship.

Both of these requirements must be fulfilled in most workers' compensation statutes. There are some cases that might meet one or the other requirement but not both; that is, injury will occur in the course of employment but will not arise out of employment, or vice versa; injuries arise out of employment but do not occur in the course of employment. For this reason the workers' compensation adjudication may depend on both requirements being separately satisfied. However, there are exceptions, again, depending on the state's rules and statutes, which may have redefined the original principle of *arising out of and in the course of employment*.

Some states liberally interpret the *arising out of and in the course of employment*; consequently, it is imperative to have an understanding of the workers' compensation statute that applies to the state at hand. A good source of explanation for any state statue is the attorney with whom the LNC works. There are also several Internet sites that give access to the complete statutes, rules, and regulations of each state. These sites are invaluable when dealing with jurisdictional differences and understanding the application to a particular claim issue.

Arising out of employment is sometimes the more difficult of the two considerations to determine. This concerns the "cause" of the injury. In the workers' compensation context, cause is not the same as "proximate cause," which is used in tort claims for determination of liability. It also does not depend on whether or not the injury is foreseeable, as in tort claims. The determination of "cause" in workers' compensation is based on the level of risk and its association with employment (Jones, 1998).

For example, a cocktail waitress working at a hotel restaurant in a city with a high crime rate may be at higher risk for sexual assault. If a sexual assault should occur in the hotel's public restroom, the employee can claim a compensable work injury even though she is neither performing the duties of her work or is in the scope of her employment at the time of the assault. The court will rule that the assault arose out of employment because the employment exposed the employee to a higher risk of crime (Jones, 1998).

Another example of an injury or condition *arising out of employment* is the case of a worker who dies of a sudden cerebral vascular accident (CVA) while at work. The death of the worker does not arise out of employment because the individual's medical illness exists regardless of employment (Jones, 1998). The CVA was not a result of employment; it was a coincidence that could have occurred anywhere. If using the *but for* example, the CVA could have occurred at any time or place with any activity. When there are very difficult medical issues regarding the exact nature of an injury that appears to *arise out of employment*, the assistance of an LNC is valuable.

"But for the Employment"

Sometimes the use of "*but for* the employment" can guide determination of causation (Jones, 1998). If the injury or condition is the same for which the general public is exposed *but for* certain aspects of employment, the injury or condition is considered a result of employment. For example, an employee that is running errands for her employer is caught in a thunder shower and is electrocuted by a fallen electrical wire as she steps out of her car. Even though the event did not arise out of her employment activities and was an event caused by the natural laws of nature, *but for* the fact that she was in the course of employment at the time, the injury would not have occurred. The injury would then be considered compensable.

Role of the LNC in Evaluating Workers' Compensation Claims for the Defense Attorney

The determination of a medically treated injury or condition may seem to arise out of employment when reviewed by a nonmedical person. This may happen because the employee's supervisor or employer files a worker's compensation claim without asking appropriate questions like "What were you doing at the time of the accident?" and "Where did the accident occur and at what time did it occur?" The place, time, and description of the incident are vital to determining if the claim is compensable. After the claim is filed, a claim's adjuster is assigned to investigate the claim. If the facts of the incident do not match up, or if there are any questions regarding whether or not the injury or condition arises out of employment, the adjuster may request review by a medical specialist.

Many insurance companies, third-party administrators, and large companies employ NCMs who may assist with determination of causality or compensability. The NCM working in the specialty area of workers' compensation is usually an important part of the claim team because of the need for clinical expertise and analytical, problem-solving skills. If the claim is one that has the potential for high medical and indemnity exposure, the claim adjuster may anticipate litigation and seek the services of an attorney.

The NCM working in a workers' compensation claim office may work telephonically with the attorney assigned to the file. However, the NCM may be unable to provide the amount of time that is necessary when working with litigated workers' compensation claims. The attorney and claim adjuster can best meet the needs of a potentially high dollar claim by requesting the assistance of an LNC.

In regard to the two nurse specialty areas, case management and legal nurse consulting, both have separate certification specifications. Both specialty areas require analytical and research skills; thus, an NCM may be capable of working as an LNC and vice versa without obtaining certification assuming each has the skills and experience for the defined specialty area. However, the certification requirement for case management has increasingly become a prerequisite for nurses who are employed by insurance companies, and it is likely that the growth of the LNC specialty practice area will see similar demands. A recent study by White and Hall (2006) reports an evolving trend for the NCM working in the specialty area of workers' compensation to manage complex patient populations, which requires sophisticated knowledge of specialty practice. This trend is exemplified by the changes that were made in the 2005 Texas workers' compensation statutes requiring the healthcare network's utilization review be performed only by a licensed medical professional with a CCM designation (Texas Department of Insurance, 2008). The LNC may also see a trend toward obtaining sophisticated knowledge in order to successfully practice in workers' compensation.

The LNC in a workers' compensation defense case may be employed by either the insurance company or a defense law firm that works with one large or several small insurance companies. The LNC hired by a large insurance company usually works in an office where the company's staff counsel resides for that jurisdiction. The LNC's work activities and reporting structure are directly connected with the attorneys and legal team in that office rather than with the claims' adjusters who reside in the insurance company's claim office. Therefore, the relationship of the defense law firm to the insurance company may be one of an employee or a completely separate business entity while the LNC may be an employee of the insurance company, employee of the defense law firm, or a contracted employee to the defense law firm. However, it seems that most insurance companies do not contract for LNC services because of budget and financial constraints. As stated previously, the in-house NCM may be requested to work in an LNC role.

Some law firms provide consulting work to large companies in regard to insurance matters and some provide consulting at the administrative level where the interests are focused more on insurance regulation or providing representation in cases related to administrative proceedings. Other law firms work independently to provide legal defense work in workers' compensation litigation for large companies that are not in the insurance business. Regardless of the defense law firm's client relationship or the type of business entity, the position of LNC has become increasingly valuable because of the need to examine the medical component of the claim and assist with compensability decisions.

There are time constraints in workers' compensation that are inflexible. Payment of indemnity for lost time from work and payment for medical expenses are critical. These must be paid according to specific time frames noted and enforced by state statute. If payment is not made in a timely manner, the insurance company can be fined by the labor commission or labor board. Generally, payments can be made to avoid penalties as payment to the injured worker is not an admission of liability (Devenny & Morgan, 2008). The payor source retains the right to deny coverage or compensability if the claim is later found to be noncompensable.

Because medical treatment determines future settlement awards as well as current expenses, the amount of exposure related to the costs of medical treatment is a critical decision at the end of determining compensability or causation. Combined with indemnity for lost time from work, workers' compensation claims can be ultimately very costly to the employer and insurer. Cost controls are vital in today's economic arena where the cost of medical treatment is at record highs. The use of an LNC can be very helpful in cost containment for defense firms working with companies to limit medical exposures in cases that are not within the scope or arise out of employment.

Another area in which the LNC can help limit financial exposure of a claim is by reviewing medical records to determine if the original injury has expanded. Expansion of injuries or extent of injury questions have to be addressed so that the claim's medical and disability exposure is contained to the original injury. Insurance companies want to pay for compensable injuries and will pay generous benefits for successful outcomes in order that the injured worker returns to work in the same capacity as before the injury. However, the insurance company should not be expected to pay for anything outside the scope of the injury.

If it appears that the accident did occur, but the injury or condition is not consistent with the mechanism of injury, the claim handler must determine what is likely to have occurred. Based on the LNC's knowledge of anatomy and physiology, medical treatment guidelines, and time frames for resolution of medical conditions, a prospective determination can be made regarding cause of the injury or if the injury arises out of employment.

Case Example 21.1: Spider Bite

In this case (Hand, 2008b), an employee reports to work on Monday morning and tells his supervisor that a spider bit him on the leg while at work the previous Friday afternoon. Upon questioning, the employee reports that he first noticed the "spider bite" on Saturday morning and today the area has become more painful and red. Although the employee did not actually see a spider, he assumes that the lesion is a "spider bite" and that it occurred last Friday when removing debris from a building where he was working. The employer writes up an injury report, submits a worker's compensation claim, and sends the injured worker to the emergency room.

At the emergency room, the injured worker is given a prescription for antibiotics and taken off work for 5 days. The emergency room discharge orders state that the employee is to be re-evaluated by his primary-care physician in 5 days. Two days later, the employee becomes very ill and is admitted to the hospital for incision and drainage of an infected wound.

The medical records describe the wound as being deep with necrotic tissue. The damage to the underlying tissue is extensive and a skin graft is necessary. The employee undergoes two incisions and drainage procedures while in the hospital and is administered intravenous antibiotics. While hospitalized, the employee is diagnosed with adult-onset diabetes mellitus.

In the meantime, the employee's worker's compensation claim is being reviewed by the employer's insurance company. The questions related to this claim are "Did the injury occur in the course of employment and did the injury arise out of employment?" The assigned claim's adjuster makes a decision to deny the claim based on lack of evidence that the incident occurred while the employee was at work and in the course of his job duties. The employee could have been at home when the spider bite occurred since the incident was reported after a weekend and, if at work, the spider bite could have occurred at any time including times when the employee was not engaged in his work activities.

The claim's adjuster must also consider the financial exposure of the spider bite claim. At this point, the claim poses significant financial exposure because costs now include emergency room visits, several days of hospitalization, surgeries, intravenous antibiotic medications, possible home health services for continued IV medications, and wage replacement. Due to age and any comorbidity diseases, healing may be compromised and expenses further increased. Furthermore, the injured worker is a laborer who is not qualified for modified work duties.

Several weeks later, the injured worker, who has received some wage replacement checks, receives a letter that the claim has been denied. The letter states that the indemnity payments will stop and medical coverage will not be available. The injured worker calls his employer who explains that the insurance company did not accept the claim because there was no evidence that the "spider bite" occurred while he was working. Furthermore, if the spider bite did occur at work this is considered an ordinary event of life because the employee is at no higher risk of injury than any other ordinary person that receives a spider bite.

The injured worker retains an attorney who specializes in workers' compensation law. The attorney immediately files for a contested hearing in order to get the plaintiff's claim reviewed. The attorney informs the claim's adjuster that upon acceptance of the contested claim, he will file against the insurance company a lawsuit for breach of contract or bad faith. A bad faith lawsuit can result in damages for the plaintiff if the claim's adjuster unreasonably denies a claim. The adjuster has the duty to provide good faith and fair dealing in regard to the insurance policy contract. To do otherwise is a breach of the duty of good faith and may be a breach of fiduciary duty, as well (Jones, 1998).

Having received the notice of representation from the attorney with potential for a bad faith lawsuit, the claim's adjuster requests the claim be assigned to an attorney and an LNC to assist with the issues of causality and compensability.

The nurse reviews the employee's medical records and researches information regarding brown recluse spider bites. The LNC then prepares a report for the attorney explaining that the plaintiff is at higher risk for obtaining a brown recluse spider bite than the general public because his particular job duties, on the alleged day of injury, involved removing old debris from a vacant room in a building. The LNC reports that this particular geographical area of the country is indigenous to the brown recluse spider, and although the plaintiff could have been bitten by a spider anywhere, *but for* the fact that he was working in an environment where a brown recluse spider is known to inhabit, this places the plaintiff at a higher risk. This claim will more than likely be found compensable by the state's workers' compensation judge.

The LNC not only confirms the likelihood of the spider bite incident arising out of employment and in the course of employment, but reviews the medical records for progression of the illness or disease, extent of injury, current treatment plan, future treatment expected, and disability time frame. The information provided by the LNC allows the plaintiff to obtain workers' compensation benefits owed as well as prevents potentially severe legal problems and expenses.

Case Example 21.2: Carpal Tunnel Syndrome

In this case (Hand, 2008a) a 50-year-old woman is hired by a company that provides typing services of medical reports for several doctor's offices. She is a consistently hard worker who is not only fast, but accurate. A month after being hired, she reports pain in both wrists, with greater pain in the left compared to the right. A workers' compensation claim is filed and she is evaluated by a doctor of her choice.

The doctor obtains electrodiagnostic studies confirming bilateral median nerve compression or carpal tunnel syndrome (CTS). The claim's adjuster understands the relationship of repetitive injury and CTS, but the employee has only worked for the employer 4 weeks. A CTS claim can be expensive with permanency and future disability.

The injured worker or employee reports that prior to this employment, she was working in a retail store part-time and prior to that, she was self-employed for 12 years as a medical transcriptionist. The claim's adjuster denies the claim based on the statutory definition of CTS as an occupational disease, the length of time the claimant worked for the insured being insufficient to cause or aggravate the diagnosis of CTS, and the electromyelogram (EMG)/nerve conduction veolocity (NCV) findings identifying chronic changes that take longer than 4 weeks to develop. In this case, CTS did not arise out of the employment.

The employee obtains an attorney. The claim's adjuster sends the claim to an attorney to assist with the pending litigation. The defense attorney asks for consultation from the LNC who questions whether the diagnosis of CTS may have a relationship to the employee's previous self-employment activities when she worked 12 years as a medical transcriptionist. The LNC obtains current and all prior medical records and finds notes from the primary-care physician documenting the employee's complaints of bilateral hand and wrist pain. The assessment by the primary-care physician is "possible CTS." The LNC reviews the chronology and determines that the reports discussing CTS are written 3 months before the employee began working for the retail store.

Another fact found in the review of records is that the employee only worked 6 weeks for the retail store. Her job duties did not involve repetitive movements of her hands or wrists. Again, the records document that the diagnosis of CTS was first made during the time she was self-employed as a medical transcriptionist. The LNC reviews the workers' compensation statutes and finds that CTS is defined as an occupational disease rather than a repetitive-trauma injury and confirms the definition with the attorney.

Some states classify CTS as an occupational disease rather than a repetitive-trauma injury, as with this case, and applicable under state statute. The date the condition is first made known to the injured worker is documented in the medical records. The LNC gives the information to the claim's adjuster explaining that the diagnosis of CTS was first made during the time the employee was self-employed. The CTS did not *arise out of the* employee's current employment and no aggravation of the condition has occurred. The claim is successfully denied.

Most states have had to distinguish between injuries that have worsened by using different terms so that the responsibility for compensability is clear, that is, compensation is sought from either the current employer or the employer who provided compensation for the original injury. The terms commonly used are "aggravation" and "reoccurrence or exacerbation." Aggravation is defined as a worsening of a prior condition caused by a new injury and a new claim opened.

Aggravation of a preexisting repetitive-trauma injury is generally addressed in the workers' compensation statutes as related to the last place the injurious action occurred (Jones, 1998). Reoccurrence or exacerbation is defined as a deterioration of an injury or condition as part of the normal progression of the injury or disease and the existing claim is reopened.

This case points out the importance of how occupational disease and cumulative trauma are defined by the individual state statute. The LNC will need to be knowledgeable about injury versus occupational disease determination and other details of a claim such as if the disease or condition worsens naturally or through aggravation.

Role of the LNC in Evaluating Workers' Compensation Claims for the Plaintiff's Attorney

The most important factor affecting the value of a worker's compensation claim will be the strength of the medical evidence supporting the injuries and disability of the injured worker. The injured worker usually seeks attorney representation when there is a dispute, or potential dispute regarding causation, extent of injury, or fear that benefits and rights will not be protected. As discussed previously, the injured worker releases the right to a tort claim for damages under workers' compensation. There are some circumstances involving third-party lawsuits for negligence or intentional negligence claims that can result in tort damages; however, for most workers' compensation plaintiff cases, the attorney's involvement is primarily to protect the injured worker and assure that all benefits are received.

In some states, the injured worker can settle their workers' compensation claim for any future medical treatment, disability, or future loss of wages. In these cases, the injured worker can obtain a large lump sum settlement or some other type of financial payment such as an annuity. In other states, there is no provision in the statute for settlement of future wage loss and medical treatment. As noted earlier, the state of Texas allows for lifetime medical benefits for the work-related injury. Disability is decided strictly on permanent disability determination based on an impairment rating (Texas Department of Insurance, 2008). Since there are no settlement provisions in the Texas workers' compensation statutes, there is generally no need to retain the services of an attorney as long as other provisions of the rules and regulations are not in question or dispute. In Texas, the injured worker has access to the services of an ombudsman who will work to intervene on his behalf to the Texas Industrial Board.

In states where the claims can be settled and in all states where future medical costs will be enormous because of catastrophic injury, the LNC can provide assistance in evaluating and assisting the plaintiff attorney with workers' compensation cases. Most plaintiff attorneys practice in several areas related to personal injury and do not limit their practice solely to the workers' compensation practice area. This obviously provides more opportunities for employment for the LNC when the plaintiff attorney has several practice area specialties.

Most plaintiff law firms with a large workers' compensation case load employ paralegals to assist with the paperwork and communication (Devenny & Morgan, 2008). The communication in workers' compensation cases involves working with employers, injured workers, families, and physicians. A paralegal provides case management activities for a specified caseload that is most likely restricted to administrative functions such as filing claims and responding to notice of claims. Although the paralegal may be responsible for obtaining and reviewing medical records, the function is usually for the purpose of itemizing billing statements and providing a chronology of all the medical providers and records. The LNC's expertise is usually necessary for analysis of the medical records and contributing to the other vital medical components of litigation.

In preparing and completing depositions, the attorney needs to understand all crucial medical points that affect current and future disability as they relate to medical problems that result from the accident, injury, or condition. Also, there is the need, regardless of settlement opportunities, to understand what future treatment is anticipated and the extent of disability. The LNC may perform the initial interview with the injured worker or accompany the attorney during the initial interview.

There are several extremely important questions that are important in the initial evaluation of a plaintiff's work injury:

1. Mechanism of the injury—how did the injury occur? What is your job? What were you doing? What is the name of your company and the name and phone number of your supervisor?
2. When did the injury occur? Date and time
3. Did you report the injury? Date and time
4. To whom did you report the injury? Did you tell anyone else about your injury or symptoms?
5. Do you know if your supervisor filed the injury form with the state? Date filed
6. Was there a coworker or supervisor who witnessed the injury? Name(s)
7. How soon after the injury, did symptoms begin? Date and time
8. When did you seek medical care? Date and time, name of facility, name of doctor, diagnosis, treatment, prescription, return date
9. Does your employer have a list of doctors from which the injured worker can choose for medical treatment?
10. Were you told where to go for treatment?
11. Have you been evaluated by your own physician?
12. Have you been removed from work? When and for how long? Obtain a copy of any disability or off-work notes given to the claimant from the physician

After these initial questions are asked, the LNC will focus on other medical- and vocational-related questions. The LNC can use observation skills to determine if there are any current symptoms that are causing obvious discomfort and alterations in the injured worker's movement, speech, or cognition. Finally, the LNC can determine if there is a third-party liability or any other potential cause for actions like retaliatory discharge or discrimination. Before ending the interview, the LNC should obtain the injured worker's signature on a medical authorization to disclose health information.

Workers' compensation cases are accepted on a contingency basis, so there is no payment required by the injured worker. In fact, the decision to accept the case is not based on an expected amount of settlement as in personal injury cases. In all states, the plaintiff attorney is paid a percentage, usually up to 20%, of the injured worker's weekly wage (Jones, 1998). There may be other legal reimbursement fees by the insurance company based on the state's statute. Therefore, the attorney is able to have an income from each worker's compensation case until settlement or maximum medical improvement is reached.

Unfortunately, sometimes, the benefit of keeping the injured worker off-work and disabled can be a monetary incentive to all parties involved in the plaintiff's worker's compensation case. This is not in the best interest of the injured worker. If the employer can accommodate the worker to perform other work activities that are within the allowable work restrictions, the injured worker benefits psychologically and physically by returning to employment activities.

The LNC working for the plaintiff attorney will need to continue to provide proper ethical considerations as an advocate for the injured worker in spite of the tendency to extend the benefits of the injured worker.

Workers' compensation benefits are available until the person is brought back to the preinjury level or maximum medical improvement, as long as this occurs within the time parameters set by the states' rules (Jones, 1998). For example, in Texas, the injured worker can receive temporary, permanent, or partial income benefits for 104 weeks. After this period, an impairment rating will need to be obtained in order to continue to receive additional income benefits. If the impairment rating is over 15% of the whole body, further supplementary benefit for up to 401 weeks can be awarded (Texas Department of Insurance, 2008). In contrast, Pennsylvania's workers' compensation statutes set the maximum time that an injured worker can receive temporary partial disability benefits at 500 weeks while total disability benefits can be received for 104 weeks (Pennsylvania Department of Labor and Industry, 2001).

Role of the LNC in Catastrophic Injury

In cases of catastrophic injury, benefits in all states continue for life. If there are financial settlements for future medical and/or disability, these are usually provided in some type of financial structure, such as annuities that pay out over the life of the injured worker and dependents. Each state has very specific rules guiding catastrophic injury lifetime benefits. It is imperative that the insurance company and plaintiff attorney assist the injured worker toward utilizing these lifetime benefits in the most effective way. The LNC for the catastrophically injured plaintiff will advocate for all medical evaluations, providers, facilities, caregivers, supplies, and necessary equipment that will promote comfort while allowing as much independence as is possible. The LNC should have a life care plan for the plaintiff that is realistic in that expectations and expenses are provided and changes can be made when necessary. A life care plan needs to be reviewed annually in order to make sure the components of the plan provide for all future expectations. It is possible that the LNC will be the only case manager for the catastrophic injured worker. Advocacy for the injured worker will need to be kept in the forefront even after the acute time of the injury has passed because the insurer may decide to cut medical costs in ways that would be detrimental to the injured worker or family.

The LNC who works for a defense attorney or insurance company is likely to perform many of the same evaluations and assessments as with any other case, with the exception that more time may be devoted to the catastrophic case. The extent of injury in a catastrophic injury may be the area that the LNC has to continually update by reviewing current medical reports on a regular basis. Limiting the injury to only that which is related requires medical expertise and research abilities so that medical treatment and services continue to be medically reasonable and necessary for any medical problems that are caused or indirectly result from the catastrophic injury. For example, an injured worker sustains a spinal cord injury as a result of a fall while installing a new roof. The spinal cord is severed at L4–L5 resulting in paraplegia. One-and-a-half years later, the claim's adjuster is told that the primary-care physician is requesting a drug treatment program for the paraplegic worker who apparently has been abusing narcotic medications. The claim's adjuster is uncertain if the payment for a drug treatment program is the responsibility of the insurer and consults with the defense attorney who asks the LNC to determine whether or not the current use of narcotic medications is prescribed for pain from his workers' compensation injury. (The question of *but for* may help: "*But for* the injury, the injured worker would not be taking narcotic medication.")

In reviewing the medical records, the LNC determines that prior to the injury the worker was taking several different narcotic medications prescribed by two different physicians for migraine headaches. After the injury, the injured worker continued to obtain prescriptions for migraine headaches and obtained additional narcotic prescriptions from the works' compensation physician for back pain. The injured worker obtained narcotic prescriptions from multiple physicians. Although the drug treatment program may be medically necessary to treat the injured worker's addiction to narcotics, the question is whether or not narcotic addiction resulted from the injury. The LNC's research on narcotic addiction and review of the injured worker's medical records show that the addiction process likely started before the injury; therefore, the treatment for drug addiction is not related to the injury.

Summary

Workers' compensation litigation is a complex but challenging practice area for the LNC. Workers' compensation statutes and administrative agencies vary from state to state. Changes in statutes occur frequently so that the LNC who chooses this practice specialty area must be able to access appropriate information on a regular basis. Fortunately, there are basic principles that provide the foundation for those working with workers' compensation litigation. Understanding these principles, the LNC can work for either the plaintiff or defense attorney to provide considerable medical expertise that will be valuable for a successful outcome of the claim.

The ability to work with defense attorneys in law firms employed specifically to litigate workers' compensation claims involves partnership and teamwork between the claims' adjuster and attorney. The atmosphere of teamwork is appealing to the LNC for executing and delivering expert information in an interactive environment. Equally rewarding is working with the plaintiff attorney in workers' compensation litigation as the focus is centered on the medical and disability needs of the injured worker. This personal focus adds to the rewarding challenges of the LNC who works in the workers' compensation specialty area.

References

Devenny, L., & Morgan, J. (2008). *Workers' compensation practice for paralegals.* Durham, NC: Carolina Academic Press.

Hand, J. (2008a). *Carpal tunnel syndrome,* personal, October 17, 2008.

Hand, J. (2008b). *Spider bite,* personal, October 17, 2008.

Jones, J. (Ed.). (1998). *Principles of worker's compensation claims* (2nd ed.). Malvern, PA: Insurance Institute of America.

Louisiana Government. (2008). *Louisiana administrative code, Title 40: Workers' compensation administration* (chap. 55, p. 229). Department of Administration, Office of the State Registry. Retrieved October 17, 2008, from OSR website: http://doa.louisiana.gov/osr/lac/40v01.doc

Pennsylvania Department of Labor and Industry. (2001). *The Pennsylvania Workers' Compensation Act 57 of 1996.* http://www.dli.state.pa.us/landi/cwp/view.asp?a=185&q=217906. Bureau of Workers' Compensation Information. Retrieved October 17, 2008, from Commonwealth of Pennsylvania government services website: http://www.dli.state.pa.us/landi/lib/landi/laws-regulations/wc/wcact.pdf

Texas Department of Insurance. (2008). *The Texas Workers' Compensation Act, 80th Legislature, 2007.* Retrieved October 17, 2008, from TDI website: http://www.tdi.state.tx.us/wc/act/doc/act80.pdf

White, P., & Hall, M. E. (2006). Mapping the literature of case management nursing. *Journal of the Medical Library Association, 94*(2 Suppl). Abstract retrieved October 17, 2008, from http://ww.pubmedcentral. hih.gov/articlerender.fcgi?artid=463029

Additional Readings

Anchor, K. N., Shmerling, J. E., & Anchor, J. M. (Eds). (2002). *The catastrophic injury handbook: Understanding vocational, economic, legal, and clinical aspects of complex physical and mental trauma*. Kendall/Hung Publishing Co.

Anderson, B. J., & Cocchiarella, L. (Eds.). (2004). *Guides to the evaluation of permanent impairment* (5th ed.). USA: American Medical Association.

Markham, J. (Ed.). (1991). *Medical aspects of claims* (1st ed.). Malvern, PA: Insurance Institute of America.

Resources

Jasper, M. (2008). *Workers' compensation law*. Oxford University Press.

Larson, A., & Larson, L. (2000). *Larson's workers' compensation, Desk edition* (3rd ed.). Albany, NY: Matthew Bender and Company, Inc.

Reed, P. (Ed.). (2005). *The medical disability advisor: Workplace guidelines for disability duration* (5th ed.). Westminster, CO: Reed Group Publisher.

Work Loss Data Institute. (2008). *Official disability guidelines* (16th ed.). Encinitas, CA: Work Loss Data Institute (WLDI).

Internet Resources

U.S. Department of Labor Office of Workers' Compensation Programs. http:/www.dol.gov/eas/regs/compliance/owcp/wc.htm

The International Association of Industrial Accident Boards and Commissions. http://www.iaiabc.org/links.htm

Workers' Compensation Administrators Directory. http://www.comp.state.nc.us/ncic/pages/wcadmdir.htm

Test Questions

1. Which one of the following is not an underlying principle in workers' compensation statutes?
   A. Prompt payment of benefits
   B. Each state decides how to administer workers' compensation statutes
   C. Employer's negligence
   D. No-fault system

2. What are three benefits injured workers receive from workers' compensation?
   A. Medical, death, and indemnity benefits
   B. Medical, indemnity, and job security benefits
   C. Medical, job security, and vocational benefits
   D. Medical, vocational, and legal benefits

3. Compensability is a term that refers to
   A. Payment for all injuries and conditions that occur while working
   B. Payment for all accidents and injuries regardless of fault
   C. Determining if injured worker has been accepted for workers' compensation benefits
   D. Determining whether or not the injury or occupational disease is covered under the state's worker's compensation statute

4. The LNC may assist with determining whether or not the injury is compensable by
   A. Review of the medical records to make sure treatment is related to the injury
   B. Review of the medical records to determine if the injured worker has any preexisting conditions
   C. Review of the medical records to determine if the injury or condition results from the performance of work activities while working for the employer
   D. Review of the medical records to make sure treatment was preauthorized

5. The LNC working for the plaintiff attorney may assist with obtaining important information vital to the work injury by asking the plaintiff all of the following except
   A. Did your supervisor cause you to have the accident?
   B. Do you know if your supervisor filed a claim with the state?
   C. Did anyone witness the accident?
   D. Did you report the injury to your supervisor?

Answers: 1. C, 2. A, 3. D, 4. C, 5. A

Chapter 22

Surgical and Anesthesia Case Evaluation

Dana Jolly, BSN, RN, LNCC and Carolyn Pytlik, BSN, RN, CRNA

Contents

Objectives

- Describe the Standards of Care and Scope of Practice for anesthesia and surgical practice
- Define anesthesia
- Discuss the surgical process from preoperative testing through postanesthesia care including other areas where anesthesia is administered (e.g., obstetrics)
- Identify anesthesia and surgical practitioners who have a duty to the patient
- Identify critical documents required for surgical case evaluation
- List three types of common surgical complications
- Discuss major differences between surgical and obstetrical anesthesia legal cases
- List three types of experts that may testify in an anesthesia case

Introduction

Surgery is a common medical intervention in the United States with well over 50 million surgical procedures being performed annually. It is estimated that up to two-third of adverse events in hospitals are attributable to surgical care (Regenbogen et al., 2007). Taking this into consideration, it is not surprising that surgical care is commonly litigated. The Bureau of Justice Statistics estimated about half of medical malpractice trials were brought against surgeons (Cohen, 2001). The surgical environment demands quick decision making in a multifaceted setting. A recent study by Harvard researchers showed most technical errors occur in routine operations performed by experienced surgeons (Regenbogen et al., 2007). Surgical errors can include consequences throughout the continuum of surgical care—from preoperative care to postoperative follow-up. It is important to remember as one analyzes surgical cases, not every bad outcome is the result of negligence. Coincidental complications happen everyday without negligence.

Legal nurse consultants (LNCs) routinely assist attorneys, risk managers, and insurance providers in distinguishing between a bad outcome resulting from negligence versus a known risk of the procedure. An LNC can prove to be invaluable to the litigation team by providing education on surgical case analysis. During the discovery process, the LNC has access to interrogatories and deposition testimony along with the medical record giving him/her a considerably richer body of information from which to draw conclusions regarding the delivery of care and its outcomes.

Evaluating surgical cases is complex for many reasons. Surgery and anesthesia are highly specialized, technical fields. Each specialty has multiple subspecialties, making the analysis of this type of care a challenge. Compounding this challenge is the multitudes of healthcare providers (HCPs) with different levels of education involved in the care of the patient during this dynamic process. Standards of care (SOC) and scope of practice are different for each of these providers with some overlap. Identifying HCPs' duties to the patient, potential breaches in that duty, and causation is a vital role for the LNC.

Anesthesia

Anesthesia, or *anaesthesia*, [both spellings are correct] is defined as the loss of sensation with or without loss of consciousness. The word is derived from the Greek word anaisthēsiā, meaning insensibility or without feeling. Anesthesia denotes a temporary and reversible lack of awareness (e.g., a general anaesthestic), or a blocking of pain sensations involving a specific part of the body such as a spinal, regional, or epidural anesthetic. The administration of anesthesia allows patients to undergo surgical, obstetrical, or other procedures without the pain and distress that would otherwise occur.

Each year, more than 30 million people in the United States undergo some form of medical treatment requiring anesthesia. Anesthesia care is not confined to surgery alone. Anesthesia care also refers to activities that take place before, during, and after an anesthetic is given. Anesthesia can be administered by an anesthesiologist, a Certified Registered Nurse Anesthetist (CRNA), Anesthesiologist Assistants (AAs), and other practitioners, including dentists, trained in anesthesia techniques. The term anesthetist describes one who administers anesthesia.

There are three basic types of anesthesia:

■ General anesthesia produces a loss of consciousness and sensation throughout the entire body
■ Regional anesthesia produces a loss of sensation to a specific region such as an extremity, or the lower part of the body
■ Local anesthesia produces a loss of sensation to a small specific area of the body

Surgical Case Evaluation

Areas of Practice

Surgery takes place in a variety of settings: hospitals, physician offices, and free-standing ambulatory surgery centers. There is a wide variety of HCPs involved in surgical procedures regardless of the setting in which they are performed.

Anesthesia providers practice in every setting in which anesthesia is delivered including traditional surgical suites, obstetrical delivery rooms, critical access hospitals, ambulatory surgical centers, endoscopy centers, and pain management practices. They also administer anesthesia in offices of dentists, podiatrists, ophthalmologists, plastic surgeons, fertility specialists. They are found in civilian facilities as well as U.S. military, Public Health Services, and the Department of Veterans Affairs (Table 22.1).

Scope of Practice

The scope of practice for each of these providers is customarily dictated by statutory state law, known in some states as a practice act. Secondary to state law is facility policy, which is more specific to the HCP's role within that particular facility. Scope of practice policies are often

Table 22.1 Divisions of Departments of Surgery

Cardiothoracic

General

Neurosurgery

Obstetrical/gynecological

Oncology

Oral/maxillofacial

Orthopedics

Pediatric

- Surgeons further specialize in various areas, that is, general, cardiothoracic, urologic, neurosurgery, etc.

Plastic/reconstructive

Trauma

- Burn
- Critical care

Thoracic

Urology

Vascular

Disclaimer: Departments of Surgery are unique to their facility. This is an example of how a division may be organized.

required by regulatory agencies, such as the Joint Commission. National credentialing organizations for anesthesia providers set forth the scope of practice for their members as well.

CRNAs may work under the direction of an anesthesiologist or an independently licensed practitioner (surgeon, dentist) or work independently while anesthesia assistants work with and under the supervision of anesthesiologists.

The anesthesiologist or anesthetist may provide anesthesia care preoperatively and postoperatively as well as during surgery. This includes evaluating the medical health and risk factors of the patient before surgery (preoperative), consulting and working with the surgical team, providing pain control and support of life functions during surgery (intraoperative), supervising care after surgery in the postoperative area. They also provide anesthesia care as well as medical expertise in other settings outside of the surgical suite.

Anesthesia providers also have the medical background to deal with many emergency situations such as airway management, cardiac and pulmonary resuscitation, and advanced life support. As consultants, they play an active role in stabilizing and preparing the patient for emergency surgery.

Standard of Care

SOC, as previously described in this text, is a dynamic entity. It is based on a reasonable practitioner's knowledge and experience, which are based on their education and clinical expertise. LNCs can find professional guidelines of care for surgical team members among their various professional organizations, facility policy and procedures, and literature such as textbooks and journal articles. As our science and technology is constantly changing, the guidelines for caring for surgical patients may also change. When analyzing surgically related cases, it is important to keep in mind the timing of the alleged negligence and research guidelines for the same time frame,that is, if the event took place in 2008, research 2008 guidelines.

Professional organizations that provide scope of practice and SOC guidelines for their members include the medical and nursing boards in the states in which the provider is licensed. As anesthesia providers may also be nationally certified by their professional organizations including the American Association of Nurse Anesthetists (AANA), American Board of Anesthesiology (ABA), American Society of Anesthesiologists (ASA), and American Association of Anesthesiologist Assistants (AAAA), members further adhere to those standards.

Surgical Team

The surgical team is divided into two categories—sterile and nonsterile. Surgeon, surgical assistant, scrub, and surgical technician are sterile. Circulator, anesthesia provider, and other providers such as perfusionists and observers are nonsterile.

Surgeon(s)

The surgeon is the "captain of the ship" and in charge of the operating room (OR); thereby, the surgeon is ultimately responsible for the patient related to the surgical procedure. Typically, there is one attending surgeon; however, there can be more than one operating surgeon. This might occur during a complex procedure or if a surgeon has limited experience or when two different systems require surgery such as total abdominal hysterectomy and umbilical hernia repair. A consulting surgeon may be involved when a complication such as organ laceration or perforation occurs. Attending surgeons routinely have assistants who are physicians, surgical residents or specially trained registered nurses, RN First Assistants (RNFA). When evaluating surgical claims, it is important to investigate the surgeon's employer, which is usually their practice. Surgeons are rarely employed by the facility in which they perform surgery. The legal doctrine of respondeat superior comes into play—an employer's responsibility for an employee's action within the scope of their employment. It is part of the LNC role in evaluating surgically claims to identify potential defendants.

Anesthesia

The anesthesia team includes anesthesiologists, Board Certified Anesthesiologists, anesthesia residents, CRNAs, Student Registered Nurse Anesthetists (SRNAs), AAs as well as the supporting anesthesia technicians, Certified Anesthesia Technicians or Certified Anesthesia Technologists.

Anesthesiologists are medical doctors (MDs), or osteopathic doctors (DOs) who are trained in anesthesiology and specialize in the practice of anesthesia. Board certification for anesthesiologists by the Board of Anesthesiology is voluntary; however, most healthcare facilities require Board certification within a set period of time to ensure continued employment or contracts.

CRNAs are Registered Nurses, trained in anesthesiology who specialize in the practice of anesthesia. AAs are allied HCPs who are trained and specialize in anesthesiology. The anesthesia team involved in a surgical case could consist of any number or combination of the above providers, depending on the complexity of a case.

Nursing Staff

There are several different intraoperative nursing providers.

RN First Assistant

RNFA is an expanded role within the specialty of perioperative nursing requiring specialized education. Certification is recommended by the professional organization, Association of Perioperative Registered Nurses, but not required. Their practice, depending on the scope of nursing defined by their state, may include use of surgical instruments or medical devices, retracting, cutting tissue, providing hemostasis, and suturing.

Remembering respondeat superior, it is important to identify the RNFA's employer who can be the surgeon, the surgeon's practice, the facility or the RNFA themselves.

Circulator

The circulating nurse (circulator) is a registered nurse who is responsible for the patient during surgery (AORN Position Statement on One Perioperative Registered Nurse Circulator Dedicated to Every Patient Undergoing a Surgical or Other Invasive Procedure). The circulator plans, implements, and evaluates the surgical nursing care. Their primary focus is patient safety. "At a minimum, one perioperative registered nurse circulator should be dedicated to each patient undergoing a surgical or other invasive procedure and is present during that patient's entire intraoperative experience" (AORN Position Statement on One Perioperative Registered Nurse Circulator Dedicated to Every Patient Undergoing a Surgical or Other Invasive Procedure). As with other professional nurse roles, the circulator may delegate certain tasks but retains accountability. The scope of responsibility of the circulator includes the scrub role (AORN Position Statement on the Role of the Scrub Person). The circulator's practice usually includes verification of consent and surgical site with the patient, positioning patient for surgery, application of surgical equipment such as grounding pads, creating the perioperative nursing record, assisting surgical providers throughout the procedure, passing additional items to the sterile field, ensuring surgical counts are correct, accompanying the patient to the postanesthesia care unit (PACU), and giving report to the postanesthesia care provider. Circulators are typically employed by the facility in which they work. An exception to this may be a nurse placed in the facility through a temporary nurse agency or traveling nurse company. The opinions of the court regarding the employer in these circumstances vary among states.

Surgical Technician

Surgical technicians are allied healthcare professionals working under the supervision of the circulator and/or surgeon. The role of the surgical tech varies. They can function in the scrub role or as a nonsterile member of the surgical team. Surgical techs require specialized education and training. Typically, they attend a 2-year accredited academic program. Certification is available but is not required for the role. Typical duties include prepping the patient (clipping hair, assisting with positioning), draping the patient, and processing specimens passed from the surgical field. Surgical technicians are typically employed by the facility in which they work. However, they may be employed by the surgeon or surgeon's practice with whom they work.

Scrub

Registered nurses, licensed practical nurses, and surgical technicians can all function in the scrub role. The scrub assists the surgeon by maintaining sterile and aseptic technique (AORN Position Statement on Allied Health Care Providers and Support Personnel in the Perioperative Practice Setting), organizing the surgical instruments for use by the surgeon, passing instruments, equipment, and supplies to the surgeon or surgical assistant, preparing and passing medications to the surgeon or surgical assistant, performing surgical counts, operating suction equipment, and receiving specimens from the surgical field. Scrub nurses or techs are typically employed by the facility in which they practice. However, they may be employed by the surgeon or surgeon's practice with whom they work.

Other

Perfusionist

Perfusionists operate the cardiopulmonary bypass machine. Cardiopulmonary bypass maintains the physiologic and metabolic requirements of the patient during nonheart beating procedures, usually open heart surgery, heart transplantation, lung transplants, implantation of ventricular assist devices, etc. Management of intra-aortic balloon pumps, extracorporeal membrane oxygenation (ECMO), and anticoagulation monitoring also fall into the responsibilities of the perfusionist. This role requires specialized training and expertise. Perfusionists may be employed by the facility in which they practice, the surgeon, or surgeon's practice with whom they work or practice privately.

Observers

Medical device representatives (sales representatives, technicians, clinical consultants) provide technical support to surgical providers. They should not provide direct patient care nor should they enter the sterile field unless they are specially trained and the facility policy approves it (AORN Position Statement on the Role of the Health Care Industry Representative in the Perioperative/Invasive Procedure Setting). When delivering patient care or in the sterile field, the representative is under the supervision of the surgeon (AORN Position Statement on the Role of the Health Care Industry Representative in the Perioperative/Invasive Procedure Setting). Other common observers during surgery include students and staff in training. Patients should be notified of the possibility of the presence of a representative or other observer during the informed consent process. Patients can disallow any observer during their surgery by stating so on their consent form.

Surgical Operative Records

The surgical process begins with a patient's presentation to a surgeon, routinely or emergently, and ends with recovery from anesthesia. Regardless of the procedure performed, there are common records documenting this process.

Notes on electronic medical records: "Electronic medical records metadata allow for creation of detailed physician profiles and will likely be used increasingly to discredit physicians during medical malpractice litigation" (McLean, Burton, Haller, & McLean, 2008).

Consents

The topic of informed consent is covered elsewhere in this text and will not be repeated here; however, how informed consent relates to surgically related litigation follows. The process of informing patients of the risk, benefits, and alternatives to surgical and anesthesia procedures is a dynamic communication between the physician and the patient. While the physician may document the occurrence of the discussion, the specifics of the communication are not detailed in that note. Typically, an LNC will see something like "... risks, benefits and alternatives of ____ procedure were explained to the patient who understands and agrees to proceed." The dynamic nature of the informed consent process makes a negligence claim based solely on informed consent difficult for plaintiff counsel to prove. It essentially comes down to the physician's version of the process versus the patient's version of the process, a "he said–she said" scenario. A signed consent form further complicates failure to obtain informed consent claims. Usually, failure to obtain informed consent is combined with a medical malpractice claim. When the process of informed consent is pertinent to a claim, evidence of the process can be found in the surgeon's office notes, preoperative and intraoperative nurses' notes, anesthesia notes, physician orders, and the consent forms themselves, both surgical and anesthesia.

Anesthesia Consent Form

State-by-state requirements regarding the use of a separate anesthesia informed consent form vary. The medical records might not always include a consent form for anesthesia separate from that of the operative consent or the facility's admission consent form.

A standarized, anesthesia-specific consent form provides the best documentation of the anesthesia informed consent discussion. The content and format may vary slightly depending on the type of anesthesia practice. It is generally a one-page document identifying the significant risks of anesthesia and providing information such as other available anesthesia options. If there is more than one page to the anesthesia consent, it should be verified that all pages have been included in the records as well as that signatures are in place. There are some situations encountered with anesthesia consents that can compromise the necessary level of informed consent. These could include the patient's pain level or mental state.

Preoperative

For routine surgery, the patient is seen by the surgeon in the office, most likely the result of being referred by another provider. The surgeon takes a complete history, performs a complete physical assessment, refers the patient for appropriate clearances, for example cardiology, and ensures the appropriate testing is performed. Many times the surgeon refers the patient to the primary-care provider for this type of testing, which may include basic lab studies (complete blood count (CBC), chemistry, coagulation). Depending on the age of the patient and history, an electrocardiogram (EKG) or cardiac stress testing may be done. The informed consent process for the surgical procedure is initiated during this visit and a plan is made regarding the type and timing of surgery.

Likewise, for any surgery requiring anesthesia, the patient is seen by the anesthesiologist who also takes a complete history, performs a basic physical assessment, and reviews the pertinent preoperative diagnostic testing. The anesthesia provider may order additional testing such as lab studies or an EKG. The informed consent process for anesthesia is initiated and a plan is made regarding the type of anesthesia to be used.

In true surgical emergencies, time is critical. Patients may go directly to the OR without complete assessments and/or documents. This is considered reasonable care under the right circumstances. Examples could include dissecting aortic aneurysm, or trauma involving internal bleeding causing hemodynamic instability. There are also surgeries that are considered urgent. In urgent situations, the patient is more stable and assessments including history and physical assessment, pertinent lab studies, and informed consent can be completed but may be abbreviated.

Day of Surgery

Whether routine or emergent, the patient presents to the preoperative area. Patient safety is the focus of this area.

Preoperative Nurses' Notes

In most instances, a preoperative checklist is used to ensure that the appropriate safety measures have been discussed and communicated with the surgical team.

- Patient identification: Verification of the patient's identity is made prior to placing the armband on the patient. Once the armband is in place, all surgical providers verify it is correct when they evaluate the patient in this area.
- Allergies: Allergies are reviewed and documented on the checklist. An allergy band is applied. Both the checklist and the allergy band should have the name of the allergen—medication, food, or substance—and the specific reaction, if known.

- Review of consents: The preoperative nurse, circulating nurse, and anesthesia provider all review the consent forms. In some cases, the consent form is signed in the preoperative area. The informed consent process, completed by the surgeon, is done prior to the patient's arrival. The preoperative nurse verifies that the process has occurred; the patient has no questions and is able to describe the planned procedure before he/she signs the consent form. The anesthesia provider may perform the informed consent process in the preoperative area.
- Verification of the operative site: In an effort to avoid wrong-site surgery, surgical sites are marked in indelible ink in the preoperative area. In cases of unmarkable sites, an armband can be used. Participants in this process are the patient, preoperative nurse, surgeon, and circulator. Each provider verifies the operative site and documents this verification.
- Verification of NPO status, medications taken/not taken: Surgeons, anesthesia providers, preoperative nurses, and circulators all verify NPO status and medications taken/not taken on the day of surgery. In emergent situations, the timing of the last meal and its contents are verified with the anesthesia preoperative documentation. Anesthesia delivery techniques are dictated by NPO status of the patient.
- Preoperative vital signs including pain score, height, and weight.
- Baseline assessment: This is not meant to be a complete physical assessment. Level of consciousness including orientation, lung sounds, cardiac, and skin assessments are made.
- Monitoring:
  - EKG
  - SaO_2
  - Blood glucose
  - Hemoglobin
  - Urine pregnancy test
- Foreign objects inventoried/removed (dentures, partials, jewelry)
- Responsible person contact information
- Timing:
  - Arrival to area
  - Medications given by preoperative nurse
  - Vital signs
  - IVs started or infusing
  - Departure to OR
- Fall risk assessment
- History and physical (H&P) signed off by surgeon: H&Ps less than 30 days old but older than 24 hours must be verified by the surgeon as unchanged. Any changes may be handwritten on the H&P. H&Ps older than 30 days must be rewritten.

Preoperative Anesthesia Notes

The purpose of prescreening anesthesia cases is to evaluate and optimize the patient's fitness for anesthesia. A complete physical assessment at this time is part of a proactive approach to preventing possible complications by anticipating them. Final decisions regarding the urgency of surgery and the type of anesthesia may be made after consultation between the surgeon(s), consulting physicians, anesthetist, *and* the patient. Any medical issues that can be resolved should be done during this preoperative assessment phase. Referrals to other healthcare specialists and additional testing may take place at this time.

The preoperative assessment process involves consideration as to whether or not the patient is in the best possible state of health consistent with his/her organic illness and the necessity of the operation and its urgency. Notations should be made as to whether existing medical issues have been resolved.

The most common classification is that of patient classification number recommended by the ASA. The preoperative anesthesia assessment should always include the careful consideration of at least the following factors:

Identification of the patient after reviewing the patient's test results and health history including the following:

- Cardiac history (angina, heart attack, hypertension, family history of cardiac problem).
- Respiratory status (asthma, emphysema, apnea).
- Neurological conditions (stroke, epilepsy).
- Previous exposure to anesthesia (family anesthesia history as well as patient's).
- Immune system deficiencies (hepatitis, immunizations, inadequate clotting or excessive bleeding).
- Esophageal or stomach conditions (reflux, hiatal hernia, heartburn, ulcers, eating disorders).
- Medication and treatment history including herbal supplements and over the counter medications.
- Allergies to medicines, eggs, seafood, or latex.
- Teeth (any loose teeth, dentures, bridgework)
- The airway including the Mallampati classification: The Mallampati classification system is used to predict how difficult it will be to intubate the patient, and assess the physical airway. The Mallampati classification system may be displayed as diagrams as well as a number of Classes I–IV with a Class I describing a predicted easy intubation to a Class V, which would be predicted to be most difficult. These determinations are made by a physical inspection of the patient's oropharyngeal area.
- Concurrent illness.

A classification system is used by anesthesia providers to establish a fitness for anesthesia.

Designations of Class I (healthy and fit), Class II (mild systemic conditions), Class III (severe condition), Class IV (constant threat to life or incapacitating), or Class V (not expected to live). An E added to any of these designates an emergent surgery.

The anesthesia preoperative record and the anesthesia intraoperative record can generally be found together in the patients operative record.

Intraoperative

Operative Note

The attending surgeon is responsible for documenting the surgical procedure in an operative note. There are two operative notes in the medical record. One is handwritten either on a preprinted form document or in the progress notes, and one is dictated. The handwritten note is a short-hand version of the dictated note. Both include preoperative and postoperative diagnoses, actual procedure performed, name of the attending surgeon and any assistants, estimated blood loss, complications, and disposition of the patient. The dictated note details the indication for the surgical procedure and a detailed description of the procedure itself. This section, usually called

"Description" contains details regarding the incision, technique, equipment used, findings, surgical counts, and any complications. This is the "meat" of the report. If surgical technique is at issue in a potential negligence claim, this is where the LNC needs to focus.

10/25/1999   **Central Vermont Medical Center Example Anesthesia Record**   Page 1 of 2

Surgical Diagnosis:	Case Times:	Patient: SAMPLE CASE
CHOLECYCTITIS	18:33 **Start Anesthesia**	ID: 1212345 **Sex:** Male In-Patient
APPENDICITIS	19:07 **Start Surgery**	**DOB:** 12/12/1912 **Age:** 86 Years
Procedure(s):	20:11 **End Surgery**	**Weight:** 68.2 kg 150.0 lb **BSA:** 1.8
LAP CHOLECYSTECTOMY AND CHOLANGIOGRAM	20:20 **End Anesthesia**	**Height:** 173 cm 68 in **BMI :** 22.9
LAPAROSCOPIC APPENDECTOMY	18:47 **Induction**	**ASA:** 3 Elective
	18:50 **Intubation**	**Preop Vitals:** BP-160/88 HR-78 RR-24 Temp-37.0
	107.0 **Total Minutes**	**NPO Status:** NPO per Instructions OR # 2

Anesthesia Provider(s):   **E-Signed**
1: DOE, JOHN MD   06/10/2008 20:17:36
2:
3:

Surgeon(s):
Primary: SMITH, J MD
Assistant: JONES, T MD
Assistant:

Anesthetic Techniques:
(X) General   ( ) MAC
( ) Spinal   ( ) Bier Block
(X Epidural   ( ) Nerve Block

( ) Cardiopulmonary Bypass
( ) Controlled Hypotension
( ) Hemodilution

Lab: ( ) See Patient's Record   **ABG:**

Hct: 42	Sodium: 140	pO2: 62	
Hb: 13.1	Potassium: 38	pCO2: 42	
WBC: 9100	Glucose: 110	pH: 7.42	
Plts: 234	BUN: 12	HCO3: 28	
PT: NL	Creatinine: 1.0	BE: 4	
PTT: NL	Calcium: 9	FiO2: RA	

(X) ECG Done (X) CXR Done (X) TS/TC Done

Physical/Airway Exam:

Mallempati	2
Heart&Lungs Nrml	(X)
Irregular Rhythm	( )
Murmur	( )
Rhochi	( )
Wheezes	( )
Decreased BS	( )
Anterior Larynx	( )
Small Mouth	( )
Large Tongue	( )
Poor Jaw ROM	( )
Poor Neck ROM	( )
Dentures/Partials	( )
Edentulous	( )
Poor Dentition	(X)
Missing Teeth	( )
Chipped Teeth	( )
Overbite	( )
Caps	( )

Past Medical History:	Current Meds:	Allergies:	Anesthetic History:	Surgical History:
COPD	SEE PATIENT RECORD	PCN	DELAYED AWAKENING	BLEEDING
SMOKER		SULFA	POST OP NAUSEA VOMITING	
ABNORMAL EKG		CODEINE		
DAILY ETOH				
CARDIOMIOPATHY				

Intravenous Lines & Invasive Monitors:

Line	Size	Side	Site	In-Place
IV #1	20 Gauge	Right	ARM	(X)
IV #2	16 Gauge	Left	HAND	( )
IV #3				( )
IV #4				( )
Arterial 1	20 Gauge	Left	RADIAL	(X)
Arterial 2				( )
Central				( )
Swan	8 French	Right	INT JUGULAR	(X)

Airway Circuits:
(X) Anesthesia Machine Checked and Suction Available
(X) Semi-Closed   (X) Nasal Prongs
( ) Closed Circuit   ( ) O2 Mask
( ) Bains   ( ) Venti-Mask
(X) Artificial Nose   ( ) T-Piece
(X) Heated Humidifier   ( ) Non-Rebreather Mask

Monitors Used:
(X) Alarms Enabled
(X) NIBP
(X) O2 Sat
(X) A-Line   (X) ETCO2   (X) Agent
(X) CVP   (X) EKG   (X) Spirometry
( ) EEG   (X) ST Segments   (X) Swan Ganz
(X) PNS   (X) Esoph Probe   ( ) TEE
(X) FIO2   ( ) Precord Steth   (X) Temperature

Patient Position(s) Used During Case:
(X) Supine   ( ) Semi-Fowler
( ) Lithotomy   ( ) Sitting
( ) Left Lateral Decubitus   ( ) Trendelenberg
( ) Right Lateral Decubitus   ( ) Reverse Trendelenberg
( ) Prone   ( ) Axillary Roll
( ) Jacknife   ( ) Extra Padding

Arms
(X) Arms < 90 Degrees
( ) Left Arm @ Side
( ) Right Arm @ Side
Eye Care
(X) Eyes Taped Closed
( ) Eye Lubrication

Accessories:
( ) Blood Recovery System   (X) In-Line Filter
( ) Doppler   ( ) Rapid Fluid Infuser
( ) Fluid Warmer   **Warming Blanket(s)**
( ) Heating Lamp(s)   (X) Air Blanket
(X) Humidifier   ( ) Water Blanket
( ) Infusion Pump(s)

Airway Management:
Induction
( ) Mask Induction
(X) IV Induction
(X) Pre O2
( ) Rapid Sequence
(X) Cricoid Pressure
Airways
(X) Oral Airway
( ) Nasal Airway

Tube
Type: ETT
Size: 8.0
Route: Orally
Depth: 22
Cuffed (X) (Inflated to 5)
Attempts: 3

Methods
(X) Direct Laryngoscopy
( ) Blind Technique
( ) Fiberoptic Scope
(X) Tube Changer Stylet
( ) Wire Stylet
(X) Fast Track LMA
( ) Awake Technique
( ) In Place On Arrival

Blade
Blade Type: Curved
Blade Size: 4

Visualization
No Cords / No Arytenoids
Mask Ventilation
Adequate

Confirmation
(X) Endtidal Carbon Dioxide
(X) Bilateral Breath Sounds
(X) Tube Secured
Comment
Anterior larynx, poor neck extension, poor mouth opening. Failed DL. Success with Fast Track.

Regional Anesthetic(s)

Block 1: EPIDURAL	Block 2:	Block 3:
Time: 18:45 Attempts: 1	Time:	Time:
Needle: 18 GA 3.5" HUSTED	Needle:	Needle:
Location: L3-4	Location:	Location:
Position: Sitting	Position:	Position:
Amount: 3 CC TEST DOSE	Amount:	Amount:
Local: .5% BUPIVACAINE + EPI	Local:	Local:
Comment: Without Heme, CSF or paresthesias. All doses in divided increments. Catheter depth at skin - 10 cm	Comment:	Comment:

Post-op Note: ( ) No compaints or apparent complications from anesthesia   ( ) See Progress Notes   Printed on 06/10/2008

10/25/1999   **Central Vermont Medical Center Example Anesthesia Record**

PATIENT: Sample Case   ID: 1212345

CASE TIME:	-	18:40	-	18:50	-	19:00	-	19:10	-	19:20	-	19:30	-	19:40	-	19:50	-	20:00	-	20:10	-	20:20	-	20:30
GASES & AGENTS FI-OXYGEN PCT	-	-	66	55	55	52	51	50	48	50	48	48	49	51	50	49	50	48	48	60	90	-	-	-
AIR FLOW LPM																								
O2 FLOW LPM	3NP	3NP	4	4	4	1	1	1	1	1	1	1	1	1	1	1	1	1	1	1	1	8	1	8
N2O FLOW LPM	-	-	4	4	4	1	1	1	1	1	1	1	1	1	1	1	1	1	1	0	1	0	-	-
FI-N2O PCT	-	-	40	50	46	50	50	48	48	49	48	47	46	48	48	49	51	50	55	40	20	-	-	-
FE-N2O PCT	-	-	35	48	40	48	48	47	46	45	44	42	42	44	43	43	48	46	50	36	15	-	-	-
FI-AGENT PCT	-	-	D1.1	D6.0	D7.1	D7.7	D6.8	D7.0	D7.0	D7.0	D7.0	D6.9	D7.0	D6.8	D6.8	D4.0	D2.0	D2.0	D0.0	D6.8	D6.8			
FE-AGENT PCT	-	-	3.4	4.6	6.0	6.8	6.5	6.4	6.0	6.2	6.4	6.2	6.3	6.2	6.2	6.5	6.4	4.5	2.0	0.5				
FI-CO2 MM HG																								
CASE TOTALS FE-CO2 MM HG	-	34	35	29	42	41	35	34	35	34	33	33	32	32	34	31	33	34	34	40	41	-	-	-
EEG																								

	CASE TOTAL	-	18:40	-	18:50	-	19:00	-	19:10	-	19:20	-	19:30	...
2.00	VERSED mg	2.00	-											
10.00	FENTANYL cc	1.00	-	9.00										
125	PENTOTHAL mg	-	-	125										
10.00	EPHEDRINE mg	-	-	-	10.00									
10.00	NORCURON mg	-	8.00						2.00					
1000	CEFAZOLIN mg			1000										
5.00	ENLON PLUS cc												5.00 (at ~20:10)	

	Infusions													
Total	NITROGLYC u/K/M	-	1	-->-	-->-	-->-	-->-	-->-	-->-	-->-	-->-	-->-	-->-	...
Total														
Total														
Total														
Total	Input-Output													
	LACTATED RINGRS	800	-	-	-	-	1000							
375 ml	Urine Output	-	-	-	-	-	-	-	150	25	-	-	-	... (100 near 20:20)
200 ml	Est Blood Loss	-	-	-	-	-	-	-	-	150	-	-	-	... (200 near 20:20)
	Other Losses													

		-	18:40	-	18:50	-	19:00	-	19:10	-	19:20	-	19:30	-	19:40	-	19:50	-	20:00	-	20:10	-	20:20	-	20:30
	TEMP C. DEGREES	-	36.9	-	36.7	36.7	36.9	36.7	36.7	36.4	36.4	36.2	36.1	35.9	35.6	35.5	35.4	35.5	35.4	35.3	35.2	35.3	-	-	-
	TIDAL VOLUME CC	-	-	-	1200	805	1106	893	790	800	805	815	810	800	804	803	812	804	800	805	250	340	-	-	-
	PIP CM H2O	-	-	-	25	32	21	23	19	22	23	22	21	24	24	23	22	24	22	23	-	-	-	-	-
	CVP MM H2O	-	6	-	3	6	7	7	2	-	6	-	8	8	10	8	8	10	8	6	6	-	-	-	-
	PA SYS BP MM HG	-	21	-	20	27	31	29	29	28	26	27	25	24	22	23	24	26	28	24	25	24	-	-	-
	PA DIA BP MM HG	-	10	-	10	16	16	16	15	14	14	15	12	12	10	11	11	18	17	14	13	14	-	-	-
	PA WEDGE MM HG	-	4	-	16			12			14			9			15			12			-	-	-
	CARD OUTPUT LPM	-	3.5	-	4.1		3.3				4.5			4.1			4.6			4.8			-	-	-
	EEG																								
	BP-SOURCE CODE	-	A	A	A	A	A	N	A	A	A	A	A	A	A	A	A	A	A	A	A	A	-	-	-
	HR-SOURCE CODE	-	E	E	E	E	E	E	E	E	E	E	E	E	E	E	E	E	E	E	E	E	-	-	-
	ECG RHYTHM	-	SR	SR	SR	SR	SR	SR	SR	SR	SR	SR	SR	SR	PVCs	SR	SR	PVCs	SR	SR	SR	SR	SR	SR	-

Graph (left Y-axis 0–220, right Y-axis 0–110; X-axis time 18:35 to 20:25)

Left axis marks: 220, 200, 180, 160, 140, 120, 100, 80, 60, 40, 20
Right axis marks: 110, 100, 90, 80, 70, 60, 50, 40, 30, 20, 10, 0
X-axis marks: 18:35, 18:45, 18:55, 19:05, 19:15, 19:25, 19:35, 19:45, 19:55, 20:05, 20:15, 20:25

* Drug given incrementally

All drugs given IV unless stated otherwise

Legend:
- ▼ BP-sys (0-220)
- ▲ BP-dia (0-220)
- ✕ HR (0-220)
- ● O2 Sat (0-100)
- □ RR (0-100)
- ○ ETCO2 (0-220)

DATA SOURCE:
N=NIBP BP
A=A-LINE BP
E=ECG HR
P=OXIM HR

AGENT CODES:
D=DESFLURANE
E=ENFLURANE
H=HALOTHANE
I=ISOFLURANE
S=SEVOFLURANE

COMMENTS:

18:33- ARRIVED OR, ID CONFIRMED, RE-EVALUATED, MONITORS APPLIED
18:34- ARRIVED FROM ICU WITH ART LINE AND SWAN IN PLACE
18:50- ANTIBIOTIC PER SURGEON REQUEST
19:02- NASAL GASTRIC TUBE INSERTED PER REQUEST
19:04- FOLEY CATHETER INSERTED
19:55- CLOSING

Perioperative Notes (Circulator)

There is a wealth of information documented by the circulating nurse before, during, and immediately after any surgical procedure. This lengthy document is usually titled "Perioperative notes" or "Perioperative nurses' notes/record," etc. Preoperative activities, such as consent verification, surgical-site verification, and surgical time-out information are found here. Surgical positioning, equipment used, tourniquet times, and implant information are part of this document. Times, which can be critical during surgical negligence claims, are found here: patient arrival time, the time the patient entered OR, surgeon arrival time, start and end of surgery, and the time the patient left OR. There is a roster of all people in the OR—the circulator, scrub, surgical technician, surgeon, assistants, anesthesiologist, anesthetist, observers, relief personnel for the nursing and anesthesia staff along with times of the relief. Surgical count records including information such as who participated, what was counted, and the outcome of the count are included. Surgical count sheets may be separate from the perioperative nurses' notes. Some facilities do not keep these count sheets as part of the permanent record. How the patient is transferred from the OR table to the stretcher or bed, transport to PACU, etc. are all part of this note.

The role of the anesthesia provider in the OR is to create the most ideal conditions for a safe and successful surgery by providing continual medical assessment and treatment of the patient. This is accomplished by (1) controlling the patient's level of consciousness and pain control, (2) continuously monitoring the patient's vital functions and vital signs, and (3) maintaining body temperature and body fluid balance. Anesthesia providers are responsible for the medical management and anesthetic care of the patient throughout the duration of the surgery. The anesthesia provider must carefully match the anesthetic needs of each patient to that patient's medical condition, responses to anesthesia, and the requirements of the surgery.

Many things may occur during the surgical experience. The anesthesia records should reflect the anesthesia care activities including placement of the monitoring equipment, the induction process, medications given, the maintenance of anesthesia levels, fluids given, the patient's responses to all interventions, continual monitoring of the vital signs, and the emergence phase of the anesthesia.

While the operative report for the surgery documents the activities surrounding the surgery itself, the anesthesia operative records document the frequent assessment and treatment of the patient's health. The anesthesia or operative record is one the most concentrated collection of information that you may encounter in reviewing medical records. It is usually easy to identify as it contains a grid in which the vital signs are recorded, but it can be difficult to read because of the great amount of information written in a small area on a single page.

Perfusionist Flowsheet

The perfusionist's role is very specific as described earlier in this chapter. Perfusionists typically use a flowsheet to document the specifics about the machine(s) they are responsible for, the patient's physical response including lab values and vital signs, machine readings and timing of events, etc. This can be a handwritten or computerized document. The perfusionist flowsheet may not be part of the initial set of requested records. Because it contains vital information regarding a specific portion of a surgical procedure, the perfusionist's record is critical for a thorough analysis of any surgical negligence claim regardless of the focus of the claim; provided, of course, a perfusionist was involved.

Logs

Should a negligence claim focus on surgical specimens, a specimen log is kept, which contains information on the person responsible for handling the specimen, timing of drop-off and pick-up, destination, etc. This log is not part of the patient's medical record and will need to be specifically requested. Likewise, laws governing destruction of these types of documents vary, if they exist at all. Specimen logs are routinely destroyed. Therefore, if an LNC finds a need to review such a log, notifying the attorney as soon as possible is helpful.

Postoperative

Following surgery, the anesthesia providers and circulators transfer the care of the patient to the post anesthesia recovery unit (PACU), formerly referred to as recovery room. The anesthesia provider and the circulator provide a report of the course of the surgery and anesthesia and transfer responsibility for patient care to the PACU staff. It is here that the patient is allowed to emerge fully from the effects of the anesthesia under the watchful eyes of skilled nursing personnel with anesthesia provider consultation immediately available.

When the patient is sufficiently recovered from the effects of the anesthesia, the PACU nurses decide when the patient is ready to move to the next level of care, unless the patient has problems requiring the anesthesiologist to intervene.

Postanesthesia Care Unit

The PACU flowsheet is the main record of the immediate postoperative period for the patient. The attending anesthesiologist or their designee remains responsible for the patient during the stay in the PACU. There are two phases of anesthesia recovery, aptly referred to as Phase I and Phase II. Phase I is the immediate intensive care level during which the patient emerges and awakens from anesthesia. Airway management and pain control are the focus of this phase. Frequent monitoring is required including assessments of vital signs, breathing pattern, level or consciousness, pain score, intake and output, and interventions such as oxygen therapy, and medication administration. Initially, the PACU nurse receives report from the anesthesia provider and the circulator. The patient's initial presentation, timing, and accompanying personnel are documented on all three records: perioperative nurses' notes, anesthesia record and PACU flowsheet. Discrepancies in the timing of arrival and condition of the patient upon arrival should be evaluated. A patient's recovery from anesthesia is multifactorial including age, type of anesthesia used, comorbidities, surgical procedure performed, etc.

Phase II is a lower level of care where monitoring is less frequent and the focus shifts to readiness to be discharged. Inpatients are assessed based on the level of care to which they will discharged, that is, ICU or floor. Ambulatory setting assessments focus on the patient's readiness for discharge home. Once deemed ready for discharge from any PACU setting, an anesthesiologist is responsible for the discharge of the patient (Freeley & Macario, 2005). This is called a 'sign out' signifying the patient has recovered from anesthesia sufficiently to progress to the next level of care.

In ambulatory surgery centers and free-standing surgery centers, patients are discharged home with written discharge instructions and equipment such as splints, braces, girdles, etc. Discharge instructions are reviewed with the patient and a responsible person, and are signed, indicating understanding of the instructions. Equipment is applied by the circulator or PACU nurse, and care and removal instructions are included in the discharge instructions. Indications to notify the surgeon and follow-up plans are also a part of discharge instructions. The discharge period can be critical for potential negligence claims. Some centers maintain a copy of the signed discharge instructions in the patient's chart. Additionally, surgeons usually have their own standard set of discharge instructions, which can be requested during discovery.

Overview

Surgically related negligence claims are unique for several reasons. The most obvious reasons are the plaintiff is in an altered state of consciousness; friends and family are not present during the procedure and recovery; and the completion of the medical record (evidence) is completed by the defendants or their colleagues. Although surgical procedures themselves are technically similar, no two sets of facts are similar. Thus, an LNC's approach to surgical case analysis must be individualized.

Screening Surgical Cases

When evaluating surgically related cases, a complete set of medical records is required, but rarely available at the initial analysis. Making a list of what records the LNC had available at the time of the report and what is missing is a valuable tool for the attorney and their staff. As records come in, updates can be made to the original report. It is important to understand the allegation(s) of negligence before beginning the case analysis. Having this knowledge helps the LNC to focus on critical documents. As with other types of medically related litigation, the LNC may find evidence of additional negligence, and identify additional providers who may be liable or additional damages to consider. The case facts dictate what the critical documents are; however, case analysis requires careful review of the entire surgical process.

Preoperative Events

Questions to ask include was the surgery necessary? Was the preoperative workup appropriate and complete? Were preoperative testing results reviewed by appropriate providers, that is, CXR reviewed by the surgeon, EKG reviewed by cardiologist and/or anesthesiologist? Was the informed consent process documented? Were any details regarding that process noted? Was the patient appropriately referred for preoperative clearance, for example, cardiology? In the preoperative area, were the proper checks and balances performed—patient identified, surgical site verified, allergies noted, etc.?

Intraoperative

Patient Safety

Patient safety is the focus of the surgical team. When analyzing surgical cases, carefully review the perioperative nurses' notes. Information regarding proper patient identification technique, surgical-site verification, surgical time-out procedure and participants, placement of grounding pad, and electrocautery equipment is all part of this document.

Technique

The majority of surgical cases focus on the surgeon's technique during the procedure. An expert surgeon's opinion will be required should a negligence claim move forward; however, the LNC plays a critical role in evaluating potential negligence claims. As noted above, the dictated operative report contains the details regarding the surgical technique, equipment used, and surgical findings. If a complication occurs, the dictating surgeon will describe the event in this section. Typically, this is done in vague terms. LNCs will need to educate themselves on the basics of the technique and known complications of the specific procedure in order to provide the attorney with the knowledge they need to decide to pursue or defend a potential claim. There are a wealth of resources on the web, in medical school libraries, and bookstores. The appendix lists some of these resources.

Postoperative

Was the patient monitored appropriately? Were complications noted in a reasonable time? Was the care of the complication(s) appropriate? For example, the blood pressure of the postoperative colon resection patient is low with a compensatory tachycardia. The PACU nurse notes the abnormalities, and notifies the anesthesiologist covering the unit within 5 min who orders a fluid bolus. The patient's vital signs, monitored every 5–15 min, stabilize.

Common Allegations in Surgical Cases

Most surgical errors are related to intraoperative events related to manual errors such as inadvertent laceration of an organ and/or judgment errors resulting in inappropriate or untimely procedures such as failure to timely treat a liver laceration (Regenbogen et al., 2007). Following is a discussion on some of the most common allegations in surgical cases. This is not meant to be an all-inclusive discussion, but merely intended to provide the reader with an overview of common allegations with some examples.

Failure to Diagnose

Examples of delayed diagnosis or failure to diagnose include inadvertent organ injuries during surgery, anastomosis leaks, and failure to promptly intervene. It is critical for the LNC to know the inherent risks of surgical procedures as injuries to organs in close proximity to the surgical field are known and accepted risks. In contrast, injury to organs or vessels not in close proximity to the surgical field should be closely scrutinized. Pertinent questions to ask when investigating such claims include when the injury was noted and how it was treated. For instance, was the injury immediately noted and repaired or was it diagnosed later in the postoperative period? Similar issues are relevant in cases regarding anastomotic leaks. Examples of failing to intervene in a timely manner include leaking aortic aneurysm, ruptured appendix, and injuries related to trauma. Timing and presenting symptoms and signs in these types of cases are critical as is the diagnostic workup. Examples of contributing factors to delayed diagnosis or failure to diagnose allegations include improper diagnostic testing and misinterpretation of testing.

Improper diagnostic testing will most commonly be related to errors in the preoperative workup, but errors in diagnostic testing can certainly occur throughout the surgical process. In routine surgery, a patient presents to a surgeon for a surgical consultation. Part of the consultation is routine diagnostic testing consisting of laboratory studies, EKG, chest x-ray, and depending on the patient's history, cardiac clearance. Anesthesia also evaluates the patient preoperatively and reviews the test results and gives orders as necessary. Guidelines for preoperative testing vary based on a patient's history, age, type of procedure being planned, etc. Resources at the end of the chapter provide information on such guidelines. Diagnostic testing is imperative in the trauma patient. Failure to carry out appropriate diagnostic studies in this population may result in missed injuries, which can prove fatal.

It is difficult to think of an example when misinterpretation of test results is not a breach in the SOC. However, misinterpretation does not always cause damage to the patient. Whenever a patient has an unexpected outcome, it is wise for the LNC to review diagnostic testing to ensure results were interpreted correctly. Misinterpretation can lead to not only delayed diagnosis or failure to diagnose, but also wrong or unnecessary surgery. A patient was incorrectly diagnosed with esophageal cancer when the pathology slides were misinterpreted. He had major complications from an unnecessary esophagogastrectomy, leaving him permanently disabled.

Failure to Assess

Failing to properly assess surgical patients is usually related to breakdown in basic patient safety procedures. Failing to assess patient identification, surgical procedure, and site leads to surgeries being performed on the wrong patient, the wrong location, or the wrong organ. A surgical time-out is now required for most surgical procedures. These types of cases garner high-profile media attention and attention from accrediting organizations such as the Joint Commission.

Administering the wrong medication is also related to patient safety procedures. The scrub nurse is responsible for drugs used by the surgeon as the scrub is responsible for instruments and supplies passed to the surgeon. A recent study noted a high percentage of PACU medication errors were related to patient controlled analgesia pump programming (Hicks, Sikirica, Nelson, Schein, & Cousins, 2008). Verification of the "five rights" applies to all medication administration during the surgical process. If the wrong drug is given, LNCs should examine injuries related to the medication and ensure clear causation of those injuries.

Adverse drug reactions related to allergies may or may not be medical malpractice. Documentation of allergies is found in the surgeon's office chart, the preoperative checklist, the anesthesia preop and intraoperative record, the perioperative nurses' notes and the PACU flowsheet. Administering a drug the patient is known to be allergic to is certainly a breach in the SOC. However, this breach does not always cause damage. If there is no damage, there is no medical malpractice claim. In other instances, a patient has never been exposed to the allergen, a surgical prep solution, for instance. Thus, the patient and the HCP had no way of knowing of the allergy. In these cases, the prompt recognition of the reaction and appropriate treatment are where the LNC should focus. Careful review of preoperative records documenting allergies is essential. Further, follow-up on the reaction and the identification of the allergen by a physician specializing in allergy medicine are important.

Latex allergy is becoming more common as the public's exposure increases. Facilities are moving toward latex-free environments to protect the patient's safety and decrease worker's exposure. If a patient is noted to be sensitive or allergic to latex, precautions are sometimes noted in the circulator and PACU record. There may not be documentation regarding specific precautions taken. The LNC may need to review that particular facilities policy and procedures regarding latex allergy. Comparison to the guidelines in the medical literature is an important step in this type of case analysis.

Timing of Therapy

Delayed treatment is another complex issue to investigate. The surgical process involves a multitude of HCPs and patient safety is a primary focus. It takes time to move the patient along the continuum of care. Documentation related to patient safety, diagnostic testing, preoperative assessments, and the flow of the OR all need to be carefully evaluated by the LNC in claims of this nature.

Failure to Monitor

Failure to monitor is a broad allegation and is one of the most common claims in medical malpractice cases. Surgical counts, equipment, and a variety of complications all fall under this category.

The circulator is responsible for ensuring that the surgical instrument (needles, knife blades, clips, etc.) and sponge counts are correct. The scrub and the circulator perform the count and document the process on the count sheet, which is a part of the medical record. The circulator then informs the surgeon of the results of the surgical count. Some procedures can use hundreds of items that require counting. Another caveat to surgical counts is that the nurses perform the count but the surgeon actually uses the items. Individual hospital policies and procedures vary on operative counts. If there is a discrepancy, x-rays are taken and the patient may need to be re-explored. The circulator and scrub and their employer are named as defendants in these types of cases. The surgeon, being the "captain of the ship" and the one actually using the items, can also be named as a defendant. Res Ipsa Loquitor, a legal doctrine, with the literal meaning "the thing speaks for itself," can be applied in cases of retained surgical instruments or supplies. Application of this legal doctrine is important as it shifts the burden of proof from the plaintiff to the defense. Medical experts are not required to testify to SOC in such cases. Causation experts, however, may prove helpful. Retained foreign objects require an additional surgery with all inherent risks. LNCs analyzing these cases should pay close attention to the special damages as some patients have little or no symptoms or sequelae related to the retained foreign object, thereby complicating plaintiff attorney's decision to pursue costly litigation.

The OR is a volatile environment for many reasons making the risk of fire inherent. The Food and Drug Administration estimates that 100 surgical fires occur each year (AORN Position Statement on Fire Prevention). Surgical fires are preventable, thereby making patient injuries resulting from surgical fire preventable. The components of the "fire triangle," an ignition source, fuel source and oxidizer, are abundantly present in the OR environment (ECRI). Fuel sources include drapes, gauze, prep solutions, and the patient's hair and body (AORN Position Statement on Fire Prevention). Common ignition sources are the electrocautery and laser. Anesthesia gases such as oxygen and nitrous oxide act as accelerants (AORN Position Statement on Fire Prevention). Communication among the surgical team is essential in keeping the elements of the fire triangle separate and thus preventing fire. Anesthesia and the rest of the surgical team need to be aware when commonly used ignition sources are being used, and surgery needs to be aware when combustion sources are in use by anesthesia such as in mask ventilation or nasal oxygen.

To prevent skin injury, great care is taken in positioning the patient. Despite this care, skin injuries, pressure ulcers, and burns do occur. Burns are typically related to electrical equipment and may go unnoticed until the surgical drapes are removed. The OR nursing staff and ultimately the surgeon are responsible for positioning the patient. Prolonged pressure due to immobility is a common problem. Add to this the pooling of fluids and shearing forces and it is easy to see why pressure ulcers occur. These injuries can prolong morbidity and extend hospitalization, thereby increasing special damages. The LNC needs to be aware of appropriate positioning and padding recommended during the specific procedure, which can be found in the medical literature. It is also important to take into account any comorbidities and the general preoperative condition of the patient as these are significant factors.

Bleeding is a well-known risk of surgery. Questions to consider in these types of cases include during what period of the surgical process was bleeding problematic? Was it intraoperative or post-operative? When and how was excessive blood loss identified? Was it identified in a timely manner? Were appropriate interventions initiated such as crystalloid and colloid replacement, increasing monitoring of vital signs and output, etc.? What was the response of the interventions? Was the blood loss communicated in a timely manner to the appropriate HCP, that is, surgeon, anesthesiologist? Careful scrutiny of the anesthesia and PACU records will be required for these types of cases. LNCs may find it helpful to create a time-line or a graph to show multiple simultaneous events, such as a drop in blood pressure and a large chest tube output followed quickly by an infusion of Hespan.

Nerve injuries are frequently the subject of negligence claims because of their impact on the daily lives of patients. They are not, however, always associated with medical malpractice. Nerve injuries are usually related to compression by a surgical instrument or by stretching of the nerve. Generally, a nerve injury caused by this mechanism is not considered malpractice as it can be a known surgical risk. However, complete transection is usually considered malpractice. LNCs looking into nerve injuries should examine descriptions of surgical positioning and technique, as well as postoperative notes describing the nerve, if such notes exist. Patients suffering from nerve injuries frequently require prolonged follow-up and therapy by multiple providers along with assistive devices. A life care plan may be helpful in some cases.

Deep vein thrombosis (DVT) and pulmonary embolism (PE), potentially fatal conditions, while known risks of surgery can be prevented with antithrombolytics and mechanical methods such as sequential compression devices. "Failure to perform a risk assessment and to provide appropriate venous thromboprophylaxis in surgical patients is considered negligent" (Scurr & Scurr, 2007). Certain surgeries carry a higher risk for DVT and PE such as orthopedic procedures. LNCs evaluating cases related to these conditions should focus on the preoperative coagulation studies and anticoagulation therapy, use of blood reinfusion, postoperative orders for antithrombolytics and/or thromboprophylaxis, timing of application of mechanical devices, compliance with mechanical devices.

Respiratory and circulatory assessment is a prime focus in the PACU. Narcotics and sedatives are routinely administered to patients in the PACU. Commonly used anesthetic agents can have a delayed effect of suppressing respirations further necessitating close monitoring of the respiratory status. Most negligence claims in the PACU relate to failure to monitor or communicate. A patient's status can change rapidly in this high volume, fast paced environment. Monitoring includes frequent assessments of respiratory effort, chest expansion, oxygen requirements, and oxygen saturation. Guidelines regarding PACU care are available from the American Society of PeriAnesthesia Nurses (ASPAN).

Surgical-site infections are unfortunately a relatively common surgical complication. Negligence in such cases can be difficult to prove as cultures of the OR are rarely taken, and thus proving the microbe causing the infection came from the OR due to poor sterile technique or sterile processing of the equipment is challenging. However, focusing on the timely diagnosis and treatment with appropriate antibiotics is worth looking into for the LNC reviewing such cases. Was infectious disease consulted? Was the monitoring of the wound appropriate—for instance, was the wound cultured and antibiotic therapy adjusted based on the culture results? Was the course of antibiotics appropriate? Was the patient compliant with the antibiotic regimen? Another issue to consider is prophylactic antibiotics. This is an area that continues to be debated in the medical literature.

Antibiotic prophylaxis within 1 hour prior to surgical incision is considered important in helping to decrease the incidence of surgical-site infections (Hawn et al., 2008). Sources vary on the optimal timing of prophylactic antibiotic administration.

Postoperative follow-up by the surgeon may also give rise to allegations of substandard care. The surgeon must be attentive to the patient and provide him/her with the proper monitoring following surgery until discharge from the hospital. If signs and symptoms are not addressed appropriately, a delay or failure to diagnose a potentially serious or fatal condition may occur. Was follow-up appropriate for the procedure performed? If a handoff occurred, were pertinent issues communicated? Evidence of this can be seen in the receiving physician's notes—were they focusing on the prior issues? Were changes in conditions addressed appropriately? Did the surgeon review all pertinent diagnostic testing? Was the patient compliant with instructions and follow-up?

Failure to Communicate

Lack of informed consent falls under this category. As previously discussed, lack of informed consent is usually a part of a negligence claim rather than being the whole claim. The reason is the dynamic process of informed consent and the "he said–she said" of the evidence. Consequently, malpractice claims of lack of informed consent are rarely settled in favor of the plaintiff.

Whose responsibility is it to follow up on diagnostic testing? It is the ordering physician's. An example could be wound cultures. As these tests take several days to complete, a patient may be discharged making follow-up more complex. Does the lab maintain documentation related to the notification of a physician of abnormal lab values? It is clear that the nurse has a duty to report abnormal results to the physician. Was the notification timely? If the lab called a critical value to the nurse, does the lab documentation match the nurses' documentation regarding timing of notification? How about radiology studies? In some cases, it is clear that there is a duty to report abnormal findings in a timely fashion, that is, call the ordering physician. In others, it is not so clear; for instance, when a lung nodule is noted on a preoperative chest x-ray on a patient undergoing knee arthroplasty. The radiologist notes the nodule and his recommendation for follow-up. The orthopedic surgeon does not note the recommendation and the patient is lost to follow-up until he presents with stage IV lung cancer.

Handoff is a term to describe the transfer of care from one HCP to another such as when anesthesia gives report to the PACU nurse. This is a time when there can be ambiguity of responsibility, that is, duty to the patient (Regenbogen et al., 2007). To compound this, there is virtually no evidence of the information exchanged during handoffs. Usually, an LNC will see written in the medical record, "report given to oncoming nurse, M. Mason RN" or "report received from CRNA." Examine the record carefully for patient history, vital signs, intake, and output on the PACU record, which can give an indication of what the PACU nurse was told by the anesthesia provider. Depositions are also a good source of information on this point.

Communication is the key of the healthcare team. The medical record is a vital communication tool. HCPs are responsible for the information contained in the medical record. For instance, a house officer is asked to see a patient during the night for foot pain. The house officer documents this visit noting an erythematic ulceration on the toe of a diabetic patient. Pain medication is prescribed and the house officer refers care of the ulcer to the attending physician. The attending physician wrote his progress note the following day directly under the house officer's note but made no reference of the ulcer. Several days pass without mention of the ulcer by the attending physician. The patient eventually required an amputation.

Failure to communicate is frequently found in verbal communication. This is much harder to prove as there is little, if any, evidence of verbal communication other than the notation of notification. For example, "Dr. Smith notified of patient's condition." What does that mean? What was Dr. Smith told? Another example is residents failing to notify attending physicians about critical events or when one attending physician is handing off to another attending physician.

For patients recovering from anesthesia, PACU nurses notify the anesthesiologist of changes in patient's condition. When reviewing communication practices, it is important to keep in mind that the providers did not have the advantage of hindsight.

Common Allegations in Anesthesia Cases

The safety record for present-day anesthesia has greatly improved. Anesthesia is one of the few specialties that have enjoyed lower insurance premiums. Some of the reasons include improved monitoring devices, safer anesthesia agents and equipment, and increased training of anesthesia providers. Complications, nevertheless, can still occur.

Anesthesia has significant inherent complications, which are discussed preoperatively with the patient and/or family. The patient assumes certain risks when undergoing surgery and anesthesia. As many inherent risks exist in anesthesia, the occurrence of malpractice rests in failure on the part of the provider to monitor, diagnose, respond, communicate, or treat correctly and in a timely manner.

Obstetrics anesthesia carries one of the great liabilities in anesthesia as it is a practice where the provider will have two or more patients at the same time. This anesthesia care may include providing pain relief with epidural or spinal blocks for the mother, while managing the life functions of both the mother and the baby. The expectation level is very high with obstetrics, with everyone anticipating a perfect delivery and a perfect baby.

The allegations of anesthesia claims range from chipped teeth and other dental injuries to death. Some of the other complications inherent to anesthesia include the following:

- Adverse reactions to medications or anesthesia agents
- Cardiac arrest
- Myocardial infarction
- Hypoxia leading to brain damage
- Nerve injuries
- Awareness under anesthesia
- Pulmonary embolism
- Aspiration of stomach contents or other fluids
- Pneumonia
- Bronchospasm
- Damage to throat, vocal cords, or esophagus
- Pneumothorax
- Eye injuries
- Hypovolemia
- Hematoma
- Epidural or spinal headaches
- Inadvertent intravenous injection of local anesthetic

Billing Analysis

When evaluating surgical cases, part of the analysis should include the billing. The LNCs knowledge of nursing prepares them for this role. An LNC can efficiently review billing records identifying related costs, billing errors, HCPs, diagnoses, etc. Private practitioners such as surgeons, anesthesiologists, and radiologists will submit separate bills for their services. Facility bills will include charges for supplies, OR time, anesthesia time, etc. OR and anesthesia time is billed by the minute. Amounts billed for these services should coincide with the times on the perioperative and anesthesia records. Nursing, surgical technician/scrub and perfusionist services are usually part of the OR charges and not itemized. Billing practices vary among facilities.

References

AORN Position Statement on Allied Health Care Providers and Support Personnel in the Perioperative Practice Setting. http://www.aorn.org/PracticeResources/AORNPositionStatements/Position_Health CareProvidersAndSupportPersonnel/ (accessed August 23, 2008).

AORN Position Statement on Fire Prevention. http://www.aorn.org/PracticeResources/AORNPosition Statements/Position_FirePrevention/ (accessed August 23, 2008).

AORN Position Statement on One Perioperative Registered Nurse Circulator Dedicated to Every Patient Undergoing a Surgical or Other Invasive Procedure. http://www.aorn.org/PracticeResources/ AORNPositionStatements/Position_RegisteredNurseCirculator (accessed August 21, 2008).

AORN Position Statement on the Role of the Scrub Person. http://www.aorn.org/PracticeResources/ AORNPositionStatements/Position_ScrubPerson/ (accessed August 23, 2008).

AORN Position Statement on the Role of the Health Care Industry Representative in the Perioperative/ Invasive Procedure Setting. http://www.aorn.org/PracticeResources/AORNPositionStatements/Position_ HealthCareRepresentative/ (accessed August 23, 2008).

ASA. Anesthesia and me, American Association of Anesthesiologists. Retrieved August 23, 2008, from http:// www.asahq.org/patientEducation/Anes%20&%20Me%20Checklist.pdf

Cohen, T. H. (2001). Medical malpracitce trials and verdicts in large counties. Bureau of Justice Statistics Civil Justice Data Brief April 2004; U.S. Department of Justice Bureau of Statistics. http://www.ojp. usdoj.gov/bjs/abstract/mmtvlc01.htm (accessed August 21, 2008).

ECRI. The patient is on fire: A surgical fire primer. http://www.mdsr.ecri.org/summary/detail.aspx?doc_id= 8197&q=surgical+AND+fire+AND+prevention (accessed August 27, 2008).

Euliano, T. (2008). Mallinpati evaluation. Retrieved September 7, 2008, from http://www.anest.ufl.edu/at.

Freeley, T. W., & Macario, A. (2005). The postanesthesia care unit. In R. D. Miller (Ed.), *Miller's anesthesia* (6th ed.). Maryland Heights, MD: Churchill Livingstone.

Hawn, M. T., Itani, K. M., Gray, S. H., Vick, C. C., Henderson, W., & Houston, T. K. (2008). Association of timely administration of prophylactic antibiotics for major surgical procedures and surgical site infection. *Journal of the American College of Surgery*, 206(5), 814–819.

Hicks, R. W., Sikirica, V., Nelson, W., Schein, J. R., & Cousins, D. D. (2008). Medication errors involving patient-controlled analgesia. *American Journal of Health System and Pharmacology*, 65(5), 429–440.

International Federation of Nurse Anesthetists. Nurse anesthesia worldwide: Practice, education and regulation (PDF). Retrieved August 24, 2008.

Iyer, P. (2008). Decoding anesthesia records. Retrieved September 3, 2008, from http://www.medleague. com/Articles/medical_records/anesthesia_records.htm

Iyer, P., & Aiken, T. (2001). *Nursing malpractice*. Tucson, Arizona: Lawyers & Judges Publishing Company.

Jurin-Semo. (1999, December). *Anesthesia billing compliance: A practical approach* (Vol. 63). Retrieved September 9, 2008, from http://www.asahq.org/Newsletters/1999/12_99/bill1299.html

Kuc, J. (2006). Perioperative records. In P. Iyer, B. Levin, & M. A. Shea (Eds.), *Medical legal aspects of medical records*. Tucson, Arizona: Lawyers and Judges Publishing Company.

McLean, T. R., Burton, L., Haller, C. C., & McLean, P. B. (2008). Electronic medical record metadata: uses and liability. *Journal of the American College of Surgery, 206*(3), 405–411.

Miriam Webster dictionary online. Retrieved August 24, 2008.

Regenbogen, S. E., Greenberg, C. C., Studdert, D. M., Lipsitz, S. R., Zinner, M. J., & Gawande, A. A. (2007). Patterns of technical error among surgical malpractice claims: An analysis of strategies to prevent injury to surgical patients. *Annals of Surgery,246*(5), 705–711. http://www.medscape.com/viewarticle/565857_1 (accessed August 21, 2008).

Rodden, D., & Dlugose, D. (2007). Nurse anesthesia malpractice issues. In P. Iyer & B. Levin (Eds.), *Nursing malpractice* (3rd ed.). Tucson, Arizona: Lawyers and Judges Publishing Company.

Scurr, J. R., & Scurr, J. H. (2007). Is failure to provide venous thromboprophylaxis negligent? *Phlebology, 22*(4), 186–191.

The American Board of Anesthesiology. (2008). Retrieved September 1, 2008, from http://www.theaba.org/index.shtml

Professional Associations

American Academy of Anesthesiology Assistants (AAAA): http://www.anesthetist.org/
American Association of Nurse Anesthetists (AANA): http://www.aana.com/org/
American Board of Anesthesiology (ABA): http://www.theaba.org/
American College of Surgeons (ACOS): cos.org/scriptcontent/index.cfm
American Society of Anesthesiologists (ASA): http://www.asahq.org/
American Operating Room Nurses (AORN): http://www.aorn.org/
American Society of PeriAnesthesia Nurses (ASPAN): http://www.aspan.org/
Association of Surgical Technologists (AST): http://www.ast.org/

Resources

Preoperative Testing

- http://www.emedicine.com/med/topic3172.htm

Wrong-Site Protocol

- http://www.jointcommission.org/NR/rdonlyres/E3C600EB-043B-4E86-B04E-CA4A89AD5433/0/universal_protocol.pdf
- http://www.jointcommission.org/NR/rdonlyres/4CF3955D-CD1F-4230-86C5-D04485CAFBEA/0/IG_final.pdf

Fire and Burn Prevention

- http://www.mdsr.ecri.org/summary/detail.aspx?doc_id=8271&q=surgical+AND+burns
- http://www.mdsr.ecri.org/summary/detail.aspx?doc_id=8185&q=surgical+AND+burns
- http://www.mdsr.ecri.org/summary/detail.aspx?doc_id=8203&q=surgical+AND+burns
- http://www.mdsr.ecri.org/summary/detail.aspx?doc_id=8202&q=surgical+AND+burns
- http://www.mdsr.ecri.org/Default.aspx

References

AORN Position Statement on Allied Health Care Providers and Support Personnel in the Perioperative Practice Setting. http://www.aorn.org/PracticeResources/AORNPositionStatements/Position_HealthCareProvidersAndSupportPersonnel/ (accessed August 23, 2008).

Association of Surgical Technologists. *Surgical technology: A growing career.* Littleton, CO: Association of Surgical Technologists. http://www.ast.org/pdf/GrowingCareer.pdf (accessed August 23, 2008).

Greenberg, C. C., Regenbogen, S. E., Studdert, D. M., Lipsitz, S. R., Rogers, S. O., Zinner, M. J. et al. Patterns of communication breakdowns resulting in injury to surgical patients. *Journal of American College of Surgery, 204*(4), 533–540.

Iyer, P. A., & Aiken, T. D. (2001). *Nurisng malpractice* (2nd ed.). Tucson, Arizona: Lawyers & Judges Publishing Company.

Test Questions

1. Which of the following is **most** important in the surgical arena?
   A. Detailed knowledge of surgical roles
   B. Ability to think quickly and critically
   C. Ability to count instruments
   D. Ability to delegate

2. LNC assist attorney in determining which of the following?
   A. The legal standard to apply in OR cases
   B. The statute of limitations
   C. Distinguishing inherent risk from bad outcomes
   D. When to send a subpoena

3. Which of the following represent types of anesthesia found in surgical case notes? **Choose all that apply.**
   A. Regional anesthesia
   B. General Anesthesia
   C. Local anesthesia
   D. Parathesia

4. The standard of care for surgical cases can be found in which of the following? **Choose all that apply.**
   A. Facility policies and procedures
   B. Newspapers
   C. Peer reviewed literature
   D. State Practice Acts

5. The term "Captain of the Ship" refers to which of the following?
   A. The surgeon
   B. The anesthesiologist
   C. The surgical team
   D. The Navigator

Answers: 1. B; 2. C; 3. A, B, C; 4. A, C, D; 5. A

Chapter 23

Issues in Residential and Community-Based Care

Laura E. Fox, MSN RN, CDDN, CLCP
and Dawn D. Nash, RN, LNCC

Contents

Residential Care for Individuals with Developmental Disabilities

Objectives

- To define the trends for long-term care for individuals with developmental disabilities (DD)
- To describe two roles of the LNC in assisting attorneys with long-term care cases for individuals with DD
- To identify areas in long-term care for individuals with DD who need monitoring by the legal nurse consultant (LNC)

Introduction

Residential care for people with developmental disabilities (DD) requires special expertise and knowledge for the legal nurse consultant (LNC). The LNC needs to know about the unique needs of people with DD, including healthcare issues. The LNC needs knowledge on the residential care system for people with DD, the various options available, the regulatory agencies, and standards of practice. The residential care system for people with DD is a field unto itself that varies from state to state. Because people with DD represent a diverse group, the residential setting needs to be able to provide for individualized needs that are dynamic and changing over a person's life. The

LNC in this field needs experience with the medical and legal aspects of long-term care specific for individuals with DD.

The LNC is often contacted by an attorney when an individual or groups of individuals with DD living in residential care sustain an injury or insult. These injuries may have occurred because the care was believed to be substandard. The attorneys often cite nursing home and/or hospital standards of care and are unaware that most people with DD reside in the community and in small group homes that are regulated at the local, state, and/or federal level. These standards are not nursing home or hospital standards and the same standards of care cannot be applied. The LNC will need to be aware of the trends in long-term care for individuals with DD, the applicable standards of care, the different types of facilities, and issues that frequently arise.

Definitions

DD is a broad term that refers to a variety of conditions and describes an individual's functional limitations in society and daily life. According to the Developmental Disabilities Assistance and Bill of Right Act Amendments (2000) a DD is a chronic, severe disability, which

- Is attributable to a mental or physical impairment of a combination of mental and physical impairment
- Occurs before the individuals reaches age 22
- Is likely to continue indefinitely
- Results in substantial functional limitations in three or more of the following areas of major life activity: (i) self-care, (ii) receptive and expressive language, (iii) learning, (iv) mobility, (v) self-direction, (vi) capacity for independent living, and (viii) economic self-sufficiency
- Reflects an individual's need for a combination and sequence of special, interdisciplinary or generic care, individualized supports, or other forms of assistance that are of lifelong or of extended duration and are individually planned and coordinated

The federal definition of DD is based on an individual's functional abilities with self-help skills and/or activities of daily living (ADL). The federal definition of DD encompasses many different disabilities, which may include cognitive disabilities, physical disabilities, or both, including but not limited to, autism, Down syndrome, cerebral palsy, spina bifida, mental retardation (MR), and epilepsy. According to the Administration on DD, there are approximately 4.5 million individuals with DD in the United States (Administration on Developmental Disabilities, 2008).

There is no single standard definition of DD. The federal definition of DD is not uniformly accepted, and the states use different definitions for DD based on the federal law. Many states use a diagnosis of MR as the primary eligibility criterion. The Diagnostic and Statistical Manual of Mental Disorders 4th edition defines MR as subaverage general intellectual functioning and significant limitations in adaptive functioning in two skills areas. Subaverage intellectual functioning is defined as an IQ of about 70 or below, approximately 2 standard deviations below the mean, starting before the age of 18 (American Psychiatric Association, 2000). By using this definition, only individuals with MR are eligible for services, and individuals with cerebral palsy and/or seizure disorders without the diagnosis of MR may not be eligible for state DD services and supports. In California, the Lanterman Act defines a developmental disability as that starts before the age of 18 (California Lanterman Developmental Disabilities Services Act, 1976). Using this definition, an individual who receives a diagnosis of traumatic brain injury from a motor vehicle accident at the age of 20 would not be eligible for services and supports through the California DD system.

Because people with DD represent a diverse group and the definition incorporates many different conditions and disabilities, it is important that the LNC should be aware of the individual's diagnoses and the definition for services where the individual resides. DD is a more specific definition than chronic conditions or the term "disabilities" (ANA, 2004). People with DD often need a combination of developmentally appropriate, interdisciplinary and individualized supports and services throughout their life. This information will be further needed when the LNC evaluates the level of care and individualized services in the community.

Overview of Residential Care

For many years, people with DD were isolated from the community and either lived at home or were sent away to large State Institutions often called State Developmental Centers. People with DD were seldom mainstreamed in the community. By the mid- 20th century, the focus was on normalization and providing care in the least restrictive environment. Normalization is used "to provide a supportive environment for persons with intellectual and DD to make decisions regarding ADL and to live as close as possible to the norms and patterns in the mainstream of the society in which they reside" (ANA, 2004, p. 53). The concept of normalization and living in the least restrictive environment started to replace the idea of segregated institutional settings for people with DD located in the outskirts of the community.

A major deinstitualization effort took place in the 1980s. This effort was fueled by media investigations exposing poor conditions in institutional settings and resulted in federal class action litigation demanding the people with DD be integrated into community settings. The transition from state institutions to the community varied from state to state (Nehring, 2003; Smith, 2006). Class action litigation continues to be a major force influencing community care options.

Olmstead v. L.C. (1999) is considered a landmark Supreme Court ruling in support of community care for people with DD. In this case, two women living in a State Institution in Georgia, determined to be appropriate for community care placement, were denied residential placement. The State argued that it was unable to afford to provide these services. The decision by the Supreme Court in *Olmstead v. L.C.* under Title II of the Americans with Disability Act (ADA) of 1990 stated that unnecessary institutional segregation constitutes discrimination that cannot be justified by a lack of funding. States are required to place individuals with DD in community settings when (1) the State's treatment professionals have determined that community placement is appropriate; (2) transfer from institutional care to the least restrictive environment is not opposed by the individual; and (3) the placement can be reasonably accommodated, taking into account the resources available to the State and the needs of others with mental disabilities. *Olmstead* requires the states to address community care in light of ADA integration. The aftermath of the *Olmstead* decision has resulted in many class action lawsuits for people with DD to receive long-term care services in the community. Litigation also addresses the issue of waiting lists that result in a denial of services. In 2006, 42 states reported that 64,990 persons with DD were on waiting lists for residential services (Braddock, Hemp, & Rizzolo, 2008). The States cite that these services are not being provided because they lack adequate funds. Other lawsuits are being filed for individuals with DD who challenge the Medicaid services that they did or did not receive in the community.

Residential and Community Care Settings

There are many available residential and long-term care options for people with DD. These settings include State Developmental Centers, often called State Institutions, Intermediate Care Facilities for the Mentally Retarded (ICF/MR), and Home and Community-Based Service (HCBS) Waiver Homes. These small ICF/MRs and HCBS Waiver homes are often called group homes. Group homes are funded by a variety of sources; however, the vast majority is funded by Medicaid, using a combination of federal and state funds. There has been a continual increase in residential out-of-home placements with an increase of 4.8% in 2004–2005 with 536,476 people with DD in residential care (Braddock et al., 2008).

The large State Developmental Centers were the backbone of the DD model. They offer a centralized model of services provided by the State. However, as the trend in long-term care for individuals with DD shifted to community and small group home-like settings, the State Developmental Centers have been closed or downsized. The individuals remaining have profound DD that require extensive medical care, including 24-hr nursing care, or significant behavioral concerns (Palley & Van Hollen, 2000). Males made up the majority of the population (Pouty, Smith, & Larkin, 2007). In 2006, 42 states continued to have state-operated institutions, while eight states and the District of Columbia no longer have these state-operative institutional facilities (Braddock et al., 2008). The majority of people with DD now reside in the small group home settings such as the ICF/MRs and the HCBS Waiver program.

The ICF/MR statute was enacted in 1971 from the Social Security Act (PL 92-223). It is based on a medical model and requires "active treatment." The ICF/MRs must comply with federal regulations found at 42 CFR Part 483, Subpart I, Sections 483, 400–493.490 and specified in eight areas that include management, client protections, facility staffing, active treatment services, client behavior and facility practices, healthcare services, physical environment, and dietetic services (wwwcms.hhs.gov). There are currently 7400 ICF/MRs in the United States serving 129,000 people (Department of Health & Human Services, 2008). Many of these people have MR, are also nonambulatory, have seizure disorders, behavior problems, mental illness, are visually and/or hearing impaired, or have a combination of these conditions. ICF/MRs range in size and may be large facilities or small six-bed homes. With the trend for smaller homelike settings, there has been a decline in the larger settings, and a growth in six people or less for ICF/MRs (Braddock et al., 2008). ICF/MRs may be operated by the State, or by private agencies, and may be for-profit or nonprofit. ICF/MRs are always residential and are regulated by the federal ICF/MR Standards through the Center for Medicare and Medicaid Services.

The HCBS Waiver program was designed for people with DD to remain in the community with supports, without having to meet all the federal regulations of the ICF/MRs. Congress first authorized the HCBS Waiver program in 1981 as an alternative to the ICF/MR program. Section 1915 (c) of the Social Security Act enables the State to request a waiver of applicable federal Medicaid requirements to provide community support services for those individuals who would have required institutional care. The residential model is generally limited to four or fewer individuals in the residential home. The program needs to demonstrate cost neutrality, as the cost for Waiver services must not exceed the cost of the institution. The HCBS Waiver is now the principal Medicaid program for people with DD. In fiscal year 2007, the HCBS Waiver exceeded $20 billion and paid for 5.2 times as many people with DD as the ICF/MR Waiver (Lakin, Prouty, Alba, & Scott, 2008).

The State agencies receive the HCBS Waiver funding for services and private agencies; both for-profit and nonprofit agencies provide the direct services. To receive the HCBS Waiver funds, a state submits an application to Health and Human Services (HHS), identifies the target population, identifies the number of people they will serve, and list the services that will be provided. Federal regulations specify that the State should have (1) adequate standards for all providers of services and (2) assurance that any state licensure of certification requirements for providers of waiver services are met. States must annually report on the implementation, monitoring, enforcement of their health and welfare standards, and the HCBS Waiver's impact on the health and welfare of the individuals.

The HCBS Waiver offers a cornucopia of community-based services and supports for people with DD, which may include case management, habilitation training, various professional therapies, behavior management, etc. These services and supports are determined by the needs of the individual, and they differ between states, and only some of the options are funded by each state (Braddock et al., 2008). Regulations are less prescriptive, allowing for "person-centered and person-driven" planning, focusing more on outcomes, rather than meeting a prescribed treatment approach. Oversight of the HCBS Waiver program is often decentralized among a variety of agencies, and rarely is one agency accountable for the overall quality of care provided. Some waiver service providers are regulated by state licensing agencies, others by private accreditation organizations, and yet others operate under a contract or other agreements with a state agency, with the vast majority provided by nonstate agencies (Pouty et al., 2007).

Current Issues

The smaller residential settings (ICF/MR and HCBS) are based on the normalization model. Adults with DD have rights and responsibilities, like the general population; however, they may need additional supports to live safely and successfully in the community. They work either independently or in sheltered settings or day programs and are not at home during daytime. They may have different diagnoses and different strengths and needs for services and supports. The residents have opportunities to interact with the community and work on independent skills. The residents have annual goals often outlined in an Individualized Habilitation Plan or Individualized Service Plan. They have regular visits to physicians and/or specialists. Residents have rights, which often have to be negotiated within the guidelines of the residential home. People with disabilities need to receive services in the settings of their choices. Bannerman, Sherldon, Sherman, and Harchik (1990) described personal choices as the rights of people with DD to eat too many doughnuts.

Adults with DD have the same medical issues as the majority of the population. They may have additional concerns and increased healthcare needs based on their functioning abilities and/or based on their diagnosis. People with DD, like the general population, often struggle with chronic conditions such as obesity, diabetes, high blood pressure, etc., and these issues may be further exacerbated by their functional limitations, for example, if the person is nonambulatory. They may also have extra medical issues, such as individuals with Downs Syndrome, who show physical signs of aging often 20 years earlier, including Alzheimer's (Service & Hahn, 2003). People with DD have the same age-related impairments and illness as people without disabilities. As our society ages, this population will also age, and will need healthcare services, including preventative health assessment.

The aging of our society directly influences the demand for residential services. As the population ages, there will be an increased need for out-of-home long-term residential care services for all persons, including individuals with DD. Currently, the majority of individuals with DD are living at home, with their aging parents (Palley & Van Hollen, 2000; Parish & Lutwick, 2005). It is anticipated that the future demand for services will far exceed the supply. The DD system competes with the general population for services and supports, including the need for care providers and community homes. The states have been experiencing an increase in the number of individuals with DD seeking community-based services, and have been unable to keep up with the growing demand (Smith, 2006). It is anticipated that this trend will continue.

Regulations on the Federal and State Level

Attorneys who contact an LNC generally want information regarding the standard of care. Frequently, the situation that occurs is that a person with DD has a change in his/her medical condition, which goes unrecognized or is ignored by the residential facility, and by the time the facility responds, the person has sustained an injury or, at worst, has died.

However, a simple scenario of reporting a change in the medical condition is complicated. For example, if the person with DD has communication difficulties, or is nonverbal, he will have limited ability to communicate a change or discuss symptoms with his care providers. His care providers will need to look at overt signs, such as weight gain/loss, intake and output, including changes with bowel or bladder, fever, etc. They will also need to look at more subtle signs such as grimacing with pain, lethargy, or change in behavior. The care providers will need to know their client and need skills in understanding and interpreting the signs and signals that the individual with DD uses to communicate his wants and needs.

As the majority of people with DD live in the group home setting (ICF/MRs and HCBS Waivers), and most are run by private companies that contract with the state, the LNC will need to determine the applicable state regulatory agency. This will assist with identifying the standards expected from the state agency. The LNC may also need to examine the statutes and regulations including those from Medicaid and/or Medicare. Portions of the basic information on laws, regulations, and compliance information are found on the website for the Centers for Medicare and Medicaid Services (CMS) (www.cms.hhs.gov).

Each State determines the settings and regulations for supporting people with DD. Because services are often decentralized, it is important for the LNC to be aware that different agencies are involved in the service delivery system. Most residential homes are privately run, receiving service funding from the state. Some state agencies include DD in their name, while others may be linked to Mental Health with one state agency that provides the umbrella for services for people with DD, mental health, and substance abuse. The National Association of State Directors of Developmental Disabilities Services (NASDDS) provides a list of the state agencies involved in providing services (www.nasdds.org). Another source for obtaining information is the National Dissemination Center for Children with Disabilities (NICHY), which provides information on various state resources, including agencies (www.nichcy.org).

Although the system is implemented differently in each state, every state has a designated department to address the needs of people with DD. President John F, Kennedy, in the 1960s, established the Office of Mental Retardation, which later became the Administration on Developmental Disabilities (ADD). The ADD, a Federal agency, is located within the United States Department of Health and Human Services with four grant programs responsible for working with their respective state governments and communities. Each state has a State Council on DD and an associated agency responsible for DD services and supports. Each state has a Protection and Advocacy (P&A) system, with attorneys available to protect the legal rights of individuals with DD. P&A has been involved with class action litigation, especially with deinstitutionalization, and ensuring community-based living options and supports are available and accessible. Each state has a University Center for Excellence in DD (formerly called University Affiliated Programs) that provides centers for learning, research, and clinical experience for students in the field of DD. Each state has a Project of National Significance, a discretionary program providing funding for national initiatives and technical assistance.

Facility Information

On the facility level, it will be important to obtain the policies and procedures of the facilities to determine compliance. Facility policies and procedures provide information not only on what the expectations are for the facility but also for the staff. To work in a facility, the staff generally receives some type of training on the DD population, first aid, medication administration, etc. It is important to remember that the direct care staff working in the residential home is generally not medically trained. They are instructed in basic signs and symptoms and taught to report medical changes to their supervisors and/or designated staff.

People with DD may have medications for chronic conditions such as seizures, psychotropic medications for behavioral issues, and medications for gastro esophageal reflux. They are often on multiple medications with many potential side effects and adverse reactions. The staff needs knowledge regarding medication and side effects, how to report changes in condition, and to whom to report when changes occur. In addition, psychotropic medications cannot be used as a chemical restraint, and each resident must have a plan of care to avoid abuse of these medications and a written plan of treatment.

Medications may be administered by nursing staff or they may be delegated to the direct care staff. Medication administration by nonnursing staff varies greatly from state to state. For example, medication aides in Virginia are required to receive a minimum of 32 hr of classroom instruction and pass a written and practical (skill demonstration) exam. The medication aide will then be able to assist with the self-administration of medication to individuals and is not expected to perform any tasks or procedures involving a medication that requires professional training and education such as that in the field of nursing. The training program is conducted by a designated licensed healthcare provider who has received training in the medication aide management course approved by the Board of Nursing (Kirkpatrick, 2000). Interestingly, this medication training program is the same program for staff working in assisted living.

In the residential setting, each resident has a formal chart, but it is quite different from a hospital chart. The residents live there and their care needs are regular and routine. The chart may contain admission information and initial assessment, history, medications, physician's orders, resident's rights, individualized habilitation plan or Individualized Service Plan with annual goals, etc. If the resident has been in the facility for many years, the charts are routinely thinned and only current information may be provided in the chart. Daily notes are often communicated informally in logbooks written for staff coordination. An incident report is written if an unusual incident has occurred, and an action plan should be noted.

Nursing Standards

The LNC will also need to determine the involvement of nursing. Nursing care in all settings and programs is dictated by the need and health status of the individual with DD. In some settings the resident may receive direct and daily nursing care by a licensed registered nurse or a licensed professional nurse, and in other settings they may receive care of a much more episodic nature. Most HCBS Waiver homes are structured with minimal nursing oversight.

Each State's Nurse Practice Act determines the scope and practice of nursing care, including what functions are performed by nursing and which tasks can be delegated. In addition, there is the American Nurses Association (ANA) Scope and Standards of Practice for Intellectual and DD Nursing (2004). DD nursing encompasses a lifetime care for people of different ages with different care needs and in various settings. DD Nursing Practice (Aggen et al., 1995, 2008) has also established standards of practice. These standards provide direction for the professional nurse in every setting, in which people with DD receive nursing services and supports and a general framework for evaluation. Nurses in the field of DD have had the opportunity to become certified since 1994. Certification requires nursing experience (4,000 hr working in the field of DD in the last 5 years), ongoing continuing education specific to DD, and a peer-reviewed examination.

Role of the LNC

The LNC may assist the attorney in various ways. As this is a very specialized field, the LNC will need experience in the field of DD and long-term care. The LNC may be involved in the role of an educator, and build the attorney's knowledge base about DD, the diverse population, various diagnoses, and specifically an individual's care needs. In this role, the LNC will discuss the types of the residential care setting for people with DD and how long-term care differs from the acute care hospital setting and the nursing home setting. The LNC may be involved as a consultant to examine the case, evaluate the standard of care, obtain information, such as policies and procedures, and assist with determining if the standard of care has been met. The LNC may need to develop a time line to determine the sequence of events including staff involvement to determine negligence or errors of omission. The LNC may be involved as an expert witness with expertise in the field of DD. In this testifying role, the LNC will educate the judge and jury. The LNC may also be involved in class action lawsuits using the expertise and knowledge in the field of DD.

Case Examples

Medication Administration

When the majority of people with DD lived in the large state institutions, service delivery was based on the medical model, and nursing staff were available and responsible for daily assessment and medication administration. People with DD now live in a variety of settings, and there may or may not be a nurse available to administer medications. In addition, many people with DD have self-care deficits, which may include communication difficulties, oral motor difficulties, hand-eye coordination problems, cognitive difficulties, and deficits in fine and gross motor skills (Barks, 1994). These self-care deficits contribute to their inability to self-administer medications, which is compounded because of the need for multiple medications with many adverse effects. The area of medication administration is ripe for errors in all settings, including settings for people with DD.

Medications are often administered in bubble packs, where daily medication is inserted in a blister from the pharmacy. Medication needs to be checked using the six rights of medication administration (the sixth right being right documentation), and medication needs to be checked with the physician order. The person administering medication needs familiarity with the medication, purpose, dose, side effects, etc.

A clinical nurse specialist working in a residential ICF/MR setting once received a call from the staff working in a residential facility because the staff had administered medication at the wrong time, and the medication was Theragran M (a multivitamin). Obviously, this was not an area of concern, except for education, as the staff needed education on what medication was being administered, side effects, etc. Another time, this clinical nurse specialist was called when the morning staff administered the same medication that the night staff had (duplicate dose). This medication error occurred because the night staff had not documented the medication doses, and the morning staff administered medication without noticing it was the wrong date and time. The physician was contacted and the individuals were monitored during the day without any further incidents. The results could have resulted in hospitalization, medical appointments, and worse, as many individuals were on seizure medication with tight therapeutic dose levels.

Wrongful Death

When an individual with DD condition meets an early death, the LNC may be contacted to determine if there was any negligence at the facility. The LNC will need to determine the standards of care and whether or not standards of care were followed. This situation may be further complicated when an individual with DD has a medical condition and that could contribute to the early demise. The LNC will need to examine standards of care, federal, state, and local standards, facility records, and level of care needs, in addition to knowledge of the individual with DD.

A choking incident is often a common liability issue. Individuals with DD often have self-care deficits, including oral motor difficulties. Mobility may also play a factor in feeding and medication administration. For example, an individual with spastic quadriplegia cerebral palsy may have difficulty in sitting in an upright position and need proper positioning in order to avoid aspiration. If an individual with DD has an injury and/or death related to a choking incident, the LNC will need to evaluate the case for merit. The LNC that reviews the records needs extensive knowledge about DD, understanding of the medical needs, the aging process including physiological and psychological changes, and the special concerns for individuals with DD. The LNC will need knowledge on the difference between normal processes and bodily insult. While the plaintiff attorney will cite neglect and wrongful death due to breach in the standard of care, the defense attorney will often state that death does not necessary mean impropriety and can occur from natural causes, especially as people with DD are classified as a vulnerable population with a reduced life expectancy compared with the typical population.

The following example provided is a clear violation of the standard of care resulting in an untimely and early death (wrongful death) of a young individual. The plaintiff, who had cerebral palsy and intellectual disabilities, lived in an ICF/MR in Texas from June 1, 1992 to her death on April 16, 1998. When the plaintiff fell in a hallway and defecated on the floor on April 12, 1998, the aide poured a mixture of undiluted bleach and another cleaning compound on the floor, left the plaintiff on the floor for at least an hour, and did not wash the bleach off the plaintiff. The plaintiff was not seen by the facility's doctor until 17 hr after the incident. She was later diagnosed with extensive chemical burns covering 40% of her body and died from these complications on April 15, 1998. A wrongful death and survival suit for compensatory and punitive damages was filed by her family, later amending it to include ongoing neglect and abuse (*Wright v. Res-care*, 2002).

Abuse and Neglect

Individuals with DD are considered a vulnerable population and are at risk for abuse and neglect at all ages. Women with DD are considered at high risk for sexual abuse as they often may be unwilling victims, or at the other extreme, be overly friendly without knowing the effect on others. Training programs are conducted and sexuality awareness is taught, but this population is vulnerable to abuse and neglect.

The following is a recent example of an assault case. In determining these cases, the issue is often whether the residential home had knowledge of a staff's violent history, or should have known, and if the residential home exercised ordinary care to protect its residents from the assault.

The plaintiff, described in court documents as a severely handicapped person, nonverbal, wheelchair dependent, and legally blind, lived in a residential facility for the DD in Rhode Island. She suffered a severe bruise that extended from the vagina to the rectum. She was examined at the hospital, and police were notified; however, there were no criminal charges filed. A civil action was filed alleging intentional and negligent conduct on the staff. The judge found that plaintiffs failed to produce any evidence of assault and there was no negligence as the plaintiffs failed to offer any evidence or expert testimony that the injury was caused by a breach of the standard of care. The plaintiffs appealed and the ruling was affirmed in the Rhode Island Supreme Court (*Broadley v. Rhode Island*, 2008).

In another example, the direct care staff was involved in a criminal charge of elderly and dependent adult abuse. This plaintiff, a 51-year-old individual with DD with limited verbal skills and wheelchair dependent, resided in a residential facility for the DD in California. On May 4, 2004, she was seated in the shower and the water heater broke, causing a scalding and third-degree burns over 60% of her body. The aide did not report this to her supervisor for 2 hr. The plaintiff was airlifted to Santa Clara Hospital and is currently nonverbal and gastrostomy tube-dependent, reporting a $3,000 per day care in a subacute setting. The aide was arrested for elderly and dependent adult abuse, later pled guilty, served jail time and probation, and was banned from working in other healthcare facilities. The case was eventually settled (*Rodriguez v. Res-Care*, 2004).

Other Case Examples

In this case, the staff clearly did not follow the standard of care and were negligent, and their negligence caused injuries to the resident.

The plaintiff, a 33-year-old-woman with DD, resided in an assistive living facility, called a personal care home, in Pennsylvania. Her mother was contacted and was notified that her daughter was either sick or pretending to be sick. The mother found her daughter screaming and crying with a soiled diaper and diarrhea. The mother cleaned her daughter without staff assistance, and informed the staff that her daughter was sick. No one at the Ivy Ridge facility responded. The mother took her daughter to the hospital where she was admitted for viral gastroenteritis, fecal impaction, and dehydration. She was discharged three days later. The court, upheld a jury verdict, and found the Ivy Ridge breached its duty of care by neglecting the plaintiff (*Ruta v. Ivy Ridge Personal Care Center*, 1995).

In a recent case, an individual with DD was scalded during bathing. Interestingly, it was alleged by the defense that the resident had turned on the water of the bath causing his own injury. The 42-year-old plaintiff was described as having severe mental disabilities, was nonambulatory, nonverbal with cerebral palsy, and resided in a residential facility for the DD in Indiana. He sustained first- and second-degree burns to his lower body when placed in a bath of scalding hot water in 2000. The estate of the plaintiff was awarded $1.5 million in damages, on January 2008, to provide for his ongoing care needs. This was considered one of the largest jury verdicts in Madison County's history (McGrath, 2008).

Summary

People with DD represent a diverse group of people with different ages and abilities and they may reside in various residential settings in the community. The LNC in this field needs a solid clinical foundation in DD and healthcare issues, in addition to an understanding of the residential setting options, and standards and regulations on the federal, state, and local level. This will continue to be a growing field as the population ages, and will provide both opportunities and challenges for the LNC involved in residential care.

References

Administration on Developmental Disabilities. (2008). *ADD fact sheet*. Retrieved July 27, 2008, from http://www.acf.hhs.gov/programs/add/Factsheet.html

Aggen, R. L., Broda, T., Brown, K., Kurlick, M., Lester, N., & Tupper, L. (2008). *Standards of developmental disabilities nurses practice*. Eugene, OR: Developmental Disabilities Nurses Association.

Aggen, R. L., DeGennaro, M. D., Fox, L., Hahn, J. E., Logan, B. A., & VonFumetti, L. (1995). *Standards of developmental disabilities nurses practice*. Eugene, OR: Developmental Disabilities Nurses Association.

American Nurses Association. (2004). *Intellectual and developmental disabilities nursing: scope and standards of practice*. Silver Spring, MD; nursebooks.org, the publishing program of ANA.

American Psychiatric Association. (2000). *Diagnostic and statistical manual of mental disorders* (4th ed.). Washington, DC: American Psychiatric Association.

Bannerman, D. J., Sheldon, J. B., Sherman, J. A., & Harchik, A. E. (1990). Balancing the right to habilitation with the right to personal liberties: The rights of people with developmental disabilities to eat too many doughnuts and take a nap. *Journal of Applied Behavior Analysis*, *23*, 79–80.

Barks, L. (1994). Approaches to medication administration. In S. P. Roth & J. S. Morse (Ed.), *A life-span approach to nursing care* (pp. 193–218). Baltimore: Paul H. Brookes.

Braddock, D., Hemp, R., & Rizzolo, M. C. (2008). *The state of the states in developmental disabilities 2008*. Washington, DC: American Association on Intellectual and Developmental Disabilities.

California Lanterman Developmental Disabilities Services Act. (1976). Welfare and Institutions Code, Section 4512 (a).

Department of Health & Human Services. (2008). *Intermediate care facilities for the mentally retarded (ICFs/MR)*. Retrieved July 28, 2008, from http://www.cms/hhs.gov/CertificationandComplianc/09_ICFMRs.asp

Developmental Disabilities Assistance and Bill of Right Act Amendments. (2000). P.L. 106-402 (42 U.S.C. 15002 Sec.102).

Kirkpatrick, M. A. (2000). A resource guide for medication management for persons authorized under the Drug Control Act. Virginia Department of Social Services, Commonwealth of Virginia.

Lakin, K. C., Prouty, R., Alba, K., & Scott, N. (2008). Twenty-five years of Medicaid home and community based services (HCBS): Significant milestones reached in 2007. *Intellectual and Developmental Disabilities*, *46*(4), 325–328.

McGrath, S. (2008, January 28). Update: Jury award $1.5 million to man who was scalded. *The Herald Bulletin*. Retrieved March 10, 2009, from http://www.hearaldbulletin.com/local/local_story_02811829html/resources_printstory

Melodye Broadley, Guardian for Linda Sue: Broadley et al. v. *State of Rhode Island* et al., 2007-80-Appeal. (PC 97-387) (2008).

Nehring, W. M. (2003). History of the role of nurses caring for persons with mental retardation. *The Nursing Clinics of North America, 38*(2), 351–372.

Olmstead v L.C. (98-536), 527 U.S. 581 (1999).

Palley, H. A., & Van Hollen, V. (2000). Long-term care for people with developmental disabilities: A critical analysis. *Health and Social Work, 25*(3), 181–189.

Parish, S. L., & Lutwick, Z. E. (2005). A critical analysis of the emerging crisis in long-term care for people with developmental disabilities. *Social Work, 50*(4), 345–354.

Pouty, R. W., Smith, G., & Larkin, K. C. (2007). *Residential services for persons with developmental disabilities: Status and trends through 2006.* Minneapolis: University of Minnesota, Research and Training Center on Community Living, Institute on Community Integration.

Rodriguez. v. Res-Care. San Mateo County Superior Court Case No. 114740. B (2004).

Ruta v. Ivy Ridge Personal Care Center, Inc. 29 Philadelphia 185 (1995).

Service, K. P., & Hahn, J. E. (2003). Issues in aging: The role of the nurse in the care of older people with intellectual and developmental disabilities. *The Nursing Clinics of North America, 38*(2), 91–312.

Smith, G. A. (2006). *Status report: litigation concerning home and community services for people with disabilities.* Human Services Research Institute. Retrieved August 27, 2008, from http:www.hrsi.org/doc/litigations052906

Wright v. Res-Care, U.S. Dist. LEXIS 4507 (5th Cir. June 2, 2002).

Resources

Issues in Residential and Community-Based Care-Developmental Disabilities

Administration on Developmental Disabilities (ADD)

The Federal agency that is responsible for the implementation and administration of the Developmental Disabilities Assistance and Bill of Rights Act. ADD is located within the United States Department of Health and Human Services and is part of the Department's Administration for Children and Families.

http://www.acf.hhs.gov

American Association on Intellectual and Developmental Disabilities (AAIDD)

Formerly called the American Association on Mental Retardation, AAIDD is the oldest and largest interdisciplinary organization of professionals involved in the field of intellectual and developmental disabilities.

http://www.aaidd.org

American HealthCare Association (AHCA)

AHCA is a nonprofit association of state health organizations and represents nonprofit and for-profit assisted living, nursing facility, developmentally disabled and subacute care providers. They focus on providing quality care to elderly and individuals with developmental disabilities in long-term care facilities and the services include information, education, legislative, and regulatory and public affairs. They also provide information on trends and government financing of long-term care.

http://www.ahcancal.org

ARC

The ARC (formerly the Associated for Retarded Citizens) is the largest community-based organization for people with intellectual and developmental disabilities. It provides services and support for families and individuals through local and state chapters.

http://www.thearc.org

Centers for Medicare and Medicaid Services (CMS)

The United States Department of Health and Human Services administers the Medicare, Medicaid and State Children's Health Insurance Program. There is extensive information available for laymen and healthcare professionals, including laws, regulations, and compliance information. CMS establishes the standards for the operations of facilities that receive funds under the Medicare or Medicaid Program. Information on home and community-based programs and ICF/MRs are also available.

http:www.cms.hhs/gov

Developmental Disabilities Nurses Association (DDNA)

DDNA is a national organization for nurses specializing in the field of developmental disabilities. The organization provides education, networking, certification, and advocacy and has developed standards for developmental disabilities nursing practice. They offer certification in the field of nursing and developmental disabilities, annual conferences and have local and state chapters.

http://www.ddna.org/

Easter Seals

Easter Seals is a community-based health agency for children and adults with disabilities for over 90 years. They have offices providing services and supports in most states. Recently, Easter Seals' was involved in the Living with Autism Study conducted in 2008.

www.easterseals.com

National Association of State Directors of Developmental Disabilities Services (NASDDDS)

A nonprofit organization established in 1964 in order to improve and expand the public services available to individuals with intellectual and other developmental disabilities. They assist state agencies in developing effective service delivery systems. They provide listings of the developmental disabilities state agency and contact information.

http://www.nasddds.org

National Dissemination Center for Children with Disabilities

NICHY is the center that provides information on programs and services for infants, children, and youth with disabilities, including information on special education laws, agencies, resources, and research.

http://wwww.nichcy.org

Protection and Advocacy (P&A)

P&A agencies are congressionally mandated, legally based disability rights agencies available at the national and state level. They provide legal representation and other advocacy services to all people with disabilities whether they reside at home or in residential facilities. P&A monitors, investigates, and attempts to remedy any adverse conditions.

http://www.napas.org

University Centers for Excellence in Developmental Disabilities Education, Research, and Service

Formerly known as the University Affiliated Programs, these centers were established in 1963 and are located in universities in every state. The University Centers offer an interdisciplinary training team in advanced practice specializing in clinical excellence services, research, and programs in the field of developmental disabilities and help prepare the future generation to be involved in the field of developmental disabilities.

http://www.aucd.org

United Cerebral Palsy (UCP)

Founded in 1949, this national organization mission is to advance the independence, productivity, and full citizenship of people with disabilities. State UCP services may include housing, therapy, assistive technology training, early intervention programs, individual and family support, social and recreation programs, community living, state and local referrals, employment assistance, and advocacy.

http://www.ucp.org

Test Questions

1. The LNC in the role of the educator can assist the attorney by
   A. Reviewing the Nurse Practice Act
   B. Obtaining information on policy and procedures
   C. Detailing the differences between nursing home and community care regulations
   D. Becoming an expert witness

2. Trends and growth in long-term care for people with developmental disabilities include
   A. HCBS Waiver Homes
   B. Intermediate Care Facilities for the Mentally Retarded
   C. Depopulation of the State Developmental Centers
   D. All of the above

3. The LNC in this field needs knowledge on the various legislative regulations for long-term care. A good source is found at
   A. Developmental Disabilities Assistance Act and Bill of Rights
   B. Centers for Medicare and Medicaid Services
   C. Developmental Disabilities Nurses Association
   D. Easter Seals

Answers: 1. C, 2. A, 3. B

Assisted Living
Objectives

- To describe an overview of Assisted Living, including the assisted living facility (ALF) philosophy, services available, and the clients it serves
- To list the varied legal and regulatory requirements related to Assisted Living Facilities
- To define the LNC role in assisting with an Assisted Living case, or in acting as an expert witness

Introduction

The Assisted Living portion of this chapter will focus on residential and community-based care issues for individuals who reside in assisted living facilities (ALF). Although assisted living residents are generally from the elderly segment of the population, individuals with developmental disabilities also reside successfully in assisted living residences. The rationale for separating assisted living from the Nursing Home/Long-Term Care chapter is that there is a significant difference in the federal and state regulations and the nursing scope of practice for assisted living. The LNC must understand this difference when assisting the attorney in cases involving assisted living residents.

Overview of Assisted Living

Historical Perspective

Assisted living is a senior housing concept originally developed in Scandinavia during the 1970s, combining residential housing for the elderly, with personal care services. Assisted living first emerged in the United States during the mid-1980s (Thayer, 2003). Initially, there were residential care facilities commonly known as board and care facilities. Board and care facilities provided nonmedical care and supervision and were sometimes located in the private homes of the service providers (Pratt, 2004). Board and care providers admitted residents who required minimal assistance with ADL and required no nursing services. As the resident's physical condition deteriorated, it would necessitate a transfer to a skilled nursing facility or nursing home resulting in decreased occupancy. To address the decrease in occupancy, many board and care providers began accepting and retaining residents requiring more assistance with ADL and more than occasional nursing services (Murer, 1997).

Assisted living ultimately evolved into a long-term care alternative for seniors requiring more assistance than is available in a retirement community, but do not need the intense medical and nursing care provided in a skilled nursing facility. The primary goal of Assisted Living then and now is to provide a setting in which individuals obtain those services needed to allow them to live with as much independence and dignity as possible (Pratt, 2004).

Assisted Living environments range from shared one-room accommodations to apartments complete with kitchens and living rooms. For most providers, Assisted Living means providing housekeeping services, meals, laundry, transportation, and limited licensed nursing services and/or oversight, including the administration of medication (Murer, 1997). Residences may be free standing or housed with other residential options, such as independent living or skilled nursing care. They may be operated by nonprofit or for-profit companies. Most facilities have between 25 and 120 units. There is no single blueprint, because consumers' preferences and needs vary widely (ALFA, 2008).

Definition of Assisted Living

The National Center for Assisted Living (NCAL) reports that Assisted Living settings have been known by as many as 26 different names, including residential care, personal care, adult congregate care, boarding home, and domiciliary care (Pratt, 2004). Even government and industry leaders cannot agree on a precise definition. The CMS defines Assisted Living as "a type of living arrangement in which personal care services, such as meals, housekeeping, transportation, and assistance with ADL, are available as needed to individuals who still live on their own in a residential facility." In most cases, the residents of these facilities pay regular monthly rent, with additional fees for other supportive services (GAO, 2004).

The Assisted Living Federation of America's (ALFA) definition of an Assisted Living residence is "a special combination of housing, personalized assistance and healthcare designed to respond to the individual needs—both scheduled and unscheduled—of those who require help with ADL and the instrumental activities of daily living (IADL). IADL include using the telephone, getting to locations beyond walking distance, grocery shopping, preparing meals, doing laundry, taking medications, and managing money" (GAO, 2004).

Philosophy of Care

Assisted Living's philosophy of care as described by AARP (American Association of Retired Persons)—Assisted Living is the maximization of residents' personal dignity, autonomy, independence, privacy, and choice; provision of home-like environment; accommodation of residents' changing care needs and preferences; minimization of the need to move when care needs increase; with the involvement of families and communities (AARP, 2008). The LNC should understand that unlike other medical models found in most healthcare settings, assisted living is based on a social model of care, with a holistic approach.

Demographics and Scope of Services

There are approximately 36,000 state-licensed Assisted Living Facilities housing approximately 900,000 older Americans and individuals with disabilities (GAO, 2004). The typical assisted living resident is a female, 75–85 years old, who is mobile, but needs assistance with two to three ADL. Of the residents who currently live in Assisted Living Facilities, 81% need help with one or more ADL, and 93% need help with IADL (Podrazik & Stefanacci, 2005). In the 2004 General Accounting Office (GAO) Report, 25% of Assisted Living residents required assistance with three or more ADL and 86% of the residents required or accepted assistance with medication. Nearly half of all assisted living residents lived at home prior to moving to the facility, while nearly one-third came from another ALF, nursing facility, or a hospital (GAO, 2004). The average length of stay in an Assisted Living residence is about 27 months. Upon discharge from Assisted Living, 34% of the residents will move into a nursing facility, 30% will have expired, and the remaining will move home or to another location (NCAL, 2008).

While the vast majority of residents are elderly persons with some level of healthcare needs, Assisted Living is also becoming the environment of choice for those with Alzheimer's or other dementias, with many Assisted Living residences having dedicated Memory Care or Alzheimer's units. Recent studies conducted by the Alzheimer's Association concluded that at least half of Assisted Living residents have some degree of cognitive impairment, though most of them do not live in specialized dementia units (Alzheimer's Association, 2008).

Residents in need of end-of life care prefer to have the hospice benefit provided in their Assisted Living residence, although not every state allows hospice residents this right. Finally, it is conceivable that, within the near future, special care for Assisted Living residents will go beyond dementia care to encompass intravenous medication therapies, respiratory therapies, and rehabilitation.

Legal and Ethical Issues

Regulations and Licensure

The LNC must consider all related federal, state, and local regulations related to Assisted Living when conducting a legal review of an Assisted Living case. Skilled nursing facilities have been heavily regulated for decades; it is only in the past few years that Assisted Living Facilities have been regulated to any significant degree. As the Assisted Living focus moves from housing to medical services, it will eventually be viewed and regulated as a healthcare provider (Murer, 1997).

In most states, Assisted Living is licensed as a "single entity that provides housing and services to residents." However, in a growing number of states, a model of Assisted Living has emerged in which the housing and services are separate. In this model, the building is not licensed, but instead makes arrangements with "licensed service agencies" to provide services to the residents. The "licensed service agency," also known as a Home HealthCare agency is regulated under state and federal law. In the unlicensed housing arrangement, the building is subject to the relevant building codes, fire codes, and other requirements for multiunit housing. The state may also require the building to be registered. Registration involves a much lower level of oversight than licensure and may require only that the building file a registration form, for example, and provide a disclosure statement to residents (Wright, 2007).

An ALF must also comply with the same regulations related to the Fair Housing Act, Occupational Safety and Health Act (OSHA), Life Safety Code, requirements of the Equal Employment Opportunity Commission (EEOC), and the Family Medical Leave Act (FMLA) (Pratt, 2004). The LNC when reviewing a case related to Assisted Living should reference the Federal Acts listed, and also carefully evaluate state laws and regulations affecting licensing, resident rights, and housing, as applicable.

As noted, there are federal laws that impact Assisted Living, but oversight of Assisted Living occurs primarily at the state level. While states vary in their approach to regulating Assisted Living, most have comprehensive regulations in place. In those states, surveyors conduct regularly scheduled inspections. To ensure that Assisted Living Facilities correct the deficiencies cited during the survey, states may require the facility to prepare a formal written plan of correction. In addition, these states may conduct reinspections and impose financial penalties, license revocations, and criminal sanctions (GAO, 2004).

The LNC will benefit from an understanding of the state-specific Assisted Living regulations and definitions when reviewing an Assisted Living case. Research of these regulations can be exhaustive as there is no one central agency or section of state law that encompasses all aspects for all states. The NCAL Assisted Living State Regulatory Review is a resource that is updated annually and is based on the applicable statutes and regulations in each state. It can be a valuable resource for the LNC in researching state specific information related to 21 state specific categories.

Staff Requirements/Qualifications/Training

Staffing levels are much less controlled by regulation in Assisted Living than in other levels of long-term care. Whereas one Assisted Living community may offer care specialized for individuals with dementia, another community may focus on providing services for residents with lower acuity needs. Each facility must have the right number of trained and awake staff on duty and they should be present at all times to meet residents' needs and to carry out the facility's emergency and disaster preparedness plan (ALW, 2003).

All states require skilled nursing facility administrators to be licensed, but not so with Assisted Living administrators. An increasing number of jurisdictions are requiring their licensure, but there is little uniformity in those requirements. In most states that have licensed Assisted Living administrators, the requirements are significantly less rigorous than for skilled nursing facility administrators (Pratt, 2004).

Assisted Living Facilities must ensure that personnel working in their facility perform duties only within the scope of that State's Nurse Practice Act, or other professional licensing or practice requirements. The professional scope and standards of practice as established by the ANA, National Gerontological Nursing Association (NGNA), and the American Assisted Living Nurse's Association (AALNA) should be adhered to in all aspects of Assisted Living nursing functions. In general, staff should be knowledgeable regarding basic changes in aging, geriatric drug pharmacology, falls prevention, incontinence care, ADL skills, communication techniques, dementia care, and recognition of acute illness/delirium. Assisted Living Facilities have a duty to retain staff that is capable of monitoring a resident's well-being and determining when significant medical, cognitive, and functional changes have occurred and evaluation by a qualified medical professional is necessary (Podrazik & Stefanacci, 2005). Staff should receive proper orientation and training and performance evaluation to be conducted no less than annually.

There is a call for a federal system for criminal background checks and state requirements regarding convictions that would disqualify individuals from providing services in Assisted Living Facilities and recommends the establishment of a national registry of individuals with histories of abuse (ALW, 2003).

Medication Management

An important concern in the administration of Assisted Living Facilities is how residents' medications are managed and administered. Research has shown that Assisted Living residents take an average of eight medications per day (ALFA, 2008). Assisted Living regulations span the gamut from requiring all residents to be capable of self-administration to allowing unlicensed staff to administer some medications under a licensed staff member's supervision. Many states allow the staff to assist residents with their medication. "Assistance" being interpreted to include verbal reminders, opening the medication container, placing the medication in the patient's hand, and even guiding the resident's hand to his/her mouth (Murer, 1997).

When reviewing an Assisted Living case, the LNC should be familiar with Assisted Living state requirements and the State's Nurse Practice Act scope of practice guidelines concerning medication administration. Knowledge of state pharmacy laws is also very important. Such issues as drug storage regulations and dispensing requirements could alter the nature of the program. Packaging policies also vary from state to state (Donovan, 1997). The facility should provide ongoing training of medication assistants on a regular basis to ensure competence. Medication administration policies and procedures are vital to medication administration safety and consistency (Podrazik & Stefanacci, 2005). One area that has received attention has been training for medication aides. More states are allowing unlicensed staff, provided they are adequately trained, to assist in the administration of medications.

Licensed nurses are the gatekeepers for the medication program. The nurses' overall responsibility for administration of medication as licensed professionals remains the same as for any setting: receiving medication orders, checking for allergies, ordering medications from the pharmacy, validating correctness of labels, assessing effectiveness, documenting and reporting adverse reactions, and policing the quality assurance component of administration—in short, ensuring that the right medication is given at the right time to the right individual (Donovan).

Determining appropriateness of self-administration of medications by an Assisted Living resident is a nursing process that requires a "judgment call" based on the nurse's education and experience in caring for the geriatric population. Before a resident can participate in self-administration of medications, the nurse must ensure that he/she first demonstrates competency (mental and physical) in self-administration of medications, and the ability to remain compliant with prescribed drug regimens. This is accomplished through a standardized assessment conducted by the licensed nurse focusing on such abilities as dexterity, comprehension, recall, and visual acuity. The assessment is applicable to oral medications, inhalers/nebulizers, dermal patches, topical ointments, and occasionally injections. The medication self-administration assessment should be conducted upon admission, and at a minimum annually, or with change in condition and results documented on a standardized form, which is maintained in the medical record.

More complicated routes of administration, such as suppositories and injections, are generally the responsibility of the nurse unless the resident has demonstrated capability for these. Some residents may have self-administered insulin for many years, but it must be determined that they still have the dexterity to draw up the insulin and adequate vision to read the units. For the resident who does not successfully pass the assessment, medications are delivered in the traditional manner and a reassessment is rescheduled.

Resident Rights

Many states already address to varying degrees the rights of ALF residents, in ways that are often similar to, if not the same as, rights afforded to nursing home residents. Residents of Assisted Living do not check their rights at the door upon moving into an Assisted Living community. To assume that an individual cannot continue to have the same rights to privacy, independence, and decision making no matter where they live is discriminatory. Participation of a guardian or responsible party is facilitated to ensure that the rights of cognitively impaired residents are preserved. The NCAL advocates that residents' rights should include the right to

- Privacy
- Be treated at all times with dignity and respect
- Control receipt of healthcare services
- Control personal finances
- Retain and have use of personal possessions

- Interact freely with others both within the assisted living residence and in the community
- Freedom of religion
- Organize resident councils

Consumer Disclosure

Consumer disclosure is essential in assisting consumers with understanding the differences among Assisted Living communities and to select the one that best meets the needs of their loved one. The decision to reside in an ALF should be an informed choice with providers fully disclosing their programs, services, and fees, so that the resident and the family can make an informed choice about where to live. There should be a decision-making process that involves the provider, the resident/resident's family, and the physician to make the decision. This decision includes end-of-life planning.

Providing consumers with the information and tools they need to make the best choice possible about where to live is also a recent legislative trend. Residency/admission agreements have improved through legislation addressing information that should be included in these agreements. In addition to the admission/residency agreement, many states now require Assisted Living providers to disseminate disclosure documents to prospective residents and families, which include information about facility services, costs, policies that impact residents, limitations on care delivery, and the move-in and move-out processes (ALFA, 2008).

Consumers need this information to be not only complete and accurate, but also presented in a timely way and in a form that they can understand. Consumers rely on facility information that they receive in various ways, including marketing brochures, facility tours, and interviews with providers. Often, the marketing materials, contracts, and other written materials that facilities give to consumers are vague, incomplete, or misleading. A facility's written materials often do not contain key information, such as a description of services that are not covered or available at the facility, the staff's qualifications and training, circumstances under which costs might change, assistance residents would receive with medication administration, facility practices in assessing needs, or criteria for discharging residents if their health changes (GAO, 2004).

Residency/Admission Agreement

Clearly defined contractual obligations to residents in the written residency/admission agreement represent the important first step in preventing or limiting liability in Assisted Living. Residency/admission agreements can be highly state specific, especially in states that license or otherwise regulate ALFs. In part, the residency/admission agreement is a housing rental contract. Thus, it must comply with federal, state, and local housing and landlord/tenant laws. The housing portion of the agreement covers the type of accommodation, the fee schedule, payment terms, deposits, the period the agreement is in effect, etc. A review of the residency/admission agreement by the LNC is essential in preparing an Assisted Living case.

The second part of the residency/admission agreement pertains to the health-related or other personal supportive services provided. Minimum state licensure requirements must be included, as applicable. Resident rights and responsibilities should also be listed. The facility is legally obligated to deliver the services promised in the residency/admission agreement (HRC, 1997). Assisted Living facilities should provide specific, comprehensive, and straightforward information in the residency/admission agreement. The residency/admission agreement should be consistent with oral and written communications made to residents and family members as part of the facility's marketing program. Residents should have the opportunity for a preadmission review of the residency/admission agreement's terms. The residency/admission agreement should include

- The term of the agreement/contract
- Comprehensive description of services provided for a fee basis
- Comprehensive description of and the fee schedule for services provided on an ala-carte basis
- Temporary absence policy
- Process for initial and subsequent assessments and the development of individualized service plans based on these assessments
- Description of all circumstances and conditions under which the ALF may require the resident to be involuntarily transferred, discharged, or evicted
- An explanation of the resident's right to notice; the process by which the resident may appeal the decision, and a description of relocation assistance offered by the facility
- A description of the ALF's process for resolving complaints or disputes
- A list of appropriate consumer/regulatory agencies
- A description of the procedures a resident must follow to terminate the agreement
- Detailed preadmission disclosures regarding advance directives, specialized programs of care, and end-of-life care
- Requirements related to resident finances (Thayer, 2003)
- Verbiage to avoid claims of discrimination including the range of services offered, facility rules, and extent to which accommodation is available (HRC, 1997)

Resident Assessments/Individualized Service Planning

For an aging adult, a move to an ALF often signals some medical, cognitive, or functional need, which makes a comprehensive assessment crucial. It offers the opportunity to provide optimum interventions designed to maintain independence and prevent existing conditions from deteriorating. All residents entering an ALF should have a baseline evaluation of their physical, medical, and psychological needs completed by a qualified, licensed, and independent practitioner. Residents should receive periodic reassessment to determine if care needs have changed (Podrazik & Stefanacci, 2005).

The foundation of resident-centered care is the Individualized Service Plan (ISP), which is also known as a care plan, service plan, or resident goal plan. The ISP is designed to meet the individual needs and preference of each resident. The ISP is developed after an assessment process that takes into account not only what services the resident needs, but what they want as well. The ISP is completed by a licensed nurse and is prepared in conjunction with the resident, family, and staff (ALFA, 2008).

Negotiated Risk Agreements

The concept of negotiated risk has been suggested as a mechanism for Assisted Living programs to balance residents' personal autonomy with the provider's duty to protect the residents from harm. Examples in which negotiated risk has been suggested involve situations such as a resident in an ALF repeatedly departing from a medically prescribed diet or failing to take ordered medications. Negotiated risk in Assisted Living has been compared with the legal and ethical doctrine of informed consent. In Assisted Living, however, the prerogative to refuse unwanted interventions applies not to discrete medical procedures, but to ongoing health-related, dietary, and residential interventions that compromise an Assisted Living arrangement.

Although the theory has not been tested directly in court, proponents of negotiated risk would be available as a defense to a negligent action if a defendant were able to prove that a plaintiff voluntarily and knowingly assumed the risk of certain conduct that might otherwise be deemed negligent. Or, even if the provider was found negligent, liability might be reduced to the degree of the plaintiff's own contributory negligence. The assumption of risk, however, is predicated upon the resident or a legally authorized surrogate being capable of a deliberate and voluntary choice.

Negotiated risk is a new approach to managing resident-related risk. This will not provide full protection from provider liability and may be inappropriate if the risk of harm is very high. As one attorney puts it, "residents may assume risk in theory, but hold the facility responsible in practice." Negotiated risk, properly understood and applied, can fill some of the void in providing an analytic tool and mechanism by which providers and residents can assess and accommodate certain unusual situations.

Negotiated risk, while a useful tool, should play a relatively limited role in day-to-day operations of the ALF. Providers always have responsibility to their residents—imposed by regulation, licensure, and community expectations—which they cannot avoid or "negotiate away." Likewise, even though the philosophy of assisted living is to promote resident autonomy and choice, resident rights are not unlimited (Bianculli, 1999).

Litigation

As with skilled nursing facilities, assisted living residences have the potential for many of the same legal actions related to negligence and medical malpractice. Many of the traditional health and safety risk areas for long-term care related to medication errors, accident or fall injuries, elopement, smoking, and suicide are also evident in assisted living. Also equipment-related causes (e.g., wheelchairs tipping, legs collapsing on commodes, safety belts loosening, and unsafe electric wheelchair use) are other risk areas. Negotiated risk factors into this area, as many of the assisted living residents want to manage their own actions in spite of the risk involved.

Abuse, neglect, and misappropriation of resident funds are other areas that have been cited in recent assisted living cases. Additionally, an ALF would also be subject to any aspect of the Fair Housing Act, OSHA, Life Safety Code, and Americans with Disabilities Act.

LNC's Role in Trial Preparation or as an Expert Witness

The LNC participating in an Assisted Living case has many areas of research and review that should be considered. These efforts should include a review of the ALF's operational processes and policies related to services, environment, consumer protections (including resident rights, contracts, and risk negotiation), and management responsibilities.

Services: Resident screening should have occurred before move- in. In addition, each resident should have undergone a comprehensive assessment for health, psychosocial, and cognitive status. This would have ensured that the facility was able to meet the resident's needs and served as a basis for the development of an individualized service plan (ISP). Information from the resident's physician and documents such as guardianship papers, powers of attorney, living wills, and do-not-resuscitate orders also should have been obtained at the time of admission. The individualized service plan should have been developed with the assistance of the resident and/or designated agent. The individualized service plan should have included the scope, frequency, and duration of services and monitoring, and it should have been responsive to the resident's needs and preferences. The individualized service plan should have been reviewed at routine intervals after move in and annually thereafter, or as the resident's needs or preferences change.

Environment: A safe, homelike environment should have been provided for all residents. This environment should support choice, independence, privacy, comfort, and individuality. Life Safety Code review reports conducted by state, county, or local authorities should be obtained and reviewed for violation of safety requirements by the LNC.

Consumer protections: Residents' records should have been kept confidential and released only with consent. In addition, providers should have ensured residents' choices and the right to autonomy for as long as possible, even if that meant taking some risks. Residents should have shared responsibility for decisions affecting their lives and have been fully informed of their rights and responsibilities. A copy of the Resident Right statement provided to the resident should be obtained and reviewed by the LNC.

Contracts and agreements: The most significant document in the resident's stay at the ALF is the residency/admission agreement. The LNC and the attorney must review the document signed by the resident assuring that it encompasses all of the facility's commitments and actual practices, including the criteria and procedures for admission, on-site transfers, and discharge. Payment information should be comprehensive and include: rate structure and payment provisions for both covered and noncovered services; an explanation of billing, payment, and credit policies; criteria for determining level of service and additional charges; fees and payment arrangements for third-party providers; provisions for payment during absences; and the facility's policy for residents who can no longer pay for services. The admission/residency agreement is used by the LNC in citing what should have been provided to the resident by the facility when writing reports or testifying.

Negotiated risk: When a resident wanted to engage in potentially risky behavior, such as service refusal, a negotiated risk agreement should have been initiated, following open discussions with management and family members about the consequences of the resident's choice. If the resident's mental or physical condition changed substantially, the negotiated risk agreement should have been reviewed. The LNC should obtain copies of the operational policies, procedures, and forms related to Negotiated Risk.

Staffing: The facility should have maintained sufficient qualified staff members capable of meeting scheduled and unscheduled resident needs at all times. The LNC should obtain copies of the facility staffing patterns for the time period applicable to the case. The facility should provide ongoing training for the staff on how to monitor changes in residents' physical, cognitive, and psychosocial conditions. In facilities serving residents with dementia, direct-care staff should receive dementia-specific training each year. The LNC should also review the ALF's orientation and training outlines and attendance documentation, job descriptions, organizational chart, determination of position and skill knowledge, and hiring practices, including background and reference checking processes.

Advertising: Facilities must be vigilant about advertising specific features if they cannot ensure 100% service or compliance. Quality-of-care claims or "overselling the product" can leave a facility vulnerable to a lawsuit if they cannot be evidenced through documentation. Examples of such claims include: "Meadow Acres Assisted Living provides the best care possible care," "24-h assistance provided," "around-the-clock support designed to meet the individual personal care needs of residents," "24-h supervision," "Meadow Acres supports aging in place; no need to ever move again." Advertising or brochures contain verbal statements that promise residents and families services that cannot be delivered. For example, "Our security system will keep your mom from eloping." If the facility does not provide a locked unit, this claim is untrue (Peterson, 2005). The LNC should obtain copies of all marketing materials for the time period of the case, including copies of informational recordings that would be listened to while an applicant was waiting on the telephone for assistance.

Statements of deficiencies from past state health department surveys can be used to contradict such statements and can lend support to plaintiff's claims. The LNC can assist the attorney with the review of state survey reports to identify negative resident outcomes that could be blamed on the facility rather than on the resident's age or preexisting medical problems. The survey reports provide a roadmap for the plaintiff's liability case at the trial and for the recovery of compensatory damages.

Operational documents: The LNC should obtain resident care and administrative policies and procedures for operation of the facility related to all services provided by the facility including

- Administrator—continuing education; responsible person designated in the absence of the administrator
- Admission, transfer, discharge, discharge planning, and referral services
- Resident assessments and care plans
- Resident records—content and storage
- Personal care services—including assistance with ADL, assistance with seeking health care and associated transportation when indicated, obtaining functional aids or equipment, clothing, as well as maintenance of personal living quarters
  - Nursing, social, dietary, and activity services, including
  - Protocols to use in the event of serious health threatening conditions, emergencies, or temporary illness. These protocols must include designation of a practitioner for each resident and notification of an appropriately licensed professional in the event of an illness or injury of a resident
  - Provision for pharmacy and medication services developed in consultation with a consultant pharmacist that include assisting residents in obtaining medications from a pharmacy, storage of medications, medication administration, disposing of medications that are discontinued or expired, and allowing the resident to be responsible for self-administration based on an assessment of the resident's capabilities with respect to this function
  - Fire safety including fire drills, fire evacuation plans, and drills

Finally, the LNC must understand the specific State's Nurse Practice Act as it related to the scope of practice; delegating medical and nursing services as tasks (especially medication administration and health or crisis interventions); premises of delegation; and supervision by an RN of unlicensed persons performing assisted living tasks. Each person involved in the delegation process is accountable for his/her own action; supervision is inherent—if an RN decides to delegate, he/she is responsible for supervising the delegate and his/her actions, whether the RN is physically present or not. An RN may assign an LPN to monitor for the RN, but the RN must be available for consultation and direction; and finally, per most State Nurse Practice Acts, the functions of assessment, evaluation, and nursing judgment cannot be delegated.

Summary

An LNC can be invaluable in providing the attorney with an overview and understanding of the complex world of assisted living. Being able to articulate the differences between long-term care and assisted living requirements, having a knowledge base of the assisted living services and philosophy, and having the ability to analyze the clinical aspects of an assisted living case are the reasons why an LNC would be an essential part of the legal team.

References

Alzheimer's Association. (2008). Website content available at www.alz.org

American Association of Homes and Services for the Aging (AAHSA). (1999). In R. A. Gulyas, (Ed.), *Operational practices in assisted living,* Washington, DC.

American Association of Retired Persons (AARP)(2008). Website content available at www.aarp.org

Assisted Living Federation of America (ALFA) (2008). Website content available at www.alfa.org.

Assisted Living Workgroup (ALW). (2003). *Assuring quality in assisted living: Guidelines for federal and state policy, state regulation, and operations.* US Senate Special Committee on Aging Report, April 29.

Bianculli, J. (1999). Negotiated risk in assisted living. In *AAHSA operational practices in assisted living* (chap. 8, pp. 157–179), Washington, DC: AAHSA—American Association of Homes and Services for the Aging.

Donovan, J. (1997). *Managing medications in assisted living,* Nursing Homes, July–August 1997. Cleveland, Ohio: Vendome Group.

General Accounting Office (GAO). (2004). *Assisted living: Examples of States efforts to improve consumer protections.* GAO Report Number GAO-04-684, May 27.

HRC Volume 3—Long-term Care 1. *Overview of long term care risks.* Published by ECRI, Plymouth Meeting, PA, January 1997.

Murer, M. (1997, July–August). *Assisted living: The regulatory outlook.* Nursing Homes, July–August 1997. Cleveland, Ohio: Vendome Group.

National Center for Assisted Living (NCAL). (2008). *2008 State regulatory review,* Prepared by: Karl Polzer. National Center for Assisted Living, Washington, DC.

National Center for Assisted Living (NCAL). (2008). Website content available at www.ncal.org

Peterson, S. (2005). *Developing risk management protocols in assisted living: Assisted living has its own litigation traps for the unwary,* Nursing Homes Magazine, November 2005. Cleveland, Ohio: Vendome Group.

Podrazik, P., & Stefanacci, R. (2005, March–April). *Negotiating the complexities of the long term care continuum.* Assisted Living Consult, Doylestown, PA: HealthCom Media.

Pratt, J. (2004). *Long term care, long-term care: Managing across the continuum* (2nd ed.) Sudbury, MA: Jones and Bartlett Publishers, Inc.

Rubinger, H., & Gardner, R. (2003). *Assisted living's first steps toward uniformity: Assisted living workgroup submits recommendations to congress.* Continuing Care, July/August.

Thayer, J. *Written statement of jan thayer on behalf of the national center for assisted living.* Federal Trade Commission/Department of Justice—Hearing on Long Term Care/Assisted Living, For the Hearing Record, Submitted June 11, 2003.

Wright, B. (2007, April). *AARP Study: #2007-08: Assisted living in unlicensed housing: The regulatory experience of four states.*

Resources

Assisted Living Federation of America (ALFA), www.alfa.org.—The ALFA monitors legislative and regulatory proposals in all 50 states. The information is updated weekly and is an excellent way for the ALFA to stay on top of what is being proposed across the country. In addition, the ALFA continues to be a resource for best practices and examples of successful laws and regulations.

U.S. Senate Special Committee on Aging—www.senate.gov. Assisted Living Workgroup (ALW) 381-page report, entitled Assuring Quality in Assisted Living: Guidelines for Federal and State Policy, State Regulation, and Operations.

Center for Excellence in Assisted Living| (CEAL)—www.theceal.org. ALW report to congress in April 2003 recommended that a National CEAL be formed and funded to serve as an ongoing source of information and guidance to states regulating assisted living.

American Assisted Living Nurses Association (AALNA), www.alnursing.org

American Nurses Association (ANA), www.nursingworld.org

Test Questions

1. Which of the following services would be available in an assisted living facility?
   A. Medication administration
   B. Hospice care
   C. Assistance with ADL
   D. All of the above

2. Which of the following statements about assisted living regulatory requirements is NOT true?
   A. All assisted living administrators are licensed by the state
   B. An assisted living facility must comply with OSHA and Life Safety Code
   C. Most states have regulations in place regarding assisted living facilities and services
   D. Medication can be administered by unlicensed staff

3. Select the answer that would NOT describe a staff member's roles and responsibilities in an assisted living facility
   A. Nurse Practice Act
   B. Job description
   C. Federal Nursing Home regulations
   D. Individualized Service Plan

4. Which of the following would be an essential element when reviewing an Assisted Living case?
   A. Admission/residency agreement
   B. Marketing materials
   C. Individualized Service Plan
   D. All of the above

Answers: 1. D, 2. A, 3. C, 4. D

Appendix 1

Glossary

Kathleen A. Morales, RN, C, BSN

Second Edition
Bruce Kehoe, JD and Sherri Reed, BSN, RN, LNCC

Access: Approach to electronic information through any storage medium. When used in relation to the term online, it implies the availability of suitable telecommunications, plus user IDs and passwords for the online host system.

Access to medical and exposure records standard: One of the standards developed by the Occupational Safety and Health Administration in order to provide the employee with a possible exposure to, or who uses toxic substances or harmful physical agents in the workplace, with the right to access employee exposure records and any analyses of employee medical and exposure records provided all employee identifiers have been removed.

Accident: An unexpected or sudden event.

Accidental injury: Usually defined in the applicable state statute and may include an injury that arises out of and in the course of employment or injuries by a third party.

Account balance: Difference between debit and credit sides of an account.

Account debtor: Person who is obligated on an account, chattel, paper, or general intangible.

Account payable: A debt owed by an enterprise arising in the normal course of business dealings and which has not been replaced by a note payable of a debtor. A liability representing an amount owed to a creditor usually arising from purchase of merchandise or materials and supplies; not necessarily due or past due.

Account receivable: A debt, owed to an enterprise, which arises in the normal course of business dealings and is not supported by negotiable paper. A claim against a debtor usually arising from sales or services rendered which is not necessarily due or past due.

Account rendered: An account made out by the creditor and presented to the debtor for his examination and acceptance. When accepted, it becomes an account stated.

Account settled: An agreed balance between parties to a settlement.

Account stated: An account accumulating additions to another account.

Accountability: An obligation of providing or being prepared to provide an account of one's actions.

Accountant: Person who works in the field of accounting and is skilled in keeping books or accounts; in designing and controlling systems of account. This person is also skilled in designing and controlling systems of account and in giving tax advice and preparing tax returns.

Accreditation: The act of granting credit or recognition, especially with respect to an education institution maintaining applicable standards.

Action level: *OSHA* and *NIOSH* expression of a health or physical *hazard* indicating the level of a harmful or *toxic* substance/activity which requires medical surveillance increased industrial hygiene monitoring, or biological monitoring. Levels are generally set at one-half of the *permissible exposure limit* (*PEL*), but the actual level may vary from standard to standard. The intent is to identify a level at which the vast majority of randomly sampled exposures will be below the PEL. For example, if the 8-hr time-weighted average (TWA) for noise levels equals or exceeds 85 decibels (dB) in a department, the employees must be included in a hearing conversation program according to OSHA's Occupational Noise Exposure Standard (29 CFR 1910.95).

Activities of daily living (ADL): Daily physical functions allowing independence living, including bathing, dressing, eating, toileting, walking or wheeling, and transferring in and out of bed.

Acute coronary syndrome: A continuum of disease processes including life-threatening cardiac conditions such as unstable angina, non-systole (ST) segment elevation myocardial infarction (MI) and ST segment elevation MI.

Address: (1) A label or number that identifies a database disk location where information is stored in the computer; (2) May also refer to the location of a host computer on an online network.

Administrative controls/work practice controls: A method of controlling hazards using management practices, such as training and education or job rotation to limit exposure.

Admission/residency agreements: Clearly defined contractual obligations to residents aimed at preventing or limiting liability in assisted living settings. Admission agreements can be highly state-specific, especially in those licensed by a State agency or otherwise regulating assisted living facilities (ALFs). In part, the admission agreement is a housing rental contract and must comply with federal, state, and local housing and landlord/tenant laws. The housing portion of the agreement covers the type of accommodation, the fee schedule, payment terms, deposits, the period the agreement is in effect, etc. The second part of the contract pertains to the health-related or other personal supportive services provided. The facility is legally obligated to deliver the services promised in the admission agreement. Residents should have the opportunity for preadmission review of the contract's terms.

Advanced cardiac life support (ACLS) provider: A healthcare professional that is certified as a basic life support (BLS) provider and passes additional certification to enhance resuscitation skills in an adult cardiopulmonary emergency. These skills include cardiopulmonary resuscitation (CPR), airway management, cardiac rhythm recognition, emergency medication administration, and the use of treatment algorithms.

Advanced directives: A written statement of an individual's preferences and directions regarding health care aimed at protecting a person's rights should he or she becomes mentally or physically unable to choose or communicate his or her wishes.

Adverse drug reaction (ADR) reports: Summaries of adverse experiences with a specific product reported to the Food and Drug Administration.

Adverse event (AE): Any untoward change in health or medical status, such as a new medical occurrence, or a change (such as an exacerbation) in a preexisting medical condition. If an AE occurs during the course of a study the medical condition does not have to be considered as related to the study drug or device to be termed an AE. The AE must be evaluated by the investigator (not the study coordinator) to examine the relationship of the study drug and designate the results as possibly related, probably related, definitely related, or definitely not related.

Advice protocols: Written guidelines and established protocols for evaluating the urgency of patient problems and differentiating cases requiring emergency intervention from those better addressed through office visits or home care.

Affidavit: Sworn, voluntary statement of fact or declaration.

Affidavit of merit (medical malpractice): A formal sworn statement of fact, signed by the attorney or an expert, stating that the named malpractice case is meritorious as set forth by state law.

Affirmative defense: A defense to a cause of action (claim) for which the defendant has the burden of proof. Comparative negligence is an example of an affirmative defense.

Aggravation: Usually implies a separate incident worsening a previously injured anatomical region.

AHCPR: Agency for Health Care Policy and Research. Currently known as The Agency for Healthcare Research and Quality (AHRQ); established standards of practice for a variety of patient-care issues.

AHRQ: Agency for Healthcare Research and Quality (formerly AHCPR). Goal is to improve the quality, safety, efficiency, and effectiveness of health care for all Americans. Research empowers more informed decisions and improves the quality of healthcare services. AHRQ was formerly known as the Agency for Health Care Policy and Research (AHCPR).

Allegations: The claims, statements, or assertions made by a party to a legal action or a potential legal action declared as a matter of fact. These assertions may be incorporated in the complaint or the answer.

Alzheimer's disease: The single most common cause of dementia, Alzheimer's, is a progressive and irreversible organic disease, typically occurring in the elderly. Characteristic brain cell degeneration leads to a progression from forgetfulness to severe memory loss and disorientation, lack of concentration, loss of ability to calculate numbers, increased severity of all symptoms and significant personality changes.

American Board of Nursing Specialties (ABNS): A not-for-profit organization with a Membership Assembly and an Accreditation Council governed by elected representatives. Specialty nursing certification is the formal recognition of specialized knowledge, skills, and experience demonstrated by the achievement of standards identified by a nursing specialty to promote optimal health outcomes.

American Legal Nurse Consultant Certification Board (ALNCCB): The American Association of Legal Nurse Consultants (AALNC) Certification Board responsible for developing the budget, determining eligibility criteria for the certification examination, auditing applications for compliance with the criteria, and setting fees and maintenance criteria for renewal of certification. The ALNCCB maintains the examination's validity, reliability, and legal defensibility.

ANA: American Nurses Association. National Association of Nurses.

Analysis and issue identification: As an LNC standard, analysis of data to identify the healthcare issues related to a case or claim.

Anesthetist: One who administers *anesthetics*.

Annotation: Critical or explanatory note or body of notes added to a text such as highlighting, drawing circles, underlining, etc. on an exhibit.

Answer: The formal written statement made by a defendant in response to the complaint, setting forth the grounds of his defense.

Aortic dissection: A violation to the aorta, such as a tear, allowing blood to leak between the layers of the wall of the aorta, forcing the layers apart, resulting in a life-threatening vascular emergency. Dissection can occur above or below the original site of the tear. For example, a thoracic aortic dissection occurs when there is a violation to the internal layer of the aorta allowing blood to leak between the medial and adventitial layers.

APA 5 format: The Publication Manual of the American Psychological Association (5th ed.). Used as a reference for manuscript citations.

Appeal: The process by which a party asks a higher court to review an adverse decision by a lower court.

Apportionment of liability: Assigning a percentage of the total negligence to each culpable party (e.g., a jury may find the plaintiff 20% liable, one defendant 30% liable, and another defendant 50% liable).

Arbitration: Informal hearing held before a neutral third party who renders a decision and issues an award.

Arbitrator: Disinterested third party chosen by the parties or appointed by the court to render a decision.

Arising out of employment: Caused by some circumstance of the employment.

Arraignment: The stage of the criminal process in which the defendant is formally informed of the charges and is allowed to enter a plea.

Assault: Threat or use of unlawful, intentional injury upon another.

ASCII: American Standard Code for Information Interchange. Pronounced "askee" (e.g., ASCII is a code for representing English *characters* as numbers, with each letter assigned a number from 0 to 127; e.g., the ASCII code for *uppercase* M is 77). Most computers use ASCII codes to represent *text*, which makes it possible to transfer *data* computer to another.

Assessment: (1) As an LNC standard, a collection of data to support the systematic assessment of healthcare issues related to a case or a claim; (2) The first step of the nursing process during which data is gathered and examined in preparation for the second step, diagnosis.

Assigned risk: A risk underwriters prefer not to insure but, because of state law or otherwise, must insure. The coverage is assigned to a pool of handlers in turn.

Assisted living facility (ALF): Assisted living facilities are for people needing assistance with activities of daily living (ADLs) but wishing to live as independently as possible for as long as possible. Individual apartments may or may not have a kitchenette. Facilities offer 24-hr on-site staff, congregate dining, and activity programs. Limited nursing services may be provided for an additional fee.

Attorney–client privilege: The protection of communication between the attorney and the client, which is made for furnishing or obtaining professional legal advice; the privilege that allows the client to refuse to disclose and to prevent any other person from disclosing confidential communications between the client and attorney (Black's Law Dictionary, 1991).

Attorney work product: Materials protected from discovery including materials prepared by an attorney in anticipation of litigation, such as private memoranda, written statements of witnesses, and mental impressions of personal recollections prepared or formed by an attorney in anticipation of litigation or for trial.

Audit trails: The capability to identify who entered or altered data in a computer system, which field the information was located, and the date and time.

Authorization: The process by which permission is granted by the plan for a member to receive a treatment or service by a healthcare provider.

Autonomy: The right to self-determination and independence. Autonomy pertains to decisions individuals make to serve their interests.

AVI: Audio video interleave. File format for *Microsoft's Video for Windows*.

Award: A decision rendered by an arbitrator or a panel of arbitrators. If the parties are satisfied with the arbitrator's award, a judgment is entered.

B-Reader: A licensed radiologist who received special training and experience in reading x-rays for the purpose of identifying lung disease, such as asbestosis and silicosis. Certified physicians have passed the National Institute for Occupational Safety and Health (NIOSH) B-Reader Examination for proficiency in the classification of chest radiographs for the pneumoconiosis. Each B-Reader is required to recertify at 4-year intervals.

B&B: Bowel and bladder. For example bowel and bladder incontinence or training.

Back file: A portion of a database or directory separate from the original file. Used as a backup for information in case it is lost or deleted.

Backup and recovery: Sometimes referred to as DBAR (disaster backup and recovery) the necessary computer programs written to ensure that data is not lost during nightly processing or any disaster, which would prevent normal computer access and function.

Bad faith: Activity designed to mislead or deceive another or to avoid fulfilling some duty or contractual obligation.

Banana peel effect: Refers to the possibility a progression of the preexisting condition(s) could be primarily responsible for the plaintiff's postaccident health status, not the alleged injury.

Basic life support (BLS) provider: One who is certified to recognize and respond to life-threatening conditions such as myocardial infarction (MI), choking, and respiratory arrest, and can provide cardiopulmonary resuscitation (CPR) and operate an automatic external defibrillator (AED). A BLS provider can be a healthcare provider, or a layperson.

Bates stamping: Organizational labeling system, which places a number on medical and legal documents.

Battery: The unlawful use of violence against another; harmful or offensive contact.

Benchmarking: Serving as a standard of reference or comparison.

Beneficence: An ethical view in which the right action is to protect the patients and to provide treatment that promotes the good of the individual.

Beyond a reasonable doubt: The degree of certainty required for a juror to legally find a criminal defendant guilty. The proof must be so conclusive and complete that all reasonable doubts of the fact are removed from the mind of the ordinary person.

Bias: Inclination; prejudice.

Bill of Particulars: A legal document in which the plaintiff sets forth the specific negligence and damage claims.

Billable hours: Hours worked in direct relationship to the project at hand.

Biomechanics: Mechanics as applied to the body and its responses to various forces.

Bit: A binary digit, that is, either 0 or 1; the smallest storage unit for data in a computer.

Blocked account: Placement of a conservatee's money in a bank or other financial institution, which cannot be withdrawn without court approval.

Blood borne pathogens standard: One of the standards developed by the Occupational Safety and Health Administration in order to limit workers' occupational exposure to blood, bodily fluids, and other potentially infectious materials.

BMP: Bitmap. The *standard format* used in the *Windows environment.*

Board and care homes: Also known as Residential Care Facilities for the Elderly (RCFE) are residential private homes licensed by the Department of Social Services to provide services to seniors. Most accept no more than six residents with at least one caregiver on-site at all times to assist residents. Group living arrangements meet the needs of people who cannot live independently, but do not require nursing facility services and offer a wider range of services than independent living options. Most provide help with activities of daily living. In some cases, private long-term care insurance and medical assistance programs will help pay for this type of living.

Bond: An obligation or promise such as when a judge requires a conservator of the estate guarantees there will be no loss to the conservatorship estate if the money is mismanaged or taken by the conservator. The bonding agency will reimburse the estate for any loss, dishonesty, or negligence. The bonding company may then sue the conservator to repay the loss.

Book of business: The specific type(s) of insurance products an insurance company might provide. For example, a company may have a book comprised of 50% automobile, 40% workers' compensation, and 10% group life and health.

Boolean logic: Consists of logical operators also referred to as Boolean operators (AND, OR, and NOT), which allow a searcher to create logical search statements or sets showing relationships (e.g., Meperidine or Demerol®).

Breach of contract: Failure to perform a promise or to comply with a term of a contract.

Brief: A formal written presentation of an argument including the main points, supporting precedents, and evidence.

Burden of proof: The duty to demonstrate a greater weight of evidence in civil cases. The jury is instructed to find for the party demonstrating the stronger evidence or "a preponderance of the evidence," regardless of how slight the edge may be.

Business Plan: A written document that details a proposed or existing business. It includes a description of the business, defines its purpose, develops a marketing and financial plan, and a plan for its implementation and management.

Byte: A group of bits sufficient to define a character. Usually represents 8 bits but 10 bits are used per character for online transmission.

Capitation: A specific dollar amount for the coverage of cost of health care delivered per person. It is usually a negotiated per capita rate paid periodically, usually monthly, to a healthcare provider for the delivery of services to a covered member. In most situations, the provider receives a specific amount of money each month for every member who has selected that provider as their primary caregiver. The provider is paid the capitation rate for each assigned member, regardless of whether or not the member receives any services from the provider during the time period.

Cardiopulmonary resuscitation (CPR): A restoration of cardiac output and pulmonary ventilation following cardiac arrest and apnea, using artificial respiration and chest compressions.

Carrier: A company providing insurance.

Case mix and acuity: Mix of types of cases in a caseload/workload determining how much time and intervention is needed for effective management.

Catastrophic injury: Injury or illness that permanently alters an individual's functional status.

Catastrophic loss: Loss of an extraordinary large value.

Cause of action: A claim in a lawsuit with specific elements that must be proven. For example, to state a cause of action for negligence, there must be sufficient proof of the four elements of negligence. The plaintiff has the burden of proof regarding these elements.

Center for Medicare and Medicaid (CMS): Formerly the U.S. Health Care Financing Administration (HCFA), CMS is an element of the Department of Health and Human Services, which finances and administers the Medicare and Medicaid programs. Among its responsibilities are establishing standards for the operation of nursing facilities receiving funds under the Medicare or Medicaid programs and administering the *Medicare, Medicaid, SCHIP* (State Children's Health Insurance), and other health-related programs.

Certificate: Demonstrates knowledge of course content, typically is offered at the completion of an educational process. Certificates are accessible to newcomers as well as experienced professionals, and are often awarded by for-profit institutions and programs. Certificates indicate completion of a course or series of courses with a specific focus, not a degree granting program. Course content is determined by the specific provider or institution and is not standardized, so quality may vary with different providers.

Certification: The formal recognition of the specialized knowledge, skills, and experience demonstrated by the achievement of standards identified by a nursing specialty to promote optimal health outcomes.

Certified Emergency Nurse (CEN): A nurse who is proficient in the specialty of emergency nursing and has passed a national certification examination produced by the Board of Certification of the Emergency Nurses' Association. Certification as an emergency nurse measures the attainment of a defined body of knowledge pertinent to the specialty of emergency nursing.

Certify: (Of a court) to issue an order allowing a class of litigants to maintain a class action; to create (a class) for purposes of a class action.

CFR: Code of Federal Regulations. Codification of the general and permanent rules published in the Federal Register by the executive departments and agencies of the Federal Government. It is divided into 50 titles that represent broad areas subject to federal regulation, such as those governing nursing homes. Each volume of the CFR is updated once in a calendar year and is issued on a quarterly basis.

Chronological chart summary: A written document, which consists of a verbatim summary of pertinent information from medical records. The summary includes the date and the page number of the referenced information.

Citation: The bibliographic information (author, title, publication, volume, date, pages) in a complete reference; often used synonymously with the term "reference."

Claim: The allegation of a right to recover for a loss such as one that is covered by an insurance policy.

Claimant: The individual petitioning for, or receiving benefits.

Claims analysis data: Data compiled through the analysis of legal claims including type of legal claim filed, prevailing party, and financial payout, in an effort to identify trends in litigation.

Claims consultant: Person designated to represent the insurance company in investigations and negotiations in order to reach an agreement on the amount of a loss or the insurer's liability.

Claims management: Records and notifications of specific claims and loss history gathered to reduce the overall cost of claims.

Claim processor: Carrier's employee responsible for handling claims as they are received from patients and providers.

Claims specialist/adjuster: The independent agent or insurance company employee who investigates claims, sets insurance reserves, and settles claims against the insured.

Client: The purchaser of services.

Clinical pathways: A precalculated plan of routine services usually required by a patient for a given disease based on average medical recovery outcomes.

Clinical trials: Premarketing evaluations of a drug or medical device performed by the manufacturer to determine the safety and effectiveness of the drug or device.

CMS 1500 (HCFA 1500): A standard claim form for submission of charges.

CNA: Certified Nursing Assistant. An unlicensed staff member providing personal care such as bathing, dressing, changing linens, transporting, and other essential activities. CNAs are trained, tested, certified, and work under the supervision of a nurse as regulated by each state.

Coefficient of friction (COF): A measurement of friction (or the degree of slipperiness) of a surface such as a floor. On ice and on wet and oily surfaces, the COF is low (.10). Excellent traction is at a COF of .40–.50 or more. "Slip resistant" is defined a COF of .50.

Copayment: A sharing in the cost of certain covered expenses on the part of the insured on a percentage basis.

Code of ethics: A set of guidelines designed to define acceptable behaviors for members of a particular group, association, or profession.

Cold calls: A sales and marketing term used for making contact with a potential client, usually by telephone, to solicit new business.

Collaboration: As it applies to the LNC, the LNC works with legal professionals and healthcare professionals when necessary.

Collateral sources: Benefits received from sources other than any and all benefits received from successful litigation.

Collegiality: As it applies to the LNC, the LNC shares knowledge and contributes to the development of peers, colleagues, and others.

Command language: Instructions entered by a searcher directing the computer retrieval program to perform specific tasks or operations. The command languages vary by vendor system and symbols may be utilized.

Common law: In general, a body of law developed and derived through judicial decisions rather than legislative enhancements.

Communication: The transmission and reception of information.

Companion care: Nonmedical services provided in the resident's home. Examples include, but are not limited to, helping the senior with everyday activities, making meals, grooming, ensuring safety, etc. No medical care is provided.

Comparative negligence: A proportional division of the damages between the plaintiff and the defendant in a tort action according to their respective share of fault contributing to the injury.

Competent: Duly qualified; answering all requirements; having sufficient capacity, ability, or authority; possessing the requisite physical, mental, natural, or legal qualifications; able; adequate; sufficient; capable; legally fit.

Complaint: The original or initial pleading by which an action is commenced under codes or rules of civil procedure. It is the pleading setting forth a claim for relief.

Complex litigation: Usually involves many parties in numerous related cases, and often in different jurisdictions. This involves large numbers of documents, witnesses, and extensive discovery requiring judicial management generally assigned to the same judge.

Concept: A term used to describe a phenomenon or group of phenomena.

Concept analysis: The method for examining attributes and characteristics of a concept as a foundation for theory development.

Concept derivation: A process in which a previously defined concept from a parent field is transposed to a new field then redefined as a new concept in the new field.

Conceptual framework: A categorization or classification of a mental image.

Conciliation: Adjustment and settlement of a dispute in a friendly, nonantagonistic manner.

Concordance: An index showing the context in which words occur.

Confidentiality: The duty to keep private all information provided by a client or acquired from other sources before, during, and after the course of the professional relationship. This includes information from the client's medical records.

Conflict of interest: A situation where one person has information that may potentially be used to influence a case and cause harm, injury, or prejudice to the client.

Congregate housing: Originally designed in a 1978 federal law to provide subsidized housing-with-services to seniors and the disabled. Housing may be partially covered by government agencies and charitable organizations. Similar to independent living, congregate housing provides convenience or supportive services such as meals, housekeeping, and transportation in addition to rental housing.

Connect time: The time between log-on to a database and/or termination. It is one of the primary components of online searching costs.

Conservatee: A person who a judge has deemed unable to care for himself or herself or to manage financial affairs and for whom a conservator is appointed.

Conservator: Person or organization appointed by the court to act as the legal representative, guardian, protector, or preserver of a person who is mentally or physically incapable of managing his or her financial or personal affairs.

Conservator of the estate: A person or organization who the court appoints to handle the financial affairs of an individual (conservatee) deemed unable to do so for themselves.

Conservator of the person: A person or organization who the court appoints to handle the personal care and protection of a person (conservatee) whom a judge has decided is unable to do so.

Consulting or reviewing expert: An expert offering an opinion on a particular subject, but not expected to testify at trial.

Consumer disclosure: Specific information that must be provided to a prospective consumer prior to signing a service contract.

Consumer expectation test: Used in product liability to determine whether the product is negligently manufactured or whether a warning on the product is defective. The product is considered defective if a reasonable consumer would find it defective. Test helps to establish a reasonable, widely accepted minimum expectations about the circumstances under which product should perform safely.

Contingency fee: A fee arrangement in which the attorney receives a percentage of the plaintiff's settlement or verdict.

Continuing care retirement communities (CCRC): A residential community for the remainder of one's life, with a choice of services and living situations. Seniors move between independent living, assisted living, and nursing home care based on needs. A written agreement or long-term contract between the resident and the community offers a continuum of housing, services, and a healthcare system, commonly all on one campus or site. Typically, CCRC require a significant payment (called an endowment) prior to admission, then charge monthly fees.

Contract: Voluntary agreement creating legally binding responsibilities for the parties named in it to facilitate predetermined amount or type of service or work to be performed for a specific reason or period of time.

Contractor: One who contracts to perform a work for another party; the person who retains the control of the means, method, and manner of the project result.

Contributory negligence: Negligent conduct by the plaintiff contributing to injury.

Controlled vocabulary: An authorized listing of subject headings or descriptor strings used by indexers to assign subject terminology to items described in records in a database or in files.

Coverage: The assurance against losses provided under the terms of a policy of insurance. It is used synonymously with the term insurance or protection.

CPT: Current Procedural Terminology. A systematic listing of descriptive terms and corresponding five-digit codes for reporting services and procedures performed by medical providers.

Credentials: Degree credentials (e.g., BS, MS, PhD, JD) awarded upon completion of a particular educational program. Licensure credentials (RN, LPN) are awarded based on completion of a specified educational program and the successful passing of a national licensure exam. Credentials required or designated by specific states are similar to licensure credentials, but are usually beyond basic licensure and designate authority and recognition to practice at a more advanced level in state (APN, APRN, ARNP, CNS), and are based on meeting certain criteria that may include advanced education or work experience (ANCC, 2008). National certifications are credentials awarded by a nationally recognized, usually accredited, certifying body, such as the LNCC, accredited by the American Board of Nursing Specialties.

Credentialing: A review process to approve a provider applying for a contract with a health plan.

Credibility: Worthy of belief; must be preceded by establishment of competency (legally fit to testify).

Crime: Performance of an act that is forbidden by law or the omission of an act required by law.

Criteria: Variables known to be relevant; measurable indicators of the standards of clinical nursing practice.

Cross-Jurisdictional Advocacy: An LNC who manages care interventions for clients in differing jurisdictions by bridging the paradigms of law and health care for the purpose of reducing conflict and producing change.

Culture brokering: The act of bridging, linking, or mediating between groups or persons of differing cultural backgrounds for the purpose of reducing conflict or producing change.

Cumulative trauma: An injury or illness that occurs over a period of time, for example, carpal tunnel syndrome.

Current procedural terminology: The American Medical Association's listing of descriptive terms and identifying codes for reporting medical services and procedures performed by physicians to provide a uniform language that accurately describes medical, surgical, and diagnostic services.

Curriculum vitae: A more formal, academically oriented resume listing presentations, publications, professional associations, and continuing education, as well as work experience.

Custodial care: Nonmedical assistance with activities of daily living, preparation of special diets, and self-administration of medication that do not require constant attention of medical personnel. Providers of custodial care are not required to undergo medical training.

Damage mitigation: Actions or steps reducing or limiting the damage resulting from an event.

Damages: A pecuniary compensation or indemnity, which may be recovered in the courts by any person who has suffered loss, detriment, or injury, whether to his person, property, or rights, through the unlawful act or omission or negligence of another. A sum of money awarded to a person injured by the tort of another.

Database: An organized collection of data in electronic form, generally related by subject, concept, or idea (e.g., MEDLINE, TOXLINE, CHEMLINE).

Declarant: A person who makes a declaration; one who makes a sworn statement.

Declaration of Helsinki: International guidelines for investigators conducting biomedical research involving human subjects. Recommendations, adopted by the 18th World Medical Assembly in Helsinki in 1964, include procedures to ensure subject safety in clinical trials.

Deductible: A preset amount that each insured must pay toward the cost of treatment before benefits go into effect.

Defective design: A drug or device, which is not reasonably safe for its intended use or a use that may be reasonably anticipated.

Defective manufacture: A product not reasonably safe as a result of the manner in which it is manufactured, existing when the product left the manufacturer's control.

Defendant: The person or entity against whom a lawsuit is brought.

Defense client: Any entity referred to as the defense client of the LNC. The LNC may work with one or more entities in assisting the defense in a professional liability case. These entities may include the healthcare provider defendants, the defense attorney, an insurance company, a third-party administrator, or a self-insured company.

Defense team member: The individuals working on behalf of the defense. The team may include the trial attorney, associate attorneys, LNCs, expert witnesses, and other consultants.

Delta V: Change in velocity; the difference between the speed just prior to the impact and the speed immediately after the impact. A low velocity motor vehicle crash is one with a delta V approximately 10 mph or less. The greater the delta V, the greater the forces, and the greater the likelihood of severe injury. An accident reconstructionist will calculate the delta V(s) in a collision.

Demand letter: A letter by one party requesting the recipient take some action such as settlement of the case.

Dementia: Progressive mental disorder affecting memory, judgment, and cognitive powers; severe and enduring impairment of mental function and global cognitive abilities in an alert individual. Behaviors can include confusion, wandering, and outbursts of aggression. One type of dementia is Alzheimer's disease.

Dementia special care units/memory care units: Separate areas of assisted living or nursing facilities set up to meet needs of residents with dementia and to protect residents without dementia.

Demonstrative evidence: Evidence in the form of objects (maps, diagrams, or models) with no probative value itself but is used to illustrate and clarify the factual matter at issue broadly.

Deposition: Pretrial sworn testimony of parties or others, such as witnesses to elicit information about the claims and defenses. Deposition testimony may be used for various purposes at trial (e.g., to impeach a witness). Depositions are conducted outside of the courtroom, usually at a law firm.

Derivative claim: The claim of an injured party's spouse, child, or parent for damages resulting to them, which may include one or more of the following: loss of companionship; loss of services; and expenses incurred.

Descriptor: A word or phrase used to describe a subject, concept, or idea.

Designated nonparty: A party deemed responsible for all or part of damages not named in the suit.

Developmental disability (DD): A diverse group of severe chronic conditions due to mental and/or physical impairments in language, mobility, learning, self-help, and independent living. Developmental disabilities may occur up to 22 years of age and usually last throughout a person's lifetime. Those affected have limitations in three or more of the following areas: self-care, receptive and expressive language, learning, mobility, self-direction, capacity of independent living, economic self-sufficiency.

Diagnosis: The second step of the nursing process, during which data are analyzed and pulled together for the purpose of identifying and describing health status (strengths, or actual and potential health problems).

Diagnostic-related groups (DRG): A patient classification scheme to provide a means of relating the type of patients a hospital treats, (its case mix), to the costs incurred by the hospital. DRGs are based on the principal diagnosis, secondary diagnosis, surgical procedures, age, sex, and discharge statuses of the patients treated, and are the foundation of reimbursement to hospitals by the Medicare program.

Digitalization: The process of making a 2D or 3D exhibit into a computer file format to be stored and retrieved from a disc on a computer. This allows easy access, quick retrieval, and simplified method of transporting exhibits.

Disbursements: Attorney's out-of-pocket expenses incurred on behalf of a specific case (e.g., expert witness fees or copying charges for medical records).

Disclosure: Communication of information regarding the results of a diagnostic test, medical treatment, or surgical intervention.

Disclosure of adverse events: The forthright and empathetic discussion of clinically significant facts between providers of care, patients, and/or their representatives about the occurrence of an adverse event that resulted in patient harm or could result in harm in the foreseeable future.

Discoverable: Subject to pretrial finding; previously unknown but may be learned by pretrial or acquisition of knowledge from opposing side.

Discovery: Pretrial devices used by one party to obtain facts and information about the case from the other party in order to assist in trial preparation.

Disk: A circular, hard or floppy, plate coated with magnetic material used to store digital or machine-readable data.

Do-not-resuscitate order (DNR): An order by a physician following the discussion with and informed consent by a legally competent patient or the patient's legal representative, which orders healthcare providers NOT perform procedures necessary for sustaining the patient's life. A DNR order is frequently initiated by the patient's living will or the legal representative's medical power of attorney.

Docket: A brief, formal record of the proceedings in a court of justice.

Docket control order: Order from a judge outlining deadlines for discovery, etc.

Domains: (1) Territories shaping practice; (2) Group of *computers* and *devices* on a *network* administered as a unit with common rules and procedures. Within the *Internet*, domains are defined by the *IP address*. All devices sharing a common part of the IP address are said to be in the same domain; (3) In *database* technology, domain refers to the description of an *attribute's* allowed values. The physical description is a set of values the attribute can have, and the semantic, or logical, description is the meaning of the attribute.

Dose–response: The process of quantifying the relationship between the level of exposure and increased risk of adverse effects such as cancer.

Downloading: The practice of copying data in electronic form on a computer, which may then be manipulated or stored permanently on a personal computer.

DRG (Diagnosis-related group): A classification scheme whose patient types are defined by patient's diagnoses or procedures and in some cases, by the patient's age or discharge status.

DRI: Defense Research Institute, the international membership organization for civil litigation defense attorneys.

Drug formulary: A listing of medications preferred for use by the health plan. An "open" or "voluntary" formulary will cover both formulary and nonformulary drugs and a "closed" formulary covers only those drugs in the formulary. The patient must pay for any drugs purchased by the patient not listed on a closed formulary, even if the ordering physician specifies the drug and even when no generic or alternative form exists.

Dual relationships: Potential conflict of interest due to prior, or concurrent, relationship with a client. Conflict in case manager relationships with client and payer source.

Durable Power of Attorney for Health Care (DPAHC): A legal document in which a competent person gives another person (called an attorney-in-fact) the power to make healthcare decisions for him or her if unable to make those decisions. A DPA can include guidelines for the attorney-in-fact to follow in making decisions on behalf of the incompetent person.

Duty: An action or observation expected to occur once a relationship has been established between two people, such as healthcare provider and patient.

DVERT: Domestic Violence Emergency Response Team. Works in partnership with community agencies to address domestic violence.

E/M: Evaluation and Management. Current procedural terminology (CPT) codes representing services most frequently performed by medical providers (e.g., office, emergency department, inpatient visits).

eCommunity: A virtual group primarily interacting via communication media such as newsletters, list serves, etc. such as the AALNC eCommunity.

Ectopic pregnancy: Implantation of a fertilized egg outside the endometrial cavity, most often in a fallopian tube (95% of the time). If the fetus continues to grow, the fallopian tube will eventually rupture causing potential life-threatening hemorrhage.

ED overcrowding: Emergency Department Overcrowding. Any situation involving an influx of patients to the emergency department, taxing the department's resources and services beyond its capacity. Examples include disaster situations, mass casualty incidents, and multiple victims from a motor vehicle crash.

Education: As it applies to the LNC, educational activities are ongoing and pertain to the LNCs practice area.

Eggshell plaintiff: A fragile plaintiff with significant preexisting conditions affecting the risk as well as the recovery from injury.

Employee: One who is engaged in paid services of another.

Engineering controls: The preferred method of controlling hazards; removes the hazard at its source or in the pathway of transmission before reaching the worker, such as elimination of a hazardous substance rather than depending on the worker to control the hazard.

Enterprise risk management (ERM): Structured and analytical process focusing on identifying and estimating the financial impact and volatility of a defined portfolio of risks.

Entrepreneur: One who organizes, manages, and assumes the risks of a business or enterprise, usually self-employed.

EPO: Exclusive Provider Organization. A managed care organization in which the providers are exclusive to the plan and its membership.

ERISA: Employee Retirement Income Security Act of 1974. A law designed to protect the rights of employees who receive employer-provided benefits such as pensions, deferred retirement income, and healthcare benefits such as health maintenance organizations (HMOs), long-term and short-term disability coverage.

Errata sheet: A document containing corrections to the text of the deposition.

Ethics: (1) As it applies to the LNC, the ANA Code for Nurses with Interpretive Statements and the AALNC Code of Ethics guides the LNC; (2) The systematic investigation of questions about right and wrong. Ethics involves critical analysis of different views of right and wrong with particular attention paid to the underlying values of each view, its coherence and consistency, and its implications in actual situations.

Euthanasia: The act, by commission or omission, of painlessly ending the life of persons suffering from incurable and distressing disease as an act of mercy.

Evaluation: The fifth step of the nursing process, during which the extent of goal achievement is determined; each of the previous four steps are analyzed to identify factors enhancing or hindering progress. The plan of care is modified or terminated as indicated.

Exacerbation: A temporary increase in symptoms related to a preexisting condition, usually after an injury but recedes to its former level within a reasonable period of time.

Excess (insurance) coverage: Insurance coverage when damages reach a certain level. This is also the function of umbrella coverage. Excess coverage may involve an additional insurance carrier.

Exclusions: Noted services or conditions, which the policy will not cover.

Exclusive remedy: Worker's compensation benefits are the sole source of recovery against the employer so that tort recovery is excluded.

Exemplary damages: Also known as punitive damages; an award made to the plaintiff for the purpose of punishing the defendant when oppressive, malicious, or fraudulent conduct is involved.

Exhibit: A document or object produced and identified in court as evidence; a document labeled with an identifying mark (as a number or letter) and appended to a writing (as a brief) to which it is relevant; something exhibited; an act or instance of exhibiting.

Experience: The history of injuries or accidents, which is used for substantiating the setting of a current premium amount.

Expert: A person possessing the knowledge, skills, and expertise concerning a particular subject who is capable of rendering an opinion.

Expert fact witness: One who by virtue of special knowledge, skill, training, or experience is qualified to provide testimony to aid the fact finder in matters exceeding the common knowledge of ordinary people, but does not offer opinions on the standard of care.

Expert witness: A witness (as a medical specialist) who by virtue of special knowledge, skill, training, or experience is qualified to provide testimony to aid the fact finder in matters exceeding the common knowledge of ordinary people.

Exposure: The maximum amount of money an insurer could spend on one claim (often coincided with the policy limit).

Exposure records: Documentation of environmental workplace monitoring or measuring of a toxic substance or a harmful agent or biological monitoring, which directly assesses the absorption of a toxic substance or a harmful physical agent.

External standards: Standards stemming from sources such as state nurse practice acts, state boards of nursing, federal organizations, independent, not-for-profit organizations, such as the Joint Commission, professional nursing organizations, and nursing literature and continuing education programs.

Fabricate: To invent; to devise falsely.

Fact witness: One not named as a defendant in a lawsuit, who has knowledge of events that have occurred.

Failure mode effects analysis (FMEA): A proactive analysis to look at a particular process and identify ways it might fail as opposed to a postevent evaluation. The first step defines the process to be analyzed and finds evidence-based data to support analysis. A multidisciplinary team then breaks the process into subprocesses and identifies failure modes for each followed by the assignment of risk priorities. An analysis of each failure mode leads to recommendations for improvement and corrective action.

Federal question jurisdiction: A term used in the U.S. law of civil procedure to refer to the situation in which a U.S. federal court has subject matter jurisdiction to hear a civil case because the plaintiff has alleged a violation of the Constitution, laws, or treaties of the United States.

Federal rules of civil procedure: Body of procedural rules that govern all civil actions in U.S. District Courts and after which most of the states have modeled their own rules of procedure.

Federal Rules of Evidence: Rules governing the introduction of evidence in proceedings, both civil and criminal, in federal courts. While they do not directly apply to suits in state courts, the rules of many states have been closely modeled on these provisions (e.g., Federal Rules of Civil Procedure and Federal Rules of Criminal Procedure).

Field: An area of a unit record used to store a defined category of data.

Field case management: Case management services provided face to face through visits with the client at home, in an inpatient setting, and at treatment provider's offices.

File: A collection of related records. The term is often used as a synonym for database; sometimes used to refer to part of a database structure.

Five C's of communication: Elements representing effective communication skills: clear, concise, complete, cohesive, and courteous.

Floppy disk: A thin, flexible disk with a magnetic surface used to store computer programs and data. Available in two sizes —3.5 or 5.0 in.

Food and Drug Administration (FDA): U.S. government agency established for the provision of regulations and guidelines for compliance with the Food, Drug, and Cosmetic Act.

Forensic science: Science applied to answering legal questions by the examination, evaluation, and exploration of evidence.

Foreseeability: The implication damages must be the foreseeable or reasonably anticipated result of substandard practice of the defendant healthcare provider.

Free text: A method by which a searcher may select the terms on which searching will be performed without the requirement of matching them to a controlled vocabulary list or thesaurus; also referred to as "text words."

G (force of gravity or "G"): Unit of measurement of a load caused by acceleration or deceleration. One *G* is the force holding objects to the Earth. A person on a roller coaster experiences more than 1*G* while a jet pilot might experience as much as 6*G* in a turn. Acceleration/deceleration in an accident subjects the occupants to increased *G*. The *G* in a motor vehicle collision are calculated by an accident reconstructionist.

Gatekeeper: The secretary, paralegal, or other personnel who take and screen calls for the professional.

General acceptance test: A standard for the admissibility of expert testimony. Expert testimony based on a scientific technique is inadmissible unless the technique has been accepted as reliable by the relevant scientific community.

General damages: Also referred to as noneconomic damages. General damages are nonpecuniary damages recognized as compensable, but on which the law is unable to place a dollar amount. Examples of general damages are "pain and suffering" and "loss of consortium."

Gigabyte: The largest unit of mass storage used in common parlance. One gigabyte is equal to 1,000 megabytes, 1 billion bytes, or 500,000 pages of information; used in huge computer storage depots by major vendors of online databases.

Goal-oriented planning: The identification of a goal and the steps it will take to reach goal, including objectives, leadership, target date, resources, training, support, budget, communication, and evaluation.

Gopher: A service providing a menu-like interface to voluminous amounts of information available on the Internet. The data in "Gopherspace" may be efficiently browsed using a Gopher client.

Grand jury: A body of people randomly selected in a manner similar to trial jurors whose purpose is to investigate and inform on crimes committed within its jurisdiction and to accuse (indict) persons of crimes when it has discovered sufficient evidence to warrant holding a person for trial.

Grandfather: A legal term exempting people or transactions previously existing prior to a new rule or regulation taking effect.

Guardian: A person lawfully invested with the power and charged with the duty of taking care of and managing the property and rights of another person who for defect of age, understanding, or self-control is considered incapable of administering his or her own affairs.

Guardianship: A person appointed by a court to assist with the personal or legal affairs of an individual who is unable to make their own decisions. The law regards a person as being unable to make personal decisions if he or she lacks sufficient understanding or capacity to make or communicate responsible decisions concerning him/her. Guardianship can be shared by one or more individuals. Generally, the duties of a guardian are to determine where the ward should live, arrange for necessary care, treatment, or other services for the ward, and ensuring basic daily personal needs for the ward including clothing, food, and shelter are met. A guardian may manage financial matters for the benefit of the ward.

A court may appoint a limited guardian to provide particular services for a specific length of time.

Guideline: A resource tool to assist employers in recognizing and controlling hazards. It is voluntary and not enforceable, as are standards; also a process of client care management that has the potential of improving the quality of clinical and consumer decision-making; includes assessment and diagnosis, planning, intervention, evaluation, and outcome.

Hard disk: A rigid storage device coated with a magnetic surface on which computer programs and data may be stored. Typical capacities for personal computers range from 5 to 120 megabytes.

Hardware: The equipment and computers used in data storage and processing systems.

Hazard communication standard: One of the standards developed by the Occupational Safety and Health Administration in order to prevent workplace illness and injury to workers exposed to hazardous chemicals by providing information to employees about chemical hazards.

HCFA: Health Care Finance Administration. Involved in regulating nursing homes (now Centers for Medicare and Medicaid Services).

Health Care Common Procedural Coding System (HCPCS): Often pronounced "*hick-picks*," HCPCS is a standardized coding system describing specific medical services, supplies, and equipments. Level I refers to the physician's *Current Procedural Terminology* and is maintained by the American Medical Association. Level II is an alphanumeric code set for medical services not included in Level I, such as durable medical equipment, prosthetics, orthotics, and supplies.

Health Care Directive: A written legal document allowing one to appoint another person (agent) to make healthcare decisions should he or she is unable to make or communicate decisions.

Healthcare Power of Attorney: The appointment of a healthcare agent to make decisions when the principal becomes unable to make or communicate decisions.

Healthcare provider defendants (HCPD): Any of the individuals involved in providing care for the plaintiff who are alleged to have fallen below the standard of care resulting in the claimed damages. These defendants may include physicians, nurses, therapists, pharmacists, and similar care providers.

Health Maintenance Organization (HMO): Groups of participating healthcare providers (physicians, hospitals, clinics) who provide medical services to enrolled members of group health insurance plan.

HIPPA: The Health Insurance Portability and Accountability Act of 1996 established privacy and security standards to protect a patient's healthcare information. In December of 2000, the Department of Health and Human Services issued final regulations governing privacy of this information under HIPPA.

Hired gun: A person hired to handle a difficult problem. In the legal arena, a person who may be perceived as someone who will provide any desired testimony for a price.

Hits: See "Postings."

HMO: Health Maintenance Organization. This type plan is based on the premise of preventative medicine and management of dollars spent for the healthcare benefits of its members.

Home Health Agency (HHA): Otherwise known as a "licensed service agency," an HHA is a public agency or private nonprofit organization, certified under Section 1861(o) of the Social Security Act, primarily engaged in providing skilled nursing care and other therapeutic services in private homes, assisted living facilities, and adult family care homes.

Services may be provided by a nurse, occupational, speech or physical therapist, social worker, or home health aide.

Home health aide: An unlicensed person who provides personal care under the direction of nursing or medical staff to help elderly, convalescent, or disabled persons live in their own homes instead of healthcare facilities. Duties may include bathing, dressing, grooming, or light housekeeping services.

Home healthcare conditions of participation: Minimum health and safety conditions that must be met by providers in order to begin and continue to participate in the Medicare Home Health Care program.

Homebound: Medicare criteria for home healthcare services require patients leave home for medical care or for short and infrequent nonmedical reasons and that such trips require a "substantial effort."

Hospice: Hospice/palliative care provided to enhance the life of the dying person often provided in the home by health professionals. Many nursing facilities and acute-care settings also offer hospice services. Hospice care is typically offered in the last 6 months of life and emphasizes comfort measures and counseling to provide emotional, social, spiritual, and physical support to the dying patient and family. Care neither prolongs life nor hastens death. Bereavement and counseling services are available to families before and after a patient's death.

HTML: HyperText Markup Language. The authoring *language* used to create *documents* on the *World Wide Web* defines the structure and layout of a web document by using a variety of *tags* and *attributes*.

Hypermedia: Similar in concept to hypertext except it also includes multimedia capabilities such as sounds and graphics related to the subject.

Hypertext: A hypertext document contains live links, to related pieces of information (e.g., in a hypertext document about photography, selecting a link or button from the word "camera" sends the reader to a related document including both terms and concepts).

ICD-9CM: International Classification of Diseases and Clinical Modification. These are three-digit codes, required by Medicare Part B referring to a disease with an additional number of up to two decimal places for specificity.

ID code: Identification code. Code issued by a vendor to individual users for identification.

IDEX: Identifying and indexing. A company that provides research and storage of information on expert witnesses using public records.

IDT: Interdisciplinary team; consists of the nurse, physician, and therapists.

Impeachment: To discredit the witness by presenting information that conflicts with testimony.

Implementation: As an LNC standard, implementation of the plan of action. Actual performance of interventions identified in the care plan. Direct patient care is coordinated with other healthcare providers. Examples are health teaching, direct patient care, medical treatments, medications, and dressing changes. Interventions serve to achieve established goals and are communicated by documenting and reporting. Interventions may not be planned as when critical thinking skills are used to respond to an unexpected crisis.

Implied consent: Implied from conduct rather than expression. A consent form is not signed, but patient's actions or circumstances surrounding the procedure or treatment at issue indicate consent; that is, filling a prescription, getting blood drawn, etc.

Improper joinder: Joining of unrelated defendants in single lawsuit.

In camera: To the judge only; in the judge's private chambers; all spectators excluded.

In-house LNC: Usually references LNC's working within a law firm, insurance company, etc.; typically salaried, full-time employment.

In the course of employment: Engaged in work-related or incidental activities at the time and place required by the employment.

***In vitro* study:** "In glass"; a biologic or biochemical process occurring outside a living organism.

***In vivo* study:** "In life"; a biologic or biochemical process occurring within a living organism.

Incident: A broad term used to describe any occurrence not consistent with routine hospital activities.

Incompetency: A relative term that may be employed as meaning disqualification, inability, or incapacity, and it can refer to lack of legal qualifications or fitness to discharge the required duty and to show want of physical or intellectual or moral fitness; unqualified to testify; inadmissible; inability; or incapacity.

Indemnity: To restore the party that has had a loss to the same financial position as before the loss occurred.

Impairment rating: An estimate of percentage of loss sustained to the injured body part. Impairment ratings are determined based on guidelines published by the American Medical Association (AMA).

Independent contractor: A person working for an entity under contract, not an employee of the contracting entity. The contracting entity does not pay unemployment, disability, or workers' compensation insurance or withhold taxes from payments to the person; a legal nurse consultant who works independently as a consultant or testifying expert, not as an employee.

Independent living: Residential living setting for elderly or senior adults that may or may not provide hospitality or supportive services. Under this living arrangement, residents lead an independent lifestyle requiring minimal or no extra assistance. It also includes government-subsidized rental-assisted or market-rate apartments and cottages.

Independent LNC: A legal nurse consultant whose LNC practice is independent of a law firm, insurance company, hospital, etc. Frequently works solo, either as an expert witness or as a behind-the-scenes consultant for multiple attorneys in a small business venture charging hourly fees for service.

Independent Medical Examination/Insurance Medical Examination (IME): An examination requested by the carrier to determine appropriateness of medical care to date, causality of work/accident related injury, length of disability, and work status.

Indictment: A formal accusation from a grand jury of a criminal offense made against a person.

International Classification of Diseases: An international standard diagnostic classification for epidemiological, health management purposes, and clinical use published by the World Health Organization (WHO). The ICD classification is used to code and classify mortality. The ICD together with a Clinical Modification (CM) is used to code and classify morbidity data.

Individual Retirement Account (IRA): Individuals with earned income are permitted, under certain circumstances, to set aside a limited amount of such income per year for a retirement account. The amount so set aside can be deducted by the taxpayer and is subject to income tax only upon withdrawal. The Internal Revenue Code limits the amount of this contribution can be deducted for adjusted gross income depending upon (1) whether the taxpayer or spouse is an active participant in an employer-provided qualified retirement plan and (2) the magnitude of the taxpayer's adjusted gross income before the IRA contribution is considered (I.R.C. §219).

Individualized Service Plan (ISP): A working plan defining the resident's goals and strategies for recovery complied by the case manager, the resident, and family.

Individuals with disabilities: A person with a physical or mental impairment, which substantially limits one or more major life activities.

Informed consent: The process of disclosure of information, usually regarding proposed medical or surgical treatment, by healthcare professionals to a competent patient who is presumed to have the capacity to understand the information and a decision by patient based on the information received. An agreement to do something or to allow something to happen only after all the relevant facts are known.

Informed Consent Form: A document outlining and fully explaining a research study including required elements. The form is to be approved by the Institutional Review Board designated for the particular jurisdiction of study location and investigator, prior to presentation to the potential study participant. The study subject is to read, sign, and date this form prior to performance of designated study procedures, to indicate acceptance to voluntarily participate in the study. The subject is considered as enrolled into a study at the time the consent form is signed and dated by the participant.

Informed consent in research: An aspect of research in which consent of the subject is obtained after the subject is informed about the possible risks and benefits of participating in the research study. The process is similar to that of informed consent for medical decisions, but includes additional information that must be understood by the subject, such as what is known or not known about aspects of the research study and their effects.

Informed refusal: The right of a patient to refuse treatment or diagnostic tests after the physician/healthcare provider has informed the patient of all the risks and likely outcomes of the choice to refuse treatment or testing.

Inherent risk: A risk of a complication or condition that is existent in and inseparable from the medical procedure or treatment.

Institutional Review Board (IRB): A standing committee in a hospital or other facility charged with responsibility for ensuring the protection of the rights and welfare, safety, and well-being of human subjects involved in research.

Instrumental activities of daily living (IADLs): More sophisticated activities of daily living including using the telephone, getting to locations beyond walking distance, grocery shopping, preparing meals, doing laundry, taking medications, and managing money.

Insurance: A contract for the provision of coverage for services, injuries, or damages as set forth in the conditions, types, and terms of the contract.

Insurer: The party agreeing to reimburse another party for loss by designated contingencies.

Integrity: The distinctive element of being honest; the soundness or moral principle and character, as shown by one person dealing with others in the making and performance of contracts and fidelity and honesty in the discharge of trusts. Firm adherence to a code, especially moral or artistic.

Intellectual property: Refers to copyrights, trademarks, and patents.

Intensity of service/severity of illness (IS/SI): Description of how sick a patient is and the level of healthcare services the patient requires.

Interfacing: The ability to send and/or receive information from one computer system to another.

Intermediate Care Facility/Mentally Retarded (ICF/MR): Residential program with a primary purpose—the provision of health and/or rehabilitation services to individuals with mental retardation (an individual with subaverage intellectual functioning who is defined as an IQ of 70 or below) or related conditions receiving care and services under the Medicaid program.

Internal standards: Institutional standards stemming from internal sources such as policies and procedures, professional job descriptions, or internal educational materials.

(The) Internet: The name given to the worldwide collection of data networks which all speak the TCP/IP network protocol or language.

Internet work: A collection of two or more distinct networks joined together typically using a router to form a larger "network of networks."

Interrogatories: A set or series of written questions about the case submitted by one party to the other party or witness. The answers to the interrogatories are usually given under oath; that is, the person answering the questions signs a sworn statement that the answers are true.

Intrapreneur: A nurse who creates innovation within the healthcare organization through the introduction of a new product, a different service, or simply a new way of doing something.

IPA: Individual Practice Association. Physicians contract with one or more specific plans and provide services to patients for an agreed-upon rate and bill the plan on a fee-for-service basis.

Item bank: References certification test items (questions), which have been developed by the Item Writing Committee and are ready for use, but which have not yet been used on the certification exam.

Job analysis: Process of looking at a job to determine physical requirements needed to perform the essential functions of the job.

Joinder: Uniting of parties or claims in a single law suit.

JPEG: Joint Photographic Experts Group (pronounced "jay-peg"). JPEG is a glossy data compression technique for color images. Although it can reduce files sizes to about 5% of their normal size, some detail is lost in the compression.

Justice: The principle of ethics involving the obligation to be fair to all persons. Distributive justice is the allocation of a good as fairly as possible. The good of health care is distributed on the basis of need, which means some people will get more than others because their need is greater.

Kantianism: This view holds that consequences do not make an action right or wrong. The moral rightness of a person's actions is dependent upon whether or not those actions uphold a principle, regardless of outcome.

Keogh Plan: A designation for tax deductible retirement plans available to self-employed taxpayers. Such plans extend to the self-employed tax benefits similar to those available to employees under qualified pension and profit sharing plans. Yearly contributions to the plan (up to a certain amount) are tax deductible.

Key words: Single words or terms of importance in an article drawn from titles, abstracts, subject headings, or any part of a record, which is used for indexing.

Kilobyte: The most common memory storage unit quoted. It is 1,000 bytes or approximately one-half page of single-spaced, printed material.

Leadership: The office, position, or capacity of a leader who gives guidance and has the ability to lead or exert authority.

Learned intermediary: The person with knowledge who prescribes the drug to the patient. The learned intermediary doctrine provides that manufacturers of prescription drugs and medical devices discharge their duty of care to patients by providing warnings to the prescribing physicians.

Learned treatises: Documents including facts, standards, methods, and principles of care; typically textbooks.

Legal assistant: A person qualified by education, training, or work experience, employed by an attorney, who performs specifically delegated substantive legal work for which a lawyer is responsible.

Legal causation: Causation in fact and foreseeability or the "but for" test (see proximate cause).

Legal Nurse Consultant Certified (LNCC): The Gold Standard of Legal Nurse Consulting Certification, accredited by American Board of Nursing Specialties (ABNS). Not an entry level exam, the qualifications to sit for the AALNC's exam include active licensure as an RN, at least 5 years experience as a practicing RN, and 2,000 hr of qualified LNC practice within the previous 3 years.

Legal writing: Writing pertaining to, or intended to be used in, the legal process; in style and execution it need not differ from other writing.

Level I Trauma Center: A healthcare facility or center with dedicated resources to the care of trauma patients 24 hr a day, 7 days a week. Level I is the highest level, with the most available resources, as designated by the American College of Surgeons. Level I trauma centers should have resources including, but are not limited to, a dedicated trauma service, a trauma director, in-house 24-hr surgeon availability, emergency resuscitation equipment for patients of all ages, a performance improvement program, coordination and/or participation in community prevention programs.

Liability: Any legally enforceable obligation. In insurance, this usually is associated with a monetary value.

Liberty interest: An interest recognized as protected by the due process clauses of state and federal constitutions.

Lien: A right or claim against an asset (e.g., Medicare may have a right to reimbursement of healthcare benefits it paid for treatment of the injury giving rise to the lawsuit from the damages recovered in lawsuit).

Life safety code: Federal fire safety requirements and other environmental standards ensuring residents' physical safety; addresses construction, protection, and occupancy features necessary to minimize danger from fire, smoke, heat, and toxic gases; establishes minimum criteria for fire evacuation plan to allow prompt escape.

Life-sustaining medical treatment: Medical treatment that sustains a person's life functions, including respiratory and cardiopulmonary functions, preventing the person's body from reaching a state where it is declared legally dead.

Limits: The amount the payer covers.

Litigation: A lawsuit, legal action, including all proceedings therein. Contest in a court of law for the purpose of enforcing a right or seeking a remedy (e.g., a judicial contest, a judicial controversy, a suit at law).

Living will: A legal document in which a competent person directs in advance that artificial life-prolonging treatment not be used when there is no reasonable expectation from recovery from extreme physical or mental disability.

Logical operators: Also called Boolean operators (see Boolean logic).

Loss control: An application of techniques designed to minimize loss in a cost-effective manner.

Loss of Chance: A theory of recovery in medical malpractice cases for a patient's loss of chance of survival or loss of chance of a better recovery. This theory applies where the patient is suffering from a preexisting injury or illness aggravated by the alleged negligence of the healthcare provider to the extent that (1) the patient dies, when without negligence there might have been a substantial chance of survival or (2) the patient survives, but the actual recovery is substantially less than it might have been absent the alleged malpractice.

Loss of consortium: A claim brought by the spouse of an injured party for loss of the benefits of companionship caused by the injuries suffered in the accident.

Loss prevention: A program seeking to reduce or eliminate the chance of loss or the potential severity of a loss.

Mainframe: A very large computer, which has many megabytes in the central processing unit, or CPU. Because it can store many gigabytes of disk memory, it may act as a host computer, which controls searches from instructions or commands from many remote terminals.

Mallampati Classification: Used to predict the ease of *intubation*. Determined by looking at the *anatomy* of the *oral cavity*, visibility of the base of *uvula*, *faucial pillars* (the arches in front of and behind the tonsils), and *soft palate*.

Malpractice: Misconduct, negligence, or failure to properly perform duties according to professional standards of care.

Marginalization: Peripheralization, to be situated on the border or edge so membership in dual domains.

Markup: See "Annotation."

Mass tort: A civil wrong injuring many people. Examples include toxic emissions from a factory, the crash of a commercial airliner, and contamination from an industrial waste-disposal site.

Material risk: Risk that if the patient were informed about, could influence the patient's decision to consent to the proposed treatment or procedure.

Material Safety Data Sheet (MSDS): Documentation provided by the manufacturer, which provides valuable information about the chemical, including a brief summary about the hazards and personal protective equipment required when working with the chemical.

MCO: Managed Care Organization. Examples are Health Maintenance Organization (HMO), Exclusive Provider Organization (EPO), Individual Practice Association (IPA), or Preferred Provider Organization (PPO). All types of MCOs utilize healthcare cost containment methods such as providing care within a specific network of providers and facilities, utilization management, and case management.

MDS: Minimum Data Set. A national tool used to assess the resident's needs and used to determine reimbursement.

Mechanism of Injury: The way in which an injury was sustained.

Mediation: A problem-solving process involving a neutral third party who facilitates the parties in reaching a resolution but lacks authority to render a decision.

Mediator: A neutral third party who assists the parties in negotiating a compromise.

Medical Durable Power of Attorney (MDPA or MDPOA): Document designating another person, called an agent to make medical decisions. The agent makes any and all medical or other healthcare decisions with the physician. The MDPA can cover more healthcare decisions than a living will/advance directive does and is not limited to terminal illness. The MDPA can be revoked by the issuer at anytime. It can become effective immediately, or it can become effective when the issuer is unable to make medical independent decisions.

Medical review panel process: Requires the submission of a medical malpractice claim to a medical review panel for its opinion prior to the institution of the judicial action.

Medical surveillance: Required monitoring of specific exposures conducted to protect workers from adverse health effects of exposures to hazards in the workplace and to ensure ability to perform job activities.

Medicare set asides: Recommended method to protect Medicare's interests by allocating a portion of a settlement, for example, workers compensation, for future medical expenses under the Medicare Secondary Payer (MSP) laws. The amount of the set aside is determined on a case-by-case basis and reviewed by the Centers for Medicare and Medicaid Services (CMS) when appropriate.

Megabyte: One million bytes, 1,000 kilobytes, or 500 pages of data.

Memo of Understanding: A document of agreement between parties with a shared commitment. Depending on the wording, may have the binding power of a contract; may be synonymous with a letter of intent.

Meningeal signs: Refers to signs and symptoms signifying possible meningeal irritation, raising the index of suspicion for a diagnosis of meningitis. Signs include nuccal rigidity, spinal rigidity, Kernig's sign, and Brudzinski's sign. Besides meningitis, other possible causes are subarachnoid hemorrhage, fossa tumor, and increased intracranial pressure.

Mentor: A wise legal advisor, trusted teacher, or guide.

Middle range theory: Believes in the necessity for sociological theory constructed between "minor working hypotheses" and "master conceptual schemes." Theories are more limited in scope, with less abstraction, and reflect practice.

Mitigate: To lessen or reduce.

Mitigation of damages: Claim that plaintiff has responsibility to minimize the adverse impact of his injury and, therefore, his failure to do so should reduce the amount awarded to him by the damages would have been avoided had he done so. This claim is typically used in the context of a defendant's assertion that plaintiff's award should be reduced by a prior act/omission of plaintiff (e.g., failure to wear a seat belt) because it would have lessened the injury, or because a treatment (e.g., a medicine, physical therapy, or a surgical procedure) is available to cure plaintiff's condition or diminish the effects of it.

Model: A mental image; a conceptualization of a phenomenon.

Model cases: The process of defining and identifying exemplars to illustrate a concept.

Modem: Modulator–demodulator. It is a device that allows a terminal to interface with the telecommunications network and converts the electrical or digital signals of a terminal.

Morality: Refers to the common societal conceptions of what is right and what is wrong. Our morality and morals are reflected in how we live, the decisions we make, and what we hold as valuable.

Motion: An application to a court or judge for the purpose of obtaining a rule or order direction of some act to be done in favor of the applicant.

Motion in limine: A pretrial motion that requests the court to issue an interlocutory order, which prevents an opposing party from introducing or referring to potentially irrelevant, prejudicial, or otherwise inadmissible evidence until the court has finally ruled on its admissibility.

Motivation: A conscious or unconscious need, drive, etc. incites a person to some action, behavior, or goal.

MPEG1: Moving Picture Experts Group. Pronounced "m-peg." The term also refers to the family of digital video compression standards and file formats developed by the group. MPEG generally produces better-quality *video* than competing formats, such as *Video for Windows*, *Indeo*, and *QuickTime*. MPEG files can be decoded by special hardware or by software.

NANDA: North American Nursing Diagnosis Association. Organization involved in developing and promoting the use of nursing diagnoses.

National Committee for Quality Assurance (NCQA): An independent, nonprofit organization evaluating healthcare coverage provided by insurers and managed care organizations (MCOs) by reviewing the clinical outcomes of its members, contracting practices, and member satisfaction surveys. Successful accreditation by the NCQA is considered a standard by which MCOs can be compared. Accreditation also implies a higher standard of service.

National Institute for Occupational Safety and Health (NIOSH): One of three separate bodies created by the OSH Act to administer the major requirement of the Act. The role of this agency is to conduct research, education, and training.

Native resolution: In referring to a projector's resolution, it is common to refer to "true" or "native" resolution. If a projector's native resolution is 800 × 600, the actual number of physical pixels on the display device is 800 × 600. The projector needs to match the resolution of the computer. Resolution is usually quoted in two numbers with the first number referring to the number of pixels from side to side across the screen and the second number referring to the number of pixels vertically from top to bottom.

Natural language: A language using natural speech (words) rather than symbols.

NCQA: National Committee for Quality Assurance. An independent, nonprofit organization evaluating healthcare coverage provided by insurers and managed care organizations (MCOs) by reviewing the clinical outcomes of its members, contracting practices, and member satisfaction surveys. Successful accreditation by the NCQA is considered a standard by which MCOs can be compared. Accreditation also implies a higher standard of service.

NEC: Not Elsewhere Classifiable. Indicates the condition specified does not have a separate more specific listing; used only in Volume 2 of the ICD-9.

Negligence: A failure to act as an ordinary prudent person or "reasonable man" would do under similar circumstances. Four elements of negligence must be proved in order for there to be a viable medical malpractice claim; (1) A duty must be owed to the patient. This duty usually occurs when the healthcare provider accepts responsibility for the care and treatment of the patient; (2) A breach of duty or standard of care by the professional for the type of specialty and particular type of treatment either by an act of omission or commission causing damage to the patient; (3) Proximate cause/or causal connection must be evident between the breach of duty and the harm or damages to the patient/plaintiff; (4) Damages or injuries suffered by the plaintiff. May be any of the following including but not limited to loss of love and affection; loss of nurturance, pain and suffering; mental anguish; emotional distress; loss of chance of survival; disfigurement; past, present, and future medical expenses; past, present, and future loss of wages; premature death; and loss of enjoyment of life.

Negligent referral: Referral to an inappropriate or unsafe resource, or one from which the case manager may stand to gain monetarily.

Negotiated risk agreements: Comparable to the legal and ethical doctrine of informed consent, the agreement accommodates the choices and potential risks of remaining in the residence. In assisted living the prerogative to refuse unwanted interventions applies not to medical procedures, but to ongoing health-related, dietary, and residential interventions.

Netiquette: Etiquette (manners) on the Internet.

Network: A collection of computers linked together by a physical medium (wires, microwaves, etc.) for transmission of data between computers or "nodes" on the network.

Network protocol: The set of rules or "language" used by computers on a network to communicate (e.g., Novell IPX, Appletalk, and TCP/IP).

Networking: Meeting and establishing a network of other like professionals to enhance information exchange and business relationships.

Newton's law's of motion: Three basic laws of physics utilized to determine if the mechanism of the claimed injury existed in the subject incident.

NIC: Nursing Interventions Classification. Method of placing interventions in a taxonomy.

No-fault system: Under a no-fault system, each party's own insurance covers the damages (up to policy limits regardless of which party is at fault); restricts the ability of accident victims to sue others for their injuries.

NOC: Nursing Outcomes Classification. Method of placing outcomes in a taxonomy.

Nonbillable hours: Hours worked not directly relate to the client/customer's project; hours spent in administrative or other support areas of a business project.

Noneconomic damages: As opposed to economic damages such as wages, noneconomic damages are for intangible harm such as pain, suffering, loss of companionship, and loss of consortium. In some states, laws limit (cap) the amount of noneconomic damages that can be recovered for torts.

Nonparty witness: A witness who is not a plaintiff or defendant or employee or agent of a plaintiff or defendant.

NOS: Not Otherwise Specified. Used only in Volume 1 of the ICD-9, when the available information does not permit assignment to a more specific code.

Notice of Intent: Document sent to a healthcare facility, which puts facility on notice that a party has initiated legal action against the facility.

NPA: Nurse Practice Acts. State laws govern nursing practice, and in some cases, nursing education, protecting the safety and welfare of the public.

Nursing facility (NF): A designation under the Medicare program for long-term care facilities providing a more intensive level of medical, rehabilitation, or nursing care required only to assist residents with activities of daily living such as eating, dressing, bathing, etc. An NF may be either freestanding or a distinct unit of a larger healthcare facility. Effective October 1, 1990, under the *Omnibus Budget Reconciliation Act of 1987* (OBRA), the skilled nursing facility (SNF) and intermediate care facility (ICF) designations were eliminated from the Medicaid program and a single designation of NF was substituted.

Nursing process: An organized, systematic method of giving individualized nursing care focused on identifying and treating unique responses of individuals or groups to actual or potential alterations in health.

Objection: Legal format for not allowing testimony into evidence based on various legal reasons such as form of question, hearsay, or privilege.

OBRA: Omnibus Budget Reconciliation Act of 1987. Changed the standard of care in nursing homes by defining minimum standards.

Occupant kinematics: The movement of the occupants of a vehicle due to the motor vehicle collision.

Occupational and environmental health nurse (OEHN): A professional licensed nurse whose specialty area of practice is the worker and the work environment.

Occupational disease: A disease that is gradually contracted in usual and ordinary course of employment and caused by the employment.

Occupational Noise Exposure Standard: One of the standards developed by the Occupational Safety and Health Administration in order to protect workers from hearing impairment when there is significant noise exposure.

Occupational Safety and Health Act (OSH Act): Federal legislation enacted in 1970 requiring employers to provide safe and healthy working conditions for employees.

Occupational Safety and Health Administration (OSHA): One of three separate bodies created by the OSH Act to administer the major requirements of the Act. The role of this agency is to set and enforce safety and health standards; provide training outreach and education; establish partnerships; and encourage continual process improvement in workplace safety and health.

Offline printing: Printed records generated at the mainframe after the user has logged off the computer system. They are usually mailed or faxed to the user.

Offline searching: Computer processing of a search after the user has entered the appropriate strategy and has logged off the system.

Ombudsman: An official or semiofficial office or person to which people may come with grievances connected with the government. The ombudsman stands between and represents the citizen before the government.

Online: The term describes the status of a searcher conversing with the host computer in the interactive mode.

Open account: An account not finally settled or closed, but is still running or open to future adjustment or liquidation. Open account, in legal as well as in ordinary language, means indebtedness subject to future adjustment, and which may be reduced or modified by proof.

Open book pelvic fracture: An unstable anterior compression fracture of the pelvis, often resulting from a heavy impact, such as a motorcycle accident. Bilateral separation anteriorly and posteriorly gives an appearance of an open book. This can be an open or closed fracture and is a potentially life-threatening injury due to the possibility of severe hemorrhage. Surgical reconstruction may be needed prior to rehabilitation.

Opt-out: Deadline set, typically by the court after a class action is certified as to when one may voluntarily decide to not participate in a class action; after the date passes, plaintiffs who have not opted-out will be bound by the decisions of the court.

Ostensible authority: Doctrine of law whereby a hospital is liable for the negligence of an independent contractor if the patient has a rational basis to believe the independent contractor is a hospital employee, for example, a physician in the emergency department.

Outcomes: Result of medical treatment and medical case management services. These should be measurable.

Outcomes and Assessment Information Set (OASIS): Federal monitoring system for Home Health Agencies. Quality information collected from Medicare home healthcare patients and submitted regularly to fiscal intermediaries who analyze the data in order to implement quality initiatives and calculate Medicare payments for services.

Outcome identification: As an LNC standard, the identification of desired activities as related to the healthcare issues of a case or claim.

Paradigm: The body of values, commitment, beliefs, and knowledge shared by members of a profession.

Paralegal: A person qualified by education, training, or work experience for employment by an attorney and who performs specifically delegated substantive legal work for which a lawyer is responsible.

Partnership: A business owned by two or more persons, which is not organized as a corporation. For income tax purposes, a partnership includes a syndicate, group, pool, or joint venture, as well as ordinary partnerships. Partnerships are treated as a conduit and are, therefore, not subject to taxation. The various items of partnership income, gains and losses, etc. flow through to the individual partners and are reported on their personal income tax returns.

Password: A unique set of characters assigned to a user for security purposes to grant access to specific databases.

Paternalism: An extension of beneficence. Paternalism is the view that professionals understand patients' best interests better than patients do and are entitled to act on behalf of the patient's well-being even when the patient does not agree.

Pathognomic or Pathognomonic: Particular sign that is *diagnostic* for a particular *disease* whose presence means, beyond any doubt, that a particular disease is present.

Payroll tax: A type of tax collected by deduction from an employee's wages. Federal, state, and half of the social security tax is paid by employees, with the social security tax matched by the employer.

PDF: Portable Document Format. A file format developed by Adobe Systems to prevent unauthorized alterations and ensure integrity of document. PDF captures formatting information from a variety of *desktop publishing applications*, making it possible to send formatted documents and have them appear on the recipient's *monitor* or *printer* as they were intended.

Pediatric advanced life support provider: A healthcare professional who is certified as a basic life support (BLS) provider and passes additional certification to enhance their resuscitation skills in a pediatric cardiopulmonary emergency. These skills include cardiopulmonary resuscitation (CPR), airway management, cardiac rhythm recognition, emergency medication administration, and the use of treatment algorithms.

Peer-reviewed: Process used by professions for monitoring and regulating member practice.

Percentile: Value of a variable below which a certain *percent* of observations fall. For example, the 20th percentile is the value (or score) below which 20% of the observations may be found. The term percentile and the related term *percentile rank* are often used in *descriptive statistics* as well as in the reporting of scores from norm-referenced tests. Results arranged in sequence from highest to lowest, with resulting range containing 100% of the total received. 80th and 90th percentile are actual results that are higher than (or equal to) 80% or 90% of all results in the range, respectively.

Performance appraisal: Evaluation of a practice of the in relation to professional standards and relevant statutes and regulations.

Persistent vegetative state: An enduring state of grossly impaired consciousness, as after severe head trauma or brain disease, in which an individual is incapable of voluntary or purposeful acts and only responds reflexively to painful stimuli.

Personal care: Care for someone who is disabled or is otherwise unable to care for themselves rendered by a nurse's aide, dietician, or other health professional. These services include assistance in walking, getting out of bed, bathing, toileting, dressing, eating, and preparing special diets.

Personal protective equipment (PPE): Devices worn by workers to protect against hazards in the workplace, such as the use of earplugs or earmuffs in high noise areas or gloves for protection against blood or other body fluid exposures.

Personal protective equipment standard: One of the standards developed by the Occupational Safety and Health Administration in order to provide information on the types of protection available for employees where engineering and administrative controls were not available or effective in reducing occupational hazards.

Perspective: The way members of a group characterize, define, and view a situation.

Phenomena: An aspect of reality that is sensed or experienced.

PIP: Personal Injury Protection. Coverage by the client's own auto insurance carrier for medical expenses; dictated by state auto law and amount of coverage purchased.

Plaintiff: A person who brings an action; the person who complains or sues in a civil action and is so named on the record. A person who seeks remedial relief for an injury to rights; it designates a complainant.

Planning: As an LNC standard, formulation of a plan of action. The third step of the nursing process. In this step, specific measures are identified to put into action based upon the initial assessment.

Pleading: A formal written statement filed with a court by parties in a civil action, such as a complaint or an answer containing the formal allegations by the parties of their respective claims and defenses. Under rules of civil procedure, the pleadings consist of a complaint, an answer, a reply to counterclaim, a third-party complaint, and a third-party answer.

PMPM: Per Member Per Month. The formula by which utilization management calculates average utilization and cost for each member of the plan.

Position statement: Consensus statements providing the generally accepted opinions of a group.

Postings: The number of citations or references retrieved as a result of a search. Synonymous with "Hits."

Power of Attorney (POA): A legal document granting one person authority to act as an agent or attorney-in-fact for the grantor including financial or real-estate transactions.

Power point: A Microsoft software slide presentation software program commonly used for computer-based presentations containing text and/or graphics.

PPO: Preferred Provider Organization. Members receive benefits at a discounted rate as long as they utilize only the providers who have a contract with the plan.

PPS: Prospective Payment System. Payment system, such as DRGs, which pays on historical data of case mix and regional differences.

Practice analysis: A study and analysis of critical skills and concepts needed to be proficient in the specialty, as identified by nurses practicing in the specialty. A practice analysis is a critical early step in creating a certification exam to accurately reflect specialty practice, serving as the exam blueprint. This periodic analysis is required to meet American Board of Nursing Specialties (ABNS) standards and maintain accreditation.

Preadmission screening: Conducted by trained state or county preadmission screening teams, the preadmission screen includes an assessment of functional, social, medical, and nursing needs in order to determine if admission to a nursing facility or selection of other community-based care services (i.e., assisted living) is appropriate for Medicaid eligible recipients.

Premium: The amount of money paid to an insurer in return for insurance coverage.

Preponderance of the evidence: Standard of proof that is more probable than not; just over 50% of the evidence favors the party.

Principal investigator (PI): An individual, usually a physician, with appropriate qualifications (eligibility usually evaluated and determined by an IRB and/or pharmaceutical sponsor) who is responsible for the research study trial conduct.

Private case management: Case managers hired privately by individuals and families.

Proactive: Planned action toward a goal.

Probable cause: Standard used to determine if a crime has been committed and if there is sufficient evidence to believe a specific individual committed it.

Probate court: The department of each county's superior court dealing with probate conservatorships, guardianships, and the estates of people who have died.

Probate system: Court system that addresses issues of conservatorships, guardianships, and estate planning of deceased; responsibility for making decisions to protect a minor or dependent adult's life and property.

Procedure creep: Billing for a higher level of service than provided. See "Upcoding."

Procedures: A series of recommended actions for the completion of a specific task or function. Procedures may be either specific to an institution or applicable across settings.

Process server: One who serves papers on parties.

Product liability: Concept in the law holding a manufacturer responsible for the article placed on the market. A tort arising out of defective products, including medical devices and medications.

Profession: An occupation requiring considerable training and specialized study. Professionals experience a high level of dedication and an acceptance of responsibility for the quality of their work. Society holds professionals in a position of high regard, with a high level of accountability in their practices.

Professional: A person with a specialized training in a field of learning, art, or science.

Professional code of ethics: Rules governing the conduct of an organization and its members.

Profit and loss: The gain or loss arising from goods bought or sold, or from carrying on any other business, the former of which, in bookkeeping, is placed on the creditor's side; the later on the debtor's side.

Properties of the nursing process: Purposeful, systematic, dynamic, interactive, and flexible.

Provider: The party providing services and supplies to the beneficiary.

Proximate cause: An act or omission found to be a substantial factor in bringing about or failing to prevent an injury.

Psychometric testing standards: Postadministration testing analysis to ensure that the certification exam questions are directly related to the roles of experienced professions who meet eligibility criteria perform successfully on the examination. Statistical analysis indicates high consistency of performance of individual candidates throughout the examination.

Punitive damages: Also known as exemplary damages. Punitive damages exceed the amount intended to make the plaintiff whole and are awarded with the intent to punish the defendant, to set an example, and to deter future behavior considered "outrageous." Most jurisdictions determine if punitive damages can be awarded and often set a cap on the amount of punitive damages awarded.

Qualification: Quality or circumstance is legally or inherently necessary to perform a function.

Qualified individual with a disability: A person who with reasonable accommodation can perform the essential functions of the job.

Qualities and traits: Characteristics personifying the behaviors of an individual.

Quality assurance: Ongoing program to objectively and systematically monitor and evaluate quality and resolve identified problems.

Quality improvement: Focuses on processes or systems contributing to or distracting from outcomes.

Quality of practice: Evaluation of the quality and effectiveness of practice.

RAI: Resident Assessment Instrument. Consists of the *Minimum Data Set* (MDS), Resident Assessment Protocol (RAP), and the care plan.

RAP: Resident Assessment Protocol. Defines the problems identified through the use of the MDS.

Rating: The quantifying of an insured or group's activity or experience.

Reader-friendly writing: Writing tailored to the audience and the purpose, attempting to minimize the effort required by the reader; typically characterized by brevity, clarity, simplicity, and structure.

Reasonable accommodation: The Rehabilitation Act of 1973 requires the employer to take reasonable steps to accommodate the individual with a disability unless it causes the employer undue hardship.

Recording and reporting of occupational injuries and illness standard: One of the standards developed by the Occupational Safety and Health Administration in order to identify high-hazard industries and permit employees to be aware of their employer's safety record.

Records: Groups of related elements which, when handled as units, make up files.

Redaction: The act of deleting identifying information, as in "redacting the names of patients."

Refereed journal: A professional journal publishing material only after comprehensive review by the author's peers.

Reference: See "Citation."

Referral: The process of sending a member to a second care provider for a consultation, second opinion, or further diagnosis and treatment of an existing condition.

Reflective reaction: Incorporates thought and action with reflection to analyze actions.

Reinsurance carrier: Provides insurance for insurance companies. It is a way by which a primary insurance company transfers or cedes some of the financial risk the company assumes to another insurance company, the reinsurer.

Request for admissions: Written statements of fact concerning the case, which are submitted to an adverse party and which the party is required to admit or deny; those statements which are admitted will be treated by the court as having been established and need not be proven at trial.

Request for production: A formal written request compelling a party to produce materials subject to discovery rules.

Res ipsa loquitur: Latin for "The thing speaks for itself." The mere facts provide information supporting negligence.

Reserves: Funds set aside for a catastrophically injured client by an insurance company to provide for anticipated care needs and expenditures for which they are responsible. Monies set aside by the insurance company for the future expenditures on a claim based on an educated projection.

Resident assessment: Baseline evaluation of assisted living facility resident's medical, cognitive, functional, and psychological needs completed by a qualified, licensed, independent practitioner. Completed prior to admission and every 6 months to determine if care needs have changed. Assessment is maintained in each resident's record at the Assisted Living Facility.

Resident assistant (RA): Unlicensed personnel who generally work in assisted living residences and provide direct personal-care services to residents. They are not certified CNA. Depending on the state, this position is also available in some nursing facilities.

Residential care facility: Group living arrangements designed to meet the needs of those who cannot live independently, but do not require nursing facility services. These homes offer a wider range of services than independent living options. Most provide assistance with the activities of daily living. In some cases, private long-term care insurance and medical assistance programs will help pay for this type of service.

Resource management: As it applies to the LNC, the LNC selects expert assistance on the needs of the case or the claim.

Respite care: Temporary, scheduled short-term nursing facility (NF) care provided to an individual needing this level of care but who is normally cared for in the community. The goal of scheduled short-term care is to provide relief for the caregivers while providing NF care for the individual. Short-term stay beds used for respite care must be distinct from general NF beds.

Respondeat superior: Latin for "Let the superior make answer"; employer liability for employee's wrongful actions within the scope of employment.

Restatement (Third) tort products liability Section 6: A statement that a prescription drug or medical device is not reasonably safe due to defective design. If the foreseeable risks of harm posed by the drug or medical device are sufficiently great in relation to its foreseeable therapeutic benefits, the reasonable healthcare providers, knowing of such foreseeable risks and therapeutic benefits, would not prescribe the drug or medical device for any class of patients.

Retainer: The act of withholding what one has in one's own hands by virtue of some right. In the practice of law, when a client hires an attorney to represent him, the client is said to have retained the attorney. This act of employment is called the retainer.

Risk: A chance of loss. Risk is a variation in possible outcomes existing in any given situation or event. Risk may include two categories: (1) objective; variations exist in nature and are the same for all individuals facing the same situation and (2) subjective; an individual's estimation of the objective risk.

Risk management: A process to identify, evaluate, and take corrective action against potential or actual risks to patients, visitors, employees, or property.

Root cause analysis (RCA): A process designed to uncover how and why something happened and to identify ways to prevent it from happening again. The four-step process includes data collection, organization of contributing factors, identification of the root causes, and recommendations for corrective action.

RUG: Resource Utilization Group. Calculated based on the MDS to help to determine reimbursement.

Rule 702: A federal rule of evidence governing the admissibility of expert testimony.

RVS: Relative Value System. Coded listing of professional services with unit values to indicate relative complexity as measured by time, skill, and overhead costs. Third-party payers typically assign a dollar value per unit to calculate provider reimbursement. Procedure/service is assigned a value multiplied by cost factor.

S corporation: A small business corporation with a statutorily limited number of shareholders, and under certain conditions, has elected to have it taxable income taxed to its shareholders at regular income tax rates. I.R.C. §1361 et seg. S corporation status usually avoids the corporate income tax and the shareholders can claim corporate losses. In terms of legal characteristics under state law, "S" Status Corporation is no different than any other regular corporation.

SART: Sexual Assault Response Team. Group of professionals who minimize the trauma for sexual assault victims seeking medical and legal assistances. Coordination of the investigation process reduces repeated questioning for the victim and to increase effective collection and preservation of evidence. SART members typically include emergency department medical personnel, law enforcement, and a sexual assault advocate. (Other partners may include representatives from state forensic labs, public health departments, victim–witness programs, prosecution offices, crime victim compensation offices, child/adult protective services, organizations serving victims from underserved populations and social and human services.)

Search statement: A user-entered instruction combining key terms and Boolean operators to retrieve a set of citations or records.

Search strategy: The selection of an essential set of planned search statements.

Securing: The protection portion of a computer system that prevents access to sensitive material.

Self-insured companies: Companies or businesses set aside a fund to cover potential business liability losses instead of insuring against such a loss through a separate insurance company.

Sentinel event: An unexpected occurrence of variation involving death, serious physical or psychological injury, or risk thereof. Serious injury specifically includes loss of limb or function. The phrase "or risk thereof" includes any process variations for which a recurrence would carry a significant chance of a serious adverse outcome.

Sepsis: The most common kind of distributive shock caused by an overwhelming systemic infection resulting in cellular destruction, microvascular occlusion, and systemic vasodilatation.

Shadow jury: Acts as a surrogate for the real jury by sitting in a courtroom whenever the real jury is present and agrees to be interviewed at regular intervals during a trial.

Sick building syndrome: Term used to describe the cluster of symptoms found to occur in office environments, particularly in sealed buildings with centrally controlled mechanical ventilation.

Software: Computer program or sets of computer-readable messages/language instructing a computer to perform specified tasks.

Sole proprietorship: A form of business in which one person owns all the assets of the business in contrast to a partnership, trust, or corporation. The sole proprietor is solely liable for all the debts of the business.

Special damages: Out-of-pocket expenses incurred by the plaintiff as a result of the negligence.

Special Needs Trust: Also known in the United States as a Supplemental Needs Trust, this type of trust is created to ensure that beneficiaries who have a physical or mental disability can enjoy the use of property that is intended to be held for their benefit. When properly drafted, the assets in the trust are not considered countable assets for the purpose of qualification for certain governmental benefits and are intended to provide supplemental and extra care over and above that which the government provides.

Staffing requirements: Required staff, which may be based on patient-care demands at particular times or on the number of residents. The federal Nursing Home Reform Act (NHRA) in the Omnibus Budget Reconciliation Act (OBRA) of 1987 requires nursing homes to provide sufficient staff and services to attain or maintain the highest possible level of physical, mental, and psychosocial well-being of each resident. Total licensed nursing requirements are converted to hours per resident day (HPRD). The NHRA also sets minimum staffing levels for registered nurses (RNs) and licensed practical nurses (LPNs), and a minimum educational training for nurse's aides (NAs). Medicare and Medicaid certified nursing homes are required to have an RN director of nursing (DON); an RN on duty at least 8 hr a day, 7 days a week; a licensed nurse (RN or LPN) on duty the remainder of the time; and a minimum of 75 hr of training for NAs. In facilities with less than 60 residents, the law allows the DONs to also serve in the capacity as the RN on duty.

Standard: A model accepted as correct by custom.

Standard of care: The degree of care a reasonably prudent person should exercise under the same or similar circumstances. In the case of a professional (e.g., nurse, doctor, lawyer), it is the degree of care a reasonably prudent person in profession should exercise under the same or similar circumstances.

Statute: A formal written enactment of a legislative body, whether federal, state, county, or city. A particular law enacted or established by the will of the legislative department of the government.

Statute of limitations: Time frame in which a plaintiff must commence litigation. Specific period of time between an occurrence and the filing of the lawsuit. In malpractice claims, this is usually when the party claiming injury first discovers or should have discovered the injury.

Statutory: Relating to a statute.

Stop word list: A list of terms ignored for online searching, such as articles and prepositions.

Strict liability: Doctrine by which the one who sells any product in a defective condition deemed unsafe to the user or consumer or to their property is subject to liability for physical harm or property damage; the plaintiff must prove that the product was in a condition not contemplated by the ultimate consumer, which would make the product unreasonably dangerous.

Sub Rosa: A technique of investigation using videotape surveillance of a plaintiff or claimant; carried out by a private investigator for the defense.

Subcontract: An agreement between a party of the original contract and a third party.

Subcontractor: One who has entered into a contract, express or implied, for the performance of an act with the person who has already contracted for its performance. One who takes from the principal or prime contractor a specific part of the work undertaken by the principal contractor.

Subpoena: A command to appear at a certain time and place to give testimony upon a certain matter.

Subpoena Duces Tecum: A command to appear at a certain time and place to give testimony upon a certain matter; a process by which the court commands a witness who has in his possession or control some document or paper pertinent to the issues of a pending controversy, to produce it at the trial.

Sullivan v. Edward Hospital: The 2004 court decision that affirmed the profession of nursing involves a unique body of knowledge and expertise, and nurses are the most appropriate experts to testify to nursing standards of care.

Summary judgment: The process by which a court decides, based on evidence presented by the defendant, no genuine issue of material fact exists for a jury to consider. Therefore, the court dismisses the case against the defendant as a matter of law and the case does not go to trial.

Summary plan description (SPD): An overview of the benefits elected by a plan member, detailing what the member can expect to be covered by the plan, and possibly, what is not covered. The structure and wording of SPDs is stipulated in Employee Retirement Income Security Act of 1974 (ERISA).

Summons and Complaint (or Petition): A document setting forth allegations against the defendant(s) which the plaintiff intends to prove. The document is formal notification and initiates the legal action against the plaintiff. The method of instituting a legal proceeding and notification of such action to all concerned parities is regulated by the individual.

Tax: A charge by the government on the income of an individual, corporation, or trust, as well as the value of an estate or gift. The objective in assessing the tax is to generate revenue to be used for the needs of the public.

Taxonomy: A common language in event reporting for use in and across organizations to promote reliable and accurate information.

Technical nurse consultant: A nurse possessing advanced skills and expertise in the use of computerized presentations for legal proceedings.

Telecommunications: Transmission of voice or data by means of telephone networks or carriers.

Telephonic case management: Coordination of services provided through telephone contact only.

Terminal: An electronic device for transmitting to and receiving signals from a computer.

Terminal illness: A medical practitioner's term for an incurable or irreversible disease and which will, with a high degree of probability, cause the death of a patient within a relatively short period of time.

Testifying expert: An expert capable of rendering an opinion as a potential trial witness.

Testimony: Spoken or written evidence by a competent witness under oath.

Text word: A single word that appears in the title or abstract of a citation, which may be used as a search tool rather than, or in addition to, the subject terms (such as MeSH terms) assigned by an indexer. Also see "Free text."

(The) Joint Commission: An independent, not-for-profit organization, whose mission is to continuously improve the safety and quality of care provided to the public through the provision of healthcare accreditation and related services supported by performance improvement in healthcare organizations. The Joint Commission accredits and certifies more than 15,000 healthcare organizations and programs in the United States. Joint Commission accreditation and certification is recognized nationwide as a symbol of quality reflecting an organization's commitment to meeting certain performance standards.

Theory: A conceptualization of an aspect of reality for the purpose of describing phenomena. Concepts are interrelated in a coherent whole for some purpose.

Theory development: The process or integrated approach by which theory is developed including the evolution of an idea, the concept analysis, the proposal of a framework and theoretical definition, substantiation through research, and critique of the theory.

Third-party administrator (TPA): A person or company hired to oversee and resolve claims and actions. TPAs are often utilized by large self-insured companies such as health maintenance organization or large healthcare conglomerates to handle claims against the company.

Third-party claim: Action against a negligent third party.

Third-party counterclaim: A separate cause of action in which a defendant asserts against a third person or party.

TIF or TIFF: Tagged Image File Format. One of the most widely *supported file formats* for *storing bit-mapped* images on *personal computers*. TIFF *graphics* can be any *resolution*, and they can be black and white, *gray-scaled*, or color.

Time management: A method of efficiently using energy, space, and time to enhance task completion.

Time-weighted average (TWA): The average exposure to a contaminant or condition (such as noise) to which workers may be exposed without adverse effect over a period such as in an 8-hr day or 40-hr week. For example, average levels and duration of noise exposure over the work shift to give an equivalent 8-hr exposure.

Tort: A civil wrong or injury other than breach of contract.

Total quality management: Process used to improve the ability to satisfy customer expectations, based on the belief that quality is a positive strategy for growth and integrated into the business plan.

Toxic tort: A civil wrong arising from exposure to a toxic substance, such as asbestos, radiation, or hazardous waste. A toxic tort can be remedied by a civil lawsuit (usually a class action) or by administrative action.

Tracking: Following and monitoring the awareness of a direction or idea.

Trauma bays: Treatment rooms in an emergency department (ED) equipped and dedicated to the care of trauma patients who arrive in the ED.

Trauma nurse core course (TNCC): A course produced by the Emergency Nurses Association in 1986 to serve as a standard of practice for nurses who provide care for patients who have sustained traumatic injuries.

Trending: Maintaining a consistent way or direction.

Trial consultant: A consultant employed or hired to assist with trial preparation, typically through the preparation of witnesses and parties for testifying at trial. Trial consultants may also assist in jury selection, through the creation of a profile of desirable jurors. Trial consultants often have background education in psychology and/or communication.

Trier of fact: Judge, arbitrator, or juror.

Truncation: To shorten by or as if by cutting off. For example, "various kidney conditions" truncated "nephr" would retrieve all terms that use "nephr" as the root, such as nephritis, nephrology, nephropathy, etc. May also serve as a means of retrieving words sharing a common root or stem. For example, to limit a lengthy abstract. The phrase "Abstract truncated at 250 words" may appear at the end of an abstract.

Trust: A property interest held by one person (the trustee) at the request of another (the settler) for the benefit of a third party (the beneficiary); fiduciary relationship involving a trustee who holds trust property for the benefit or use of a beneficiary.

Trustee: A person or an institution managing the assets for the benefit of someone else, for example, the consevatee.

U&C: Usual and Customary. A fee defined as the charge for health care consistent with the average rate or charge for identical or similar services in a certain geographical area.

UB-92: Universal Bill 1992. The form used by hospital-based providers to bill for services.

Unbundling: Breaking a single service into its multiple components to increase total billing charges.

Underwriting: The analysis done for accepting insurance risk and determining the amount of insurance the company will write on each risk.

Upcoding: The process of assigning a code representing a more complex or involved service than actually provided and thus receives a higher reimbursement.

Update service: A periodic online search of a previously selected topic. The search strategy is stored and activated periodically (e.g., monthly or quarterly) to provide new citations. Also known as "Selective Dissemination of Information" or "SDI."

URC: Usual, Customary, and Reasonable. A method for determining benefits by comparing the charges of one provider to like charges of others in the same area and specialty.

Utilitarianism: The ethical view that the right action is that which promotes a greater balance of good over harm for everyone concerned in a situation.

Utilization management: A method employed by the insurance and managed care industry to track and manage the use of medical benefits by covered beneficiaries. It is a formal assessment of medical necessity, efficiency, appropriateness of healthcare services and treatment plans. This assessment can occur prior to, during, and after delivery of services.

Utilization review: A process of evaluation of health care based on medical necessity and appropriateness. Utilization review can include preadmission review, concurrent review, discharge planning, and retrospective review.

Vaccine Injury Compensation Program: Created in 1986, the National Vaccine Injury Compensation Program (VICP) was established as a no-fault alternative to the traditional tort system for resolving vaccine injury claims providing compensation to people found to be injured by certain vaccines. The U.S. Court of Federal Claims decides who will be paid.

Vendor: A service company storing databases electronically making them available, via telecommunications, to clients for a fee.

Venture capital: Funding for new companies or others embarking on new or turnaround ventures, which entails some investment risk but offers the potential for above average profits. Venture capital is often provided by firms specializing in financing new ventures with capital supplied by investors interested in speculative or high-risk investments.

Veracity: The principle of telling the truth without deception.

Vicarious liability: Vicarious liability occurs when the law, in certain limited instances, imposes liability on a principal for the acts or omissions of an agent.

Vision statement: Articulation of a view of a realistic, credible, attractive future for the organization.

Voir dire: The questioning of prospective jurors by a judge and attorneys in court.

Warranty: An assurance by the manufacturer that the product is merchantable or fit for the purpose for which it was sold.

WAV or WAVE: The *format* for storing sound in *files* developed jointly by *Microsoft* and *IBM*. Support built into *Windows 95* making it the *de facto standard* for sound on personal computers.

Whistleblower: An employee who reports an employer wrongdoing to a government or law enforcement agency.

Welfare plans: Benefit plans including insurance or healthcare coverage, long- and short-term disability coverage, and life insurance benefits.

Witness: One who is called on to be present at a transaction so as to be able to testify to its occurrence.

Word: When capitalized, short for *Microsoft Word*. A word processing software.

Worker's compensation: Federal- and State-mandated insurance program providing medical care and wage loss replacement when a worker is injured in the course of employment.

World Wide Web (WWW): A collection of hypermedia documents residing on computers (web servers) located all over the Internet linked together in a "world wide web" of information. A web browser (such as Mosaic or Lynx) is needed to gain access to the World Wide Web.

Wrongful death: Type of legal theory argued on behalf of a deceased person's beneficiaries alleging death was attributable to the willful or negligent act of another.

Wrongful life: Refers to a type of medical malpractice claim brought on behalf of a child, alleging the child would not have been born but for negligent advice to, or treatment of, the parents.

Appendix 2

Acronyms

Lori Barber, RN, MN, LNC

AANLCP	American Association of Nurse Life Care Planners
AANLCPCB	American Association of Nurse Life Care Planners Certification Board
AAOHN	American Association of Occupational Health Nurses
ABEM	American Board of Emergency Medicine
ABNS	American Board of Nursing Specialties
ABOHN	American Board for Occupational Health Nurses
ACEP	American College of Emergency Physicians
ADA	Americans with Disabilities Act
ADL	Activities of Daily Living
ALF	Assisted Living Facility
ANA	American Nurses Association
ARN	Association of Rehabilitation Nurses
CCM	Certified Case Manager
CCMC	Commission for Case Manager Certification
CCRC	Continuing Care Retirement Communities
CDC	Centers for Disease Control and Prevention
CDMS	Certified Disability Management Specialist
CDMSC	Certification of Disability Management Specialists Commission
CEN	Certified Emergency Nurse
CERT	Comprehensive Error Rate Testing
CFR	Code of Federal Regulations
CHCC	Commission on Health Care Certification
CHIP	Children's Health Insurance Program
CLCP	Certified Life Care Planner
CM	Case Management
CMS	Centers for Medicare and Medicaid Services
CMSA	Case Management Society of America

CNA	Certified Nursing Assistant
CNLCP	Certified Nurse Life Care Planner
COHN	Certified Occupational Health Nurse
COHN-S	Certified Occupational Health Nurse-Specialist
CPT	Current Procedural Terminology
CRC	Certified Rehabilitation Counselor
CRCC	Commission on Rehabilitation Counselor Certification
CRRN	Certified Rehabilitation Registered Nurse
CTS	Carpal Tunnel Syndrome
CVA	Cerebral Vascular Accident
DD	Developmental Disability
DHHS	Department of Health and Human Services
DOI	Department of Insurance
DOJ	Department of Justice
DOL	Department of Labor
DOT	Department of Transportation
DP	Discharge Planning
DPAHC	Durable Power of Attorney for Health Care
DRG	Diagnostic Related Groups
ED	Emergency Department
EEOC	Equal Employment Opportunity Commission
EMS	Emergency Medical Services
EMTALA	Emergency Medical Treatment and Active Labor Act
ENA	Emergency Nurses Association
EPA	Environmental Protection Agency
ESA	Employment Standards Administration
FAA	Federal Aviation Administration
FBI	Federal Bureau of Investigation
FDA	Food and Drug Administration
FI	Fiscal Intermediary
FIFRA	Federal Insecticide, Fungicide, and Rodenticide Act
FLSA	Fair Labor Standards Act
FMCSA	Federal Motor Carrier Safety Administration
FMLA	Family and Medical Leave Act
FRA	Federal Railroad Administration
FRE	Federal Rules of Evidence
FTA	Federal Transportation Administration
GAO	Government Accountability Office
HCPCS	Healthcare Common Procedural Coding System
HHA	Home Health Agency
HIPAA	Health Insurance Portability and Accountability Act
HMO	Health Maintenance Organization
IADL	Instrumental Activities of Daily Living
ICD	International Classification of Diseases
ICF	Intermediate Care Facility
ICF/MR	Intermediate Care Facility/Mentally Retarded
ICHCC	International Commission on Healthcare Certification

IDEA	Individuals with Disabilities Education Act
IME	Independent Medical Examination
ISP	Individualized Service Plan
IW	Injured Worker
JCAHO or "JC"	Joint Commission on Accreditation of Healthcare ("Joint Commission")
LNC	Legal Nurse Consultant
MAC	Medicare Administrative Contractors
MDPA	Medical Durable Power of Attorney
MIP	Medicaid Integrity Program
MMIS	Medicaid Management Information System
MSA	Medicare Set-Aside Allocation
MSDS	Material Safety Data Sheet
MSP	Medicare Secondary Payer Statute
MVA	Motor Vehicle Accident
NACOSH	National Advisory Committee on Occupational Safety and Health
NCCA	National Commission for Certifying Agencies
NCLEX	National Council Licensure Examination
NCM	Nurse Case Manager
NCSBN	National Council of State Boards of Nursing
NF	Nursing Facility
NIOSH	National Institute for Occupational Safety and Health
NLC	Nurse Licensure Compact
OBRA	Omnibus Budget Reconciliation Act
OCR	Office for Civil Rights
ODEP	Office of Disability Employment Policy
OEHN	Occupational and Environmental Health Nurse
OHN	Occupational Health Nurse
OIG	Office of the Inspector General
OSH Act	Occupational Safety and Health Act
OSHA	Occupational Safety and Health Administration
OSHRC	Occupational Safety and Health Review Commission
PHMSA	Pipeline and Hazardous Materials Safety Administration
PIP	Personal Injury Protection
POS	Point of Service
PPE	Personal Protective Equipment
PPO	Preferred Provider Organization
PRO	Peer Review Organization
QIO	Quality Improvement Organization
RA	Resident Assistant
RAC	Revenue Audit Contractor
RN	Registered Nurse
RNCB	Rehabilitation Nursing Certification Board
S-CHIP	State Children's Health Insurance Program
SM	Safety Management
SNF	Skilled Nursing Facility
SSDI	Social Security Disability Insurance
TNCC	Trauma Nursing Core Course

TWA	Time-Weighted Average
TWCC	Texas Workers' Compensation Commission
UCR	Usual, Customary, and Reasonable
UIM	Underinsured Motorist
UM	Uninsured Motorist
UR	Utilization Review
USDHHS	United States Department of Health and Human Services
USDOL	United States Department of Labor
WC	Workers' Compensation
WHD	Wage and Hour Division
WPA	Whistleblower Protection Act
WPS	Worker Protection Standard

Index